T0142348

New Perspectives in End-User Development

Fabio Paternò · Volker Wulf
Editors

New Perspectives in
End-User Development

 Springer

Editors
Fabio Paternò
ISTI - C.N.R
Pisa
Italy

Volker Wulf
Universität Siegen
Siegen
Germany

ISBN 978-3-319-86827-1   ISBN 978-3-319-60291-2 (eBook)
DOI 10.1007/978-3-319-60291-2

Printed on acid-free paper

This Springer imprint is published by Springer Nature
The registered company is Springer International Publishing AG
The registered company address is: Gewerbestrasse 11, 6330 Cham, Switzerland

Preface – New Perspectives in End-User Development: Elaborating Upon a New Research Paradigm

More than a decade ago, we postulated that the design goals of human–computer interaction will evolve from *easy-to-use* to *easy-to-develop* applications (Lieberman et al., 2006). Recent trends show that this challenge is more important than ever. We need to design environments that allow users who do not necessarily have a background in programming to develop or modify their applications, with the ultimate aim of empowering them to flexibly employ digital services.

Since the origins of computing, hardware and software architectures have become more sophisticated, higher-level programming languages have been invented, and computer programming has evolved into a profession whose practices diverged from those of end users. The emergence of a (global) software industry was based on some interesting related aspects:

(a) development of ever more powerful hardware – following Moore's law for long time
(b) abstracting programs from the particularities of the hardware they ran on
(c) creating layered software architectures with well-defined interfaces to build upon each other
(d) abstracting software design from the particularities of specific work practices that the Information Technology (IT) artefacts were supposed to support

These developments contributed to the emergence of affordable and widely applied digital services. While in the beginning computing was restricted to rather few work domains in natural science, engineering, and accounting, we are now in the situation that IT is penetrating all aspects of life for a steadily increasing part of the world's population. So, the design of computer applications interacts with social practices in a vast variety of domains (Wulf et al., 2017). However, the software industry is still based on a division of labour between program creation at design time and use at run time.

With the increased spread of digital services and their resulting deep interaction with social practices, the traditional division of labour has become problematic, mainly for two reasons:

(1) Modern societies have become more and more differentiated in their patterns of life. Therefore, requirements for IT artefacts are very diverse and specific to individual application domains. The differentiated nature of software requirements is difficult to fully extract at design time for reasons of (a) problems in understanding the detailed social practices in all application domains, (b) lacking manpower in terms of software developers, and (c) economic efficiency.
(2) Social practices change rather dynamically. This is due to increasingly more dynamic environments in which organizations and individuals act. Moreover, the appropriation of digital services artefacts may impact social practices, individual qualifications and preferences, and may once again lead to new requirements for them.

The field of end-user development (EUD) emerged as an approach to overcoming these issues. In challenging the existing division of labour, EUD enables domain experts to (re-)design their applications in use – often at run time. In line with the Lieberman et al. (2006) definition, we suggest that:

> End-User Development should be understood as a set of methods, techniques, and tools that allow users who are acting as non-professional software developers of a specific application environment at some point to create, modify or extend an IT artefact.

The "development" concept in the term EUD has sociotechnical implications and thus indicates an important interdependency: on the one hand, it requires design environments enabling end users to modify their digital services; on the other hand, by appropriating the design environment, end users can potentially further develop their skills and practices. The immaterial property of software offers high-level technical flexibility in the sense that its functionality can be modified at any time – at least in theory.

EUD strives to change the traditional labour organization in the software industry by adding tools for end users to modify existing and to develop new applications. Existing software development cycles are still too slow to quickly respond to rapidly changing user needs of variegated categories of users, and professional developers often lack the needed domain knowledge to address such requirements, especially in pervasive modern applications (Ghiani et al., 2017). End users are generally neither skilled nor interested in adapting their applications at the same level as software professionals. So, EUD tools need to be appropriately crafted at application design time to anticipate technical flexibility that will be needed during their use.

Moreover, given new trends in hardware production, EUD does not even need to be understood as restricted to software. Technologies such as 3D printing or laser cutting enable end users to even modify aspects of hardware artefacts in use – thus also starting to challenge the traditional division of labour in hardware production (Ludwig et al., 2017).

The second aspect of the interdependency regards an emancipatory perspective on the development of human actors' capabilities and social practices. Engaging in adapting IT artefacts involves learning on the users' part and may lead to their personal and collective development. For an explicit investigation into this relationship see Dittrich et al. (in this volume), who discuss two cases of EUD in the context of organizations that depend on an IT infrastructure to provide their services. In both cases, EUD was used not only to personalize technical support but also to maintain and evolve the organizations' infrastructure. Thus, EUD was in both cases a constituent part of the innovation capability of the organizations. Therefore, EUD also has a societal dimension since it enables the codesign of work places as well as the full participation of citizens in the emerging Information Society (Fischer et al. in this volume).

Possibilities for EUD need to be intentionally designed into the application environment. Since EUD environments do not typically allow users to fundamentally redesign software architectures, EUD requires foreseen in which aspects of an applications' functionality will remain stable over time (Stiemerling et al., 1997; Stevens et al., 2006). Cabitza and Simone (in this volume) suggest a layered perspective on the architectural design of malleable applications. Wulf et al. (2008) explored opportunities for such architectures in the context of a component-oriented software paradigm.

One important issue is how to design the tools to support application personalization, specifically the level of complexity to offer from a user's point of view. The literature provides different classification schema of the technical means by which end users could be enabled to modify their IT artefacts (e.g. Henderson & Kyng, 1991; Morch et al., 2004). Lieberman et al. (2006) distinguish broadly between parameterization and customization as well as program modification and creation.

It is generally assumed that an EUD-friendly design environment should enable a seamless move from the usage mode of interaction towards an adaptation mode (Wulf & Golombek, 2001). Additionally, the different levels of adaptations should be designed in a way that the transition towards higher levels of complexity is supported. MacLean et al. (1990) suggested the design metaphor of a "gentle slope of complexity." AI techniques, for example, adaptivity may play a role in enabling the different transitions and support certain EUD activities. They typically result in mixed forms of interactions where adaptive features can support interaction but users can still take the initiative in the development process and may provide interesting results.

Since EUD is a sociotechnical activity, it requires analysing how to empower development in its interdependent sociotechnical aspects. Blackwell et al. (in this volume) aim to categorize the differences among end-user developers from a psychological perspective. Future work will address the design implications of such investigations.

There is definitively a collaborative dimension in EUD activities (Mørch & Mehandjiev, 2000; Wulf, 1999; Kahler, 2001). Actors learn from each other and cooperate when conducting EUD. A routinization of such collaborative patterns can lead to a division of labour among end users in conducting adaptations and sharing tailored artefacts of different types and levels of complexity. Supporting collaborative patterns in EUD is also an interesting theme in design research. This line of research includes recommendations and awareness mechanisms for finding suitable EUD expertise as well as reusable artefacts. EUD-related communities allow end users to share EUD-related knowledge and artefacts with their peers (Costabile et al., 2003; Pipek & Kahler, 2006; Draxler & Stevens, 2011).

There are other approaches to differentiate the division of labour in the software industry by involving users more intensively into the design process; examples of such approaches are Open Source Development, Software Ecosystems, Prototyping, Participatory Design, Agile methods (see, for instance, Diaz et al. in this volume). However, they all focus on design time activities.

EUD is an activity with sociocultural implications, depending on place, time, and people involved. This is particularly true with the explosion of mobile technologies, which has made it possible for people to access their applications from a variety of contexts of use that differ in terms of available devices, things, and services, and that require specific actions when various types of events occur. Differences in EUD practice are likely to develop for different application scenarios, cultures, and languages. These differences may relate to who is in control of EUD activities, the relation between individual and collaborative EUD, and how communities of end-user developers are organized.

At the same time, theory-oriented research in EUD has a long history and may also contribute to the community's efforts towards engineering and reengineering software applications. For example, deSouza (in this volume) discusses the use of Semiotic Engineering to stimulate design-oriented EUD research from a specific conceptual perspective. The chapter by Burnett et al. (in this volume) discusses how theoretical foundations may facilitate the transferability of insights beyond individual tools to the creation of generally applicable methods and principles for other researchers to draw upon.

Comparing the current technological scenario with the state of the art when the first EUD book was published in 2006, the most important technological revolution has been the advent of the Internet of Things. Our life is now characterized by the presence of a multitude of sensors, objects, and devices. This technological trend has posed new challenges for EUD as well. Paternò and Santoro (in this volume) discuss a framework that provides opportunities to identify important aspects to be considered when analysing EUD in Internet of Things domains. In this area, Diaz et al. (in this volume) discuss tools to support the ideation, design, and early prototyping of augmented experience.

This book also presents examples of how EUD research has expanded into specifically interesting and emerging domains: Menestrina and De Angeli discuss how computer games can benefit from a EUD approach, in particular those games designed for a purpose other than entertainment; Valtolina and Barriccelli report on their experience with an EUD framework to support the "quantified self" concept during sport activities; Morch et al. speak about their experience concerning EUD and learning in the 3D virtual world Second Life; Reuter et al. discuss how EUD can support the gathering and assessment process of data from social networks in emergency situations.

From a technological perspective, the Web is the most diffuse and penetrating technological infrastructure. Various mashup environments have been proposed to support the development of new applications starting with components of existing ones. Ardito et al. show how they can be exploited within a three-layer meta-design model. In this area, Aldalur et al. provide a review of Web Augmentation technologies (aimed at improving existing Web applications) as tools and techniques for EUD.

New application domains and emerging new technologies drive innovations in EUD. A key question is how to evaluate these innovations. Tetteroo and Markopulos (in this volume) and Ludwig et al. (in this volume) suggest that innovative EUD solutions need to be explored in practice. While laboratory evaluations or short-term rollouts can be found rather frequently in the literature, these methods do not provide a sufficient understanding regarding the appropriation of EUD technologies in social practices and how these technologies should be improved to encourage such practices (Wulf et al., 2017). Tetteroo and Markopulos discuss challenges pertaining to field deployments based on their experiences in the healthcare sector, coming up with some possible guidelines for the evaluation of EUD technologies.

Overall, we can see that in the last ten years there have been considerable research efforts to establishing the new EUD paradigm in all its different methodological aspects and application domains. Several chapters of this book report on long-term research strategies conducted by individual groups. For example, Myers et al. (in this volume) report on their efforts aiming to better understand how end users think about their tasks, and how to support them to express those tasks in ways closer to the way they think.

While we have better understood certain concepts and design implications of the EUD paradigm, we also realize that generally applicable solutions are (still) missing, important new application domains are materializing (e.g. customizing robot behaviour, personalizing ambient-assisted living, adapting smart home objects), and further research is required to identify how to exploit the potentialities of the EUD paradigm. In this context, we will have to better understand how to apply given insights to new problem domains.

So, we hope you will join us in this fascinating research endeavour!

References

Costabile, M.F., Fogli, D., et al. (2003). Building environments for end-user development and tailoring. In *IEEE symposia on human centric computing languages and environments*, Auckland.

Draxler, S., & Stevens, G. (2011). Supporting the collaborative appropriation of an open software ecosystem. *Computer supported cooperative work (CSCW), 20*(4–5), 403–448.

Ghiani, G., Manca, M., Paternò, F., Santoro, C. (2017). Personalization of context-dependent applications through trigger-action rules. *ACM Transactions on Computer-Human Interaction, 24*(2), Article N.14, April 2017.80). Programs, Life Cycles, and Laws of Software Evolution. IEEE 68.

Henderson, A., & Kyng, M. (1991). There's no place like home: continuing design in use. In J. Greenbaum, M. King, *Design at work - cooperative design of computer systems* (pp. 219–240). NJ, USA: L. Erlbaum Associates Inc. Hillsdale.

Kahler, H. (2001). *Supporting Collaborative Tailoring*. Roskilde: Department of Communication, Journalism and Computer Science, Roskilde University.

Lieberman, H., Paternó, F., Wulf, V. (Eds.). (2006). End user development. London: Springer.

Lieberman, H., Paternò, F., Klann, M., Wulf, V. (2006). End-user development: an emerging paradigm. In Lieberman, H., et al. (Eds.), *End user development* (pp. 1–8). London: Springer.

Ludwig, T., Boden, A., Pipek, V. (2017). 3D printers as sociable technologies: taking appropriation infrastructures to the internet of things. *Transactions on CHI, 24*(2), 17:1–17:28.

MacLean, A., Carter, K., Lövstrand, L., Moran, T. (1990, April 1–5). User-tailorable systems: pressing the issue with buttons. In *Proceedings of the conference on computer human interaction (CHI '90)* (pp. 175–182). Seattle: ACM-Press.

Mørch, A.I., & Mehandjiev, N.D. (2000). Tailoring as collaboration: the mediating role of multiple representations and application units. *Computer Supported Cooperative Work, 9*(1), 75–100.

Mørch, A. I., Stevens, G., Won, M., Klann, M., Dittrich, Y., Wulf, V. (2004). Component-based technologies for end-user development. *Communications of the ACM, 47*(9), 59–62.

Pipek, V., & Kahler, H. (2006). Supporting collaborative tailoring. In H. Lieberman, et al. (Eds.), *End user development* (pp. 315–354). London: Springer.

Stevens, G., Quaisser, G., Klann, M. (2006). Breaking it up: an industrial case study of component-based tailorable software design. In H.Lieberman, F. Paternò, V. Wulf, *End user development* (pp. 269–294). London: Springer.

Stiemerling, O., Kahler, H., Wulf, V. (1997). How to make software softer - designing tailorable applications. In *Proceedings of the ACM symposium on designing interactive systems (DIS 97), 18. - 20.8.1997* (pp. 365–376). Amsterdam, NL: ACM-Press.

Wulf, V. (1999). "Let's see your Search-Tool!" - collaborative use of tailored artifacts in groupware. In *Proceedings of GROUP '99* (pp. 50–60). New York: ACM-Press.

Wulf, V., & Golombek, B. (2001). Direct activation: a concept to encourage tailoring activities. *Behaviour & Information Technology, 20*(4), 249–263.

Wulf, V., Pipek, V., Randall, D., Rohde, M., Schmidt, K., Stevens, G. (Eds.). (2017). *Socio informatics – a practice-based perspective on the design and use of IT artefacts*. Oxford: Oxford University Press.

Wulf, V., Pipek, V., Won, M. (2008). Component-based tailorability: Enabling highly flexible software applications. *International Journal of Human-Computer Studies, 66*(1), 1–22.

Contents

Contributors

Ignacio Aedo Universidad Carlos III de Madrid, Madrid, Spain

Iñigo Aldalur University of the Basque Country (UPV/EHU), San Sebastián, Spain

Antonella De Angeli University of Lincoln, Lincoln, United Kingdom

Carmelo Ardito Università degli Studi di Bari Aldo Moro, Bari, Italy

Barbara R. Barricelli Università degli Studi di Milano, Milan, Italy

Laura Beckwith Configit, Atlanta, GA, United States

Andrea Bellucci Universidad Carlos III de Madrid, Madrid, Spain

Alan F. Blackwell University of Cambridge, Cambridge, United Kingdom

Johan Bolmsten World Maritime University, Malmö, Sweden

Margaret Burnett Oregon State University, Corvallis, OR, United States

Federico Cabitza University of Milano Bicocca, Milano, Italy

Jill Cao Oregon State University, Corvallis, OR, United States

Valentina Caruso Swiss Federal Institute for Vocational Education and Training, Zollikofen, Switzerland

Kerry Chang IBM, Armonk, NY, United States

Maria Francesca Costabile Università degli Studi di Bari Aldo Moro, Bari, Italy

Julian Dax University of Siegen, Siegen, Germany

Giuseppe Desolda Università degli Studi di Bari Aldo Moro, Bari, Italy

Oscar Díaz University of the Basque Country (UPV/EHU), San Sebastián, Spain

Paloma Díaz Universidad Carlos III de Madrid, Madrid, Spain

Yvonne Dittrich IT University, Copenhagen, Denmark

Jeanette Eriksson Malmö University, Malmö, Sweden

Shannon Ernst Oregon State University, Corvallis, OR, United States

Gerhard Fischer University of Colorado, Boulder, CO, United States

Daniela Fogli University of Brescia, Brescia, Italy

Valentina Grigoreanu Microsoft, Washington, DC, United States

Melissa M. Hartley West Virginia University, Morgantown, WV, United States

William Jernigan Oregon State University, Corvallis, OR, United States

Marc-André Kaufhold University of Siegen, Siegen, Germany

Mary Beth Kery Carnegie Mellon University, Pittsburgh, PA, United States

Andrew J. Ko University of Washington, Seattle, WA, United States

Todd Kulesza Microsoft, Washington, DC, United States

Toby Jia-Jun Li Carnegie Mellon University, Pittsburgh, PA, United States

Thomas Ludwig University of Siegen, Siegen, Germany

Panos Markopoulos Eindhoven University of Technology, Eindhoven, Netherlands

Maristella Matera Politecnico di Milano, Piazza Leonardo da Vinci, Milano, Italy

Zeno Menestrina University of Trento, Povo, Italy

Anders I. Mørch University of Oslo, Oslo, Norway

Brad A. Myers Carnegie Mellon University, Pittsburgh, PA, United States

Alannah Oleson Oregon State University, Corvallis, OR, United States

Stephen Oney University of Michigan, Ann Arbor, MI, United States

Philippe Palanque University of Toulouse, Toulouse, France

Fabio Paternò CNR-ISTI, HIIS Laboratory, Pisa, Italy

Antonio Piccinno University of Bari "Aldo Moro", Bari, Italy

Volkmar Pipek University of Siegen, Siegen, Germany

Christian Reuter University of Siegen, Siegen, Germany

Carmen Santoro CNR-ISTI, HIIS Laboratory, Pisa, Italy

Chris Scaffidi Oregon State University, Corvallis, OR, United States

Carla Simone University of Siegen, Siegen, Germany

Clarisse Sieckenius de Souza Semiotic Engineering Research Group (SERG), PUC-Rio, Rio de Janeiro, Brasil

Daniel Tetteroo Eindhoven University of Technology, Eindhoven, Netherlands

Stefano Valtolina Università degli Studi di Milano, Milan, Italy

Marco Winckler University of Toulouse, Toulouse, France

Volker Wulf University of Siegen, Siegen, Germany

YoungSeok Yoon Google, Mountain View, CA, United States

Making End User Development More Natural

Brad A. Myers, Andrew J. Ko, Chris Scaffidi, Stephen Oney,
YoungSeok Yoon, Kerry Chang, Mary Beth Kery and Toby Jia-Jun Li

Abstract When end users approach a development task, they bring with them a set of techniques, expressions, and knowledge, which can be leveraged in order to make the process easier. The *Natural Programming Project* has been working for over twenty years to better understand how end users think about their tasks, and to develop new ways for users to express those tasks that will be more "natural," by which we mean closer to the way they think. Our chapter in the previous book covered the first 10 years of this research; and here we summarize the most recent 10 years. This includes studies on barriers that impede EUD, and a new tool that helps with the understanding and debugging barriers by showing developers *why* their program has its current behavior. We also describe a tool that we created to

B.A. Myers (✉) · M.B. Kery · T.J.-J. Li
Carnegie Mellon University, Pittsburgh, PA, United States
e-mail: bam@cs.cmu.edu

M.B. Kery
e-mail: mkery@andrew.cmu.edu

T.J.-J. Li
e-mail: tobyli@cs.cmu.edu

A.J. Ko
University of Washington, Seattle, WA, United States
e-mail: ajko@uw.edu

C. Scaffidi
Oregon State University, Corvallis, OR, United States
e-mail: scaffidc@eecs.oregonstate.edu

S. Oney
University of Michigan, Ann Arbor, MI, United States
e-mail: soney@umich.edu

Y. Yoon
Google, Mountain View, CA, United States
e-mail: youngseokyoon@google.com

K. Chang
IBM, Armonk, NY, United States
e-mail: kerry.chang@ibm.com

© Springer International Publishing AG 2017   1
F. Paternò, V. Wulf (eds.), *New Perspectives in End-User Development*,
DOI 10.1007/978-3-319-60291-2_1

help EUDs input, process, and transform data in the context of spreadsheets and web pages. Interaction designers are a class of EUDs that may need to program interactive behaviors, so we studied how they naturally express those behaviors, and then built a spreadsheet-like tool to allow them to author new behaviors. Another spreadsheet tool we created helps EUDs access web service data without writing code, and extends the familiar spreadsheet to support analyzing the acquired web-based hierarchical data and programming data-driven GUI applications. Finally, EUDs often need to engage in *exploratory programming*, where the goals and tasks are not well-formed in advance. We describe new tools to help users selectively undo past actions, along with on-going research to help EUDs create more efficient behaviors on smartphones and facilitate variations when performing data analysis.

Keywords Spreadsheets · exploratory programming · data analysis · the Natural Programming Group

1   Introduction

The Natural Programming group at Carnegie Mellon University (CMU) has been working for nearly 20 years on applying methods from Human-Computer Interaction (HCI) in order to make programming easier. We have applied this research to professional developers (Myers, Ko, LaToza, & Yoon, 2016), to learners who are trying to become professional developers, and to end-user developers (EUDs). Our key strategy is to study the target developers to understand what their current problems are, and then try to design new languages and tools that will address those problems. We try to make programming be a more "natural" process for the developers, by which we mean *closer to the way the developers think about their tasks*. The goal is to reduce the size of the gulfs of execution and evaluation as articulated by Don Norman (1988) – to make it easier for developers to implement what they have in mind and to understand the state of their program. This is also motivated by the *cognitive dimension* of "Closeness of Mapping," which says: "The closer the programming world is to the problem world, the easier the problem-solving ought to be" (Green & Petre, 1996). The Natural Programming methodology helps us understand how to bring those worlds closer together.

In the early days of the Natural Programming project, as reported in our chapter for the previous version of the *End User Development* book, we studied how non-programmers think about programming tasks, and used that knowledge to develop a more usable programming language for children (Pane & Myers, 2006). This chapter summarizes our work since then that has been focused on EUDs:

- We studied learners and identified debugging as a key stumbling block, which has been surprisingly ignored in many previous tools for EUDs (Ko, Myers, & Aung, 2004). We developed a new tool called the "Whyline" which helps EUDs answer a key question – *why* did or didn't something happen with a program (Ko & Myers, 2004).
- Most of the data on which EUDs' code operates are richly structured, yet mostly must be operated on as strings. The "Topes" system allows EUDs to express the constraints and structure of their data (Scaffidi, Myers, & Shaw, 2008).

- One class of EUDs that our group has addressed are interaction designers, who often must now program in HTML/CSS/JavaScript in order to achieve their desired behaviors. We first studied how interaction designers think about their tasks (Myers, Park, Nakano, Mueller, & Ko, 2008; Ozenc, Kim, Zimmerman, Oney, & Myers, 2010), and then designed a new tool, called **InterState** that tries to enable a more natural way for interaction designers to express those behaviors (Oney, Myers, & Brandt, 2014).

- Spreadsheets remain a key tool for EUDs to do data analyses, but much modern data now comes from web services in hierarchical XML or JSON formats. We developed the "Gneiss" tool to enable EUDs to create their own data analysis and web applications using hierarchical data from web services using familiar spreadsheet languages and interaction techniques (Chang & Myers, 2014a, 2014b, 2016).

- Much programming by EUDs and professionals is *exploratory*, in that the developer does not necessarily know the correct code to write before starting, and therefore must try out different code, often by *backtracking* or reverting old code (Yoon & Myers, 2014). However, there is surprisingly little support for this exploration in programming environments. We are studying this problem as part of a large, multi-institution project called "Variations to Support Exploratory Programming" (http://www.exploratoryprogramming.org/). One approach is to facilitate *undoing* of the unwanted edits. The "Azurite" tool supports selective undo, to allow developers to go back and undo edits while retaining desired edits that happened afterwards (Yoon, Koo, & Myers, 2013; Yoon & Myers, 2015). One application of this is *regional undo*, where all the edits for a selected section of code can be undone without affecting any other code.

- A current project is looking at better support for data scientists in their exploratory programming. Many data scientists are EUDs, using languages such as Excel, R, or Python, and often need to try out different algorithms, libraries and parameter values, for which there is little support. The "Variolite" tool provides many features, including light-weight variants, to support EUD explorations (Kery, Horvath, & Myers, 2017).

- Finally, another new project, called "Sugilite," supports EUD on mobile phones, especially to help with complex and repetitive multi-app tasks. This multimodal system can learn how to perform arbitrary tasks using third-party Android apps from the user's demonstration, and generalizes the automation by finding parameters and their possible alternative values from the users' verbal commands and the third-party apps' UI structures (Li, Azaria, & Myers, 2017).

The following sections discuss these projects in more detail.

2 Whyline

One of the most difficult tasks in end user development is *debugging*, or trying to find the code in a program that is causing an unwanted behavior. In our lab, we wanted to discover novel ways of making debugging easier, faster, and more successful. To begin, we asked *how do EUDs think about debugging?*

To find out, we observed many EUDs trying to fix bugs, and discovered many slow, unproductive strategies (Ko & Myers, 2005; Ko, Myers, Coblenz, & Aung, 2006). Less experienced EUDs would just read their code and change things they thought *might* be wrong. This often introduced *new* defects, rather than resolving the original ones. More experienced EUDs used breakpoint debuggers to step through a program's execution, looking for where it deviated from the expected behavior. For non-trivial programs, this involved inspecting thousands of lines of code, which required so much vigilance that many EUDs skipped right over the bug. The most experienced EUDs *guessed* what the defect might be and set breakpoints to see if their guess was right. If it was, or if it was close, this was effective – unfortunately, the space of possible defects was often so large, most guesses were wrong, and these EUDs had to spend minutes, if not hours discovering that their hypothesis was incorrect. When we compared these strategies to those of novices and professionals, we found that even experienced professional developers guessed wrong the first time (but were faster at investigating their hypotheses).

In all of these observations, we noticed one recurring trend: every search for a defect began with a question about *program output* such as "Why didn't that animation start?," "Why did this error dialog appear?," or "Why is this button disabled?" We realized that EUDs were starting their search with something they were certain about – the faulty output – and trying to retrieve information about its causes. This led to a compelling idea: what if EUDs could ask these "why" and "why not" questions directly and a tool could simply answer them by showing the *causes* of the faulty output?

Our breakthrough insight was that programs *specify* the output they produce in the form of API calls: programs have print statements, they call graphics rendering libraries, they call audio libraries, and so on. What our tool had to do was identify these output statements and then present a user interface for EUDs to select which output they wanted to ask "why" and "why not" about.

We built our prototype for the Alice programming environment, which enables EUDs to create interactive 3D virtual worlds (Ko & Myers, 2004). As Fig. 1 shows, our interface, which is called the Whyline, lets EUDs pause the program, click on a "why" menu that contained all of the possible program's output, and then select a question. To answer "why" questions, the Whyline keeps a detailed execution history that stores the *data* and *control* dependencies of every instruction executed in the program, allowing the Whyline to identify every upstream cause of a selected program output, and display those causes to help EUDs find the source of the unwanted output. To answer "why not" questions, the Whyline analyzes the static control dependencies that prevented the desired output statement from executing, showing all of the conditions that were not satisfied that would have enabled the output to execute. Fig. 1 shows an example of a "why not" explanation.

Did the Whyline actually help? Over the course of several studies (Ko & Myers, 2004, 2009), the answer was clearly yes, showing that EUDs using the Whyline could localize defects anywhere from 2 to 8 times faster than EUDs using conventional breakpoint debuggers. Our results showed these increases in

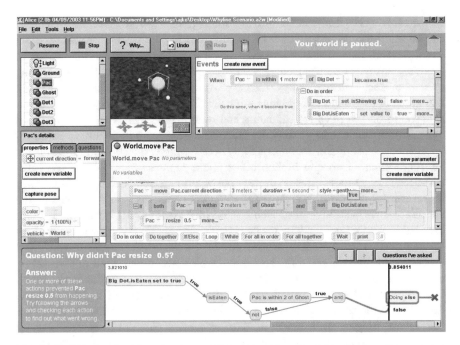

Fig. 1 The Whyline for Alice, showing an EUD asking why a Pac Man character did not resize, as expected. The Whyline explains that that it would have resized, but the condition that guarded the behavior was false

debugging speed were due to a change in the structure of an EUD's debugging task: rather than having to iteratively guess the defect and check if they were correct, EUDs could work backwards from something they were *certain* was wrong directly to the source code that caused it. The Whyline prevented speculation, and instead encouraged EUDs to focus on facts. Further, we found that the Whyline's benefits generalize beyond EUDs and can also be effective in helping more experienced developers debug Java programs (Ko & Myers, 2010). Thus, our initial observations of EUDs' bug fixing strategies informed the design of a technique that is useful for both EUDs and for traditional developers.

3 Topes

Much of the data that EUDs deal with must be represented in programming systems as strings, including names, job titles, part numbers, ID numbers, locations, etc. In fact, according to one study, 40% of spreadsheet cells contained non-numeric, non-formula textual data (Fisher & Rothermel, 2004). Software applications offer poor support for operating on these data, so EUDs must write their own code for working with them. Parsing, categorizing, validating, and reformatting these data can be difficult for several reasons. First, each category can be multi-format in that each of its instances can be written several different ways. Second, many useful categories are probabilistic rather than binary – each category can include questionable values that are unusual yet still valid. During user tasks, such unusual strings often are worthy of double-checking, as they are neither obviously valid nor obviously invalid. Third, each category is application-agnostic in that its rules for validating and reformatting strings are not specific to one software application – rather, its rules are agreed upon implicitly or explicitly by members of an organization or society. For example, a web form might have a field for entering Carnegie Mellon office phone numbers like "8-5150" or "412-268-5150." EUD tools offer no convenient way to create code for putting strings into a consistent format, nor do they help users create code to detect inputs that are unusual but possibly valid, such as "7-5150" (since CMU office phone numbers rarely start with "7"). The result is that end-users must often manually clean up their data, or leave the data unchecked.

In order to help users with their tasks, we created a new kind of abstraction called a "tope" and a supporting development environment (Scaffidi et al., 2008). Each tope describes how to validate and reformat instances of a data category. Topes are sufficiently expressive for creating useful, accurate rules for validating and reformatting a wide range of data categories commonly encountered by EUDs. By creating and applying topes, EUDs can validate and reformat strings more quickly and effectively than they can with other techniques. Tope implementations are reusable across applications and by different people, highlighting the leverage provided by EUD research aimed at developing new kinds of application-agnostic abstractions. The topes model demonstrates that such abstractions can be successful if they model a shallow level of semantics, thereby retaining usability without sacrificing usefulness for supporting users' real-world goals.

The Topes system includes tools that allow EUDs to define their own categories, including checking whether a string is of the desired format, and ways to convert strings into various valid formats. For example, in Fig. 2, the user is defining two variations of a "person name," which share the same parts. The system will use this definition to generate code for use in spreadsheets and web pages for validating and transforming strings representing person names. For constraints that are "almost always" true, the system will generate warnings instead of errors for violations. In a small user study, EUDs were able to create such definitions and the system proved highly effective at helping EUDs to create abstractions for validating strings.

4 InterState

Creating a good user interface requires more than carefully arranging the graphical elements that define its appearance. It also requires defining the interface's *behavior* – how it reacts to user input and other events. Although sketches and drawing software

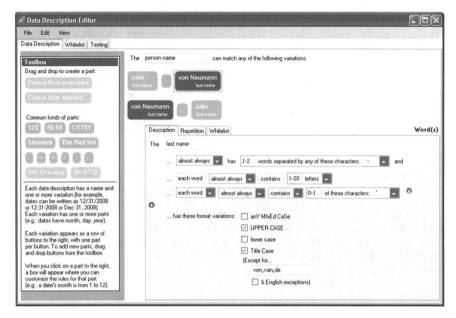

Fig. 2 Dragging and dropping a prototype's icon from the Toolbox creates a new part, and the editor also supports drag/drop rearrangement of parts as well as copy/paste. Users can click the example in a part's icon to edit it, while clicking other parts of the icon displays widgets for editing its constraints, which are shared by every instance of the part. Clicking the "+" icon adds a constraint while clicking the "x" icon deletes the constraint

make it relatively straightforward to define an interface's appearance, correctly implementing its behavior requires programming skill. The event-callback model, which most user interface frameworks rely on to define interface behaviors, has several drawbacks that make it inappropriate for EUDs (Meyerovich et al., 2009; Myers, 1991; Oney, Myers, & Brandt, 2012). We explore how to enable interaction designers who are EUDs to program behaviors themselves by extending the spreadsheet model of programming.

In order to explore a more usable way for EUDs to define interactive behaviors, we started with studies on how non-programmers naturally describe interactive behaviors (Park, Myers, & Ko, 2008). We also conducted workshops to better understand communication barriers between interaction designers and developers (Ozenc et al., 2010). Based on the results of those studies, we iteratively designed a new framework for letting interaction designers define GUI behaviors, called the *state-constraint framework*. This framework combines *constraints* – which allow developers to define relationships among elements that are maintained by the system – and *state machines* – which track the status of an interface. In the state-constraint framework, developers write interactive behaviors by defining constraints that are enforced when the interface is in specific states (Oney et al., 2012, 2014). We implemented the state-constraint framework

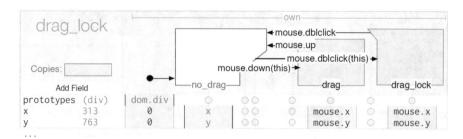

Fig. 3 An illustration of a basic InterState object, named drag_lock. Properties, which control drag_lock's display, are represented as rows (e.g. x, and y). States and transitions are represented as columns (e.g. no_drag, drag, and drag_lock). An entry in a property's row for a particular state specifies a constraint that controls property's value in that state; while drag_lock is in the drag state, x and y will be constrained to mouse.x and mouse.y respectively, meaning drag_lock will follow the mouse while dragging. Note that in this example, when the user performs a double click to initiate drag lock, the drag_lock object does enter and then leave the drag state intermittently as a result of the mouse.down and mouse.up events that are fired during a double click

in InterState (Oney et al., 2014), an interactive spreadsheet-like graphical environment for EUDs.

InterState reduces the number of control structures that new developers need to learn in order to write UI behaviors. Developers can express UI behaviors using simple expressions – which are like spreadsheet equations – that define constraints and transitions among states. InterState's visual notation concisely represents interactive behaviors as a table whose rows are properties and whose columns are states. This visual notation allows developers to see which events affect a property by scanning the property's row and which properties an event affects by looking at that event's column, as Fig. 3 illustrates.

InterState also includes a *live editor* that helps reduce the "gulf of evaluation" in determining the effects of a change, which has been shown to be a significant barrier for both EUDs and experienced developers. In InterState, edits are immediately reflected in the running application and changes in runtime state and property values are highlighted in the editor, which enables quick experimentation and parameter tuning. The live editor also allows the developer to always have a running application by "localizing" errors. This means that only the parts of the program that depend on problematic expressions are not executed, which avoids confronting EUDs with dozens of syntax and runtime errors.

A comparative laboratory study indicated that InterState can be effective in helping users who do not have prior UI programming experience understand and modify code. Even developers with JavaScript experience were significantly faster at understanding and modifying UI code in InterState compared to using JavaScript (Oney et al., 2014). Further, in order to test InterState's scalability, we implemented several complex user interfaces, finding that by many metrics (such as number of control structures and amount of space), InterState's implementation is more concise than the alternative JavaScript implementation.

5 Gneiss

Today, more and more data are moving to the cloud, and many companies provide *web services* that let people access web data programmatically. Web services allow developers to make custom use of various kinds of online data. Many web services also provide computational services that can analyze or transform the user's data. While web services are powerful tools that make the data and computing ability of the cloud available to people, using these web services currently requires significant programming expertise and effort.

The creation of Gneiss[1] was motivated by prior literature that shows that even professional developers found it difficult to use web services and often required learning new language features or libraries to complete their tasks (Zang, Rosson, & Nasser, 2008). Prior literature also showed that some EUDs want efficient ways to do custom data analysis that use multiple online data sources (Lin, Wong, Nichols, Cypher, & Lau, 2009). In Gneiss, we explored extending the spreadsheet model to support using web service data, since spreadsheet programming is popular among users of all programming levels from EUDs to professional developers and data analysts.

Gneiss makes contributions in extending spreadsheets to support new programming tasks that help EUDs work with online data. First, Gneiss introduces new UIs and interaction techniques to the familiar spreadsheet environment to enable users to send data to and retrieve data from web services without writing conventional code. Gneiss has a left pane (Fig. 4 at 1) that lets users load JSON data from REST web services. The user can send data from arbitrary spreadsheet cells by replacing any part of the web API with spreadsheet cell name (see Fig. 4 for an example), and extract data from the returned document in the left pane to the spreadsheet by selecting a field and dragging it to a spreadsheet column. Using the returned document's structure and the user's selection as an example, Gneiss will extract other similar fields in the document for the users, eliminating the need to write queries in languages such as XPath to select the desired data. Leveraging the spreadsheet's live programming, changes in spreadsheet cells used in a web service call will trigger Gneiss to immediately send a new API request using the cell's new value and in turn update the spreadsheet data. This makes a spreadsheet into an interactive platform for querying cloud data (Chang & Myers, 2014b).

Gneiss further enables spreadsheet users to create interactive web applications that can use and modify spreadsheet data (Chang & Myers, 2014a). Gneiss's right pane (Fig. 4 at 3) is a web interface builder where the user can create web pages by dragging-and-dropping GUI elements from the right bar and editing the properties of an element in a table (Fig. 4 at 4 and 5). In Gneiss, each GUI element property in the web application is treated as a spreadsheet cell, so it can reference other

---

[1]Gneiss is a type of rock, pronounced like "nice." Here it stands for **G**athering **N**ovel **E**nd-user **I**nternet **S**ervices using **S**preadsheets.

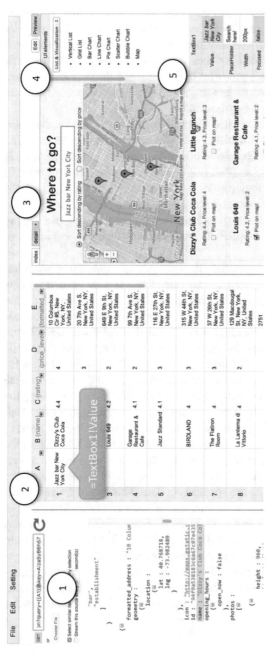

Fig. 4 Gneiss's user interface. (1) is the source pane where the user can load a web API in the URL box and view the returned JSON document. The user can send spreadsheet data to a web service by replacing parts of the web API with spreadsheet cell names. Here the user sends spreadsheet cell A1 to the web service as the value of the query parameter using the syntax {(A1)}. The user can extract fields from the returned JSON document to the center spreadsheet (2) by drag-and-drop. Here, spreadsheet column B-E hold four different fields extracted from the returned document in (1). (3) is the web interface builder where the user can create a web application by dragging-and-dropping GUI elements from the right toolbar (4) to the output page. The user can view and edit a selected GUI element's properties in (5). Here, (5) shows the properties of TextBox1 which is the search box in the output page. The textbox's Value property changes dynamically based on what the user enters in it (currently "Jazz bar New York City"). In the spreadsheet, cell A1 is set to be the value of the search box using the formula =TextBox1!Value, which is then sent to the web service in (1) as the query term to retrieve new data. GUI element properties in (3) can also use spreadsheet data as their values. For example, here the bold text in the grid list is set to show the data in spreadsheet column B using a spreadsheet formula

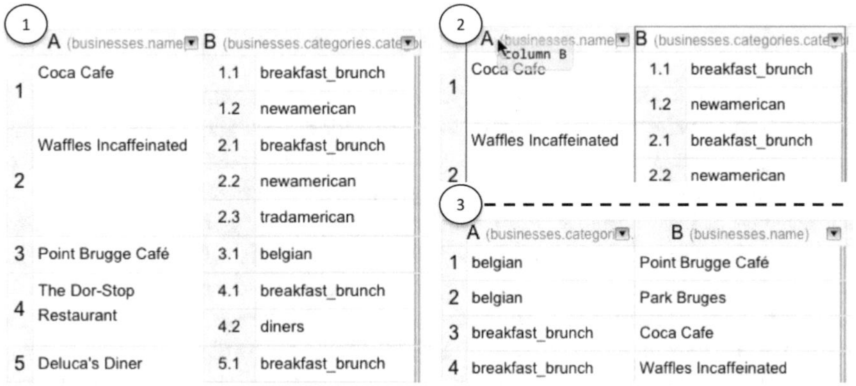

Fig. 5 Gneiss visualizes hierarchies in data using nested spreadsheet cells, and lets users restructure the data by any field by drag-and-dropping a column to a different location. Here, (1) shows a structured document of restaurant data grouped by restaurant names. The user can restructure this document to instead view the data by restaurant categories by dragging the categories column to the front of the names column (2 and 3)

spreadsheet cells and use functions to compute its value, and also be referenced in spreadsheet cells and functions to compute new values. This allows the use of spreadsheet languages to construct two-way data flow between a web page and a spreadsheet whose data can be local or from web services. Gneiss further introduces *interactive properties* in web GUI elements whose values change live based on how the user interacts with the elements. This enables the user to program many kinds of interactive behaviors in a web application, such as to search, sort, filter and visualize data using GUI controls, using spreadsheet languages without needing to write conventional event handler code (Chang & Myers, 2014a).

Finally, since most modern web services return hierarchical data such as JSON and XML data, we also extend spreadsheets to support hierarchical data, with control over how they are shown and manipulated in the spreadsheet (Chang & Myers, 2016). Gneiss introduces a new method to visualize hierarchical data as a spreadsheet using the relative hierarchical relationships among data in adjacent columns. Under this new visualization method, reshaping, regrouping, and joining hierarchical objects in a spreadsheet can be done using simple interaction techniques (see Fig. 5). This model also extends spreadsheet languages, sorting and filtering to support selecting and manipulating data by its hierarchies, allowing the user to calculate summaries of data using spreadsheet formulas without the need of pivot tables. In our user study, Gneiss helped spreadsheet users who were EUDs complete data exploration tasks that involve restructuring and joining two hierarchical JSON documents almost two times faster than Excel, and they even outperformed experienced programmers writing JavaScript or Python code doing the same tasks (Chang & Myers, 2016).

6 Azurite

Since developers are human, they often make mistakes while writing code. In other cases, developers intentionally make temporary changes to the code, either as an experiment or to help with debugging. As a consequence, developers often need to *backtrack* while coding, meaning that they revert their code back to an earlier state at least partially. For example, developers try out different values for various parameters. When developers try to learn an unfamiliar API, they might try writing some code and running it to see if the code works as expected, and if it does not, they backtrack and try something else. Backtracking support is much needed in *exploratory programming* (Sheil, 1983), where the correct solution to the given problem is not well known or when there are multiple potential solutions with their own strengths and weaknesses. Moreover, recent studies show that EUDs need easy access to past versions of their code as reference when rewriting parts of their code (Henley & Fleming, 2016; Kuttal, Sarma, & Rothermel, 2011).

However, we noticed that modern development tools for EUDs and professional programmers alike do not provide enough support for backtracking. The linear undo model used in development tools is not suitable for all situations. Notably, users can only undo the most recent edits, which can be very inconvenient when they realize their mistake after making some other changes that they want to keep. Another option is to use version control systems such as Subversion or Git, but backtracking is supported in these tools only if the desired code is already committed to the system, and version control is rarely used by EUDs (Grigoreanu, Fernandez, Inkpen, & Robertson, 2009).

To provide better backtracking support for developers, we first asked, *when and how do developers backtrack?* To answer this, we observed developers completing simple programming tasks in our lab, interviewed and surveyed developers about their backtracking experience, and finally collected and analyzed developers' coding logs while they are working on their own projects. Developers felt that backtracking happens quite frequently, and they had problems while backtracking, such as failing to locate the right code to be backtracked (Yoon & Myers, 2012). Our log analysis detected about 10 backtracking instances per hour, and for 34% of those backtracking situations, developers performed them manually by deleting or retyping code, confirming that there are backtracking situations not very well supported by existing tools (Yoon & Myers, 2014).

So how could we support backtracking better? One insight we had was that a *selective undo* in editors could help solve these backtracking problems. Users could use selective undo to revert only specific edits from the past, without affecting the following, more recent edits. Inspired by prior research in selective undo in the area of drawing editors (Berlage, 1994; Myers, 1998), we developed our tool Azurite[2], which is a selective undo tool that works in the Eclipse code editor.

---

[2]Azurite is a blue mineral, and here stands for **A**dding **Z**est to **U**ndoing and **R**estoring **I**mproves **T**extual **E**xploration.

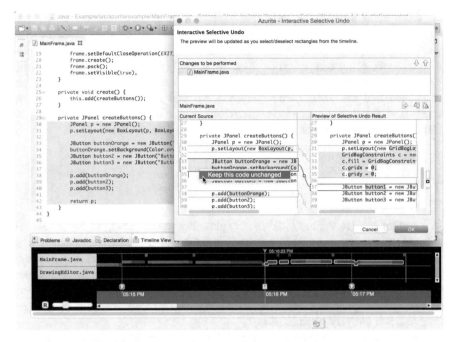

Fig. 6 An example screenshot of Azurite running in the Eclipse IDE. At the bottom, a timeline visualization of recent code changes is provided. The user is currently using the "Interactive Selective Undo" dialog, which is one of the more sophisticated selective undo features of Azurite

Although Eclipse is a tool mostly used by professional developers, the ideas explored in Azurite are relevant to EUD environments as well, since EUDs perform exploratory programming (Henley & Fleming, 2016; Kuttal et al., 2011), and must enter and edit their code.

Fig. 6 shows an example screenshot of the Azurite tool. The *timeline visualization*, shown at the bottom of Fig. 6, is the most basic user interface of Azurite, where the users can see the code change history by scrolling through it, select some past edits, and use the selective undo command (Yoon et al., 2013). All the fine-grained code changes are automatically tracked by the Azurite system, without users needing to manually commit their code. However, an important question still remains: how can users effectively and accurately find and select the desired edits which are to be undone?

The observations from our lab study showed that developers remember certain aspects about the code edits that they want to undo. Our goal was to provide a more natural way for users to express what they remember about the code changes. To this end, Azurite supports a rich set of user interfaces for selective undo besides the timeline visualization. One of the most popular form of selective undo Azurite provides is *regional undo*, where users can select some region of code in the editor and use a keyboard shortcut to perform selective undo directly on only that region. This feature was driven by our observation that users often remember the *location* of the code changes they want to undo (Yoon & Myers, 2015). With these selective undo features implemented, we evaluated whether Azurite actually helps developers perform backtracking better. Through a controlled lab study with 12 developers, we confirmed that the users could quickly learn and use the features during the study, and the Azurite users completed the given backtracking tasks twice as fast compared to when not using Azurite (Yoon & Myers, 2015).

7 Variolite

In a current project, we are looking at exploratory programming in the context of *data scientists*. The term "data scientist" is open-ended (and often disputed who exactly it includes), but here we use it simply to encompass a broad range of people who write programs to work with data. Analyzing data and using techniques such as machine learning is increasingly important to many professions, including, for example, engineering, medicine, marketing, and research. Individuals in these diverse fields are very often EUDs.

Current tools for data science include GUI-based tools like SPSS or WEKA for relatively straightforward analyses. For more complex data manipulation, individuals often turn to programming, using languages such as Excel, MatLab, R, or Python. While much recent research has gone into making GUI-based tools (mostly for machine learning) more accessible to EUDs (Amershi, Cakmak, Knox, & Kulesza, 2014; Yang et al., 2013), the act of coding in this context is less studied. A few recent studies of professional programmers (Hill, Bellamy, Erickson, & Burnett, 2016) and machine learning experts (Patel, 2013) working in data science tasks have pointed to real struggles that experts faces with exploratory programming.

When "what code should I implement?" or "what is the precise goal of my code?" are questions that cannot be answered at the start of a project, *exploratory programming* is a way of understanding the problem better through a trial-and-error approach with code. In a concrete sense, this means changing code, parameters, and data to test out new ideas until something works. With data science in particular, this process is unfortunately not always straightforward code development. *Non-linear* iteration (Patel, 2013) where an attempt that failed in the past may be fruitful in the future is quite common. For this reason, data scientists often try, and struggle, to keep track of their experiments (Hill et al., 2016). Experimentation can cause code to be more and more unstable, as new chunks of code are added, tested, discarded, and run on different sets of input files. As developers try to answer complex questions with their data, ideas tried so far can be difficult to keep track of and confusion and logic errors are very real threats (Hill et al., 2016; Patel, 2013). Understanding these coding practices and developing new kinds of supports for exploration are crucial to making this kind of work more accessible to EUDs.

To investigate this problem more closely, we approached 10 data scientists and interviewed them about their recent projects (Kery et al., 2017). We grounded these discussions by viewing and discussing artifacts that went with their projects, such as their code, data, file folders, and notes. We followed this with a survey of an additional 60 data scientists.

What does it mean to develop exploratory code? We found that developers currently use ad-hoc strategies for keeping track of their experiments' code and data. For example, developers in our study often rely on commenting and copying code, as well as keeping around old code to facilitate "versioning" of different ideas within the same file. For instance, in order to try different variations of an algorithm, one participant used copy-and-paste to create functions such as "analyis1," "analysis2" and alternated which one was run. Another participant used code comments to alternate their code's execution, sometimes in complex sets of code switched "on" or "off" using a code comment symbol. Through the survey, we found that informal versioning techniques such as these are widely used. Furthermore, we found that even among data scientist who actively use version control software (VCS) systems such as Git or SVN for *other* kinds of work, they predominantly chose to rely on informal techniques, rather than a VCS, for exploratory code.

Finding ways to support data scientists' needs with versioning and experiment-tracking may help make their explorations more robust. Informal versioning that data scientists currently rely on allows them to perform interactions which typical VCSs currently do not support. For example, a data scientist using simple copy/paste and text commands can create versions of any size chunk of code, whereas standard VCS only support versions at the file level. Furthermore, with informal techniques, there is a far lower learning curve for EUDs who do not know VCS, since they can simply leverage their text editing skills to explore variants, rather than learning a new tool.

We created Variolite,[3] an extension to the Atom editor, to investigate new kinds of support for data science versioning (Kery et al., 2017). In Variolite (Fig. 7), a developer can select any size piece of code and issue the command "wrap in variant." This wraps the code chunk in a box, which can be tabbed, similar to a web browser, to keep different local versions of that code on different tabs. We used participatory design for Variolite by showing initial sketches of potential design ideas to data scientists and getting their feedback. In a preliminary usability test of an implemented version of Variolite with 10 participants, who were a mix of novice and advanced developers, the majority found this interaction usable and desirable. We are continuing work on Variolite, and are investigating new ways to support data scientists in their exploratory code.

---

[3]Variolite, which is a kind of rock structure, here stands for **V**ariations **A**ugment **R**eal **I**terative **O**utcomes **L**etting **I**nformation **T**ranscend **E**xploration.

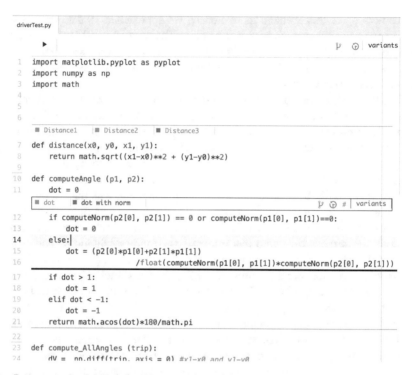

```
driverTest.py

    ▶                                                          ⅋   ⊙   variants
1   import matplotlib.pyplot as pyplot
2   import numpy as np
3   import math
4
5
6
    ■ Distance1    ■ Distance2    ■ Distance3
7   def distance(x0, y0, x1, y1):
8       return math.sqrt((x1-x0)**2 + (y1-y0)**2)
9
10  def computeAngle (p1, p2):
11      dot = 0
    ■ dot    ■ dot with norm                              ⅋   ⊙   #   variants
12      if computeNorm(p2[0], p2[1]) == 0 or computeNorm(p1[0], p1[1])==0:
13          dot = 0
14      else:|
15          dot = (p2[0]*p1[0]+p2[1]*p1[1])
16                      /float(computeNorm(p1[0], p1[1])*computeNorm(p2[0], p2[1]))
17      if dot > 1:
18          dot = 1
19      elif dot < -1:
20          dot = -1
21      return math.acos(dot)*180/math.pi
22
23  def compute_AllAngles (trip):
24      dV = np.diff(trip, axis = 0) #x1-x0 and y1-y0
```

Fig. 7 A screenshot of Variolite. Here are two variant boxes. An outer box wraps the distance and computeAngle functions, and has three versions "Distance1," "Distance2," "Distance3" that the user can flip among with tabs. The inner variant box has two versions "dot," and "dot with norm." Versioning that is visible within the text editor is meant to be more accessible to novices and EUDs

8 Sugilite

In recent years, mobile phones have evolved from being solely communication devices into ubiquitous tools that support a wide range of computing tasks, including information seeking, game playing, entertainment, and navigating. Mobile devices have exceeded PCs in internet usage (O'Toole, 2014) and have become the main computing device for many users (Smith, 2015). Thus, it is increasingly important to study how end-user development can be applied to enable end-users to create automations to help perform personalized computing tasks on mobile devices. In this section, we report on our ongoing project to create a new EUD tool named SUGILITE[4] (Li et al., 2017) to enable EUDs to automate mobile tasks using a Programming by Demonstration (PbD) approach

---

[4]Sugilite is named after a purple gemstone, and here stands for **S**martphone **U**sers **G**enerating **I**ntelligent **L**ikable **I**nterfaces **T**hrough **E**xamples.

Fig. 8 Screenshots of SUGILITE: (a) the conversational interface; (b) the recording confirmation popup; (c) the recording disambiguation/operation editing panel; and (d) the viewing/editing script window

(Cypher et al., 1993; Myers, McDaniel, & Wolber, 2000) combined with a conversational agent.

Tasks on mobile devices are often performed using mobile apps. Each app usually has limited functionality within a single domain. As a result, complex tasks often require the use of *multiple* apps (Sun, Chen, & Rudnicky, 2016). For example, planning a dinner event may require steps like searching for a restaurant, viewing the transportation options, determining scheduling information, making the actual reservation, and entering information into a calendar, where each step is performed with a different app. However, coordinating multiple apps is particularly challenging on mobile compared to on a computer due to the small screen size and limited support for multi-tasking and cross-app data sharing. For the most common scenarios of cross-app usage, the developers of the apps may implement features to support a few built-in data sharing mechanisms (e.g. the "Share To" button to share data from Photo Gallery to Messenger or Social Media Apps) or the API of services (e.g. Google Maps showing Uber fare estimates in the results). Nevertheless, the "long tail" of personalized mobile computing tasks are mostly not supported directly. This is where EUD can play an important role in enabling the users to create their own automations for repetitive mobile tasks in order to improve their efficiencies in mobile computing.

The SUGILITE system uses the Programming by Demonstration (PbD) approach. It has a multi-modal interface where the user can give a verbal command to execute an automation through a voice conversational interface (Fig. 8a), while making demonstrations (Fig. 8b, c) and editing existing scripts (Fig. 8c, d) using direct manipulation. In the background, SUGILITE detects the apps' user interface hierarchical structures, such as the menu tree, for all the activities that users visit. Then, SUGILITE combines the voice command, the actions recorded, and an analysis of the app's structures to infer generalizations of the script. This allows SUGILITE to learn a generalized script for the task from a single demonstration. SUGILITE also provides error handling and checking mechanisms that allow the user to demonstrate new steps to enable the script to handle new situations at runtime.

A major advantage of SUGILITE and the PbD approach compared to other Mobile EUD systems is that SUGILITE can automate tasks using *any* third-party Android app (with a few exceptions noted in the paper (Li et al., 2017)). It also enables the users to demonstrate directly in the interfaces of the third-party apps that they are already familiar with, which is particularly useful for EUDs.

In a lab study, 19 participants with various levels of programming experience (including seven non-programmers) were able to use SUGILITE to create automations for four tasks derived from common real-world smartphone usage scenarios with an 85.5% completion rate. No significant difference in either completion rate or completion time was found between participant groups with different levels of programming experience. The result also showed that for our four example tasks, using SUGILITE to automate tasks is more efficient timewise than using direct manipulation if a repetitive task is to be performed for more than 3 to 6 times (Li et al., 2017).

9   Lessons Learned and Implications for the Future

Here we collect some observations on EUD from our over twenty years of research in this area.

- Studying the target group of EUDs to investigate their *natural* ways to describe their tasks and procedures can reveal novel ways that the development system might operate. For example InterState's design was motivated by research into non-programmers' natural language descriptions of interface behaviors. Other design and evaluation methods from the human-computer interaction (HCI) area also have proven useful in improving our systems (Myers et al., 2016).
- Many of the problems that end user developers face are problems that professional developers face as well (Ko & Myers, 2005; Ko et al., 2006). The difference is that EUDs face them at a smaller scale and often with less experience, less effective strategies, and different motivation (Ko et al., 2011). Because of this overlap, our work has shown that it is often possible to make breakthroughs in professional developer tools by first starting with smaller scale EUD tools. For example, the ideas behind Gneiss, the Whyline, and InterState have been shown to benefit both EUDs and professional developers.
- Although debugging is just as important for EUDs as it is for professional developers, many EUD tools do not provide adequate debugging support. Even for the EUD tools that provide some debugging support, they often use the same techniques and metaphors as professional debugging tools. While teaching EUDs appropriate strategies is a great idea (Loksa et al., 2016), tools for EUDs can do a lot more to help with debugging, as shown by the Whyline.

- Although spreadsheets are an old tool, they are still a favorite EUD platform, and can be extended to support EUDs in several areas. We have presented three enhancements of spreadsheets – Topes, InterState and Gneiss, which extend what spreadsheets can process to more expressive strings, stateful formulas, web services and hierarchical data.
- Most EUDs use exploratory programming and write code that they may know they do not intend to keep, or which they plan to edit frequently, but this process is not supported by today's tools. Ideas such as visualizing edit history, selective undo, and light-weight variants have been shown to help.

10 Conclusions and Future Work

The Natural Programming Project has been studying end-user development and creating novel ways for end-users to create and debug their programs for many years, with much exciting research in progress. The "natural programming" approach has proven to be a useful way to understand the target users' real needs and what might be the appropriate ways to solve them. Across this work, we have found that supporting EUDs in all of these settings has required the same basic process: (1) understand what is difficult about a task, and then (2) identify ways of changing that task through new kinds of analyses and data.

For the future, we will continue to strive to produce a "gentle-slope system" where getting started with programming will be easy for EUDs, and there will be no walls that prevent them from learning what is needed to expand the kinds of programs they can build (Myers, Hudson, & Pausch, 2000). While we have made progress, research is still needed across all the topics mentioned above. In addition, the recent rise in computing power has made more powerful machine learning techniques such as deep learning possible, which computer scientists have leveraged to create artificial intelligence capable of complex tasks including driving automobiles, categorizing videos (Clark, 2012), learning games (Muncy, 2016), and doing science (Buchen, 2009). End-user programmers, each with their own unique and diverse needs and context, could potentially benefit from new systems enabling them to create artificial intelligences of their own. As the computing power of machines grows ever closer to that of animals, programming could some become as "natural" as training a dog.

Acknowledgements This article grows out of over 20 years of work by the Natural Programming group by more than 50 students, staff and postdocs in addition to the authors, and we thank them all for their contributions. The work summarized here has been funded at least by SAP, Adobe, IBM, Microsoft, Yahoo! and multiple NSF grants including CNS-1423054, IIS-1314356, IIS-1116724, IIS-0329090, CCF-0811610, IIS-0757511, and CCR-0324770. Any opinions, findings and conclusions or recommendations expressed in this material are those of the authors and do not necessarily reflect those of any of the sponsors.

References

Amershi, S., Cakmak, M., Knox, W. B., Kulesza, T. (2014). Power to the people: the role of humans in interactive machine learning. *AI Magazine, 35*(4), 105–120.

Berlage, T. (1994). A selective undo mechanism for graphical user interfaces based on command objects. *ACM Transactions on Computer Human Interaction. ACM Transactions on Computer Human Interaction, 1*(3), 269–294.

Buchen, L. (2009). Robot makes scientific discovery all by itself. *Wired UK Online.* https://www.wired.com/2009/04/robotscientist/.

Chang, K., & Myers, B.A. (2014a, October 5–8). Creating interactive web data applications with spreadsheets. In *UIST'14: ACM Symposium on User Interface Software and Technology* (pp. 87–96). Honolulu, Hawaii.

Chang, K., & Myers, B.A. (2014b, July 28–August 1). A spreadsheet model for using web service data. In *VL/HCC'14: IEEE Symposium on Visual Languages and Human-Centric Computing* (pp. 169–176). Melbourne, Australia.

Chang, K., & Myers, B.A. (2016, May 7–12). Using and exploring hierarchical data in spreadsheets. In *Proceedings CHI'2016: Human Factors in Computing Systems* (pp. 2497–2507). San Jose, CA.

Clark, L. (2012). Google's artificial brain learns to find cat videos. *Wired UK Online.* https://www.wired.com/2012/06/google-x-neural-network/.

Cypher, A., Halbert, D. C., Kurlander, D., Lieberman, H., Maulsby, D., Myers, B. A., Turransky, A. (1993). *Watch what I do: programming by demonstration.* Cambridge, MA: MIT Press.

Fisher, II, M., & Rothermel, G. (2004). *The EUSES spreadsheet corpus: a shared re-source for supporting experimentation with spreadsheet dependability mechanisms.* Lincoln: University of Nebraska. Technical Report 04-12-03.

Green, T. R. G., & Petre, M. (1996). Usability analysis of visual programming environments: a 'cognitive dimensions' framework. *Journal of Visual Languages and Computing, 7*(2), 131–174.

Grigoreanu, V., Fernandez, R., Inkpen, K., Robertson, G. (2009, September 20–24). What designers want: needs of interactive application designers. In *IEEE Symposium on Visual Languages and Human-Centric Computing, VL/HCC'09* (pp. 139–146). Corvallis, Oregon.

Henley, A.Z., & Fleming, S.D. (2016, September 4–8). Yestercode: improving code-change support in visual dataflow programming environments. In: *VL/HCC'16: IEEE Symposium on Visual Languages and Human-Centric Computing.* Cambridge.

Hill, C., Bellamy, R., Erickson, T., Burnett, M. (2016). Trials and tribula-tions of developers of intelligent systems: a field study. In *VL/HCC'2016: IEEE Symposium on Visual Lan-guages and Human-Centric Computing* (pp. 162–170). Denver, CO.

Kery, M.B., Horvath, A., Myers, B.A. (2017, May 6–11). Variolite: supporting exploratory programming by data scientists. In *Proceedings CHI'2017: Human Factors in Computing Systems* (pp. 1265–1276). Denver, CO.

Ko, A. J., Abraham, R., Beckwith, L., Blackwell, A., Burnett, M., Erwig, M., et al. (April, 2011). The state of the art in end-user software engineering. *ACM Computing Surveys, 43*(3), Article 21 44 pages.

Ko, A.J., & Myers, B.A. (2004, April 24–29). Designing the whyline, a debugging interface for asking why and why not questions about runtime failures. In *Proceedings CHI'2004: Human Factors in Computing Systems* (pp. 151–158). Vienna, Austria.

Ko, A. J., & Myers, B. A. (2005, February). A framework and methodology for studying the causes of software errors in programming systems. *Journal of Visual Languages and Computing, 16*(1), 41–84.

Ko, A.J., & Myers, B.A. (2009, April 4–9). Finding causes of program output with the java whyline. In *CHI'2009: Human Factors in Computing Systems* (pp. 1569–1578). Boston, MA.

Ko, A. J., & Myers, B. A. (2010, August). Extracting and answering why and why not questions about java program output. *ACM Transactions on Software Engineering and Methodology (TOSEM), 20*(2), Article 4 36 pages.

Ko, A.J., Myers, B.A., Aung, H.H. (2004, September 26–29). Six learning barriers in end-user programming systems. In *IEEE Symposium on Visual Languages and Human-Centric Computing (VL/HCC)* (pp. 199–206). Rome, Italy.

Ko, A. J., Myers, B. A., Coblenz, M., Aung, H. H. (2006, December). An exploratory study of how developers seek, relate, and collect relevant information during software maintenance tasks. *IEEE Transactions on Software Engineering, 33*(12), 971–987.

Kuttal, S.K., Sarma, A., Rothermel, G. (2011). History repeats itself more easily when you log it: versioning for mashup. In *IEEE Symposium on Visual Languages and Human-Centric Computing (VL/HCC)* (pp. 69–72). Pittsburgh, PA.

Li, T., Azaria, A., Myers, B. (2017, May 6–11). SUGILITE: creating multimodal smartphone automation by demonstration. In *Proceedings CHI'2017: Human Factors in Computing Systems* (pp. 6038–6049). Denver, CO.

Lin, J., Wong, J., Nichols, J., Cypher, A., Lau, T. A. (2009). End-user programming of mashups with vegemite. *Proceedings of the 14th International Conference on Intelligent User Interfaces* (pp. 97–106). Sanibel Island, FL: ACM.

Loksa, D., Ko, A. J., Jernigan, W., Oleson, A., Mendez, C. J., Burnett, M. M. (2016). Programming, problem solving, and self-awareness: effects of explicit guidance. *Proceedings of the 2016 CHI Conference on Human Factors in Computing Systems* (pp. 1449–1461). Santa Clara, CA: ACM.

Meyerovich, L. A., Guha, A., Baskin, J., Cooper, G. H., Greenberg, M., Bromfield, A., et al. (2009). Flapjax: a programming language for Ajax applications. *SIGPLAN Notices (Proc. OOPSLA'2009), 44*(10), pp. 1–20. 1640091.

Muncy, J. (2016). Making AI play lots of videogames could be huge (No, Seriously). *Wired UK Online.* https://www.wired.com/2016/04/videogames-ai-learning/.

Myers, B.A. (1991, November). Separating application code from toolkits: eliminating the spaghetti of call-backs. In *UIST'91: ACM SIGGRAPH Symposium on User Interface Software and Technology* (pp. 211–220). Hilton Head, SC.

Myers, B.A. (1998, April). Scripting graphical applications by demonstration. In *SIGCHI'98: Human Factors in Computing Systems* (pp. 534–541). Los Angeles, CA.

Myers, B. A., Hudson, S. E., Pausch, R. (2000, March). Past, present and future of user interface software tools. *ACM Transactions on Computer Human Interaction, 7*(1), 3–28.

Myers, B. A., Ko, A. J., LaToza, T. D., Yoon, Y. S. (2016, July). Programmer are users too: human centered methods to improve software development. *IEEE Computer, 49*(7), 44–52.

Myers, B., McDaniel, R., Wolber, D. (2000, March). Programming by example: intelligence in demonstrational interfaces. *Communications of the ACM, 43*(3), pp. 82–89.

Myers, B.A., Park, S.Y., Nakano, Y., Mueller, G., Ko, A. (2008, September 15–18). How designers design and program interactive behaviors. In *2008 IEEE Symposium on Visual Languages and Human-Centric Computing, VL/HCC'08* (pp. 185–188). Herrsching am Ammersee, Germany.

Norman, D. A. (1988). *The design of everyday things.* New York: Doubleday.

Oney, S., Myers, B.A., Brandt, J. (2012, October 7–10). ConstraintJS: programming interactive behaviors for the web by integrating constraints and states. In *UIST'2012: ACM Symposium on User Interface Software and Technology* (pp. 229–238). Cambridge, MA.

Oney, S., Myers, B.A., Brandt, J. (2014, October 5–8). InterState: a language and environment for expressing interface behavior. In *ACM Symposium on User Interface Software and Technology, UIST'14* (pp. 263–272). Honolulu, Hawaii.

O'Toole, J. (2014, February 28). Mobile apps overtake PC Internet usage in U.S. *CNN Money.* http://money.cnn.com/2014/02/28/technology/mobile/mobile-apps-internet/.

Ozenc, K., Kim, M., Zimmerman, J., Oney, S., Myers, B. (2010, April 10–15). How to support designers in getting hold of the immaterial material of software. In *CHI'2010: Human Factors in Computing Systems* (pp. 2513–2522). Atlanta, GA.

Pane, J. F., & Myers, B. A. (2006). More natural programming languages and environments. H. Lieberman, F. Paterno, V. Wulf (Eds.). *End-User development* (pp. 31–50). Dordrecht: Springer.

Park, S., Myers, B., Ko, A. (2008, September 15–18). Designers' natural descriptions of interactive behaviors. In *2008 IEEE Symposium on Visual Languages and Human-Centric Computing, VL/HCC'08* (pp. 185–188). Herrsching am Ammersee, Germany.

Patel, K. D. (2013). *Lowering the barrier to applying machine learning.* Seattle, WA: University of Washington. PhD Dissertation.

Scaffidi, C., Myers, B., Shaw, M. (2008, May 10–18). Topes: reusable abstractions for validating data. In *ICSE'08: International Conference on Software Engineering* (pp. 1–10). Leipzig, Germany.

Sheil, B. (1983, February). Environments for exploratory programming. In *Datamation*. Reprinted in in "Papers on Interlisp-D," Sheil, B.A. and Masinter, L.M., eds., Xerox PARC Tech Report CIS-5.

Smith, A. (2015, April 1). U.S. smartphone use in 2015. *Pew Research Center.* http://www.pewinternet.org/2015/04/01/us-smartphone-use-in-2015/.

Sun, M., Chen, Y.N., Rudnicky, A.I. (2016, March 10). Learning user intentions spanning multiple domains. In *Proceedings of IUI 2016 Workshop on Interacting with Smart Objects (SmartObjects 2016)*. Sonoma, California.

Yang, H., Pupons-Wickham, D., Chiticariu, L., Li, Y., Nguyen, B., Carreno-Fuentes, A. (2013). I can do text analytics!: designing development tools for novice developers. In *CHI'2013: Human Factors in Computing Systems* (pp. 1599–1608). Paris, France.

Yoon, Y.S., Koo, S., Myers, B.A. (2013, September 15–19). Visualization of fine-grained code change history. In *IEEE Symposium on Visual Languages and Human-Centric Computing (VL/HCC'13)* (pp. 119–126). San Jose, CA.

Yoon, Y.S., & Myers, B.A. (2012, June 2). An exploratory study of backtracking strategies used by developers. In *Cooperative and Human Aspects of Software Engineering (CHASE'2012), An ICSE 2012 Workshop* (pp. 138–144). Zurich, Switzerland.

Yoon, Y.S., & Myers, B.A. (2014, 28 July–1 August). A longitudinal study of programmers' backtracking. In *IEEE Symposium on Visual Languages and Human-Centric Computing (VL/HCC'14)* (pp. 101–108). Melbourne, Australia.

Yoon, Y.S., & Myers, B.A. (2015, May 16–24). Supporting selective undo in a code editor. In *37th International Conference on Software Engineering, ICSE 2015* (vol. 1; pp. 223–233). Florence, Italy.

Zang, N., Rosson, M.B., Nasser, V. (2008). Mashups: who? what? why? In *CHI'08 Extended Abstracts on Human Factors in Computing Systems* (pp. 3171–3176). New York, NY.

A Practice-Oriented Paradigm
for End-User Development

Thomas Ludwig, Julian Dax, Volkmar Pipek and Volker Wulf

Abstract What is end-user development (EUD) and when does a user become an end-user developer? Since the concept of EUD encompasses methods as well as practices of appropriating technology, it is not easy to answer these questions and several researchers already dealt with these issues. Within our chapter we suggest to conceptually extend our understanding of both EUD and the end user (developer). We draw on experiences we gained from past research exploring EUD in practice. We reflect upon the concepts of "gentle slope of complexity," "tailoring languages" and "appropriation" which we situate within the broader concept of "infrastructuring." We claim that EUD is given whenever an end user starts modifying the permanent aspects of an application (soft- or hardware) and, thus, starts climbing the tailorability mountain – or in our words, the tailorability staircase – and switching to a higher level to perform a specific practice. In our newly developed terminology this very moment, called "point of infrastructure," is characterized by a break-down in the current practices which leads an end user to becoming an end-user developer.

Keywords End-user development · practice · appropriation · infrastructuring · gentle slope of complexity

T. Ludwig (✉) · J. Dax · V. Pipek · V. Wulf
University of Siegen, Siegen, Germany
e-mail: thomas.ludwig@uni-siegen.de

J. Dax
e-mail: julian.dax@uni-siegen.de

V. Pipek
e-mail: volkmar.pipek@uni-siegen.de

V. Wulf
e-mail: volker.wulf@uni-siegen.de

© Springer International Publishing AG 2017   23
F. Paternò, V. Wulf (eds.), *New Perspectives in End-User Development*,
DOI 10.1007/978-3-319-60291-2_2

1   Introduction

What is end-user development (EUD), and when is a user considered an end-user developer? What kind of development practices does an end user have to perform? Answering these questions requires an exploration of the origins of EUD. When exactly the discourse around EUD emerged is hard to say. While Paternò (2013) argues, EUD emerged with the rise of graphical applications, Burnett and Scaffidi (2013), on the other hand, argue EUD dates to the 1980s when the first personal computers (then known as microcomputers) appeared. As Burnett and Scaffidi (2013) reason EUD emerged at this time because personal computers were inexpensive enough that companies could provide increasingly larger numbers of employees with one and the machines had sufficient processing power to compile or interpret new code written in higher programming languages. Computers soon came to include innovative new hardware such as the mouse and powerful graphics cards (the latter of which enabled graphical user interfaces and therefore direct manipulation). The number of computer-using employees rapidly increased and came to encompasses "managers, accountants, engineers, home makers, teachers, scientists, health care workers, insurance adjusters, salesmen, and administrative assistants" (Burnett & Scaffidi, 2013). The work tasks of these groups or actors are rather differentiated and always change, which means that software needs are consequently differentiating and changing as well. However, professional software engineers are unable to meet all of these (contextual) needs due to capacity reasons and their limited domain knowledge (Burnett & Scaffidi, 2013). At the same time, end users usually do not have training in professional programming languages, formal development processes, or modeling and diagramming notations and are therefore not able to tailor and appropriate software according their specific requirements (Burnett & Scaffidi, 2013).

End-user development tries to help solve the mismatch between end users' high and specific domain knowledge but limited programming expertise. In particular, it enables end users to design, tailor and customize software's user interface and functionality. Through EUD, end users can tailor and appropriate software systems to fit their requirements more closely than would otherwise be possible. In this context, tailoring is defined as any "activity to modify a computer application within its context of use" (Won, Stiemerling, & Wulf, 2006); it can be a simple or complex activity (Burnett & Scaffidi, 2013). However, multiple definitions exist in relation to what EUD is, who the end-user developers are and at what point end users achieve developer status. Within this chapter, we review the understandings and specific characteristics of EUD and the end user (Sect. 2). Based on the concepts of the gentle slope of complexity (MacLean, Carter, Lövstrand, & Moran, 1990) and infrastructuring (Sect. 3), we conceptually extend the current EUD discourse with a practice-oriented and hardware-related perspective. We provide a slightly changed understanding of the end-user developer and the moment at which EUD occurs from a practical perspective (Sect. 4). Finally, we use our extended and practice-based understanding to outline some problems and future perspectives related to EUD (Sect. 5).

2 EUD and the Gentle Slope of Complexity

Definitions of EUD have been provided at various junctures, including the most prominent ones of the mid-1990s (Nardi, 1993), early 2000s (Lieberman, Paternò, Klann, & Wulf, 2006) and today (Fischer, Fogli, & Piccinno, 2017). One of the most influential definitions of EUD can be found in Nardi's book *A Small Matter of Programming* (Nardi, 1993). The book does not mention "end-user development" per se ("end-user computing" is utilized instead), but the work was – and still is – popular within the EUD community. Nardi (1993) makes a strict differentiation between an end user and a professional programmer: "It is helpful to understand that a key difference between professional programmers and end-users is that programmers like computers because they get to program, and end-users like computers because they get to get their work done. End-users are not 'casual,' 'novice,' or 'naive' users; they are people such as chemists, librarians, teachers, architects, and accountants, who have computational needs and want to make serious use of computers, but who are not interested in becoming professional programmers" (Nardi, 1993). End users do not set out to write a computer program; they want to do something – and to accomplish their task (or to perform it more efficiently), they need to create a program. Paternò (2013) describes it as follows: "End users have specific goals in their own domains, which are not related to software development."

When focusing on the term "programming," Nardi (1993) dismisses the idea of characterizing it as a behavior because a "definition of programming that refers to detailed behavior is likely to be technology-specific." She instead defines programming utilizing its objective to "create an application that serves some function for the user" (Nardi, 1993). Lieberman et al. (2006) introduce a perspective in which EUD encompasses "a set of methods, techniques, and tools that allow users of software systems, who are acting as non-professional software developers, at some point to create, modify, or extend a software artifact." From Lieberman et al.'s (2006) perspective, EUD focuses not only on programming itself (cp. Nardi, 1993) but also on the methods, techniques and tools that support the act of programming. In addition to program creation and modification, Liebermann et al. (2006) include parameterization and customization as important end-user activities. By parameterization or customization, they mean "activities that allow users to choose among alternative behaviors (or presentations or interaction mechanisms) already available in the application. Adaptive systems are those where the customization happens automatically by the system in reaction to observation the user's behavior" (Lieberman et al., 2006). In contrast to parameterization or customization, they define program creation and modification as "activities that imply some modification, aiming at creating from scratch or modifying an existing software artifact" (Lieberman et al., 2006). Their definition therefore broadens the scope of EUD by expanding program creation to include software modification and extensions, which is the main differentiation between end-user programming (EUP) and EUD (Burnett & Scaffidi, 2013).

Most recently, Ko et al. (2011) provide definitions for programming, EUP and end-user software engineering. They do not define EUD itself and instead utilize

Lieberman's definition (2006), which states that EUD "also focuses on the use and adaptations of software over time, and focuses on elements of the software lifecycle beyond the stage of creating a new program." Ko et al. (2011) clearly distinguish EUD from professional programming and consider a program as "a collection of specifications that may take variable inputs and that can be executed (or interpreted) by a device with computational capabilities." They note that the "variability of input values requires that the program has the ability to execute on future values, which is one way it is different from simply doing a computation once manually" (Ko et al., 2011).

The two main aspects of EUP are (1) repeatability and optionally and (2) abstraction from a single case. A program can be executed multiple times; it may also be generic enough to take variable inputs. This crisply defines what programming actually is and clearly distinguishes between *programming* and *use*, which previous definitions did not. Ko et al. (2011) also provide insights into the end-user programming vs. programming issue, suggesting that the former be viewed as "programming to achieve the result of a program primarily for personal, rather public use." The distinction they make is that in end-user programming, the "program itself is not primarily intended for use by a large number of users with varying needs" (Ko et al., 2011).

Fischer et al. (2017) put the concept of EUD on a more general level and argue that the "real impact of EUD transcends the developments to create new technologies but transform cultures by empowering all people to become active contributors in personally meaningful activities." They therefore broaden the scope of EUD and argue that meta design could be applied to enable appropriate conditions for "putting owners of problems in charge by defining the technical and social conditions for broad participation in design activities" (Fischer et al., 2017).

On an operational level, most of the EUD definitions rely on the concept of the "gentle slope of complexity" (MacLean et al., 1990), which is a core and widely cited component of EUD research (Costabile, Fogli, Mussio, & Piccinno, 2006; Ko et al., 2011; Lieberman et al., 2006; Paternò, 2013; Rode, Rosson, & Pérez Quinones, 2006; Spahn & Wulf, 2009; Wulf, Pipek, & Won, 2008). It originally "characterizes the relationship between the amount of skill required and tailoring power using a mountain climbing analogy." As Burnett and Scaffidi (2013) summarize, "at each increased level of complexity, users have more ability to redesign the interaction and functionality of an application. At the most basic level, tailoring encompasses specifying parameters to an existing application in a way that changes its behavior at a high level of granularity. [...] Once tailoring begins to involve creating full-fledged programs in order to extend the functionality of an application, the activity seamlessly encompasses end-user programming."

Figure 1 shows the relationship between people's skill in tailoring an application and the tailoring power that this skill grants them. In the left graph, MacLean et al. (1990) present a typical tailorable application, using the EMACS text editor as an example; the right graph shows the system they develop around the concept of on-screen buttons (MacLean et al., 1990). Typical applications feature steep

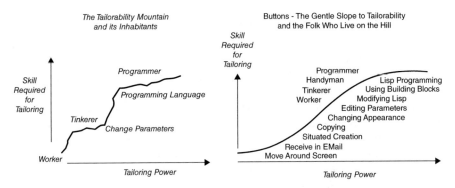

Fig. 1 Steep and gentle slopes of tailorability (MacLean et al., 1990)

slopes that require a user to acquire a relatively high amount of additional skill to achieve only a modest increase in his or her tailoring power.

The high amount of skill required to achieve an increase of tailoring power leads to two challenges: (1) the steep slopes are barriers to skill acquisition and (2) people with similar skill levels form relatively isolated groups. These groups include "workers," who are traditional end users who utilize – but do not modify – a system; "tinkerers," who modify a system through parameterization; and the actual "programmers." These groups "inhabit" different terraces on the "tailorability mountain." In the "Buttons" system (MacLean et al., 1990) and other EUD systems, "'smoothing off' the mountain should allow people with different skills to intermingle more and so communicate better with each other." The goal of EUD is to achieve this "smoothing off" by creating systems that provide a smooth learning curve – in other words, a gentle slope of complexity.

Related to this gentle slope is the idea of "layered tailoring languages" (Won et al., 2006), which essentially describes various regions on the "tailorability mountain" as different layers of programming and user interface languages. Following Henderson and Kyng (1991), Wulf (1999) describes three levels of complexity in tailoring: choosing between alternatives of anticipated behavior, constructing new behavior from existing pieces and altering an artifact (i.e. changing the source code). The different levels of complexity lead to the implementation of programming and user interface languages that correspond to these levels. There have been other, approaches to categorize different kinds of tailoring. A prominent one – which is analogous to the one from Wulf (1999) is the categorization into three levels of end-user tailoring by Mørch (1997). Mørch (1997) gives a detailed overview about these three levels and defines them as (1) *Customization*: "Modifying the appearance of presentation objects (UI-widgets like buttons and text boxes), or editing their attribute values by selecting among a set of predefined configuration options." (2) *Integration*: Integration "[…] goes beyond customization by allowing users to add new functionality to an application […]" by "[…] linking together predefined components within or across the application." (3) *Extension*: "Extension is an approach to tailoring where the functionality of an application is improved by adding new code."

3   Social Aspects of EUD: Appropriation and Infrastructuring

Modern work environments mainly use information systems as their basic *work infrastructures* (Pipek & Wulf, 2009) that are shaped and "used across many different locales and endures over long periods" (Monteiro, Pollock, Hanseth, & Williams, 2013). The term infrastructure arose from the Latin infra (below) and structura (assemblage) and comprises all the basic structures which are needed for the operation of a society. Based on its early definitions and referring to List (1841), Jochimsen (1966) defined infrastructure as "the sum of material, institutional and personal facilities and data which are available to the economic agents and which contribute to realizing the equalization of the remuneration of comparable inputs in the case of a suitable allocation of resources, that is complete integration and maximum level of economic activities." While some researchers follow this techno-centric perspective on infrastructural approaches to information systems (Dourish, 1999; Edwards, Newman, & Poole, 2010; Tanenbaum, 2002), others outline the social aspects of an infrastructure, such as that the users inevitably reshape a new infrastructure *during use*, and should always be considered as "designers." The most prominent exponents of this socio-technical perspective on infrastructure are Star and Ruhleder (1996). Besides just looking on the physical entities, they also took the role of the actors as well as their relationships into account.

When considering work-related information systems, Pipek and Wulf (2009) have outlined their infrastructural aspects such as interconnectedness, complexity, layer approach and standardization, as well as (in-)visibility in use. A work infrastructure, therefore, does not necessarily cover only technological systems, but – in accordance to Star and Ruhleder (1996) – also the "entirety of devices, tools, technologies, standards, conventions, and protocols on which the individual worker or the collective rely to carry out the tasks and achieve the goals assigned" (Pipek & Wulf, 2009).

When EUD is considered from a practical viewpoint, users often discover ways to utilize technologies that were not anticipated by the professional software developers and engineers as they attempt to manage their own understanding of sophisticated "new" technologies in the context of their existing (and changing) practices (Dalton, MacKay, & Holland, 2012). Based on two long-term studies on the evolution of usages of collaborative software in a German authority and in a network of freelancers in the field of consulting, Pipek (2005) utilize the concept of appropriation as the sense making of a software while it is being used in practice. He argues that "besides activities to configure the software to fit into the technological, organizational and individual work context of the users ('Tailoring'), there is a larger area of technology-related communication, demonstration and negotiation activities aimed at establishing a shared understanding of how a software artefact works and what it can contribute to the shared work context" (Pipek, 2005). For an account on the historic emergence of the concept see Stevens and Pipek (2017).

De Souza (2017) also takes a socio-technical point of view by developing the concept of semiotic engineering (de Souza, 1993) as a new theoretical basis for EUD research. She argues that within semiotic engineering the "activities performed by end users during, and by means of, software development are primarily related to a particular kind of computer-mediated social communication, rather than to algorithmic problem solving and program coding." Such an understanding explicitly privileges the social dimensions of programming and development instead of the logic and cognitive ones.

These understandings have their roots in the established literature of computer-supported cooperative work, in which appropriation is associated with the process of users fitting new technologies into their practices in situ by both adopting and adapting them (Balka & Wagner, 2006; Dourish, 2003; Mackay, 1990; Stevens, Pipek, & Wulf, 2009). The concept of appropriation goes deeper than that of the initial concepts of customization or tailoring of software in that it can encompass fundamental changes in practice and embraces the possibility of users adopting and using a technology in completely new ways (Pipek, 2005). Pipek (2005) focuses on developing appropriation support functionalities for connecting users of one tool, while other researchers (Draxler & Stevens, 2011; Draxler, Stevens, Stein, Boden, & Randall, 2012) look at ensembles of tools and suggest an appropriation framework that would also address the developers' interest in improving the technology and its underlying infrastructure.

A further example that underpins the concept of appropriation was outlined by Spahn, Dax, Yetim, and Pipek (2017), in which company staffers were given access to a tool which allowed them to create so-called widgets. Widgets are small, interactive applications for displaying data. The intended use for these widgets was to help employees in accomplishing business tasks and widgets were used that way for the most part. For example, one staffer created a widget for quickly looking up how many spare kinds of a particular type are in stock and how many are in production. However, one staffer created a birthday widget for keeping track of his colleague's birthdays. Both users have used the same tool as well as the same underlying technology, but for a purpose not intended by the designers of this technology.

Pipek and Wulf (2009) broaden the scope of EUD and understand the entire reshaping of a work infrastructure and the practice of "re-conceptualizing one's own work in the context of existing, potential, or envisioned IT tools" (Pipek & Wulf, 2009) as *infrastructuring* (Fig. 2). By introducing this term to refer to all activities that that lead to discovering and developing the usage of an entire infrastructure and contribute to successfully establishing usages of information infrastructures, Pipek and Wulf (2009) want to "avoid confusion with classic notions of design as design-before-use performed by professional designers." Based on a long-term study about the introduction, appropriation, and removal of a groupware infrastructure in a German state government, they have unconvered cases of infrastructuring and developed a design-oriented version of the infrastructuring as a new kind of technology development methodology that does not use a successfully designed product as its anchor, but rather the successful establishment of technology usage in the context of a given practice context (over time, Y axis in Fig. 2). The major aspect of this concept is that the dual perspective on IT usage from both the infrastructural layers of work development as well as the infrastructural layers of technology development and its specifics such as culture of design on the one hand and culture of (technology) use on the other hand.

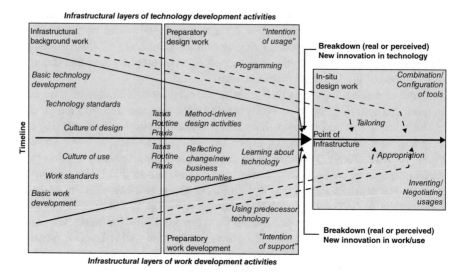

Fig. 2 Infrastructural layers of technology development activities (Pipek & Wulf, 2009)

Cabitza and Simone (2017) utilize the concept of infrastructuring and introduce the Logic of Bricolage (LoB) as a theoretical framework for the development of malleable systems. The LoB conceives of malleability as a first-level affordance to be "put in full control of the end users to empower them in appropriating and adapting their applications at different (potentially any) level of detail." The LoB's "clear separation of the technical infrastructure from the platform allows an alternative views of the standardization problem, one of the main issue concerning infrastructures" (Cabitza & Simone, 2017).

One important characteristic of infrastructuring as a technology development methodology (Fig. 2) is the "point of infrastructure" (PoI), which is the moment in which a (group of) practitioner(s) understand(s) that the current use of a technological infrastructure needs to be reconsidered (Pipek & Wulf, 2009). A PoI does not happen arbitrarily when a practice is being performed. Instead, specific factors are likely to trigger this reconsideration and that a dependency between a (work) practice and its supporting (work) infrastructure has developed previously and hence becomes largely invisible to the actors engaging in the practice in question. This dependency is what causes the reconsideration, based on four motivational forces (Pipek & Wulf, 2009):

- Actual infrastructure breakdown: The infrastructure is not able to deliver the service it is expected to provide, often because parts of the technologies have become inoperable (e.g. power failure when trying to stream a video).
- Perceived infrastructure breakdown: The infrastructure does provide its service technologically, but not to the level of expectations of its user (e.g. the low quality of a stream video in a mobile network when there is limited bandwidth available).
- Extrinsically motivated practice innovation: The framing conditions or the task and goals associated with a practice have changed in a way that it is impossible

to maintain the old practice (e.g. a video streaming platform develops a new pricing/subscription scheme and the customer requires a new device to be accompanied with new process documentation).

- Intrinsically motivated practice innovation: The framing conditions, tasks and goals associated with a practice remain unchanged, but practitioners discovered the potential for performing the practice in a new way, possibly because it is more cost efficient, simpler, quicker, or simply more fun (e.g. equipping the home with new sensor and management technology to be able to start streaming a video two minutes after arrival in the living room).

The concept of infrastructuring suggests that this initial impulse gives rise to a period of technology configuration, tailoring and convention development in which the "last mile of technology development" is mainly performed by (not necessarily technologically skilled) practitioners until finally the usage of a new technology has been successfully established (Pipek & Wulf, 2009).

With the rise of ubiquitous technology as well as the vision of an Internet of Things, new types of (physical) technology assemblies became available. The materiality (of the often called cyber-physical systems) poses a new dimension for EUD research, as it is not clear in how far insights from software can be easily transferred or adapted to the mixed domain of hardware *and* software. Ludwig, Tolmie, et al. (2017) and Ludwig, et al. (2014) conducted an empirical study within two different communities, illustrating how 3D printer users appropriate these "new" technologies for their purposes, and what practices are entailed in order to face several hardware breakdowns, unexpected effects concerning the printing material, unintuitive modeling tools and complex configurations.

The empirical study reveals as a main take away message that most of the practices users reported were highly socially embedded in the sense that the appropriation of the 3D printer was strongly enabled by cooperative informal learning and coordination in the context of playful experimentation. Such motivations are scarcely unique or new. A variety of material practices around hobbies in particular, such as working with wood or baking pastries, can show similar creative aspects. During those ludic moments in 3D printing, much experimenting is done, considerably in excess of perusal of the literature, which only seems to happen occasionally. This is why the understanding of the printers is mostly limited to operational handling. Those difficulties in understanding are compounded by the identifying, locating and fixing problems encountered in the printing process e.g. matching them conceptually to hardware, software or external factors. Solutions are sought both internally and externally. Internally, face-to-face conversations with colleagues are preferred. Attempts at preserving the knowledge resulted in a collaborative blog, which is maintained and read only very irregularly. This is because the entries have to be made by hand after a print and entail a post-hoc overhead.

In addition to the internal practices, users often search for problem solutions in bulletin boards and follow discussions on the web. This search however, poses a problem in itself, concerning domain specific slang and wording. On platforms such as Thingiverse or similar websites, 3D models themselves are central rather

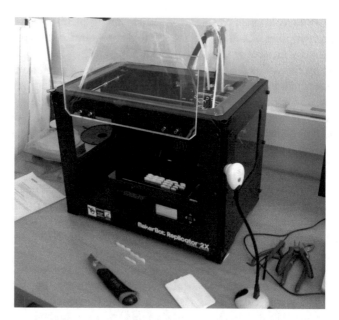

Fig. 3 Webcam to monitor the hardware (Ludwig, Boden, & Pipek, 2017)

than solution processes, or how to print a model or best practices. This helps the users at times, but it does not support the appropriation of 3D printers and its entire process – they are faced with similar problems during subsequent prints and have to try to identify the problems de novo.

Ludwig, Tolmie, et al. (2017), Ludwig et al. (2014) have found evidence for appropriation activities in the sense that the end-users modified their machines (e.g. installation of cameras to monitor the current printing status, Fig. 3) in ways the manufacturers did not plan for, but could be incorporated in future generations of their machines.

4   An Extended Conceptual Framework for EUD in Practice

To identify who the end-user developer is as well as when a development occurs, and therefore to conceptualize a new definition of EUD, we have presented an overview of currently available definitions and understandings as well as related work. While Nardi (1993) describes end users as individuals who would like to accomplish some specific task (which is not programming), Lieberman et al. (2006) characterize them as users of a software system who are aided by EUD methods and techniques in creating, modifying or extending software. However, Lieberman et al. (2006) do not clearly distinguish between EUD and general computer use. Many everyday computing tasks could be characterized as parameterization or customization. The question what EUD is – compared to general computer use – and what an end-user developer is – compared to a regular user – cannot be answered

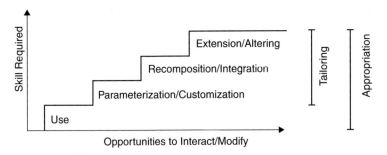

Fig. 4 The concept of tailoring levels and language layers applied to the tailorability mountain

clearly by using these definitions. Slightly exaggerated, one could respond to the question, who end-user developers are with "people who do EUD" according to these definitions. When we base our understanding of EUD on tailoring as well as software systems alone, the differences between usage and programming as well as between the notions of design before and during usage are considered particularly poorly.

One of our aims is therefore to provide a way to separate EUD from activities that are not EUD and end users who are not end-user developers – although these activities and user types are often a fluent transition in practice. The tailorability mountain and gentle slope of complexity (MacLean et al., 1990), language layering (Won et al., 2006; Wulf, 1999) and the three levels of tailoring are well known and central concepts in EUD. We want now to extend the understanding of end-user-development beyond software to any kind of tools. In recent years, the EUD community concerned itself more and more with hardware and IoT (Kubitza & Schmidt, 2015; Ludwig, Boden, et al., 2017). Therefore, we aim to formulate an understanding of EUD which is independent of software GUIs and programming languages, as the others are.

By applying the theoretical concept of appropriation and methodological framework of infrastructuring we enhance the tailorability mountain (Fig. 4) now looking more like a tailorability staircase, which we feel is closer to reality for most EUD activities and systems. The "gentle slope" can be achieved by making the steps small and helping people from one step to the next (like a staircase) – through software system appropriation as well as (hardware-related) infrastructuring. This mountain is not only concerned with tailorability, but also with the general concepts of use and appropriation. The four levels are defined as follows:

- *Use:* Use of a tool in its default configuration, as it was provided by the vendor and without any modifications.
- *Parameterization/Customization:* Parameterization of a tool by selecting from different options provided by the vendor.
- *Recomposition/Integration:* Adding new functionality to a tool by integrating it with other tools or recombining existing components of a tool.
- *Extension/Altering:* Adding new functionality to a tool by extending it, creating new components and adding them to a tool or altering the already existing components it is made of.

The methods used in the upper two levels – Recomposition/Integration and Extension/Altering are some form of programming language in software-related EUD. In physical EUD, the methods used on these two levels are other physical tools like a screwdriver or a hammer, raw material like plastic or wood and other end-products like a lamp or a camera. To illustrate this, we build on the two examples above: The 3D-printing case as an example of a physical tool (Ludwig, Boden, et al., 2017) and the user-defined widgets as an example of a software tool (Spahn et al., 2017).

The *Use-level* of a 3D-printer is simply printing a 3D artefact with the default configuration. (We acknowledge this may not be the most realistic scenario given the current state of 3D-printing technology and systems.) Then a serious shortcoming that became apparent in the study of how users operate their 3D printer is that the 3D printer itself is effectively a kind of black box for end-users and lacks descriptions of method and functionality. That is, users have no overall picture of how it works. This became especially crucial when errors during the printing process occurred and the users often were not able to identify or locate problems due to the high context-dependency of those issues (e.g. the impact of sunlight to black printing material). To address this PoIs the end users aim to gather as much contextual and environmental data as possible and to gather detailed information about the behavior of the 3D printer itself that goes far beyond the kind of information provided by the machinery's manufacturer.

At the *Parameterization/Customization-level*, the end users (together with researchers) implemented a ReplicatorG plugin that sniffs all data during the printing process, for instance, the extruder temperature, the platform temperature, all the extruder movements or the 3D model itself in STL format. To gather further information about the socio-material context, they set up an Arduino board with different sensors for measuring e.g. the temperature, brightness, humidity and vibration (Fig. 5). The end users further deployed the webcam to monitor the printing process, which represents tailoring at the Recomposition/Integration-level. Further, if a user had added a second printing nozzle to the printer to print

Fig. 5 Arduino for gathering socio-material context

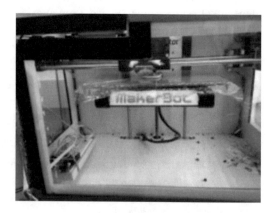

3D-models in two different colors, this is an instance of working on the *Extension/Altering* level – but we did not reach this state during the study.

To illustrate the different levels on the EUD-system described in Spahn et al. (2017) we must first go into more detail about the system. One example is an "employee in the procurement department of [a company]" who "[…] needs to access certain information related to material many times a day. For instance, he needs to identify a specific spare part by its material number and finding out about the quantity currently in stock and the quantity already scheduled for production" (Spahn et al., 2017). This is the *Use-level* of the system, where the user just uses standard functionality of the underlying SAP enterprise resource planning system. However, the user has some problem when using the system: "To get a first overview of the status of the spare part, the employee could determine a rather fixed set of information which she considers to be highly relevant for her work context. […] [This] information is widely spread within the GUI of the SAP ERP application, and users have to gather it in a cumbersome manner." These problems constitute an "infrastructure breakdown" (as described above) – the user is not able to perform the work task at hand.

In this case, *the Parameterization/Customization-level* provide by the ERP system does not help the user in addressing this breakdown as it does now allow GUI customization to a degree which would allow the user to view all relevant information on one screen. Spahn et al. (2017) now provide a system for creating widgets shown in Fig. 6. Using this system, users can use building blocks to create widgets which allow them to view the information they need. Building and integrating the widgets takes place on the level of *Recomposition/Integration*. The *Extension/Altering* level

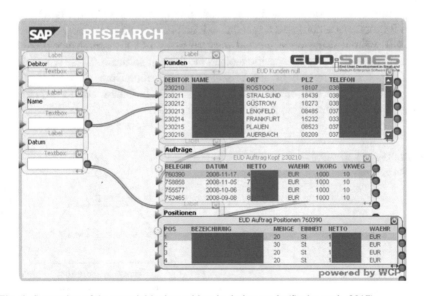

Fig. 6 Screenshot of the material lookup widget in design mode (Spahn et al., 2017)

would be reached, if the users would change or extend the underlying Java or ABAP source code to build their own GUIs.

In general, the differences between *Use* and *Parameterization/Customization* are highly contextual, but we make a distinction here for simplicity. It is also important to note that the same programming language, physical tool or raw material can be used in more than one of the tailorability levels as defined by Henderson and Kyng (1991) and that multiple programming languages, physical tools and materials can be used on one layer. The obvious advantage is that users do not need to learn different, maybe more complex tools and (programming) languages to be able to customize their infrastructure. Each layer grants the user more opportunities to interact, build and modify, but is more complex. The different languages allow the user to switch between metaphors and programming paradigms. On the "way up," each layer is slightly more flexible and powerful and adds possibilities to solve problems in certain ways – but it is also often harder to learn and use. However, these ways of learning and using strongly dependent of the end user's experience.

We thus extended the EUD discourse with a conceptual model that combines established concepts and our enhanced tailorability mountain with the ideas of infrastructuring and appropriation support to encompass a practical perspective on all of the diverse research interests of the EUD community (focusing on a software as well as hardware ecosystem). We have dubbed this model the "EUD pyramid" (Fig. 7).

This EUD pyramid shows how different kinds of tools correspond to the tasks that can be accomplished using those tools. The top level, "Practice," signifies a single task that a user might perform, such as 3D printing or performing ERP tasks. As Nardi (1993) notes, EUD enables a user to accomplish a specific task that he or she could not otherwise do (or do as well) without programming. In our definition, this is not only true for software and programming, but for tools generally. EUD enables users (of tools) to accomplish a specific task that they could not otherwise do (or do as well) without using more general purpose tools. EUD accomplishes this oftentimes by providing domain specific tools in the form of software. These where developed e.g. for the domain of enterprise systems (Spahn, Dörner, & Wulf, 2008), groupware (Wulf, 1999) or research (Dax et al., 2015). Others aim to be useful in many domains (Ardito et al., 2014; Mørch et al., 2004).

Fig. 7 The end-user development pyramid

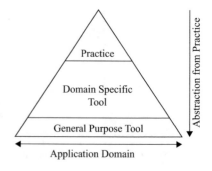

As an example which illustrates the different levels of the pyramid, we can consider a simple image editor. In the case of the image editor, a practice might be drawing a house. The second level, "Domain Specific Tool," corresponds to a group of related tasks, which are all the tasks that an image editor enables an end user to do (e.g. clicking on a house button or using lines and squares). The lowest level, "General Purpose Tool," corresponds to all the tasks that the computer can generally do.

Another (no software-related) example for the different levels of the pyramid is the practice of cutting out cookies from dough. A domain specific tool for cutting the dough is a cookie cutter. A general-purpose tool which can serve the same function is a knife. The knife can be used for many more applications then cutting cookies, but it is harder to cut a snowman shape with a knife then with a snowman-shaped cookie cutter. Keeping such broader ways of thinking in mind, the pyramid becomes increasingly generic in nature from top to bottom (i.e. from a domain expert's viewpoint); from bottom to top, it becomes more domain specific (i.e. from a professional programmer's perspective). Using the above example of drawing a house, the top level is concerned with one concrete instance of a house; in the middle level, the "first-class objects" are lines or shapes in general; and on the lowest level, the tool is completely agnostic to the application. In other words, the tools are increasingly abstracted from the domain of interest to the end user at the bottom of the pyramid.

Based on such an extended (more general) conceptualization, we define a practice-oriented and more inclusive understanding of EUD as follows: "end-user development occurs whenever an end user has to switch to a more abstract level, which is further away from his/her, practice to fulfill a specific task." The moment of recognizing that an end user has to switch to a lower (more abstract) level of practice (and therefore become an end-user developer) is usually driven by a PoI. The context is important within our understanding, as EUD strongly depends on an end user's knowledge about the system itself. The same activity may constitute EUD for one user but just be "normal use" for another. Engaging in EUD means climbing the tailorability mountain – or in our words the tailorability staircase – and therefore switching to a more abstract level of practice.

5   Conclusion and Outlook

We have described the concepts of the gentle slope, language layering and appropriation and applied these definitions to EUD activities beyond software-related ecologies and programming. We discussed these concepts in the contexts of appropriation and infrastructuring. Based on two examples (Ludwig, Boden, et al., 2017; Spahn et al., 2017), we applied these concepts to the practical experiences we gained over the last years to derive an extended understanding of EUD. Of course, our conceptually extended understanding of EUD has also some drawbacks and limitations and there are still open research questions.

A gentle slope is more pleasant to climb than a steep one, but a steep slope provides a shorter path to the top. If the tools at the foot of the mountain (i.e. a domain-specific visual language) stop providing value to people who have mastered the tools at the top (i.e. Java), those individuals have wasted time in learning things they are never going to use again. Moreover, if each layer is more powerful than the one before, why should users not always utilize the most powerful tool they have mastered? This question has to be answered by providing EUD tools that are so well suited to their specific tasks or practices that they are easier to use than the more general-purpose ones – even for users who have already mastered those more abstract tools.

Another related drawback is that switching between layers that use different paradigms and metaphors requires re-learning. This drawback is connected with an increasing need for abstractions. While abstractions are generally preferable as they hide underlying details, and allow users to interact on a level closer to their practices, coming up with appropriate abstractions that work and do not "leak" their underlying implementation is challenging. Leaking the underlying levels is problematic as it requires the end-user developer to understand not only the current layer but also underlying ones. This is contrary to the core idea of gentle slope of complexity, where uses do not have to understand the whole system to modify it. Abstraction is always a tradeoff between flexibility and tailorability as well as between complexity and often also performance.

With regard to our notion of infrastructuring informed EUD more research is needed to understand how to support both infrastructuring activities and appropriation from an end-user perspective. How could designers and professional programmers anticipate functionality for appropriation practices that are needed at a later time? Indeed, a discourse on how to support appropriation infrastructures already exists (e.g. Draxler & Stevens, 2011; Pipek & Wulf, 2009; Stevens, 2009; Stevens, Pipek, & Wulf, 2010); however, related studies deal with handling the software tool instead of the entire set of development practices.

Another open research question focuses on how to support cooperative approaches to allow end-user developers to cooperatively climb the gentle slope of complexity. Appropriation encompasses highly cooperative activities, but how to integrate the cooperation and learning between end users into the development process also remains an open question. First attempts for example were made by Ludwig, Schneider, and Pipek (2017) who apply the concepts of collaborative visualization to integrate end users into development practices.

A last open issue focuses on the applicability of EUD in the "Internet of things" era (Markopoulos, Nichols, Paternò, & Pipek, 2017; Paternò & Santoro, 2017). Although our understanding provides space for the interweaving of digital and physical technology, new EUD technologies are needed to be considered and adapted to new ways of emerging development. In this context, initial approaches are already aiming to conceptualize hardware-related appropriation infrastructures (Ludwig, Boden, et al., 2017; Ludwig et al., 2014) and moving towards an Internet of Practices (Ludwig, Tolmie, et al., 2017).

References

Ardito, C., Francesca Costabile, M., Desolda, G., Lanzilotti, R., Matera, M., Piccinno, A., et al. (2014). User-driven visual composition of service-based interactive spaces. *Journal of Visual Languages and Computing*, 25(4), 278–296. doi:10.1016/j.jvlc.2014.01.003.

Balka, E., & Wagner, I. (2006). Making things work: dimensions of configurability as appropriation work. In *Proceedings of the 2006 20th anniversary conference on computer supported cooperative work* (pp. 229–238). ACM. doi:10.1145/1180875.1180912.

Burnett, M.M., & Scaffidi, C. (2013). End-user development. In *The Encyclopedia of Human-Computer Interaction, 2nd Ed.* Retrieved from https://www.interaction-design.org/encyclopedia/end-user_development.html.

Cabitza, F., & Simone, C. (2017). Malleability in the hands of end users. In F. Paternò & V. Wulf (Eds.). *New perspectives in end-user development* (pp. 137–164). Cham: Springer.

Costabile, M. F., Fogli, D., Mussio, P., Piccinno, A. (2006). End-user development: the software shaping workshop approach. *End User Development*, 183–205.

Dalton, N., MacKay, G., Holland, S. (2012). Kolab: appropriation & improvisation in mobile tangible collaborative interaction. *Proceedings of the designing interactive systems conference* (pp. 21–24). Newcastle: ACM New York. doi:10.1145/2317956.2317960.

Dax, J., Ludwig, T., Meurer, J., Pipek, V., Stein, M., Stevens, G. (2015). FRAMES - a framework for adaptable mobile event-contingent self-report studies. In *Lecture Notes in Computer Science (including subseries Lecture Notes in Artificial Intelligence and Lecture Notes in Bioinformatics)* (vol. 9083). doi:10.1007/978-3-319-18425-8_10.

de Souza, C. S. (1993). The semiotic engineering of user interface language design. *International Journal of Man-Machine Studies*, 39, 753–773. doi:10.1006/imms.1993.1082.

de Souza, C. S. (2017). Semiotic engineering: a cohering theory to connect EUD with HCI, CMC and more. In F. Paternò & V. Wulf (Eds.). *New perspectives in end-user development* (pp. 269–306). Cham: Springer.

Dourish, P. (1999). *Software infrastructures* (ed. Beaudouin-Lafon, M.). Computer Supported Co-operative Work. Retrieved from https://www.lri.fr/~mbl/Trends-CSCW/references.html.

Dourish, P. (2003). The appropriation of interactive technologies: some lessons from placeless documents. *Computer Supported Cooperative Work*, 12(4), 465–490. doi:10.1023/A:1026149119426.

Draxler, S., & Stevens, G. (2011). Supporting the collaborative appropriation of an open software ecosystem. *Computer Supported Cooperative Work*, 20(4–5), 403–448. doi:10.1007/s10606-011-9148-9.

Draxler, S., Stevens, G., Stein, M., Boden, A., Randall, D. (2012). Supporting the social context of technology appropriation: on a synthesis of sharing tools and tool knowledge. In *Proceedings of the 2012 ACM annual conference on human factors in computing systems – CHI '12* (pp. 2835–2844). doi:10.1145/2207676.2208687.

Edwards, W. K., Newman, M. W., Poole, E. S. (2010). The infrastructure problem in HCI. *Proceedings of the conference on human factors in computer systems (CHI)* (pp. 423–432). Atlanta, GA: ACM.

Fischer, G., Fogli, D., Piccinno, A. (2017). Revisiting and broadening the meta-design framework for end-user development. In F. Paternò & V. Wulf (Eds.). *New perspectives in end-user development* (pp. 61–98). Cham: Springer.

Henderson, A., & Kyng, M. (1991). There's no place like home: continuing design in use. In J. Greenbaum & M. Kyng (Eds.), *Design at work cooperative design of computer systems* (pp. 219–240). Lawrence Erlbaum Associates. Retrieved from http://books.google.co.kr/books?hl=ko&lr=&id=BCGM7GQFyqYC&oi=fnd&pg=PA219&dq=There's+no+place+like+home&ots=BghnneB4l0&sig=WdDuQAUfHZ6jfWoLQEQ2V6p-lYo.

Jochimsen, R. (1966). *Theorie der Infrastruktur, Grundlagen der marktwirtschaftlichen Entwicklung*. Tübingen: J. C. B. Mohr. (Paul Siebeck).

Ko, A. J., Abraham, R., Beckwith, L., Blackwell, A., Burnett, M., Erwig, M., et al. (2011). The state of the art in end-user software engineering. *ACM Computing Surveys*, 43(3), 1–44.

Retrieved from http://search.ebscohost.com/login.aspx?direct=true&db=aph&AN=703416 36&site=ehost-live.

Kubitza, T., & Schmidt, A. (2015). Towards a toolkit for the rapid creation of smart environments. In P. Díaz, V. Pipek, C. Ardito, C. Jensen, I. Aedo, A. Boden (Eds.), *End-user development SE – 21* (vol. 9083, pp. 230–235). Springer International Publishing. doi:10.1007/978-3-319-18425-8_21.

Lieberman, H., Paternò, F., Klann, M., Wulf, V. (2006). End-user development: an emerging paradigm. *End User Development SE - 1*, *9*, 1–8. doi:10.1007/1-4020-5386-X_1.

List, F. (1841). *Das nationale System der politischen Ökonomie*. Stuttgart: Cotta Verlag.

Ludwig, T., Boden, A., Pipek, V. (2017). 3D printers as sociable technologies: taking appropriation infrastructures to the internet of things. *ACM Transactions on Computer-Human Interaction (TOCHI)*, *24*(2).

Ludwig, T., Schneider, K., Pipek, V. (2017). Integration of empirical study participants into mobile data analysis through information visualization. In *Proceedings of the international symposium on end-user development (IS-EUD). Lecture notes in computer science.* Eindhoven: Springer.

Ludwig, T., Stickel, O., Boden, A., Pipek, V. (2014). Towards sociable technologies: an empirical study on designing appropriation infrastructures for 3D printing. In *Proceedings of DIS14 designing interactive systems* (pp. 835–844). Canada: Vancouver. doi:10.1145/2598510.2598528.

Ludwig, T., Tolmie, P., Pipek, V. (2017). From the internet of things to an internet of practices. In *Proceedings of 15th European conference on computer-supported cooperative work – exploratory papers*. Sheffield: Reports of the European Society for Socially Embedded Technologies. doi:10.18420/ecscw2017-10.

Mackay, W. E. (1990). Patterns of sharing customizable software. In *Proceedings of the 1990 ACM conference on computer-supported cooperative work* (pp. 209–221). Los Angeles, CA: ACM New York. doi:10.1145/99332.99356.

MacLean, A., Carter, K., Lövstrand, L., Moran, L. (1990). User-tailorable systems: pressing the issues with buttons. In *Proceedings of the Conference on Human Factors in Computer Systems (CHI)* (pp. 175–182). Seattle, Washington: ACM New York.

Markopoulos, P., Nichols, J., Paternò, F., Pipek, V. (2017). Editorial: end user development for the internet of things. *Transactions on Human Computer Interaction (ToCHI)*, *24*(2).

Monteiro, E., Pollock, N., Hanseth, O., Williams, R. (2013). From artefacts to infrastructures. *Computer Supported Cooperative Work: The Journal of Collaborative Computing (JCSCW)*, *22*(4), 575–607. doi:10.1007/s10606-012-9167-1.

Mørch, A. (1997). Three levels of end-user tailoring: customization, integration, and extension. In M. Kyng & L. Mathiassen (Eds.). *Computers and design in context* (pp. 51–76). Cambridge, MA: MIT Press. Retrieved from http://dl.acm.org/citation.cfm?id=270318.270321.

Mørch, A. I., Stevens, G., Won, M., Klann, M., Dittrich, Y., Wulf, V. (2004). Component-based technologies for end-user development. *Communication ACM*, *47*(9), 59–62. doi:10.1145/ 1015864.1015890.

Nardi, B. A. (1993). A small matter of programming: perspectives on end user computing. SIGCHI Bulletin 26. doi:10.1145/191642.1047947.

Paternò, F. (2013). End user development: survey of an emerging field for empowering people. *ISRN Software Engineering*, *2013*, 1–11. doi:10.1155/2013/532659.

Paternò, F., & Santoro, C. (2017). A design space for end user development in the time of the internet of things. In F. Paternò & V. Wulf (Eds.). *New perspectives in end-user development* (pp. 43–60). Cham: Springer.

Pipek, V. (2005). *From tailoring to appropriation support: negotiating groupware usage.* University of Oulu. Retrieved from http://herkules.oulu.fi/isbn9514276302/isbn9514276302.pdf.

Pipek, V., & Wulf, V. (2009). Infrastructuring: toward an integrated perspective on the design and use of information technology. *Journal of the Association for Information Systems (JAIS)*, *10*(5), 447–473.

Rode, J., Rosson, M. M. B., Pérez Quinones, M. A. (2006). End user development of web applications. End User Development, 161–182. doi:10.1007/1-4020-5386-X.

Spahn, M., Dax, J., Yetim, F., Pipek, V. (2017). Enabling users of enterprise systems to mashup resources and develop widgets. In V. Wulf, V. Pipek, D. Randall, M. Rohde, K. Schmidt, G. Stevens (Eds.), *Socio informatics – a practice-based perspective on the design and use of IT artefacts*. Oxford University Press.

Spahn, M., Dörner, C., Wulf, V. (2008). End User Development of Information Artefacts: A Design Challenge for Enterprise Systems. Proceedings of European Conference on Information Systems (*ECIS*). 190.

Spahn M., Wulf V. (2009). End-User Development of Enterprise Widgets. In: Pipek V., Rosson M.B., de Ruyter B., Wulf V. (eds). End-User Development. IS-EUD 2009. *Lecture Notes in Computer Science*, (vol. 5435, pp. 106–125). Springer, Berlin, Heidelberg.

Star, S. L., & Ruhleder, K. (1996). Steps toward an ecology of infrastructure: design and access for large information spaces. *Information Systems Research*, 7(1), 111–134. doi:10.1287/isre.7.1.111.

Stevens, G. (2009). *Understanding and designing appropriation infrastructures: artifacts as boundary objects in the continuous software development*. University of Siegen. Retrieved from http://dokumentix.ub.uni-siegen.de/opus/volltexte/2010/433/.

Stevens, G., & Pipek, V. (2017). Making use: understanding, studying, and supporting appropriation. In V. Wulf, V. Pipek, D. Randall, M. Rohde, K. Schmidt, G. Stevens (Eds.), *Socio informatics – a practice-based perspective on the design and use of IT artefacts*. Oxford University Press.

Stevens, G., Pipek, V., Wulf, V. (2009). Appropriation infrastructure: supporting the design of usages. In B. De Ruyter, V. Pipek, M. B. Rosson, V. Wulf (Eds.). *Proceedings of the 2nd international symposium on end-user development* (vol. 5435/2009, pp. 50–69). Heidelberg: Springer. doi:10.1007/978-3-642-00427-8.

Stevens, G., Pipek, V., Wulf, V. (2010). Appropriation infrastructure: mediating appropriation and production work. *Journal of Organizational and End User Computing*, 22(2), 58–81. doi:10.4018/978-1-4666-0140-6.ch012.

Tanenbaum, A.S. (2002). *Computer networks (4th Edition)*. Prentice Hall. Upper Saddle River, New Jersey.

Won, M., Stiemerling, O., Wulf, V. (2006). Component-based approaches to tailorable systems. *End User Development SE – 6, 9*, 115–141. doi:10.1007/1-4020-5386-X_6.

Wulf, V. (1999). "Let's see your search-tool!"—collaborative use of tailored artifacts in groupware. In *GROUP* (pp. 50–60). Retrieved from http://www.ncbi.nlm.nih.gov/entrez/query.fcgi?db=pubmed&cmd=Retrieve&dopt=AbstractPlus&list_uids=8290831043742281329related:cS4KV-jyDnMJ.

Wulf, V., Pipek, V., Won, M. (2008). Component-based tailorability: enabling highly flexible software applications. *International Journal of Human-Computer Studies.*, 66(1), 1–22. doi:10.1016/j.ijhcs.2007.08.007.

A Design Space for End User Development in the Time of the Internet of Things

Fabio Paternò and Carmen Santoro

Abstract This paper discusses the issues raised by the Internet of Things for end user development of interactive applications, and how they can be addressed. In such technological setting, applications have to adapt to various types of contextual events, which can be related to users, devices, environments, and social relationships. This calls for environments supporting the development of applications able to cope with dynamic sets of people, objects, devices, and services. The article discusses the characterizing concepts of such environments and their underlying motivations by analysing various solutions proposed to support them and their main design issues. We describe the relevant concepts and discuss how to make them understandable by people without programming experience. One result of this work is a design space, which identifies the main features that should be addressed to support Internet of Things applications using EUD approaches. Such a design space can be used as the basis for comparative discussion amongst various approaches. The analysis provided can also inform the design and development of new tools, and stimulate discussion on current research challenges.

Keywords End user development · Internet of Things · context-dependent applications

1 Introduction

The design and development of flexible software able to match the many possible users' needs is a difficult challenge. One of the main problems is that it is almost impossible to identify all the requirements at design time, since they are often not static (user needs are likely to change over time), and designers also have to

F. Paternò (✉) · C. Santoro
CNR-ISTI, HIIS Laboratory, Pisa, Italy
e-mail: fabio.paterno@isti.cnr.it

C. Santoro
e-mail: carmen.santoro@isti.cnr.it

© Springer International Publishing AG 2017
F. Paternò, V. Wulf (eds.), *New Perspectives in End-User Development*,
DOI 10.1007/978-3-319-60291-2_3

consider the wide variability of the possible contexts of use. In recent years, the explosion of mobile and Internet of Things technologies has made it possible for people to access their applications from a variety of contexts of use. In this scenario, it is nearly impossible for professional designers and developers to guarantee a good fit between the initially designed system and the actual user needs at any given time. As a result, it is important to design software through methods and tools capable of dynamically and quickly responding to new requirements without spending vast amounts of resources, and able to consider that boundaries between design-time and run-time have become more and more blurred.

End User Development (EUD) is a research field that focuses on enabling people who are not professional developers to design or customize their interactive applications (Lieberman, Paternò, Klann, & Wulf, 2006). Indeed, nowadays users are becoming ever more familiar with ICT technology and they are increasingly capable of using existing tools to create simple applications by themselves. However, since such people usually lack the training of professional software developers, it is simply not possible to use traditional programming environments and methodologies for software development.

The topics related to EUD have already been investigated to some extent in recent years, however, up to a few years ago the main EUD approaches have mainly considered desktop-based applications, such as spreadsheets, unable to adapt to the changing context of use (Paternò, 2013). Only recently have some proposals been put forward to address EUD through mobile technologies. However, the Internet of Things (Atzori, Iera, & Morabito, 2010) introduces further issues such as the need to design how to react to dynamic events that can be generated through a variety of sensors, objects, services, and devices.

If we want to find some relevant aspects in the early end-user development literature before such technology was available, we should look at environments that allowed developers to consider highly interactive applications. In such cases, events were related to user interactions and application functionalities. Alice[1] is a good example of this type of environment. It supports end user development of 3D animations. In particular, it allows users to access lists of events corresponding to user interactions or some specific animation state and indicate what the corresponding event handler should be. HANDS (Pane, Myers, & Miller, 2002) is an environment with similar goals, more oriented to children. It uses the cards metaphor: all objects in HANDS are represented by cards, which have user-defined properties, while the program execution, that is, the manipulation of cards, is represented by an agent. HANDS allows users to select one event from seven predefined event types and indicate the corresponding actions for which it provides some possible operations ("Add," "Sorted," "Sum," "Greatest_Item," etc...). These two important contributions were designed for development in desktop systems and did not consider the variety of events that can be triggered in modern ubiquitous settings.

In the Internet of Things (IoT) vision, "smart" physical objects are networked together, able to interact and communicate with each other, with human beings and/or

---

[1]http://jupiter.plymouth.edu/~wjt/foundations/alice/Alice05.pdf

with the environment to exchange data and information "sensed" about the environment, reacting autonomously to events in the physical world, and influencing it by running processes that trigger actions and perform services. According to Gartner,[2] there will be nearly 26 billion devices on the Internet of Things by 2020. In this scenario, immense amounts of data can be generated by sensor and communication infrastructures that are growing by orders of magnitude, and IoT applications need to address extremely contextualized user needs. Indeed, one of the primary concerns of IoT is the heterogeneity of devices, sensors, actuators, and services involved in the relevant domains. EUD foresees the use of meaningful logical abstractions and metaphors to abstract out low-level details and make users focus only on relevant aspects, thus facilitating the participation of end-users in the development process.

In order to support EUD of Internet of Things-enabled context-dependent applications we need to consider that context can vary on aspects related to **users** (e.g. tasks, preferences, emotional state), **technology** (e.g. devices, modalities supported, connectivity), **environment** (e.g. light, noise, place), and **social aspects** (e.g. networks, social relationships), and only end users can know the most appropriate ways their applications should react to contextual events. However, to reach such a broad audience of users, authoring environments should be almost transparent to them, presenting a very low threshold to get started, while allowing users to attain high value and even complexity of the software they create or customize. In this way it would be possible to avoid the need to involve in the process people with high developer skills, with the benefit of faster development, better control over the application functionality and improved user experience.

EUD is expected to bring several benefits to the IoT domain. Indeed, giving end-users the adequate tools to create IoT applications is a way to ensure that people's needs will be adequately addressed, and it is also a way to shift innovation from software companies to end users. In addition, EUD foresees the use of intuitive abstractions and metaphors to reduce the cognitive burden associated to handling the multitude and heterogeneity of things, devices, sensors, actuators, services involved in IoT-related domains, and thus support more easily end-user participation in the development process. Furthermore, the use of meaningful abstractions in EUD, in terms of relevant concepts, metaphors, programming styles, vocabularies and intuitive notations should allow different stakeholders (e.g. professional software developers, domain experts, and users) to comprehensively handle the system and also to communicate ideas and concepts. Moreover, EUD is expected to allow users to do more (and more easily) with their existing devices and things within their homes or at work: in other words, EUD for IoT should allow for higher control, more confidence, and better personalisation support. Considering that IoT spams a disparate range of domains, this approach will be key to support the long tail of requirements of IoT end user developers.

In this paper we first discuss metaphors and programming styles for EUD, in particular those more relevant in the IoT field, also providing a discussion of research work that have exploited them. Next we move on to present the proposed

---

[2]http://www.gartner.com/newsroom/id/2684616

design space, which can be used for comparative analysis. Lastly, we draw some conclusions and mention potential areas that can be object of future research.

2 Metaphors and Programming Styles

We identified two levels for classifying the various techniques that have been mainly used so far in the EUD-related area. One level is represented by **metaphors**, i.e. concepts which do not have any specific connections with the programming world, but rather have a precise meaning in the real world. As such, metaphors' meaning is generally quite familiar to generic users who, by analogy, apply and transfer to the development world the knowledge that the metaphor concept has in the real world. In this way, metaphors provide users with easily understandable cognitive hints expected to facilitate the creation or customisation of an application by decreasing the learning effort needed by a non-professional user to manipulate programming concepts and artefacts. For instance, using the jigsaw metaphor each software component is seen as a piece of a puzzle and the shapes of the various pieces provide the cognitive hints needed to understand the possible compositions.

The second level identified – **programming styles** – is more connected with the programming world and with the need to identify specific interaction paradigms and programming techniques aimed at making end user development easier. At this level we included *programming by example, trigger-action –based approaches, natural language* techniques, *spreadsheets, mashups, mock-up –based* and *tangible programming techniques*. It is worth noting that neither level is specific to IoT and, as such, such techniques could be applied to different domains. In the following sections we analyse work in the state of the art which exploited the above concepts, with particular attention to application to the IoT domain (Fig. 1).

2.1 Metaphors

Various metaphors have been considered in this area, Davidyuk, Sanchez, Gilman, and Riekki (2015) discuss the use of some of them. Using the **pipeline metaphor**, applications are represented graphically as directed graphs where nodes correspond to elementary services or activities, and links (i.e. pipelines) connect them. Pipelines can also be organized in complex structures, for example by using logic binary operators connecting nodes, and they can have various implementations depending on how such nodes are represented. Often they are rendered through icons associated with high-level functionalities, with some output and input ports representing the input and the output data, and the application development mainly consists in indicating from where such functionalities receive input and where they send the results of their processing. Realinho, Romão, and Dias, (2012) have proposed IVO (Integrated Virtual Operator), an event-driven workflow/pipeline framework for allowing end users to develop context-aware mobile applications.

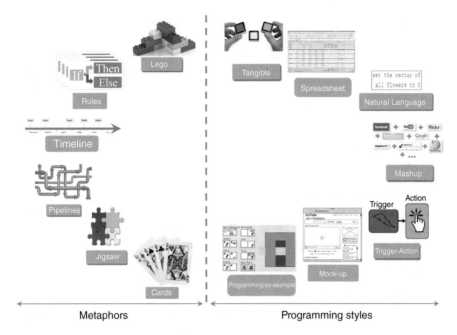

Fig. 1 Metaphors and programming techniques considered in EUD approaches

Using IVO, users build such applications by creating workflows that determine the application behaviour when a specified context is detected. An IVO application is therefore described as a set of workflows that are triggered when some contexts are checked. The workflows are created by combining the available building blocks, which represent the various actions that can be performed by an application. The pipeline metaphor is a visual paradigm which allows for modelling the behaviour of complex applications. However, despite its expressiveness, the use of this metaphor can be problematic when the number of graphical elements and their connections increases, thereby making the resulting diagram difficult to interpret.

In the **jigsaw puzzle metaphor**, each software component is seen as a piece of a puzzle and the shapes of the various pieces provide the cognitive hints needed to understand the possible compositions. Thus, non-expert users can easily associate each puzzle piece with the component it represents. This metaphor has been used in various environments. First, Scratch[3] proposed it for supporting children in learning programming concepts, in particular in creating interactive applications with multimedia content. AppInventor[4] then exploited such metaphor to support the development of functionalities triggered by events in an app user interface. While this metaphor supports more complex configurations than the pipeline

---

[3]http://scratch.mit.edu

[4]http://appinventor.mit.edu/explore/

metaphor, one disadvantage is that it has limited expressiveness. Indeed, the pieces of the puzzle have a limited number of interfaces (i.e. sides), thereby restricting the set of possible programming expressions. While in Scratch and AppInventor puzzles pieces are used to represent low-level programming constructs, in Puzzle (Danado & Paternò, 2014), they have been exploited to support development of Internet of Things applications on smartphones: the elements are associated with high-level functionalities that can also control actuators. Thus, Puzzle has been designed to facilitate the composition of various pieces through a touch interface for a screen with limited size. Each puzzle piece represents a high-level functionality that can be composed, and its shape and colours indicate the number of inputs and outputs, as well as the information type they can communicate. Thus, the tool provides a usable solution but it is limited to the composition of functionalities for which a puzzle piece has been provided. A similar approach has been investigated also in MicroApp (De Lucia, Francese, Risi, & Tortora, 2012), which exploits graphical composition of common functionalities offered by phone applications, such as taking an image through the camera and saving it, retrieving the contact list, and sending an email. However, in order to work it requires each action or service to expose a description that enables automatically generating the MicroApp puzzle-based user interface. Among commercial systems, Zipato[5] exploits the jigsaw metaphor for rule composition. A variation of the jigsaw metaphor is the *tile-based approach* (Cavallaro, Nitto, Furia, & Pradella, 2010), which allows building programs by combining graphical units (tiles). Although each tile can be combined only with other specific tiles, the shapes of the tiles do not limit the connections. Another variation of the jigsaw metaphor is the *join-the-dots metaphor*, where the editing canvas presents a set of individual devices that are available in the environment. Each device is shown as the centre of a cluster, while the surrounding nodes represent services accessible from the environment. Users create compositions by linking one service to the desired destination device. This metaphor has been applied in the editor of the Platform Composition prototype (Pering, Want, Rosario, Sud, & Lyons, 2009). The main advantages of this metaphor is the simplicity of its visual representation, as only services and devices available for composition are visualized.

Timeline is another relevant metaphor that has been considered in the EUD area. It basically provides a temporal reference along which events/objects are aligned, so helping in organising relevant information in a chronological order. Timelines are typically represented by a line on which various elements are graphically positioned, thus, in timelines temporal relationships (between e.g. events) are basically represented as spatial relationships. TagTrainer (Tetteroo et al., 2015) is an approach exploiting timelines for EUD. TagTrainer enables caregivers to develop rehabilitation exercises for patients with hand or arm mobility problems based on the manipulation of everyday objects. It is designed to create training programs consisting of sequential activities: the workspace located in the center of the screen displays a timeline containing the sequence of all actions associated with the objects involved

---

[5]www.zipato.com

in the exercise, and, depending on the selected action (e.g. "Place object"), a window on the right side gives the possibility to specify relevant properties, such as the exact location where the object has to be placed at a given time.

Rules represent another used metaphor in the EUD area. The underlying idea is to specify the system behaviour by using a number of if-then statements expressing how the system should behave when specific situations occur. One of the first proposals using rules for EUD was iCAP (Dey, Sohn, Streng, & Kodama, 2006), which introduced the possibility to create if-then rules to support personalization of dynamic access to home appliances. Recently, due to relevancy of contextual dynamic aspects that can potentially affect the behaviour of applications in IoT-based environments, rule-based approaches are receiving increasing interest since end users can easily reason about context and express in rules the desired behaviour of their applications by describing how the application should react to specific events occurring in the context. However, rule-based approaches can become difficult for non-programmer users when complex rules have to be expressed, since e.g. a correct formulation of logical expressions implies the knowledge of some key concepts (e.g. Boolean operators, priority of operators) that could not be always intuitive for non-professional software engineers. Rules can be realised using various programming techniques: in TARE (Ghiani, Manca, Paternò, & Santoro, 2017) rules are expressed using a trigger-action syntax and also by providing a representation in natural language.

2.2 Programming styles

Spreadsheets have proven enormously popular with personal computer users as they provide a concrete, visible representation of data values, as well as powerful features like the possibility to apply formulas to cells, which quickly allow users to solve simple problems within their domain of interest (Burnett, Yang, & Summet, 2002). However, they do not seem suitable to address more dynamic environments such as IoT applications.

The programming style based on user interface **mock-ups** as design tools (Beaudouin-Lafon & Mackay, 2002) has long been considered due to its intuitiveness and effectiveness, and various tools for rapid prototyping for early stages of design, and iterative and evolutionary prototyping have been proposed. They can still be useful in IoT domains as well.

One programming style relevant for EUD is based on **natural language**, a way of programming using a subset of constructs expressed in natural language which should model user's intents. An example approach exploiting this programming style can be found in the work of Perera, Aghaee, and Blackwell (2015), which analysed how a natural language approach can support the definition of policies to manage the home environment. The authors considered the "sticky note" technique for defining the tasks requiring information exchange between IoT appliances and services. The findings revealed mainly that: the average number of words per note was relatively small; people in general adjust their language depending on the type of addressee (human vs. machine); and their technical background affects the way users communicate with machines. Natural language has also been exploited in *composition screens*, where users are able to specify the connections of services and devices for concrete applications, such as in the InterPlay prototype (Messer et al., 2006). InterPlay relies on visual "verb-object-target" constructions which resemble pseudo-English sentences. Users specify a task by first selecting a "verb" (i.e. a command), then an "object" (i.e. content) and, finally, a "target" (i.e. a device). While this approach offers an intuitive user interface, users are only able to trigger the automated composition of the tasks defined in the system at design time. AppsGate (Coutaz & Crowley, 2016) is an EUD prototype which has been deployed in real domestic environments. Its goal is to support end-users defining their own semantics concerning the use of devices and services available at home. AppsGate consists of a server and a set of Web clients. The server is structured in two abstraction levels (one application-agnostic and another one application-specific), and uses OSGi to support the dynamic appearance and disappearance of devices. In order to allow users to express the intended behaviour, a pseudo-natural language is used to express rules that are specified in terms of conditionals (which can regard states and events) and actions. The underlying tool supports a feedforward mechanism to facilitate users in expressing their rules without being burdened by an excessively complicated syntax. In addition, AppsGate also analyses the difficult problem of how to support debugging in EUD environments, by providing the possibility to run programs using a virtual date and time.

Another relevant approach in this area is represented by **tangible interfaces**, where a person interacts with digital information through the physical environment. An example of tangible interactive environment for EUD is in (Truong, Huang, & Abowd, 2004), where they used the fridge magnet metaphor: it mimics refrigerator magnets where the magnets offer a set of words that users can arrange into phrases. It also provides an interface for automated capture and playback (which allows users to replay events that were automatically recorded in the home).

From a HCI perspective, **mashup** refers to a composition of contents and/or features from several sources that determines new client-side interactive applications. For instance, Web mashups can combine data, presentations and functionalities from different Web sites into a novel, single Web application. Various approaches have been put forward in this area. The approach illustrated in (Desolda, Ardito, Matera, & Piccinno, 2015) for mashing up smart things (sensors, actuators) relies on domain-specific customization of the platform. In mashup approaches the basic point is to facilitate new compositions amongst existing components, while a more flexible approach would be to add incrementally new contextual rules for modifying the original behaviour of the interactive application. In (Aghaee & Pautasso, 2014) the authors describe the design and evaluation of NaturalMash, an EUD tool for enabling non-professional users to create mashups by using a subset of natural language expressions, which are associated with mashup components beforehand. They also provided an evaluation in which they compared the expressive power of

NaturalMash with other state-of-the-art mashup environments, showing that their tool offers a good level of expressive power compared with other tools.

IoT is characterized by the presence of a variety of sensors in contexts containing dynamic sets of devices, people, and services. Thus, applications able to exploit such situations need to be informed of the various changes in order to adapt accordingly. This has stimulated renewed interest in **trigger-action programming**, an approach which is mainly based on event-condition-action (ECA) rules. Triggers can be associated with events and/or conditions. Events are instantaneous changes that occur at some point, while conditions define specific contextual states. For example "when the user enters home" is an event since it refers to a state change, while "when the user is at home" indicates a condition corresponding to the state associated with the user being at home. Huang and Cakmak (2015) discuss current Trigger-Action Programming trends and issues. In particular, they found that the distinction between relevant concepts is a source of problems, since users can have difficulties interpreting the difference between events and conditions or between the possible types of actions (for example extended actions, which automatically revert back to the original state after some time, and sustained actions, which do not revert to the original state automatically). Misunderstandings can cause undesired behaviours (e.g. unlocking doors at the wrong time or causing unintended energy waste). Lucci and Paternò (2014) have analysed how three Android apps support this type of programming. Such tools categorize triggers and actions differently according to users' objectives. Their analysis indicates further requirements, for example that EUD tools for IoT should allow the combination of more than one trigger and more than one action in the same rule.

EUD based on trigger-action rules is expected to allow users to do more (and more easily) with their existing devices and things by softening the boundaries between "end users" and "professional developers" as well as between design done before use and software adaptation done at runtime. By specifying customisation rules, users should be able to get better personalisation support and more satisfaction in the use of their context-dependent IoT-based applications. This type of solution can thus contribute to creating technological infrastructures that can successfully establish their usage in practise (Pipek and Wulf, 2009) if they are able to address the specific challenges for obtaining low threshold and high ceiling environments. In (Ghiani et al., 2017) the authors present TARE (Trigger-Action Rule Editor), an environment that allows end users to customize the context-dependent behaviour of their Web applications through the specification of trigger-action rules. The environment is able to support end-user specification of flexible behaviour, including an underlying infrastructure able to detect available devices and objects and possible contextual changes to achieve the desired behaviour. The resulting environment supports the dynamic creation of application versions more suitable for specific contexts of use. An example of its use in a real environment (a students' home) is reported in (Corcella, Manca, and Paternò, 2017).

Another environment that aims to support the development of rule-based reactive applications is IFTTT. It uses the textual syntax "IF This Than That" to specify the scheduling of execution of a certain action (That), and the occurrence of a specified event (This). Its distinguishing feature is that, besides being able to express "recipes" that concern and make changes in the hosting device, IFTTT communicates with widely used Web services, thus allowing the automatic execution of functions related to the internal state of apps such as Facebook, Instagram, Box, Ebay, YouTube and others. In the mobile version the process of creating a recipe is done sequentially through some guided steps. A recent study (Ur, McManus, Ho, & Littman, 2014) found that trigger-action programming can express most desired behaviour in order to customize smart home devices. They evaluated the uniqueness of the 67,169 trigger-action programs shared on IFTTT.com, finding that real users have written a large number of unique trigger-action interactions. Finally, they conducted a 226-participant usability test of trigger-action programming, finding that inexperienced users can quickly learn to create programs containing multiple triggers or actions obtained by extending the IFTTT language, which has limited possibilities, since it only supports applications with only one trigger and one action. This shows that this approach seems suitable to support EUD of context-dependent applications, but needs to be improved in order to allow users to express various desired combinations of events and corresponding actions. Another interesting point of (Ur et al., 2014) is that it shows that the approach based on IFTTT can address emerging Internet of Things (IoT) applications as well. In such applications "smart" physical objects are thought as networked together, able to interact and communicate with each other, with human beings and/or with the environment to exchange data and information "sensed" about the environment, and thereby able to react autonomously to events in the real world, and influence it by running processes that trigger actions and perform services. The availability of mobile tools to perform real time checks of the configuration of on-site visual interactive systems is deemed essential in (Kubitza, Thullner, & Schmidt, 2015) to accelerate the so-called "change and re-try cycles." An example tool for configuring smart environments is described in (Kubitza & Schmidt, 2015). It aims to facilitate physical prototyping by hiding the complexity that arises when many different technologies are combined together. The tool is structured so as to separate the management of devices, events and rules, and mainly targets people with some programming experience since the rules are based on JavaScript.

a CAPpella (Dey, Hamid, Beckmann, Li, & Hsu, 2004) is a desktop tool aiming to address context-dependent applications. It applies the **programming-by-example** style in which the user does not provide the specification of the program but just furnishes examples of sequences of interactions from which the environment understands what the corresponding expected general behaviour is. In this case a user demonstrates context-aware behaviour that includes both a situation and an associated action, and trains the environment on this behaviour over time by giving multiple examples. Once the systems has been trained, the user can run the application, which will then perform the demonstrated action whenever it detects the demonstrated situation. An attempt to apply the programming-by-example paradigm to a mobile development environment is "Keep Doing It" (Maues & Barbosa, 2013), which provides the possibility of identifying context-dependent adaptation rules in the ECA format according to the history of user interactions. The rules are represented through a natural language subset using "when," "if" and imperatives verbs. An example rule is: "When a wired headset is connected, if my phone is unlocked, launch the Google Play Music application." A different application of the programming-by-example relevant for IoT is Improv (Chen & Lin, 2017), which aims to support end users in dynamically defining cross-device interactions in order to leverage the capability of additional devices. Thus, users first demonstrates the target UI behaviour using the native input on the primary device. Improv parameterizes the user-demonstrated behaviour. Then, the user demonstrates the input on an accessory device, and Improv associates it with the parameterized behaviour so that the user can obtain the same original application behaviour through the cross-device interaction demonstrated.

3 Design Space

Based on our analysis of metaphors and programming styles, we have identified a logical framework to better understand and compare work in this area. It is composed of seven logical dimensions.

- **Platforms**. The platform supported for the development activities. Traditionally it has been the desktop, but other platforms are being increasingly considered, e.g. mobile, even in combination. e.g. desktop and mobile together (Chen & Lin, 2017);
- **Domains**. An indication of the relevant application domains which the concerned EUD approach can be applied to. The domain can vary depending on the case; in the IoT area examples of application domains often considered are home automation, ambient assisted living, rehabilitation;
- **Events**. In this dimension we consider the types of events that can have an impact on the behaviour of IoT applications. They can concern not only interaction events (i.e. events occurring when interacting with the application), but also contextual events (i.e. those associated to aspects such as user, technology, surrounding environment and social relationships) occurring in the current context of use;
- **Metaphors**. The metaphor dimension aims to analyse the type of representations and interactions adopted in order to make intuitive the specification of the intended application behaviour;
- **Programming styles**. This dimension refer to the programming techniques aimed at making end user development easier for the non-professional user.
- **Actions**. This level describes which type of changes to the application behaviour the EUD environment allows. Different types of actions can be identified, e.g. those performed in appliances (to change the state of actuators), user interface modifications (to change e.g. its presentation, content or navigation), execution of functionalities (e.g. access to an external service like a weather forecast service);

- **Event Compositions/Operators**. This dimension analyses the possibility to build composite expressions of events. Events can be combined in various manners, by using e.g. Boolean operators or temporal operators;
- **Action Compositions/Operators**. This dimension analyses the possibility to build composite expressions of actions. Constructs similar to those occurring in programming languages can be used (e.g. sequence, for, while, if).

Such dimensions can be useful to analyse proposals for EUD environments and think about possible new solutions. Table 1 provides an example of how our logical framework can be used to analyse various proposals. For the sake of brevity we only consider a small set of tools, which have been identified to show different ways to address the design space dimensions.

The first dimension is dedicated to the *platform* supported for the development activities: it can be desktop (as in Alice, HANDS, a CAPpella, TagTrainer) or mobile devices (as in Keep Doing it) or both (as in Puzzle, IFTTT, TARE, AppsGate). As for the application *domains*, some are more oriented to specific sectors (e.g. HANDS for children's animations), while others are more general-purpose (e.g. IFTTT). Regarding the *events*, all the approaches consider interaction events, whereas much fewer approaches consider the full range of event types (interaction, user-related, environment-related, technology-related, social relationships -related), i.e. IFTTT and TARE.

As for the *metaphors*, the most used approaches for addressing IoT domains seem the rule-based one (e.g. IFTTT, TARE, AppsGate) for its immediate way to handle their typical reactive behaviour, and the one based on some subset of natural language (see e.g. Alice and HANDS) for its intuitiveness. The most used *programming styles* were natural language (in Alice, HANDS and AppsGate it was used in an exclusive manner, in TARE it was used in combination with rules), programming by demonstration (a Cappella, Keep Doing it), and the trigger-action approach (IFTTT and TARE).

Regarding the range of *actions* covered by the approaches, it is addressed in a variety of ways and also depends on the considered application domain: TagTrainer is focused on rehabilitation exercises, IFTTT allows users to connect to a predefined set of existing applications, TARE allows the customization of existing Web IoT Applications, AppGate focuses on the home domain, while KeepDoing it aims to extend the possibilities of automating smartphones' tasks. In particular, they cover the modification of the application UI (Alice, Hands exclusively focus on such aspects on desktop platforms), but also consider mobile applications (Keep Doing It, Puzzle), up to covering smart environments and IoT-based settings, especially with the most recent approaches (see e.g. TARE, TagTrainer andAppsGate).

In addition, the possibility of *composing events* in EUD environments has been considered only in a few approaches (a CAPpella, Keep Doing It, TARE and TagTrainer), where in any case a limited set of Boolean operators among AND, OR, NOT have been supported. Instead, *action composition* has been supported in almost all approaches with a few exceptions (namely: IFTTT and AppsGate).

Looking at this table some observations can be derived, also in terms of potential areas that require further research in the near future. For example, while all the

Table 1 Analysis of related work according to the proposed framework

EUD environment	Alice	HANDS	a CAPpella	Keep doing It	Puzzle	IFTTT	TARE	TagTrainer	AppsGate
PLATFORM	Desktop	Desktop	Desktop	Mobile	Mobile/Desktop	Mobile/Desktop	Mobile/Desktop	Desktop	Mobile/Desktop
DOMAIN	Multimedia animations	Multimedia animations for children	Context-dependent behaviour (e.g. meeting rooms)	Context-dependent smartphone applications	Automate sequences of actions	Composition of various existing Web services	Context-dependent Web IoT applications	Rehabilitation	Home
EVENTS	Interact. Technol.	Interact. Technol.	Interact. Environ.	Interact. User Environ. Technol.	Interact. User Environ. Technol.	Interact. User Environ. Technol. Social	Interact. User Environ. Technol. Social	Interact. User	Interact. Environ. Technol.
METAPHOR	Storyboard	Cards	Timeline	Rules	Jigsaw	Rules	Rules	Timeline	Rules
PROGRAMMING STYLE	Natural language	Natural language	Programming by demonstration	Programming by demonstration		Trigger-action	Trigger-action +Natural Language		Natural language
ACTIONS	Handlers associated to interaction events	Handlers associated to interaction events	Smart environment actions	Smartphone tasks	Actions for application UI, objects, appliances, and devices.	Changes in the device, activate Web services and apps	Actions for application UI, objects, appliances, and devices.	Exercises/actions for physical objects	Behaviour of devices and services available at home
EVENTS COMPOSITION OPERATOR			AND	AND NOT			AND OR	AND	
ACTIONS COMPOSITION OPERATORS	Do together Do together If else While Loop Wait	And Not Or	And	And	Loop		Sequence	Sequence	

approaches consider interaction events, only a few approaches address (at various levels) proper contextual events (e.g. those connected with user, environment, technology, and social aspects). This can be explained with the fact that in the past the initial focus was mainly limited to the events raised by the interactive application, while in more recent years the increasing availability and affordability of various devices and sensing technologies has stimulated the development of context-dependent applications, whose behaviour can be affected by events occurring in the surrounding context. Therefore, the inclusion of various types of contextual events has been mainly considered only in more recent approaches, and thus a more complete coverage of such events in future work would be advisable.

Regarding the actions, we observe a trend similar to the one identified for events: initially the focus was on actions just affecting the interactive application; later on, with the increasing diffusion of IoT technologies and related smart applications, the focus was extended to include actions controlling not only the application but also devices, actuators, physical objects and appliances that can be available in the considered context.

In addition, apart from a few exceptions, the possibility to compose events and corresponding actions is generally very limited, some approaches even do not support their composition at all (as it happens with IFTTT). Therefore, further effort in enabling end users to specify complex expressions of triggers and actions should be pursued because this would provide users with the possibility to specify more flexible behaviours.

However, especially when dealing with complex expressions of triggers (e.g. events and conditions) and actions, there are further aspects that need to be better analysed. As it has been previously highlighted (Huang & Cakmak, 2015), rule-based approaches (and, in particular, trigger-action–based rules) could raise some ambiguity in the interpretation of rules, due to potential inaccuracies in end users' mental models. For instance, interpretation problems can occur when it is not clear whether actions occurring in a rule should be explicitly reverted or not (by using e.g. another rule) as soon as the involved triggers do not hold anymore. This requires further analysis and investigation of the different types of triggers and actions that can be included in complex expressions, in order to avoid such interpretation issues in future EUD tools.

The problem of intuitive composition of logical expressions by end users has also been studied in (Metaxas & Markopoulos, 2017), where an established theory of mental models has been used to guide the design of interfaces for natural programming so that people can find easy to comprehend and manipulate logical expressions. According to such mental model theory people find it easier to conceptualize logical statements as a disjunction of conjunctions (an OR of AND's), as opposed to other logically equivalent forms. Thus, (Metaxas & Markopoulos, 2017) presented a tool which is expected to facilitate end-users in programming context-dependent behaviour using quite complex logical expressions. Although this work represents a useful contribution to facilitate natural programming by decreasing the cognitive load associated with the specification of complex logical expressions, further studies are needed to further elaborate on these key aspects.

Finally, another interesting aspect (yet not fully developed in the EUD area) is how people can test and possibly assess whether the modified/created behaviour of the application actually resulted in the expected one. This need is especially relevant in IoT domains where incorrect behaviour of applications or actuators can eventually have safety-critical consequences (e.g. in the elderly assistance domain and in the home domain). If we consider rule-based approaches, a way to reduce the likelihood of errors in the specification of rules is to allow users to simulate the conditions and the events that can trigger a rule and the effects that they will bring about. An example of this approach can be found in TARE, where users can check the rules (e.g. by simulating them) in order to identify possible errors or conflicts in their specifications, or directly execute them in the current context of use. In this way it should be possible to receive information helpful to find the causes of the undesired behaviour detected and eventually fix them. However, although debugging support could represent an important aid for improving the correctness of the resulting applications, most EUD environments do not include debugging aids for such users (Coutaz & Crowley, 2016) since for non-professional end users debugging becomes especially difficult. Therefore, another possible area that can be subject of possible further investigation is the one dedicated to improve such kind of support in EUD tools.

4 Conclusions

In this paper we have presented a design space, which identifies the main features that should be addressed to support End User Development for Internet of Things applications. The presented conceptual framework is useful to facilitate a better understanding of the important aspects to consider when design EUD environments for IoT, and can be used as the basis for comparative analysis amongst various approaches and inform discussion about areas that can be further investigated.

The discussion about solutions for supporting low threshold/high ceiling specifications of events and actions compositions has still some open points, which require further research work.

Additional aspects that are currently starting to emerge include the possibility for people to test/simulate the behaviour of the IoT applications obtained with the EUD tool in order to assess whether it actually results in the expected one, with the additional possibility to receive information helpful for finding the causes of any undesired behaviour detected and fixing it.

References

Aghaee, S., & Pautasso, C. (2014). End-user development of mashups with natural mash. *Journal of Visual Languages and Computing, 25*(4), 414–432.

Atzori, L., Iera, A., Morabito, G. (2010). The internet of things: a survey. *Computer Networks, 54*(15), 2787–2805. doi:10.1016/j.comnet.2010.05.010.

Beaudouin-Lafon, M., & Mackay, W. (2002). Prototyping tools and techniques. In J.A. Jacko & A. Sears (Eds.), *The human computer interaction handbook* (pp. 1006–1031). Hillsdale, NJ: L. Erlbaum Associates Inc.

Burnett, M., Yang, S., Summet, J. (2002). A scalable method for deductive generalization in the spreadsheet paradigm. *ACM Transactions on Computer-Human Interaction, 9*(4), 253–284.

Cavallaro, L., Nitto, E. D., Furia, C. A., Pradella, M. (2010). A tile-based approach for self-assembling service compositions. In R. Calinescu (Ed.), *Proceedings of the 15th IEEE international conference on engineering of complex computer systems (ICECCS'10)* (pp. 43–52). Oxford: IEEE Computer Society.

Chen, X., & Lin, Y. (2017). *Improv: an input framework for improvising cross-device interaction by demonstration.* New York, NY: ACM TOCHI.

Corcella, L., Manca, M., Paternò, F. (2017). Personalizing a student home behaviour. In *Proceedings IS-EUD 2017, LNCS 10303* (pp. 1–16). Cham: Springer Verlag.

Coutaz, J., & Crowley, J.L. (2016, May–June). A first person experience with end-user development for smart home. *IEEE Pervasive Computing, 15*(2), 26:39.

Danado, J., & Paternò, F. (2014). Puzzle: a mobile application development environment using a jigsaw metaphor. *Journal of Visual Languages and Computing, 25*(4), 297–315.

Davidyuk, O., Sanchez, I., Gilman, E., Riekki, J. (2015, December). An overview of interactive application composition approaches. *Open Computer Science, 5*(1), 2299–1093. doi:10.1515/comp-2015-0007. ISSN (Online).

de A. Maues, R., Barbosa, S.D.J. (2013). Keep Doing What I Just Did: Automating Smartphones by Demonstration. *Proceedings of the 15th international conference on human-computer interaction with mobile devices and services,* MobileHCI 2013 (pp. 295–303). New York, NY: ACM. ISBN: 978-1-4503-2273-7. doi:10.1145/2493190.2493216

De Lucia, A., Francese, R., Risi, M., Tortora, G. (2012). Generating applications directly on the mobile device: an empirical evaluation. In *Proceedings of the International Working Conference on Advanced Visual Interfaces (AVI '12)* (pp. 640–647). New York, NY, USA: ACM. doi:10.1145/2254556.2254674

Desolda, G., Ardito, C., Matera, M., Piccinno, A. (2015, April 19). Mashing-up smart things: a meta-design approach. In *Proceedings of workshop on end user development in the internet of things era – CHI '15 EA* (pp. 33–36). Seoul.

Dey, S. K., Hamid, R., Beckmann, C., Li, H., Hsu, D. (2004). A CAPpella: programming by demonstration of context-aware applications. In *Proceedings of the SIGCHI Conference on Human Factors in Computing Systems (CHI '04)* (pp. 33–40). New York, NY, USA: ACM. doi:10.1145/985692.985697

Dey, A.K., Sohn, T., Streng, S., Kodama, J. (2006). iCAP: interactive prototyping of context-aware applications. *Pervasive,* 254–271.

Ghiani, G., Manca, M., Paternò, F., Santoro, C. (2017). Personalization of Context-Dependent Applications Through Trigger-Action Rules. *ACM Transactions on Computer-Human Interaction, 24*(2), Article 14, 33 pages. DOI: 10.1145/3057861.

Huang, J., & Cakmak, M. (2015). Supporting mental model accuracy in trigger-action programming. *Proceedings of the 2015 ACM international joint conference on pervasive and ubiquitous computing (UbiComp '15)* (pp. 215–225). New York, NY: ACM. doi:10.1145/2750858.2805830.

Kubitza, T., & Schmidt, A. (2015). Towards a toolkit for the rapid creation of smart environments. *IS-EUD, 9083,* 230–235.

Kubitza, T., Thullner, S., Schmidt, A. (2015). VEII: a toolkit for editing multimedia content of interactive installations on-site. *Proceedings of the 4th ACM International Symposium on Pervasive Displays, 2015* (pp. 249–250). New York, NY, USA: ACM.

Lieberman, H., Paternò, F., Klann, M., Wulf, V. (2006). End-user development: an emerging paradigm. In H. Lieberman, F. Paternò, V. Wulf (Eds.), *End-user development (Human-Computer Interaction Series)* (pp. 1–8). Netherlands: Springer.

Lucci, G., & Paternò, F. (2014). Understanding end-user development of context-dependent applications in smartphones. In *HCSE* (pp. 182–198). Heidelberg: LNCS Springer Verlag.

Messer, A., Kunjithapatham, A., Sheshagiri, M., Song, H., Kumar, P., Nguyen, P., et al. (2006, March). InterPlay: a middleware for seamless device integration and task orchestration in a networked home. In *Proceedings of the 4th annual IEEE conference on pervasive computing and communications (PERCOM'06)* (pp. 296–307). Pisa: IEEE Computer Society.

Metaxas, G., & Markopoulos, P. (2017). Natural contextual reasoning for end users. *ACM Transactions on Computer-Human Interaction, 24*(2), Article 13. doi:10.1145/3057860.

Pane, J.F., Myers, B.A., Miller, L.B. (2002). Using HCI techniques to design a more usable programming system. *Proceedings of 2002 IEEE Symposia on Human Centric Computing Languages and Environments (HCC 2002)* (pp. 198–206). doi:10.1109/hcc.2002.1046372

Paternò, F. (2013). End user development: survey of an emerging field for empowering people. *ISRN Software Engineering, 2013*, Article ID 532659, 11 pages.

Perera, C., Aghaee, S., Blackwell, A.F. (2015). Natural notation for the domestic internet of things. In *Proceedings IS-EUD* (pp. 25–41). Cham: Springer Verlag.

Pering, T., Want, R., Rosario, B., Sud, S., Lyons, K. (2009, May). Enabling pervasive collaboration with platform composition. In H. Tokuda et al. (Eds.), *Proceedings of the 7th international conference on pervasive computing (Pervasive'09), LNCS 5538* (pp. 184–201). Nara: Springer.

Pipek, V., & Wulf, V. (2009). Infrastructuring: toward an integrated perspective on the design and use of information technology. *Journal of the Association for Information Systems (JAIS), 10*(5), 447–473.

Realinho, V., Romão, T., Dias, A.E. (2012). An event-driven workflow framework to develop context-aware mobile applications. In *Proceedings of the 11th International Conference on Mobile and Ubiquitous Multimedia (MUM '12)*. ACM, New York, NY, USA, Article 22, 10 pages. doi:10.1145/2406367.2406395

Tetteroo, D., Vreugdenhil, P., Grisel, I., Michielsen, M., Kuppens, E., Vanmulken, D., et al. (2015). Lessons learnt from deploying an end-user development platform for physical rehabilitation. In *Proceedings of the 33rd annual ACM conference on human factors in computing systems (CHI '15)* (pp. 4133–4142). New York, NY: ACM. doi:10.1145/2702123.2702504.

Truong, K.N., Huang, E.M., Abowd, G.D. (2004). CAMP: a magnetic poetry interface for end-user programming of capture applications for the home. In *Proceedings of Ubicomp* (pp. 143–160). Heidelberg: Springer.

Ur, B., McManus, E., Pak Yong Ho, M., Littman, M. L. (2014). Practical trigger-action programming in the smart home. In *Proceedings of the 32nd annual ACM conference on human factors in computing systems (CHI 14)* (pp. 803–812). New York, NY, USA: ACM. doi:10.1145/2556288.2557420

Revisiting and Broadening the Meta-Design Framework for End-User Development

Gerhard Fischer, Daniela Fogli and Antonio Piccinno

Abstract Our contribution will review, analyze, discuss, and synthesize the research work done over the last 10 years exploring *meta-design* as a major framework for *end-user development* (EUD). The overriding perspective of our approach is grounded in the basic assumptions that (1) designers can prompt and support change in a community of practice, but they cannot predetermine it and (2) design and use mutually shape one another in iterative, social processes. The chapter argues and provides evidence that EUD should not be restricted to create new technologies but its most important and far-reaching impact will be to *transform cultures* by empowering all people to become active contributors in personally meaningful activities. The individual sections discuss and describe our basic framework, EUD applications in different domains, new conceptual developments that broadened the concept of meta-design, the identification of design trade-offs and drawbacks, and design guidelines. All of these activities have contributed to revisiting and broadening the meta-design framework for end-user development.

Keywords Design · meta-design · participatory design · transformative cultures · cultures of participation · co-evolution · socio-technical systems · design methodologies · design guidelines · design drawbacks and trade-offs

G. Fischer
University of Colorado, Boulder, CO, United States
e-mail: gerhard@colorado.edu

D. Fogli
University of Brescia, Brescia, Italy
e-mail: daniela.fogli@unibs.it

A. Piccinno (✉)
University of Bari "Aldo Moro", Bari, Italy
e-mail: antonio.piccinno@uniba.it

© Springer International Publishing AG 2017
F. Paternò, V. Wulf (eds.), *New Perspectives in End-User Development*,
DOI 10.1007/978-3-319-60291-2_4

1   Introduction

In earlier developments, *End-User Development (EUD)* was conceived as "a set of methods, techniques, and tools that allow users of software systems, who are acting as non-professional software developers, at some point to create, modify, or extend a software artifact" (Lieberman, Paternò, Klann, & Wulf, 2006). However, if one analyses the variety of proposals in the EUD field in international journals or in the proceedings of the five editions of the International Symposium on EUD held up so far, such a definition is too restrictive. Due to the many possibilities provided by technology (e.g. Web 2.0 and 3.0, Internet of Things, smart appliances and devices), the term EUD today should be conceived as a broader umbrella, including methods, situations, and socio-technical environments allowing and empowering end users "to express themselves and being independent of high-tech scribes."

One influential framework for supporting EUD is *meta-design* (Fischer & Giaccardi, 2006) empowering all stakeholders (including end users) to be actively engaged in the *continuous development* of personally meaningful socio-technical systems (Fischer & Herrmann, 2011).

Historically, software design was initially dominated by professionals. *Professional-dominated design* is a methodology founded on the belief that professional experts understand the users' needs (Rittel, 1984). At design time, they create artifacts which users "have to live with" at use time. While professional-dominated design has its place, it often creates systems that are at odds with users' interests, needs, and background knowledge. Successively, *user-centered design* (Norman & Draper, 1986) has been a major step forward to transcend the limitations of professional-dominated design by analyzing the interests, needs, and background knowledge of users and envisioning how users are likely to use an artifact. Then, to better cope with the users' needs and include them into the design, *participatory design* (PD) (Schuler & Namioka, 1993) focused on system development at design time by involving end users more deeply in the design process as co-designers by empowering them to propose and generate design alternatives themselves. It requires the social inclusion and active participation of the users at design time by bringing developers and users together to envision the contexts of use. But, despite the efforts at design time, systems need to evolve at use time to fit new needs, account for changing tasks, deal with a great variety of subjects, contexts and evolving needs, and incorporate new technologies, making meta-design a necessity.

This chapter explores how this conceptualization of EUD supported by meta-design was advanced over the last decade. As indicated in Fig. 1, the different sections describe

- the impact of EUD on transforming cultures and some specific developments exploring and supporting this transformation process;
- a description of applications in different domains that were influenced by meta-design;
- new conceptual developments that broadened the concept of meta-design;
- the identification of design trade-offs and drawbacks that need to be carefully considered.

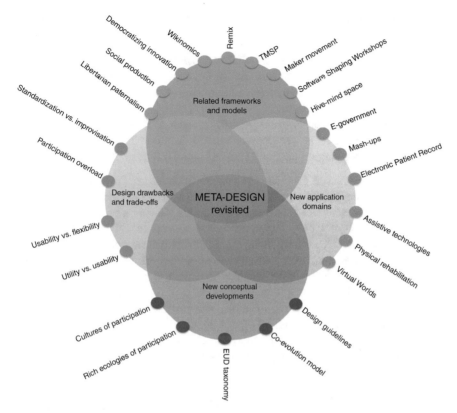

Fig. 1 An overview of the structure of our contribution

Fig. 1 synthesizes the structure of our contribution; while design guidelines proposed by various scholars to realize the conceptual developments above and cope with trade-offs and drawbacks are finally presented.

2 End-User Development: From Creating Technologies to Transforming Cultures

EUD is instrumental for "the ability to reformulate knowledge, to express one-self creatively and appropriately, and to produce and generate information rather than simply to comprehend it" (National Research Council, 1999). It appeals to diverse audiences by supporting them in designing and building their own artifacts by situating computation in new contexts, by generating content, and by developing tools that democratize design, innovation, and knowledge crea-tion (von Hippel, 2005). This broad vision of EUD complements and transcends a *technological perspective* of EUD (Burnett & Scaffidi, 2013) that is closely related to:

- *End-User Programming (EUP)* that empowers and supports end users to program (with techniques such as: programming by demonstration, visual programming, scripting languages, and domain-specific languages) (Lieberman, Paternò, & Wulf, 2006); and
- *End-User Software Engineering (EUSE)* that adds to EUP support for systematic and disciplined activities for the whole software lifecycle (including: reliability, efficiency, debugging support, and version control) (Burnett, 2009).

In other words, EUD provides the enabling conditions for putting owners of problems in charge by defining the technical and social conditions for broad participation in design activities (Fischer, 2013). In this view, in a broader and updated definition, EUD is not only important in the context of software systems (the primary focus of EUP and EUSE), but it "encompasses methods, techniques, methodologies, situations, and socio-technical environments that allow end users to act as professionals in those domains in which they are not professionals." Examples can be found in software systems, as well as in many other technological fields. In 3D modeling, for example, non-professional designers can today easily create their models and 3D print them to obtain the desired physical artifacts; or family members can easily create and control their smart home by using cheap off-the-shelf devices, smart objects and smartphones. Such a new perspective aims at seeing EUD more than a mere technique or tool, but includes conditions that allows end users to actually do EUD, easily and continuously, by taking advantage with respect to the traditional counterparts and finding this convenient and engaging during the time. This slightly differs, but includes, the definition given in the chapter by Ludwig et al. based on the concepts of the "gentle slope of complexity" (Ludwig, Dax, Pipek, Wulf, 2017).

An early inspiration for conceptualizing EUD as a transformational culture was articulated by Ivan Illich with *convivial systems* envisioned to "give each person who uses them the greatest opportunity to enrich the environment with the fruits of his or her vision" (Illich, 1973).

2.1 Meta-Design: Framing and Supporting EUD as a Cultural Transformation

Meta-design derives from the observation that designing a system that can sufficiently anticipate all possible uses in advance (that is, when the system is created) is an impossible task. This idea led for example to the downfall of expert systems and of closed systems in general (Fischer & Scharff, 2000). Closed systems typically create a sharp separation between design and use; however, providing functionality of interactive systems that is fixed when the system is created has important implications on how it will be used. As a consequence, it has been estimated that 40–60% of a system's cost over its lifetime is spent after the original system design is finished, not only to cope with the traditional need of "maintenance," but rather to carry out all those enhancement activities whose need is noticed by domain experts during the use of the system (Fischer & Scharff, 2000).

To this end, meta-design promotes the design of open systems that users can modify and evolve at use time (Henderson & Kyng, 1991). As open systems are used, users will encounter mismatches and opportunities serving as potential sources for new insights and new understandings, and giving rise to the *co-evolution* between system and users (Costabile, Fogli, Mussio, & Piccinno, 2007; Fogli & Piccinno, 2013a). Therefore, meta-design as "design for design after design" is a fundamentally different design methodology compared for example to user-centered design and participatory design, which substantially promote "design for use before use" (Binder et al., 2011; Ye & Fischer, 2007). Indeed, the latter approaches force all the design intelligence to the earliest part of the design process, when everyone knows the least about what is really needed. In a world that is not predictable, meta-design allows taking into account improvisation, evolution, and innovation by including the emergent and making it an opportunity for more creative and adequate solutions to problems (Fischer & Giaccardi, 2006). For these reasons, meta-design is an interdisciplinary activity, bringing together multiple perspectives from different stakeholders and areas of expertise: from designers having specific knowledge in mathematics, computer science, and engineering, but who are ignorant of the problem domain, to end users, who are experts in the problem domain, but ignorant of the domain of software solutions (Fischer, 2000). Such a "symmetry of ignorance" (Rittel, 1984) (or "asymmetry of knowledge") can be an advantage for social creativity instead of an obstacle for design. This is particularly true for ill-defined problems, whose solution cannot be delegated to professional software developers, but requires that end users, as owners of problems, be put in charge. For example, in an *interview with a geoscientist* of the University of Colorado reported in (Fischer, Nakakoji, & Ye, 2009), it emerged that this end user, after a three months period in acquiring programming knowledge, spent an hour every day on average in the development of software for data analysis. This was necessary, since there was not any suitable software available and explaining the needs to a software developer was not possible due their variability as the research progressed. Therefore, the geoscientist, even though not considering himself a software developer, arrived at accepting software development as an essential task of his daily work. A meta-design approach would have probably been better suited to such a situation, by involving the geoscientist in the design of an open system to be shaped to his own needs at use time, without requiring him to spend three months learning a programming language. Such an approach would be even more useful in other domains (such as the medical one), in which domain experts are not interested and not motivated to invest time in learning technical skills that are not directly related to their work, rather they are willing to manipulate building blocks that make sense to their work practice (Cabitza & Simone, 2017).

In summary, meta-design does not only encompass the study and development of enabling technologies for EUD, but also and above all sustaining a *cultural transformation* (Benkler, 2006; Fischer, 2013; von Hippel, 2005). Therefore, the primary objective of meta-design is to allow and support end users to become end-user developers of their systems, where, nowadays, the term "system" denotes all the software and hardware components such as smartphones, smart watches, interactive displays, as well as the low cost devices that contribute to create the so-called Internet of Things (Barricelli & Valtolina, 2015; Cabitza, Fogli, Lanzilotti, & Piccinno, 2016).

2.2 Integrating and Relating Meta-Design with other Frameworks

Framing meta-design as a cultural transformation from *closed systems* (designed at design time and fixed at use time) to the design of *open systems* that users can modify and evolve at use time relates meta-design with a number of other frameworks summarized in Table 1 and briefly described below.

Libertarian Paternalism. An interesting perspective and framework for EUD is provided by the book "Nudge: Improving Decisions about Health, Wealth, and Happiness" (Thaler & Sunstein, 2009). The fundamental concept explored in the book is *libertarian paternalism*. The *libertarian* aspect of their approach "lies in the straightforward insistence that, in general, people should be free to do what they like and to opt out of undesirable arrangements if they want to do so" (p. 5). The *paternalistic* objective is grounded in the claim that "it is legitimate for choice architects to try to influence people's behavior in order to make their lives longer, healthier, and better" (p. 5). *Nudges* are defined by choice architects trying to

Table 1 Overview of related frameworks

Framework	Relationship to meta-design
Libertarian Paternalism	Providing evidence for the different ways how control can be divided between designers and end users
Social Production	Illustrating the possibilities and the power how individual autonomy can lead to interesting new artifacts
Democratizing Innovation	Allowing professional amateurs to do things because they want to do them
Wikinomics	Supporting mass collaboration
Remix	Indicating the intellectual property challenges with evolving artifacts
Technology Mediated Social Participation	Representing a model for new scientific communities
Maker Movement	Technology-based extension of a "Do-it-Yourself (DIY)" culture

motivate people to engage in certain actions and behavior. The role of choice architects is closely related to the role of meta-designers who create contexts in which users can provide content. By providing rich seeds (Fischer & Ostwald, 2002), they impose structures that affect the choices and actions of users, making a certain level of paternalism inevitable. The approach provides evidence and arguments about the importance of good defaults especially for activities that users consider personally of minimal relevance: users welcome a default rule and prede-fined functionality making life simpler and easier and protecting them from parti-cipation overload (see Sect. 5.2) and against their own mistakes.

Social Production. Benkler (2006) provides an elaborate framework and argu-ments that the most important aspect of the networked information economy is the possibility for reversing the *control focus* of the industrial information economy by enriching individual autonomy. This objective will be achieved by creating environments built less around control and more around facilitating action. He differentiates between passive (e.g. television) and active (e.g. open source, Wikipedia, Second Life) media (see Sect. 4.1). In active media, users are restricted to the role of consumers limited to selecting finished goods they can consume from a pre-defined range of options whereas in active media users are treated as active, creative human beings, capable of solving their own problems and building their own fantasies, alone and in affiliation with others.

Democratizing Innovation. Von Hippel (2005) provides evidence from a broad range of different domains that users (supported by improvements in com-puter and communication technology) increasingly can develop their own new artifacts and services. His case studies demonstrate that users (acting as profes-sional amateurs – "pro-ams" – (Leadbeater & Miller, 2004)) who innovate can develop exactly what they want, rather than relying on designers of manufacturers to act as their agents or scribes. Additionally, individual users (acting as power users, local developers, and gardeners (Nardi, 1993)) do not have to develop everything they need on their own: they can benefit from innovations developed and freely shared by others.

Wikinomics. Tapscott and Williams (2006) in their book "Wikinomics: How Mass Collaboration Changes Everything" explore what the Web 2.0 (O'Reilly, 2005) and mass collaboration (Cress, Jeong, & Moskaliuk, 2016) means for busi-ness and technology. They describe and analyze a number of success stories (including Wikipedia, open source, and LEGO) and introduce a number of con-cepts such as "prosumers" (indicating that users today often being "producers" in one context and "consumers" in another one). While the book analyzes success stories based on wiki-based environments, it does not mention that many efforts engaging users in participation (including their own effort that readers edit their book or write a chapter of it) did not succeed providing evidence for the empirical finding that "most wikis are dead at arrival."

Remix. Lessig (2008) in his book "Remix: Making Art and Commerce Thrive in the Hybrid Economy" analyzes participatory cultures (as promoted and sup-ported by meta-design) from an *intellectual property perspective*. He distinguishes between two cultures: (1) a RO ("Read/Only") culture dominated by consumption, and (2) a RW (Read/Write) culture in which all people contribute to the re-creation and evolution of an existing culture by remixing existing components to create new ones. He discusses specifically the importance of "amateur creativity" (Leadbeater & Miller, 2004) in a RW culture (resembling the creativity of end users in an EUD culture) and how to avoid that this creativity is restricted by copyright regulation.

Technology Mediated Social Participation (TMSP). TMSP (http://tmsp.umd. edu) represents a movement (sponsored by the U.S. National Science Foundation) aiming to develop a scientific research agenda and educational recommendations for creating a cohesive community that generates the foundational science, engineering, and graduate training necessary for a new era of social participation technologies by empowering individuals to become active in local and global communities with a focus on exploring questions of how to motivate participation, increase social trust, and promote collaboration (Shneiderman, 2009).

Maker Movement. A basic belief and objective underlying the community of Makers is that the movement will end the monopoly of mass manufacturing just as the Internet ended the monopoly of mass media (Anderson, 2012). It creates a culture that represents a technology-based extension (with 3D printers, laser cutters, microcontrollers, etc.) of the "Do-it-Yourself (DIY)" culture (as it has existed in numerous other domains such as home improvement activities). It emphasizes learning-through-doing in social environments by highlighting informal, networked, peer-led, and shared learning motivated by interest and fun.

2.3   Methodologies and Models Extending the Meta-Design Framework

The meta-design framework has inspired some methodologies for modeling and developing systems for EUD. Two of such extensions will be briefly described.

Software Shaping Workshop (SSW). The SSW is a design methodology based on the meta-design framework to model EUD-enabling systems (Costabile, Fogli, Mussio, & Piccinno, 2006; Costabile et al., 2007). The idea underlying this methodology is that software environments should be designed in analogy with artisan workshops, where traditional artisans, such as blacksmiths and joiners, extract the necessary tools to perform their activities from a repository, put them on a bench to do their work and finally set back in the repository those ones not useful anymore. In this way, artisans shape their work environments to their needs by using all and only the tools needed in a *specific* situation. By analogy, a SSW is designed as a virtual workshop, in which end users find a set of virtual tools useful to carry out their activities and shape their environment and tools by adapting them to their current needs, without the burden of using a traditional programming language. In SSW, end users manipulate objects and tools through a suitable domain-oriented visual language, and unwittingly create software programs (Costabile, Mussio, Parasiliti Provenza, & Piccinno, 2008), through which they later perform the necessary computations. In the SSW approach, users play two distinct roles, which should be supported by two types of SSWs. The former is that of end users who perform their work activities; the latter refers to domain experts, who are called on to design the SSW for end users in collaboration with other experts, e.g. software engineers, graphic designers, and HCI experts. End users will use *application SSWs*; whilst, the workshops used by domain experts to perform their design activities are called *system workshops*. The other members of the design team are supported by system workshops as well; all application and system workshops are customized to the culture and skills of their users. The designed interactive system results in a hierarchical network of SSWs, each specific for a community of users (Costabile et al., 2007). The network encompasses three levels: (1) the *meta-design level*, where software engineers shape the tools and the system workshops to be used in the next level; (2) the *design level*, where HCI experts and domain experts use their system workshops to design, implement, and validate the application workshops devoted to end users; and (3) the *use level*, where end users of the different sub-communities use their application workshops and cooperate to achieve a task.

The SSW methodology encourages software designers to become *meta-designers* by involving all stakeholders in system design. In SSW, all stakeholders can make contributions that will be available to the other stakeholders for evaluation and feedback, in order to eventually converge to a common design. In light of these considerations, meta-design has been conceived in (Costabile, Fogli, Mussio, & Piccinno, 2005) as "a technique, which provides the stakeholders in the design team with suitable languages and tools to foster their personal and common reasoning about the development of interactive software systems to support user work." This definition complements that of Fischer and Giaccardi, who conceive meta-design as a conceptual framework for defining and creating socio-technical infrastructures in which new forms of collaborative design can take place (Fischer & Giaccardi, 2006).

Hive-Mind Space (HMS) Model. The HMS model (Zhu, 2012; Zhu, Barricelli, & Iacob, 2011; Zhu, Mussio, & Barricelli, 2010) is an evolution of the SSW methodology specifically oriented to support collaborative and creative design activities of multidisciplinary design teams. Hive Mind models in general focus on the collective intelligence (the hive mind) of people collaborating to pursue a common goal. They rely on the metaphor that people may collaborate within a community as a swarm of bees (Kelly, 1995), where each member of the community interacts locally, according to local rules, with a limited number of other community members, and the global behavior of the community emerges from local interactions. The HMS blends the general Hive Mind models and the SSW approach to support collaborative design and to foster creativity among design teams. The HMS model considers group activities, collective intelligence, and social creativity; whilst, from the SSW approach, the HMS model retains the three-level structure of the SSW network and enriches the workshops with tools for communication with other members of the same community and with other communities involved in the design collaboration. To this end, the HMS model introduces a central communication channel, called *digital boundary zone*, that allows the exchange and management of so-called *digital boundary objects* (Zhu et al., 2010) consisting of software artifacts to represent what stakeholders mean during a collaboration activity. The HMS model supports a *Community of Interest* (CoIs) (Fischer, 2001) composed of a set of *Communities of Practice* (CoPs) (Wenger, 1998; Wenger, McDermott, & Snyder, 2002). Indeed, the HMS model, as well as the SSW approach, offers different workshops for various CoPs involved in collaborative design, each one localized to the CoP's culture, role and platform in use. Furthermore, the architecture proposed for the HMS model has an open under-development structure: further levels could be added to the network and at each level new CoPs can collaborate if needed. In order to evaluate the HMS model and provide some concrete guidelines for its implementation, the MikiWiki meta-design environment has been developed (Zhu, Vaghi, & Barricelli, 2011). It is a structured programmable wiki that encompasses a hierarchical page organization made of pages and folder pages. Communication features are made available in MikiWiki as underdesigned "nuggets" (e.g. *chat, comment, wall*, and *notify* nuggets), which also represent the seeds (Fischer et al., 2001) for promoting system appropriation and modification. Users can easily start using and remixing existing nuggets, while power users may modify them, thus introducing new behaviors. MikiWiki has been applied in a variety of case studies, including the support of co-located meetings for the collaborative design of original mobile applications, such as the creativity barometer (Zhu & Herrmann, 2013).

The above conceptualizations define and support the role of meta-designers as professionals (1) using their own creativity to produce socio-technical environments in which other people can be creative and (2) defining the technical and social conditions for broad participation in design activities, which are as important as creating the software artifacts themselves.

3 Exploring Applications in Different Domains from a Meta-Design Perspective

This section presents some applications in different domains for which a meta-design perspective has been adopted. It is based on specific case studies (discussed in more detail in other publications) illustrating how meta-design has allowed modeling problems in innovative ways and putting end users in charge with the help of socio-technical mechanisms enabling EUD activities. They are all examples of system design to support human-problem interaction, rather than human-computer interaction (see design guidelines listed in Sect. 6). However, it is worth noticing that tools developed in the case studies were not deployed, but remained at an academic proofs-of-concept level; therefore, no consideration about consequences of long-term participation within related communities will be provided.

3.1 E-government

Meta-design and EUD techniques have been applied in the e-government domain pursuing two main objectives: (1) supporting municipality clerks in performing content authoring tasks by paying attention to the accessibility of the underlying web-oriented code (Fogli, 2009; Fogli, Colosio, & Sacco, 2010); and (2) supporting the same users in the creation of online e-government services devoted to citizens (Fogli & Parasiliti Provenza, 2011, 2012).

In the first case, a Content Management System (CMS) was extended to allow end users creating accessible web content (e.g. tables that could be easily accessed by visually impaired people) without being aware of performing software development, that is, creating proper HTML code. The extended CMS allowed users to accomplish tasks by simply editing content or selecting some content from available choices; the system then generated the correct HTML code by exploiting the content provided by the user. In the case of e-government service creation, a meta-design approach structured in two main phases was adopted: (1) a bottom-up activity was carried out, starting from the analysis of current services made available by the municipality, with the aim of defining a meta-model of e-government services; and (2) an EUD environment that allowed civil servants to create instances of the meta-model was developed; this environment allowed creating XML documents, without being aware of that, and these documents were automatically interpreted to generate web applications that implemented e-government services (see Fig. 2).

Both objectives were achieved after the observation of the daily tasks of end users (civil servants) and their usual approach to the use of computer systems; in this way, a fill-in form interaction style was provided in both solutions, given that administration tasks often consist in the compilation of paper-based forms. In the case of service creation, the interaction style was combined with a wizard design pattern that reflected the structure of the service to be created. Indeed, according to libertarian paternalism (Sect. 2.2), the civil servants should not have had so

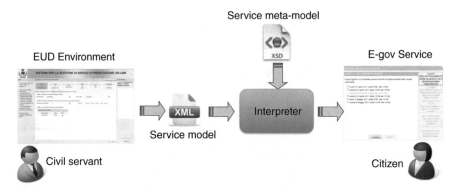

Fig. 2 EUD approach to e-government service creation

much freedom (and consequent responsibility) to modify the layout of the service pages or the structure of the service. In this way, service analysis and model-based design of EUD techniques remained in control of the software developers, as well as the consequent development of the fill-in forms that allowed civil servants to create online services.

In both cases, the rational for participation of civil servants consisted in becoming more independent from IT people for editing web site content and defining e-government services respectively. An EUD approach to this field was indeed been recognized by the domain experts as a way to improve work practice, in terms of effectiveness and efficiency, especially in those small or rural government agencies that cannot afford the budget necessary to employ software professionals or pay for software consultants. In this sense, EUD in the e-government domain can be conceived as a social production framework (Benkler, 2006) (Sect. 2.2), which contributes to enrich individual autonomy by making people capable of solving their own problems.

3.2 Mash-ups

From the end users' perspective, the development of web-based interactive systems is a demanding task. Perfectly in line with a democratized innovation (von Hippel, 2005), a common technique addressing this problem are mash-ups, i.e. the creation of Web applications through the composition of available Web services, without requiring skills in computer programming. Cappiello and colleagues present DashMash (Cappiello et al., 2011), an end-user oriented platform enabling inexperienced users to compose their own mash-ups, in the form of dashboards exploiting company-internal services operating on data warehouses and public APIs.

The work in (Ghiani, Paternò, & Spano, 2011) proposes an approach, based on direct manipulation, which allows end users to create mash-ups by using web components extracted from existing web applications, such as Amazon or eBay. Other EUD tools for mash-ups are based on annotation features (e.g. Avola, Bottoni, & Genzone, 2011; Dittrich, Madsen, & Rasmussen, 2011).

A recent mash-up platform, EFESTO, enables end users to create interactive workspaces by exploiting visual composition paradigms that accommodate the end-user mental model. With EFESTO end users create "live mash-ups" where information is dynamically extracted from heterogeneous data sources and visualized and manipulated into visual templates (Desolda, Ardito, & Matera, 2016). Besides the composition paradigm for end users, one of the most relevant features of EFESTO is the possibility to exploit the data available in the Linked Open Data cloud. In fact, this mash-up platform allows end users to extend a Web service with the so-called "polymorphic data source" built on top of the Linked Open Data cloud. It is called polymorphic because it provides mutable information with respect to the data sources of which it is composed (Desolda, 2015).

Following a RW culture, instead of a RO one, mash-up platforms can be regarded as EUD environments able to foster user creativity in defining tools for personalized search and data analysis, and, at the same time, transform end users from consumers of a variety of Web services into producers of Web applications suitable to their work practice or personal needs.

3.3   Electronic Patient Records

Patient records are official artifacts with which medical and paramedical personnel preserve the memory or knowledge of facts and events that occurred in a hospital ward (Berg, 1999). The patient record is a many-sided document: it is available to several different people, with different skills, background and expertise. They are not only physicians and nurses, but also patients and their relatives; thus patient records must have the ability to speak different "voices" to convey different meanings according to people using it (Cabitza & Simone, 2009). A patient record is composed of a number of modules, each one containing specific patient data; hospital personnel in different wards are usually only interested in a subset of such modules. The employees use the modules to accomplish their specific tasks: for example, the reception staff records personal data at the acceptance of patients into the hospital; physicians examine other modules to make a diagnosis; nurses record medications and patients' parameters; and so on.

The development of the Electronic Patient Record (EPR) must take into account the various stakeholders involved in the EPR management and their different needs and personal (visual) languages. In the study reported in (Costabile et al., 2009), five different stakeholders have been identified: (1) *practice managers*, who decide the modules to be taken into account for the hospital; (2) *head physicians*, who are responsible for the specific EPR (subset of modules) for the ward; (3) *physicians*, using the EPR into their ward; (4) *nurses*, who fill the EPR; and (5) *administrative staff* who manages patient admission and billing. This is a typical situation that can be found in any hospital. In particular, the head physician has the responsibility of the definition of the EPR to be adopted in her/his ward, and currently must transfer her/his EPR specification to IT personnel or software consultants for successive implementation.

The SSW methodology described in Sect. 2.3 has been applied for the development of a novel concept of EPR, tailored to the ward's needs and to the different stakeholders' preferences and practices (Costabile et al., 2007, 2008). In particular, the hierarchical and interconnected structure of SSWs has allowed implementing the concept of libertarian paternalism (Sect. 2.2). At the *meta-design level* foreseen by the SSW methodology a team composed of software engineers, HCI experts and physicians designed the software environments for the different stakeholders, as well as the data modules, which are the basic components of the EPR. At the design level, software environments allowing each head physician to design the EPR for her/his ward by directly manipulating data modules in her/his software environment have been created, without depending anymore on "high-tech scribes," but sharing control on the system with them (see design guidelines in Sect. 6). In this case, physicians and nurses of a specific ward are the end users, while the head physician is the end-user developer in charge of creating the EPR for them.

3.4 Supporting People with Cognitive Disabilities

People with cognitive disabilities represent a "universe of one" problem (Carmien & Fischer, 2008, 2010). They often will have several different disabilities and each specific combination of cognitive, motoric, sensory, and psychological impairments together define a need for deeply customized assistive technology such that a solution for one person will rarely work for another. The "universe of one" conceptualization includes the empirical finding that (1) *unexpected islands of abilities* exist: users can have unexpected skills and abilities that can be leveraged to ensure a better possibility of task accomplishment; and (2) *unexpected deficits of abilities* exist often occurring in otherwise high functioning individuals. Accessing and addressing these unexpected variations in skills and needs, particularly with respect to creating task support, requires an intimate knowledge of the user that *only caregivers* can provide.

The fundamental challenge derived from supporting the "universe of one" requirement is that it demands highly specific systems that we tried to achieve with a *meta-design approach*.

The *Memory Aiding Prompting System* (MAPS) (Carmien, 2006) represents a socio-technical environment based on a meta-design framework by providing the caregivers the design power to modify and evolve the technical systems according to the needs of individual users. To accommodate unexpected issues at use time, systems need to be *underdesigned* (Brand, 1995) by providing a context and a background against which situated cases can be interpreted thereby allowing the "owners of problems" to create the solutions themselves at use time.

Supporting people with cognitive disabilities represents a *multi-tiered proxy design problem*, since the end users (the persons with cognitive disabilities) cannot act as end-user developers, but only their caregivers can exercise this role. Some problems are characterized by the presence of end users that may not be able to express their needs, requiring additional stakeholders to articulate such needs and act as end-user developers on behalf of them and for them (see the proposed taxonomy of EUD activities in Sect. 4.3).

The challenge of MAPS was to design tools flexible enough to adapt to the unique needs of people with cognitive disabilities. The system was developed as a platform able to provide a prompting system for individuals with cognitive disabilities, along with an editing tool that allowed caregivers to design prompting scripts (Fig. 3). It was aimed to support the independence and safety of people with cognitive disabilities in their daily activities, such as going to a grocery store or taking

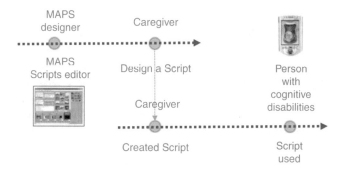

Fig. 3 MAPS: empowering caregivers to act as designers

a bus. Participation was motivated by the fact that creating a specific environment by caregivers helped the people with cognitive abilities. Furthermore, like in other applications previously described, participation was facilitated by domain-oriented interaction support: indeed, designing a system for a unique use could be learnt and done with a reasonable time investment, thus coping with the trade-off between cultures of participation and participation overload (see Sect. 5.2).

MAPS included: (1) an editor to enable the caregiver (usually a family member) to edit, store, and reuse multimedia scripts for prompting instructions to support different daily tasks (i.e. sequences of video and verbal instructions); (2) a shared information space for storing script images and sounds, user and task modeling meta-data, and a repository of tested scripts to be used as templates by other caregivers using the editor; and (3) a PDA-based device that prompted instructions to support the persons with cognitive disabilities in the accomplishment of their daily tasks.

Multi-tiered proxy design problems push further in the direction of adopting meta-design approaches, since all involved stakeholders must be provided with suitable languages and tools to foster their participation in the development of software and hardware systems that support end users (Costabile et al., 2007).

3.5   Physical rehabilitation

The PhD research of Daniel Tetteroo (2013, 2015) explored the design, development, and deployment of an end user extensible physical rehabilitation technology (called TagTrainer). The thesis provides a socio-technical perspective on the merits and issues related to the deployment of an EUD system in the context of physical rehabilitation therapy requiring personalized exercises, due to the high diversity in patients and their corresponding treatment needs.

TagTrainer is a tangible, interactive training platform for arm-hand rehabilitation exercises focused on relearning daily activities, such as manipulating cutlery and cups, in patients who experienced a stroke (Tetteroo, Seelen, Timmermans, & Markopoulos, 2014). It consists of four parts: (1) one or more interactive boards that can give audio-visual feedback and are able to detect RFID-tagged objects; (2) a collection of objects with RFID-tags attached to them; (3) the TagTrainer Exercise Creator, which supports therapists in creating and modifying exercises to be executed on the board; and (4) the TagTrainer Patient Interface, which allows therapists to manage personalized exercise programs by providing patients with feedback about their progress. From a preliminary study, it emerged that therapists are not information workers and usually do not rely on ICT for delivering treatment to patients; however, a cultural transformation could be fostered through TagTrainer, which allowed therapists to become end-user developers, without the need to learn any programming language.

The PhD thesis describes the user-centered and participatory design process adopted for TagTrainer development; and it presents four studies in which TagTrainer was deployed in the context of rehabilitation clinics. The aim of these studies was to evaluate the acceptance of TagTrainer, to probe the feasibility of therapists as end-user developers of training exercises (supported by a meta-design environment based on a closely related architecture as illustrated in Fig. 3 for MAPS), and to identify factors that influence the uptake of EUD practices. In particular, it has been observed how therapists varied in engagement as exercise creators: indeed, they played different roles, either (re-)using existing exercises or creating new ones, depending on their attitudes, age, and experience with information technology, as anticipated by cultures of participation theory introduced in (Fischer, 2011) (see Sect. 4.1). The research effort centered on TagTrainer identified some key challenges for enabling EUD practices (see Tetteroo & Markopoulos, 2017) in clinical settings. This by aligning with the organization model, guiding end-user developers to ensure usability and software quality of their creations (see design tradeoffs discussed in Sect. 5), and providing features for retrieval and sharing of solutions created by end-user developers (Tetteroo et al., 2014).

3.6   Virtual worlds

Research conducted by Benjamin Koehne (Koehne, Redmiles, & Fischer, 2011) (closely related to the research by Mørch and colleagues (Caruso, Hartley, & Mørch, 2015; Mørch, Caruso, Hartley, 2017)) employed meta-design based theories in *virtual worlds* specifically by contrasting massively-multiplayer online role-playing games such as "Lord of the Rings Online" with open-ended virtual worlds such as "Second Life." The research employed ethnographic methods to explore the following research objectives:

- develop *additional examples* of meta-design for worlds that have no laws and boundaries;
- support the *empowerment of end users* that are not initially interested or motivated to conduct design practice;

- assess the *duality* between virtual worlds and meta-design, i.e. how does meta-design affects practices in *virtual worlds* and vice versa; and
- analyze the *support for meta-design* in both unique environments, focusing on the benefits and shortcomings of the gaming-oriented and the open-ended environment under study.

Some of the findings of this research can be summarized as follows:

- Virtual worlds offer an opportunity to study the effects of collaboration on the way casual users move through rich ecologies of participation (see Sect. 4.2). Technical scaffolding systems alone are not sufficient. Instead, social community components need to make collaboration tools more accessible and attractive for casual users.
- Current open-ended virtual worlds (such as Second Life) provide means for extensions through source code modification which only technical people will be able to do. Additional mechanisms supporting meta-design would empower end users to extend these systems with additional capabilities.

4   New Conceptual Developments

This section explores some of the concepts related to the meta-design paradigm that emerged or were refined in the last decade. Table 2 briefly summarizes such concepts, while the next subsections discuss them in more detail.

Table 2 Concepts related to meta-design

Concept	Description
Cultures of participation	A shift from a consumer culture to cultures of participation, in which all people are provided with the socio-technical means for participation, has been observed in commercial systems and scientific works.
Rich ecologies of participation	Beyond the roles of consumer and designer, other roles of end users have been identified in literature; this led to identify richer ecologies of participation in software development.
Taxonomy of EUD activities	Different types of EUD activities have been identified and classified as individual EUD, public inward EUD and public outward EUD.
Co-evolution model	A model describing the interaction and co-evolution of users and systems is proposed; it takes into consideration all the different types of EUD foreseen in the EUD taxonomy.

4.1   Cultures of Participation

The rise in *social computing* (based on social production and mass collaboration) has facilitated a shift from *consumer cultures* (specialized in producing finished artifacts to be consumed passively) to *cultures of participation* (in which all people are provided with the means to participate and to contribute actively in personally meaningful problems) (Fischer, 2011; Jenkins, 2009).

Cultures of participation are facilitated and supported by a variety of different technological environments (such as: the participatory Web ("Web 2.0") (O'Reilly, 2005), table-top computing and domain-oriented design environments (Arias, Eden, & Fischer, 2016)); all of them contributing in different ways to the aims of engaging diverse audiences, enhancing creativity, sharing information, and fostering the collaboration among users acting as active contributors and designers. They democratize design and innovation (von Hippel, 2005) by shifting power and control towards users, supporting them to act as both designers and consumers ("prosumers") (Tapscott & Williams, 2006) and allowing systems to be shaped through real-time use.

The following design requirements derived from the meta-design framework support cultures of participation as follows:

- *Making changes must seem possible:* Contributors should not be intimidated and should not have the impression that they are incapable of making changes; the more users become convinced that changes are not as difficult as they think they are, the more they may be willing to participate.
- *Changes must be technically feasible:* If a system is closed, then contributors cannot make any changes; as a necessary prerequisite, there needs to be possibilities and mechanisms for extension.
- *Benefits must be perceived:* Contributors have to believe that what they get in return justifies the investment they make. The benefits perceived may vary and can include: professional benefits (helping for one's own work), social benefits (increased status in a community, possibilities for jobs), and personal benefits (engaging in fun activities).
- *The environments must support tasks that people engage in:* The best environments will not succeed if they are focused on activities that people do rarely or consider of marginal value.
- *Low barriers must exist to sharing changes:* Evolutionary growth is greatly accelerated in systems in which participants can share changes and keep track of multiple versions easily. If sharing is difficult, it creates an unnecessary burden that participants are unwilling to overcome.
- *Defining the role of meta-designers:* Meta-designers should use their own creativity in developing socio-technical environments in which other people can be put in charge. They must be willing to share control of how systems will be used, which content will be contained, and which functionality will be supported.

Cultures of participation support users as active contributors who can transcend the functionality and content of existing systems. By facilitating these possibilities, *control* is distributed among all stakeholders in the design process. There is evidence that shared control will lead to more innovation (von Hippel, 2005): "Users that innovate can develop exactly what they want, rather than relying on manufacturers to act as their (often very imperfect) agents." (A similar argument surfaced in the interview with the geo-scientist described earlier). Cultures of participation erode monopoly positions held by professions, educational institutions, experts, and high-tech scribes (Fischer, 2002). Drawbacks and trade-offs associated with cultures of participation are discussed in Sect. 2.

4.2   Rich Ecologies of Participation

Users and developers are commonly considered two distinct groups of people. Nowadays, with the Web 2.0 and the widespread use of web-based software systems, the sharp distinction between users and developers is quickly disappearing since users are more and more involved in the development of interactive (web-based) systems. An example is given by Google Sites and the many other similar platforms that today allow even naïve users to have an active role in the development of web sites suited to their needs. This results in a continuum ranging between end users as passive consumers to meta-designers (Fischer & Giaccardi, 2006). In some cases, the same individuals play different roles: sometimes they are and want to be consumers, in other situations they prefer to be designers. Therefore, the terms "consumer" and "designer" cannot be considered as attributes of a person, but as roles in a specific context. More generally, several virtual organizations of end users exist in which richer ecologies of participants can develop according to their own needs (Preece & Shneiderman, 2009). A deeper understanding of these ecologies leads to identify further roles beyond the traditional ones: *professional amateurs* (Leadbeater & Miller, 2004), *prosumers* (Tapscott & Williams, 2006), *power users, local developers*, and *gardeners* (Nardi, 1993), *bricolant-bricoleur* (Cabitza & Simone, 2015). Such roles need to be exploited to create multi-faceted computational environments (Myers, Ko, & Burnett, 2006) tailored to the interests, needs and expertise of different stakeholders (see for instance the SSW methodology and HMS model discussed in Sect. 2.3), in order to also support *migration paths* among the different roles (Fischer, Piccinno, & Ye, 2008).

The meta-designer role is usually intended for those professionals who are in charge of creating "open systems at design time that can be modified by their users, acting as co-designers, requiring and supporting more complex interactions at use time" (Fischer & Herrmann, 2011). The work of Cabitza, Fogli, and Piccinno (2014b) extended this definition by introducing a distinct role for her/his social counterpart, that is the role of the *maieuta designer*.[1] On the one hand, the meta-designer is regarded more as a technical role: he/she is in charge of designing the EUD environment and all those tools by which end users could carry out their EUD activities. On the other hand, the maieuta designer can be considered as someone in charge of designing the EUD-enabling environment by creating the *social conditions* for end users to become developers of their own system. These social conditions include: (1) sustaining end users to appropriate the design culture and the technical notions necessary for system development; (2) involving as many end users as possible in the process of continuous refinement of the system, by stimulating their participation and providing tools supporting their collaboration; and (3) facilitating the migration from the role of passive user to that of end-user developer. For these reasons, such a designer has been called a "maieuta," that is, someone who is able to apply the Socratic method of making people acquire notions, motivations, and self-confidence to undertake challenging tasks.

The maieuta designers are the persons who guarantee the long-term sustainability of an EUD project. Indeed, they should be identified within a community as someone who could make all community members become progressively independent from the IT professionals. One of their main tasks is to design (or better "co-design") initiatives in which to promote the EUD project and transfer to the community members the underlying values and concepts (i.e. empowerment, co-production, appropriation, cultures of participation, etc.). For example, the maieuta designer can devise simple mechanisms to foster participation and build a real culture of participation by creating proper motivation strategies, e.g. by exploiting gamification mechanisms (Benzi, Cabitza, Fogli, Lanzilotti, & Piccinno, 2015), and by creating collaboration infrastructures (e.g. by setting up social media associated with the EUD project to stimulate contributions and moderate communication among community members).

4.3 EUD Taxonomy

The new developments that occurred in the EUD field in the last ten years have led research scholars to analyze the new concepts, roles, and artifacts developed around EUD. To this aim, an EUD taxonomy has been proposed in (Cabitza, Fogli, & Piccinno, 2014a). In this taxonomy, a classification of EUD into *individual EUD* and *public EUD* is proposed (see Fig. 4). Individual EUD encompasses all those activities that are concerned with the creation, modification or extension of a software artifact for personal use only (therefore, individual EUD overlaps with End-User Programming (Myers et al., 2006)). Typical examples of individual EUD are spreadsheet programming for macro creation or modification, and scripting environments,

---

[1]From "maieutic," the adjective relating to the method used by Socrates of eliciting knowledge in the mind of a person by interrogation and insistence on close and logical reasoning (http://dictionary.com).

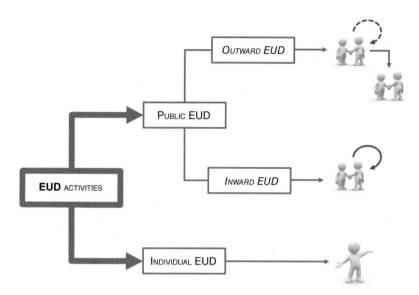

Fig. 4 A taxonomy of EUD activities

like R and MATLAB, for statistical computing and data visualization (used by biologists, geologists and other scientists to analyze and display their data autonomously).

Public EUD denotes all those situations where end users either create or configure software artifacts that are used by *other* people belonging to the same community (because they are colleagues and co-workers) or belonging to a different community (because they work in a different department). In both cases, public EUD means that the outcome of the EUD activity is aimed at being shared and publicly available to others than the end user involved in the programming activity. The main difference between public and individual EUD is then the explicit intention behind the development effort: either making something intended to be shared or not.

Public EUD can be further specialized into *inward EUD* and *outward EUD*. In the former case, the people carrying out the EUD activity work for a community they also belong to, as in the case of Electronic Patient Records mentioned before (Costabile et al., 2007, 2008). In inward EUD, activities are intended to support members of small teams and groups of people sharing sets of conventions, assumptions, and practices, i.e. communities of practice (Wenger, 1998; Wenger et al., 2002). In this case, one member or a group of members of the community carries out the EUD activities, possibly engaging a conversation with software professionals over time, according to a *mutual development* approach (Andersen & Mørch, 2009): they work for the proficiency of the community itself, given their (often tacit) knowledge of the characteristics and skills of its members. In the outward EUD case, the EUD activity is aimed at building and improving tools that have to be used across different communities or, even, in other communities. Therefore, at least two communities (forming a community of interest (Fischer, 2001)), are involved and there is no guarantee that those who carry out EUD activities will also take advantage of the product of these activities. For example, in the e-government case (see Sect. 1) (Fogli & Parasiliti Provenza, 2011, 2012), the civil servants are in charge of creating e-government services for the citizens, whereas in the Memory Aiding Prompting System (see Sect. 3.4) (Carmien & Fischer, 2010), caregivers develop and customize prompting systems for persons with cognitive disabilities. Therefore, in public outward EUD, the quality of the software artifacts created by the end-user developers is more important than in individual and public inward EUD (see design tradeoffs in Sect. 5.5).

The objective of deepening the meaning implicit in the taxonomy is twofold. On the one hand, it suggests that there exist different "types" of end-user developments, and thus different meta-design frameworks, methods, and techniques should be considered for sustaining the activities of the end-user developers. On the other hand, it focuses on public EUD that is more and more pervading our daily life, but that has not received so far enough attention by the EUD community (this is true especially for outward EUD).

4.4 Co-evolution Model

EUD encompasses techniques and applications that empower end users to develop and adapt systems creating foundations for the co-evolution of users and systems (Costabile et al., 2007). To model this phenomenon, the *Interaction and Co-Evolution (ICE)* model (proposed in Costabile, Fogli, Marcante, & Piccinno, 2006) encompasses three cycles: the user-system interaction cycle, the task-artifact co-evolution cycle, and the organization-technology co-evolution cycle. The inner cycle emphasizes that two different interpretation processes occur inside the human and the machine, which may become the source of usability problems and are related to the communication gap existing between users and designers at design time. The task-artifact co-evolution cycle recalls a well-known phenomenon described by Carroll and Rosson (Carroll & Rosson, 1992), namely that the software artifacts created to support some user's tasks usually suggest new possible tasks and that, to support these new tasks, new artifacts must be created. The outer cycle regards the co-evolution phenomenon according to a wider view: since technological advances provide designers with new possibilities for improving interactive systems once they are already in use, these possibilities may change users' work habits, thus making their social and work organization evolve itself with technology.

The ICE model is suitable to individual EUD, whilst an extended model, ICE^2, has been proposed in (Fogli & Piccinno, 2013a) to deal with public inward and outward EUD. Here, since end-user developers develop for others, they need to interact easily with an EUD environment to create, modify, or adapt software systems devoted to end users. Therefore, the ICE^2 model encompasses the end-user developer role, and three additional cycles model the mutual influence that systems and technology have with end-user developers and respective organizations.

Figure 5 illustrates the ICE^2 model presented in (Fogli & Piccinno, 2013a). The left-hand side of the figure corresponds to the ICE model previously

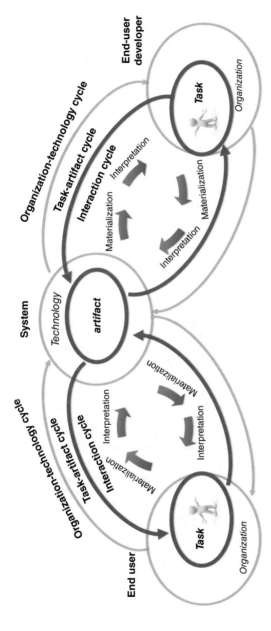

Fig. 5 The ICE^2 model

mentioned; it describes a process that is influenced by the specular process involving end-user developers, which is described by the right-hand side of the figure. The artifact can be regarded as a boundary object (Star, 1989) between the community of end users and that of end-user developers. It consists of the software system devoted to the end users and of the EUD tools used by end-user developers to generate and/ or adapt the software system for end users. Different kinds of interaction between the two co-evolution processes occur at use time. They are discussed in (Fogli & Piccinno, 2013a) with the help of some case studies.

5 Identifying Design Drawbacks and Trade-Offs Associated with Meta-Design

This section will examine some of the most important design trade-offs associated with meta-design. They are first summarized in Table 3 and then analyzed in the following sub-sections.

Table 3 Design trade-offs related to meta-design scenarios

Trade-off	Description
Standardization vs. Improvisation	Tension between improvisation that encompasses innovation and creativity and the need for providing standard applications easy to distribute and maintain.
Cultures of participation vs. Information, participation and collaboration overload	Cultures of participation can cause (1) information overload (by generating more information), (2) participation overload (by engaging people to act as active contributors), and (3) collaboration overload (by requiring coordination activities between the numerous contributors).
End-user driven evolution vs. Lack of continuity and synergy	End user-driven evolution is no guarantee for success because: (1) there is a lack of continuity over time, and (2) professional developers and users did not collaborate.
Usability of EUD products vs. flexibility of EUD tools	Guaranteeing the usability of the software artifacts created by end-user developers should be counterbalanced by a lack of flexibility in their creation/adaptation possibilities.
Utility vs. usability of EUD products	Some EUD projects should privilege utility whilst other should focus more on the usability of the results of EUD activities (i.e. EUD products); the "type" of EUD (see EUD taxonomy) may determine the choices in setting up the socio-technical conditions for EUD.

5.1   Standardization versus Improvisation

Meta-design creates inherent tensions, for example, between standardization and improvisation. The SAP Info (July 2003, page 33) argues to reduce the number of customer modifications (Fischer & Giaccardi, 2006, p. 446): "every customer modification implies costs because it has to be maintained by the customer. Each time a support package is imported there is a risk that the customer modification may have to be adjusted or re-implemented. To reduce the costs of such on-going maintenance of customer-specific changes, one of the key targets during an upgrade should be to return to the SAP standard wherever this is possible." Finding the right balance between standardization (which can suppress innovation and creativity) and improvisation (which can lead to a Babel of different and incompatible versions) has been noted as a challenge in open-source environments (Raymond & Young, 2001), in which forking has often led developers in different directions.

5.2   Transcending Consumer Cultures versus Information and Participation Overload

More and more information is available in the current digital society, coming from social networks, smart sensors and actuators, personal mobile systems, and web-based applications (e.g. there are approx. 1.5 Million Apps available for iPhones and Android phones). Better support environments (such as: search engines, recommender systems, aggregators systems, and context-aware applications based on user and task models) are needed to cope with this *information overload* (Fischer, 2012).

Cultures of participation (see Sect. 4.1) have as a downside that they are contributing to a *participation overload* problem. People are more and more required to personally take care of their bank accounts, travel arrangements, retirement plans, etc. All these activities are manifestations of the DIY society. E-participation, e-democracy, wikis, open source software and EUD environments represent other situations where end users are asked to participate with their opinions, votes, interests, knowledge and expertise. In addition, users are asked to participate in peer-support communities, collaboratories, and crowdsourcing environments.

Participation overload is one of the most serious problems for meta-design. The following design trade-offs should be taken into account:

- for *personally irrelevant problems,* individuals should not be forced to act as an active contributors in cases in which they want to be consumers; people do not enjoy freedom of choice, and specifically in complex and unfamiliar domains, active choosing can be a burden, not a benefit (in the libertarian paternalism framework (see Sect. 2.2) the paternalism dimensions should be emphasized);

- for *personally meaningful problems*, individuals should not be restricted to act as consumers in situations where they want to be active contributors and decision makers. In such situations, environments should support engagement, promote learning, and participation. The rationale for this is provided by the following observation: "The experience of having participated in a problem makes a difference to those who are affected by the solution. People are more likely to like a solution if they have been involved in its generation; even though it might not make sense otherwise" (Rittel, 1984).

To cope with the participation overload problem, existing *methods* such as rich seeds, reuse, redesign, and remixing need to be further improved and extended. *Support environments*, such as construction kits and domain-oriented design environments providing high-level building blocks and allowing users to express themselves in their own language should be studied and developed.

5.3   Lack of Continuity and Lack of Synergy

The Oregon Experiment, a housing experiment at the University of Oregon, instantiating the concept of end user-driven evolution, served as an interesting case study that end user-driven evolution is no guarantee for success (Alexander, 1975). The analysis of its unsustainability indicated two major reasons: (1) there was a lack of continuity over time, and (2) professional developers and users did not collaborate, so there was a lack of synergy. These findings led to postulate the need for methods and techniques for maintaining high the interest in the user-driven evolution activities during the time and making developers and users engage in intense collaborations. The first aspect regards *long-term sustainability*, i.e. the need for taking high the interest of users when they are involved as contributors in the evolution, even after that any expert has left them alone.

With design rationale captured, communication enhanced, and end-user modifiability supported, developers have a rich source of information to evolve the system in the way users really need it. This leads to address a new issue that is the *perception of relative advantage*: for an innovation to have an impact on the daily life of its users it is important that these latter ones perceive the new thing as giving them a clear advantage with respect to the traditional counterparts whatever these are (Emani et al., 2012).

As has been outlined in Sect. 4.2, in a richer ecology of participants, the role of the maieuta designer is to make the community around an EUD system progressively more independent from the professionals (Cabitza et al., 2014b). In other words, the maieuta designer is the person who is in charge of designing the EUD-enabling environment by creating the *social conditions* for end users to become developers of their own system and guaranteeing the long-term sustainability of the end-user driven evolution of the system at hand.

The more and more involvement of end users in the evolution of the system brings different stakeholders, including consultants, designers internal to the organization and end users, to collaborate among themselves to shape the system. This means that such stakeholders need to face fundamental challenges in learning how to communicate and in building a shared understanding. Such a *lack of synergy* emerged also because during time, users and environments evolve. Collaborative design has emerged as a response to the needs felt by various organizations of adapting software to specific environments and users. Visual mediation mechanisms for collaborative design, development and evolution of software have been proposed to provide a means to improve communication and cooperation among all stakeholders involved in the design process (Ardito et al., 2011).

5.4   Usability of EUD Products versus Flexibility of EUD Tools

Several companies are more and more requiring information systems that are flexible enough to be adapted to the variety of their users, e.g. employees, business analysts, customers, and providers (Dörner, Heß, & Pipek, 2007). EUD methods have been proposed as a solution for developing flexible systems, which can be adapted to the different needs directly on behalf of end users. However, such end users have no or few competencies in information technologies and often are not willing to acquire them; therefore, the software engineering community has raised many doubts on the effectiveness of the EUD approach, by underlying the important role played by skilled, professional software developers to guarantee software correctness, efficiency, maintainability, and security (Harrison, 2004). For these reasons, the End-User Software Engineering (EUSE) research addresses the issue of software quality in EUD (Burnett & Scaffidi, 2013). Literature works in this area propose methods oriented to non-professional software developers to carry out requirement analysis and specification, system design and reuse, code debugging, verification and testing. However, there is a further and important issue related to EUD, that is the usability of the software artifacts developed by end users (Fogli & Piccinno, 2013b). EUSE mainly considers EUD as an activity targeted to create programs for personal rather than public use, thus distinguishing it from professional programming (Ko et al., 2011); in this view, usability may not be an issue. However, if we consider public outward EUD (see Fig. 4), where end-user developers create and adapt programs for others (sometimes belonging to another community), usability of the results of the EUD activity could become a problem. This is due to the fact that end-user developers are neither professional developers nor HCI experts, and may have a vague understanding of the usability concept. The idea proposed in (Fogli & Piccinno, 2013a, b) to cope with this problem does not conceive EUD as direct creation of code on behalf of end-user developers, but as the instantiation of a meta-model that represents a domain-dependent class of software applications for end users. Therefore, usability of the resulting environments is achieved through a meta-design activity, carried out by a multi-disciplinary design team including domain experts, which is aimed at defining the conceptual model of the resulting applications, the meta-model subsuming them and proper EUD tools for instantiating the meta-model in a easy way by end-user developers. To guarantee usability, the types of available EUD activities should be restricted and end-user developers' creativity could be limited as a consequence. In summary, a trade-off would emerge between the flexibility of EUD tools and the usability of systems resulting from EUD activities.

5.5   Utility versus Usability of EUD Products

Another design trade-off that has been observed in different contexts is that between *utility* and *usability* of software applications. In Grudin (1992), Grudin highlighted that in in-house and internal system development emphasis is usually put on utility since software artifacts are built according to the functional needs of the company; whilst, in commercial projects, usability is more important, since one of the priorities is to facilitate system acceptance by users and thus promote the diffusion of the system.

This trade-off is revived in meta-design and is concerned with utility and usability of EUD products. Recalling the EUD taxonomy described in Sect. 4.3, if one considers individual EUD and public inward EUD, the activities of end-user development encompass system adaptation and extension to increase effectiveness of the individual user and/or of his/her community; therefore, emphasis in these cases should be mainly put on utility. On the other hand, in public outward EUD, end-user developers create or adapt a software artifact by constantly taking into account the requests of the end users belonging to a different community.

As a consequence the socio-technical conditions that meta-designers (and maieuta designers) must create are different for these two situations. To support end-user developers in individual EUD and public inward EUD, meta-design must focus on the design of EUD tools and infrastructures for communication within the community (Dittrich, Bolmsten, & Ericksson, 2017); furthermore, proper training of the end-user developers must be taken into consideration, both in terms of programming methods and languages and of software engineering methods for guaranteeing software quality (as EUSE prescribes). On the other hand, in public outward EUD, not only tools supporting end-user developers must fit their characteristics, skills and background, but also the artifacts created for end users by the end-user developers must be usable. Thus, in this case, EUD techniques must be based on domain-specific concepts inspired to daily work practices and enriched with proper mechanisms for making artifact creation easier and code generation transparent, as well as for guaranteeing the creation of usable artifacts. Therefore, in this case, end-user developers should be supported no more with training in programming, but rather with user-friendly and visually engaging EUD systems, along with motivation strategies to foster end-user developers' participation in effectively doing EUD.

6   Design Guidelines

The above mentioned conceptual developments and analyzed trade-offs and draw-backs led the research on EUD, meta-design, and co-design to look for design guidelines for domain experts and for designing in use.

Among them, the set of guidelines for *domain experts* (representing end users who are experts in domains other than software design) proposed in (Fischer et al., 2009) include:

- *Support human-problem interaction.* Domain experts are interested in solving their problems, rather than in interacting with computers, therefore design must support human-problem interaction, rather than human-computer interaction. This can be achieved by increasing domain specificity, as in the case of domain-oriented design environments (Arias et al., 2016) and the various Software Shaping Workshops (see Sect. 2.3) (Costabile et al., 2006, 2007).
- *Underdesign for emergent behavior. Underdesign* (Brand, 1995) relates to meta-design, in that it creates design spaces where users can create solutions suitable to their contingent needs allowing them to explore problems and solutions not envisioned at design time. Systems should be underdesigned so that users do not treat them as finished products but view them as continuous beta versions that are open to incorporate emergent design behaviors during use.
- *Enable legitimate peripheral participation.* Newcomers to a community must be able to engage in *legitimate peripheral participation* (Lave & Wenger, 1991) through transparent policies and procedures for incorporating user contributions into the software systems. To this aim, the system architecture must support rich ecologies of participation (see Sect. 4.2), in order to support newcomers in progressively difficult and independent tasks, so that they can start participating peripherally and move on gradually to take charge of more difficult tasks.
- *Share control.* Meta-designers must share control on the system with the participating users. Users can play different roles, depending on their level of involvement, and thus have their own responsibility and authority. When users change their roles in the community by making frequent and substantial contributions (Fischer et al., 2008), they should be granted with more authority in the decision-making process that shapes the system. This helps sustain user participation and system evolution: users become stakeholders, acquire ownership in the system, and will likely make further contributions; granting authority attracts (new) users who want to influence system development and encourages them to contribute.
- *Reward and recognize contributions.* Fostering user participation in system use and development requires paying attention to users' motivations. Human beings do not act only for material gain but also for psychological well-being, social integration and connectedness, social capital, recognition, and reputation (Benkler & Nissenbaum, 2006). Motivation is derived from users' satisfaction in their involvement by shaping the software system to solve their problems, and can be positively reinforced and amplified when the community's social structure and conventions reward and recognize the contributions of users.

- *Foster reflective communities*. The knowledge relevant to a complex design problem is usually distributed among many domain experts. Fostering reflective communities becomes a fundamental goal of meta-design (Arias et al., 2016) and can be achieved by creating proper mechanisms for collaboration among domain experts, who may bring controversial perspectives to the problem solution. This requires facilitating a shared understanding among domain experts, by allowing them to bring their different knowledge sources and equally contribute to the creation of new insights, new ideas, and new artifacts.

The set of guidelines for designing in use (Maceli & Atwood, 2011) are derived from the literature on *co-design* (in which designers and users collaboratively are shaping a system over time) and include:

- *Connect with other people with similar needs, both nearby and far away*. This principle would like to encourage designers to focus on how users can use the system to connect with other people, and how they might extend the system to satisfy this requirement.
- *Reach out and converse with other people in real-time, while they are using the system*. This principle emphasizes how users can have live experiences and conversations with other people, who could be not only other users within or outside their community, but also designers or users acting as designers. This principle also suggests paying attention to the emergent use of chat and microblogging tools to facilitate backchannel conversations.
- *Combine it with other tools and systems they use regularly*. The idea suggested by this principle is regarding a system as only one piece of a larger, evolving puzzle and not assume it to be something on which the user is totally focused for all the time. Users interact with several tools and systems on a daily basis and often at the same time. The possibility offered by mashups (see Sect. 3.2) to combine different data sources and programming interfaces to create novel tools is suggested as a possible way to address this need.
- *Begin using it quickly, without a lot of help or instruction*. This principle is related to the general and traditional theme of system usability; it is aimed at envisioning ways in which users could begin using a system quickly, by potentially becoming able to act as designers with a limited effort.
- *Tailor it to their personalized needs*. This principle regards tailorability as fundamental to support users to act as designers. Both adaptivity (the system may tailor itself on the basis of recurrent user interactions) and adaptability (the user consciously performs tailoring actions) are considered successful solutions to provide users with the necessary tools for system modification when new needs arise during its use.

With respect to the meta-design guidelines mentioned before, these principles are especially aimed at providing a frame for users and designers to communicate changes across the system lifecycle to foster co-evolution of system and users.

7 Conclusion

Providing all citizens with the means to become co-creators of new ideas, knowledge, and products in personally meaningful activities presents one of the most exciting innovations and transformations with profound implications in the years to come. This objective characterizes *the vision behind EUD as a cultural transformation*, which complements and transcends the traditional technological perspective of EUD (Burnett & Scaffidi, 2013) mainly oriented to engage and support people in programming activities.

To make this vision a reality, the EUD research community needs to establish (1) new theoretical frameworks (the chapter by Clarisse S. de Souza in this volume argues that Semiotic Engineering can provide a unified theoretical framing for various EUD-related topics (de Souza, 2017)), (2) new discourses and shared languages about concepts, assumptions, values, stories, metaphors, design approaches, and (3) new learning theories, such as those aimed at promoting computational thinking (Brennan & Resnick, 2012; Kafai, 2016). End users (by claiming ownership in personally meaningful problems) should be empowered to design, build, and evolve their own artifacts and meta-designers should create environments to foster *cultures of participation*. These objectives will support all citizens to situate computation in new cultural and material contexts with the support of socio-technical environments that democratize design.

New information and communication technologies have been heralded as the major driving forces behind innovations in working, learning, and collaborating. But many approaches have had only a minor impact by being conceptualized primarily as technology-centered developments. *Technology alone does not determine social structure: it creates feasibility spaces for new social and cultural practice.* Changes in complex environments are not only dictated by technology; rather, they are the result of an incremental shift in human behavior and social organization and, as such, require the *co-design of social and technical systems*.

In an EUD culture supported by meta-design, individuals acting as designers will acquire a new mindset: they are no longer passive receivers of knowledge, but instead are active researchers, designers, and communicators of knowledge. Knowledge is no longer handed down from above, but instead is constructed collaboratively in the contexts of work.

Meta-design provides the enabling conditions for putting owners of problems in charge by defining the technical and social conditions for broad participation in design activities. It addresses the challenges of fostering new mindsets, new sources of creativity, and cultural changes to create foundations for innovative societies. The foremost objective of meta-design is empowering humans (albeit not all of them, not at all times, not in all contexts) to be and act as designers in personally meaningful activities (Fischer, 2011).

Acknowledgements The authors would like to thank Stefan Carmien, Benjamin Koehne, Monica Maceli, Anders Mørch, Yunwen Ye, Daniel Tetteroo, and Li Zhou, who (based on their own research related to meta-design) provided us with important insights and findings in response to a questionnaire.

References

Alexander, C. (1975). *The oregon experiment*. New York: Oxford University Press.
Andersen, R., & Mørch, A. (2009). Mutual development: a case study in customer-initiated software product development. In V. Pipek, M. B. Rossen, B. deRuyter, V. Wulf (Eds.). *End-user development* (pp. 31–49). Heidelberg: Springer.
Anderson, C. (2012). *Makers - the new industrial revolution*. New York: Crown Business.
Ardito, C., Barricelli, B. R., Buono, P., Costabile, M. F., Piccinno, A., Valtolina, S., et al. (2011). Visual mediation mechanisms for collaborative design and development. In C. Stephanidis (Ed.). *Universal access in human-computer interaction. Design for all and eInclusion* (vol. 6765, pp. 3–11). Berlin: Springer. doi:10.1007/978-3-642-21672-5_1.
Arias, E. G., Eden, H., Fischer, G. (2016). *The envisionment and discovery collaboratory (EDC): explorations in human-centered informatics*. San Rafael, CA: Morgan & Claypool.
Avola, D., Bottoni, P., Genzone, R. (2011). Light-weight composition of personal documents from distributed information. In M. F. Costabile, Y. Dittrich, G. Fischer, A. Piccinno (Eds.). *End-user development* (vol. 6654, pp. 221–226). Berlin: Springer. doi:10.1007/978-3-642-21530-8_17.
Barricelli, B. R., & Valtolina, S. (2015). Designing for end-user development in the internet of things. In P. Díaz, V. Pipek, C. Ardito, C. Jensen, I. Aedo, & A. Boden (Eds.), *End-user development* (vol. 9083, pp. 9–24). Springer International Publishing. doi:10.1007/978-3-319-18425-8_2.
Benkler, Y. (2006). *The wealth of networks: how social production transforms markets and freedom*. New Haven: Yale University Press.
Benkler, Y., & Nissenbaum, H. (2006). Commons-based peer production and virtue. *Political Philosophy, 14*(4), 394–419.
Benzi, F., Cabitza, F., Fogli, D., Lanzilotti, R., Piccinno, A. (2015). Gamification techniques for rule management in ambient intelligence. In B. De Ruyter, A. Kameas, P. Chatzimisios, I. Mavrommati (Eds.), *Ambient intelligence* (vol. 9425, pp. 353–356). Springer International Publishing. doi:10.1007/978-3-319-26005-1_25.
Berg, M. (1999). Accumulating and coordinating: occasions for information technologies in medical work. *Computer Supported Cooperative Work, 8*(4), 373–401. doi:10.1023/A:1008757115404.
Binder, T., De Michelis, G., Ehn, P., Jacucci, G., Linde, P., Wagner, I. (2011). *Design things*. Cambridge, MA: MIT Press.
Brand, S. (1995). *How buildings learn: what happens after they're built*. New York: Penguin Books.
Brennan, K., & Resnick, M. (2012). New frameworks for studying and assessing the development of computational thinking. In *Proceedings of annual meeting of the American Educational Research Association (AERA'12)* (pp. 1–25). Vancouver.
Burnett, M. (2009). What is end-user software engineering and why does it matter? In V. Pipek, M. B. Rossen, B. deRuyter, V. Wulf (Eds.). *End-user development* (pp. 15–28). Heidelberg: Springer.
Burnett, M., & Scaffidi, C. (2013). End-user development. In M. Soegaard, R. F. Dam (Eds.). *The encyclopedia of human-computer interaction, 2nd*. Aarhus: The Interaction Design Foundation. Available at http://www.interaction-design.org/encyclopedia/end-user_development.html.

Cabitza, F., Fogli, D., Lanzilotti, R., Piccinno, A. (2016). Rule-based tools for the configuration of ambient intelligence systems: a comparative user study. *Multimedia Tools and Applications*, 1–21. doi:10.1007/s11042-016-3511-2.

Cabitza, F., Fogli, D., Piccinno, A. (2014a). "Each to his own": distinguishing activities, roles and artifacts in EUD practices. In L. Caporarello, B. Di Martino, M. Martinez (Eds.). *Smart organizations and smart artifacts* (vol. 7, pp. 193–205). Switzerland: Springer International Publishing. doi:10.1007/978-3-319-07040-7_19.

Cabitza, F., Fogli, D., Piccinno, A. (2014b). Fostering participation and co-evolution in sentient multimedia systems. *Journal of Visual Languages and Computing*, *25*(6), 684–694. doi:10.1016/j.jvlc.2014.10.014.

Cabitza, F., & Simone, C. (2009). LWOAD: a specification language to enable the end-user develoment of coordinative functionalities. In V. Pipek, M. B. Rosson, B. de Ruyter, V. Wulf (Eds.). *End-user development* (vol. 5435, pp. 146–165). Berlin: Springer. doi:10.1007/978-3-642-00427-8.

Cabitza, F., & Simone, C. (2015). Building socially embedded technologies: implications about design. In V. Wulf, K. Schmidt, D. Randall (Eds.). *Designing socially embedded technologies in the real-world* (pp. 217–270). London: Springer. doi:10.1007/978-1-4471-6720-4_11.

Cabitza, F., & Simone, C. (2017). Malleability in the hands of end users. In F. Paternò & V. Wulf (Eds.). *New perspectives in end-user development* (pp. 137–164). Cham: Springer.

Cappiello, C., Matera, M., Picozzi, M., Sprega, G., Barbagallo, D., Francalanci, C. (2011). DashMash: a mashup environment for end user development. In S. Auer, O. Díaz, G. A. Papadopoulos (Eds.). *Web engineering* (vol. 6757, pp. 152–166). Berlin: Springer. doi:10.1007/978-3-642-22233-7_11.

Carmien, S. (2006). *Socio-technical environments supporting distributed cognition for persons with cognitive disabilities*. PhD Thesis, Computer Science Department, University of Colorado, Boulder. http://www.scarmien.com/papers/dissertation_sm.pdf.

Carmien, S., & Fischer, G. (2008). Design, adoption, and assessment of a socio-technical environment supporting independence for persons with cognitive disabilities. *Proceedings of CHI 2008: ACM conference on human factors in computing systems* (pp. 597–607). New York, NY: ACM Press.

Carmien, S., & Fischer, G. (2010). Beyond human-computer interaction: meta-design in support of human problem-domain interaction. In M. Banich, D. Caccamise (Eds.). *Generalization of knowledge: multidisciplinary perspectives* (pp. 331–349). New York: Psychology Press.

Carroll, J. M., & Rosson, M. B. (1992). Getting around the task-artifact cycle: how to make claims and design by scenario. *ACM Transactions on Information Systems*, *10*(2), 181–212. doi:10.1145/146802.146834.

Caruso, V., Hartley, M. D., Mørch, A. I. (2015). End-user development in second life: meta-design, tailoring, and appropriation. In P. Díaz, V. Pipek, C. Ardito, C. Jensen, I. Aedo, A. Boden (Eds.). *End-user development: 5th international symposium, IS-EUD 2015, Madrid, Spain, May 26-29, 2015. Proceedings* (pp. 92–108). Cham: Springer International Publishing. doi:10.1007/978-3-319-18425-8_7.

Costabile, M. F., Fogli, D., Marcante, A., Mussio, P., Parasiliti Provenza, L., Piccinno, A. (2008). Designing customized and tailorable visual interactive systems. *International Journal of Software Engineering and Knowledge Engineering*, *18*(3), 305–325. doi:10.1142/S0218194008003702.

Costabile, M. F., Fogli, D., Marcante, A., Piccinno, A. (2006, May 23–26). Supporting interaction and co-evolution of users and systems. In *Proceedings of international conference on advanced visual interface* (pp. 143–150). Venice, Italy. doi:10.1145/1133265.1133294.

Costabile, M. F., Fogli, D., Mussio, P., Piccinno, A. (2005, September 20–24). A meta-design approach to End-User Development. In *Proceedings of IEEE symposium on visual languages and human-centric computing (VL/HCC)* (pp. 308–310). Dallas, TX. doi:10.1109/VLHCC.2005.7.

Costabile, M. F., Fogli, D., Mussio, P., Piccinno, A. (2006). End-user development: the software shaping workshop approach. In H. Lieberman, F. Paternò, V. Wulf (Eds.). *End user development* 9, (183–205). Dordrecht: Springer. doi:10.1007/1-4020-5386-X_9.

Costabile, M. F., Fogli, D., Mussio, P., Piccinno, A. (2007). Visual interactive systems for end-user development: a model-based design methodology. *IEEE Transactions on System Man and Cybernetics Part A-Systems and Humans*, *37*(6), 1029–1046. doi:10.1109/TSMCA.2007.904776.

Costabile, M. F., Mussio, P., Parasiliti Provenza, L., Piccinno, A. (2008, May 28–30). Advanced visual systems supporting unwitting EUD. In *Proceedings of international conference on advanced visual interfaces (AVI)* (pp. 313–316). Naple, Italy. doi:10.1145/1385569.1385621.

Costabile, M. F., Mussio, P., Piccinno, A., Ardito, C., Barricelli, B.R., Lanzilotti, R. (2009, September 10–12). End-user development in the medical domain. In *Proceedings of 15th international conference on distributed multimedia systems (DMS)* (pp. 10–15). San Francisco Bay, CA.

Cress, U., Jeong, H., Moskaliuk, J. (Eds.) (2016). *Mass collaboration and education.* Heidelberg: Springer.

Desolda, G. (2015). Enhancing workspace composition by exploiting linked open data as a polymorphic data source. In E. Damiani, J. R. Howlett, C. L. Jain, L. Gallo, G. De Pietro (Eds.). *Intelligent interactive multimedia systems and services* (pp. 97–108). Cham: Springer International Publishing. doi:10.1007/978-3-319-19830-9_9.

Desolda, G., Ardito, C., Matera, M. (2016). EFESTO: a platform for the end-user development of interactive workspaces for data exploration. In F. Daniel, C. Pautasso (Eds.). *Rapid mashup development tools: first international rapid mashup challenge, RMC 2015, Rotterdam, The Netherlands, June 23, 2015, revised selected papers* (pp. 63–81). Cham: Springer International Publishing. doi:10.1007/978-3-319-28727-0_5.

de Souza, C. S. (2017). Semiotic engineering: a cohering theory to connect EUD with HCI, CMC and more. In F. Paternò & V. Wulf (Eds.). *New perspectives in end-user development* (pp. 269–306). Cham: Springer.

Dittrich, Y., Bolmsten, J., Eriksson, J. (2017). End user development and infrastructuring – sustaining organizational innovation capabilities. In F. Paternò & V. Wulf (Eds.). *New perspectives in end-user development* (pp. 165–206). Cham: Springer.

Dittrich, Y., Madsen, P., Rasmussen, R. (2011). Really simple mash-ups. In M. F. Costabile, Y. Dittrich, G. Fischer, A. Piccinno (Eds.). *End-user development* (vol. 6654, pp. 227–232). Berlin: Springer. doi:10.1007/978-3-642-21530-8_18.

Dörner, C., Heß, J., Pipek, V. (2007, September 10–14). Improving information systems by end user development: a case study. In *Proceedings of European conference on information systems (ECIS)* (pp. 783–794). St. Gallen, Switzerland.

Emani, S., Yamin, C. K., Peters, E., Karson, A. S., Lipsitz, S. R., Wald, J. S., et al. (2012). Patient perceptions of a personal health record: a test of the diffusion of innovation model. *Journal of Medical Internet Research*, *14*(6). doi:10.2196/jmir.2278.

Fischer, G. (2000). Symmetry of ignorance, social creativity, and meta-design. *Knowledge-Based Systems*, *13*(7–8), 527–537. doi:10.1016/S0950-7051(00)00065-4.

Fischer, G. (2001). Communities of interest: learning through the interaction of multiple knowledge systems. In *Proceedings of 24th annual information systems research seminar in Scandinavia (IRIS'24)* (pp. 1–14). Ulvik, Norway.

Fischer, G. (2002). Beyond 'couch potatoes': from consumers to designers and active contributors. *FirstMonday*, *7*(12), http://firstmonday.org/issues/issue7_12/fischer/. doi:10.5210/fm.v7i12.1010.

Fischer, G. (2011). Understanding, fostering, and supporting cultures of participation. *Interactions*, *18*(3), 42–53. doi:10.1145/1962438.1962450.

Fischer, G. (2012, May). Context-aware systems: the 'right' information, at the 'right' time, in the 'right' place, in the 'right' way, to the 'right' person. In G. Tortora, S. Levialdi, & M. Tucci (Eds.), *Proceedings of the conference on advanced visual interfaces (AVI 2012)* (pp. 287–294). Capri: ACM.

Fischer, G. (2013). End-user development: from creating technologies to transforming cultures. In Y. Dittrich, M. Burnett, A. Mørch, D. Redmiles (Eds.). *End-user development* (vol. 7897, pp. 217–222). Berlin: Springer. doi:10.1007/978-3-642-38706-7_16.

Fischer, G., & Giaccardi, E. (2006). Meta-design: a framework for the future of end user development. In H. Lieberman, F. Paternò, V. Wulf (Eds.). *End user development* 9, (427–457). Dordrecht, The Netherlands: Springer. doi:10.1007/1-4020-5386-X_9.

Fischer, G., Grudin, J., McCall, R., Ostwald, J., Redmiles, D., Reeves, B., et al. (2001). Seeding, evolutionary growth and reseeding: the incremental development of collaborative design environments. In G. M. Olson, T. W. Malone, J. B. Smith (Eds.). *Coordination theory and collaboration technology* (pp. 447–472). Mahwah, NJ: Lawrence Erlbaum Associates.

Fischer, G., & Herrmann, T. (2011). Socio-technical systems: a meta-design perspective. *International Journal of Sociotechnology and Knowledge Development (IJSKD)*, 3(1), 1–33. doi:10.4018/jskd.2011010101.

Fischer, G., Nakakoji, K., Ye, Y. (2009). Metadesign: guidelines for supporting domain experts in software development. *IEEE Software*, 26(5), 37–44. doi:10.1109/MS.2009.134.

Fischer, G., & Ostwald, J. (2002). Seeding, evolutionary growth, and reseeding: enriching participatory design with informed participation. In *Proceedings of the participatory design conference (PDC'02)* (pp. 135–143). Sweden: Malmö University.

Fischer, G., Piccinno, A., Ye, Y. (2008). The ecology of participants in co-evolving socio-technical environments. In P. Forbrig, & F. Paternò (Ed.). *Engineering interactive systems (Proceedings of 2nd conference on human-centered software engineering* (vol. LNCS 5247, pp. 279–286). Heidelberg: Springer.

Fischer, G., & Scharff, E. (2000). Meta-design: design for designers. In *Proceedings of 3rd conference on designing interactive systems: processes, practices, methods, and techniques* (pp. 396–405). New York City, NY. doi:10.1145/347642.347798.

Fogli, D. (2009). End-user development for e-government website content creation. In V. Pipek, M. B. Rosson, B. de Ruyter, V. Wulf (Eds.). *End-user development* (vol. 5435/2009, pp. 126–145). Berlin: Springer. doi:10.1007/978-3-642-00427-8.

Fogli, D., Colosio, S., Sacco, M. (2010). Managing accessibility in local e-government websites through end-user development: a case study. *Universal Access in the Information Society*, 9(1), 35–50. doi:10.1007/s10209-009-0158-z.

Fogli, D., & Parasiliti Provenza, L. (2011). End-user development of e-government services through meta-modeling. In M. F. Costabile, Y. Dittrich, G. Fischer, A. Piccinno (Eds.). *End-user development* (vol. 6654, pp. 107–122). Berlin: Springer. doi:10.1007/978-3-642-21530-8_10.

Fogli, D., & Parasiliti Provenza, L. (2012). A meta-design approach to the development of e-government services. *Journal of Visual Languages and Computing*, 23(2), 47–62. doi:10.1016/j.jvlc.2011.11.003.

Fogli, D., & Piccinno, A. (2013a). Co-evolution of end-user developers and systems in multi-tiered proxy design problems. In Y. Dittrich, M. Burnett, A. Mørch, D. Redmiles (Eds.). *End-user development* (vol. 7897, pp. 153–168). Berlin: Springer. doi:10.1007/978-3-642-38706-7_12.

Fogli, D., & Piccinno, A. (2013b). Enabling domain experts to develop usable software artifacts. In P. Spagnoletti (Ed.). *Organizational change and information systems* (vol. 2, pp. 419–428). Berlin: Springer. doi:10.1007/978-3-642-37228-5_41.

Ghiani, G., Paternò, F., Spano, L. D. (2011). Creating mashups by direct manipulation of existing web applications. In M. F. Costabile, Y. Dittrich, G. Fischer, A. Piccinno (Eds.). *End-user development* (vol. 6654, pp. 42–52). Berlin: Springer. doi:10.1007/978-3-642-21530-8_5.

Grudin, J. (1992). Utility and usability: research issues and development contexts. *Interacting with Computers*, 4(2), 209–217. doi:10.1016/0953-5438(92)90005-Z.

Harrison, W. (2004). From the editor: the dangers of end-user programming. *IEEE Software*, 21(4), 5–7. doi:10.1109/MS.2004.13.

Henderson, A., & Kyng, M. (1991). There's no place like home: continuing design in use. In J. Greenbaum, & M. Kyng (Eds.). *Design at work: cooperative design of computer systems* (pp. 219–240). Hillsdale, NJ: Lawrence Erlbaum Associates, Inc.

Illich, I. (1973). *Tools for conviviality*. New York: Harper and Row.

Jenkins, H. (2009). *Confronting the challenges of participatory cultures: media education for the 21st century*. Cambridge, MA: MIT Press.

Kafai, Y. B. (2016). From computational thinking to computational participation in K–12 education. *Communications of the ACM, 59*(8), 26–27. doi:10.1145/2955114.

Kelly, K. (1995). *Out of control: the new biology of machines, social systems, and the economic world*. Boston, MA: Addison-Wesley Longman Publishing Co., Inc.

Ko, A. J., Abraham, R., Beckwith, L., Blackwell, A., Burnett, M., Erwig, M., et al. (2011). The state of the art in end-user software engineering. *ACM Computing Surveys, 43*(3), 1–44. doi:10.1145/1922649.1922658.

Koehne, B., Redmiles, D., Fischer, G. (2011). Extending the meta-design theory: engaging participants as active contributors in virtual worlds. In M. F. Costabile, Y. Dittrich, G. Fischer, A. Piccinno (Eds.). *End-user development (Third International Symposium, Torre Canne, Italy, June)* (vol. LNCS 6654, pp. 264–269). Heidelberg: Springer.

Lave, J., & Wenger, E. (1991). *Situated learning: legitimate peripheral participation*. New York: Cambridge University Press.

Leadbeater, C., & Miller, P. (2004). *The Pro-AM revolution — how enthusiasts are changing our economy and society*. London: Demos.

Lessig, L. (2008). *Remix: making art and commerce thrive in the hybrid economy*. New York: Penguin Press.

Lieberman, H., Paternò, F., Klann, M., Wulf, V. (2006). End-user development: an emerging paradigm. In H. Lieberman, F. Paternò, V. Wulf (Eds.). *End user development* (vol. 9, pp. 1–8). Dordrecht: Springer. doi:10.1007/1-4020-5386-X_1.

Lieberman, H., Paternò, F., Wulf, V. (Eds.) (2006). *End user development* 9, Dordrecht: Springer. doi:10.1007/1-4020-5386-X_9.

Ludwig, T., Dax, J., Pipek, V., Wulf, V. (2017). A practice-oriented paradigm of end-user development. In F. Paternò & V. Wulf (Eds.). *New perspectives in end-user development* (pp. 23–42). Cham: Springer.

Maceli, M., & Atwood, M. E. (2011). From human crafters to human factors to human actors and back again: bridging the design time – use time divide. In M. F. Costabile, Y. Dittrich, G. Fischer, A. Piccinno (Eds.). *End-user development* (vol. 6654, pp. 76–91). Berlin: Springer. doi:10.1007/978-3-642-21530-8_8.

Mørch, A., Caruso, V., Hartley, M. M. (2017). End-user development and learning in second life: the evolving artifacts framework with application. In F. Paternò & V. Wulf (Eds.). *New perspectives in end-user development* (pp. 333–358). Cham: Springer.

Myers, B. A., Ko, A. J., Burnett, M. M. (2006). Invited Research Overview: End-User Programming. *Proc. of CHI '06 Extended Abstracts on Human Factors in Computing Systems* (pp. 75–80), Montréal, Québec, Canada. doi:10.1145/1125451.1125472.

Nardi, B. A. (1993). *A small matter of programming*. Cambridge, MA: The MIT Press.

National Research Council (1999). *Being fluent with information technology*. Washington, DC: National Academy Press.

Norman, D. A., & Draper, S. W. (1986). *User centered system design; new perspectives on human-computer interaction*. Hillsdale, NJ: L. Erlbaum Associates Inc.

O'Reilly, T. (2005). What is web 2.0 - design patterns and business models for the next generation of software. http://www.oreillynet.com/pub/a/oreilly/tim/news/2005/09/30/what-is-web-20.html.

Preece, J., & Shneiderman, B. (2009). The reader-to-leader framework: motivating technology-mediated social participation. *AIS Transactions on Human-Computer Interaction, 1*(1), 13–32.

Raymond, E. S., & Young, B. (2001). *The cathedral and the bazaar: musings on linux and open source by an accidental revolutionary*. Sebastopol, CA: O'Reilly & Associates.

Rittel, H. (1984). Second-generation design methods. In N. Cross (Ed.). *Developments in design methodology* (pp. 317–327). New York: John Wiley & Sons.

Schuler, D., & Namioka, A. (1993). *Participatory design: principles and practices*. Hillsdale, New Jersey: Lawrence Erlbaum Associates, Inc.

Shneiderman, B. (2009). National initiative for social participation. *Science, 323*(5920), 1426–1427.

Star, S. L. (1989). The structure of ill-structured solutions: boundary objects and heterogeneous distributed problem solving. In L. Gasser, M. N. Huhns (Eds.). *Distributed artificial intelligence* (vol. II, pp. 37–54). San Mateo, CA: Morgan Kaufmann Publishers Inc.

Tapscott, D., & Williams, A. D. (2006). *Wikinomics: how mass collaboration changes everything*. New York, NY: Portofolio, Penguin Group.

Tetteroo, D. (2013, June). TagTrainer: a meta-design approach to interactive rehabilitation technology. In *End-user development: fourth international symposium* (pp. 289–292). Copenhagen, Denmark.

Tetteroo, D. (2015). *End-user adaptable rehabilitation* (Ph.D. Dissertation), Eindhoven University of Technology.

Tetteroo, D., & Markopoulos, P. (2017). EUD survival "in the wild": evaluation challenges for field deployments and how to address them. In F. Paternò & V. Wulf (Eds.). *New perspectives in end-user development* (pp. 207–230). Cham: Springer.

Tetteroo, D., Seelen, H., Timmermans, A., Markopoulos, P. (2014). Rehabilitation therapists as software creators?: Introducing end-user development in a healthcare setting. *International Journal of Sociotechnology and Knowledge Development (IJSKD), 6*(1), 36–50. doi:10.4018/ijskd.2014010103.

Thaler, R. H., & Sunstein, C. R. (2009). *Nudge — improving decisions about health, wealth, an happiness*. London: Penguin Books.

von Hippel, E. (2005). *Democratizing innovation*. Cambridge, MA: MIT Press.

Wenger, E. (1998). *Communities of practice — learning, meaning, and identity*. Cambridge, UK: Cambridge University Press.

Wenger, E., McDermott, R. A., Snyder, W. (2002). *Cultivating communities of practice: a guide to managing knowledge*. Boston, MA: Harvard Business Press.

Ye, Y., & Fischer, G. (2007). Converging on a "science of design" through the synthesis of design methodologies (CHI'2007 workshop). http://swiki.cs.colorado.edu:3232/CHI07Design/3.

Zhu, L. (2012). *Hive-mind space: a meta-design approach for cultivating and supporting collaborative design* (PhD). Università degli Studi di Milano, Milano.

Zhu, L., Barricelli, B. R., Iacob, C. (2011). A meta-design model for creative distributed collaborative design. *International Journal of Distributed Systems and Technologies (IJDST), 2*(4), 1–16. doi:10.4018/jdst.2011100101.

Zhu, L., & Herrmann, T. (2013). Meta-design in co-located meetings. In Y. Dittrich, M. Burnett, A. Mørch, D. Redmiles (Eds.). *End-user development: 4th international symposium, IS-EUD 2013, Copenhagen, Denmark, June 10-13, 2013. Proceedings* (pp. 169–184). Berlin: Springer. doi:10.1007/978-3-642-38706-7_13.

Zhu, L., Mussio, P., Barricelli, B. R. (2010). Hive-mind space model for creative, collaborative design. In *Proceedings of 1st DESIRE network conference on creativity and innovation in design* (pp. 121–130). Aarhus, Denmark.

Zhu, L., Vaghi, I., Barricelli, B. R. (2011). *A meta-reflective wiki for collaborative design. Proc. of Proceedings of the 7th International Symposium on Wikis and Open Collaboration – WikiSym '11* (pp. 53–62), Mountain View, California. doi:10.1145/2038558.2038569.

A Three-Layer Meta-Design Model for Addressing Domain-Specific Customizations

Carmelo Ardito, Maria Francesca Costabile, Giuseppe Desolda
and Maristella Matera

Abstract Meta-design has been proposed as a model to design systems able to support End-User Development (EUD). Meta-design means "design for designers." Differently than in traditional design, professional developers do not directly create a final application, but they build software environments thorough which non-technical end users, acting as co-designers, are enabled to shape up the application while they are using it. Allowing end users to participate to the creation of their applications, by modifying or even creating from scratch software artifacts, is very challenging. To make this possible, end users have to be provided with software environments customized to their specific domain, which they can easily understand and use. In order to cope with domain specificity, this chapter presents a new meta-design model that specifically addresses the customization to a domain of interest. Customization, performed by domain experts possibly in collaboration with professional developers, becomes the key activity to provide non-technical end users with software environments that are adequate to their knowledge and needs, thus allowing them to actually become co-designers of their applications. The model is illustrated by describing its successful application to the design of a mashup platform that allows end users to create new applications by integrating data and functionality taken from different resources. The customization of the platform to different domains, such as Cultural Heritage and Technology Enhanced Learning, is discussed.

Keywords Meta-design · End-User Development · Mashup platform

C. Ardito (✉) · M.F. Costabile · G. Desolda
Dipartimento di Informatica, Università degli Studi di Bari Aldo Moro, Via Orabona 4,
Bari 70125, Italy
e-mail: carmelo.ardito@uniba.it

M.F. Costabile
e-mail: maria.costabile@uniba.it

G. Desolda
e-mail: giuseppe.desolda@uniba.it

M. Matera
Dipartimento di Elettronica, Informazione e Bioingegneria, Politecnico di Milano,
Piazza Leonardo da Vinci 32, Milano 20134, Italy
e-mail: maristella.matera@polimi.it

© Springer International Publishing AG 2017   99
F. Paternò, V. Wulf (eds.), *New Perspectives in End-User Development*,
DOI 10.1007/978-3-319-60291-2_5

1   Introduction

Meta-design is a model often applied to designing systems supporting End-User Development (EUD) (Costabile, Fogli, Mussio, & Piccinno, 2007; Fischer & Giaccardi, 2006; Fischer, Giaccardi, Ye, Sutcliffe, & Mehandjiev, 2004). It promotes the active involvement of software engineers and end users in a continuous cycle of development, use and evolution of systems. As defined by Fischer et al.: "Meta-design extends the traditional notion of system development to include users in an ongoing process as co-designers, not only at design time but throughout the entire existence of the system" (Fischer et al., 2004). The meta-design model encompasses different activities: *meta-design* activities consist of designing software environments; this leads to the next activities of *design and use*, where end users complete the design of the final application and use it. Meta-design is in line with the so-called culture of participation (Díez, Mørch, Piccinno, & Valtolina, 2013; Fischer, 2011; Jenkins, 2009), which has received a lot of attention as it promotes a shift from consumer cultures, where produced artifacts are passively consumed, to participatory approaches that greatly exploit computational media to support collaboration and communication. The aim behind this design model is to provide end users with the means to become co-creators of new ideas, knowledge and products that can effectively satisfy their specific needs (Porter, 2008).

Following this line of action, in this chapter we show how the original meta-design model is refined by explicitly modeling all those activities that enable domain experts, possibly in collaboration with professional developers, to customize general tools to the domain of interest. Customization is indeed instrumental to provide non-technical end users with software environments that are adequate to their knowledge and needs and that actually allow them to perform EUD activities. In the new model we therefore devise three different types of activities that conceptually can be organized in three different layers.

The chapter also discusses the application of the new model to the customization of a mashup platform. In the last years we have indeed worked extensively on *fostering the adoption, in real contexts and by non-technical end users, of mashup platforms enabling EUD*. Such class of tools accommodate very well EUD, as they allow end users to create new applications by integrating functions and content exposed by remote services and Web APIs. By means of two case studies in Cultural Heritage and Technology Enhanced Learning, this chapter illustrates how the three-layer meta-design model allowed us to customize a general mashup platform for its use in the two domains.

The adoption of mashup platforms in real contexts is largely debated (see for example (Casati, 2011)). So far, the research on mashup highlighted several advantages that can favor EUD. For example, the possibility to start from ready-to-use components certainly mitigates the complexity of creating a new application from scratch and can be also faced, under given assumptions, by non-technical end users who do not know how to program and do not want to be forced to do it. However, several disadvantages also emerged, for example in relation to the difficulties for end users in understanding and using the notations to compose resources, to the inadequacy of available components with respect to the end-user needs, and to the difficulty of adding new components into the composition platforms (Namoun, Nestler, & De Angeli, 2010). Our position, which also derives from observing people adopting our tools during field studies, is that these disadvantages occur because the proposed platforms are too "general," claiming that one single design might satisfy the requirements of many domains. We therefore propose domain customization as a solution to make meta-design still more effective in creating platforms that really fit the end-user needs. This position is also in line with the guidelines proposed in (Fischer, Fogli, & Piccinno, 2017).

This chapter is organized as follows. Sect. 2 illustrates the background of this research by discussing related work. Sect. 3 presents the three-layer meta-design model and illustrates how it has driven the development of the mashup platform according to an open architecture that specifically favors customization activities. Sect. 4 reports two case studies that show how the platform was used in two application domains, after a proper customization to each one of such domains. Sect. 5 concludes the paper.

2 Background and Related Work

In this section, we discuss the background of this article along two main dimensions, namely meta-design as a design model to support EUD and mashup platforms as tools for fostering user-driven innovation. The goal is to push end users to evolve from passive consumers of software to active producers of new knowledge and products.

2.1 Meta-Design to Foster EUD

Traditionally, the life cycle of interactive systems distinguishes between design time and use time. At design time, system developers create a system that should satisfy the requirements they collected about end users' needs and objectives. At use time, end users exploit the system to accomplish their tasks. Design frameworks are based on the assumption that major design activities end at a certain point; then use time begins and people use the system. *Participatory design* was introduced to take into account the participation of end users in the design process (Schuler, 1993). It was based on the rationale that users are experts of the application domain, thus a system can be effective only if these experts are allowed to participate in its design, highlighting their needs and expectations. In participatory design, end users are members of the design team, but no tools are provided to let them create or modify software. EUD started the trend toward a more active involvement of end users in the overall software design, development, and evolution processes, to allow them becoming co-designers of the tools and products they will use. This does not imply transferring the responsibility of good system design to them. It actually makes the work of professional developers even more difficult, since: (a) it is still their responsibility to ensure the quality of the software artifacts created by end users (Ko et al., 2011), and (b) they have to create proper tools that support end users in these new roles of designers and developers.

The design of systems that enable EUD activities thus requires a different design paradigm, called *meta-design*, which literally means "design for designers" (Costabile et al., 2007; Fischer et al., 2004). It consists of two types of activities that might also alternate: *meta-design* activities are performed by professional developers, who create the design environments that allow the diverse stakeholders to participate in the creation of the final applications; *design* activities consist of designing the final applications and are performed by end users, and possibly other stakeholders, by using the design environments devoted to them. The two activities are not clearly distinct and are executed several times in an interleaved way because the design environments evolve, both as a consequence of the progressive insights the different stakeholders gain into the design process, and as a consequence of the feedbacks provided by end users working with the system in the field.

Since several years, Costabile et al. have been working on the creation of software infrastructures that support EUD activities (Costabile, Fogli, Fresta, Mussio, & Piccinno, 2003; Costabile, Fogli, Mussio, & Piccinno, 2006; Costabile et al., 2007; Costabile, Mussio, Parasiliti Provenza, & Piccinno, 2009). They defined a design approach that allows a team of stakeholders to cooperate in the design, development, use and evolution of interactive systems. The approach is based on a meta-design model, because it prescribes that, instead of developing the final interactive system as in traditional design approaches, professional developers design software environments for the different communities of stakeholders involved in the creation of the system. Such stakeholders will use such environments to carry out specific tasks at use time, and as a side effect they will also contribute to the design and evolution of the interactive system (Costabile et al., 2009). These software environments are called *Software Shaping Workshops* (SSWs or briefly workshops). The term *workshop* comes from the analogy with an artisan's workshop (e.g., the joiner's or the smith's workshop), i.e., the workroom where the artisan finds all and only those tools necessary to carry out her/his activities. According to the metaphor, the different software environments provide all and only the tools necessary to their users to perform their specific activities, as well as interaction languages tailored to their users' culture, defined by formalizing the traditional user notations and system of signs (Iverson, 1980). In the original definition, and in particular in (Costabile et al., 2006, 2007), the SSW model distinguished three levels of activities: (1) design by software engineers; (2) design by different communities of experts of the application domain or of experts of human factors; (3) use by different communities of end users. The design by software engineers is actually meta-design according to the definition provided in

(Fischer & Giaccardi, 2006; Fischer et al., 2004). Moreover, since the focus is on EUD, it is implicit that some communities operate at both level 2 and level 3, i.e., they perform both design and use of an application, at use time.

By applying the SSW model to real cases, it was soon realized that domain experts often need to perform meta-design. Several case studies are reported in (Ardito, Buono, Costabile, Lanzilotti, & Piccinno, 2012), which show that meta-design is not only performed by software engineers, but some domain experts have often to shape software artifacts that are used by other communities of experts and/or end users to design other artifacts. Specifically, most of such meta-design activities perform customization to a specific domain, in order to tailor generic tools to the needs of non-technical end users. In (Cabitza, Fogli, & Piccinno, 2014a, 2014b), Cabitza et al. introduce the "domain developer", i.e., a domain expert actively involved in the creation of artifacts more suitable for end users and the tasks in the work domain at hand. The three-layer meta-design model presented in this chapter makes explicit the customization activities, which are crucial for making EUD possible.

Fisher proposed the model called SER (Seeding, Evolutionary and Reseeding) (Fischer, 1998). Instead of building a complete system at design time, system design starts from seeds, which are developed by meta-designers in a participatory team involving end users. A subsequent evolutionary growth follows, and then a reseeding phase occurs. The seeding phase concerns the definition of the initial prototype, which will be used by end users to perform their activities. The reseeding is performed by meta-designers to modify the initial state of a software artifact, on the basis of the evolutions determined by end users. The evolving system continually alternates between periods of unplanned evolutions by end users and periods of deliberate restructuring and enhancement. Customization to a specific domain is not explicitly addressed.

Other authors present meta-design as an approach supporting end users to tailor the tools they use. Maceli and Atwood discuss that end users often adapt systems by a trial-and-error strategy (Maceli & Atwood, 2011). Koehne et al. show that meta-design is instrumental to provide useful tools for involving end users in the design of virtual worlds, such as online role-playing games like "Lord of the Rings Online," and open-ended virtual world like "Second Life" (Koehne, Redmiles, & Fischer, 2011). Sutcliffe and Papamargaritis suggest that customization is successful for "seeding" the adoption of EUD tools and propose the use of a configuration environment based on generic conceptual models of problem domains (Sutcliffe & Papamargaritis, 2014).

2.2   User-Driven Innovation by Web Mashup

Meta-design can be fruitfully exploited for the design of *Web mashup* (simply called *mashup*) platforms. As also remarked in (Fischer et al., 2017), given their component-based nature, mashups intrinsically favor EUD and meta-design. Mashups are "composite" applications constructed by integrating ready-to-use functions and content exposed by public or private services and Web APIs (Daniel & Matera, 2014). Mashups were initially exploited in the context of the consumer Web to rapidly create applications reusing programmable APIs and content scraped out from Web pages. Soon, the potential of such lightweight integration practice emerged in various domains. Several mashup platforms have been proposed in the last years to allow end users to visually compose data and services taken from different sources, so that they can satisfy their information needs (e.g., see Aghaee & Pautasso, 2014; Danado & Paternò, 2014; Daniel & Matera, 2014; Ghiani, Paternò, Spano, & Pintori, 2016; Mehandjiev & de Angeli, 2014). Very often these platforms are general, i.e., they do not show any specificity with respect to given domains. As observed in (Casati, 2011), the lack of specificity is a problem when platforms have to be adopted by users without expertise in computer programming. Methodologies are therefore needed to create platforms that, although designed to be generic, can be then effectively specialized when adopted in specific application domains.

Mashup development resembles service composition, a development practice traditionally covered by powerful standards and technologies that, however, can only be mastered by IT experts (Ro, Xia, Paik, & Chon, 2008). What makes mashup development different from plain Web service integration is the possibility, deriving from recent Web technologies, to merge ready-to-use resources at the client-side, thus with reduced efforts and without the need of complex integration platforms. Mashup development also emphasizes novel issues, such as the composition at different layers of the application stack of heterogeneous resources that make use of different technologies. In particular, the integration at the presentation layer is the most innovative aspect enabling the creation of full-fledged Web applications whose user interface (UI) can be easily obtained by synchronizing the UIs of different ready-to-use components. If supported by adequate tools, mashup development can be an alternative to service composition that goes towards the dream of a "programmable Web" (Maximilien, Wilkinson, Desai, & Tai, 2007) even by end users without any knowledge in programming.

Because of its intrinsic value as development practice to let end users produce new value, mashup composition is in line with the so-called "culture of participation" (Fischer, 2010); users are enabled to evolve from passive consumers of applications to active co-creators of new ideas, knowledge, and products. There is indeed a specific driver at the heart of the user participation to the mashup phenomenon: *user-driven innovation*, that is, the desire and capability of users to develop their own things, to realize their own ideas, and to express their own creativity (Von Hippel, 2005). According to recent works published in literature (Ardito, Costabile, Desolda, Latzina, & Matera, 2015; Latzina & Beringer, 2012), there is also an increasing need to replace fixed applications with *elastic environments* that can be shaped up flexibly, to accommodate different situational needs. New design principles are emerging to promote paradigms where end users can access contents and functions through different devices and flexibly use and compose such resources in several situations and across several applications. If the composition activity turns out to add significant new value, the advantage for the users is that they co-create effective applications matching exactly their needs. Additionally, an interesting side effect is that the providers of the original resources can integrate the user innovation back into their core products (Iyer & Davenport, 2008) and improve their services, in order to fulfill users' requirements without the need of carrying out the iterative experimentation generally required to identify requirements and develop and test a new product. In this new process, the end users are entirely in charge of these aspects because they are enabled to create solutions that closely meet their needs.

Such innovation potential requires adequate approaches and tools for enabling mashup by non-technical end users (Daniel & Matera, 2014). However, the research on mashups has been focusing especially on enabling technologies and standards, with little attention on easing the mashup development process. Research teams and industrial players tried to define simplified composition paradigms, mostly based on visual notations and lightweight design and execution platforms running on the Web. A number of tools have been proposed that offer composition paradigms based on graphical notations, which abstract relevant mashup development aspects and operations. The user defines diagrams to express the internal logic of a mashup, without writing code. However, many of such tools failed because they resulted non adequate for end users (Casati et al., 2012; Namoun et al., 2010). One of the main reasons is that they lack intuitive abstractions (Burnett, Cook, & Rothermel, 2004; Liu, Huang, & Mei, 2007). To support the user-driven innovation potential, the challenge is indeed to let users concentrate on the conception of new ideas, rather than on the technicalities beyond service composition. In other words, users should be enabled to easily access resources responding to personal needs, integrate them to compose new applications, and simply run such applications without worrying about what happens behind the scenes.

To achieve this goal, one direction is to restrict mashup platforms to a well-defined domain the user is comfortable with. General-purpose platforms are not adequate to the needs of specific application domains and specific end users. Some studies on composition approaches indeed showed that too general plat-forms are not used with satisfaction by end users (Casati, 2011; Namoun et al., 2010). This represents an obstacle to a wider adoption of such platforms by non-technical people, who need to interact with tools and notations they are familiar with (e.g., see Costabile et al., 2006, 2007). In order to develop generic platforms that can be valid in different domains, it is fundamental to design platform archi-tectures able to support the easy customization of the platform. This is what our extension to the meta-design model supports.

3   A Three-Layer Meta-Design Model for a Mashup Platform

Since 2012, we have been developing a mashup platform where end users, at use time and according to their needs, can select and integrate content into Interactive Workspaces (IWs). The platform may be accessed through different devices, such as a desktop computer, a mobile device or a large multi-touch display; it shows content retrieved by dynamically querying Web data sources registered into the platform, and allows the users to select pertinent content items to fill-in *visual templates*, i.e., visualization skeletons through which users easily organize and instantiate with data their IWs. In other words, the visual templates are the "containers" in which raw data (i.e., content) retrieved from Web sources are shown in the visual interface (Ardito et al., 2015). Examples of visual templates are a map showing geo-referenced data, a list of items, a chart of values. A live programming paradigm let the users see immediately the effect on any composition action, having the possibility to assess directly the progressive definition of the final application. Users can therefore easily explore any feature offered by the platform and easily go back when they are not satisfied with their choice.

The result of the visual composition is an XML-based representation of the IW, which the user can store on the platform server and download anytime and anywhere for its execution on different devices. The schema specifies the selected services, the way they are queried in order to create the desired mashup, and how the mashup results are displayed through rendering elements of the visual template.

3.1 The Three-Layer Meta-Design Model

The mashup platform we developed is not tied to any specific domain. Indeed, a key feature of the platform is that it provides mechanisms for customization to specific usage domains. The only way to offer a composition paradigm and resources adequate to end users of a specific application domain is to capitalize on their domain knowledge. Thus, the general tools and interaction elements have to be customized to the domain of interest. To make this possible, the platform adopts a stratification into different design (and meta-design) layers where different stakeholders contribute to the creation of different artifacts (Fischer et al., 2004). The involvement of domain experts is instrumental for a successful customization.

As represented in Fig. 1, the top layer refers to a meta-design activity performed by *professional developers* (likely a multi-disciplinary participatory team), who design and develop the design environments for the other stakeholders. The team also develops *visual templates*, by using Web technologies (for example HTML and JavaScript) or specific languages for other devices (e.g., Java for Android). Visual templates are important ingredients for the successive customization, since customized visualizations can reflect the knowledge domain.

The middle layer refers to another meta-design activity, *Domain customization*. Domain experts, possibly collaborating with professional developers (not necessarily the same that act at the first level), customize the general-purpose tool resulting from the activities at the top layer. Domain experts are familiar with the types of information end users would retrieve, the manipulations they would perform and the most suitable visualizations. Thus, they exploit a platform tool, called

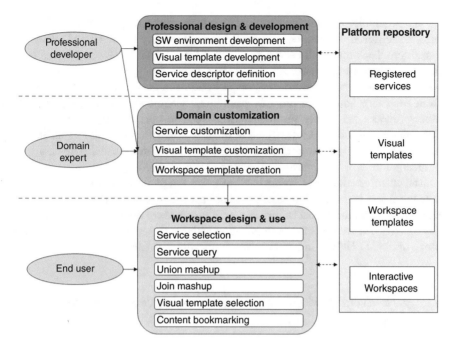

Fig. 1 The three-layer meta-design model; the middle layer is devoted to the customization to the domain of interest

Workspace composition environment, to register services, compose registered services by exploiting data-composition operations (like join and union), select how to materialize service results by means of visual templates (e.g. map, list, graph) (Matera, Picozzi, Pini, & Tonazzo, 2013). Domain experts perform these technical activities in a way that is suitable for their skills. However, they do not have the skills and expertise to perform more complex customization activities like the registration of more sophisticated services (e.g. the ones requiring complex authentication mechanisms, proprietary technologies), advanced service compositions, the development of new and domain-specific visual templates, as well as the development of workspaces skeletons (i.e., pre-defined, typical aggregations of services). This is the reason why another environment, more devoted to advanced activities, is available for professional developers that integrate the domain experts' requests in the general-purpose tool.

At the bottom layer, end users finally design, use and update their IWs. This means that they start by a customized version of the mashup tool, which provides a selection of services composed and visualized according to the customization activity. In addition, in order to satisfy personal and situational needs, end users can manipulate content extracted from the registered services, for example, by using the union and join of different result sets. They can also associate different visualizations to the composed content and bookmark content in order to save it.

The possibility for end users to select pertinent services, query them and aggregate the retrieved content, and especially the opportunity to define and customize visual templates makes the entire approach *elastic*. So far, software systems have been conceived as pre-packaged sets of data, functionality, and visualizations that somebody else (the software developer) builds for us. *Elastic systems* diverge from such idea and try to promote paradigms where contents, functionality and access devices are totally decoupled from specific contexts of use and can be determined at use time. Elasticity is, in other words, an opportunity to accommodate multiple and variable contextual needs, moving the responsibility to end users of creating their own applications (Latzina & Beringer, 2012).

The customization is performed before using the platform in a new application domain; it can be later re-executed to satisfy specific needs emerging later, e.g., to register or to combine further services, as it emerges by the platform usage in the field. In Sect. 4, we illustrate customization activities by means of examples of the usage of a real platform in two different application domains.

3.2   Architecture for Mashup Platforms Implementing the Meta-Design Model

Adequate software architectures are needed, in order to make concrete the meta-design model illustrated above. We here report the architecture of EFESTO (Desolda, Ardito, & Matera, 2016), the mashup platform that we have designed with the specific purpose of supporting a meta-design methodology. The platform architecture complies with a separation of concerns so that the layers managing the different aspects of mashup creation and execution (presentation, logics, data) are decoupled. This means that each aspect, if needed, can be easily adapted to the application domain.

Separation of concerns is facilitated especially by the compositional nature of the platform. Being a mashup platform, EFESTO is indeed conceived for the integration of heterogeneous services. This openness facilitates the customization of the platform with respect to the characteristics and needs of specific communities of end users. Customization, for example, occurs by selecting and registering into the platform services and data sources (public or private) that, for any different domain, can provide content able to fulfill specific users' information needs. Service registration is kept as simple as possible, so that even non-technical users can possibly add new services if needed. Indeed. Except for particular cases, service registration requires the user to input, by means of visual forms, the service URI and the value of some search keys for executing basic service queries. Then the XML specification, i.e. the *Service Descriptor*, is automatically generated by the system and stored in the *Repository Server* (Desolda, 2015). A further customization activity performed by domain experts consists of reducing the initial data set of a registered service, so that only the attributes of interest for a specific domain are available to end users.

In EFESTO different *Visual templates*, which play the role of visualization containers (Cappiello, Matera, & Picozzi, 2015), can be easily introduced to represent metaphors and interaction paradigms that best suit the background and the needs of the addressed end users. Through visual templates, domain experts define how the content dynamically retrieved by querying a service will be visualized in proper visualization containers to be then adopted by end users to create their IWs. Visual templates, available in the *Repository Server*, provide end users with a schematic representation of how data extracted from services will be organized, i.e., aggregated and visualized. They also provide data integration schemas, as they determine how the involved data sources are queried and the resulting data integrated.

This schematic representation can be easily modified to reflect domain specificity. Providing a new visual template implies defining a new HTML template or a new View for execution on an Android smart phone. At composition time, by visually associating selected service attributes to visual template fields, the end user defines a projection of the only attributes of interest. In addition, if the attributes associated to a single visual template element are selected from multiple services, then the structure of the visual template determines a global integration schema mapping the attributes of single services into an integrated data set. In few words, to operate on data, end users actually manipulate visual representations that can be easily modified to accommodate the end-user mental model.

The overall organization of the platform is represented in Fig. 2. Thanks to the adoption of a live programming paradigm, end users create their IW through the

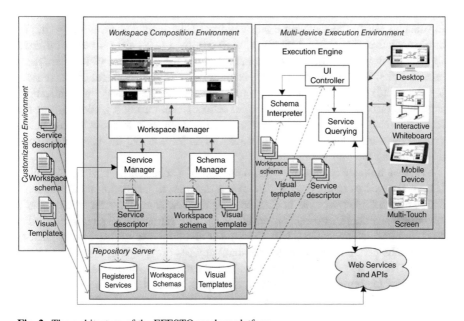

Fig. 2 The architecture of the EFESTO mashup platform

Workspace Composition Environment, an HTML/JavaScript Web application that allows them to execute composition actions and immediately see the result, i.e., a running application. A *Workspace Manager* intercepts the visual mapping and synchronization actions performed by an end user. Through its *Schema Manager* module, such actions are automatically translated into elements of a *Workspace schema*, expressed in an XML-based domain specific language (Cappiello et al., 2015), which describes the service queries, the association of the query results with specific visual templates, and possible synchronizations among different visual templates.

The execution of an IW can occur on the device where it was created, as well as through an *Execution Environment* running on a different device (right side of Fig. 2). An *Execution Engine*, possibly implemented through any Web or device-native technology, interprets the Workspace schema (*Schema Interpreter*) and instantiates the adopted visual templates (*UI controller*), by rendering the corresponding user interface and filling the visual elements with data requested to the involved services (*Service Querying*). It is worth noting that the Model-Driven Architecture paradigm on which our approach is based allows the user to generate *one* platform independent model, representing the structure, in terms of integrated data sources and data visualizations, of the composed application, and to pervasively execute it on *different* devices and in *different* contexts of use.

4 Customization to Specific Application Domains

In order to verify the usefulness and validity of the extended meta-design model implemented in our mashup platform, we performed two field studies in different application domains. One study was carried out in the context of visits to archaeological parks. Two professional guides composed a mashup application for retrieving content relative to an archaeological park using a desktop application, accessible through a PC placed in his/her office. Later, during a guided visit of the archaeological park, two guides use the mashup application to show the content to visitors by using a large interactive display when introducing the visit and a tablet device during the tour in the park.

Another field study, performed in a context of Technology-Enhanced Learning (TEL), allowed us to analyze the use of the platform in a situation where students learn about a topic presented in class by their teacher, complementing the teacher's lecture by searching information on the Web. The retrieved information can also be communicated and shared with the teacher and the other students using interactive whiteboards, desktop PCs and personal devices (e.g., laptop, tablet and smartphone). These two studies are reported in details in (Ardito et al., 2014). The description in the next two subsections emphasizes the customization activities performed before the actual studies.

4.1   Customization in a CH Context

In order to customize the mashup platform to the Cultural Heritage context, in particular to provide support to the activities of professional guides, we worked in a team that included two professional developers with HCI expertise and two guides with a long experience of conducting visit in archaeological parks. They met twice to perform various activities.

During the first meeting, the guides explained the way they usually organize a visit. The briefing phase performed before the actual tour through the ruins is fundamental. It aims at both introducing visitors to the history of the archaeological park and providing some preliminary information. It is usually carried out in front of a large panel showing the map or an aerial photography of the park. This phase would greatly benefit from making the panel interactive and able to show multimedia content related to the topics described by the guide. The team agreed that the debriefing should be supported by an interactive workspace displayed on a large display. Multimedia content (Web pages, images and videos) retrieved beforehand by the guide from the Web could be displayed as icons on a map.

After the meeting, the professional developers performed a first step of customization of their Interactive Workspaces (IW) by registering in the platform services like Google Search, Wikipedia, Google Images, FlickR and YouTube. In addition, developers integrated the map visual template by including the Google Maps service that, beyond the map, also provides some business logic; for example, it displays further details of a place by clicking on the corresponding pin on the map.

During the second meeting, the two guides had the possibility to directly perform a second step of customization using a desktop application, accessible through a PC placed in their office. First, they decided which services should be synchronized with the map, in order to show service data as pin on the map when a search was performed. Second, they saved favorites contents relative to the archaeological park of Egnathia (in Southern Italy) in a specific container with lists of items. Lastly, both the guides and the developers decided that the same interactive workspace should be made available on a tablet carried out by the guide, so that it could be accessed during the tour (Fig. 3).

Once the platform was customized, few days later the guides experimented the mashup platform with a large interactive display (46-inch) and a tablet device (7-inch) during two guided visits of the archaeological park, involving 28 visitors. To introduce the visit, the professional guides interacted with the IW they created, in order to "enhance" their presentation of the history of the park. The IW was then executed on a large interactive display available at the entrance of the park museum (Fig. 4a). Media contents, such as photos, videos, and wiki pages associated with park locations to be visited during the guided tour were represented by an icon and a title placed on a map centered on the park. By tapping on an icon, a pop-up window visualizes the corresponding media. During the park tour, the

Fig. 3 A guide performing the customization of the platform

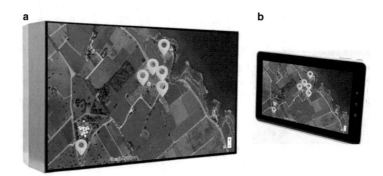

Fig. 4 IW for the archaeological park of Egnathia visualized on a large interactive display (a) and on tablet (b)

guides accessed their IW on the tablet (Fig. 4b), in order to show photos, videos and other information when appropriate.

The study showed a general appreciation of the use of IW in the context of the visit and interesting insights emerged. The guides acknowledged the support of the mashup platform in composing the application and organizing the material for the visit. However, they complained about the scarce material they were able to find when searching the services available in the platform. This is a problem common to all service-based applications, which have to rely on content made available by third-parties. To limit this problem, more sensible services should be added into the platform; they can be further third-parties' services, if any responding to the user needs exists, but they can also be local and ad-hoc created collections of contents, maintained by domain experts and even fed by end users themselves by adding self-produced material. Also, since the services used for the study at the Egnathia park are Web 2.0 resources, the guides could publish online their own material (e.g., videos, pictures, Wikipedia pages) that can thus be easily accessed through the mashup platform. This of course requires a more intensive use of the system by the guides, since they have to realize which content is missing and to enrich consequently their public online collections.

It also emerged that guides would like to have the possibility of switching among different visualizations, according to the specific task they are performing. For example, it happens quite often that they want to refer to buildings or venues located in a different park. In this case, they are forced to navigate in the map for localizing the other park, which could be very far, and then show the content. Thus, they want the possibility to organize these contents, which cannot be positioned on the park they are currently visiting, in a different visual template, even a simple folder tree like the one used by Windows™ operating system they are familiar with.

4.2   Customization in a TEL Context

The platform was also validated in a Technology Enhanced Learning (TEL) context. Nowadays, schools are provided with different computing devices, not only desktops but also different types of tablets and interactive whiteboard. Teachers and students are increasingly using such devices in their daily activities. The experience on TEL of some of the authors of this paper showed that, if used with proper techniques and tools, technology may be a valid support to learning and can even encourage people to become more active in their learning activities (Ardito, Costabile, De Angeli, & Lanzilotti, 2012). The proposed platform has a great potential to be one of such supporting tools.

The customization of the platform to the TEL domain was performed by a team of two professional developers with HCI expertise and two high school teachers. They met four times to perform various activities. Other activities were performed in between two consecutive meetings.

In the first two meetings, important information to identify new services to be registered was collected. Teachers illustrated their current use of technology in their school. Teachers and students regularly use Google Drive tools to support the activity of sharing and integrating information they find on the Web using students' laptops or tablets. The teacher organizes a Google Drive folder in subfolders, each related to a class topic. Web pages, images, videos, presentations, or part of them that the teacher has selected for her/his class are pasted into a document and saved in a folder, which is shared with students. In addition, each student has a folder on Google Drive (named with his/her name), containing his/her documents, some of which are shared with other students and with the teacher, others are only in view modality for other people. In class, the teacher uses the interactive white board, in order to show and discuss the contents available in the folder of that specific topic. A blank document is opened, in which s/he writes the titles of the topics that students will further deepen. Students individually perform their searches in the laboratory or at home and create documents that contain links to content on the Web and/or portions of Web documents that are copied and pasted in a new document. Each student saves these documents in the personal folder in the class folder. Back to classroom, the teacher, through the interactive whiteboard, examines and discusses with students the documents produced by them. During the discussions, the two teachers realized that, while Google Drive only permits manual operations to copy and paste into a new document text, images and links to Web pages, videos, etc., the mashup platform should be valuable in performing, in particular, the following activities: (1) creating more sophisticated search tools by composing data coming from different services; (2) updating the content returned by the components by simply re-running their queries; (3) organizing contents in appropriate visual templates. At the end of the second meeting, the team agreed that the teacher's class should be supported by multimedia content (Web pages, images, videos, presentations) retrieved beforehand by the teacher from the Web. Thus, the services Google Search, Wikipedia, SlideShare, Google Images, YouTube and Vimeo were registered in the platform.

In the third meeting, teachers customized the platform by registering new services (e.g. Wikipedia, SlideShare). They were able to manipulate content, performing join and union of services, primarily using various types of lists to visualize the results. They asked for having the possibility to save the current results of the composed services somewhere, replicating the classical operation they were used to do: they copy and paste the results of their searches in a document in Google Drive. This opened a discussion within the team. Teachers understood the different behavior of a widget in the workspace. Indeed, once a user, acting on that widget, performs a query, the original sources are accessed, but the results may be different than those obtained with a previous query on the same widget. This has many advantages, but the teachers explained that sometimes, when they find an interesting result, they want to keep it to show later to their students. In order to satisfy this requirement, the final decision was to implement in the platform a very primitive container, a kind of folder, in which they can save the results of a specific query. This "Favourite" folder was indeed implemented in the platform.

In the fourth and last meeting, teachers finalized the customization of the platform by refining the services and saving some contents in the favorite container. However, some concerns aroused about the appropriateness of the content visualization allowed by the "Favourite" container for supporting class activities. At the end, the teachers insisted on having a different visual template, such as a *concept map*, which permits to organize and structure the retrieved contents according to learning concepts and their relationship. Therefore, the design team specified the requirements of this new visual template so that a first prototype could be available.

The use of the customized platform was carried out at a high school in Southern Italy. It was organized over three days and involved a class of 16 students

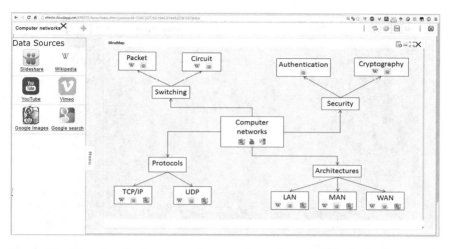

Fig. 5 The Interactive Workspace on *Computer Networks* created by the teacher using a desktop PC

(9 females, 19-year-old on average) and a teacher. The first day, using a PC in his office, the teacher composed an IW relative to a specific topic, i.e., *Computer Networks*, searching and including content about *Protocols*, *Architectures*, *Switching* and *Security* retrieved from the registered services. The retrieved contents were saved and organized in the concept map container (see Fig. 5).

Two days later, the teacher taught a class supported by the IW visualized on an interactive whiteboard. The teacher very effectively presented the different contents; he visualized them using the concept map container, with which he was familiar. At the end, he divided the students in groups of 2–3; each group was assigned the task of creating an IW about a specific *Computer Networks* sub-topic, e.g., *Protocols*, *Packet Switching*, *Latency Period*. After a brief individual training session, all the groups accessed the laboratory to carry out their assignments.

Next day students presented in class their group work using a interactive whiteboard (see Fig. 6). The list container, used by students to organize the content they retrieved, proved very poor for presentation purposes. In particular, the list visualization makes difficult the identification of a specific content to be illustrated.

Students agreed that the concept map would be a better visual template, even if they did not realize this during the workspace composition. A group of students proposed a visual template in which contents could be organized in different folders; it is evident that this derived from the influence of Google Drive on their mental model. In general, they agreed on the value of more flexibility in organizing the interactive workspace. The provided visual templates should also be empowered with functionality that permits ordering, filtering and searching actions.

Fig. 6 A student presenting the Interactive Workspace of her group organized as a list of contents and visualized on an Interactive White Board

4.3 Discussion

The studies conducted in the Cultural Heritage and in the Technology Enhanced Learning domains (see Ardito et al., 2014 for more details) demonstrated how the customization activities allowed domain experts to take advantage of their domain knowledge to adapt the general-purpose mashup platform to the specific end-user requirements in those domains. Customization was functional to foster the adoption of mashup platforms in real contexts, also favoring the "seeding" of such EUD tools in a specific domain.

Besides allowing us to assess the advantages of the customization activities introduced in the meta-design model, the studies demonstrated that the platform is sufficiently easy to use and users felt quite supported in accomplishing their tasks. Most participants appreciated the value of the platform in enabling easy and effective integration of content retrieved on the fly from online APIs. Low response time of the platform was indicated as a negative aspect, but this was due to the very poor technology infrastructure available both at the archaeological park and at the school lab. In other studies that we performed to evaluate the platform, none ever complained about this problem.

Participants highlighted the lack of collaboration tools, such as chats or forums. Other remarks also concerned distributed collaborative creation of components and functions to annotate them services, widgets and information items. In earlier versions of the platform (Matera et al., 2013) we already included these functions, thus their provision would be possible. They were not made available during the study as our main focus was on the adequateness of the composition paradigm.

The studies also revealed new requirements that mashup platforms should feature to foster their adoption in real contexts. First, the users expressed the need to "manipulate" data extracted from services. They highlighted that through the platform they could not perform much more than visualizing data, modifying visualizations, and inspecting data details. They would instead appreciate functions to make the displayed information *actionable*, i.e., suitable for being manipulated according to their task goals. For example, in the content retrieval task, beyond composing services and choosing how to visualize retrieved content, participants also wanted to perform ordering, filtering, or selecting a specific part of a content item, possibly annotating the selected parts with comments. A suggestion came out about the adoption of the *mind map* as further visual template, because teachers are familiar with it and it is indeed appropriate in the learning domain where concept relationships are very significant.

Second, they needed to satisfy complex information needs by gathering data from the entire Web - not only from pre-packaged components. Inspired by these requirements, the most recent version of EFESTO offers: (1) a set of tools to organize, visualize and manipulate extracted data according to specific functions (Ardito et al., 2015); (2) a new "polymorphic" data source that exploits the Linked Open Data cloud (Desolda, 2015); (3) visual mechanisms to integrate data retrieved from different data sources (Ardito et al., 2014). Further studies have been planned to assess the benefit of these new features.

5   Conclusion

This chapter presented a three-layer meta-design model to build systems that enable EUD and that leverage domain specificity to provide end users with tools that really make sense in real contexts of use. The peculiarity is the introduction of additional methodological activities, which address the customization of systems to specific domains. This customization is performed by domain experts, possibly in collaboration with professional developers.

Although the studies were conducted in two specific domains, we are confident that the proposed methodology can be effectively applied to the customization of any domain. Our current work is devoted to further refining the customization activities. For this purpose, following a bottom-up approach, we are applying the methodology for customizing the mashup platform to other domains, in particular home automation to support the elderly. This domain poses some more challenges: even the composition paradigm needs to be revised, as also smart objects needs to be composed and synchronized with Web services. Some preliminary results however already confirmed the effectiveness of the three-layer design model and the adequateness of the architecture organization of the EFESTO platform.

Acknowledgments This work is partially supported by the Italian Ministry of University and Research (MIUR) under grants PON03PE_00136_1 - "DSE - Digital Services Ecosystem" and CTN01_00128_111357 - "SHELL - Cluster Smart Living Technologies".

References

Aghaee, S., & Pautasso, C. (2014). End-user development of mashups with naturalmash. *Journal of Visual Languages & Computing, 25*(4), 414–432.

Ardito, C., Bottoni, P., Costabile, M. F., Desolda, G., Matera, M., Picozzi, M. (2014). Creation and use of service-based distributed interactive workspaces. *Journal of Visual Languages & Computing, 25*(6), 717–726.

Ardito, C., Buono, P., Costabile, M. F., Lanzilotti, R., Piccinno, A. (2012). End users as co-designers of their own tools and products. *Journal of Visual Languages & Computing, 23* (2), 78–90.

Ardito, C., Costabile, M. F., De Angeli, A., Lanzilotti, R. (2012). Enriching exploration of archaeological parks with mobile technology. *ACM Transactions on Computer-Human Interaction, 19*(4), 1–30. Article 29.

Ardito, C., Costabile, M. F., Desolda, G., Lanzilotti, R., Matera, M., Picozzi, M. (2014). Visual composition of data sources by end users. In *Advanced visual interfaces (AVI '14), Como, Italy* (pp. 257–260). New York: ACM.

Ardito, C., Costabile, M. F., Desolda, G., Latzina, M., Matera, M. (2015). Making mashups action-able through elastic design principles. In P. Díaz, V. Pipek, C. Ardito, C. Jensen, I. Aedo, A. Boden (eds.). *End-user development - IS-EUD 2015* vol. LNCS 9083, (pp. 236–241). Berlin Heidelberg: Springer.

Burnett, M., Cook, C., Rothermel, G. (2004). End-user software engineering. *Communications of the ACM, 47*(9), 53–58.

Cabitza, F., Fogli, D., Piccinno, A. (2014a). "Each to his own": distinguishing activities, roles and artifacts in EUD practices. In L. Caporarello, B. Di Martino, M. Martinez (eds.). *Smart organizations and smart artifacts: fostering interaction between people, technologies and processes* vol. 7, (193–205). Cham: Springer International Publishing.

Cabitza, F., Fogli, D., Piccinno, A. (2014b). Fostering participation and co-evolution in sentient multimedia systems. *Journal of Visual Languages & Computing, 25*(6), 684–694.

Cappiello, C., Matera, M., Picozzi, M. (2015). A UI-centric approach for the end-user develop-ment of multidevice mashups. *ACM Transactions on the Web, 9*(3), 1–40.

Casati, F. (2011). How end-user development will save composition technologies from their con-tinuing failures. In M. Costabile, Y. Dittrich, G. Fischer, A. Piccinno (eds.). *End-user devel-opment - IS-EUD 2011* LNCS vol. 6654, (4–6). Berlin Heidelberg: Springer.

Casati, F., Daniel, F., Angeli, A. D., Imran, M., Soi, S., Wilkinson, C. R., et al. (2012). Developing mashup tools for end-users: on the importance of the application domain. *International Journal of Next-Generation Computing, 3*(2), 144–172.

Costabile, M. F., Fogli, D., Fresta, G., Mussio, P., Piccinno, A. (2003). Building environments for end-user development and tailoring. In *IEEE symposium on human centric computing lan-guages and environments (HCC'03)* (pp. 31–38). Auckland, New Zealand: IEEE Computer Society.

Costabile, M. F., Fogli, D., Mussio, P., Piccinno, A. (2006). End-user development: the software shaping workshop approach. In H. Lieberman, F. Paternò, V. Wulf (eds.). *End user develop-ment* (pp. 183–205). Dordrecht, The Netherlands: Springer.

Costabile, M. F., Fogli, D., Mussio, P., Piccinno, A. (2007). Visual interactive systems for end-user development: a model-based design methodology. *IEEE Transactions on Systems, Man, and Cybernetics - Part A: Systems and Humans, 37*(6), 1029–1046.

Costabile, M. F., Mussio, P., Parasiliti Provenza, L., Piccinno, A. (2009). Supporting end users to be co-designers of their tools. In V. Pipek, M. Rosson, B. de Ruyter, V. Wulf (eds.). *End-user development - IS-EUD 2009* vol. LNCS 5435, (70–85). Berlin Heidelberg: Springer.

Danado, J., & Paternò, F. (2014). Puzzle: a mobile application development environment using a jigsaw metaphor. *Journal of Visual Languages & Computing, 25*(4), 297–315.

Daniel, F., & Matera, M. (2014). *Mashups - concepts, models and architectures.* Berlin Heidelberg: Springer-Verlag.

Desolda, G. (2015). Enhancing workspace composition by exploiting linked open data as a polymorphic data source. In E. Damiani, R. J. Howlett, L. C. Jain, L. Gallo & G. De Pietro (Eds.), *Intelligent interactive multimedia systems and services - IIMSS '15* 40, (97–108). Cham: Springer.

Desolda, G., Ardito, C., Matera, M. (2016). EFESTO: a platform for the end-user development of interactive workspaces for data exploration. In: F. Daniel, C. Pautasso (Eds.), *Rapid mashup development tools.* Communications in Computer and Information Science. Vol 591 (pp. 63–81). Cham: Springer.

Díez, D., Mørch, A., Piccinno, A., Valtolina, S. (2013). Cultures of participation in the digital age: empowering end users to improve their quality of life. In Y. Dittrich, M. Burnett, A. Mørch, D. Redmiles (eds.). *End-user development - IS-EUD 2013* vol. LNCS 7897, (pp. 304–309). Berlin Heidelberg: Springer.

Fischer, G. (1998). Seeding, evolutionary growth and reseeding: constructing, capturing and evolving knowledge in domain-oriented design environments. *Automated Software Engineering, 5*(4), 447–464.

Fischer, G. (2010). End user development and meta-design: foundations for cultures of participation. *Journal of Organizational and End User Computing, 22*(1), 52–82.

Fischer, G. (2011). Understanding, fostering, and supporting cultures of participation. *Interactions, 18*(3), 42–53.

Fischer, G., Fogli, D., Piccinno, A. (2017). Revisiting and broadening the meta-design framework for end-user development. In F. Paternò & V. Wulf (eds.), *New perspectives in end-user development* (pp. 61–98). Cham: Springer.

Fischer, G., & Giaccardi, E. (2006). Meta-design: a framework for the future of end-user development. In H. Lieberman, F. Paternò & V. Wulf (eds.), *End user development* (pp. 427–457). Dordrecht, The Netherlands: Springer.

Fischer, G., Giaccardi, E., Ye, Y., Sutcliffe, A., Mehandjiev, N. (2004). Meta-design: a manifesto for end-user development. *Communications of the ACM, 47*(9), 33–37.

Ghiani, G., Paternò, F., Spano, L. D., Pintori, G. (2016). An environment for end-user development of web mashups. *International Journal of Human-Computer Studies, 87*(C), 38–64.

Iverson, K. E. (1980). Notation as a tool of thought. *Communications of the ACM, 23*(8), 444–465.

Iyer, B., & Davenport, T.H. (2008). Reverse engineering: Google's innovation machine. *Harvard Business Review, 86*(4).

Jenkins, H. (2009). *Confronting the challenges of participatory culture: media education for the 21st century.* Cambridge, MA: MIT Press.

Ko, A. J., Abraham, R., Beckwith, L., Blackwell, A., Burnett, M., Erwig, M., et al. (2011). The state of the art in end-user software engineering. *ACM Computing Surveys, 43*(3), 1–44.

Koehne, B., Redmiles, D., Fischer, G. (2011). Extending the meta-design theory: engaging participants as active contributors in virtual worlds. In M. F. Costabile, Y. Dittrich, G. Fischer, A. Piccinno (eds.). *End-user development - IS-EUD 2011* vol. 6654, (pp. 264–269). Berlin Heidelberg: Springer.

Latzina, M., & Beringer, J. (2012). Transformative user experience: beyond packaged design. *Interactions, 19*(2), 30–33.

Liu, X., Huang, G., Mei, H. (2007). Towards end user service composition. In: *Computer software and applications conference (COMPSAC '07)*, Beijing, China, 24–27 July (pp. 676–678). IEEE.

Maceli, M., & Atwood, M. E. (2011). From human crafters to human factors to human actors and back again: bridging the design time – Use time divide. In M. F. Costabile, Y. Dittrich, G. Fischer, A. Piccinno (eds.). *End-user development - IS-EUD 2011* vol. 6654, (pp. 76–91). Berlin Heidelberg: Springer.

Matera, M., Picozzi, M., Pini, M., Tonazzo, M. (2013). PEUDOM: a mashup platform for the end user development of common information spaces. In F. Daniel, P. Dolog, Q. Li (eds.). *Web engineering - ICWE '13* vol. LNCS 7977, (pp. 494–497). Berlin Heidelberg: Springer.

Maximilien, E. M., Wilkinson, H., Desai, N., Tai, S. (2007). A domain-specific language for web APIs and services mashups. In B. Krämer, K.-J. Lin, P. Narasimhan (eds.). *Service-oriented computing – ICSOC 2007* vol. LNCS 4749, (pp. 13–26). Berlin Heidelberg: Springer.

Mehandjiev, N., & de Angeli, A. (2014). Guest editors introduction: representations and environments for user-driven development of service applications. *Journal of Visual Languages & Computing*, 25(4), 251–252.

Namoun, A., Nestler, T., Angeli, A. (2010). Conceptual and usability issues in the composable web of software services. In F. Daniel, F. M. Facca (eds.). *International conference on web engineering - ICWE 2010 workshops - revised selected papers* vol. LNCS 6385, (pp. 396–407). Berlin Heidelberg: Springer.

Namoun, A., Nestler, T., De Angeli, A. (2010). Service composition for non-programmers: prospects, problems, and design recommendations. In: *IEEE European conference on web services (ECOWS '10), Ayia Napa, Cyprus* (pp. 123–130). Washington, DC: IEEE Computer Society.

Porter, J. (2008). *Designing for the Social Web*. Thousand Oaks, CA: New Riders Press.

Ro, A., Xia, L.-Y., Paik, H.-Y., Chon, C. (2008). Bill organiser portal: a case study on end-user composition. In S. Hartmann, X. Zhou, M. Kirchberg (eds.). *Web information systems engineering – WISE 2008 workshops* vol. LNCS 5176, (pp. 152–161). Berlin Heidelberg: Springer.

Schuler, D. (1993). *Participatory design: principles and practices*. Hillsdale, NJ: L. Erlbaum Associates.

Sutcliffe, A., & Papamargaritis, G. (2014). End-user development by application-domain configuration. *Journal of Systems and Software*, 91, 85–99.

Von Hippel, E. (2005). *Democratizing innovation*. Cambridge, MA: MIT Press.

End-User Developers – What Are They Like?

Alan F. Blackwell

Abstract End-user developers are identified by their difference from (ordinary) developers. This difference is both a matter of definition, and an essential starting point for investigation. So the question arises *how* are they different? Since there are so many more non-developers in the world than developers, it seems likely that the differences among end-user developers may be even larger than the difference between (ordinary) developers and end-user developers. This chapter will review these individual differences, to the extent that they have been addressed in the research literature. These differences influence and are determined by education and training, differences in professional and domestic settings, differences in personality and intrinsic motivation, and differences in work practices and habits of thinking. All of these differences between individuals present questions for future investigation in end-user development research, and also opportunities for design of tools and systems that support end-user developers in different ways.

Keywords End-user developers · work practices · professional developers · artistry

1 Introduction

An end-user developer is not a professional developer. As a definition of the phrase "end-user development," this provides a good starting point for investigation. However, when a definition is framed in negative terms like this, the attributes that we might associate with the definition will also be negative attributes. For example, we might observe that the end-user developer has not received professional training in development, is not paid for doing development, would not describe development as being her profession, and so on.

There is not necessarily any problem in a negative definition like this. After all, many people do things that are not their job, do things they are not trained for, and

A.F. Blackwell (✉)
University of Cambridge, Cambridge, United Kingdom
e-mail: afb21@cam.ac.uk

© Springer International Publishing AG 2017
F. Paternò, V. Wulf (eds.), *New Perspectives in End-User Development*,
DOI 10.1007/978-3-319-60291-2_6

121

do things without being paid for them. Such everyday activities include mundane duties (doing laundry, washing a car), DIY projects (adjusting a bicycle, shortening a pair of trousers, putting up a shelf), hobbies (making a sundial, arranging flowers, playing a violin) or games (competing at bridge, chess, or tennis). All of these are activities that might equally be done by a professional, who we pay for the pleasure of watching them at work, or just because we don't fancy doing it ourselves.

However, if there is any respect in which the tools and techniques of the non-professional "end-user" will differ from those of the professional, we need to ask more closely what end-users are really like. What motivates them to do these things? Is there any economic logic, or are they being "irrational" (in the economic sense (Harper, Randall, & Sharrock, 2016)).

Why would somebody who is not a professional developer even consider creating a piece of software? Possibilities include: because they like it; because it is immediately useful; or because they believe they will be good at it. The rest of this chapter considers each of these in turn. However, we do not assume that all end-user developers are the same. They are not only different from professional developers – they are different from each other. The main focus of this chapter, therefore, is on understanding each of these perspectives as a basis for studying such differences, in order to better understand the range of tools and techniques that might support the various different types of end-user developer in future.

2   Because They Like It … Motivation in End-User Development

Professional developers do development work because they are paid for it. This is an *extrinsic* motivation – professional workers may or may not enjoy their work, but they do it because they are paid. There are also some end-user developers who create software as part of their employment (perhaps to improve efficiency), in which case they also have an extrinsic motivation, although it is subject to a cost-benefit equation (Mehandjiev, Sutcliffe, & Lee, 2006; Wulf & Jarke, 2004). I will discuss cost-benefit models in the next section, but there is another kind of motivation – *intrinsic* motivation, when people do things just because they enjoy it, for its own sake.

The discussion in this section is based on the first systematic study of intrinsic motivation in end-user programming, taking into account the differences between people that cause some people to be motivated by different things from others. Those differences between people can be related (unsurprisingly) to different personality types. Furthermore, it is possible to describe these differences systematically, by reference to the standard psychometric basis of personality – the five factor or "Big Five" model (John & Srivastava, 1999) that builds on the reliable statistical independence found between individual factors of (1) Openness to experience, (2) Conscientiousness, (3) Extraversion, (4) Agreeableness and (5) Neuroticism (the Big Five can easily be recalled with the mnemonic O.C.E.A.N).

Aghaee, Blackwell, Kosinski, and Stillwell (2015) developed a statistical model that correlates motivations for end-user programming within the five factor

"OCEAN" model of personality differences. They based their work on a calibrated data set of over 6 million Facebook users who had volunteered to complete standardised personality questionnaires, followed by providing access to their Facebook profiles for research purposes (Kosinski, Matz, Gosling, Popov, & Stillwell, 2015). This data set had been used for many previous studies, relating various kinds of online and social data to underlying personality models (e.g. Quercia et al., 2012).

In using this data set to study motivations for end-user development, the Facebook data was used to construct a statistical model of hypothetical factors that previous literature had suggested might motivate people to do end-user programming: practical tinkering (which we describe as bricolage), creative expression (which we describe as artistry), and fascination with new technology (which we describe as technophilia). As with other MyPersonality studies (Kosinski et al., 2015), these hypothetical factors must be operationalised by constructing independent sets of Facebook likes that the researchers expect to be associated with each factor. The hypothetical factors are then tested for reliability, in terms of reliably independent correlations with the OCEAN components.

These factors, summarised in relation to Facebook likes that were correlated with them, can be seen in Fig. 1. This figure presents a dimension-reduced view of a large statistical model in which the many dimensions of the MyPersonality data set were subjected to principal components analysis (PCA) in order to characterise hypothetical motivation factors. As can be seen from the figure, it was possible to construct a PCA model in which the three hypothetical factors characterizing end-user programming were relatively orthogonal. More importantly, they were also associated with different profiles of OCEAN measures.

In the following sections, we provide narrative descriptions of these alternative intrinsic motivations for end-user development, and discuss the ways in which they were found to be reliably correlated with different personal characteristics. Note that this work has been published relatively recently, and is yet to be applied more widely. Although the hypothetical factors were found to be reliably correlated with OCEAN components using the MyPersonality data set, application to end-user programming has only been tested in two studies of 100 participants each. These studies demonstrate that the constructs do predict the experiences that end-user developers have with a single product (IFTTT), but it is not yet known whether the same constructs will predict experiences with other end-user development tools, or whether there might be further reliable constructs for intrinsic motivation in end-user development. More details of the process by which the constructs were derived, the statistical model development, and the experimental tests of their predictive power, can be found in Aghaee et al. (2015).

2.1   Bricolage

A bricoleur is a practical person, a person who takes delight in making things useful and making them work. A hacker, a fixer. Anthropologist Claude Levi Strauss borrowed the term to mean a particular kind of philosophical style. Not a

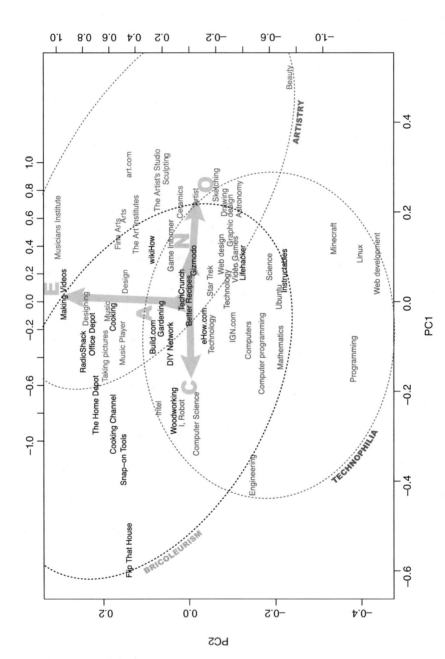

Fig. 1 Principal Components Analysis of the three sets of Facebook likes associated with end-user development motivators Bricoleurism, Technophilia and Artistry. The Five Factor Model personality components (O, C, E, A, N) are shown as vectors mapped within the same PCA space. Reproduced from Aghaee et al. (2015)

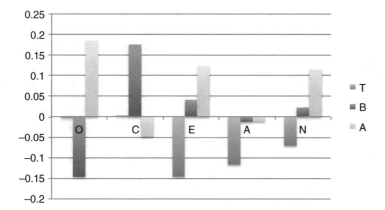

Fig. 2 BigFive personality traits profile for the three motivational factors (T: Technophilia, B: Bricoleurism, A: Artistry, O: Openness, C: Conscientiousness, E: Extroversion, A: Agreeableness, N: Neuroticism). Reproduced from Aghaee et al. (2015)

theoretician or scientist, but someone who cobbles together mash-ups, lash-ups, bodges and dodges. In France, "bricolage" has become the local word for DIY, and the weekend handy-man or -woman will visit the *Bricomart* before going home to *faire le brico*. For computer scientists, this kind of approach might reflect the worst kind of indiscipline, amateurism and unprofessionalism. It sounds like the ideal characterisation of the end-user developer.

In the study of personality correlations by Aghaee et al., as seen in Fig. 2, Bricoleurism was most significantly correlated with the big five factor of Conscientiousness. Bricoleurs are motivated by making things work, and they are likely to persist until they succeed. In contrast, bricoleurism was associated with low Openness to experience – as the editors of the Wikipedia Big Five page express this, they are practical people, preferring the plain, straightforward, and obvious over the complex, ambiguous, and subtle. When computer scientists criticize undisciplined "craft" approaches to programming (e.g. Dijkstra, 1970), it is possible that their lack of sophisticated intellectual analysis, rather than lack of discipline, is most objectionable.

In designing end-user development tools to suit the bricoleur, it seems likely that simple techniques and components, allowing for systematic assembly and testing, may be both appreciated and successful.

2.2 Artistry

People increasingly make software as an outlet for their creativity. Maker and hack-spaces are always full of enthusiasts working on art projects, and the rising enthusiasm for trends such as "live coding" and "algoraves" (Collins & McLean, 2014) suggests that we will continue to see both audiences and aspirations for people to do artistic things with software. As with most art-forms, this popularity will no doubt be associated with support for high-end software artists – professionals like Nick Rothwell and Marc Downie (Woolford, Blackwell, Norman, & Chevalier, 2010). These people have some serious skills, and unsurprisingly use high-end software tools and workstations, just as any media professional would do. However, the end-user development end of software artistry still represents the motivations of a large number of people. They might be creating interactive web pages, experimental mobile apps, competing in the demoscene (Scheib, Engell-Nielsen, Lehtinen, Haines, & Taylor, 2002), or just fooling around for their own satisfaction. Their motivation is quite different to that of the bricoleur – artists are not making something because it is useful, but for the experience it provides.

Unlike bricoleurism, artistry is most strongly correlated with the Big Five factor of Openness to experience, as seen in Fig. 2. Artists love to try out new things, whether or not they have any practical value, or even whether they work. They are curious and like adventures, quite possibly playing around with something just because it is unusual or different to what they have tried before. They are also likely to be high in Extraversion and Neuroticism. They are energetic and like mixing with people, so end-user development is far more likely to be a social activity for those motivated by artistry. Unfortunately, they might also become upset or discouraged more easily, or become anxious or stressed when technology is not working as they expect.

When we design end-user development tools for artists, it might be more important to support rapid experimentation, but with a safety net allowing users to roll back quickly when the experiments are unsuccessful. Most EUD tools focus on maintaining a minimal and stable feature set, but artists might appreciate tools in which novel capabilities emerge serendipitously or unpredictably. Appearances are important to people motivated by artistry, so both the tools and the products should aspire to higher aesthetic standards that the typical software engineering IDE. Looking at tools that software artists create for themselves, such as Downie's Field[1] or Brian Eno's Bloom[2], illustrates just how far EUD could go in thinking about the visual surface of their work.

2.3 Technophilia

Some people just love technology. They like everything to do with technology, are always keen to buy the latest gadget, or read about new and future developments. When they get a new toy, they try out all the features, to see what it can do. We all know people like this, and we probably know people who engage in end-user development just because it seems fun to see what else can be done with

---

[1]http://openendedgroup.com/field

[2]http://www.generativemusic.com

technology. For a technophile, programming is not a chore, but a technical adventure, or perhaps just an excuse to play around.

Once again, we can see in Fig. 2 that people motivated by Technophilia have a different personality profile by comparison to Artists and Bricoleurs. Opposite to artists, technophiles are low on extraversion – perhaps they are quite happy to stay in their bedrooms reading and playing with their gadgets. They are the first of our end-user types to have a strong tendency on the Agreeableness scale – but this is a negative correlation! With low agreeableness, they are less interested in other people, and may be unfriendly or uncooperative. Perhaps they will engage in online communities, but only for what they can get out of it, not for chitchat or to make friends. They are, however, more likely to be low in neuroticism, tending to be emotionally stable and less likely to be upset.

In designing end-user development tools for technophiles, compatibility with other new technologies is likely to be important, but perhaps not compatibility with other people. Although not driven by creative experimentation, they may also be less likely to be disappointed when facing challenges. Importantly for early adopters, practicality need not be a major priority, so a technophile will spend more time working on integration with other technologies, without being impatient to see practical benefits.

This discussion of the intrinsic motivation factors proposed by Aghaee et al. is based on a single publication, so should be interpreted with some caution. Reliability is dependent on the MyPersonality data set and research methods (Kosinski et al., 2015) and the two predictive experiments conducted by Aghaee et al., studying user experiences of the IFTTT tool. As the first study of *intrinsic* motivation in end-user development, it complements earlier studies of *extrinsic* motivation, for example in terms of cost-benefit analysis.

3   Because They Find It Useful … Rational Choice in End-User Development

In this section, we turn away from the *intrinsic* motivation differences between end-user developers to *extrinsic* motivation – what's in it for me? End-user development tools can clearly be useful, but the specific way this utility becomes apparent also differs between people.

Many end-user developers, writing programs for their own use, do so in order to automate some routine procedure that they would otherwise have to carry out manually. The routine manual procedure might involve repetitive calculations, routine decisions, or searching and filtering data sets. However, the amounts of data or repetition involved in an end-user development application are likely to be relatively small, simply because situations involving really high volume data processing are more likely to justify the employment of a professional programmer. Organisations may well be able to assess the financial costs of having such work done by an end-user rather than a software specialist (e.g. Mehandjiev et al., 2006; Wulf & Jarke, 2004).

Whether or not an organizational case is made, if an individual end-user developer is automating a procedure that they would otherwise have to complete manually, this involves a *personal* cost-benefit calculation. On the benefit side, how much manual processing effort will be saved if the task can be successfully automated? On the cost side, how much effort will be involved in creating the automated solution? The "effort" is unlikely to involve strenuous physical effort. Instead, it is *attentional* effort – the amount of time that the user must spend concentrating on the data or on the program, in order to complete the task.

This kind of end-user development, automating tasks that the same person would otherwise have to complete manually, can therefore be described as an "attention investment" (Blackwell, 2002). The promise of attention investment is that a relatively small amount of concentration right now (to write the automation program) will result in a larger saving of concentration in future (through completing the automated task without further attention from the user).

The *amount* of attention involved is not simply the number of minutes or hours to be saved, but rather the amount of *effort*. Writing a program does involve considerable concentration, when compared to routine data processing tasks. Many people might therefore choose to complete their work manually (involving relatively little concentration) rather than engaging in end-user development, with the higher levels of concentration that this will require. The decision of whether to engage in end-user programming therefore depends on how different people make this judgment.

In addition to estimating the relative amounts of concentration involved in choosing a manual or automated approach, the end-user also has to take into account the risks that might be involved. Investment of attention in order to receive future benefits through time saving is similar to financial investment for future benefits, because investment in the future always carries a degree of uncertainty or risk. Perhaps the amount of manual processing to be done in future will be less than estimated, in which case the investment might not be paid back? Perhaps it will take longer to write the automation program than expected, in which case the immediate costs will be too high relative to future savings? Perhaps the program will not handle all cases automatically, in which case there will continue to be future costs of manually processing the exceptions? In the worst case, unsuccessful automation might even make things worse, if the automated program runs out of control, creating further problems that need to be fixed. Such things are less likely to happen with manual processing, because the problems can be recognised as they happen, and fixed immediately.

This attention investment process, although long-established as a significant aspect of human factors in end-user development, is closely related to recent interest in behavioural economics, popularised as the "nudge" theory (Leonard, Thaler, & Sunstein, 2008). The core principle of behavioural economics is that people make cost-benefit decisions in all areas of their lives, based on a trade-off between immediate costs and future benefits. The "nudge" strategy suggests that people often make decisions on the basis of short-term convenience that might be worse for them in the long term. It would therefore be in their own interests if somebody (such as a paternalistic government) "nudged" them to behave in the right way, for their own good.

The attention investment model of end-user development has been used to justify a related design strategy, in which users might be encouraged to consider a programming approach to their tasks, rather than continuing with manual task completion. It was applied, for example, in the domain of spreadsheet debugging in the form of *surprise-explain-reward* – by drawing the user's attention to a potential bug, where they had previously assumed that the spreadsheet was correct, they would be nudged out of their complacency by this surprise. If they follow up on the surprise by taking the time to look at an explanation (rather than just carrying on with their previous plan), they should receive a "reward" telling them how much valuable time they have saved by fixing the bug (Wilson et al., 2003).

A similarly nudge-based strategy seemed promising (and still seems promising) as a user interface pattern for programming-by-example systems. If the user really is carrying out repetitive manual tasks rather than choosing to automate them, then the system should be able to detect the regularity in those tasks, and suggest an automated alternative. Cypher's *Eager* (1991) was one of the first prototypes implementing this principle, with a cartoon character "eagerly" offering to help the user by automating repeated operations that the user had been performing in the Apple Finder. Of course, a related approach later became very unpopular indeed, with the now proverbial *Clippy* character that was included in versions of Microsoft Office, and whose offers of help were often irrelevant or unwelcome. Users are easily able to recognise the implicit paternalism in these offers of assistance, and resent them when they are poorly informed. Future machine learning algorithms, exploiting larger volumes of data about user behaviours, should in future make it more straightforward to derive good quality generalisations for use in automating end-user tasks.

These opportunities for incidental end-user development will continue to rely on better understanding of the specific reasons for individual user choices, as well as on technical capabilities for accurate and reliable automated assistance. Systems will not be able to anticipate the broader context of a user decision. For example, what if this is the last day before a user leaves the company? It is extremely unlikely that they will want to develop a new solution to save future manual processing effort. What if they are just in a bad mood, or alternatively, what if they have time to spare, having intended for many months to try out a new programming feature, and decide to use it just for the experience, despite little likelihood of practical benefit? Successful approaches to end-user development should allow users to make such decisions according to the broader context of personal costs, risks, and benefits that only they are aware of, rather than assuming that they will act rationally in accordance with the financial or organizational goals of others.

Nevertheless, users will be better supported in making such decisions if the information available to them does provide accurate estimates of cost, risk and benefit. This is currently an untouched area of EUD research. People implicitly make judgments about cost of concentration all the time. Sometimes a person might drive her car fast, concentrating hard in order to avoid other traffic, manoeuvre around slower cars, accelerate and brake etc. At other times, she might just want to relax, staying in the slow lane, driving at a steady pace while thinking about other things. Different people make different choices, for different reasons. In order to make those choices well, they need better information about costs, risks and benefits. Furthermore, such information should not be costly to absorb. If it were necessary for the user to read complex documentation, or provide additional information about future plans, such activities would themselves take extra concentration! Designing for end-user development, according to attention investment principles, requires subtle design cues and clever visual design, providing users with access to information about available capabilities, but without increasing cognitive and attentional load.

From a research perspective, it is important to consider how the design principles appropriate for the support of end-user development might differ from those of conventional user interface design. The golden rules of user interface design, in the modern era of graphical user interfaces and touch screen interaction, are those of direct manipulation – the data that the user is working with should always be visible on the screen, operations should act directly on that data, the effects should be immediately visible, and they should be immediately reversible (Shneiderman, 1982). At first, these principles seem to make sense from an attention investment perspective. The cost of action is low, the risks are low, and the user does not need to spend much time deciding how to act. Unfortunately, the benefits are also low – this is not a recipe for automation, but for manual processing.

If users want to move beyond manual processing, by engaging in end-user development, the golden rules of direct manipulation are no longer the main consideration. Whereas manual processing can be done by direct manipulation, dealing with each object in turn, automated processing happens in the future, with objects that you haven't seen yet. The actions you are specifying are not immediate, but will take place when the program executes. You can't see the effects at the time you write the program, because those effects are in the future. At a deep level, end-user development is the *opposite* of direct manipulation, so making good user interfaces for end-user development requires that we abandon some of the most fundamental principles in the user experience textbooks.

This contradiction between end-user development and conventional good practice in user experience design should perhaps come as no surprise. Before the modern user interface paradigm became established, everyday user interaction with computers resembled programming languages. The command line interface was a simple programming language, and indeed remains so today, with the close relationship between command "shells" and shell scripts. The transition from the command line to the windows, icons, menus and pointer of the graphical user interface was associated with reduced user functionality – a reality that was immediately recognised, and loudly complained about, by many professional computer users at the time. The loss of command line interfaces quickly became a serious obstacle for end-user development, because the smooth upgrade path from single commands to simple batch files and shell scripts was no longer available.

However, despite the loss of functionality, few technical experts at the time recognised how the advantages that had been gained for end-users could be formulated in terms of programming. These advantages can be clearly expressed in terms of attention investment. Although the potential benefits of automation had been lost, these had been balanced by the gains of huge cost savings (in attentional effort) and the reduction in risks that had been associated with powerful commands that often went wrong. This is not a simple story in which end-user development is good, and direct manipulation bad. Successful design of end-user development functionality requires a deep understanding of the ways that we can express future functionality, in terms of the things we are doing right now, for example as "tailoring" of an interface to better suit future usage (MacLean, Carter, Lövstrand, & Moran, 1990; Wulf & Golombek, 2001).

From this perspective, end-user development is purely a way of talking about the future. All human languages make distinctions between talking about the future – especially things in the future that are conditional on different situations and contexts – and instructions to act in the moment. Talking about the future is more complicated than simple instructions, as will be easily understood by anyone who has raised small children. A three year-old may (or may not) follow an instruction to put her toy in the toy box right now. But there is no point in telling a child of this age that they should put their toy away tomorrow. Extrinsic motivation is not the same for everyone – the measures may be comparable, but perceptions of the future differ between individuals.

4   Because They Believe They Will Be Good At It …
   Self-Efficacy and End-User Development

This final section considers the ways in which some people may be more inclined to engage in end-user development because they believe they will be good at it. As discussed in the previous section, the extrinsic rewards of end-user development are subject to constant estimation and re-evaluation. People assess the likely cost of concentrating on a programming project, and weigh this up against the likely benefit that will result, along with any associated risks. These attention investment judgments are modified by perceived risks and benefits of the technologies they work with. To follow our theme of understanding individual differences, different people perceive those risks in different ways, modified by expectations based on their own personal experience (and of course, intrinsic motivation), as well as by cultural expectations of class, race, gender and wealth.

American education researcher Mary Rowe studied the way in which cultural expectations about laboratory equipment were likely to influence learning and performance in science lessons (1978). She observed that white male students were more likely to play around with the equipment before the lesson started, and that this resulted in confidence and an attitude of ownership that naturally encouraged their experimental work in the lesson itself. Female students and ethnic minorities were more likely to hold back, reluctant to touch the equipment, gaining less benefit from the lesson that followed.

This analysis has been applied in the past to end-user development. In a study of men and women learning to use spreadsheets Beckwith, Kissinger et al. (2006) observed whether the students spent time playing around and experimenting with the system features – behaviour they described as *tinkering*. It did indeed turn out that men were more likely to spend time tinkering, and that this was associated with increased self-efficacy – confidence in their own abilities, and belief that they were likely to succeed. Self-efficacy is well-known to be closely associated with successful educational outcomes (Bandura, 1994). Those students who believe they are going to succeed, do achieve the confidence to go on and do well, while for those who believe they are going to fail, this becomes a self-fulfilling prophecy.

There is also an obvious relationship between self-efficacy and attention investment, in that those who do not believe they are likely to do well at end-user development will assess the benefits and risks in a way that discourages them from even starting. As a result, an initial difference in self-efficacy, for example related to gender expectations of technology use, may lead to a decrease in tinkering, and eventual gender-linked failure to gain benefits from end-user development. Burnett's GenderMag, which originally developed from research into self-efficacy in end-user development (Beckwith, Burnett et al. 2006), has been widely promoted as a general approach to the analysis of gender bias in user interface design (Hill, Ernst, Oleson, Horvath, & Burnett, 2016). Although most widely studied in relation to gender, it would seem likely that race, class and economic situation are equally likely to have similar effects in the context of end-user development.

A small amount of work has been carried out in relation to race and class effects in computer science education, especially among high school students. Indications from work by Margolis (2013) and others are that students from minority and lower socio-economic groups are more likely to be motivated by the potential for professional career opportunities, including experiments in which students were paid to carry out professional work (as system testers) as an extension of the educational context. This focus on professionalism is certainly welcome as an educational initiative, but does not appear directly related to end-user development concerns, where development work is carried out by non-professionals without explicitly associated financial reward.

In comparison to race and class, there has been more focus on gender expectations of programming in both educational contexts and end-user development. In the Anglo-American countries, programming is identified as a stereotypically male-gendered activity, and computer science degree programmes attract far higher proportions of male students (Margolis & Fisher, 2003). This is seen as undesirable, where there is a liberal focus on equal opportunity of education and professional attainment. Researchers with links to the end-user development community have therefore created a range of educational programming tools that are designed to be attractive to girls at about the age this stereotypical gender separation is observed. The most prominent example is Kelleher's Storytelling Alice (Kelleher & Pausch, 2006; Kelleher, Pausch, & Kiesler, 2007), which can be contrasted with educational tools that aspire to more stereotypically male interests such as robot programming (Lego Mindstorms) or rap music ("Scratch" DJ culture).

However, in contrast to educational settings, end-user development takes place in rich cultural contexts, where stereotypical gender expectations are still pervasive. Self-efficacy mixes with intrinsic motivation to produce gendered behavior in end-user development in both business learning contexts such as the use of spreadsheets (Beckwith, Kissinger et al., 2006), and also in routine home automation, where particular devices are strongly associated with particular gender roles, resulting in dramatic differences in self-efficacy and attention investment decisions (Blackwell, Rode, & Toye, 2009).

The design lessons to be drawn from considerations of self-efficacy place a new emphasis on end-user development tools as cultural artefacts, which are embedded within cultural systems of expectation. These systems might often be discriminatory or exploitative, and could perhaps be dismissed as irrelevant to this volume, on the basis that they belong in the domain of political critique rather than software engineering. Nevertheless, it is undeniably true that the individual differences in intrinsic and extrinsic motivations discussed in the first two sections of this chapter are shaped by cultural forces. We need to pay close attention to the ways in which the design of end-user development tools might reinforce social expectations, whether expressed in crude "paint it pink" visual styling, or more subtle appeals to theories of aptitude that rely on gender-linked stereotypes such as "systemizing" traits (Fine, 2010).

5 Summary

This chapter has set out an agenda for understanding individual differences in end-user development. End-user developers are not all alike, and the current audience for end-user development tools is perhaps more homogeneous than necessary. If end-user development is to become more broadly adopted, then it seems a natural conclusion that it must be extended to appeal to a broader audience. Understanding the sources of variation, and identifying the different respects in which people might be observed to differ, is therefore a critical priority for the end-user development field.

We need not assume that everyone will be good at end-user development, or even that they will want to do it at all, so aiming for a universal theory of end-user development is unnecessary and perhaps unhelpful. As an alternative, we might look for people who *are* likely to find end-user development useful, appealing, or accessible, but are different to the current assumed audience for EUD. This not only broadens our potential audience, but helps us to be inclusive, perhaps delivering new capabilities to people who had been excluded from the potential of end-user development for reasons of gender, race, class, social status or other cultural and economic factors. More qualitative empirical research would be beneficial in gaining a richer understanding of end-user developers in their specific work and leisure contexts.

Many of the observations in this chapter are explicitly linked to design opportunities and design guidance that could be used to develop new kinds of end-user development tools for broader audiences. These connections have been mentioned in passing, as they arise, but this chapter is not primarily concerned with design methods. Other chapters in this volume provide far more information about the principles and methods for creation of new end-user development tools, and readers should find it instructive to assess and apply them in the light of aspects of diversity that have been reviewed here.

References

Aghaee, S., Blackwell, A. F., Kosinski, M., Stillwell, D. (2015). Personality and intrinsic motivational factors in end-user programming. In Z. Li, C. Ermel, S. D. Fleming (Eds). *Proceedings of IEEE symposium on visual languages and human centric computing (VL/HCC 2015)*, Atlanta, GA (pp. 29–36). Los Alamitos, CA: IEEE.

Bandura, A. (1994). *Self-efficacy*. New Jersey: John Wiley & Sons, Inc.

Beckwith, L., Burnett, M., Grigoreanu, V., Wiedenbeck, S. (2006). Gender hci: what about the software? *Computer, 39*(11), 97–101.

Beckwith, L., Kissinger, C., Burnett, B., Wiedenbeck, S., Lawrance, J., Blackwell, A., et al. (2006). Tinkering and gender in end-user programmers' debugging. In *Proceedings of CHI 2006* (pp. 231–240).

Blackwell, A. F. (2002). First steps in programming: a rationale for Attention Investment models. *Proceedings of the IEEE symposia on humancentric computing languages and environments*, Arlington, VA (pp. 2–10). Los Alamitos, CA: IEEE.

Blackwell, A. F., Rode, J. A., Toye, E. F. (2009). How do we program the home? Gender, attention investment, and the psychology of programming at home. *International Journal of Human Computer Studies, 67*, 324–341.

Collins, N., & McLean, A. (2014). Algorave: A survey of the history, aesthetics and technology of live performance of algorithmic electronic dance music. In *Proceedings of 14th international conference on new interfaces for musical expression*, B. Caramiaux, K. Tahiroğlu, R. Fiebrink, A. Tanaka (Eds.). (pp. 355–359). London: Goldsmiths University.

Cypher, A. (1991). Eager: programming repetitive tasks by example. In S. P. Robertson, G. M. Olson, J. S. Olson (Eds.). *Proceedings of the SIGCHI conference on human factors in computing systems (CHI'91)*, New Orleans LA (pp. 33–39). New York: ACM.

Dijkstra, E. W. (1970). *Notes on structured programming*. Eindhoven Netherlands: Technological University.

Fine, C. (2010). *Delusions of gender*. London: Icon.

Harper, R., Randall, D., Sharrock, W. (2016). *Choice*. New Jersey: John Wiley & Sons.

Hill, C., Ernst, S., Oleson, A., Horvath, S., Burnett, M. (2016). GenderMag experiences in the field: the whole, the parts, and the workload. In A. Blackwell, B. Plimmer, G. Stapleton (Eds.). *Proceedings of the IEEE symposium on visual languages and human-centric computing*, Cambridge, UK (pp. 199–207). Los Alamitos, CA: IEEE.

John, O. P., & Srivastava, S. (1999). The Big Five trait taxonomy: history, measurement, and theoretical perspectives. *Handbook of Personality: Theory and Research, 2*(1999), 102–138.

Kelleher, C., & Pausch, R. (2006). Lessons learned from designing a programming system to support middle school girls creating animated stories. In J. Grundy, J. Howse (Eds.). *Proceedings of the IEEE symposium on visual languages and human-centric computing*, Brighton, UK (pp. 165–172). Los Alamitos, CA: IEEE.

Kelleher, C., Pausch, R., Kiesler, S. (2007). Storytelling Alice motivates middle school girls to learn computer programming. In M. B. Rosson, D. Gilmore (Eds.). *Proceedings of the SIGCHI Conference on Human Factors in Computing Systems (CHI'07)*, San Jose, CA (pp. 1455–1464). New York: ACM.

Kosinski, M., Matz, S., Gosling, S., Popov, V., Stillwell, D. (2015). Facebook as a social science research tool: opportunities, challenges, ethical considerations and practical guidelines. *American Psychologist, 70*(6), 543–556.

Leonard, T. C., Thaler, R. H., Sunstein, C. R. (2008). Nudge: improving decisions about health, wealth, and happiness. *Constitutional Political Economy, 19*(4), 356–360.

MacLean, A., Carter, K., Lövstrand, L., Moran, T. (1990). User-tailorable systems: pressing the issues with buttons. In J. C. Chew, J. Whiteside (Eds.). *Proceedings of the SIGCHI conference on human factors in computing systems (CHI'90)*, Seattle WA (pp. 175–182). New York: ACM.

Margolis, J. (2013). *Stuck in the shallow end: education, race and computing*. Cambridge, MA: MIT Press.

Margolis, J., & Fisher, A. (2003). *Unlocking the clubhouse*. Cambridge, MA: MIT Press.

Mehandjiev, N., Sutcliffe, A., Lee, D. (2006). Organisational view of end-user development. In H. Lieberman, F. Paterno, V. Wulf (Eds.). *End user development*. Berlin, Heidelberg, New York: Springer.

Quercia, D., Las Casas, D. B., Pesce, J. P., Stillwell, D., Kosinski, M., Almeida, V., et al. (2012). Facebook and privacy: the balancing act of personality, gender, and relationship currency. In N. Ellison, J. G. Shanahan, Z. Tufekci (Eds.). *Sixth International AAAI Conference on Weblogs and Social Media (ICWSM)*, Dublin (pp. 306–313). Palo Alto, CA: AAAI Press.

Rowe, M. B. (1978). *Teaching science as continuous inquiry*. 2nd ed. New York: McGraw-Hill.

Scheib, V., Engell-Nielsen, T., Lehtinen, S., Haines, E., Taylor, P. (2002). The demo scene. In T. Appolloni (Ed.). *ACM SIGGRAPH 2002 conference abstracts and applications* (pp. 96–97). New York: ACM.

Shneiderman, B. (1982). The future of interactive systems and the emergence of direct manipulation. *Behaviour & Information Technology, 1*(3), 237–256.

Wilson, A., Burnett, M., Beckwith, L., Granatir, O., Casburn, L., Cook, C., et al. (2003). Harnessing curiosity to increase correctness in end-user programming. In G. Cockton, Panu Korhonen (Eds.). *Proceedings of the SIGCHI conference on human factors in computing systems (CHI'03)*, Ft. Lauderdale, FL (pp. 305–312). New York: ACM.

Woolford, K., Blackwell, A. F., Norman, S. J., Chevalier, C. (2010). Crafting a critical technical practice. *Leonardo, 43*(2), 202–203.

Wulf, V., & Golombek, B. (2001). Direct activation: a concept to encourage tailoring activities. *Behaviour & Information Technology, 20*(4), 249–263.

Wulf, V., & Jarke, M. (2004). The economics of end-user development. *Communications of the ACM, 47*(9), 41–42.

Malleability in the Hands of End-Users

Federico Cabitza and Carla Simone

Abstract The chapter deconstructs the notion of *malleability* in regard to interactive systems, mainly seen as the affordance that the system offers to the end users to adapt (some of) the system's behaviors and structures to their contingent needs, and it positions this concept in the ambit of the different approaches that have characterized it so far in the EUD perspective. The notion of malleability adopted in this chapter lies at the core of a research line that, starting in the late '90 with the notion of Coordination Mechanism, is now focusing on a conceptual framework called Logic of Bricolage. This framework conceives of malleability as a first-level affordance to be put in the hands, i.e., in full control of the end users to empower them in appropriating and adapting their applications at different (potentially any) level of detail. The chapter illustrates how this framework has been defined on the basis of several field studies and sketches how it can be instantiated in a computational platform, AdHoc, that is currently oriented to document-based management systems. The chapter will highlight the research efforts that are still needed to make the framework more effective in supporting the collaborative bricolage of the end users.

Keywords Malleability · interactive systems · Logic of Bricolage · socio-technical dimensions of EUD

1 Introduction

The chapter presents the outcomes of a quite long research trajectory that is rooted in the CSCW stream of research and met the EUD ambit along its unfolding. There are several reasons why this was a natural event from the plain fact that

F. Cabitza (✉) · C. Simone
University of Milano Bicocca, Milano, Italy
e-mail: cabitza@disco.unimib.it

C. Simone
University of Siegen, Siegen, Germany
e-mail: simone@disco.unimib.it

© Springer International Publishing AG 2017   137
F. Paternò, V. Wulf (eds.), *New Perspectives in End-User Development*,
DOI 10.1007/978-3-319-60291-2_7

these two ambits share some of their basic tenets (Henderson & Kyng, 1992; MacLean, Carter, Lövstrand, & Moran, 1990). Among these latter ones, first the attention for the users of the technology and their work contexts as main source of inspiration for the identification of its features; second, the acknowledgment that the context of use can change for many reasons and therefore the technology has to allow for the change of its features accordingly; and finally, the conviction that activities are increasingly collaborative and therefore the related technologies must offer affordances dealing with work interdependency and collaboration.

How can CSCW and EUD be mutually supportive? On the one hand, EUD outcomes can contribute to the conception of CSCW applications by making these more suitable to be changed and thus by offering to CSCW technical and social considerations explicitly connected to this specific requirement; on the other hand, CSCW can offer to EUD a rich set of methods and case studies to better understand the very nature of cooperation thus promoting in EUD scholars the awareness of how collaborative applications have to be conceived and how the practices around their changes should be better supported.

This mutual influence can be seen under a unique perspective: moving from the traditional design approaches that are merely focused on technology delivery to design approaches that focus on the users and on technology-design-in-use, in order to account for the impossibility to anticipate all the possible usage contexts and conditions. This shift would consequently aim at enhancing user agency in the construction of the technology itself. This is the perspective taken in the research trajectory that we report in this chapter.

There is a clear element that should be factored in the feasibility of such an integrated approach in order to avoid misleading preconceptions: the kind of problem at hand. We can identify two extreme situations. In the first case, the problem is about how to make existing work practices more effective by tapping into the capabilities of the related computational technologies, and then about how to govern their adoption to minimize the risk that the above work practices are disrupted and their evolution hindered. In the second case, the problem is about how to deal with a situation in which traditional work practices are not applicable or have been proven to be ineffective, through the adoption of a prospective technology. These two situations define different contextual conditions. In the former case, the end users know the requirements of the technology all too well: their problem is that they are not in the condition to build a technology complying with those (even implicit) requirements; in the latter case, the requirements themselves are unknown, and their definition is part of the problem together with the construction of the technology addressing them (Buchanan, 1992). In this latter case, the active participation of the end users to these two activities has to be carefully planned and stimulated since sometimes different/external competences are required (Borchorst, Bødker, & Zander, 2009; Bratteteig & Wagner, 2014): to this aim, the above approach can play a role only in combination with the usage of techniques that are typical of User-Centered Design and Participatory Design (Kensing & Blomberg, 1998; Stiemerling, Kahler, & Wulf, 1997), as aptly proposed in (Hartswood et al., 2008). Both traditions, and especially the latter one, deal with situations where the participation of users cannot be taken for granted for several reasons, and it might require a specific technology that would stimulate and support the participation itself.

The real life situations are often somewhere in-between these two extremes cases: then the approach has to be open and flexible enough to be usefully applicable under many circumstances and for various purposes. The chapter by Dittrich, Bolmsten, and Eriksson (2017) shows two nice examples of this complex situation and shares our claim that the possibility to adapt the whole process (from the definition of the problem up to the construction of an interactive system) to various and ever-varying situations is based also on the capability of the realized technology to do the same: we metaphorically call this capability *malleability*.

Since in the specialist literature different terms are used to express a similar property, the paper characterizes what we mean by malleability, as how we define it has a strong impact on the following arguments. Then, a conceptual framework and architecture, which we have called *Logic of Bricolage (LOB)*, is proposed for the development of *malleable systems* in terms that are general enough to be applied to any specific application domain; its relation to the notion of *infrastructure-(ing)* is discussed to better clarify our contribution. The observation of work practices in a number of field studies served as a sort of sandbox for the progressive definition and refinement of the LOB.

The LOB is then instantiated in the case of document-based work practices (that is work practices based on the recording of information), which are (still) common in many application and organizational domains. The architecture guided the development of a prototypical platform, called AdHoc, that supports the construction of this class of systems. The conclusions of the chapter highlight the research efforts that are still needed to make that the LOB, and any similar conceptual initiative, more effective in supporting the collaborative bricolage of the end users.

2 What We Mean by Malleability

From the very beginning, the EUD research field has followed different research lines and adopted alternative approaches according to the peculiar differences among the work settings, from both the technological and the organizational standpoints. Consequently, several terms ended up by denoting the different approaches to emphasize and corroborate a specific perspective. In (Lieberman, Paternò, Klann, & Wulf, 2006; Chap. 1), the authors proposed an initial systematization of the phenomenon that encompassed different dimensions and that has been an important reference for the EUD community. We will elaborate on this effort to highlight the dimensions characterizing the notion of *malleability* that informs the conceptual framework illustrated in this chapter.

2.1   The Sociotechnical Dimension of EUD

EUD was naturally conceived in the framework of a socio-technical approach to system design: the proposed solutions are characterized by how these two aspects are taken into account. When the focus is on the tools enabling the modification of existing applications or the creation of new applications, "the main goal of EUD [solutions] is *empowering end users* to develop and adapt systems themselves" (Lieberman et al., 2006; Chap. 1), and the attention is paid to the extent end users are differently interested in (and skilled for) these activities. The functionalities that have been proposed so far to achieve these goals vary a lot in relation to the chosen perspective. For example, in (Mørch, 1997) the authors use the *tailoring* metaphor to emphasize the phenomenon of *modifiability;* this latter can be divided in increasing levels, namely: customization, integration and extension. Other proposals focus on a guided sequence of checkpoints to respect some predefined norm (Fogli, Colosio, & Sacco, 2010); or to support the modification of the predefined system behaviours by using different patterns (e.g., model-based programming, programming by examples or various kinds of user-friendly visual languages).

All of these specific solutions can be seen as part of a class of technological supports that can coexist in the same solution, to both take into account the variety of end users and to implement what is called a "gentle slope" to complexity (MacLean et al., 1990), that is to align the system to the different skills and competencies that end users may acquire within a learning curve and over time. Moreover, when there is a concern about the overall quality of a user generated application (e.g., stability, reliability, security), there are attempts to apply and adapt some software engineering methods to the case of EUD for an easier verification of the software quality during code debugging, verification and testing (Hailpern & Santhanam, 2002) or for the check of their degree of fault tolerance to internal and external failures (Voas, Charron, McGraw, Miller, & Friedman, 1997).

Modularity is often claimed as a good programming style to achieve this goal (e.g., Won, Stiemerling, & Wulf, 2006), but also other means of software development are proposed to guarantee the quality of the final product such as design patterns or abstraction and reuse techniques (Ko et al., 2011).

When the focus is on the organization of the social context in which the EUD activities themselves are to be performed, approaches are proposed such as those discussed in the Software Shaping Workshop (Costabile, Fogli, Mussio, & Piccinno, 2006) or those based on the concept of *co-realization* (Hartswood et al., 2008), or on the concept of *seeds* (Fischer & Giaccardi, 2006). The main idea of the seed concept is to conceive initial and possibly partial solutions that end users can develop further with the help of the designers. In this perspective, a crucial issue is related to the *relationship between end users and IT designers*, that is between people who possess different levels of skills in system design and development, and people that perform these activities as professionals in the IT sector (Hartswood et al., 2003). This relationship requires to give an explicit interpretation of what *empowering end users* means as an aim, but also as a high-level goal, of EUD. This problem has been addressed along different perspectives. One attempt is to classify different classes of users according to their skills and attitudes: roles such as "power user," (Lieberman et al., 2006; Chap. 1), "gardener" (Gantt & Nardi, 1992), "local developer" (Cabitza, Fogli, & Piccinno, 2014), "end-user developer" (Fogli & Piccinno, 2013), "bricolant bricoleur" (Cabitza & Simone, 2015) have been identified from both vertical and cross-sectional field studies. Another possibility is to classify different classes of (IT) professionals who should fill in the competence gap in different ways: roles such as meta-designer and maieuta-designer (Cabitza & Simone, 2015) have been identified. In (Cabitza et al., 2014) is given an articulated discussion of the roles involved in EUD as well as of the kind of activities that these roles perform and of the artifacts that are built under their responsibility.

To sum up, the territory in which EUD is called to find an adequate solution is varied: therefore the underlying approach has to make clear how the malleability requirement is interpreted, and how the relationship between end users and IT professionals is defined accordingly.

2.2 The Features of Malleability

The term malleability has been used within EUD and CSCW with different meanings.

Within the EUD discourse, Richter and Riemer (2013) limit the scope of the applicability of the malleability requirement by distinguishing between two kinds of software applications. On the one hand, they consider what they call Purpose-Specific End-User Software (PEUS). This kind of software "is introduced with the aim to solve an existing corporate problem or to immediately improve an existing user task." like, e.g., ERP or CRM; consequently it "is thus prescribed and communicated in a 'top-down' manner by the corporate management." On the other hand, there is what they called Malleable End-user Software (MEUS), whose "main characteristic [...] is its inherent flexibility and openness when enabling and supporting a wide variety of work practices without the need for technical customization." Examples of MEUS are spreadsheets, platforms like Dropbox, and (Enterprise) Social Networking platforms. However, this distinction seems questionable as it creates an undue barrier between applications that are strongly integrated in the work practices. Moreover in this case, the meaning of the term malleability denotes a property that we prefer to call *versatility*, since the use of the platforms "are open-ended and not prescribed by the software, a wide range of possible ways exist to appropriate such platforms": in fact in this case the platform remains the same but can be used to serve different purposes according to the contingent culture and needs. In addition, in (Trier & Richter, 2013) malleability is put in relation to the property of *simplicity* that is defined "as an economic quality that aims at achieving a maximum of results with given means through parsimony of elements and structural principles." Hence, in the authors' view malleability and simplicity are strongly intertwined to make software appropriation by the users more likely, or easy, to happen.

Within the CSCW field, the term malleability takes a richer connotation. The first authors to refer to malleability were probably Navarro, Prinz and Rodden, who in (Navarro, Prinz, & Rodden, 1992) wrote that "CSCW systems need be malleable and tailorable [...] both by developers and users." In the same year, Dourish in a Xerox technical report spoke of malleability in terms of *interoperability*, open-endedly *extensibility*, efficiency in a range of different circumstances, "even when those circumstances could never have been foreseen by the systems designer." However, Dourish did not specify how this ambitious goal could be reached by mere hardware and software compatibility. Some years earlier, Randall in (Randall, 1988) wrote that "systems need to be malleable in the sense that the user can appropriate them to the task at hand in ways that arise naturally in the course of activity." He also rightly noted that "the danger, however, is that as systems become more malleable, they also become more complex due to an increased range of options. This forces users to spend more time dealing with the system and less with the task at hand. In cases of well-established activities for which there is a wealth of collective experience, this danger can sometimes be avoided."

The concept of malleability that we use in this chapter is close to the socio-technical perspective that considers the "psychological fit between users and interactive systems" and to the typical CSCW and HCI concerns of "maximizing the sovereignty, creativeness and satisfaction of the final user" (Potas, 1978). We introduce these ideas by referring to a visionary work from almost 40 years ago – and of uncertain impact – because this contribution, by relating to the metaphor of the "man-machine symbiosis" coined by Licklider (1960), also introduced ideas that are central to our proposal. In Potas' words:

> systems may be structured to allow the development of command tools based on key underlying data objects and operators having relatively simple initial structure. The user could then build his command repertoire from these elements, or, if a system provided some initial set of commands built upon a basic internal command language, could redefine or enhance such commands. Malleability [regards the] richness of basic elements and structures which can be used to create small chunks incorporating immense complexity.

Independently from this seminal contribution, we also consider malleability as the capability of interactive systems to empower end users in tailoring their systems in different ways: accordingly, *malleability goes beyond versatility*. Indeed, its meaning is compatible with the idea of *logical malleability* of computer systems Moor (1985) introduced and connected with ethical concerns and with an ethics of design. In his words: "Computers are logically malleable [...] in that they can be manipulated to do any activity that can be characterized in terms of inputs, outputs, and connecting logical operations. [...] Because computers are logically malleable, they will continue to be applied in unpredictable and novel ways, generating numerous policy vacuums for the foreseeable future." On the other hand, Moor claims that malleability is not only a generator of ethical dilemmas, but also what makes computer systems less rigid "political artifacts" (Winner, 1980), that is artifacts that do have politics by either imposing or reflecting political and moral values, e.g., in the categories (Suchman, 1994) they afford and disseminate, and in the behaviors that they promote and constraint. This is because the designers' politics can be confronted, and modified (at least to some extent and in principle) at run time, by the end users themselves, if they do not fit the users' worldview or if changes made them no longer correct or applicable.

The above connotation of malleability is fully coherent with one of the basic properties of Computable Coordination Mechanisms (CCM) (Schmidt & Simone, 1996), that is constructs that had been derived from a series of field studies by observing how people define and use information artifacts in cooperative settings to support the articulation of their activities. Not only "a CM must be malleable in the sense that it supports users in specifying its behavior [...] by making local and temporary changes to [it]"; but in addition, the available building blocks (the Potas' "underlying data objects and operators") should be at the *semantic level of articulation work*: "at a semantic level, at a level of granularity, and in a modality which is appropriate for the specific work domain at hand. That is, [...] expressed in terms of categories of articulation work [...] that are meaningful to the participants involved in terms of their everyday work activities." A similar requirement is stressed in (Lieberman et al., 2006; Chap. 1): "a system's component structure [should be] designed to be meaningful for its users and [...] these users [should be] able to easily translate changes in the application domain into corresponding changes in the component structure." For these reasons we prefer to use the more comprehensive phrase *semantic level of work practices*, which includes articulation work. Accordingly, malleability aims to support *appropriation* (Wulf et al., 2015) through the suitable semantic level of the building blocks rather than by relying on the notion of simplicity. This latter is usually interpreted from the perspective of the IT designer(s) rather than from the perspective of the users' work practices, thus taking an undue and risky simplification. In so doing, malleability and appropriation reduce the danger of distraction raised in (Randall, 1988).

Finally, the concept of malleability that we use in this chapter implies the *openness* emphasized in (Richter & Riemer, 2013): as in the case of CCM, malleability entails a third level, besides those devoted to the definition and execution of an application. This level would allow for the extension and modification of the basic building blocks if new digitized practices made this necessary. Moreover, since practices and technologies mutually influence each other and co-evolve (Carroll, Kellogg, & Rosson, 1991; Fogli & Piccinno, 2013), the framework should allow end users to construct not only open but also *opennable* applications (Cabitza, Simone, & Storni, 2016). Opennable means that end users can unpack their applications (almost) at any level of detail, up to the basic building blocks that the framework makes available to them, while still remaining at the semantic level of their work practices.

This complex notion of malleability has been taken as a reference by the research we have undertaken in the recent years. We kept observing work practices in different domains to identify the required basic building blocks and their composition at the appropriate semantic level, and we tapped into the evolution of the enabling technologies that had progressively become available to test their technological feasibility. This effort allowed us to identify a more general conceptual framework that is independent of any specific application domain: this framework is generative as it defines the main constituents for the construction of more specific architectures that have to be instantiated in each domain. This framework encompasses also the characterization of the roles that the people involved in the construction activities are called to play.

3   The Conceptual Framework: The Logic of Bricolage

The leading idea in the conception of the conceptual framework that informs our proposal is the following one: in order to fully achieve the objectives of the EUD agenda we believe that it is necessary to rethink how end-user applications are conceived (Procter & Robin, 1996). Thus, the starting point is to face the problem of the relationship between end users and IT designers. As widely discussed in (Cabitza & Simone, 2015), the culture and practice of the IT designers are fundamentally based on the notion of *model*: indeed, the construction of an application is conceived as the construction of computational models at different levels of abstraction. We see in this general, widespread, and almost undisputed attitude one of the main reasons of the failure of these applications, as they are often neither useful nor usable by their target users. This occurs for two main reasons. First, these models are conceived by the IT designers: they interpret the users' needs (irrespective of how these have been collected) and transform them into functionalities of the target application. In so doing, the models incorporated in the application are almost unfamiliar to the end users and distant from their work practices; in other words the models carry "invisible programming values" (Moor, 1985). This approach affects also some of the approaches developed in the EUD ambit, as aptly reported in (Eriksson, Lindeberg, & Dittrich, 2003) where "leaving variability management to the end users" is based on their accessibility to a component architecture that is strongly integrated in the chosen programming environment. Second, and more importantly, end users do not organize their work practices in terms of conceptual models: they usually build what is instrumental to fulfil their needs by conceiving of ad-hoc information structures, often represented in traditional spreadsheets, which soon become effective *shadow tools* (Cabitza & Simone, 2014; Handel & Poltrock, 2011) working "in the shade" of official information systems; and perform actions that manipulate those information structures in what is mundanely called a *bricolage* endeavour. In (Cabitza & Simone, 2015) we reconstructed how the notion of bricolage, which has been recently reused by Rob Procter et al. (2013) in the domain of assisted living technologies, has been promoted since the early 90s by scholars belonging to the IS area and how this unorthodox position influenced our research approach. For this reason we denote our conceptual framework with the term of *Logic Of Bricolage* (LOB), also to blur the distinction between the classes of applications proposed by Richter and Riemer (2013).

According to this logic, the goal should not be to provide end users with a framework that allows them to perform increasingly complex actions on the products built with the logic of the IT designers, possibly by means of a user-friendly user interface. Rather, the goal is to provide end users with a framework that takes into account all the facets of malleability discussed in the previous section in the construction of their tools. The LOB agenda takes then a challenging and radical perspective in its goals as it proposes an approach that can be taken in the design of applications in any specific domain; but it is incremental and iterative in the way these goals are pursued as its validity has to be proven for each domain.

4   The Conceptual Architecture

The following *basic principles* are (presently) at the basis of the LOB we propose:

- To clearly separate the features that are or are not at the semantic level of work practices and then under end-user control: in other words, to distinguish between the *platform* targeted to the end users and the underlying *technological infrastructure*.
- To guarantee an adequate level of technical *opennability* and *openness* to avoid any undue barrier to changes in the usage of the platform (design-in-use).
- To consider components that are built by IT designers only when their development is outside of the competence that an end user can reasonably acquire, and to start this development from the identification of features that are at the *semantic level of end-user practices*.
- For each application domain, to identify the *functionalities* peculiar to that domain and the *composition patterns* that can make sense to the end users, possibly by trying to factorize the ones that are common to several domains.
- To define in a clear and flexible way the *roles* of the people involved in the EUD activities and their *domain of responsibility*. We identified four main roles: on the non-technical side, the *bricoleur* end user and the *maieuta* designer; and on the technical side, the *meta-designer* and the *IT professional*. The maieuta- and meta-designers play the role of mediators between the end users and the IT professionals to fulfil domain requirements and solve technical problems, respectively.

Fig. 1 summarizes the above principles in a conceptual tiered architecture where also the roles and the tasks they are mainly involved in are reported for each identified level.

In this architecture, openness and opennability are afforded to the end users by the Editors, which define, extend and combine the (basic) building blocks. In order to keep this layer as general as possible we have proposed a *grammar* (its detailed

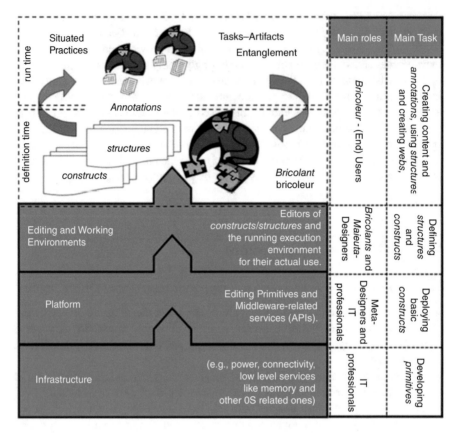

Fig. 1 The conceptual architecture

definition can be found in Cabitza & Simone, 2015) that contains productions to define, through dedicated *constructs*:

- The layout of the application *interface*;
- The *structure* of the *objects* characterizing the application domain;
- The *if-then rules* to make those objects active (Dourish et al., 2000) thorough two kinds of operators: *functional operators* characterizing the application domain (e.g., the function to compute the fluid balance of a patient or to manipulate a 3D object); and *actional operators* that reflect the work practices affecting the objects (e.g., the commands to save, move, combine, delete, augment, link, mailto).
- The *annotations* that users can link to any kind of element mentioned in the grammar: they are constituted by a *target* and a *multimedia content*.

The grammar explicitly mentions the *annotations* as a fundamental affordance offered by the platform: as already mentioned in (Lieberman et al., 2006; Chap. 1) annotations offer a way to support communication and the sharing of contextual information among the roles involved in the EUD activities and more generally involved in any cooperative activities (Cabitza, Simone, & Locatelli, 2012). In addition, annotations and if-then rules allow for the expression of another feature that is fundamental to support cooperative actors, namely various kinds of *awareness* (Schmidt, 2002): notifications to collaborators as well as the change of affordances of the objects (e.g., the usage of cues to bring the attention to relevant pieces of information).

The conceptual architecture and the related grammar support the incremental construction of a platform that does not build undue barriers between application domains, but yet still recognizes their peculiarities; and that does not raise barriers between actors with different competence and attitudes, but rather recognizes that these latter ones have to be duly taken into account, respected and possibly promoted. In fact, the platform offers the following advantages:

- To facilitate the appropriation of the technology through the presence of different levels of abstraction at which end users can construct, modify and use the combination of the basic building blocks; moreover, the attention to the appropriate semantic level creates the conditions for an easier and more effective way to document and share the blocks as well as the already constructed combinations. In other words, these latter "speak" the local jargon of the end-user community and constitute a ground (a "repertoire" as said by Wenger, 1998) where this community can record and share individual outcomes and experiences. This is an answer to the claim mentioned in (Lieberman et al., 2006; Chap. 1) that components have to be meaningful to the users.
- To make the space of action of all of the roles involved clear and, in so doing, to reduce the odds for subordinate positions by end users in the EUD "game."
- To give end users a way to show to the top management and the IT designers that an alternative way to build applications is feasible and affordable.

The LOB can be interpreted as a contribution to the effort to define paradigms for EUD that go beyond specific solutions and support the identification of conceptual frameworks guiding the construction of technologies supporting EUD. The LOB shares many of the tenets underlying the meta-design paradigm whose evolution is described in the chapter by Fischer, Fogli, and Piccinno (2017). As discussed in (Cabitza & Simone, 2015) the main difference regards a more radical view of the role of the professional designers in EUD and an explicit emphasis on malleability at the semantic level of work practices as a leading requirement shaping the construction of technological frameworks that make a correct relationship between end-users and professional designers possible.

The same requirement allows us to reformulate the EUD pyramid proposed by Ludwig, Dax, Pipek, and Wulf (2017) (see Fig. 2). In our view, end users should not be requested to learn and use any General Purpose Language (whatever it can be) for the design-in-use of their applications. Instead, they should rather be put in the condition to leverage the language they are able to use to both sustain and innovate these applications (see Dittrich et al., 2017) since this language is at the semantic level of their work practices. In this view, the EUD "staircase" can be

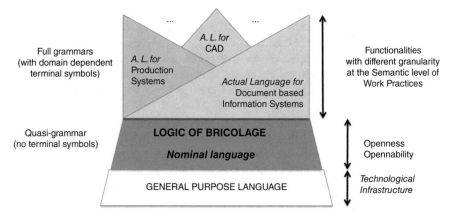

Fig. 2 The pyramid of malleability (*A.L. means Actual Language*)

climbed by the end users at their own speed by leveraging different levels of complexity (and granularity) of the technology that they develop. To achieve this goal, the formalization of that language in a generative grammar is performed in two steps: a domain independent definition of the productions that guarantee the openness and opennability of the prospective application, that is a quasi-grammar governing their construction through suitable categories (the non terminal symbols of the grammar): at this stage the grammar is capable to generate only a *nominal language*,[1] in that it only defines a space of possibility. And a domain and user-dependent definition of the full language through the identification of the necessary atomic operators and their composition laws (the terminal symbols of the grammar): at this stage the grammar is able to generate the *actual language* that the end users can use to construct functionalities at any level of granularity, according to their needs and work practices. In this view, there are as many actual languages related to the same nominal one as there are specific application domains and local practices.

Then, the LOB can be viewed as a contribution to make the notion of work infrastructure operational. This concept has been introduced to take into account the broader context in which technology is constructed and to relate to the EUD tenets (Pipek & Wulf, 2009). The LOB shares the idea that the work infrastructure is the outcome of an infrastructuring effort that involves the maintenance and innovation of the LOB architecture and of the specific applications built on top of it. Moreover, the clear separation of the technical infrastructure from the end-user

---

[1]We borrow the terms *nominal* and *actual* (used later on in the chapter) from the definition of the notation proposed in (Schmidt & Simone, 1996) to express the mentioned Coordination Mechanisms: for instance, a *task* is at the nominal level since it defines the space of possibility where different *actions* at the actual level can be done to accomplish it. The term *quasi-grammar* used in Fig. 2 is inspired by the field of urban design (Aydin & Schnabel, 2013).

realm allows for an alternative view of the standardization problem, which is one of the main issues concerning infrastructures.

At the technical infrastructure level, standardization (and all of the related issues like interoperability and compatibility) can be managed according to the ICT methods that are out of the scope of EUD: the LOB identifies a clear space of responsibility, the meta-designer and IT professional roles, for the management of the technical impact of the changes of the technical infrastructure on the domain-dependent level. At this latter level, standardization is problematic as it would imply a sort of standardization of work practices: this attempt has been proved unfeasible and harmful in a number of studies (especially in the CSCW ambit). The LOB promotes the local and collaborative development of work practices and their ICT support as a unique way to make them appropriated by the end users. The LOB also envisages a bottom-up approach to deal with the need of standardization concerning the objects that flow across local settings. In (Cabitza & Simone, 2015) we mentioned the idea of *minimal data set* to contain those basic objects whose structure and semantics have to be negotiated, and to let more articulated constructs be (automatically) reconstructed in each local setting according to its logic, in the line of the approach proposed in (Parsons & Wand, 2000). In other words, at this level standardization results from a negotiation process that defines contracts among the involved parties at any level of the organizational dimension (Simone, 2016): instead of being an imposition from above, standardization is a bottom-up collaborative process of continuous learning.

Finally, the LOB can be interpreted also as a contribution to make approaches to practice-based computing (Schmidt & Bansler, 2016; Wulf et al., 2015) operational, by stressing the need to help users in identifying and expressing the mechanisms supporting their work practices (the maieuta designer role) through the domain-dependent language. To this aim, the LOB architecture offers (at least) a technological sandbox, where prototypes and technical probes can be tested and validated.

5   Where the Logic of Bricolage Came From

The LOB distilled the above set of guiding principles for the construction of a malleable technology from the findings of a series of field studies. The settings that we had the chance to analyse were characterized by an intensive usage of (paper-based) documents that played three main roles: on the one hand, as also recognized by Berg (1999), the accumulation of information through the artifacts' progressive inscriptions; and the coordination of collaborative activities through the affordances, inscriptions, marks and signs hosted by the artifacts to promote the mutual awareness of the actors involved. In addition to these two latter roles, also the exchange of contextual information to support collaborative decision making and the continuous on-the-go learning of the involved actors. In order to emphasize and characterize this latter role in a EUD perspective, we proposed the term *knowledge artifact* (Cabitza, Colombo, & Simone, 2013). Thus, the artifacts that we observed in our field studies showed that the three above roles cannot be separated or handled in isolation (Cabitza & Simone, 2012a). In what follows, we will refer to these three indivisible roles with the phrase "work artifacts." Moreover, all these studies showed that users were ingeniously creative in trying alternative paper-based solutions that could better meet their needs of informality, flexibility and dynamicity. This led us to propose them a critical discussion and a trial in a controlled environment of some ad-hoc mock-ups and prototypes that had been inspired by their own ideas. These partial solutions paved the road for the development of the platform supporting EUD activities in the application domains where work artifacts are recognized to play a relevant role: this platform, called AdHoc, will be illustrated in some detail in the next section.

In what follows of this section, we will report on the main findings of the field studies in the healthcare domain that helped us to characterize the notion of malleability and to conceive the LOB: healthcare is an ideal domain encompassing many of the situations that can be encountered in other domains.

5.1   The Requirements and Their Technical Probes

The field studies mainly involved doctors and nurses in hospital settings and identified the requirements illustrated here below.

5.1.1   About the Information Structure

The main kind of work documents in use in a clinical setting are related to the Patient Record (PR), and it is well known how the introduction of its digitized counterpart, the Electronic Patient Record (EPR), is far from being a trivial task (Fitzpatrick & Ellingsen, 2013). For this reason the artifacts that we analysed were mainly still based on paper. As in many other ethnographic observations (e.g., Berg & Toussaint, 2003; Harper, O'Hara, Sellen, & Duthie, 1997; Schmidt, 2008), also our studies confirmed the effectiveness of this support, which is mainly based on its *flexibility* and *openness* (Fitzpatrick, 2004). The kind and the layout of the fields constituting the template of a work artifact can be easily changed, extended, printed out and put to work in a very short time. The same flexibility and openness is not achieved in EPRs (Fitzpatrick & Ellingsen, 2013); for instance doctors and nurses can only have access to templates displaying the fields that that have been *a priori* identified as the most relevant ones for each single caring phase, so as to impose layouts that are optimized according to technical visualization criteria only (Swinglehurst, Greenhalgh, & Roberts, 2012). However, it is well known that a broader context and the spatial layout of the information conveys additional meaning about and across the various inscriptions (Harrison & Dourish, 1996). Moreover, every minimal change requires a long time as the IT designers and developers of the IT vendor and provider have to be involved.

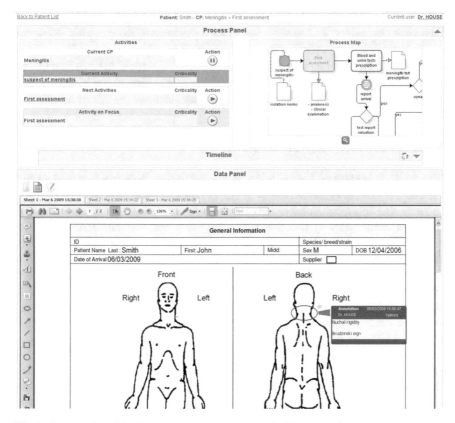

Fig. 3 A screenshot of the Pro-Doc prototype to support healthcare practices

Since the caring process often occurs in critical situations (e.g., for the kind of intervention, the heavy workload or the unexpected interruptions) often *provisional inscriptions* are used to be checked and confirmed afterwards.

It is often the case that the EPR incorporates in a visible position (typically on the front-page of the folder) a particular work artifact that contains the visual description of a caring *process*, i.e., a Clinical Pathway, especially when the intended trajectory is considered to be complex and risky, or conversely when it is rarely performed (Cabitza & Simone, 2008). This usually *graphic information* should be preserved and reproduced in a prospective EPR since professionals are used to interpret Clinical Pathways as a "plan for situated action" (Suchman, 1987). This point is critical in relation to EPR construction (as any other workflow digitalization) but it is out of the scope of this chapter: we refer to (Cabitza & Simone, 2013) for a discussion on malleability in relation to work processes.

Since the very beginning, the prototypes that we proposed to the health professionals fulfilled the above requirements at different degrees (see for example Fig. 3 taken from (Cabitza, Simone, & Zorzato, 2009)), as they reflect and support the practices established around paper-based work artifacts. Nowadays there are applications/platforms that increasingly allow for the construction of form templates that can be instantiated and filled in; moreover, the adoption of mobile devices, such as smart phones and tablets, offers interfaces that can be closer to the look-and-feel of the paper-based work artifacts. However these solutions still show a limited openness, they are not opennable and in general can be poorly integrated with more collaboration-oriented functionalities.

5.1.2 Augmenting the Work Artifacts

The work practices that we analysed in the hospital settings made it evident that the clinical work is characterized by several kinds of *redundancy*. It is not difficult to recognize this phenomenon also in other domains, such as office work. We observed *redundancy of function* when the same professionals possess competences that overlap those of other colleagues in a team to deal with the (sudden) unavailability of a human resource; *redundancy of effort* when the same action is executed more than once, typically for the sake of safety and cross-check; and *redundancy of data* when the same information appears, possibly slightly elaborated, in different points of the same work artifacts or in different work artifacts. All these kinds of redundancy should be taken into consideration in the construction of an EPR (as of any other work artifact). Let us start from the redundancy of data whose articulation in the four possible cases is summarized in Table 1. A detailed exemplification of the four cases can be found in (Cabitza, Sarini, Simone, & Telaro, 2005). For this paper it is useful to distinguish if the data are exactly the same or closely related, and if they belong or not to the same work artifact: in fact the four cases have obvious implications on the affordances that have to be offered to the end users and on the way they have to be dealt within the platform.

Redundancy of function and of effort have an impact on the flexibility by which the platform allows the various actors to play different roles (as characterized by their competences), to manage the distributed workflow of their actions to encompass repeated and repetitive actions, and to deal with the consequences of possible discrepancies in their effects and outcomes.

The practices unfolding around the work artifacts showed another kind of redundancy that would be helpful to support, as suggested also by other studies (Bringay, Barry, & Charlet, 2006; Whittaker, 2003). The work practices augment the artifacts themselves in different ways that can be grouped under two main categories: *annotations* and *conventions*. Annotations are inscriptions added to the artifacts that

Table 1 The four cases of redundancy of data

	Same Data	Correlated Data
Same artifact	Redundancy by *replicated* data	Redundancy by *derived* data
Different Artifacts	Redundancy by *duplicated* data	Redundancy by *supplementary* data

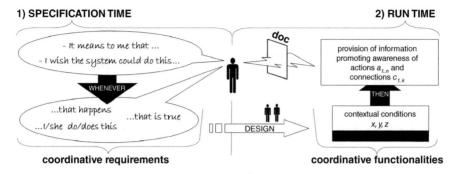

Fig. 4 The translation rules expressed in a pseudo-natural language

contribute to enrich their interpretation by the collaborating actors: for example, an exclamation mark next to a field in a document can be used to bring the attention of readers to an anomalous value. On the other hand, conventions are sort of rules that are agreed upon in a more or less explicit way by the members of a work team or organization, and that these latter apply (or expect that the others comply with) if some specific conditions have been met. For instance, the combination of specific patient's conditions have to be notified to the appropriate doctor specialist; a capital U jotted down next to an exam entry means that this should be accomplished quickly as it is urgent (Cabitza & Simone, 2007). These conventions, differently from formal rules, are not aimed at the construction of any sort/approximation of expert systems: the professionals we met in our field studies emphasized that the useful rules should only cover the relevant knowledge put to work at each step of a caring processes and could also be sometimes contradictory as they have in any case to be interpreted by the professionals involved in these processes. Thus, the role of annotations and conventions is to facilitate the collaborative interpretation of relevant events and conditions, not to prescribe behaviours.

Annotations are nowadays a function that is usually offered by document management systems, although still in a basic manner. Conversely, the possibility to make tacit conventions explicit, if users deem it necessary, to improve coordination and, as in the case of healthcare, patient safety are usually not supported. We constructed some prototypes to check the feasibility and acceptability of these affordances: for example, the Lifebook prototype (Cabitza & Simone, 2012b) offers an interface that mimics the classical sheet and the possibility to have a rich set of textual annotations; in (Cabitza & Simone, 2009) we experimented with a group of clinicians a mock-up interface to define rules in a pseudo-natural language that could be automatically translated into a machine-readable format (see Fig. 4).

5.1.3 Linking the Work Artifacts to Their Context

The redundancy of pieces of information contained in a work artifact, especially across different artifacts, points to the need to consider what we called Web of

Documental Artifacts (WOAD) (Cabitza & Simone, 2010). For this phrase, we took inspiration from the phrase "Web of Artifacts" proposed in (Bardram & Bossen, 2005), but aimed to make this notion even stronger by supporting different kinds of *relations between work artifacts*: these relations are obviously depending on the setting where the work artifacts are in use.

In the case of the healthcare settings that we have investigated, the professionals mentioned a set of relations that they would like to have embedded into a digital support such as an EPR. For instance, in (Cabitza & Simone, 2008) we observed that the subtle differences between the relationships proposed in the Clinical Document Architecture (CDA) standard were not easily accepted by a group of clinicians that would have had the possibility to define more locally meaningful relations such as: (1) "the source *because of* the target," used by clinicians to convey a strict causal relationship between two items; (2) "the source *after* the target," used by the clinicians not only in strictly temporal sense, but also to hint at a very weak or just hypothesized causal relationship between two entries; and (3) "the source *for* the target," used by clinicians to express either a justification, provide evidence supporting a decision or to make explicit an intention (Cabitza & Simone, 2008). The clinicians emphasized that the specification of these relations has to be open-ended and under their control. Moreover, in combination with the above requirement to make work artifacts active, proper rules could associate a specific behaviour with each relation, e.g., to facilitate double-checking and the propagation of information that promotes collaboration awareness.

In the healthcare domain, we observed work artifacts that flank institutional and official information systems: we already introduced the term *shadow tools* to refer to this phenomenon. Indeed, paper-based work artifacts were sometimes locally defined according to the local work practices irrespective of any kind of Hospital Information System in use or any work artifacts that were more official and imposed by the management for the sake of the standardization of the caring processes. Shadow tools impose a *double work* as the information they are built to contain has to be transferred, often only partially, to the official Information Systems. Then, a basic requirement of any support of the EUD activities around user-defined work artifacts is to have an easy and solid interface with these Information Systems. In (Cabitza & Simone, 2012c) we discussed a conceptual architecture that aims to reconcile the coordinative role of artifacts and the archival roles of the IS through the design of a meta-content layer that encompasses an awareness (promoting) manager (AM in Fig. 5).

The findings from our investigations in the healthcare and other application domains (examples of this kind can be found in (Cabitza & Simone, 2014, 2015) and of parallel studies by other authors on various kinds of artifacts (e.g., Schmidt & Wagner, 2004; Xiao, 2005) allowed us to conceive of the LOB conceptual framework described in the previous section. As a first step to check the feasibility of the translation of the framework into a concrete technology we built a platform supporting the EUD of work artifacts, and more specifically document-based artifacts.

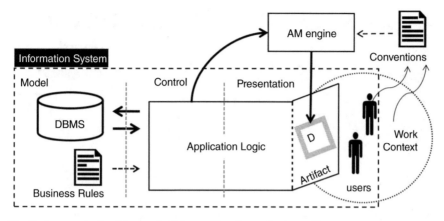

Fig. 5 A conceptual architecture bridging an IS and coordinative artifacts

6   The AdHoc Platform

The AdHoc platform allows end users to create their own work artifacts templates, and create their computationally-augmented work artifacts out of these templates. According to the LOB tenets AdHoc mirrors how users create working documents and forms from (electronic) templates existing in their everyday work practices. The name of the platform itself reflects this main requirement: end users must be able to create work artifacts *ad hoc*, that is for a specific task, also through re-use and adaptation of other documents (acting as templates) created in the same or other end-user communities. In this section we describe how the main functionalities that AdHoc offers to its users to construct malleable applications based on work artifacts reflect the LOB architecture: more details can be found in (Cabitza & Mattozzi, 2017).

In AdHoc end users can define the structure of their work artifact by creating a corresponding template in a bottom-up manner. To this aim, they have to instantiate the *layout* and *objects structure* of the general grammar that is associated with the Logic of Bricolage. We use the phrase bottom-up to hint at the fact that this process of construction is not based on any abstract data model, but rather it is performed by considering the work artifact interface as a sort of blank canvas on which end users can place writings, headings and data fields and controls, according to specific and local needs. Moreover, end users can create their own *control structures*, that is application behaviours, by which to have the platform process the document's content, change its appearance or activate other actions for sake of communication, coordination, awareness promotion and knowledge exchange. In order to both build the structural templates and attach to these latter ones the behaviours that make them active, the end users can find within the AdHoc platform the two visual editors characterizing the LOB architecture: these editors present and allow for the direct manipulation of the building blocks that closely mirror the constructs of the instantiated grammar.

Fig. 6 A screenshot from the main interface of the datom editor of the AdHoc platform

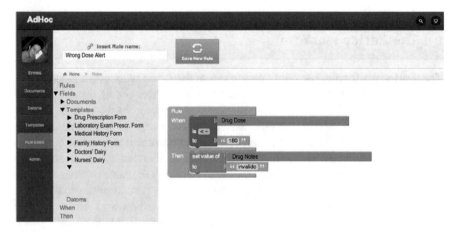

Fig. 7 A screenshot from the main interface of the rule editor of the AdHoc platform

A first visual editor (see Fig. 6) allows end users to define basic data structures, or what we call *datoms* (Cabitza & Simone, 2015) and then include them recursively in greater and more complex (layout) structures (e.g., records, folders, repositories). These datoms will contain the data that end users will consider meaningful to bind strictly together, for any reason, like the name of a drug and its prescribed dose of administration, or the name and family name of a patient.

Templates encompass sets of these datoms; documents are created by activating the corresponding template in any given context. In addition, the same datom can be re-used in different templates, thus creating different kinds of associative relations between active documents that spread the data inscribed in a document into other related documents (see (Cabitza & Mattozzi, 2017) for further details).

The second visual editor allows end users to develop the set of *if-then rules* that make documents active (see Fig. 7), and associate them with a template. In so

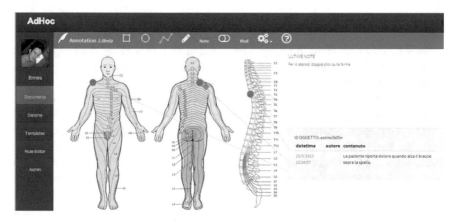

Fig. 8 A screenshot from the AdHoc interface that visualizes an annotated form

doing, any document created from the same template is endowed with the rules associated with their original template. The *then* part of the rules uses and combines the functional and actional operators of the full grammar that the users identified, possibly with the help of maieuta- and meta-designers. Combinations of operators can be named and recorded; and can be accessed and unpacked for modification, according to the opennability feature of malleability.

Finally, AdHoc integrates a tool that allows users to create n-ary associative relations between document elements, documents and annotations themselves. In Fig. 8 we show an AdHoc document, defined from a template containing an anatomic diagram. Through the annotation function the user has augmented the diagram with three markings, namely three small circles and put them in three different places of the image to indicate where the patient reported pain. Then she selected these three elements and created a textual annotation linked to these elements (target of the annotation; just anything that can be selected can become an association target, so also any portions of text. In this case, the elements are graphical markings). The annotation, depicted on the right, contains a short textual comment. Graphically AdHoc makes the anchoring between the comment and the target explicit (the thin blue lines), so that the annotation acts as a ternary relation, relating three elements of the documents together.

Then AdHoc collects in a single platform the main functionalities that have been separately discussed and validated with the users in the collection of probes presented in the previous section.

7   Conclusions and Future Work

The research trajectory described in this chapter has led to the definition of a conceptual framework for EUD infrastructures that is characterized by two main tenets. First, the infrastructure should give to the end users the possibility to construct malleable applications that they can adapt to their changing needs and contexts at any level of detail: this means that end users can construct their applications and unpack them (bricolage) by manipulating (basic) building blocks that at any level of detail make sense according to their work practices. Second, this recursive manipulation is the means by which to balance the different attitudes of the end users with the role of the professional designers involved in the construction of the applications, and by which to circumscribe the more technical intervention to the implementation of what the end users are not able to do in autonomy (i.e., the basic building blocks and constructs to combine them). The conceptual framework has been instantiated in a specific platform (AdHoc) that can be viewed as a proof-of-concept for a practice-based and open toolkit supporting the bricolage of malleable document-based applications.

The research path described above has produced some stable results but is not over. On the one hand, the AdHoc platform has to be validated in real settings to increase the quality of the user experience with its interface, including the two visual editors presented above. On a more conceptual level, the Logic of Bricolage has to be validated in application domains that are characterized by objects of different kinds: in other words, through autonomous investigations and from the literature we aim to identify the basic building blocks and the composition constructs that these potential domains would require and then to validate the expressive power of the proposed grammar.

Another relevant issue that has to be further investigated relates to what in the literature has been called *collaborative tailoring*, that is the activities that in real-work settings end users perform to deal with their (technological) problems within the communities of practice they belong to. Pipek and Kahler (2006) articulated this issue by offering a taxonomy that is based on scenarios of increasing complexity in relation to "ideas and approaches according to what actually motivates users to collaborate regarding the configuration of software tools." The approach presented in this chapter falls under the "shared tool" scenario and shares some tenets with the meta-design approach (as discussed in the previous sections): as Pipek and Kahler (2006) emphasize, there are several (technological) means that can support collaborative tailoring in this scenario such as situated communication, shared representations, models of the decisions processes and so on. A modular architecture affording several of these means is proposed in (Stevens, Pipek, & Wulf, 2010). Pipek and Kahler (2006) point also to the risk to propose, if not impose, means that would require an additional learning effort to the end-users. Without denying the value of these means, and in the aim to reduce this risk, it would be interesting to verify if collaborative tailoring could be supported by a dedicated platform based on the LOB itself: here again, the observation of the real practices is a necessary source of inspiration to identify the suitable objects and constructs, and then to instantiate the grammar and build a dedicated platform accordingly. A very preliminary attempt to deal with this aspect of EUD was illustrated in (Bandini & Simone, 2006): by taking inspiration from the practices governing the maintenance of a repertoire of software components for the sake of reuse that we observed in a IT system integration company (Cabitza et al., 2013), the idea was to augment the component-based EUD technology proposed in (Won et al., 2006) with functionalities supporting a similar behaviour. The interesting aspect of this attempt was that the observed practices were not related to any software engineering standard; instead, the professionals identified a classification of the stored components and of the relationships among them that reflected their way to minimize the effort to keep the information about the experimented software components up-to-date, and to guarantee their effective reuse. This experience shows that malleability, and then EUD, matters not only for naïve users. Rather, it raises interesting challenges for any setting, if practices are seriously taken into account as the conceptual framework proposed in this chapter aims to do.

References

Aydin, S., & Schnabel, M. A. (2013). Coding shape grammars: hints for generating a parametric design tool for large-scale urban renewal projects. In M. A. Schnabel (ed.), *Proceedings of the 47th International Architectural Science Association Conference* (pp. 177–186). Australia: The Architectural Science Association (ANZAScA).

Bandini, S., & Simone, C. (2006). EUD as integration of components off-the-shelf: the role of software professionals knowledge artifacts. End-user development: the software shaping workshop approach. In H. Lieberman, F. Paternò, V. Wulf (Eds.). *End user development* (pp. 347–369). Dordrecht, The Netherlands: Kluwer Academic Publishers.

Bardram, J. E., & Bossen, C. (2005). A web of coordinative artifacts: collaborative work at a hospital ward. In G. Mark & M. Ackerman (eds), *Proceedings of the 2005 international ACM SIGGROUP Conference on Supporting Group Work* (pp. 168–176). New York USA: ACM.

Berg, M. (1999). Accumulating and coordinating: occasions for information technologies in medical work. *Computer Supported Cooperative Work, 8*(4), 373–401.

Berg, M., & Toussaint, P. (2003). The mantra of modeling and the forgotten powers of paper: a sociotechnical view on the development of process-oriented ICT in health care. *International Journal of Medical Informatics, 69*(2), 223–234.

Borchorst, N.G., Bødker, S., Zander, P.O. (2009). The boundaries of participatory citizenship. In *ECSCW 2009, - Proceedings of the 11th European conference on computer supported cooperative work* (pp. 1–20). London: Springer.

Bratteteig, T., & Wagner, I. (2014). *Disentangling participation: Power and decision-making in participatory design.* Switzerland: Springer International Publishing.

Bringay, S., Barry, C., Charlet, J. (2006). Annotations: a functionality to support cooperation, coordination and awareness in the electronic medical record. *Frontiers in Artificial Intelligence and Applications, 137,* 39.

Buchanan, R. (1992). Wicked problems in design thinking. *Design Issues, 8*(2), 5–21.

Cabitza, F., Colombo, G., Simone, C. (2013). Leveraging underspecification in knowledge artifacts to foster collaborative activities in professional communities. *International Journal of Human-Computer Studies, 71*(1), 24–45.

Cabitza, F., Fogli, D., Piccinno, A. (2014). "Each to his own": distinguishing activities, roles and artifacts in EUD practices. In L. Caporarello, B. Di Martino, M. Martinez eds., *Smart organizations and smart artifacts - fostering interaction between people, technologies and processes* (pp. 193–205). Berlin: Springer.

Cabitza, F., & Mattozzi, A. (2017). The semiotics of configurations for the immanent design of interactive computational systems. *Journal of Visual Languages and Computing.* In press. doi:10.1016/j.jvlc.2017.01.003.

Cabitza, F., Sarini, M., Simone, C., Telaro, M. (2005). When once is not enough: the role of redundancy in a hospital ward setting. In *Proceedings of the 2005 International ACM Conference on Supporting Group Work* (pp. 158–167). New York USA: ACM.

Cabitza, F., & Simone, C. (2007). "… and do it the usual way": fostering awareness of work conventions in document-mediated collaboration. In: L. J. Bannon, I. Wagner, C. Gutwin, R. H. R. Harper & K. Schmidt (eds), *ECSCW 2007 - Proceedings of the 10th European Computer Supported Cooperative Work 2007* (pp. 119–138). London: Springer.

Cabitza, F., & Simone, C. (2008, June 17–19). Supporting practices of positive redundancy for seamless care. In *CBMS'08: proceedings of the 21th IEEE international symposium on computer-based medical systems* (pp. 470–475). Jyväskylä, Finland.

Cabitza, F., & Simone, C. (2010). WOAD: a framework to enable the end-user development of coordination-oriented functionalities. *Journal of Organizational and End User Computing (JOEUC)*, 22(2), 1–20.

Cabitza, F., & Simone, C. (2012a). Affording mechanisms: an integrated view of coordination and knowledge management. *Computer Supported Cooperative Work (CSCW)*, 21(2–3), 227–260.

Cabitza, F., & Simone, C. (2012b). Tell me another story, granpa! Requirements for sharing lived lives online. *I-Com, Zeitschrift für interaktive und kooperative Medien*, 11(3), 14–18.

Cabitza, F., & Simone, C. (2012c). "Whatever works": making sense of information quality on information system artifacts. In G. Viscusi, G. M. Campagnolo & Y. Curzi (Eds.), *Phenomenology, organizational politics, and IT design: the social study of information systems* (pp. 1–321). Hershey USA: IGI Global.

Cabitza, F., & Simone, C. (2013). Computational coordination mechanisms: a tale of a struggle for flexibility. *Computer Supported Cooperative Work (CSCW)*, 22(4–6), 475–529.

Cabitza, F., & Simone, C. (2014). "Through the glassy box": supporting appropriation in user communities. In *COOP 2014-proceedings of the 11th international conference on the design of cooperative systems, Nice (France)* (pp. 173–187). Springer International Publishing.

Cabitza, F., & Simone, C. (2015). Building socially embedded technologies: implications about design. In *Designing socially embedded technologies in the real-world* (pp. 217–270). London: Springer.

Cabitza, F., Simone, C., Locatelli, M. P. (2012). Supporting artifact-mediated discourses through a recursive annotation tool. In: C. Inpken & T. Gross (Eds), *Proceedings of the 17th ACM International Conference on Supporting Group Work* (pp. 253–262). New York USA: ACM.

Cabitza, F., Simone, C., Storni, C. (2016). Seams and sutures in IT artifacts: sewing up the socio and the technical together. *International Journal of Systems and Society (IJSS)*, 3(1), 18–31.

Cabitza, F., Simone, C., Zorzato, G. (2009). PRODOC: an Electronic Patient Record to Foster Process-Oriented Practices. In I. Wagner, H. Tellioglu, E. Balka, C. Simone & L. Ciolfi (Eds.), *ECSCW09: Proceedings of the 11th European Conference on Computer Supported Cooperative Work. 2009* (pp. 85–104). London: Springer.

Carroll, J. M., Kellogg, W. A., Rosson, M. B. (1991). The task-artifact cycle. In J. M. Carroll (ed). *Designing Interaction: Psychology at the Human-Computer Interface* (pp. 74–102). New York, NY: Cambridge University Press.

Costabile, M. F., Fogli, D., Mussio, P., Piccinno, A. (2006). End-user development: the software shaping workshop approach. In H. Lieberman, F. Paternò, V. Wulf (Eds.). *End user development* (pp. 183–205). Dordrecht: Kluwer Academic Publishers.

Dittrich, Y., Bolmsten, J., & Eriksson, J. (2017). End user development and infrastructuring — sustaining organizational innovation capabilities. In F. Paternò & V. Wulf (Eds.). *New perspectives in end-user development* (pp. 165–206). Cham: Springer.

Dourish, P., Edwards, W. K., LaMarca, A., Lamping, J., Petersen, K., Salisbury, M., et al. (2000). Extending document management systems with user-specific active properties. *ACM Transactions on Information Systems (TOIS)*, 18(2), 140–170.

Eriksson, J., Lindeberg, O., Dittrich, Y. (2003). *Leaving variability management to the end user; a comparison between different tailoring approaches*. Blekinge Institute of Technology Research Report 2003:10.

Fitzpatrick, G. (2004). Integrated care and the working record. *Health Informatics Journal*, *10*(4), 291–302.

Fitzpatrick, G., & Ellingsen, G. (2013). A review of 25 years of CSCW research in healthcare: contributions, challenges and future agendas. *Computer Supported Cooperative Work (CSCW)*, *22*(4–6), 609–665.

Fischer, G., Fogli, D., & Piccinno, A. (2017). Revisiting and broadening the meta-design framework for end-user development. In F. Paternò & V. Wulf (Eds.). *New perspectives in end-user development* (pp. 61–98). Cham: Springer.

Fischer, G., & Giaccardi, E. (2006). Meta-design: a framework for the future of end user development. In H. Lieberman, F. Paternò, V. Wulf (Eds.). *End user development* (pp. 427–457). Dordrecht: Kluwer Academic Publishers.

Fogli, D., Colosio, S., Sacco, M. (2010). Managing accessibility in local e-government websites through end-user development: a case study. *Universal Access in the Information Society*, *9*(1), 35–50.

Fogli, D., & Piccinno, A. (2013). Co-evolution of end-user developers and systems in multi-tiered proxy design problems. In Y. Dittrich, M. Burnett, A. Mørch, D. Redmiles (eds.). *End-user development* LNCS, vol. 7897, (pp. 153–168). Berlin: Springer. LNCS.

Gantt, M., & Nardi, B. A. (1992). Gardeners and gurus: patterns of cooperation among CAD users. In: P. Bauersfeld, J. Bennet & G. Lynch (eds), *Proceedings of the ACM Conference on Human Factors in Computing Systems (CHI)* (pp. 107–117). New York USA: ACM.

Hailpern, B., & Santhanam, P. (2002). Software debugging, testing, and verification. *IBM Systems Journal*, *41*(1), 4–12.

Handel, M. J., & Poltrock, S. (2011). Working around official applications: experiences from a large engineering project. In *Proceedings of the ACM 2011 Conference on Computer Supported Cooperative Work* (pp. 309–312). New York USA: ACM.

Harper, R. H., O'Hara, K. P., Sellen, A. J., Duthie, D. J. (1997). Toward the paperless hospital? *British Journal of Anaesthesia*, *78*(6), 762–767.

Harrison, S., & Dourish, P. (1996). Re-place-ing space: the roles of place and space in collaborative systems. In *Proceedings of the 1996 ACM Conference on Computer Supported Cooperative Work* (pp. 67–76). New York USA: ACM.

Hartswood, M. J., Procter, R. N., Rouchy, P., Rouncefield, M., Slack, R., Voss, A. (2003). Working IT out in medical practice: IT systems design and development as co-realisation. *Methods of Information in Medicine*, *42*(4), 392–397.

Hartswood, M., Procter, R., Slack, R., Voß, A., Büscher, M., Rouncefield, M., et al. (2008). Co-realization: toward a principled synthesis of ethnomethodology and participatory design. *Resources, co-evolution and artifacts* (pp. 59–94). London: Springer.

Henderson, A., & Kyng, M. (1992). There's no place like home: continuing design in use. In *Design at work* (pp. 219–240). L. Erlbaum Associates Inc.

Kensing, F., & Blomberg, J. (1998). Participatory design: issues and concerns. *Computer Supported Cooperative Work (CSCW)*, *7*(3–4), 167–185.

Ko, A. J., Abraham, R., Beckwith, L., Blackwell, A., Burnett, M., Erwig, M., et al. (2011). The state of the art in end-user software engineering. *ACM Computing Surveys*, *43*(3), Article 21 (April 2011), 44 pages.

Licklider, C. R. (1960). Man-computer symbiosis. *IRE Transactions on Human Factors in Electronic HFE*, *1*, 4–11.

Lieberman, H., Paternò, F., Klann, M., Wulf, V. (2006). *End-user development: an emerging paradigm* (pp. 1–8). Springer, The Netherlands.

Ludwig, T., Dax, J., Pipek, V., & Wulf, V. (2017). A practice-oriented paradigm of end-user development. In F. Paternò & V. Wulf (Eds.). *New perspectives in end-user development* (pp. 23–42). Cham: Springer.

MacLean, A., Carter, K., Lövstrand, L., Moran, T. (1990). User-tailorable systems: pressing the issues with buttons. In: J. Carrasco Chew & J. Whiteside (eds), *Proceedings of the SIGCHI conference on Human Factors in Computing Systems* (pp. 175–182). New York USA: ACM.

Moor, J. (1985). What is computer ethics? *Metaphilosophy*, *16*(4), 266–75.

Mørch, A. (1997). Three levels of end-user tailoring: customization, integration, and extension. M. King & L. Mathiassen (eds), *Computers and Design in Context* (pp. 51–76). Cambridge Massachusetts USA: MIT Press.

Navarro, L., Prinz, W., Rodden, T. (1992). Towards open CSCW systems. In *Proceedings of the third workshop on Future Trends of Distributed Computing Systems* (pp. 4–10). Los Alamitos California USA: IEEE Computer Society Press.

Parsons, J., & Wand, Y. (2000). Emancipating instances from the tyranny of classes in information modeling. *ACM Transactions on Database Systems (TODS)*, *25*(2), 228–268.

Pipek, V., & Kahler, H. (2006). Supporting collaborative tailoring. *End user development* (pp. 315–345). The Netherlands: Springer.

Pipek, V., & Wulf, V. (2009). Infrastructuring: toward an integrated perspective on the design and use of information technology. *Journal of the Association for Information Systems*, *10*(5), 447–473.

Potas, W. A. (1978). Interactive systems as if users really mattered. *Information Systems Methodology* (pp. 618–630). Berlin: Springer.

Procter, R., Greenhalgh, T., Wherton, J., Sugarhood, P., Rouncefield, M., Dewsbury, G. (2013). The ATHENE Project: the importance of bricolage in personalising assisted living technologies. *International Journal of Integrated Care (IJIC)*, *13*(7). doi:10.5334/ijic.1423.

Procter, R., & Robin, W. (1996). Beyond design: social learning and computer-supported cooperative work—some lessons from innovation studies. *Human Factors in Information Technology*, *12*, 445–463.

Randall, D. (1988). Guided tours and tabletops: tools for communicating in a hypertext environment. *ACM Transactions on Information Systems (TOIS)*, *6*(4), 398–414.

Richter, A., & Riemer, K. (2013). Malleable end-user software. *Business & Information Systems Engineering*, *5*(3), 195–197.

Schmidt, K. (2002). The problem with "awareness": introductory remarks on awareness in CSCW. *Computer Supported Cooperative Work*, *11*(3), 285–298.

Schmidt, K. (2008). *Cooperative work and coordinative practices*. London: Springer 3–27.

Schmidt, K., & Bansler, P. (2016). Computational artifacts: interactive and collaborative computing as an integral feature of work practice. In: De Angeli, A., Bannon, L., Marti, P., Bordin, S. (Eds.) *COOP 2016 Proceedings of the 12th International Conference on the Design of Cooperative Systems* (pp. 21–38). Springer International Publishing.

Schmidt, K., & Simone, C. (1996). Coordination mechanisms: towards a conceptual foundation of CSCW systems design. *Computer Supported Cooperative Work (CSCW)*, *5*(2–3), 155–200.

Schmidt, K., & Wagner, I. (2004). Ordering systems: coordinative practices and artifacts in architectural design and planning. *Computer Supported Cooperative Work (CSCW)*, *13*(5–6), 349–408.

Simone, C. (2016). Everything is permitted unless stated otherwise. Models and representations in socio-technical (re)design. In *Proceedings of the conference ITAIS 2016*. Verona, Italy. To appear in LNSOI, Springer.

Stevens, G., Pipek, V., Wulf, V. (2010). Appropriation infrastructure: mediating appropriation and production work. *Journal of Organizational and End User Computing (JOEUC)*, *22*(2), 58–81.

Stiemerling, O., Kahler, H., Wulf, V. (1997). How to make software softer—designing tailorable applications. In: S. Coles (Ed), *Proceedings of the 2nd Conference on Designing Interactive Systems: processes, practices, methods, and techniques* (pp. 365–376). New York USA: ACM.

Suchman, L. (1987). *Plans and situated actions: the problem of human-machine communication*. Cambridge: Cambridge University Press.

Suchman, L. (1994). Do categories have politics? *Computer Supported Cooperative Work (CSCW)*, *2*(3), 177–190.

Swinglehurst, D., Greenhalgh, T., Roberts, C. (2012). Computer templates in chronic disease management: ethnographic case study in general practice. *BMJ Open*, *2*(6), e001754.

Trier, M., & Richter, A. (2013). "I can simply..." - theorizing simplicity as a design principle and usage factor. In *Proceedings of ECIS 2013 Completed Research*. 72. http://aisel.aisnet.org/ecis2013_cr/72.

Voas, J., Charron, F., McGraw, G., Miller, K., Friedman, M. (1997). Predicting how badly" good" software can behave. *IEEE Software, 14*(4), 73.

Wenger, E. (1998). *Communities of practice: learning, meaning, and identity*. Cambridge, England: Cambridge University Press.

Whittaker, S. (2003). Things to talk about when talking about things. *Human–Computer Interaction, 18*(1–2), 149–170.

Winner, L. (1980). Do Artifacts Have Politics? *Daedalus, 109*(1), 121–136.

Won, M., Stiemerling, O., Wulf, V. (2006). Component-based approaches to tailorable systems. End-user development: the software shaping workshop approach. In H. Lieberman, F. Paternò, V. Wulf (Eds.). *End user development* (pp. 115–141). Dordrecht: Kluwer Academic Publishers.

Wulf, V., Müller, C., Pipek, V., Randall, D., Rohde, M., Stevens, G. (2015). Practice-based computing: empirically-grounded conceptualizations derived from design case studies. In V. Wulf, K. Schmidt, D. Randall (eds). *Designing socially embedded technologies in the real-world* (pp. 111–150). London: Springer.

Xiao, Y. (2005). Artifacts and collaborative work in healthcare: methodological, theoretical, and technological implications of the tangible. *Journal of Biomedical Informatics, 38*(1), 26–33.

End User Development and Infrastructuring – Sustaining Organizational Innovation Capabilities

Yvonne Dittrich, Johan Bolmsten and Jeanette Eriksson

Abstract Today, both businesses and public organizations need to be able to innovate and continuously develop their services and processes along with the underpinning IT infrastructure. We argue that End-User Development (EUD) becomes a necessary part of the innovation capability that underpins such service and process innovation. The book chapter presents a meta-analysis of two case studies. The analysis shows how the need for change in both cases brought about an organizationally established sustainable practice of EUD, where empowered employees cooperated with IT professionals in the development and evolution of an IT infrastructure based on flexible technologies. The chapter further discusses how such practices are supported by (participatory) organizational IT management structures and processes. Finally, it discusses how EUD in this way contributes to the innovation capability of the organization. The conclusion points to transferability of the insights gained and provides suggestions for future research.

Keywords Case studies · sustainable practise · IT management structures · technical infrastructures

1 Introduction

In most of today's organizations competition is hard. Providing for innovation and rapidly adapting to changes driven by the business and organizational environment is a matter of survival. In order to be able to organizationally sustain innovation

Y. Dittrich (✉)
IT University, Copenhagen, Denmark
e-mail: ydi@itu.dk

J. Bolmsten
World Maritime University, Malmö, Sweden
e-mail: johan.bolmsten@wmu.se

J. Eriksson
Malmö University, Malmö, Sweden
e-mail: jeanette.eriksson@mah.se

© Springer International Publishing AG 2017
F. Paternò, V. Wulf (eds.), *New Perspectives in End-User Development*,
DOI 10.1007/978-3-319-60291-2_8

capability and support the evolution of services and processes, the IT infrastructure must adapt to changes as well as provide a base for future innovations.

End-User Development (EUD) (Lieberman, Paternò, Klann, & Wulf, 2006) allows domain experts to tailor and customize their software. However, non-IT professionals are not always incentivized or even welcome to change the IT infrastructure (Dittrich, Lundberg, & Lindeberg, 2006). This chapter addresses the question of what it takes to include EUD as part of a developing and evolving IT infrastructure of an organization as a means of supporting continuous organizational innovation.

The chapter reports the re-analysis of two case studies:

- **Case 1 – The Telecom Provider**: Empirical research took place from 1999 to 2006 concerning IT support for the back office and economic unit. In long-term engagement, both the development of a tailorable application supporting specific tasks and the flexible integration of different applications were addressed (Dittrich et al., 2001; Eriksson, 2008; Eriksson & Dittrich, 2007). Though not at that time a focus of the research collaboration, the IT unit and business units worked closely together to handle the flexibility necessary to co-design work practices and technologies (Dittrich & Lindeberg, 2002, 2004).
- **Case 2 – The UN University**: Empirical research took place from 2008 to 2013 on the Participatory Design (PD) of the IT infrastructure for a university. Though the technical base was crucial for providing enough flexibility (Bolmsten, 2016), collaboration between end-user developers and the IT professionals turned out to be important as well (Bolmsten & Dittrich, 2011). To support the co-development of work and business practices and the supporting technology, participatory approaches were developed at the project and organizational level of structures and processes for participatory IT management (Bolmsten, 2016).

Both cases turned out to address EUD and flexible technical infrastructures to support organization and work practice change and innovation. In both cases, a sustained culture of EUD was developed. These similarities triggered a meta-analysis of the two cases: Yvonne Dittrich has been part of both projects as a principle investigator PhD supervisor, respectively. While engaged on the latter project, similarities between the two projects became visible. Jeanette Eriksson is one of two PhD students who worked on the telecom provider case. Johan Bolmsten completed his PhD studies while employed as an IT officer at the UN University.

Based on our meta-analysis, we recognize how flexible technologies are an enabling factor that needs to be complemented with empowered employees who are entrusted with making (design) decisions, and constructive collaboration between IT professionals and end-user developers. These three factors need to be supported and complemented by organizational structures and processes that provide a frame for organizationally accountable development and the evolution of a common IT infrastructure. The concepts, together with their interaction, can be regarded as an empirical theory grounded in the meta-analysis of the two case studies. An analytical framework is put forward that relates the observed sustained

EUD to technical, organisational and collaboration practices. In the discussion we argue that such sustained EUD becomes part of the continuous day-to-day infrastructuring that, in turn, is a central contribution to the innovative capabilities of an organisation.

The remainder of the chapter will be structured as follows: Scct. 2 discusscs related work with respect to EUD, innovation, and IT infrastructures; Sect. 3 discusses the research approach of the meta-analysis; Sect. 4 present the relevant aspects of the two case studies; Sect. 5 then discusses the findings and develops the core concepts and their relations; Sect. 6 sums up the conclusions and discusses the study's limitations as well as possibilities for future research.

2 Innovation, End-User Development, and Infrastructuring

In order to provide the necessary background to understanding the further discussion, this section discusses related work around four concepts: innovation, EUD, IT infrastructure, and infrastructuring. As innovation and infrastructuring are not commonly associated with EUD, they warrant a more comprehensive discussion. The first Subsect. 2.1 develops a modern concept of organizational innovation by relating democratized innovation to organizational processes of learning and innovation. In the organizational arena, user-driven innovation is dependent on an evolution of the enabling technical infrastructure. Subsect. 2.2 presents research on EUD that focuses on providing and using technically flexible infrastructures to support the evolution of the organization. Sect. 2.3 then presents state-of-the-art understanding of "infrastructuring" (Karasti, 2014; Karasti & Syrjänen, 2004) as a way to conceptualize the social aspect of the socio-technical design and evolution of the infrastructure that is needed to support organizational innovation.

2.1 Democratized Innovation in the Organization

Organizations have become faced with the challenge of developing and sustaining capabilities for innovation to cope with the increased pressure for change, the acceleration of globalization, and the possibilities that come with new information technologies (Ober, 2008; Orlikowski, 2002). According to Lawson and Samson (2001), an innovation capability is the "ability to continuously transform knowledge and ideas into new products, processes, and systems for the benefit of the firm and its stakeholders." At the same time, both the capability to innovate and the understanding of how to put innovations to use is a learning process that must continuously develop (Lawson & Samson, 2001).

Current developments in the understanding of and conditions for innovation provide new opportunities for organizations faced with the challenge of innovating. Using the concept of "democratizing innovation," von Hippel (2005) shows that in many cases it is the users of technology who actually take the first step that leads toward basic innovations. According to von Hippel (2005), user-centered innovation processes offer great advantages in that users can develop exactly what they need. These differ from the traditional model in which dedicated designers and engineers develop products and services. In this traditional model, the user's role is to have needs, which are funneled in design and where somebody else develops solutions (von Hippel, 2005).

This new innovation trend is supported by technological developments that enable users both to innovate IT products and services and to share their innovations. When it comes to IT, the users' ability to innovate is radically and rapidly improving in line with the quality of computer software and hardware, increased access to easy-to-use tools and components for innovation, and enriched innovation commons (von Hippel, 2005). This is illustrated, for example, by free and open source software projects, which are in many cases well developed. It is further illustrated by the potential of new internet-based innovation communities, in which individual users do not have to develop everything they need on their own: they can benefit from innovations developed and shared by others. Users joining together in networks and communities provide useful structures and tools for their interactions and for the distribution of innovations.

Different spheres of user-centered innovations can be distinguished. Von Hippel (2005) focuses on the benefits to the consumer in the marketplace of user-centered innovations, and how innovations by users provide a necessary complement and feedstock to manufacturer innovation. Companies are well advised to open their innovation models to incorporate the innovations especially of lead-users of their services and products in their business models: "if […] the information needed to innovate in important ways is widely distributed, the traditional pattern of concentrating innovation-support resources on a few individuals is hugely inefficient" (von Hippel, 2005, p. 14). Björgvinsson, Ehn, and Hillgren (2010) discuss democratized innovation from the point of view of public spheres and everyday life. They address the question of how open innovation milieus can be participatory designed for the user as a citizen, and how new constellations, issues, and ideas evolve from bottom-up and long-term collaborations among diverse stakeholders.

In this chapter, democratized innovation is discussed from the perspective of users as members of organizations. Democratized innovation, in this respect, is about the need for organizations to take advantage of the capabilities of their own members. User-centered innovation by organizational members is needed for organizations to develop new products and services as well as internal operations (Manville & Ober, 2003; Ober, 2008). Organizations need to make use of and cultivate the capabilities of their members, the communities that they are part of, and the networks that they have access to – inside and outside the organization. This is a process that involves both user-centered innovation and organizational learning of how to make use of innovations to add organizational value. Orlikowski (2002) recognizes that especially when it comes to complex organizational change, the collective capabilities of organizational members need to be drawn on, with a focus on "organizational knowing as emerging from the ongoing and situated actions of organizational members" (Orlikowski, 2002; Suchman, 1987, 2007).

The need to combine bottom-up innovation and learning processes that take their stance with organizational members is addressed by Andreu and Ciborra (1996), ranging from improvements of routines to strategic capabilities, and involves both what can be referred to as "bricolage" and "radical learning." The former relates to incremental advances through situated tinkering by organizational members to improve their everyday work, and the latter concerns bringing about radical change by becoming aware of what the context is and explicitly stepping out of the box and innovating in a new manner (Andreu & Ciborra, 1996). Combined democratized and user-centered innovation and organizational learning challenge traditional approaches to information system management, where top-down planning-oriented management schemes are not sufficient to keep up with innovation and learning pressures (Andreu & Ciborra, 1996; Ciborra, 2000).

In Eriksén (1998), shop floor IT management by users is recognized as highlighting their capabilities to cater for the development of their own software support to the benefit of the organization. How such "design in use" complements a traditional "use for design" in the user-centered development approach PD is further developed by Dittrich, Eriksén, and Hansson (2002). In the analysis of two cases of software support in a municipality and a public service one-stop-shop, respectively, they find that important development activities are going on "in the wild," which are managed by the users themselves with only a secondary dependence on IT professionals. In "From control to drift," Ciborra (2000) analyzes a number of infrastructure development projects in multi-nationals with regard to how bottom-up development initiatives are important to understanding the dynamics of corporate information infrastructures; nevertheless, such development initiatives are found to appear to be "drifting" (anarchic) compared to the wisdom of the predominate information system management approaches.

In the chapter by Cabitza and Simone (2017) a conceptual framework called the Logic of Bricolage is developed to understand the technical malleability of systems to allow end-users to both make incremental improvements and innovate new solutions. Our cases focus on socio-technical dimensions enabling such practices. The comparative analysis of our two cases shows how EUD can become an integral part of such organizational user-centered innovation. Based on the observations, the discussion section indicates how the user-centered innovation of IT infrastructures can be contained and supported by IT management structures that make EUD practices organizationally accountable.

2.2 End-User Development

EUD and end-user software engineering (Ko et al., 2011) address tools and techniques that allow non-IT experts to develop software applications, such as Excel sheets, or finalize the design of software, as when developing the filters of an e-mail reader, through an interface that is understandable to non-IT professionals. In this volume, Ludwig, Dax, Pipek, and Wulf (2017) put forward a practice-oriented definition of EUD where EUD is defined to occur whenever an end-user has to switch to a lower language layer to fulfil a specific task. An open question identified that relate to the contribution of this chapter is how to support coopera-tive approaches in order to allow end-user developers to together develop IT-support of different technical complexities. Whereas the EUD community in the US emphasizes programming language technologies to support non-IT profes-sionals, the European part of the community emphasizes the need to understand the context in which EUD takes place in order to support not only the individual end-user developer but also the sharing and evolution of the results of EUD. As the analysis presented in this chapter focuses on the deployment of EUD and sus-tainable innovation, the research on cooperation around EUD and its connection to the organizational arena is most relevant here.

From the very start, the research on EUD has not only addressed the tools and interfaces for EUD but also the sharing and cooperation around the tailoring of software. One of the very first articles, "There's no place like home: continuing design in use" by Henderson and Kyng (1992), discussed the sharing of EUD results. In "A small matter of programming," Nardi (1993) analyzes, among other things, the role of super users of customizable Computer Aided Design (CAD) software to support other users in the organization and how to quality assure and support the sharing of macros and customizations. In these early cases, the end-user developers and users cooperated around the adaptation of individual perfor-mance tools.

However, organizational and cooperative aspects became more prominent when EUD research extended into contexts where EUD tasks concerned the adaptation or provisioning of common resources or infrastructures. An early example is the research reported by Trigg and Bødker (1994) in "From implementation to design: tailoring and the emergence of systematization in CSCW." The development of a set of form letters to be shared among the employees of a public agency in Denmark was considered to be of an organizational importance that warranted an organizational process to review and approve the form letters by a committee of lawyers. Likewise, the tailoring of a common cooperation infrastructure used by ministerial employees that cooperated between Bonn and Berlin during the transi-tion of the German government to the new capital in the 1990s needed to be subject to negotiation and discussion, as EUD did not only affect individual work tools (Pipek & Kahler, 2006). Dittrich et al. (2006) mention deliberation and quality assurance in the context of configuration and customization of mission critical sys-tems as two of the central challenges for EUD in such contexts. However, the research of Wulf (1999) on the tailoring of access rights indicates that EUD can be used to implement and assure compliance with organizational strategies. To date, the research on the organizational side of EUD has, in most cases, been analytical.

Reflecting on their experiences, Pipek and Kahler (2006) provide a categoriza-tion of cooperative tailoring scenarios: most of the early projects, like that of

Henderson and Kyng (1992), fall into the shared usage scenario that requires the least coordination, whereby user groups are a self-help feature in both commercial and private contexts. The tailoring of CAD systems reported in Nardi (1993) is an example of the shared context scenario that requires better possibilities for sharing customizations, but might result in conflicts if changes to the individual tool hinder the sharing of work results. In a shared tool scenario, as in the case of form letters by a public agency (see Trigg & Bødker, 1994), the group needs to negotiate not only the adaptations but also the usage of the common tool with the adaptations.

Shared infrastructure scenarios, the last of Pipek and Kahler's (2006) categories, have been and still are the least researched scenarios. Here, tailoring results can affect configurations of other systems. The shared infrastructure scenario also provides additional challenges. The design space for EUD of an individual application is constrained by interoperability requirements. Both the cases discussed in our meta-analysis fall into this scenario. Heterogeneous user groups are dependent on each other, though they share neither a common work practice nor a common tool.

Another challenge that might also be responsible for the difficulties in researching cooperative EUD in shared infrastructure scenarios is that the evolution of shared infrastructures often involves collaboration between users, end-user developers, and IT professionals. The notion of meta-design (Fischer, 2010) has been introduced to describe the need for software engineering of EUD systems to target the design of design environments for end-user developers. Fischer (1998) also coined the term of "seeding – evolutionary growth – reseeding" to describe long-term cooperation between users and IT professionals in the context of EUD, whereby the IT professionals provide initial design environments with currently needed building blocks as a base for EUD. Over time, the dynamics of usage and EUD practices result in requirements that cannot be supported within the current state of the EUD environment. In this situation, IT professionals are required to evolve the EUD environment. Fischer's concepts have informed the design of successful EUD environments (Costabile, Dittrich, Fischer, & Piccinno, 2011).

Shared infrastructure aspects have already been discussed in earlier publications on the projects presented here: Dittrich and Lindeberg (2002) observe that in infrastructures supporting data-intensive businesses like telecommunications, the flexibility of a specific application can only be deployed when other applications in the same network and the interoperability platform are tailored accordingly (Dittrich & Lindeberg, 2002). The importance of combining EUD and professional development activities when evolving such a common infrastructure and gaining support for it has been raised in both cases (Bolmsten & Dittrich, 2011; Bolmsten, 2016; Eriksson, 2008; Eriksson & Dittrich, 2007). In our comparative analysis, we go one step further: we aim not only to understand how EUD can take place in a shared infrastructure setting but what it takes to integrate EUD and infrastructure development in order to sustain the innovation capacity of an organization.

2.3   IT Infrastructures and Infrastructuring

Infrastructures and their maintenance and evolution have been subject to discussion in their own right in the Information Systems and PD communities. Inspired by observations similar to the ones leading to Eriksén's (1998) concept of "shop floor IT management," Karasti (Karasti, 2014; Karasti & Syrjänen, 2004) developed the concept of "infrastructuring." Karasti (2014), here, refers to Star and Ruhleder's (1994, 1996) salient characteristics of information infrastructures.

Star and Ruhleder (1994, 1996) use information infrastructures to analytically target technology development that goes beyond the local project and to discuss how technology affects organizational transformation. Based on their analysis of the development of a distributed information system that served as a platform for archiving and exchanging data in a scientific community, eight characteristics of information infrastructures are described: (1) embeddedness in other social and technological structures and arrangements; (2) transparency in invisibly supporting tasks; (3) spatial and temporal reach or scope; (4) the taken-for-grantedness of artifacts and organizational arrangements, learned as part of membership in a community; (5) infrastructures shape and are shaped by conventions of practice; (6) infrastructures are plugged into other infrastructures and tools in a standardized fashion, though they are also modified by scope and conflicting (local) conventions; (7) infrastructures do not grow de novo, but wrestle with the inertia of the installed base and inherit strengths and limitations from that base; (8) normally invisible infrastructures become visible upon breakdown. These eight characteristics stress situated and socio-technical relations. The analysis of infrastructural relations provides an understanding of infrastructure development that, according to Star and Ruhleder (1994), moves away from a conception of infrastructure as a substrate of "something upon which something else runs or operates" to infrastructure as something that is constantly "in the making" (p. 252). The possibility of infrastructures as "genuine universals," where tasks to be automated are well-structured, the domain well understood, and system requirements determinable by formal a priori needs assessments, is challenged by this definition (Star & Ruhleder, 1994, 1996). In Star and Bowker (2002), the discussion is extended to implications for infrastructure development and a focus on "how to infrastructure." This includes the challenge of designing for flexibility and the need for the infrastructure designer to always be aware of the multiple set of contexts upon which her work impinges.

Karasti and Syrjänen (2004) approach infrastructures from a bottom-up point of view, compared to Star and Ruhleder (1994, 1996), who are concerned with large infrastructure projects. Through two cases in very different contexts, one community of dog hobbyists and one community of information managers within a large-scale research network, Karasti and Syrjänen (2004) develop an understanding of community PD. The community members in both of these cases exhibit common traits: a community identity through common causes, shared interests, and strong commitments. In addition, they take long-term responsibility for their work domain and for both existing systems and procedures and the development of new ones. The notion of "infrastructuring" is applied to sensitize the understanding of infrastructure maintenance and development as a procedural, ongoing, and multi-relational activity that unfolds over extended periods of time (Karasti & Syrjänen, 2004). In order to deepen the relational understanding of infrastructures, Karasti and Syrjänen (2004) also connect infrastructuring to Suchman's (1987, 2007) notion of artful integrations, which refer to hybrid systems comprising media, material, and practices. This emphasizes a "located accountability" of design, where change becomes a part of everyday practice, and further highlights design as a continuous process of inscribing knowledge and activities in new material forms.

Infrastructuring can be further understood in an organizational context through Pipek and Wulf's (2009) framework of infrastructural layers of technology development. Their framework takes a stance on the "work infrastructure" of in-situ development activities and connects these to preparatory and background related activities. In addition, work- and technology-related activities are distinguished. In the framework, infrastructure development is triggered by "points of infrastructure" at which an infrastructure becomes visible to its users (and IT professionals), either during instances of infrastructure breakdowns or local innovation. As the infrastructure becomes visible, the activities that contribute to that specific part of the infrastructure development become visible as well. This can, in turn, trigger new work and technology design in the supporting infrastructure layers, such as method-driven design activities (preparatory) and basic development of work and technology standards (background). Pipek and Wulf (2009) further highlight the role of end-users and their EUD activities, observing that any actual work infrastructure includes numerous user innovations, and that IT professionals are rarely, if ever, able to take full account of the evolution of the systems and practices involved in the local accomplishment of work goals. They further argue how a wide variety of work practices – tasks, routines, and praxes – prepare both users and professional designers for "points of infrastructure" design. In this volume, Rohde & Wulf (in, press) develop a process framework of Integrated Organization and Technology Development (OTD) to facilitate change in organizational structures and processes with their supporting IT-infrastructure. The process framework has been developed over time to support a practice-based research perspective in a number of empirical cases that are characterized by parallel development of work practice, technical, organizational systems. In Bolmsten, (2016), participatory IT management structures and processes are proposed that support the linking of different work and technology layers in organizationally accountable infrastructure development, which are independent of the support and intervention by researchers. The focus is on managing integrated technical and organizational change through empowering end-users to participatory in sustainable change processes. These proposals are taken up and further developed in this chapter.

2.4   Summary

The interrelated work on democratized innovation, organizational innovation, and learning indicates, on the one hand, that there is a need to acknowledge user innovation of the IT and work infrastructure as part of the innovation necessary for an organization to continue to perform in a changing environment; on the other hand, such user innovation is regarded as (anarchic) drift that is in contradiction to the traditional IT management frameworks (Ciborra, 2000). The observation of such "shop floor IT management activities" (Eriksén, 1998; Dittrich & Eriksén, 2002) inspired the development and exploration of the notion of "infrastructuring," as such innovation and design activities involve maintaining and evolving the IT infrastructure. EUD has been identified as a core activity in such scenarios (Bolmsten, 2016; Pipek & Wulf, 2009).

The current chapter sets out to explore what is needed to sustain EUD activities to better the organization and to correspondingly underpin EUD as an innovation capability of the organization. Sect. 3 that follows discusses the research methods before the following section presents the analysis of two cases focusing on the relevant dimensions of the resulting model.

3   Research Methods

Both case studies examined in this chapter were designed and researched as independent projects. Both of them applied Cooperative Method Development (CMD), an action research approach combining qualitative empirical research with software engineering tool, method, and process improvements (Dittrich, Rönkkö, Eriksson, Hansson, & Lindeberg, 2008) The research results of each case have been published prior to the meta-analysis undertaken for this chapter. Table 1 summarizes the fieldwork supporting the meta-analysis for both cases and the prior publication in the context of each case. The specific research method applied in each case is briefly introduced in the case descriptions. The method section here refers to the method of meta-analysis. The Subsect. 3.1 describes the meta-analysis performed. Thereafter in Subsect. 3.2, we discuss what measures we have taken to assure the trustworthiness of the research.

3.1   Meta-Analysis

The chapter aggregates qualitative research from two case studies. A common way to aggregate qualitative research is multiple case studies (Yin, 2013) or meta-ethnography (Britten et al., 2002). Multiple case studies are typically designed as such, and the cases are chosen to triangulate specific research

Table 1 Research methods and earlier results related to the two cases

Case	Research approach and focus	Initial fieldwork and material	Quality assurance of initial research	Publications
Telecom Provider	Action research and design research on the introduction of flexible technologies providing the basis for software and infrastructure evolution.	Participatory observation; design and evaluation of prototypes; individual and group interviews; document analysis	Method triangulation; researcher triangulation; member checking; rich descriptions	Dittrich & Lindeberg, 2001; Dittrich & Lindeberg, 2002; Dittrich & Lindeberg, 2003; Dittrich & Lindeberg, 2004; Dittrich et al., 2006; Dittrich et al., 2001; Eriksson & Dittrich, 2007; Eriksson, 2007; Eriksson, 2008
World Maritime University	Action research addressing technical development, IT management structures and representations mediating infrastructure projects.	Participatory observation; field notes; taped individual and group interviews; document analysis	Method triangulation; research triangulation; member checking; complete audit trail of field material	Bolmsten, 2016; Bolmsten & Dittrich, 2011; Bolmsten, 2016

questions. Meta-ethnography involves aggregating published research based on articles. This case is a hybrid between the two: research on each case took place independently of the other. Both cases are based on long-term engagement. A strict control for the sake of comparability would not have allowed us to follow the dynamics of the collaboration. Furthermore, the two cases took place one after another, and it was not anticipated that there would be common themes emerging from the research. Compared with a meta-ethnography, the meta-analysis does not only refer to the published results but is also able to take the original field material into account. Below, we describe how the meta-analysis was conducted.

Both case studies resulted in new insights about EUD, cooperation between users and organizational units, and IT professionals and their departments. Given a prior understanding of common threads in the empirical material, the researchers involved met for a brainstorming session on how innovation, IT infrastructure, and EUD were interrelated in the field material. Episodes of the respective field materials resulted in an initial identification of common themes.

This initial set of themes was used to identify relevant sections in the field material. The researchers then went back to their original analyses and the field material itself using the themes in an axial coding manner, identifying supportive

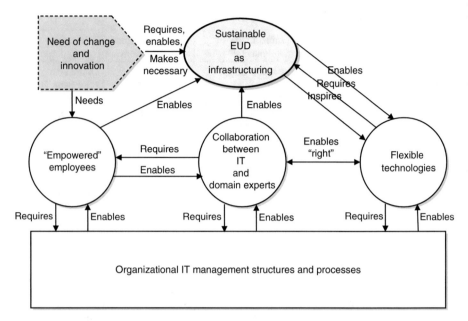

Fig. 1 Empirical theory based on two cases

and contradicting evidence. The results were used not only to refine the set of themes but also to identify relationships between these themes.

The results were again integrated, giving us a first version of Fig. 1, representing an empirical theory grounded in the two cases. The initial figure was then used as a basis for theoretical coding, resulting in a refined version of the figure and theory.

The meta-analysis informed an empirically grounded theory relating how technology, people, and organizational aspects contribute to sustainable organizational innovation capabilities.

3.2   Trustworthiness

To assure trustworthiness of the meta-analysis, on the one hand, we relied on the quality assurance of the original research detailed in Table 1; on the other hand, we worked with both data triangulation across the cases and researcher triangulation.

A comparative meta-analysis of the two cases situated in as widely differing domains as education and telecommunication, in itself provides an indication that the developed, empirically grounded theory is sound. Relating different cases to the same codes and concepts forced us to sharpen our conception.

Researcher triangulation assures that the judgments, e.g., on codes and the relationship between concepts and empirical material, are inter-subjective. The first author has been involved in both cases and is able to triangulate the main fieldworkers' analyses in both cases. Further, the cooperation between researchers not engaged in each other's cases forced us to explicate our at times tacit assumptions and to explicate the relations encountered.

Finally, we provide a thick description (Ponterotto, 2006) to allow the reader to review our analysis and discussion.

Sect. 4 presents the two cases based on the categories identified as constitutive for sustainable EUD.

4 The Two Cases

In this section, we present and analyze the two cases. For each of them, we first give an overview of the case and the major lines of research. We then present the original research approach and methods. The following subsections then focus on the need for change that was the rationale behind the observed EUD practices, the organizational characteristics that sustained EUD as an organizational practice, and finally the organizational IT management that provided a frame for this sustained EUD. An overview of these building blocks and their relations is given in Fig. 1, which illustrates our meta-analysis (see Sect. 3). Our resulting empirical theory of how the different building blocks contribute to sustainable EUD as infrastructuring is discussed further in Sect. 5.

4.1 Telecom Case: Innovating for Changing Business Practices

The telecom case was carried out in cooperation with a major telecommunication operator in Sweden. Since this line of business is characterized by rapid change, the company's information infrastructure and development processes need to support frequent change. Telecommunication operators remain competitive by, among other things, being innovative and introducing new types of services to their customers. Their business system must therefore be upgraded to continuously support these new services. In such a fast-changing world, flexible software is beneficial to prevent it from becoming obsolete. Because changes are very fast, it takes a lot of effort to keep business systems up to date. To come to terms with this problem, the telecom operator had invested in making some systems tailorable by the end-user (Dittrich & Lindeberg, 2002; Dittrich et al., 2006), and started to cooperate with the researchers of this study in this pursuit. In the beginning, the research focused on a contract and payment system – from hereon called "the payment system." To keep up with changes in the telecom market, new payment types had to be created at short notice. The payment system was used to compute payments based on contracts that were modelled in the system, and the payments were triggered by specific events. The data describing the triggering events were periodically imported from another system. It became evident that the communication and data exchange between systems constrained the flexibility of the individual applications. In a second cooperation project, we therefore focused on flexible connections in the infrastructure: the researchers developed concepts and prototypes to provide the end-users with the possibility to tailor the communication paths and data flow between different systems – a possibility to manage the system infrastructure. This second part of the cooperation focused on how to structure a tool that made it possible for end-users to manage a large infrastructure and at the same time facilitate use, tailoring, and further development of the tailoring capabilities (Eriksson, 2008).

From the very beginning, it struck us that the users were treated as equal members of the development team and engaged in tweaking the system and developing workarounds where necessary in cooperation with the IT professionals (Dittrich & Lindeberg, 2001, 2004). When so engaged, it is important that the users are aware of the possibilities and limitations of the software, so they can recognize when tailoring is not enough. The tailoring capabilities are always limited, meaning that tailoring cannot support completely unanticipated changes. The tailoring capabilities must therefore be extended, and tailoring activities must be coordinated with software evolution activities performed by IT professionals. The second study with the telecom provider (Eriksson, 2008) shows that it is possible to benefit from both user and system perspectives through collaboration between users, tailors, and IT professionals. It is necessary for users and IT professionals to collaborate closely in order to make tailorable information systems both durable and innovative to the business environment. In this way, the development of useful, sustainable software, which adapts easily to changes in an evolving environment, can be achieved.

4.1.1   Methods of Original Research

The study followed the CMD methodology and implemented two research cycles with three iterative phases: (1) understanding the problem, (2) cooperation to make improvements, and (3) implementation and evaluation. Both cycles involved the development of prototypes as part of the improvement based on the findings in the previous phase. The research approach adopted in the second phase may be termed "design science research," as the projects started out by defining the research question based on business needs and unexplored issues in the research discourse. Design research has been discussed in several papers, among others Nunamaker, Chen, and Purdin (1991), March and Smith (1995), Hevner, March, and Park (2004), and Peffers, Tuunanen, Rothenberger, and Chatterjee (2007). In 2016, Rohde, Brödner, Stevens, Betz, and Wulf (2016) published an evolved version of Design Science Research called Grounded Design (GD). In retrospective, the Telecom case can be seen as Grounded Design as the study implements the GD principles (Rodhe et al., 2016). The prototypes were iteratively developed and evaluated in cooperation with IT professionals and users at the telecom company.

In another chapter in this volume, Tetteroo and Markopoulos (2017) discuss how to evaluate successful deployment of EUD technology and how EUD should be postponed until the host technology is accepted by the users. In line with their recommendations, the prototype in the Telecom case was implemented on top of existing software. The evaluation involved not only technical issues but also addressed "how" and "why" the prototypes worked. In other words, issues such as user knowledge, collaboration, and organizational aspects were considered in the evaluation.

In both studies, the collected data were analyzed in a qualitative manner. Coding schemes were developed, taking field notes and transcripts as a starting point. For specific research questions, multiple sources of data were combined. For quality assurance, member checking and researcher triangulation were applied.

4.1.2 Need for Change

As mentioned above, the motivation to explore the use of flexible technical solutions allowing for EUD stemmed from the market competition that forced the telecom operator to devise and compute new payments to keep up with the changing telecom market. The payment system that was the subject of cooperation had several predecessors, all of which were suitable for the needs at hand but unable to scale or to provide the necessary flexibility for future development needs. Each solution supported a number of contracts and payments but failed to support innovative marketing strategies. This resulted in only part of the payments based on events being able to be handled automatically by the regular payment system. Innovative contracts and payments, which were called "extra payments," needed to be handled and computed manually once a month, just like the regular payments. The computation of the extra payments was done based on database queries and complex spreadsheets.

Each generation of the in-house developed system included the current extra payments as regular payments in the new system. Experience suggested that it was impossible to anticipate what future extra payments would look like and which details were needed. It became clear that this situation was set to continue: the competitive telecom business was forcing the company to come up with new services on a continuous basis, which consequently resulted in new types of payments that could not be handled through the system. These extra payments were based on new types of events, which meant that new types of datasets were needed. This resulted in the innovation of a new approach to not only replace manual computation but also support EUD of contract types and payments as well as user-defined assembling of data from different systems.

Besides a more flexible payment system, this required an event definer/handler that was able to communicate with any system in the infrastructure. What was needed was an infrastructure tool for inter-application communication, which could be adapted by the user. At the same time, it was essential that the tool allow for expansion of the tailoring capabilities so that new data sources could be added.

What made the telecom case special at the time was that the EUD features where not introduced to support personalization of tools or the adaptation of generic software to any specific organization, but as a continuous development of part of the IT infrastructure in order to support business innovation on a corporate level.

4.1.3   Flexible Technologies as Enablers

From the very start, the exploration of flexible technologies to support this specific area of business was at the center of the cooperation. Creating prototypes that acted as mediating artifacts enabled exploration of what was required of the flexible technology to support EUD for business critical processes. One of the central insights was that not only EUD but three different interfaces needed to be considered: the tailoring interface, the deployment interface, and the development interface.

From the study, it was determined what was required of technology to act as an enabler for innovation (Dittrich et al., 2006; Eriksson, 2008):

- Functionality for controlling and testing changes has to be integrated into the tailoring interface, and there must be sufficient technical support for the end-user to estimate and check the correctness of the computation.
- A tailorable system has to support the development of a mental model that makes a clear division between normal execution and tailoring. This mental model must be adopted in the tailoring interface and shared by users, end-user developers, and IT professionals.
- The tailoring interface also has to make the potential for unanticipated use visible. This means that the information given must, to a certain extent, exceed what is currently necessary.
- The tailoring interface can be more complex, provided that the tailoring process makes the usage easier. The tailoring interface is not used as often as the deployment interface and the tailoring itself often additionally involves careful thought.
- The developer expanding the tailoring capability should only interact with one clearly defined point in the tailorable system: that is, changes are made at one point in the system.

The flexibility for innovation of the technology was clearly recognized by the users in the business unit, both for its potential and its challenges. The following citation underpins the innovative potential of flexible technology.

> This is interesting! It opens up new opportunities. It might be like one extra payment uses another payment as a base. (User comment, evaluation session, February 24, 2004, cited in Eriksson & Dittrich, 2007)

In a discussion with the business department of the potential design of a tailoring interface, one of the business unit managers indicated an organizational problem: if a change in the business practices does not require an IT development project anymore, the deliberation on what to offer has to be taken care of by the business units (Dittrich et al., 2001). For the technology to act as an innovation enabler not only must the "right" flexibility from a business perspective be implemented but also the support functionality in terms of control and testing.

4.1.4   Collaboration Between End-User Developers and IT Professionals

One of the central findings was that end-user developers and IT professionals needed to work tightly together to make sure that the IT infrastructure allowed the company to maintain its competitive edge. The fieldwork and evaluation established that it is impossible to know what future contracts and extra payments will look like. Therefore, there will always come a time when the end-user wants to establish payment types that cannot be supported in the current system, or use data that is not yet published in an available view. In such cases, IT professionals need to step in to develop new modules, implement a new view in the system, or update existing ones, and also to publish the relevant information on how to use and tailor the system.

Another issue related to communication and cooperation between users and IT professionals concerned the decision of how much information to make available for the users to do a good job of tailoring. The users wanted to see as much information as possible, within reasonable scope. The IT professionals would rather restrict the users' options in order to have better control over the execution of the system and detach maintenance that would not necessarily impact on communication with the payment system. These two perspectives had to be negotiated. The culture of cooperation between users and IT professionals had a major impact on the evaluation of trade-offs between flexibility, usability, development effort, and change effort (Dittrich & Lindeberg, 2003).

In the telecom company, cooperation between business units and the IT unit worked very well. The users were quite aware of the limits of their own competences and knew when to consult the responsible IT professionals. All users frequently referred to IT professionals when they experienced something that was beyond them. As the IT professionals were involved in maintenance and operation of the software, they could, if needed, take over the adaptation, tailoring, and especially the testing of the changes (Dittrich & Lindeberg, 2003). Neither users nor IT professionals considered the necessary coordination and cooperation to be a serious problem.

4.1.5   Empowered Users

In the information systems and PD literature, users are often described as people with low power and influence that need to be supported in their participation; this definitely was not the case at the telecom provider. Users were equal members in the project teams and sometimes even shared project management responsibilities

(Dittrich & Lindeberg, 2004). During participatory observations at the telecom company, the high expertise of the users was acknowledged, not only with regard to their tasks but also to managing the data available in the different databases that were part of the IT infrastructure. To be able to create new kinds of payment, data had to be collected from different sources and then pruned and aggregated using algorithms implemented as spreadsheets. To map requirements regarding the task at hand demanded expertise about the available data in the different systems. The communication between different systems was normally hidden from the user in a data communication layer for the separate systems, but users nevertheless acquired the knowledge necessary to perform the assembly of data.

The prototype created in the second study helped with the exact location of the data; for example, it guided the user to which fields to use by listing them with examples of the data they contained. However, the user had to understand the sometimes quite cryptic names and know where to look for specific data. Both users and IT professionals were aware of each other's competences and the responsibilities for the different systems were clear to all parties. This contributed to transparency in the organization, whereby the users and the IT professionals knew whom to ask depending on what the question was.

Business knowledge about contracts and payments provided the basis on which the users decided what data to collect. Extensive business knowledge was a prominent feature of the results in the evaluation of the created prototype. The users' reflections on which data to collect often concerned different aspects of the business tasks. The users were also well aware of which errors could occur, that is, errors concerning the use of the prototype, the IT infrastructure, and the task. Task-specific errors were, for example, particularly important for the end-user to monitor since they could cause serious consequences for the company if they were not caught. Concern over making errors was expressed in statements like this:

> when you work as we do you must know a little about database management, you have to understand how the tables are constructed and how to find the information. And also in some way understand the consequences of or the value of the payment. In other words how you can formulate conditions and what that leads to. (User comment, evaluation session, February 24, 2004; cited in Eriksson & Dittrich, 2007).

In summary, the users' awareness of system capabilities, fellow workers' competences, and business cases made it possible for them to compile and execute data for extra payments. At the same time, users cooperated with IT professionals on equal footing in the development projects as well as the operation of the systems (Dittrich & Lindeberg, 2004). This required users to become trusted end-user developers (Eriksson & Dittrich, 2007).

4.1.6 Organizational Structures and Processes

From the very beginning of the research cooperation, it was striking how closely domain experts and IT professionals cooperated. This was partly due to the company's project model. The workspace at the telecom company was organized as open plan offices. Initially, the IT unit was co-located with some of the users, and cooperation did not only take place in meetings but also by walking over to other people and having a chat about a problem or an idea. The IT project model was a specialization of the general project model that was used for any kind of change project. The model was structured around three decision points where the company-wide project committee decided whether to continue the project: the start of a pre-study was based on a document formulating the business unit requirements. The pre-study resulted in a document describing the outcome of the project in more detail and outlining the budget and a development model. For software projects, this document was complemented by requirements' specification, a more technical implementation proposal, and a time-plan detailing implementation tasks based on the implementation proposal. The implementation proposal described the functionality of the future system at a more concrete level. This meant that it already contained a preliminary design.

The general project model required all affected organizational units to be represented both in the project team and in the steering committee. The same principle applied for users and IT professionals in the software development projects. The first study was related to a project developing a new and innovative version of the payment system. The project management of this project was shared by a general project manager from the business department and a technical project manager from the IT department. As further elaborated on in the previous articles (Dittrich & Lindeberg, 2001, 2004), the collaboration built on long-term contact and mutual appreciation.

IT professionals were not only responsible for new developments, but also for supporting operations of the system in the case of errors occurring. They also supported users, e.g., when looking for up-to-date and accurate data on which to base new payment types. The established way of cooperating across departments and the day-to-day cooperation around the operations of the system provided a sound basis for the continuous and flexible evolution of the system both through end-user tailoring and new developments.

In the studies, it could be observed that a flexible system requires an organizational structure to decide what changes can actually be reasonably implemented from a business point of view (Dittrich & Lindeberg, 2003). This requires cooperation between the IT unit and the business units around the deliberation of changes not only by IT professionals but also by end-user developers.

Further, the prototype demonstrating the possibility to tailor the interaction between other systems and the payment system showed the need for coordination across the infrastructure of the telecom provider: when preparing an extra payment, regardless of whether the process is supported by tailorable software or not, the user needs to know where to find relevant and accurate data. During some workshops, it became apparent that there was friction in the coordination between the payment system and the changes in the surrounding systems. Each one of these systems was itself the subject of both tailoring and evolution. Both users and the IT professionals addressed the necessity of communicating with other system owners and assigning responsibilities regarding the publication and updating of the connected information and kinds of data available. When one system in the IT infrastructure was changed, the changes were orally communicated to the owners as well as users of other systems that might be affected by the change. This indicates that it is important for the organization to support these kinds of communication paths.

4.2 The UN University Case: Infrastructuring in a Knowledge Organization

The second case concerns a UN-based university. The rationale of the university is the development and alignment of education and training across the member countries of a particular UN agency. Students at the university come from all over the world and stay for a 14-month master's program. The special nature of the university also implies that it does not align with the host country's legislation and framework concerning higher education. This has meant that the employees need to innovate the organizational strategies, policies, processes, and structures, and supporting IT solutions – as it turned out, with or without the assistance of IT professionals. Three such cases are reported on in a long-term action research study by Bolmsten, (2016) about sustaining PD in the organization: (1) faculty and faculty assistants working closely with IT professionals in the development of *course administration* support (such as scheduling, marking, and e-learning components); (2) the registrar also taking on the technical development of a *registry system* to support enrollment, grade reporting, curriculum quality evaluation, and student welfare and living support; and (3) an administrative assistant developing *electronic forms* and an address database. These shop floor IT management practices, where local software development takes place in close connection to daily work activities in different situated constituencies, were established approaches that predate the research study by many years.

The research focused on the increasing need for cross-organizational collaboration and integration: the enrollment process, for example, takes place not only within the registry department but has many points of integration with the faculty, where information flows back and forth; consequently, many considerations and decisions have to be made at both ends before a student is enrolled. In the same way, marking entails a work process that first involves a number of faculty and faculty assistants, and later continues at the registry department. Likewise, the working purpose of the electronic forms is not only for these to be used by the administrative department but by all departments and published in common information repositories.

The empirical research resulted in new insights about how EUD is an important contributor to the innovation capabilities of a knowledge intensive organization such as a university. The following sections describe how sustainable EUD depends on employees taking charge of their work tasks and the IT needed to support them. This, in turn, puts requirements on a flexible technical base when EUD extends from local applications to shared infrastructure, and mandates new ways of collaboration between end-user developers and IT professionals. Moreover, organizational structures and processes need to support participatory IT management to coordinate the development of an integrated technical base.

4.2.1   Methods of Original Research and Analysis for This Chapter

The empirical findings reported here are based on a PhD study (Bolmsten, 2016), where Bolmsten worked as an embedded action researcher employed as an IT professional by the university and combined action research with the daily development of software support with and for users. The research took place over the course of 5 years. Combined, the embedded nature and duration of the research provided an opportunity to understand, deliberate, and evaluate improvements of infrastructure development together with users. To guide the exposed research process, CMD was chosen as a structured methodology. CMD was appropriated beyond software engineering (1) to address PD and provide a focus on the development of the use organization, and (2) to include technical and organizational infrastructure from the users' perspective. In total, three interlinked CMD research cycles were carried out, where the findings in one CMD research cycle pushed further inquiry and improvements in a new CMD research cycle. Empirical data were recorded during day-to-day interaction through an audio and text-based research diary, complemented with participatory observations, workshops, and semi-structured interviews. This also provided a basis for triangulation of the empirical findings. In addition, off-site debriefing sessions were carried out, and in some cases complementary interviews with end-users were conducted by Dittrich. The findings reported below are based on open coding of transcribed episodes selected from the empirical material.

4.2.2   Need for Change

As mentioned above, the university is a unique and specialized agency in the UN system to which standard university regulations do not apply, such as accreditation and quality assurance frameworks. Academic and administrative staff needed to develop policies, structures, and processes, borrowing meaningful elements from different national systems and adapting them to the specific context, which includes interaction with third-party organizations providing funding for the students for their education, for example. As the IT systems also needed to support these tailored procedures, EUD and close collaboration with IT staff were crucial to developing the IT infrastructure of the UN university.

The registry system is a primary example of how to deal with this need for change. Due to its special status, there was still no accountable system in place for course, subject, credit, and grade management when the registrar joined the university 10 years after its inauguration. "Can you imagine, coming into this situation?," the registrar reflected on the situation that had confronted him. The registrar took on the creation of such a system himself, which also came to involve the technical development of the registry IT system. When analyzing the system 15 years later from a technical point of view, technical improvements could still be identified, partly due to the registrar not having been trained as an IT professional. For example, the technical database design was not optimized. However, when analyzed from a usefulness point of view, the registry system was one of the most integrated and comprehensively working systems in the organization.

Key to the continuous usefulness of the system were the development dynamics, wherein use and socio-technical development were intertwined as an often natural part of everyday work. When studying the development of the registry system, it was the day-to-day discussions that came across as most important, where the development of the technical system was discussed and negotiated in relation to its daily operation and development of work practices. The same development dynamics were observed in regard to the development of other university systems, where a piece of functionality working well or not so well in relation to the execution of a work task would lead to an in-situ discussion of how it could be improved. When interviewing a registry assistant about the development approach of the registry system, it was notable how such evolution of the registry system was an almost implicit part of her work. For example, she exemplified the nature of day-to-day development collaboration, citing an issue with menu tabs being divided into different databases in her interface "[…] you can always call him [the registrar], go in to him, and he listens […] it is not like it is small petites […] I have not thought about it before, but now when we are talking about it, it is pretty great […] and then he either says it works, if it works […]." These development dynamics would not have been possible to capture, for example, by studying a formal project management framework, which in many cases was, in fact, absent.

One of the motivations for the research resulting in a PhD thesis was the recognition that this approach has its limitations when the development of bespoke IT systems take up more and more resources and, at the same time, the need for integration becomes visible.

4.2.3   Flexible Technologies as Enablers

For the end-users to effectively participate in the development of IT support, the technology used was of importance. This became evident when EUD expanded from local development, adaptation, and configuration to encompass infrastructure development on a shared technical base. In total, three improvements to technical bases were designed as part of the action research, of which one was specifically implemented to support EUD. In order to allow for both cross-university integration and local innovation and EUD, a fourth-generation Content Management System was adapted as a technical base to host the Learning Management System and all other faculty portals. Special attention was paid to selecting a technical base that supported the integration with local tools and custom-developed modules for situated work practices. The improvements to EUD were twofold: when development took place on a shared technical base, possibilities opened up for end-user developers to exchange information and use the same datasets and modules as other local applications developed on the same technical base. This created opportunities for end-users to develop consolidated reports with interlinked information that previously resided within the confines of local departments. An example was academic reporting that used schedule data from the faculty department, grade data from the registry department, and employee data from the human resources department. Another benefit from a shared technical base was that it enabled shared investments that otherwise would not have been possible, e.g., new catalogues of pre-defined modules that could be shared, further developed, and configured by the end-users themselves in different local applications.

The shared technical base also came to prompt coordination between end-user developers and the IT staff: it became necessary to negotiate requirements for shared modules across the university. An example was the decision to have a new module for shared documents between two local application communities, which turned into a "straightjacket" for one of them as it had not been properly deliberated. For the grade notifications, the access rights needed to be configured in a more granular way than could be accommodated by the newly shared module. These experiences provided motivation for the organization as a whole to develop organizational structures and processes for proper deliberation of decisions impacting more than one department.

4.2.4   Collaboration Between End-User Developers and IT Professionals

Before the university undertook the development of an integrated IT infrastructure, IT staff had not only taken care of the administration of network servers but also supported users with the development of custom applications that required more technical expertise than they could master themselves. This cooperation became more pronounced when the shared technical base was implemented to support the integration of different local applications. The development, configuration, and maintenance of the shared technical base required the expertise of IT professionals. The empirical research showed that IT professional expertise is also needed to moderate the often complex and multi-layered negotiations between different user interests and areas of expertise that need to be accommodated: design options need to be analyzed and presented to the domain experts, and dependencies and trade-offs need to be rendered understandable so that domain experts can gain an overview of the implications of the decisions. In the university case, PD techniques and tools were experimented with for this purpose. These included rich-picture workshops (Bødker, Kensing, & Simonsen, 2004) and design workshops to support end-users from different application domains to learn about and negotiate the trade-offs of technical base decisions. However, different end-user developers had different strategies of how to relate to the organization and their IT professional colleagues: some decided to isolate their professional domain and its IT support; others included the IT professionals in their personal network and exploited their expertise where suitable (Bolmsten & Dittrich, 2011).

IT professionals also benefited from the expertise of end-user developers in their development work. End-user developers care about usability and are confronted with the problems of unusable software. This expertise came in handy for IT professionals when working with IT infrastructure tasks: end-user developers, for example, helped to recruit the right people for user participation, to prioritize issues, and to distinguish between those of them leading users to reject an application or representing "good to have" features that could wait until the IT professionals had time to attend to them.

4.2.5 Empowered Users

One of the motivations for the research was that users were in charge of the software support for academic and administrative areas: the academic vice president hired IT support personnel instead of administrative assistants to take care of the development under his guidance; administrative personnel very outspokenly rejected the design solutions (Bolmsten, 2016); and end-user developers took charge of the development of software support for their specific professional domains (Bolmsten & Dittrich, 2011).

The analysis of the empirical material (Bolmsten, 2016) shows that EUD is a professional skill that contributes to the service provisioning of the organization. It also became evident that this skill was not always adequately recognized, which could place both the individual end-user developer as well as the professional domains and co-workers that were beneficiaries of the EUD results in a vulnerable position.

The administrative assistant developing the electronic forms described herself as a "spider in the net." For the electronic forms to work she consciously had to target other staff with her development. Over time, she developed her own approach not only to gathering requirements but also to addressing lifecycle management, such as training, further development, and maintenance. She had established relationships with internal staff stakeholders and developed the know-how of whom to ask for certain requirements and how different people could contribute. She also maintained relationships with internal IT professionals and external communities with lead-users and IT professionals that could aid her development. In addition, she continuously had to develop her own technical proficiency by reading manuals and books as well as downloading and testing new applications from the Internet.

In the beginning, the professionalization of the organizational IT management especially obscured such networking-oriented EUD. The administrative assistant, however, did not let that hinder her development efforts. Instead, she described how she approached it with a "bugger that" mentality and carried on with her development regardless. Not only does such lack of recognition of EUD create personal impediments, for example, for career development, but it can also make IT systems that are important for the organization vulnerable. In addition, organizational invisibility can also risk loss of opportunities for infrastructure integrations and collaborations. This was something that was taken into consideration in the improvements' organizational decision-making structures and processes described below.

4.2.6   Organizational Structures and Processes: Participatory IT Management

The findings above triggered the development of an organizational IT management that supported both EUD and collaboration between users and professional IT-developers in more profound development projects. To this end, the changes facilitated by the action research built on the existing IT management at the WMU: the university already had a long-term tradition of committee-based IT management that involved representatives from user-, end-user developer-, IT professional-, and manager-stakeholder groups. However, being faced with increasingly complex infrastructure development, also involving an increasing number of stakeholders, called for improvements. The mandate for change that underpinned the action research was to extend the existing working shop floor IT management practices as EUD in the organizational arena. The action research contributed through structure, process, and procedure improvements to sustaining a participatory IT management for infrastructure development purposes, which can be related to democratic decision-making criteria (Dahl & Shapiro, 2015). As discussed in (Bolmsten, 2016) the proposed approach of participatory IT management consisted of:

(a) A participatory and evolutionary project management approach enabling users and end-user developers to *effectively participate* in infrastructure development spanning the realm of individual EUD domains. The project management approach was based on a combination of the Bødker et al. (2004) PD approach called MUST together with an evolutionary and agile development and implementation approach based on Floyd, Reisin, and Schmidt (1989) and Beck and Andres (2004). The importance of not adding unnecessary bureaucracy was highlighted. The project management had to be flexible in order to cope with projects of different scope. The project management model was developed and appropriated throughout the empirical research: it was first introduced to support two projects that were already ongoing. The first project was about the development of electronic forms, which already had strategic anchoring but used project management to strengthen the definition of project scope, and supported the organization and prioritization of tasks during the course of the project. In the second project, which involved a further development of course administration, the project management framework allowed project members and stakeholders to take a step back and reconsider the strategic alignment of the project. This resulted in an in-depth study of work practices and several technical prototypes that were then used to define practical development tasks that were prioritized in an evolutionary manner, using the agile component of the project management framework.

(b) PD representations that enabled users and end-user developers to acquire a thorough understanding of both work- and technology-related infrastructure design matters. These included extended versions of story cards (Beck & Andres, 2004; Kyng, 1995) that were used to communicate the implications of infrastructure development from a work practice perspective. They were co-constructed between users and IT professionals and continuously updated throughout the development as a living boundary object. In the most comprehensive project documented in the action research, the story cards were co-constructed through the use of a number of PD tools and techniques both to gain an in-depth understanding of important workflows in the current use organization and develop visions and proposals for new IT usage in regard to the registry system. Participatory observations were used to understand and document work domains and workflows, and underpinned an iterative writing process of a story card between users and IT professionals. The story cards were then mapped onto rich-pictures that were used in multi-stakeholder workshops to understand how both technical and organizational infrastructure improvements could be made. The story cards were further used in contact with IT-providers to understand how their applications provided solutions for the organization. The participatory observations and the story cards show how the original in-situ close-knit approach, where development took place in close connection to work realities, was further developed to address more complex socio-technical infrastructure developments.

(c) Processes and associated documentation to connect the local development to IT and infrastructure development. To this end, a practice based on what was referred to as business plans was developed to detail the organizational rationale of the projects. These business plans related the inline analysis of the MUST-based project management approach to the cross-organizational infrastructure development. They contributed toward users exercising control of the complete *agenda* of technical and organizational infrastructure development that affected their individual applications. The business plans were important not only in prioritizing development resources, such as the time of the IT professionals, but also in providing transparency for affected stakeholders between different but linked local applications. A typical example was how a proposed change in one part of an administrative infrastructure to consolidate databases had implications for the local of the contact database that the administrative assistant was working with. The business plans allowed for the identification and negotiation of this dependence on a pre-project and development stage, using the organizational structures and processes described next.

(d) Improved decision-making processes and procedures in the committee-based IT management. These addressed how to prepare, present, decide, and record agenda items, including the above-mentioned business plans to plan and track projects. This was of additional benefit to users, who could influence the agenda of design and development also in regard to infrastructure development. In addition, structural change was undertaken where the IT professionals were formally defined as a resource for committee-based management.

The empirical findings show that EUD and user-centered design need to be supported by a participatory IT management approach to effect the necessary change and innovation in a sustainable manner. The chair of the committee-based management described how the improvements resulted in an organized and constructive approach to planning by focusing on the "subject matter":

> then one has the subject matter, one has a presentation, the one who has prepared the case then has to focus on what is suggested [...] it is important that opinions can be put forward, subject matter arguments, and that it is documented, then that goes a long way [...] if one can come to a clear concrete decision, and if I then don't get a hearing for my view then one kind of has to accept, there has been a forum, I have put forward the arguments, and they were not approved, then one has to accept the vote of the majority.

The citation shows that decision-making in the committee-based management was actually important. Even though it was not common for decision-makers to have to resort to voting, the stakes could be high when negotiating different interests in infrastructure development. The findings provide one example of how such participatory IT management can be instantiated, but there are other possibilities as well. They also show the value of the underlying principles of (1) enabling effective participation in individual projects, (2) enabling users to gain an enlightened understanding of infrastructure design issues, (3) including a broad array of stakeholders that can (4) control the agenda, together with (5) inclusive decision-making practices for other organizations to apply.

4.3   Summary

The studies reveal similarities between the organizations in regard to EUD as a sustained organizational capability for innovation. The pressure for change makes it necessary to consciously include EUD as part of the development of the organizational infrastructure. On the one hand, this requires flexible technologies when designing specific applications and, on an infrastructure level, when connecting different applications; on the other hand, users need to be capable as well as empowered to take on EUD tasks. In order to provide the right flexibility and to take local expertise into account, we observed close collaboration between IT and domain experts in local design constituencies in both cases. The organizational IT management needs to accommodate these design constituencies with processes and structures that make the situated infrastructuring organization accountable and to coordinate EUD and infrastructure evolution.

Table 2 summarizes the analysis and allows for a comparison of how the elements of the model in Fig. 1 become manifest in the two cases.

Table 2 Summary of analysis results

Sustainable EUD factors	Telecom case	UN university case
Need for change and innovation	• Rapidly changing industry due to technology development	• Not subject to standard university regulations
	• Fierce competition, where it is important to rapidly answer to changes in the market by: (1) providing new products and services to the customers; and as an implication (2) developing internal support systems	• Needed to develop policies, structures, and processes
		• Borrows elements from national systems
		• Need for IT solutions supporting these processes
		• Need for integrated solutions
Flexible technologies	• Evolution through three interfaces: deployment, tailoring, and development	• Technical base allowing for:
	• Tailoring interface separates deployment and tailoring and allows for testing	• Custom development by IT professionals
	• Tailoring interface supports unanticipated changes	• Usage of pre-defined modules that can be configured by the end-users themselves
	• Defined points of interaction between tailoring and professional IT development	• End-users exchange information and datasets across local applications on the same infrastructure
Collaboration between IT and domain experts	• End-user developers and IT professionals need to work tightly together	• IT staff support users with custom applications requiring more technical expertise than users can master themselves
	• Understanding of each other's competencies	• Negotiations between different user interests and areas of expertise by PD workshops
	• Overlapping knowledge of professional domain, where, e.g., IT professionals support domain experts with their in-situ tailoring and adaptation	
"Empowered" employees	• Users equal members in the project teams	• Users in charge of the design and development of software support for administrative areas
	• Shared management responsibilities	• End-user developers taking charge of the development of software support for their specific professional domains
	• Developers and users are trusted in a de facto evolutionary agile development model	• User influence by competence and position

(continued)

Table 2 (continued)

Sustainable EUD factors	Telecom case	UN university case
	• Acknowledgment of users' business knowledge	
	• Developers are responsible for operations	
Organizational structures and practices	• Participatory and flexible project model	• Participatory IT management
	• Representation by all affected organizational stakeholders in both project team and steering committee	• Organizational IT management supports both EUD and collaboration between users and professional IT-developers
	• Users and developers in the same building, which stimulates quick and informal communication	• A participatory and evolutionary project management
	• IT unit and users co-located	• PD representations for users and end-user developers to understand both work- and technology-related infrastructure design
	• Coordination of infrastructure across individual applications	• Processes and documentation to relate local development to the strategic level of IT and infrastructure development
		• Decision-making procedures in the committee-based IT management

5   Discussion

This section further discusses how, in the two cases, empowered employees, tight collaboration between domain experts and IT professionals, and flexible technologies contribute to sustainable EUD as infrastructuring. Sect. 5.1 highlights the need for change that has been identified as the driver for the development of the EUD culture in the respective organization and relates the cases to the discussion on user-driven innovation and organizational innovation. Sect. 5.2 further elaborates sustainable EUD in connection to the related work. Sect. 5.3 discusses the organizational structures and processes necessary to support sustainable EUD. Finally, Sect. 5.4 further considers how important sustainable EUD is in enabling the innovative capabilities of the organizations.

5.1   Need for Change and Innovation

The two cases' area of operation is very different: where the telecommunications company needs to provide state-of-the-art technical services, the UN university provides education, research, and capacity-building. Both organizations have, however, experienced a long-term need to be innovative. The telecom company is in a constantly changing market, where the company is forced to invent new services both to retain existing customers and attract new ones. The services need to be unique to gain a market advantage. The UN university also provides services, but in terms of training, education, and capacity-building. The innovatory need stems from the university being in a unique situation that is not comparable with other universities. This implicated a need for unique administrative solutions, where standard systems did not suffice.

Despite the different organizations having different primary trades and different motivations for why innovation is necessary, we can see that their need for unique solutions is a common factor. The telecom company requires unique services to remain competitive, while the UN university needs unique solutions to address their particular situation. In both cases, therefore, unique technical support systems are required.

Both organizations have historically handled the need for change by isolated EUD initiatives. In the telecom company, the need for "extra payments" arose frequently and at short notice. This entailed both a need for EUD support in the individual "payment systems" and a technical infrastructure to support these type of activities. External circumstances push the need for constant updating and renewal of the administrative system. The UN university managed the bespoke systems through an individual initiative. For example, there was a need for a reliable academic management system to manage courses, subjects, grades, and grading, which the registrar developed on his own.

One similarity between the two cases is that the need for change and innovation is initiated by external factors. For the telecom company, this means external factors such as market forces, while the UN university need for change is initiated by the continuously developing demands of education and training from the International Maritime Organization and its member states.

The administrative support systems at both the telecom company and at the UN university must evolve over time. What made the telecom case special at the time was that the EUD features were not introduced to support personalization of tools or the adaptation of generic software to a specific organization but to continuously develop part of the IT infrastructure in order to encourage business innovation on a corporate level. What makes the UN university special is that all the knowledge of how to handle administrative issues was situated with the individual users, and to be able to elucidate the knowledge to form an infrastructure, a special kind of IT management was needed which would lead to the continuous development of the infrastructure.

The need for continuous change and innovation originated from external factors in both cases, but it demanded solutions that took their stance of origin in the situated development of end-user developers. In the telecom case, changes clearly needed to be effected at short notice, and it was the users who knew what kind of changes to the system were required and who was best positioned to perform the changes. In both cases, the need for change and innovation concerned complex socio-technical infrastructures that required the situated expertise of end-user developers to develop them. A comprehensive understanding of both current work practices and the need for change, together with technical know-how, were called for to come up with new solutions. These findings provide concrete evidence in support of the assumptions of user-centered innovation and organizational learning put forward by von Hippel (2005), Björgvinsson et al. (2010), and Orlikowski (2002), as described in the related work. In this way, the need for change is initiated by external factors but the innovative solutions are provided from the bottom up by the staff on the shop floor, which creates end-user developers. This, in turn, allows continuous change and innovation. The following Subsect. 5.2 discusses what was needed to allow both case organizations to rely on EUD as part of the continuing development of the IT infrastructure. Thereafter, the organizational structures underpinning these requirements are discussed.

5.2   Sustainable End-User Development

In both cases, the need for innovation and change was partly realized through established practices of EUD, although this took place in very different contexts. From the outset, faculty and administrators at the UN university took on EUD as part of the development of their work processes and practices, and partly due to the lack of professional IT support, as the IT department was focused on hardware and network provisioning; the EUD at the telecom provider took place in close collaboration with the respective software engineers of the IT unit. As the telecom provider was one of the pioneering companies in Sweden, software and business had to be developed hand in hand. Technical expertise among users and business knowledge among software engineers developed due to close collaboration that was supported by management. As in both cases EUD was not introduced by the researcher but was already an established practice in the organization, the comparison allows us to analyze what is needed for EUD practices to become a sustainable part of the IT development of an organization.

In both cases, users made use of standard applications for their development tasks: for example, spreadsheets provided an important tool for end-user developers in both organizations, which required interfaces to integrate results produced with the help of local tools. At the telecom provider, an interface for "extra payments" for which the necessary data were compiled "by hand" was implemented; at the UN university, the course management module supported the import of schedule and room allocation from spreadsheets. In both cases, the custom-developed software provided possibilities for end-user developers and/or IT professionals to configure and customize the individual applications. In both cases, the need for flexible integration between applications became visible. The telecom provider already had an, at that time advanced, data warehouse that allowed the sharing of data across different applications before the research cooperation was implemented. The second part of the cooperation explicitly addressed the development of customizable data exchange. From the very beginning, the research together with the UN university addressed the development of an infrastructure that was flexible enough to enable access to heterogeneous data sources to support specific, local practices. However, in both cases the deployment of flexible technology was clearly not enough to support sustainable EUD.

We observed a high level of IT expertise among the group of domain experts who undertook the EUD for the respective organizations. In the context of the telecom provider, domain experts had acquired substantial technical knowledge that enabled them to work independently with database queries and the aggregation of results in elaborated spreadsheets (Dittrich & Lindeberg, 2004). Similarly, at the UN university, especially those domain experts who took on the development supporting the whole organization and not only their individual tasks continuously had to acquire the necessary technical skills (Bolmsten & Dittrich, 2011). On their own initiative, they engaged in Internet communities to get answers to issues they were facing, read books and manuals, and participated in training courses. Whereas the IT skills and EUD by domain experts at the telecommunication provider were regarded as important and necessary to support the evolving business and to provide input into the development, however, the situation of end-user developers at the UN university depended from the outset on the organizational position of the EUD. Though EUD was wide spread in the organization, and the competence of domain experts and end-user developers was widely acknowledged, different end-user developers developed different strategies to sustain their practices.

One of the most prominent observations at the telecom provider was the close cooperation between end-user developers and IT professionals. The cooperation was based on long-term development between software engineers and domain experts. Often, the same domain experts and software engineers were involved in consecutive development projects addressing the same business domain. Between the projects, the software engineers were responsible for operations, fixed bugs, and implementing smaller changes to the software they had developed. They supported the end-user developers with their knowledge of the surrounding systems and their quality control expertise. As we mentioned above, users and developers openly discussed the need to cooperate when evaluating the prototype for flexible integration of heterogeneous databases. From the IT unit, this was an explicit strategy: one of the managers in the project emphasized that whereas technical expertise could be acquired through the use of consultancy hours, the business knowledge and the understanding of what was needed in terms of IT support was a strategic business asset. In the analysis of the end-user developers' strategies at the UN university, a lack of collaboration between end-user developers and IT professionals was shown to be problematic, both for the individual EUD and also for the organization. Collaboration with IT professionals was necessary to support a controlled and accountable integration in the IT infrastructure. In both cases, the interlacing of EUD and evolution of both individual applications and the infrastructure became visible as a matter requiring both cooperation and organizational support.

Though other studies as well as theoretical work corroborate the findings above, the comparison between the two cases allowed us to address them in a more systematic manner and gain an in-depth understanding of the technical and organizational infrastructure that is needed to support EUD. Many case studies show and discuss the IT expertise of the end-user developers, indicating that non-IT professionals can indeed competently develop software if given the right tools. Only few studies discuss the organizational support for end-user developers. Nardi (1993), for example, compares different cases of EUD of Computer Aided Design software and proposes acknowledging the contribution of the end-user developers in the organization and supporting their role through formal structures. Trigg and Bødker (1994) report that, in their case, the organization needed to re-evaluate which configuration tasks could be left to end-user developers and which needed to be discussed and decided on at an organizational level. Kanstrup (2005) discussed the role of local designers as brokers between users and IT professionals. However, our analysis shows that skills and organizational empowerment but also collaboration with the software engineers are necessary to include EUD as part of the infrastructure maintenance and evolution. Our observations regarding the cooperation between IT professionals and end-user developers support Fischer's (1998) approach to meta-design and the conceptualisation of software developments in terms of seeding, evolutionary growth, and reseeding. However, our analysis also shows that this is not the only interaction needed to support organizationally sustainable EUD. Collaboration between IT professionals and end-user developers continues between projects and only intensifies when an application is redeveloped to take care of the evolution pressure that cannot be handled by EUD alone. Similarly to Star and Ruhleder's (1994, 1996) discussion of the use of information infrastructures to target organizational transformation, our analysis extends the understanding of salient infrastructural dimensions, what triggers their development, and their relations in supporting EUD. As shown, empowering employees, collaborating with IT professionals, and flexible technologies are integral infrastructure dimensions that are necessary to sustain EUD in the organization.

Our systematic analysis further points to the need for organizational structures and processes that provide a foundation and frame for both EUD and the collaboration between IT professionals when together developing the IT infrastructure for an organization. The next Subsect. 5.3 analyzes and discusses our respective findings.

5.3   Organizational Structures and Processes

Above, we have argued that sustainable EUD underpinned the evolution of both IT and work practices to meet the requirements for change that the case organizations faced. This requires not only flexible technologies supporting the adaptability of both the individual applications and their connection but also end-user developers who are empowered with IT skills and a mandate from the organization, as well as a close collaboration between IT professionals and domain experts. To mandate the former and establish the latter, IT management strategies and processes need to be adequately designed. In this respect, the two cases differ substantially: whereas the telecom provider had established IT management structures, the research at the UN university explicitly addressed this aspect. Here, we structure the discussion on the IT management based on the elements we identified and established at the UN university and compare it with the respective elements of the IT management at the telecom provider. In the latter case, we have analyzed the IT project model and its implementation in one of the projects in detail in the article "How Use-Oriented Development can take place" (Dittrich & Lindeberg, 2004). Much of the discussion below is based on this material and analysis. The difficulty is that, at the time of the research, we only focused on the project level and did not address the organizational level. This aspect is therefore rather underdeveloped in the following discussion of the telecom case. The comparison shows that what we deemed necessary together with the UN university was actually in place, though in a different form, at the telecom provider.

In order to take into account the requirements and needs of both the users and the end-user developers, the individual project needs to be organized in a participatory manner. To this end, the IT steering group at the UN university decided on a participatory project management approach, adapting the MUST approach by Bødker et al. (2004). The PD covered by the MUST approach was complemented with an XP-oriented agile development interlacing with the PD activities. In addition, a process and documentation approach referred to as business cases detailed the relation of the individual project to the organizational IT strategy and planning. Though not using the word PD explicitly, the projects at the telecom provider implemented a participatory process. Users and developers were equal project members: after developing an implementation proposal together, which also detailed the implications for other applications in the infrastructure, the development process was an iterative one (today one would call it agile), where annotated "implementation sketches" containing both a UI draft and technical specifications served as the main boundary object (Star & Griesemer, 1989) between users and developers. In the project that was the subject of the study, project management was shared between a software engineer from the IT unit and a project manager from the business side.

To empower the project to take decisions based on the PD process on the one hand, and make sure that the dynamics in the project do not lead the project beyond what has been decided at the organizational level on the other, the connection between the project and the organizational IT management level needs to be explicitly taken care of. At the UN university, this was achieved by the PD project management approach and the "business case" document, which was decided by the IT steering committee. At the telecom provider, the implementation proposal developed in a pre-study served a similar purpose.

In order to support joint decisions by representatives of the local design constituencies and the IT professionals on infrastructure matters, the IT steering committee needed to be supported by tools and techniques to discuss the impact of individual projects as well as cross-cutting infrastructure development decisions. In order to achieve a common understanding, we used an approach of storytelling initially called "reflection papers" that was inspired by user stories (Beck & Andres, 2004; Kyng, 1995). These were co-constructed between users and IT professionals and described the technical implications routed in day-to-day use as well as EUD practices. In the telecom provider case, the implementation proposal served the same issue. Before the company-wide project committee decided on a project, a pre-study was implemented resulting in a requirements' specification, an implementation proposal, a specification of the implementation project model, and a budget. The implementation proposal also detailed the effect on other systems of the infrastructure. As in the specific case, the pre-study was not only reported to the project committee but presented in a meeting to which all affected units and groups were invited.

In order to take in the interests of the users and end-user developers in the management of the organization, the decision-making structures and processes need to be anchored with the different parts of the organization affected by the decisions. To this end, the UN university established an IT steering committee consisting of representatives of users, IT professionals, and managers, which was mandated to take decisions on IT projects. Decisions were deliberated based on the above-mentioned PD project management, representations, and the business cases for the individual projects. The agenda of the committee meetings and supportive material was published well in advance. Discussions and decisions were documented. This rendered the IT management procedures at the UN university open and accountable to the whole organization. Anyone affected by a decision had the chance to partake in the discussion either in person or through a designated representative on the committee. By comparison, the organizational IT management at the telecom provider was more comprehensive: the cross-organizational project committee did not only hold responsibility for IT-related projects; the company had a strict process organization. Any changes to existing processes were organized as projects, and all such projects were decided by the project committee.

In the book chapter "Organizational IT managed from the shop floor – Developing Participatory Design on the organizational arena," with reference to the UN university case, Bolmsten (2016) argue that in order to support an organization heavily relying on empowered domain experts to reach its objective, the IT management needs to take a participatory approach as well, and show how it is possible to leverage PD in the organizational arena. They also demonstrate that it is possible to provide organizational structures that support a bottom-up IT management in which EUD is an integrated part of organizational IT development, challenging the current standard of IT management as a top-down structure design approach (Bernard, 2005). The discussion above indicates that also in organizations that need to have an IT management of a different size and scope due to their technical infrastructure, as in the case of the telecom provider, IT management structures can be found that support bottom-up as well as top-down decision-making. We also showed that the integration of EUD and professional software development benefits from such participatory structures: these structures allow us to take into account local developments to support evolving business and work practices, making local EUD organizationally accountable. In this way, they support shop floor IT management practices (Dittrich et al., 2002; Eriksén, 1998) and can provide an organizational frame for infrastructuring, as discussed by Karasti (2014; Karasti & Syrjänen, 2004) and Pipek and Wulf (2009). The next section will take this argument one step further by contending that such structures and the sustainable EUD practices they support substantially contribute to the innovative capability of an organization.

5.4 Innovation Capabilities

In the analysis above, we can see that EUD is an important ingredient of the innovative capability of the two case organizations. In the related work section, we defined innovation capability according to Lawson and Samson (2001) as the "ability to continuously transform knowledge and ideas into new products, processes, and systems for the benefit of the firm and its stakeholders." In both cases of EUD presented here, EUD was part of the organizational practices and structures that enabled the development and evolution of IT systems to support the innovation of new services that the organization provided. As previously discussed, both the telecom provider and the UN university faced continuously high pressure to innovate. The fact that the systems were in both cases sustained over an extended period of time with a continuous dependence on improvements and extensions by end-user developers further adds to the recognition of end-user development as an innovative capability.

Not only do the cases demonstrate that, as an innovatory capability, EUD answers to organizational needs for change, but they additionally indicate which infrastructural technical and organizational structures and processes are necessary for EUD innovations to become a sustained ingredient of the innovation capabilities of an organization. When EUD expands from individual appropriation and customizations to becoming part of the cooperative development of the organization's IT infrastructure, EUD alone is not enough. End-users need a supporting technical and organizational infrastructure to innovate. At the same time, this is a reciprocal dependence, where the resulting EUD innovations are put into use as part of the very same infrastructure. The dimensions discussed in the previous two sections, in this way, constitute a socio-technical infrastructure and together underpin the organization's capability to innovate. This forms the main contribution of this chapter. An overview of these infrastructural dimensions and their relations is presented in Fig. 2 and summarized in the following claim: end-users need to be empowered through a flexible technical base, their development needs to receive professional recognition in the organization, and the collaboration between EUD and other IT professionals needs to be supported. As is further shown, these infrastructural dimensions are not statically provided; rather, end-users need to participate in decision-making structures and processes to develop them.

Especially, the organizational IT management processes were necessary to sustain EUD and the innovation capabilities through it. The UN university case

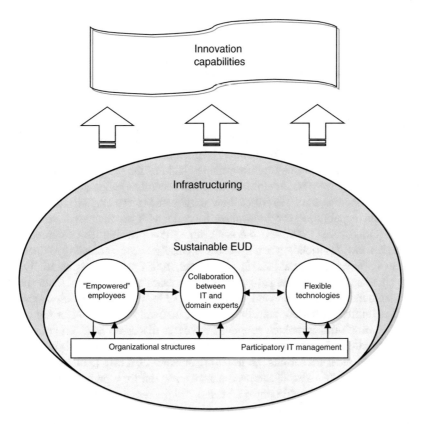

Fig. 2 Overview of infrastructural dimensions

showed that these structures needed to be maintained and unfolded together with renewal and evolution of the technical infrastructure, the corresponding changes for the EUD, and the professional development processes. The evolution of the organizational structures, the EUD processes, and the technical infrastructure development can be denoted by the term "infrastructuring," representing the continual maintenance and evolution of the organization's socio-technical infrastructure (Karasti, 2014; Karasti & Syrjänen, 2004). Especially, in the case of the long-term action research at the UN university, it was possible to follow how the process of sustaining EUD as an innovation capability unfolded over time. The needs of the administrative assistant developing the address database to collaborate with IT professionals, for example, developed over time when the address database gradually benefited from interfacing with other systems on a shared technical platform. Another example is how possible synergies arising from the integration of the Learning Management System and the registry system at the UN university prompted a new and more advanced technical base and the advancement of coordination both on a project and organizational level between end-user developers, users, IT professionals, and other stakeholders that were associated with the respective developments. At the UN university, the challenge of sustaining an innovatory EUD capability can be recognized as maintaining a local accountability of development in an expanding process of technical and organizational infrastructuring. However, the telecommunication provider case also shows that EUD of the back-end systems and the connected IT infrastructure were backed up by continuous professional development and a close collaboration between the end-user developers and the software engineers of the IT unit. Also here, the organizational IT management structures underpinned the EUD practices as well as the close collaboration between end-user developers and the IT unit. Nevertheless, the resulting professional IT practices were contested as they did not adhere to the then prevalent control-oriented state of the art in software engineering; indeed, they were much closer to the more recently evolving agile paradigm.

Previous studies have described how organizations are challenged to develop and sustain capabilities for innovation to cope with an increased pressure for change (Orlikowski, 2002). At the same time, new possibilities of democratized innovation are described, whereby users themselves can innovate products and services (Björgvinsson et al., 2010; von Hippel, 2005), which can potentially meet those challenges. The combined analysis of the cases adds empirical evidence that such democratization of innovation is also possible within organizations and that this, if carefully supported, contributes to the innovation capability of the organization. Through the combined results of the cases discussed here, it is possible to concretize how a democratized innovation capability can be realized to cope with the increased pressure for change in an organization. Ciborra (Andreu & Ciborra, 1996; Ciborra, 2000) also discusses the principal need for a process that combines bottom-up innovation and learning to make both incremental and radical improvements that range from improvements of routines to strategic capabilities. The results here show how end-user development can be positioned to meet such need for innovation and learning. The occurrence and possibilities of end-user development have been discussed before in connection to a wide range of cooperative tailoring scenarios (Pipek & Kahler, 2006). The results here connect end-user development with shared infrastructure development as a strategic capability for innovation. In addition, it has been shown how the bottom-up process of innovation and learning can be depicted as "infrastructuring" (Karasti, 2014; Karasti & Syrjänen, 2004). Where this is based on end-user development, it is a central ingredient of the innovation capability in organizations that are dependent on an IT infrastructure. The several dimensions of "infrastructuring" that are presented can, in this respect, be related to Pipek and Wulf's (2009) layers of infrastructural technology development. This ranges from how innovations are triggered by end-users – either through breakdowns or other needs for local innovation – to how end-users work together with IT professionals and other users in method-driven design activities, to the need to improve technical platforms and organizational decision structures and processes. Moreover, Sects 5.2 and 5.3 have detailed what is required with respect to technology, competences, and cooperation, and how the organizational structures need to support infrastructuring through adequate project models, collaboration tools, and decision-making procedures.

6   Conclusion

In this chapter, we have provided a comparative analysis of two cases of EUD in the context of organizations that depend on an IT infrastructure to provide their services. In both cases, EUD was not only used to personalize IT support but to maintain and evolve the organizations' IT infrastructure. EUD was in both cases a constituting part of the innovation capability of the organizations.

Based on our two cases, we indicate what is required in terms of organizational IT management to support the inclusion of EUD activities as part of IT infrastructure development in the organization and support both lasting quality in use for the domain experts and the competitive advantage of the business. Besides a flexible technical base, the EUD practices were dependent on the skills and competences of the end-user developers as well as a fruitful cooperation between end-user developers and professional software engineers.

EUD as part of organizational IT management can be expected to become more and more relevant. The need for development and evolution of organization-specific software and IT solutions continues to grow, and has already outgrown the capacity of the software developers we educate. Even if we are able to educate more software engineers, we will not be able to keep up with the growing needs of organizations. The only solution to this situation is to open up participation to end-users in the development and maintenance of their work infrastructure. At the same time, more and more software provides generic functionality and invites users to configure and combine these building blocks. Examples here are learning environments and case handling systems.

The comparison of the IT management structures and processes of the two case organizations allowed us to abstract some cornerstones for an accountable organizational frame for EUD practices as innovation capability: PD on a project level was important to communicate local needs for change and diversity; IT development projects needed to be well-connected to the embedding infrastructure so that the impacted professional and EUD practices were not disrupted; the infrastructural implications of local development were in both cases part of the deliberation process preceding decisions on IT projects; and last but not least, the organizational decision-making about the IT infrastructure supported bottom-up as well as top-down initiatives.

This points us toward a number of future research trajectories: most prominently, the mutual dependency between IT management, organizational innovation capacity, and EUD is here only touched upon, yet the comparison of the two cases provides some indication of what is needed from an IT management to support both IT-based innovation and EUD. However, additional focused case studies would allow for the development of the observed regularities into recommendations and methods. From a technical and conceptual point of view, the integration of EUD with respect to individual applications and across applications and work practices has so far not been addressed. As in the case of early EUD, industrial solutions supporting and integrating both exist but are not systematized.

It could be that the concept of meta-design needs to be complemented. Last, but not least, in both cases, the representation of infrastructures in order to visualize dependencies and deliberate new developments was an area in need of more development. At the UN university we experimented with extended user story-inspired descriptions; at the telecom company, involvement of relevant organizational stakeholders in the deliberation provided the relevant information. Here, we see the need for further research to support EUD with the means for participatory infrastructuring.

References

Andreu, R., & Ciborra, C. (1996). Core capabilities and information technology: an organizational learning approach. In B. Moingeo, A. Edmondson (Eds.). *Organizational learning and competetive advantage* (pp. 139–163). London: Sage.

Beck, K., & Andres, C. (2004). *Extreme programming explained: embrace change*. Boston MA, USA: Addison-Wesley Professional.

Bernard, S. A. (2005). *An introduction to enterprise architecture*. USA: Authorhouse.

Björgvinsson, E., Ehn, P., Hillgren, P.-A. (2010). Participatory design and "democratizing innovation". *Presented at the PDC '10: proceedings of the 11th biennial participatory design conference* (pp. 41–50). New York: ACM.

Bødker, K., Kensing, F., Simonsen, J. (2004). *Participatory IT design: designing for business and workplace realities*. London: MIT Press.

Bolmsten, J. (2016). *Sustaining participatory design in the organization-infrastructuring with participatory design*. PhD Thesis. Denmark: IT University of Copenhagen.

Bolmsten, J., & Dittrich, Y. (2011). Infrastructuring when you don't–end-user development and organizational infrastructure. In *End-user development* (pp. 139–154). Berlin Heidelberg: Springer.

Britten, N., Campbell, R., Pope, C., Donovan, J., Morgan, M., Pill, R. (2002). Using meta ethnography to synthesise qualitative research: a worked example. *Journal of Health Services Research & Policy*, 7(4), 209–215.

Cabitza, F., & Simone, C. (2017). Malleability in the hands of end users. In F. Paternò & V. Wulf (Eds.). *New perspectives in end-user development* (pp. 137–164). Cham: Springer.

Ciborra, C. (2000). *From control to drift: the dynamics of corporate information infastructures*. USA: Oxford University Press.

Costabile, M. F., Dittrich, Y., Fischer, G., Piccinno, A. (2011). End-user development - third international symposium, IS-EUD 2011, Torre Canne, Italy, June 7–10, 2011, Proceedings. Berlin and Heidelberg: Springer-Verlag.

Dahl, R. A., & Shapiro, I. (2015). *On Democracy: Second Edition*. New Haven, Connecticut, United States: Yale University Press.

Dittrich, Y., Eriksén, S., Hansson, C. (2002). PD in the Wild; Evolving practices of Design in Use. In: Binder, T., Gregory, J., Wagner, I. Proceedings of the Participatory Design Conference 2002, Malmö, Sweden. Computer Professionals for Social Responsibility, Palo Alto, California, United States, pp. 124–134.

Dittrich, Y., & Lindeberg, O. (2001). Can software development be too use oriented? Going native as an issue in participatory design. In *IRIS 24, information systems research seminar in Scandinavia*. Department of Information Systems, University of Bergen, Norway.

Dittrich, Y., & Lindeberg, O. (2002). Designing for changing work and business practices. In N. Patel (Ed.). *Evolutionary and adaptive information systems*. 1st edition (pp. 152–171). USA: IDEA Group Publishing.

Dittrich, Y., & Lindeberg, O. (2003). Designing for changing work and business practices. *Adaptive Evolutionary Information Systems* (pp. 152–171). Hershey, PA: Idea group Inc.

Dittrich, Y., & Lindeberg, O. (2004). How use–oriented development can take place. *Information and Software Technology, 46*(9), 603–617.

Dittrich, Y., Lindeberg, O., Ludvigsson, I., Lundberg, L., Wessman, B., Diestelkamp, W., et al. (2001). *Design for change.* Research Report, Blekinge Institute of Technology, Sweden, ISSN: 1103–1581.

Dittrich, Y., Lundberg, L., Lindeberg, O. (2006). End-user development as adaptive maintenance. In H. Lieberman, F. Paternò, V. Wulf (Eds.). *End user development.* 1st edition (pp. 295–313). Netherlands: Springer Verlag.

Dittrich, Y., Rönkkö, K., Eriksson, J., Hansson, C., Lindeberg, O. (2008). Cooperative method development. *Empirical Software Engineering, 13*(3), 231–260.

Eriksén, S. (1998). *Knowing and the art of IT management: an inquiry into work practices in one-stop shops.* PhD Thesis. Lund, Sweden: Lund University.

Eriksson, J. (2007). Support of Cooperative Design of End-user Tailorable Software, the 2nd IFIP Central and East European Conference on Software Engineering Techniques CEE-SET 2007.

Eriksson, J. (2008). *Supporting the cooperative design process of end-user tailoring* (Doctoral dissertation series, Blekinge Institute of Technology), 1653–2090; 2008:03.

Eriksson, J., & Dittrich, Y (2007). Combining tailoring and evolutionary software development for rapidly changing business systems - what is required to make it work? *Journal of Organizational and End-User Computing, 19*(2), 47ff.

Fischer, G. (1998). Seeding, evolutionary growth and reseeding: constructing, capturing and evolving knowledge in domain-oriented design environments. *Automated Software Engineering, 5*(4), 447–464.

Fischer, G. (2010). End user development and meta-design: foundations for cultures of participation. *Journal of Organizational and End User Computing (JOEUC), 22*(1), 52–82.

Floyd, C., Reisin, F., Schmidt, G. (1989). STEPS to software development with users (vol. 89, pp. 48–64). *Presented at the ESEC'89.*

Henderson, A., & Kyng, M. (1992). There's no place like home: continuing design in use. In J. Greenbaum & M. Kyng (Eds.), *Design at work: cooperative design of computer systems* (pp. 219–240). New Jersey, United States: L. Erlbaum Associates Inc.

Hevner, A. R., March, S. T., Park, J., et al. (2004). Design science in Information Systems research. *MIS Quarterly, 28*(1), 75–105.

von Hippel, E. (2005). *Democratizing innovation, edn.* Cambridge, MA: The MIT Press.

Kanstrup, A. (2005). Local design: an inquiry into workpractices of local it-supporters. *Department of Communications.* Denmark: Aalborg University.

Karasti, H. (2014). Infrastructuring in participatory design. In *Presented at the the 13th participatory design conference* (vol. 1, pp. 141–150). New York, NY: ACM Press.

Karasti, H., & Syrjänen, A.-L. (2004). Artful infrastructuring in two cases of community PD. In *Presented at the Proceedings of the eighth conference on Participatory design: artful integration: interweaving media, materials and practices* (vol. 1, pp. 22–30). ACM.

Ko, A. J., Abraham, R., Beckwith, L., Blackwell, A., Burnett, M., Erwig, M., et al. (2011). The state of the art in end-user software engineering. *ACM Computing Surveys (CSUR), 43*(3), 21.

Kyng, M. (1995). Making representations work. *Communications of the ACM, 38*(9), 46–55.

Lawson, B., & Samson, D. (2001). Developing innovation capability in organisations. *International Journal of Innovation Management, 05*(03), 377–400.

Lieberman, H., Paternò, F., Klann, M., Wulf, V. (2006). *End-user development: an emerging paradigm* (pp. 1–8). Netherlands: Springer.

Ludwig, T., Dax, J., Pipek, V., & Wulf, V. (2017). A practice-oriented paradigm of end-user development. In F. Paternò & V. Wulf (Eds.). *New perspectives in end-user development* (pp. 23–42). Cham: Springer.

Manville, B., & Ober, J. (2003). *A company of citizens: What the world's first democracy teaches leaders about creating great organizations.* Cambridge, MA, USA: Harvard Business Press.

March, S. T., & Smith, G. F. (1995). Design and natural science research on information technology. *Decision support systems*, *15*(4), 251–266.

Nardi, B. A. (1993). *A small matter of programming: perspectives on end user computing* (vol. xvi). Cambridge: MIT Press.

Nunamaker, J., Chen, M., Purdin, T. (1991). System development in Information Systems research. *Journal of Management Information Systems*, *7*(3), pp. 89–106.

Ober, J. (2008). *Democracy and knowledge: Innovation and learning in classical Athens*. New Jersey, United States: Princeton University Press.

Orlikowski, W. J. (2002). Knowing in practice: Enacting a collective capability in distributed organizing. *Organization science*, *13*(3), 249–273.

Peffers, K., Tuunanen, T., Rothenberger, M. A., Chatterjee, S. (2007). A design science research methodolgy for information system research. *Journal of Management Information Systems*, *24*(3), pp. 45–77.

Pipek, V., & Kahler, H. (2006). Supporting collaborative tailoring. In *End user development* (vol. 9, pp. 315–345). Dordrecht: Springer. Netherlands.

Pipek, V., & Wulf, V. (2009). Infrastructuring: towards an integrated perspective on the design and use of Information technology. *Journal of the Association for Information Systems*, *10*(5), 447–473.

Ponterotto, J. G. (2006). Brief note on the origins, evolution, and meaning of the qualitative research concept Thick Description. *The Qualitative Report*, *11*(3), 538–549.

Rohde, M., Brödner, P., Stevens, G., Betz, M., Wulf, V. (2016). Grounded design–A praxeological IS research perspective. *Journal of Information Technology*. doi:10.1057/jit.2016.5.

Rohde, M., & Wulf, V. (2017). Integrated Organization and Technology Development (OTD): a critical evaluation. In Wulf, V., Pipek, V., Randall, D., Rohde, M., Schmidt, K., Stevens, G. (Eds.), *Socio informatics – a practice-based perspective on the design and use of IT artefacts*. Oxford: Oxford University Press.

Star, S. L., & Ruhleder, K. (1994, October). Steps towards an ecology of infrastructure: complex problems in design and access for large-scale collaborative systems. *Proceedings of the 1994 ACM conference on Computer supported cooperative work* (pp. 253–264). New York, NY, USA: ACM.

Star, S., & Ruhleder, K. (1996). Steps toward an ecology of infrastructure: design and access for large information spaces. *Information Systems Research*, *7*(1), 111–134.

Star, S. L., & Bowker, G. C. (2002). How to infrastructure. In *Handbook of new media: social shaping and social consequences of ICTs* (pp. 230–245). London: Sage Publications Ltd.

Star, S. L., & Griesemer, J. R. (1989). Institutional ecology, translations' and boundary objects: amateurs and professionals in Berkeley's Museum of Vertebrate Zoology, 1907–39. *Social Studies of Science*, *19*(3), 387–420.

Suchman, L. A. (1987). *Plans and situated actions: the problem of human-machine communication* (Learning in Doing: Social, Cognitive and Computational Perspectives). New York: Cambridge University Press.

Suchman, L. A. (2007). *Human-machine reconfigurations: plans and situated actions*. Cambridge, United Kingdom: Cambridge University Press.

Tetteroo, D., & Markopoulos, P. (2017). EUD survival "in the wild": evaluation challenges for field deployments and how to address them. In F. Paternò & V. Wulf (Eds.). *New perspectives in end-user development* (pp. 207–230). Cham: Springer.

Trigg, R. H., & Bødker, S. (1994, October). From implementation to design: tailoring and the emergence of systematization in CSCW. In *Proceedings of the 1994 ACM conference on Computer supported cooperative work* (pp. 45–54). New York, NY, USA: ACM.

Wulf, V. (1999). "Let's see your search-tool!"—collaborative use of tailored artifacts in groupware. *Proceedings of the international ACM SIGGROUP conference on Supporting group work* (pp. 50–59). New York, NY, USA: ACM.

Yin, R. K. (2013). *Case study research: design and methods*. Thousand Oaks, CA, USA: Sage publications.

EUD Survival "in the Wild": Evaluation Challenges for Field Deployments and How to Address Them

Daniel Tetteroo and Panos Markopoulos

Abstract This chapter discusses methodological choices facing researchers wishing to evaluate end user development technologies. While laboratory evaluations or short term evaluations are often conducted as a way to validate an end user development technology, these do not provide sufficient guarantees regarding the adoption of end user development practices and how systems should be improved to encourage such practices. The challenges pertaining to field deployments are discussed first at an operational level and second at a teleological level where we debate what should be success criteria for such studies. Discussing previous studies and our experiences from a deployment case in the healthcare sector, we propose guidelines for the evaluation of EUD technologies.

Keywords Evaluation of EUD technologies · EUD deployment success · surveys · methodological choices

1 Introduction

A recent literature survey on research methods and purposes characterizing research studies in the field of end user development (Tetteroo & Markopoulos, 2015) has shown that field evaluations of EUD systems are relatively uncommon. Mostly, these systems are evaluated in a lab setting, an approach which while useful and sometimes a necessary prerequisite to field testing, disregards the impact of the context of actual use in which such systems would be deployed in practice. Although it is worrying that there have been only a few attempts to deploy an EUD system in the field, it is also quite understandable. After all, arranging a field deployment is usually much harder and costly than arranging a lab study. Further,

D. Tetteroo (✉) · P. Markopoulos
Eindhoven University of Technology, Eindhoven, Netherlands
e-mail: d.tetteroo@tue.nl

P. Markopoulos
e-mail: p.markopoulos@tue.nl

© Springer International Publishing AG 2017
F. Paternò, V. Wulf (eds.), *New Perspectives in End-User Development*,
DOI 10.1007/978-3-319-60291-2_9

and this is the major point throughout this chapter, evaluating the impact of an EUD deployment is far from trivial: What exactly needs to be evaluated, in order to conclude anything about the success of an EUD deployment? Which measures should be taken and which outcomes are to be expected?

This chapter discusses these methodological questions, starting with a discussion on what actually constitutes "success" in the case of EUD deployments. Then we reflect on our own deployment studies of an end-user adaptable technology for physical rehabilitation. We present a structured literature survey on previous attempts of EUD deployments, analyzing the evaluations performed and the success measures considered in those studies. Finally, we propose some guidelines for the evaluation of EUD field deployments.

2 Related Work

A recent literature survey (Tetteroo & Markopoulos, 2015) that classified research methods used in the field of End User Development (EUD), pointed out that a significant part of the work that is performed in the field of EUD (42%, of the works covered in that survey) includes an evaluation of EUD systems or parts thereof. Of course, not all of user evaluations are equal in nature; published studies apply quite diverse methods (e.g., case study, lab study) and measures. Choosing amongst these methods reflects the particular aims of the research, e.g., whether it aims to assess the usability of a system or the impact of a particular technology in the workplace, or perhaps how successful is a particular theoretical framework in guiding design, etc.

While formative evaluations are a common and, arguably, a necessary element of the design most interactive systems and therefore also EUD technologies, research articles in this field that introduce EUD technologies report summative evaluations as a means to demonstrate the success of the design effort; examples of such works are (Namoun, Wajid, Mehandjiev, & Owrak, 2012; Wong & Hong, 2007). Most often such evaluations are conducted in a laboratory setting, where test participants use the system tested on artificial tasks selected for the evaluation rather than the actual work or activities spontaneously stemming from their own interests and real life needs. Also, testing often takes place in controlled conditions rather than in the context of actual work or daily life. In these cases, success measures are often related to the usability of the tool and the efficiency with which users can complete tool-related tasks. Beyond the efficiency of the tool itself some researchers focus on the impact of specific methods, practices or functionality on the behavior of their users, e.g., (Ruthruff, Prabhakararao, & Reichwein, 2005; Tsandilas, Letondal, & Mackay, 2009). However, it is not often that research papers examine what happens if experimental EUD systems are deployed in a context of actual use. Interestingly it appears that they are also not very explicit about how they define what should be considered a successful EUD field deployment. This chapter, therefore, explores further the question of successful EUD deployments, and aims to establish a common understanding hereof amongst the members of the EUD research community.

3   Defining "Success" in Field Deployments of End User Development Technology

With regards to information technology there exists a fairly established view on how success can be defined referring to actual use and adoption of novel technologies and perhaps factors that predict it, see for example (Venkatesh, Morris, Davis, & Davis, 2003). Here we argue that transposing such concepts and criteria to EUD is not straightforward and researchers seem to hold different assumptions regarding success for EUD in the field.

3.1   What Makes EUD Special?

One could state that the deployment of an EUD system is nothing more than a specific case of software deployment in general, which brings together concerns regarding the technology, its users, and the context of deployment. For example, a successful deployment might require the technology to be functional and match the needs of its users and require it to fit the organization's goals.

However, it is important to note that from a technological perspective EUD is often an "extra" layer, an add-on to a technology that already provides some value to its users (see the Chap. 2). After all, if the essence and main purpose of a technology would be to allow for the modification, extension and creation of software artifacts, this technology would in fact be a "regular" software development environment[1]. Similarly, from a socio-technical perspective, EUD is an additional activity that users may perform, aiding them in achieving a grander core task. After all, if development would be a person's primary activity, the person would be a developer rather than a user of that technology.

In other words, the EUD component of a technology is per definition auxiliary to that host technology. This does not imply that the EUD functionality needs to be deployed separate from the host technology itself. In fact, it often forms an integral part of it, such as in the case of macro editors in office software, or level editors in games. Nevertheless, the core tasks that end users perform with these base technologies will not be EUD related.

Assuming this view on EUD, one can state that the adoption of EUD practices transcends regular use of the host technology. Where technology *use* implies the application of that technology for a core task, *EUD* requires end users to deviate from that task to engage in an activity that will presumably, eventually benefit the core task. As such, it creates additional challenges over and above those that come with the deployment of "traditional software." As with most definitions

---

[1]The discussion here steers clear from programming environments that address novice programmers with general purpose programming languages and development environments for which success criteria are very different and more similar to information systems in general.

that imply an inclusion/exclusion criterion we expect that there will be cases that do not neatly follow this rule; however, for a large majority of cases referring to the long tail of software engineering, this definition appears like a useful departure point.

In light of this view, two important questions arise when it comes to evaluating EUD deployments:

1. Does it make sense to separate the evaluation of the *EUD-part* of a socio-technical system from the *use-part*?
2. In what way could one separately evaluate the impact of EUD?

These questions are discussed later in this chapter.

3.2   How to Define "Success" of EUD?

Often, from the perspective of the EUD researcher, "success" equals the adoption of EUD practices. The rationale adopted here is often very direct: *people are using my (EUD) tool, so it must be good*. However, such adoption is usually put forward as a means towards a higher order goal, such as increased efficiency in completing repetitive tasks through the creation of macros, or the personalization of technology, etc. Given that there can be alternative ways to achieve such higher-level goals, not necessarily involving any EUD, usage as such does not equate to success. Moreover, there might even be cases in which the adoption of EUD practices indicates failure, e.g., a system is so poorly designed that end users are forced to "fix" it through EUD. In short, simply showing that EUD is actually taking place does not represent a sufficient evaluation goal.

Consider the example of a primary school teacher who aims to increase her pupils' motivation during a math class. During the class, pupils learn arithmetic by interacting with a virtual character on their tablet computers. One way to increase their motivation is by tailoring the math exercises to the personal interests of each specific student, e.g., sports, animals, cars. In this scenario, EUD deployment would be successful if the teacher would adopt EUD practices in order to create personalized training content for her pupils, eventually increasing their motivation and performance at school. It is these latter end-goals that represent success rather than engaging in EUD as such.

Although the above scenario relates to a typical EUD case (tailorability and personalization), there are other cases in which a continuous occurrence of EUD practices are in fact a sign of failure. An example class of such scenarios is the "IKEA case": the business model of this furniture supplier requires customers to assemble their own furniture. While some customers might actually enjoy the process of assembling their newly bought furniture, most customers would probably prefer pre-assembled furniture instead and only choose to construct their furniture to save costs and facilitate transport from the shop. In a similar manner, if development tasks are "offloaded" to end users that could have been handled as well (or even better) by technology providers, one can hardly consider such end user development practices signs of a successful software deployment (Fischer, 2011). The notion of a successful EUD deployment is thus strongly tied to the tasks it aims to facilitate and is application specific. Despite this high level of context dependency, successful EUD deployments have in common that they aim to maximize the value of EUD within their context, thus increasing the likelihood that EUD practices contribute to the achievement of end users' goals. In the words of Fischer et al. (see their chapter elsewhere in this book), users should be enabled *to participate and to contribute actively in personally meaningful problems.*

Some questions remain, however, such as: *How to best capture evidence of the success of an EUD deployment? What measures are best to be used?*, and *What methods are most likely to deliver the desired data?* In the remainder of this chapter, we first analyze and reflect on the evaluations performed during four EUD deployment studies in a healthcare setting. Then, we compare these evaluations to deployment evaluations performed by other researchers in previous studies. We discuss whether and how existing theoretical models can help design and interpret such evaluation studies, and from there we finally draw some general guidelines for future evaluations of EUD deployments.

4 Evaluating TagTrainer

In the following paragraphs we discuss and review a series of deployment studies concerning the customization and personalization of rehabilitation training technology by means of EUD. These studies and their findings relating to the quality of the therapy and the attitudes of the therapists are described extensively in (Tetteroo, Timmermans, Seelen, & Markopoulos, 2014; Tetteroo, Vreugdenhil, & Grisel, 2015); below we reflect on methodological aspects aiming to draw lessons of more general interest for evaluating EUD deployments. We start by introducing TagTiles, the host technology enabling tangible interaction, and TagTrainer, the EUD environment for constructing interactive exercises.

4.1 TagTiles and TagTrainer

TagTiles is an interactive board that supports tangible interaction with objects adorned with RFID tags; see Fig. 1. It encases a grid of RFID tag readers and a grid of RGB LED lights that provide visual stimuli and feedback for tangible interaction. The board can detect placement, lifting and movement of objects on its surface; interaction involves physical manipulations of the objects and audio/visual output.

TagTrainer is a software system that runs on a personal computer connected to the TagTiles board, which can be used to select, author, and execute interactive exercises for the board. TagTrainer supports upper extremity rehabilitation for neurological patients including stroke survivors, multiple sclerosis patients, spinal

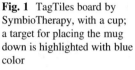

Fig. 1 TagTiles board by SymbioTherapy, with a cup; a target for placing the mug down is highlighted with blue color

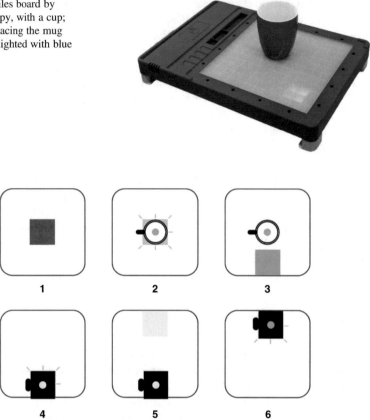

Fig. 2 Storyboard representation of a simple exercise: (1) A target (red square) lights up (2) a cup is placed on the target which turns green (3) another target lights up (blue square), (4) the cup is rotated 90° around an axis parallel to the plane (5) a final target appears (yellow square) (6) the cup is rotated the other way to touch the final target with its yellow marker. Note that the target colors correspond with the colors of the tags attached to the cup at suitable positions

cord injury patients and cerebral palsy patients. TagTrainer can help train daily living skills, e.g., opening a box, drinking from a cup, eating with knife and fork, etc., by prompting the patient to carry out relevant manipulations of such objects and by providing stimulating feedback. Typically, exercises consist of multiple iterations where a target area on the TagTiles board lights up, and the patient needs to touch this area with the appropriate side of an object (see Fig. 2).

Rather than prepackaging exercises with the interactive board, as were the first therapeutic applications for TagTiles (Lanfermann, Te Vrugt, & Timmermans, 2007; Li, Fontijn, & Markopoulos, 2008), TagTrainer provides a simple timeline based programming interface (TagTrainer Exercise Creator, see Fig. 3). Exercises can be modified or created by dragging actions (such as: "place object," "move object," etc.) onto the timeline, assigning RFID-tagged parts of an object (e.g., the

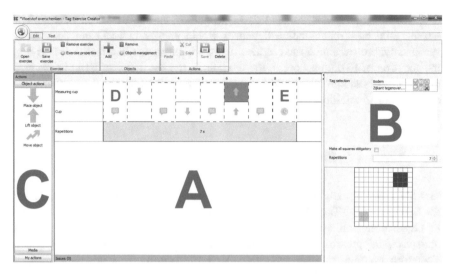

Fig. 3 The TagTrainer Exercise Creator software. The center area (A) shows the workspace with the exercise, featuring a timeline with actions associated with the objects ("measuring cup" and "cup") involved in the exercise. Properties of the selected action (in this case "lift object") such as position on the board are displayed to the right (B). Finally, additional actions can be dragged from the library (C) into the workspace to extend an exercise. Note that beyond actions involving manipulations on the board, other actions such as giving instructions (D) and pausing (E) can be used

bottom of a cup, the index finger on a glove) to these actions, and indicating corresponding target areas on the TagTiles board.

This TagTrainer Exercise Creator interface allows therapists to create exercises for each patient addressing their specific training needs and explicit requests. In a therapy session supported by TagTrainer the therapist might commence by inquiring what the patient wishes to train, rapidly create an exercise or retrieve an exercise created earlier, and then ask the patient to train for a certain duration or number of repetitions. This type of approach fundamentally changes the role of therapists; next to their role of caregivers – who instruct, monitor and encourage – they are also responsible for creating software content. Programming exercises for TagTiles is straightforward using TagTrainer, though creating such interactive applications without TagTrainer requires considerable effort and software development expertise.

5   Evaluation of TagTrainer

We chose to evaluate TagTrainer in several stages. First, TagTrainer was evaluated in a lab setting in order to ensure it was fit for use in the field (Hochstenbach-Waelen, Timmermans, & Seelen, 2012). After some improvements and participatory design activities carried out on location at a rehabilitation clinic, a series of four field deployment studies was conducted. In all these studies, we were interested in whether and how rehabilitation therapists would engage in EUD practices. More specifically, we were interested in identifying and understanding factors influencing the adoption of EUD practices in the workplace, the feasibility of EUD in the context of a rehabilitation clinic, and how technical aspects of the TagTrainer influence or hinder this feasibility.

5.1   Success Criteria

The latter study goals are mainly related to an EUD research agenda. However, for EUD to occur, TagTrainer first needed to be accepted as a technology for use in physical rehabilitation. After all, without the technology being adopted by therapists, adopting EUD practices would not be possible in the first place. Therefore, the following success criteria were used during the four case studies:

SC1. Therapists accept TagTrainer as a viable technology for arm-hand rehabilitation.
SC2. Therapists use TagTrainer in daily arm-hand therapy.
SC3. Therapists are able to perform EUD activities with TagTrainer.
SC4. Therapists perform EUD activities as part of their daily work.

5.2   Methodology

Two different methodologies were used in the evaluation of TagTrainer. For the first case study, an action research methodology (Herr & Anderson, 2014) was applied. In action research the researcher has a dual agenda of effecting a change in the context of the study (here to introduce a new form of therapy which requires a different set of responsibilities for therapists) and to study the process of change. The rationale behind applying this methodology was that it would allow us to study the adoption of TagTrainer in a clinical setting, while at the same time it would allow us to perform adjustments and modifications to better fit TagTrainer into a clinical context.

The three latter deployments adopted a case study approach, see (Yin, 2003). Though "bug" fixes and minor improvements were still performed by the researcher during these studies, significant modifications of or extensions to the system were no longer undertaken, and the participants in these studies were no longer actively participating in the development of TagTrainer or in the setting of research goals, assuming the role of a test-user rather than a co-designer or co-investigator.

The case studies were performed at three different clinics in The Netherlands and Belgium. These clinics provide physical rehabilitation to patients with stroke, spinal cord injury and multiple sclerosis. In total, 24 therapists (20 female, 4 male) participated in the studies, and both physiotherapists and occupational therapists were involved. The duration of the studies ranged from 3 weeks for the first case study, to 8 weeks for the third case study. Though from a researcher's perspective longer field studies are preferable, the study length was capped by the clinic whose business model only includes compensation for time spent with patients rather than participating in studies or creating content.

During all case studies we chose to apply a staged deployment of TagTrainer. Given that TagTrainer was new to the participants, we first introduced TagTrainer only as a technology-supported solution for providing rehabilitation training. At a later stage during the case studies, we explained to the participants the possibility to add, modify or expand upon exercises already available from the start.

The action research approach adopted in the first study helped us to quickly develop TagTrainer into a technology fit for use in a practical setting. However, the continuous presence of the first author and his active engagement with professionals on site has probably caused a compliance bias. Due to their continuous involvement in the development of TagTrainer, therapists were triggered to work with the system. Our suspicions towards this bias are strengthened by the fact that the number of EUD activities in the latter studies (where the researcher was less frequently present) was significantly lower than that of the first study. The studies and their findings are described elsewhere (Tetteroo et al., 2014, 2015), so they will not be repeated here. Rather we aim to reflect on methodological choices and limitations of the approach chosen.

5.3 Measures

In all TagTrainer deployment studies several measurements have been taken. To measure whether therapists considered TagTrainer a viable technology for arm-hand training (SC1), we administered both the UTAUT questionnaire based on the unified theory of technology acceptance by Venkatesh (2003) and the CEQ questionnaire, which measures the therapists' perception of TagTrainer as a technology suitable for arm-hand rehabilitation.

The therapists' use of TagTrainer in daily arm-hand therapy (SC2) was measured by logging all instances where TagTrainer was used, and by observing therapists during usage.

EUD activities performed with TagTrainer (SC3 and SC4) were also captured through automated logging, as all instances of exercise modification and creation were stored by the system. Additionally, a self-efficacy questionnaire constructed according to the guidelines by Bandura (2006) allowed us to capture therapists' self-confidence in performing EUD tasks, regardless of their actual performance that we captured through logging.

Finally, semi-structured interviews were used to enrich the quantitative data that was collected. They allowed us to reveal the causes of some quantitative findings and helped us to better interpret the data.

5.4 Reflection on the Case Studies

Through four case studies, we have captured large amounts of data on the deployment of TagTrainer in rehabilitation clinics. The question we consider here is, whether the methods and measures that were chosen for our evaluations have resulted in data that helps us to determine whether the implementation of TagTrainer has been successful.

Since a relative wealth of data (see Tetteroo et al., 2015) was available for measuring SC1, one would expect that it was easy to determine whether or not therapists accepted TagTrainer as a technology for rehabilitation therapy. However, the flipside of having many data sources is that these sources might support conflicting conclusions. Indeed, results from the UTAUT and CEQ questionnaires often showed a relatively favorable result for the acceptance of TagTrainer, but interview and observation data revealed a more nuanced picture. The overall picture emerging on the acceptance of TagTrainer is one of *yes, but ...*: Yes, therapists do accept TagTrainer as a technology for physical rehabilitation, given that certain boundary conditions (e.g., organizational support, technical support) are met. The important question now is whether the measures used were appropriate for measuring SC1.

As far as we know, our studies are the first in the domain of EUD where the UTAUT questionnaire was applied to measure the acceptance of the deployed solution over time. The questionnaire provided us both with new insights, and data that confirmed findings obtained from other sources (e.g., interviews). Interestingly, where theoretically the UTAUT model is supposed to carry predictive value about the use of technology, in our cases it was more useful in confirming and triangulating findings obtained from other data sources. For example, though in our studies the initial results from the UTAUT questionnaire predicted fairly good levels of acceptance (and thus technology use), the use of TagTrainer declined over the duration of our studies. Eventually, at the end of the studies, the results from the UTAUT questionnaire would confirm this development. One might be inclined to question the predictive validity of survey data. Nonetheless, we think these measures used are appropriate, and the mixed results from the different data sources show the importance of longitudinal quantitative data, which can indicate a general inclination towards a particular outcome, and qualitative data, which can provide nuance and depth to this inclination.

The outcome of SC2 was mainly measured by analyzing log files that were automatically generated by TagTrainer which helped pinpoint exactly which participants were more or less actively engaged in using TagTrainer. This allowed us to query participants during interviews on their use behavior. In this respect, it was also helpful that interviews were scheduled regularly, such that changes in usage behavior over time could be tracked and explained. Again, observations and interviews provided depth to the quantitative data, explaining not only *who* was using TagTrainer, and *when*, but also *how* and *why*.

Though a previous study (Hochstenbach-Waelen et al., 2012) had already shown that, in principle, rehabilitation experts (there students) without software expertise are able to act as creators of therapy exercises for TagTrainer, we were interested whether this finding would also hold amongst professionals in the context of a rehabilitation clinic (SC3). In this regard, especially the self-efficacy questionnaire provided useful information. Increasing self-efficacy scores on EUD related tasks aligned with actual EUD performance that was recorded in the TagTrainer log files. Once more, interviews and observations provided us with additional insights, for example as to why particular therapists seemed more (or less) skilled in EUD related tasks.

Ultimately, the question we wanted to answer through our case studies is whether therapists would adopt EUD practices as part of their daily work (SC4). Although in principle the logs combined with the data from interviews and observations provided us with the possibility to answer this question, the analysis and interpretation of this data led us to the conclusion that the success criterion may not have been well chosen in the first place.

The difficulty in measuring whether therapists adopt EUD practices *as part of their daily work* is that it is hard to define what this qualifier actually means. Taken literally, it would require therapists to perform EUD activities every single day. By the nature of the rehabilitation profession and process there are bounds to what role TagTrainer can play in therapists' daily work, so this would be an unreasonable expectation. Rather, adoption in daily work should be interpreted more broadly, meaning that therapists have embraced EUD activities as an integral part of working with TagTrainer. When EUD activities take not place on a daily basis, any evaluation on the adoption of EUD practices in this context needs to be longitudinal, before a reliable and truthful picture of therapists' EUD practices can be formed.

An additional complication to the SC4 definition is that one would expect the amount of EUD activities to decrease over time, as the set of exercises grows and the need to create even more exercises declines. So even if there would be a value for, or an understanding of therapists' engagement in EUD activities, such a value or understanding would be specific to a particular moment in time, and rather meaningless on its own.

Finally, taking a *cultures of participation*-view (Fischer, 2011) where EUD is situated in a socio-technical setting that involves multiple actors practicing various degrees of EUD, what exactly do the collected data tell us about the EUD activities taking place within the TagTrainer community in its entirety? How meaningful is it to consider the EUD activities of individual therapists, if these activities are entwined with those of other members of the community?

Concluding, in our studies we were successful in evaluating the three success conditions (SC1–3) that we regarded as instrumental for the adoption of EUD practices. Our decision to delay the introduction of EUD to the participants enabled us to record findings that may otherwise have gone unnoticed, such as the decline in TagTrainer usage after participants had been introduced to EUD. We were able to identify that it was not TagTrainer per se, but rather the organizational requirements that EUD put on our participants which hindered its usage in the later stages of our studies.

Though we were able to successfully evaluate the first three success-conditions, we were unable to get an unambiguous result regarding SC4 ("Therapists perform EUD activities as part of their daily work."). Our inability to do so is not caused by a wrongfully chosen evaluation strategy, but by a lack of clarity regarding what might constitute a successful benchmark for the adoption of EUD technology. To answer to this rather fundamental question, in the next section we present a structured literature survey on the evaluation goals, methods, measures that previous deployment studies of EUD environments have reported.

6   A Structured Literature Survey

A structured literature survey was conducted by querying the online digital libraries of ACM (dl.acm.org) and Scopus (www.scopus.com). Together these libraries include indexes of the most relevant conference proceedings and journal publications on EUD. In addition to the database searches, the proceedings of all editions of the International Symposium on End User Development (IS-EUD, (Costabile, Mussio, Parasiliti Provenza, & Piccinno, 2008; Dittrich, Burnett, Morch, & Redmiles, 2013; Pipek, Rosson, & Wulf, 2009); were manually analyzed for articles missed by the dataset search but matching the criteria of this survey. Finally, two relevant articles that had not been captured by the search were added manually. Fig. 4 provides an overview of the survey process.

6.1   Inclusion/exclusion Criteria

Articles resulting from the search were included if they were written in English, published between 1991 and June 2015 when the survey was carried out, accessible to the authors and describing actual in-the-field deployment of EUD systems. We excluded papers published before 1991, in non-English languages or describing lab-studies, usability evaluations, retrospective analyses of cases, theories, methods, etc.

6.2   Search Keywords

The databases used were queried for articles containing at least one of the following terms as keywords *end user programming, end user development, EUD*, and *meta design*. Meta-design is a *conceptual framework aimed at defining and creating social and technical infrastructures in which new forms of collaborative design can take place* (Fischer, 2007) – the term was included since work in this area is closely related to end user development.

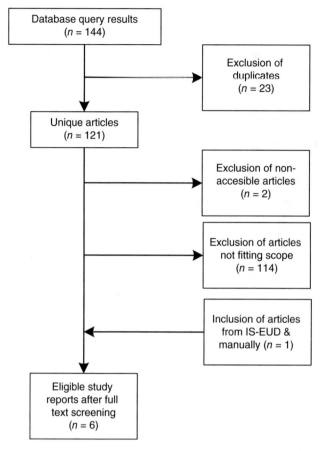

Fig. 4 Flowchart of the structured literature survey

In addition to matching one of the keywords, to filter for studies describing actual in-the-field deployments of EUD systems, articles had to include at least one of the following terms as a keyword, or in their abstracts: *deployment, case study, field study, ethnography, practices, ethnographic methods.*

6.3   Results

The combined queries returned 144 results (ACM: 31, Scopus: 113). After correcting for duplicates, 121 unique results remained. The abstracts of all candidate articles were read and compared against the inclusion/exclusion criteria. Where abstracts were found to provide insufficient information for the inclusion/exclusion decision, the full article was read. The proceedings of IS-EUD were scanned for

Table 1 Articles selected for analysis in this survey

Title	Authors	Source	Year
"Let's see your search-tool!" – On the collaborative use of tailored artifacts	Wulf, V.	Proc. GROUP'99	1999
Investigating success factors for hypermedia development tools	Bolchini, D., Garzotto, F., Paolini, P.	Proc. Hypertext'08	2008
Design, adoption, and assessment of a socio-technical environment supporting independence for persons with cognitive disabilities	Carmien, S.P., Fischer, G.	Proc. CHI'08	2008
Software development cultures and cooperation problems: a field study of the early stages of development of software for a scientific community	Segal, J.	CSCW (journal)	2009
Study of using the meta-model based meta-design paradigm for developing and maintaining web applications	De Silva, B., Ginige, A.	Proc. UNISCON'09	2009
End-user development of enterprise widgets	Spahn, M., Wulf, V.	End-user development (book)	2009
Enabling users of enterprise systems to mashup resources and develop widgets	Spahn, M. et al.		

relevant articles not covered by the database search, but no additional eligible articles were found. Most of the excluded articles, although being EUD related, did not present deployment studies. Instead, they often concerned formative (lab) evaluations and retrospective analyses of cases where EUD would already be in place. Finally, one article that was missed by the keyword search was added manually.

Six articles in total were found to be eligible for answering our research questions (see Table 1). A summarized version of these articles is given below.

Bolchini, Garzotto, and Paolini (2008) have attempted to identify *the key factors that contribute to the success of a hypermedia development tool*. They acknowledge that success factors exist on various levels, but focus on those that can be observed and are directly related to the "product." In their case study, the authors have studied the adoption of the *1001Stories* tool. This tool allows for web-based hypermedia development and has been deployed amongst Italian primary-school and high-school classes. The authors have studied the adoption of the tool through two sub-studies: the first study involved primary school children and teachers, focusing on tool and process simplicity. In this study, task-based observational user testing was used to evaluate the ease of use of the tool. Contextual inquiry was used to study the development process. Finally, a questionnaire was submitted to the participating children at the end of the study, to investigate their overall satisfaction. Their second study was *mainly devoted to investigate satisfaction, prospective adoption, and success factors on a larger statistical base* (Bolchini et al., 2008). In this study, the authors queried participating teachers through an online questionnaire. Finally, they measure the success of their tool and its deployment by assessing the following variables: *appreciation, educational benefits, prospective adoption, tool simplicity*, and *process efficiency*. Although the results of their questionnaires are generally favorable, the authors draw no conclusions about the success of their deployments.

Carmien and Fischer (2008) have studied the use of EUD practices to enhance the independence of cognitively disabled persons. They present the Memory Aiding Prompting System (MAPS), which provides caregivers the opportunity to *create scripts that can be used by people with cognitive disabilities ("clients") to support them in carrying out tasks that they would not be able to achieve by themselves* (Carmien & Fischer, 2008).The system consists of the *MAPS-DE*, an EUD environment allowing caregivers to create and share scripts, and *MAPS-PR*, a client interface for the created scripts. They present a field study with 6 participants (3 caregiver-client dyads) who have been provided with the MAPS system. The authors used several ethnographic methods to collect data, in particular participant observation and semi-structured interviews. Their goals were to (1) learn about the client's and caregiver's world and their interactions, (2) observe and analyze how tasks and learning of tasks were currently conducted, (3) understand and explicate the process of creating and updating scripts, (4) comprehend and analyze the process of using the scripts with a real task, and (5) gain an understanding of the role of meta-design in the dynamics of MAPS adoption and use. During their field study, the authors collected audio recordings, field notes and secondary artifacts. The authors are not explicit about the success of their deployment.

Segal (2009) describes the development process of scientific software as a combined effort of several "professional end user developers" (i.e., scientists who can program). The article focuses on cooperation problems arising from the professional end user development culture associated with the development project. While her article strictly speaking does not meet the inclusion criteria for this survey (since EUD is already common practice amongst these scientists), the collaborative nature of the software project described presents new challenges to the users involved and hence can be regarded as the "deployment" of a new form of EUD. The process that Segal describes is one in which professional end user developers, as part of an organized project with multiple stakeholders that belong to several organizations, develop a laboratory information management system for use in biology research. These stakeholders are: a management board, the development team (highly heterogeneous, nine members, five locations), collaborators from research groups that have the potential to share resources with the development team, and the users. The goal of the field study that Segal conducted is to illustrate how cultural influences impact cooperation in a professional end user development project. For this, she collected data through ten observations, ten interviews, twelve phone calls, numerous emails, and by consulting project documentation.

De Silva and Ginige (2009) describe the deployment of end-user extensible websites for three small and medium-size enterprises (SMEs). They draw inspiration from Fischer's meta-design theory (Fischer & Scharff, 2000) and provide the

SMEs with a first version of a website as a seed that can later be extended by the SMEs. The goal of their study was to investigate how the tool making industry in Australia, specifically the SMEs, could benefit from end-user extensible websites. The data collected is very sparse: only data on the toolmakers' perceived ability to execute maintenance tasks and a log of the maintenance activities performed by the SMEs have been collected.

Spahn and Wulf (2009) describe the deployment of their Widget Composition Platform (WCP) – a platform that allows business users to create custom widgets, tailored to their personal information needs – to three mid-sized German companies. The goal of their evaluation was to investigate questions such as: are their end users able to create widgets using WCP? Do the widgets address practical problems in real work contexts? Are advanced end users able to create and wrap enterprise resources as new services to extend the available building blocks for widget creation? What types of end users exist with regard to widget usage and development and how do they collaborate? Spahn and Wulf used interviews, observations, and questionnaires focusing on EUD-related tasks to find answers to these questions.

Volker Wulf (1999) describes the development of a component-based search tool as an extension to an existing database system. They deployed the artifact in a German government organization and studied a small group of users in depth. The goals of their evaluation were to research (1) to which extend users without programming skills would be able to tailor the search tool, (2) which division of labor would emerge between the end users and the local experts, (3) whether end users would be able to understand the components, compound components and search tool alternatives provided to them by programmers and local experts, and (4) how to support the exchange of tailored artifacts between end users and local experts. Their deployment approach was staged: first they presented the prototype to a group of participants in a workshop and performed a formative usability evaluation, after which the tool was adopted by the designers. Then, they deployed the revised tool for a period of two weeks, starting with a workshop where the tool was presented to the participants and training was provided. During this study, participants were observed in their tailoring process and the emerging problems. Finally, semi-structured interviews were held with the participants, and the tailored artifacts were copied for analysis. During all workshops and the field study, written notes were taken and transcribed directly after each session.

6.4 Evaluating EUD Deployments

As has been demonstrated by the survey, research in which researchers attempt to *create* an environment that facilitates EUD, by implementing appropriate methods, techniques and tools, as well as by shaping facilitating conditions on a psychological and social level is far less common than retrospective ethnographic studies.

Remarkably few attempts of EUD deployments were found, and the variation between them (amongst others in terms of domain, approach, scope, authors and findings) leads to believe that this aspect of EUD is currently underexplored, and the state of the art is limited to ad-hoc attempts rather than structured and planned approaches. One possible explanation for the scarcity of deployment studies is that EUD needs not necessarily be introduced as part of an orchestrated effort - involving planned investments of time and effort by end users and commitment by some form of management. Rather, suitable environments may have evolved gradually to accommodate for EUD. Still, the articles discussed in this survey show there is a need for an orchestrated deployment of EUD technology in several cases. For example, non-information workers (such as the caregivers in Carmien & Fischer, 2008) might not be aware of the possibilities that EUD environments can provide them with to address personally relevant problems. The need for organizational support for encouraging EUD practices has been also argued on the basis of the surveys by Mehandjiev, Sutcliffe, and Lee (2006) and Kierkegaard and Markopoulos (2011).

Table 2 provides an overview of the aims of the surveyed articles, and the evaluation methods that were used in these articles. Most articles are not very clear on what they expect to find when starting their deployment. Nevertheless, by "reading through the lines" it is clear that the studies had either one or both of the following goals: to evaluate a tool for EUD, or to better understand the principles that underlie EUD (see also the "research purpose" qualifications in Kjeldskov & Graham, 2003).The methods that these studies used varied, but the use of qualitative methods such as observations and interviews is common, especially amongst

Table 2 Aims and research methods used in the surveyed studies

Article	Study aims	Methods used	New tech?
Bolchini et al. (2008)	Tool evaluation	Task-based observational user testing Contextual inquiry Questionnaires	Yes
Carmien and Fischer (2008)	Understanding EUD principles	Observations Interviews	Yes
Segal (2009)	Understanding EUD principles	Observations Interviews Documentation analysis	No
De Silva & Ginige (2009)	Tool evaluation understanding EUD principles	Usage logging Questionnaires	Yes
Spahn and Wulf (2009)	Tool evaluation understanding EUD principles	Observations Interviews Questionnaires	Yes
Wulf (1999)	Tool evaluation understanding EUD principles	Observations Interviews	No

studies that focus on creating a better understanding of EUD principles. Where questionnaires were used, their aim varied from measuring tool appreciation and usability, to measuring the participants' general opinions on the use and usefulness of EUD in their domain. Interestingly, only two studies concerned the deployment of EUD as an addition to an already existing system (e.g., an extension or plugin), while the others introduced a new technology entirely. There seems to be no correlation between the deployment type and the methods used.

7 Discussion

In order to find an answer to the question *how should deployments of EUD systems be evaluated?* we have reflected on the deployment studies of TagTrainer. Further, we presented a structured literature survey on other deployment studies of EUD systems. We discuss the results of the survey and our reflections on a number of questions that are related to the evaluation of EUD deployments.

7.1 How to Best Capture Evidence of the Success of an EUD Deployment?

The studies discussed in this chapter are characterized by a great diversity in their approaches, methods, goals and results. Therefore, it is not easy to draw a conclusion about what are suitable methods for capturing evidence of successful EUD deployments. On the other hand, if we take a step back and look at how the different studies have interpreted the evaluation task, we can make some interesting observations.

Earlier in this chapter, we stated that successful EUD deployments *maximize the value of EUD within their context, thus increasing the likelihood that EUD practices contribute to the achievement of an end user's goals*. Success, by this definition, is thus strongly related to the goals that a particular end user of the EUD technology has in a particular context. As has been shown before, these goals vary greatly between different cases, and range from "allowing patients to live more independently" (therapists, Carmien & Fischer, 2008) to "developing web-based hypermedia to pass a course" (high-school children, Bolchini et al., 2008) and "running a profitable business" (De Silva & Ginige, 2009).

As much as the goals of the end users in the contexts of the surveyed studies differ, the role that EUD plays in these contexts differs as well. For example, the relative importance of an up-to-date website for an SME in (De Silva & Ginige, 2009) might be less than the importance of a working memory prompting system for the cognitive disabled in (Carmien & Fischer, 2008). SMEs will probably primarily be focused on producing and selling goods and services. Maintaining an up-to-date online presence can help to increase sales but is usually not amongst the core activities of such companies.

It can be argued that the evaluation approach, and the methods and measures used should be adapted to the role that EUD is expected to play for the end users. For example, adopting an action research approach where researchers collaborate with end users in the deployment and evaluation of an EUD environment over an extended period of time, might not be the right choice if the prospective adoption of EUD practices will remain low and infrequent (e.g., De Silva & Ginige, 2009). However, it is not always trivial to estimate the importance of EUD for the context in which it is being implemented. For example, in our own studies we expected the importance of EUD in the use of TagTrainer to be greater than it turned out to be. Though therapists indicated that providing patient-centered training content is an important consideration to them, in practice they often settled for readily available exercises (rather than ones tailored for a specific patient) from the library of exercises that we made available to them.

Since it is difficult to predict in advance what the rate of EUD adoption will be, it is sensible to adopt a staged approach in the evaluation of EUD systems. Rogers (2010) famously describes a five-stage model on the diffusion of innovations that provides us with sufficient theoretical guidance to propose suitable methods of evaluation for the different stages of EUD deployments. The five stages of his model are (adapted from Rogers, 2010, p. 169):

1. *Knowledge*, occurs when an individual is exposed to an innovation's existence and gains an understanding of how it functions.
2. *Persuasion*, occurs when an individual engages in activities that lead to a choice to adopt or reject the innovation.
3. *Decision*, takes place when an individual engages in activities that lead to a choice to adopt or reject the innovation.
4. *Implementation*, occurs when an individual puts a new idea into use.
5. *Confirmation*, takes place when an individual seeks reinforcement of an innovation-decision already made, but he or she may reverse this previous decision if exposed to conflicting messages about the innovation.

Importantly, the five stages of Rogers' model show us that at different moments during a deployment process, different factors become important for the end user in relation to the adoption of the technology that is being deployed. If we now turn the question with which we started this section - on the best way to capture evidence of successful EUD deployments - we can use Rogers' model to define for each stage what evidence could or should be collected in support of any statement on the success of an EUD deployment:

1. *Knowledge:* evaluate the end users' understanding of the EUD system being deployed e.g., its usability and functionality.
2. *Persuasion:* evaluate the end users' attitude towards the system, for example by using the UTAUT model (Venkatesh et al., 2003) or self-efficacy regarding EUD (Bandura, 2006).

3. *Decision:* evaluate whether, in the opinion of the end users, adopting EUD practices will lead to a positive outcome of the cost/benefit tradeoff related to the adoption of EUD practices (*relative advantage*, in Rogers' theory (2010)). Blackwell's Attention Investment model (Blackwell, 2002; Blackwell & Burnett, 2002) could be used to gauge this specifically for EUD.
4. *Implementation:* evaluate the EUD practices that end users develop, the role that EUD starts playing in the context in which it is deployed, and most importantly, the extent to which the EUD practices help the end user to achieve his or her goals.
5. *Confirmation:* evaluate whether the decision to (not) engage in EUD has sustained after a period of time, and if not, what has caused the end user to reverse his or her initial decision.

The advantage of designing evaluations in a staged approach, as outlined above, is that it is then possible to relate different evaluation studies to each other and we can pinpoint more precisely areas of improvements. It also protects us from setting up large, time-consuming and expensive evaluations that study EUD practices, if in an earlier stage we can detect threads for a successful deployment (e.g., usability flaws, acceptance issues). The first two stages can, in principle, even be evaluated in a laboratory setting. Finally, the structured and staged evaluation approach allows us to better compare different cases of EUD deployments. It provides us with terminology to discuss these cases in a context independent manner, and allows us to draw generalizations over several cases of EUD deployments, even if these cases themselves are context specific.

7.2   The Role of New Technology in EUD Deployments

Earlier in this chapter we limited our discussion to cases where EUD comes on top of an existing host technology (e.g., as a plugin to existing software), or is deployed simultaneously with another, new host technology (e.g., the case of TagTrainer). As we have experienced ourselves, evaluating the impact of introducing EUD in an organization while simultaneously introducing a new host technology can lead to difficulties. The impact of the introduction of the new technology might overshadow the impact of introducing EUD, thereby obscuring the effects that the introduction of EUD might have had. Further, the actual adoption of EUD practices might, in such a context, be hampered by the fact that the host technology introduced does not align with the existing practices within that context (i.e., what Rogers calls *compatibility with previously introduced ideas* Rogers, 2010).

In our own studies, we have tried to counter this bias caused by the introduction of a new host technology, by adopting a staged introduction of TagTrainer. First, the system was introduced as a technology for physical rehabilitation, without focusing on the possibility for therapists to modify or create exercises. Only later were the participating therapists instructed on the EUD possibilities that the system offered them.

The rationale was that therapists could first get used to working with TagTrainer as a new technology for physical arm-hand rehabilitation. Then, once they had adopted the technology for this purpose, they would be introduced to EUD. We assumed that through this approach, the novelty of the technology would no longer interfere with the introduction of EUD. Still, many of the issues that were raised by therapists in the later stages of our deployment studies were related to the system in general and not specifically to the possibility to modify or create exercises. Some of these issues would have such a negative impact on their perception of the system that they would abandon it completely, limiting our ability to study EUD adoption and practice.

The studies reviewed in the survey however reveal different results. Four of these articles report a simultaneous introduction of a new technology, as well as EUD, as part of their study. Still, they do not report on issues in the adoption of EUD practices arising from this simultaneous introduction, nor do they report on the occurrence of a results bias. It is possible that in some cases, such as (Spahn & Wulf, 2009), the technology that was introduced was compatible enough (see Rogers, 2010) to the technology their participants had been working with previously, that it did not cause any significant problems.

Earlier, we asked ourselves whether it is sensible to separate the evaluation of the EUD-part of an environment from the other parts. Unfortunately, this question cannot conclusively be answered from the results of our survey. The fact that none of the surveyed studies report on issues arising from the simultaneous evaluation of the technology and EUD practices does not mean that such issues do not occur. Moreover, since in our own studies we *did* encounter these issues, we believe that the answer to this question depends on the context in which the EUD system is being deployed.

8   Conclusion

Evaluating EUD deployments is far from trivial, since it is difficult to define the precise subject of evaluation and to determine which approach and which methods are suitable for such an evaluation. In this chapter, we have explored these questions by first defining what makes EUD deployments different from regular software deployments. Then, we discussed the evaluation of TagTrainer, after which we presented a literature survey on EUD deployment studies. One lesson we can draw from this survey is that evaluations of EUD deployments so far do not share a common framework and form a rather fragmented picture.

From this survey and from our own experiences, we discussed suitable ways to evaluate EUD deployment, and more specifically:

1. A staged evaluation approach, evaluating sequentially the end users' knowledge about, and acceptance of the deployed system, the tradeoffs that the end users face in considering to engage in EUD activities, the EUD practices and activities that end users develop, and finally whether these practices sustain after a longer period of time.

2. A staged implementation of the host technology (the technology to which support for EUD is added) and the EUD technology. Where the host technology is deployed next to EUD technology, the deployment of EUD technology should be postponed until the host technology has been accepted and incorporated by the end users.

We believe that if future EUD deployment studies take these suggestions into account, we can more effectively compare different studies and draw generalizable conclusions from their data.

References

Bandura, A. (2006). Guide for constructing self-efficacy scales. In Urdan, T., & Pajares, F. Eds. *Self-efficacy beliefs of adolescents.* IAP, 2006.

Blackwell, A., & Burnett, M. (2002). Applying attention investment to end-user programming. In *Proc. HCC 2002* (pp. 28–30). IEEE.

Blackwell, A.F. (2002). First steps in programming: a rationale for attention investment models. In *Proc. HCC 2002* (pp. 2–10). IEEE.

Bolchini, D., Garzotto, F., Paolini, P. (2008). Investigating success factors for hypermedia development tools. In *Proc. HT 2008* (pp. 187–192). New York: ACM.

Carmien, S. P., & Fischer, G. (2008). Design, adoption, and assessment of a socio-technical environment supporting independence for persons with cognitive disabilities. In *Proc. CHI 2008* (pp. 597–606). New York: ACM.

Costabile, M.F., Mussio, P., Parasiliti Provenza, L., Piccinno, A. (2008). End users as unwitting software developers. In *Proc. 4th int. workshop end-user softw. eng* (pp. 6–10). ACM.

De Silva, B., & Ginige, A. (2009). Study of using the meta-model based meta-design paradigm for developing and maintaining web applications. In *Int. united inf. syst. conf* (pp. 304–314). Springer.

Dittrich, Y., Burnett, M., Morch, A., Redmiles, D. (2013). *End-user development: 4th international symposium, IS-EUD 2013, Copenhagen, Denmark, June 10–13, 2013, Proceedings.* Berlin Heidelberg: Springer.

Fischer, G. (2007). Meta-design: expanding boundaries and redistributing control in design. In C. Baranauskas, P. Palanque, J. Abascal, S. D. J. Barbosa (Eds.). *Hum.-comput. interact. – INTERACT 2007* (pp. 193–206). Berlin Heidelberg: Springer.

Fischer, G. (2011). Understanding, fostering, and supporting cultures of participation. *Interactions, 18,* 42–53.

Fischer, G., & Scharff, E. (2000). Meta-design: design for designers. In *Proc. DIS 2000* (pp. 396–405). New York: ACM.

Herr, K., & Anderson, G. L. (2014). *The action research dissertation: a guide for students and faculty.* Thousand Oaks: SAGE Publications.

Hochstenbach-Waelen, A., Timmermans, A., Seelen, H., Tetteroo, D., Markopoulos P. (2012). Tag-exercise creator: towards end-user development for tangible interaction in rehabilitation training. In *Proc. EICS 2012* (pp. 293–298). ACM.

Kierkegaard, P., & Markopoulos, P. (2011). From top to bottom: end user development, motivation, creativity and organisational support. In *Int. symp. end user dev* (pp. 307–312). Springer.

Kjeldskov, J., & Graham, C. (2003). A review of mobile HCI research methods. In L. Chittaro (ed). *Hum.-comput. interact. mob. devices serv.* (pp. 317–335). Berlin Heidelberg: Springer.

Lanfermann, G., Te Vrugt, J., Timmermans, A., Bongers, E., Lamber, N., Van Acht, V. (2007). Philips stroke rehabilitation exerciser. In *Tech. aids rehabil.-TAR 2007* January 25–26 2007.

Li, Y., Fontijn, W., Markopoulos, P. (2008). A tangible tabletop game supporting therapy of children with cerebral palsy. In P. Markopoulos, B. Ruyter, W. de IJsselsteijn, D. Rowland (Eds.). *Fun games* (pp. 182–193). Berlin Heidelberg: Springer.

Mehandjiev, N., Sutcliffe, A., Lee, D. (2006). Organizational view of end-user development. In H. Lieberman, F. Paternò, V. Wulf (Eds.). *End user dev* (pp. 371–399). Netherlands: Springer.

Namoun, A., Wajid, U., Mehandjiev, N., Owrak, A. (2012). User-centered design of a visual data mapping tool. In *Proc. AVI 2012* (pp. 473–480). New York: ACM.

Pipek, V., Rosson, M.-B., Wulf, V. (2009). *End-user development: 2nd international symposium, IS-EUD 2009, Siegen, Germany, March 2–4, 2009, Proceedings*. Berlin-Heidelberg: Springer.

Rogers, E.M. (2010). *Diffusion of innovations*, 4th Edition. Simon and Schuster.

Ruthruff, J. R., Prabhakararao, S., Reichwein, J., Cook, C., Creswick, E., Burnett, M. (2005). Interactive, visual fault localization support for enduser programmers. *Journal of Visual Languages and Computing, 16*, 3–40. doi:10.1016/j.jvlc.2004.07.001.

Segal, J. (2009). Software development cultures and cooperation problems: a field study of the early stages of development of software for a scientific community. *Computer Supported Cooperative Work (CSCW), 18*, 581 doi:10.1007/s10606-009-9096-9.

Spahn, M., & Wulf, V. (2009). End-user development of enterprise widgets. In V. Pipek, M. B. Rosson, B. Ruyter, V. de, Wulf (Eds.). *End-user dev* (pp. 106–125). Berlin Heidelberg: Springer.

Tetteroo, D., & Markopoulos, P. (2015). A review of research methods in end user development. In Díaz P., Pipek V., Ardito C., Jensen C., Aedo I., Boden A. (Eds.), *End-user dev* (pp. 58–75). Springer International Publishing.

Tetteroo, D., Timmermans, A. A., Seelen, H. A., Markopoulos, P. (2014). TagTrainer: supporting exercise variability and tailoring in technology supported upper limb training. *Journal of NeuroEngineering and Rehabilitation, 11*, 140 doi:10.1186/1743-0003-11-140.

Tetteroo, D., Vreugdenhil, P., Grisel, I., Michielsen, M., Kuppens, E., Vanmulken, D., et al. (2015). Lessons learnt from deploying an end-user development platform for physical rehabilitation. In *Proc. CHI 2015* (pp. 4133–4142). New York: ACM.

Tsandilas, T., Letondal, C., Mackay, W. E. (2009). Musink: composing music through augmented drawing. In *Proc. CHI 2009* (pp. 819–828). New York: ACM.

Venkatesh, V., Morris, M. G., Davis, G. B., Davis, F. D. (2003). User acceptance of information technology: toward a unified view. *MIS Q, 27*, 425–478.

Wong, J., & Hong, J. I. (2007). Making mashups with marmite: towards end-user programming for the web. In *Proc. CHI 2007* (pp. 1435–1444). New York: ACM.

Wulf, V. (1999). "Let's see your search-tool!"—Collaborative use of tailored artifacts in groupware. In *Proc. GROUP 1999* (pp. 50–59). New York: ACM.

Yin, R. K. (2003). *Case study research: design and methods*. Thousand Oaks: SAGE Publications.

Toward Theory-Based End-User Software Engineering

Margaret Burnett, Todd Kulesza, Alannah Oleson, Shannon Ernst,
Laura Beckwith, Jill Cao, William Jernigan and Valentina Grigoreanu

Abstract One area of research in the end-user development area is known as end-user software engineering (EUSE). Research in EUSE aims to invent new kinds of technologies that collaborate with end users to improve the quality of their software. EUSE has become an active research area since its birth in the early 2000s, with a large body of literature upon which EUSE researchers can build. However, building upon these works can be difficult when projects lack connections due to an absence of cross-cutting foundations to tie them together. In this chapter, we advocate for stronger theory foundations and show the advantages through three theory-oriented projects: (1) the Explanatory Debugging approach, to help end users

M. Burnett (✉) · A. Oleson · S. Ernst
Oregon State University, Corvallis, OR, United States
e-mail: burnett@oregonstate.edu

A. Oleson
e-mail: olesona@oregonstate.edu

S. Ernst
e-mail: ernstsh@oregonstate.edu

T. Kulesza · V. Grigoreanu
Microsoft, Redmond, WA, United States
e-mail: todd.kulesza@microsoft.com

V. Grigoreanu
e-mail: valeng@microsoft.com

L. Beckwith
Configit, Copenhagen, Denmark
e-mail: laura.beckwith@gmail.com

J. Cao
comScore, Portland, OR, United States
e-mail: jillchencao@gmail.com

W. Jernigan
GE, Manhattan, KS, United States
e-mail: wdcjernigan@gmail.com

© Springer International Publishing AG 2017   231
F. Paternò, V. Wulf (eds.), *New Perspectives in End-User Development*,
DOI 10.1007/978-3-319-60291-2_10

debug their intelligent assistants; (2) the GenderMag method, which identifies problems with gender inclusiveness in EUSE tools and other software; and (3) the Idea Garden approach, to help end users to help themselves in overcoming programming barriers. In each of these examples, we show how having a theoretical foundation facilitated generalizing beyond individual tools to the production of general methods and principles for other researchers to directly draw upon in their own works.

Keywords End-user software engineering · theory foundations · theory-oriented products · EUD research

1   Introduction

Since the first book on end-user development (EUD) (Lieberman, Paterno, & Wulf, 2006), research on EUD has made significant progress. From its early beginnings focusing mostly on supporting end users' software development using spreadsheets and event-based computing paradigms, EUD research has emerged to support end-user development of web automations, mobile devices, personal information management systems, business processes, programming home appliance devices, and even internet-of-things programming. Further, EUD research now spans much more of the software development lifecycle, supporting not only creating new programs alone and collaboratively and testing/debugging them, but also designing, specifying, and reusing them. For a survey of related works, see (Ko et al., 2011).

However, EUD research as a field also has an important shortcoming: it lacks cross-cutting foundations. Although it is common to ground EUD research efforts in formative empirical studies so as to understand a particular target group of end-user developers, this (important) practice still leaves a gap: weak connections among similar EUD research projects that target different audiences or tasks. This lack of broad, cross-cutting foundations, in turn, silos our research (Burnett & Myers, 2014), making it difficult for EUD researchers to build on one anothers' shoulders in principled ways.

1.1   Theory: What It Is and How It Can Help

This is where theory can help. The essence of theory is generalization through abstraction – mapping instances of successful approaches to cross-cutting principles. In the realm of human behavior, these abstractions can then produce explanations of *why* some software engineering tools succeed at supporting people's efforts and why some tools that were expected to succeed did not.

As Shaw eloquently explains, scientific theory lets technological development pass previously imposed limits inherent in relying on intuition and experience

(Shaw, 1990). For example, her summary of civil engineering history points out that structures (buildings, bridges, tunnels, canals) had been built for centuries – but only by master craftsmen. Not until scientists developed theories of statics and strength of materials could the composition of forces and bending be tamed. These theories made possible civil engineering accomplishments that were simply not possible before, such as the routine design of skyscrapers by ordinary engineers and architects (Shaw, 1990). In computer science, we have seen the same phenomenon. Expert developers once built compilers using only their intuitions and experiences, but the advent of formal language theory brought tasks like parser and compiler writing to the level that undergraduate computer science students now routinely build them in their coursework (Aho, Lam, Sethi, & Ullman, 2006). In a more recent example, de Souza shows how semiotic theory can provide a unified theoretical underpinning for the communication aspects of a wide range of EUD projects (2017).

Opinions differ on exactly what a theory is, but as Sjoberg et al. explain, most discussions of what a theory is come down to four points: what a theory *does*, what its *elements* are, where they *come from*, and how they are *evaluated* (Sjøberg, Dybå, Anda, & Hannay, 2008). At least five types of theory have been identified from the perspective of what theory *does* (Gregor, 2006), but the types of interest to this chapter are those that explain why something happens, those that predict what will happen under different conditions, and those that prescribe how to do something. According to Sjoberg et al., scholars agree that theory's basic *elements* are constructs, relationship, and scope; and theories *come to* a given discipline by borrowing them from other disciplines (with or without adaptation along the way) or may be generated from scratch within the discipline using data collected. Sjoberg et al.'s fourth point, how theories are *evaluated*, brings up a particularly important point: theories of human behavior, which are the theories of interest to this chapter, can never be completely "proven" – because we cannot see inside humans' heads – but they can be supported or refuted through empirical evidence.

This chapter advocates for more theory-based research in the end-user development domain. Informing EUD research with theories – i.e., being good *consumers* of theory – can lead to the kinds of advantages Shaw described. In terms of Sjoberg et al.'s four points, this chapter is a consumer of theories (1) that explain, predict, or prescribe; (2) that come from other disciplines; (3) whose constructs, relationships, and scope are potentially good fits to end-user development projects; and (4) are already well supported through significant amounts of empirical evidence. Further, informing next steps of our research with principles that we can derive from our results – i.e., being good *producers* of theory – enables EUD researchers to build upon one anothers' findings effectively because the derived principles identify the new fundamentals of successful results. This chapter demonstrates this point by deriving prescriptive theories in the form of principles accompanied by a beginning body of supporting evidence.

1.2   Overview of This Chapter: Three Examples of Theory-Based Research

To illustrate EUD research from both a theory-consuming perspective and a theory-producing perspective, we present theory-oriented views of three of our recent EUD projects in the area of end-user software engineering.

End-user software engineering (EUSE) is a particular type of EUD research that focuses on the *quality* of end-user developed software (Ko et al., 2011). A significant challenge in EUSE research is to find ways to incorporate software engineering activities into users' existing workflows without requiring people to substantially change the nature of their work or their priorities. For example, rather than expecting spreadsheet users to incorporate a testing phase into their programming efforts, tools can simplify the tracking of successful and failing inputs incrementally, providing feedback about software quality as the user edits the spreadsheet program. Approaches like these allow users to stay focused on their primary goals (balancing their budget, teaching children, recording a television show, making scientific discoveries, etc.) while still achieving software quality (Ko et al., 2011).

The three EUSE examples in this chapter illustrate how starting with a theory foundation (being *consumers* of theory) facilitated our ability to not only chart a path toward new visions, but also to derive principles to guide others following similar paths in their own works (being *producers* of theory).

We will begin with Explanatory Debugging, an approach to enabling end users without backgrounds in debugging or in computer science to personalize or "debug" their intelligent assistants. Explanatory Debugging draws mainly upon Mental Model Theory (Johnson-Laird, 1983). From this foundation, we derived a set of principles to form a design-oriented theory about how to create EUD tools that support Explanatory Debugging, instantiated them in a prototype, and used that prototype to empirically evaluate the principles. The second example we discuss, Gender HCI, describes a series of theory-based works that originated in the EUSE domain to investigate how gender differences in problem solving styles come together with software for problem-solving tasks (such as end-user development tasks). It draws from several theories, most notably Self-Efficacy Theory (Bandura, 1986) and Information Processing Theory as per Meyers-Levy's Selectivity Hypothesis (Meyers-Levy, 1989; Meyers-Levy & Loken, 2015; Meyers-Levy & Maheswaran, 1991). Finally, we discuss the Idea Garden, an explanation approach designed to supplement existing end-user development environments to enable end users who are "stuck" to help themselves to overcome their barriers. As in the Explanatory Debugging approach, the Idea Garden draws from theory – here, the primary theory used was Minimalist Learning Theory (Carroll, 1990, 1998; Carroll & Rosson, 1987; van der Meij & Carroll, 1998). From these foundations, we derived principles to form a design-oriented theory for how to create Idea Garden tools for EUD environments, instantiated the principles in prototypes, and used the prototypes to empirically evaluate the principles. The evaluation of the principles served a dual role: it not only empirically evaluated the principles themselves, but also evaluated the derivation of the principles (i.e., whether we introduced problems in the course of deriving them from the original theory).

2   Explanatory Debugging

2.1   End Users Personalizing ("Debugging") Machine Learning: Foundations

An increasing amount of software includes some form of machine learning, from facial recognition to personalized search results, document classification, and media recommendation. Often these learning systems allow users to personalize their behavior by providing examples (e.g., "I really liked *Casablanca*, so recommend more movies like it") or by placing limits on the system (e.g., "Only recommend movies in the *film noir* genre").

End users change the system's logic when they personalize it in the above manners, resulting in a software artifact that is now (hopefully) more closely aligned with the way its end user expects it to behave. We term such changes "debugging" the system – a form of end-user software engineering – because they are changing the learning system to make its behavior better match their requirements.

However, debugging learning systems can be difficult, regardless of the mechanisms available to debug, because many machine learning systems are complex – their internal logic is often Byzantine, and may change after (learn from) each user action. Because of this difficulty, many learning systems do not try to empower end users to understand or debug them – instead, they act as a "black box" to the user. For example, such systems usually provide little or no explanation of their predictions. Further, if the system allows any user feedback at all about a prediction, it is usually limited to users being able to say they disagree with the system's prediction or possibly to say what the answer should be. However, users are rarely allowed to explain *why* they disagree or what the system should start or stop taking into account in its reasoning. In contrast, we subscribe to Shneiderman's viewpoint that, just as professional software developers need to understand the software they maintain and debug, end users likewise need to understand (at least some of) how the learning system works, and further, must be empowered to fix (debug) the system so that its behavior becomes more useful to their needs (Shneiderman, 1995).

To investigate how to enable ordinary users to understand such complex systems as machine learning environments, we turned to the mental model theory of reasoning. In this theory, *mental models* are internal representations that people generate based on their experiences in the real world. These models, when they are reasonably accurate, allow people to understand, explain, and predict phenomena, then act accordingly (Johnson-Laird, 1983). In the context of machine learning systems, reasonably accurate mental models should help users understand why a system is behaving in a given manner and allow them to predict how it will respond if they make specific changes to it. Given this foundation, we hypothesized that by being able to accurately predict how a learning system will respond to specific adjustments, a user with a reasonably accurate mental model will be able to debug the system more successfully than a user whose mental model is flawed.

We explored this hypothesis and investigated the accuracy and malleability of end users' mental models through a succession of user studies (Kulesza, Burnett, Wong, & Stumpf, 2015; Kulesza, Stumpf, Burnett, & Kwan, 2012; Kulesza et al., 2010, 2011; Kulesza, Stumpf, Burnett, & Yang, 2013). Critically, we found that users rarely have accurate mental models of how common machine learning systems operate, and that in the absence of explanations, these models do not improve over time through continued interaction with the system. Even brief explanations, however, were able to increase the quality of users' mental models. This increase was often matched by a corresponding increase in users' abilities to personalize the learning system to their satisfaction. Thus, the mental model theory of reasoning helped us identify the importance of explanations to interactive machine learning systems.

The mental model theory of reasoning also helped direct our research efforts as we strove to better understand how end users build mental models of machine learning systems. For example, the theory posits that mental models are "runnable," meaning that people should be able to compare the results of different actions by "running" their mental model on multiple inputs. This implied that our research should consider how much and what kind of information end users need in order to create runnable models, as well as how users might want to use the insights gained from these models to correct their learning systems.

Our Explanatory Debugging approach for interactive machine learning systems was born from these foundations. Our formative research found a significant correlation between the quality of a user's mental model and their ability to control the learning system as desired, suggesting that the better someone understands the underlying system, the better they will be able to control it (Kulesza et al., 2012). Explanatory Debugging is therefore characterized by eight principles: four for *explainability*, and four for *correctability*.

2.2 The Explainability Principles

The first four principles of Explanatory Debugging are intended to enable end users to build high-quality mental models. They must, however, be carefully balanced: there is a tension among these four principles, such that increasing some of them may cause undesirable decreases in others.

Principle 1: Be Iterative
Our formative research suggested that users personalize a learning system best if they build their mental models *while interacting with it* (Kulesza et al., 2012), and therefore that explanations should support an iterative, *in situ* learning process. For example, explanations could take the form of concise, easily consumable "bites" of information in the context of the system's recent outputs. Such incremental, situated ways of explaining can thereby allow more interested users

to incrementally attend to more of these explanations, while still allowing less interested users to incrementally attend to fewer bite-sized chunks of information, all in the context of the system's most recent actions on their behalf.

Principle 2: Be Sound

We use the term *soundness* to mean the extent to which each component of an explanation's content is truthful in describing the underlying system (Kulesza et al., 2013): does the explanation include "nothing but the truth?" Kulesza et al. detailed the impact of explanation fidelity on mental model development, finding that users did not trust – and thus, were less likely to attend to – the least sound explanations (Kulesza et al., 2013). Thus, because reducing soundness reduces the likelihood that users will invest attention toward it, Explanatory Debugging requires designing explanations that are as sound as practically possible.

One method for evaluating explanation soundness is to compare the explanation with the learning system's mathematical model. For each of the model's terms that are included in the explanation, how accurately is it explained? If those terms are derived from more complex terms, is the user able to "drill down" to understand those additional terms? The more accurately these explanations reflect the underlying model, the more sound the explanation is.

Principle 3: Be Complete

Completeness is a complement to soundness, and describes the extent to which *all* of the underlying system is included in the explanation: does it explain "the whole truth?" Thus, a complete explanation does not omit important information about the model. In our formative research, we found that end users built the best mental models when they had access to the most complete explanations, which informed them of all the information the learning system had at its disposal and how it used that information (Kulesza et al., 2013). Also pertinent is work showing that users often struggle to understand how different parts of the system interact with each other (Kulesza et al., 2011). Complete explanations that reveal how different parts of the system are interconnected may help users overcome this barrier.

One method for evaluating completeness is via Lim and Dey's intelligibility types (2009); a more complete explanation system will cover more of these intelligibility types than a less complete system.

Principle 4: Don't Overwhelm

Balanced against the soundness and completeness principles is the need to remain comprehensible and to engage user attention. Achieving this goal while maintaining reasonably high soundness and completeness is still an underexplored problem, but the following approaches provide several starting points.

Findings from (Kulesza et al., 2013) suggest that one way to engage user attention is to frame explanations concretely, such as referencing the predicted item and any evidence the learning system employed in its prediction. In some circumstances, selecting a more comprehensible machine learning model may also be appropriate. For example, a neural network can be explained as if it were a decision tree (Craven & Shavlik, 1997), but this reduces soundness because a different model is explained, and may in turn require an additional explanation of the differences between the two models. Similarly, a model with 10,000 features can be explained as if it only used the 10 most discriminative features for each prediction, but this reduces completeness by omitting information that the model uses. Still, when the differences in outcome are small, the omissions may not be problematic. Alternative approaches that embody the Explanatory Debugging principles include selecting a machine learning model that can be explained with little abstraction (e.g., Lacave & Díez, 2002, Stumpf et al., 2009, Szafron, Greiner, Lu, & Wishart, 2003) or using feature selection techniques (Yang & Pedersen, 1997) in high-dimensionality domains to prevent users from struggling to identify which features to adjust (as happened in Kulesza et al., 2011).

2.3   The Correctability Principles

Given an appropriate mental model, we posited that users would be able to correct a learning system that has somehow gone awry, such as by having not enough data or having received skewed data. To empower them to do this, we added four correctability principles to our Explanatory Debugging approach; these four correctability principles are interdependent on the four explainability principles. In other words, besides informing correctability itself, the correctability principles also reinforce – and even suggest mechanisms helpful to – instantiating the explainability principles.

Besides the mental model theory of reasoning, two additional theoretical foundations were prominent in informing correctability. The first was the *attention-investment model* (Blackwell, 2002), which posits that users will invest their attention toward something (e.g., learning a little bit more about a specific machine learning system) if they expect their benefits (e.g., time saved through better recommendations or predictions) to be greater than the costs and risks (e.g., time, effort, or potential lack of payoff) of investing their attention. This model helped us shape an interactive paradigm in which users immediately see the benefits of their feedback, with the intent of encouraging further interaction. *Minimalist learning theory* (to be more fully introduced in Sect. 4.1) also informed our approach, especially as it relates to helping users learn and work with a concept *in-situ* (van der Meji & Carroll, 1998). (Both of these foundations were also useful in informing Explainability Principle 1.)

Principle 5: Be Actionable
Both theory (Blackwell, 2002) and prior empirical findings (Bunt, Lount, & Lauzon, 2012; Kulesza et al., 2012, 2013) suggest that end users will ignore explanations when the benefit of attending to them is unclear. By making explanations actionable, we hoped to lower users' perceived (and actual) cost of attending to them by obviating the need to transfer knowledge from one part of the user interface (the explanation) to another (the feedback mechanism). Actionable explanations also fulfill three

aspects of minimalist learning (van der Meji & Carroll, 1998): (1) people are learning while performing real work; (2) the explanatory material is tightly coupled to the system's current state; and (3) people can leverage their existing knowledge by adjusting the explanation to match their own mental reasoning.

Principle 6: Be Reversible
A risk inherent in enabling users to provide feedback to a machine learning system is that they may actually make its predictions worse (e.g., Kulesza et al., 2010, Stumpf et al., 2009). Being able to easily reverse a harmful action can help mitigate that risk, which is especially important to the risk component of the attention investment model. Reversibility may also encourage self-directed exploration and tinkering, which can facilitate learning (Rowe, 1973). When combined with Principle 8, reversibility also fulfills a fourth aspect of minimalist learning (van der Meji & Carroll, 1998): helping people identify and recover from errors.

Principle 7: Always Honor User Feedback
As Yang and Newman found when studying users of smart home thermostat systems (which learn from their users to predictively adjust the home's temperature) (Yang & Newman, 2013), a system that appears to disregard user feedback deters users from continuing to provide feedback. However, methods for honoring user feedback are not always straightforward. Handling user feedback over time (e.g., what if new instance-based feedback[1] contradicts old instance-based feedback?) and balancing different types of feedback (e.g., instance-based feedback versus feature-based feedback[2]) requires careful consideration of how the user's feedback will be integrated into the learning system.

Principle 8: Incremental Changes Matter
In our formative work (Kulesza et al., 2013), participants claimed they would attend to explanations only if doing so would enable them to more successfully control the learning system's predictions, a result predicted by the attention-investment model. Thus, continued user interaction likely depends on users being able to see the incremental effects their feedback has had on the learning system's reasoning immediately after each interaction. (This is an example of closing Norman's gulf of evaluation – enabling the user to see the results of their last action to interpret the state of the system, so as to evaluate how well their expectations and intentions were met (Norman, 2002)). This principle is also related to Principle 1 (Be iterative) because our thesis is that users will develop better mental

---

[1]Instance-based feedback, also known as label-based feedback, is when a user tells a machine learning system what a specific item's predication label should be. A common example is telling a junk mail filter that a specific email message is (or is not) SPAM.

[2]Feature-based feedback is when the user tells a machine learning system which particular features of the data (e.g., which words or fields of email messages) it should or should not use in its reasoning. One example would be a user telling a junk mail filter that every message from a specific email address should always go to the junk folder.

models iteratively, requiring many interactions with the learning system. These interactions may not always result in large, obvious effects, so being able to communicate even small, incremental effects a user's feedback has had upon a learning system may be critical to Explanatory Debugging's feasibility.

2.4 EluciDebug: A Prototype of Explanatory Debugging in Action

To evaluate the Explanatory Debugging approach's viability with end users, we prototyped it in the context of text classification. We designed a prototype, which we call EluciDebug, to look like an email program with multiple folders, each representing a particular topic (Fig. 1). The prototype's machine learning component attempts to automatically classify new messages into the appropriate folder.

To support Explanatory Debugging's Soundness and Completeness principles (Principles 2 and 3), we designed our EluciDebug explanations to detail *all* of the information the classifier could potentially use when making predictions (*completeness*) and to *accurately* describe how this information is used (*soundness*). For example, the explanation shown in Fig. 2 tells users that both feature presence and folder size played a role in each prediction. The explanation shown in Fig. 3 builds on this, telling the user all of the features the classifier knows about and may use in its predictions. To make clear to users that these features can occur in

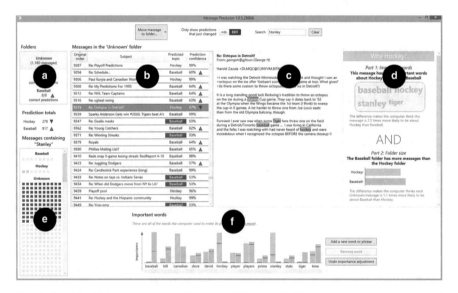

Fig. 1 The EluciDebug prototype. (A) List of folders. (B) List of messages in the selected folder. (C) The selected message. (D) Explanation of the selected message's predicted folder. (E) Overview of which messages contain the selected word. (F) Complete list of words the learning system uses to make predictions

Why Hockey?

Part 1: Important words
This message has more important words about Hockey than about Baseball

baseball **hockey stanley** tiger

The difference makes the computer think this message is 2.3 times more likely to be about Hockey than Baseball.

AND

Part 2: Folder size
The Baseball folder has more messages than the Hockey folder

Hockey:	7
Baseball:	8

The difference makes the computer thinks each Unknown message is 1.1 times more likely to be about Baseball than Hockey.

YIELDS

67% probability this message is about Hockey

Combining 'Important words' and 'Folder size' makes the computer think this message is 2.0 times more likely to be about Hockey than about Baseball.

Fig. 2 The *Why* explanation tells users how features and folder size were used to predict each message's topic. This figure is a close-up of Fig. 1 part D

all parts of the document – message body, subject line, and sender – EluciDebug highlights features in the context of each message (Fig. 1, part C).

The *Why* explanation (Fig. 2), which was inspired in part by the WhyLine for end-user debugging (Ko & Myers, 2004), is a concrete explanation and includes only information that was used for the selected prediction. This brevity is intentional; as per Principle 1, it is intended to be consumed iteratively, with users learning more about the overall system as they attend to more *Why* explanations. Such a design also supports Principle 4 by reducing the amount of information continuously shown to end users, to avoid overwhelming them with details that they may not (yet) care about.

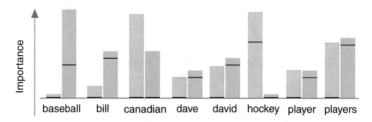

Fig. 3 The *Important words* explanation tells users all of the features the classifier is aware of, and also lets users add, remove, and adjust these features. Each topic is color-coded (here, the left, blue bar in a pair for *hockey* and right, green bar for *baseball*) with the difference in bar heights reflecting the difference in the word's probability with respect to each topic (e.g., the word *canadian* is roughly twice as likely to appear in a document about *hockey* as one about *baseball*, while the word *player* is about equally likely to appear in either topic). This figure is an excerpt from Fig. 1 part F

The *Important words* explanation (Fig. 3) is the primary actionable explanation in EluciDebug (Principle 5). Users can add words to – and remove words from – this explanation, which in turn will add those words to (or remove them from) the machine learning model's feature set. Users are also able to adjust the importance of each word in the explanation by dragging the word's bar higher (to make it more important) or lower (to make it less important), which then alters the corresponding feature's weight in the learning model. As described in (Kulesza et al., 2015), EluciDebug incorporates these corrections into its classifier in such a way that the user's feedback is always honored (Principle 7).

Finally, EluciDebug incorporates infinite undo functionality to allow the user to retrace their steps as far back as they like (Principle 6), and highlights recent changes to the classifier's predictions and certainty levels (Principle 8). The latter is especially important for motivation, because a single user correction often will not cause a classifier's predictions to change; instead, the classifier's *certainty* in predictions will shift, becoming either more or less certain. By observing these certainty changes, users can see how the system is honoring their feedback and can identify whether it is moving in the right or wrong direction.

2.5 Evaluation

We conducted an empirical evaluation to learn whether the Explanatory Debugging principles, as instantiated in the EluciDebug prototype, would indeed enable users to effectively and efficiently "debug" a machine learning system. The full details of our experiment design and procedures are enumerated in (Kulesza et al., 2015), but we present a brief summary of the results below to highlight the outcomes achievable by grounding EUSE research in theory.

Overall, Explanatory Debugging's cycle of explanations – from the learning system to the user, and from the user back to the system – resulted in smarter users

Fig. 4 Participants who used EluciDebug for 30 minutes learned approximately 50% more about how the classifier worked than control participants

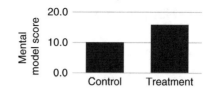

Fig. 5 Corrections provided by participants using EluciDebug (light orange) resulted in significantly more accurate classifiers than the same number of corrections provided by control participants (dark blue)

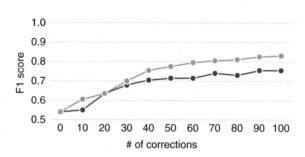

and smarter learning systems. For example, treatment participants (i.e., those using the Explanatory Debugging prototype) understood how the learning system operated about 50% better than control participants using a traditional learning system that lacked actionable explanations (Fig. 4). Further, this improvement correlated with the F1 scores of participants' classifier accuracy ($\rho[75] = .282$, $p = .013$), which were significantly more accurate (given the same number of corrections) for EluciDebug participants than for control participants (Fig. 5). Finally, participants liked Explanatory Debugging, rating EluciDebug significantly better than the control group and responding enthusiastically to the system's explanations.

We attribute these positive outcomes to Explanatory Debugging's strong theoretical foundations. The psychological theories of how people learn, understand, and invest their attention when working with interactive systems provided us the guidance to stay on an efficient research track. This guidance not only foretold our promising results, but enabled us to avoid false starts in wrong directions that might have later needed to be discarded and redone. For example, the mental model theory of reasoning guided our approach to enable ordinary end users to understand a fairly complex machine learning system. The attention investment and minimalist learning models combined with the mental model foundation to guide our research toward the correctability principles.

Finally, these theoretical foundations enabled us to think about Explanatory Debugging at the level of principles rather than systems and UI widgets, so that future approaches for different systems and situations can still leverage them. We hope that others will build upon these principles for interactive machine learning to further advance the state of the art in producing more controllable and satisfying experiences for end users than traditional machine learning systems, enabling ordinary end users to gain the most benefit from the learning systems on which they increasingly depend.

3   Gender HCI and GenderMag

In the Gender HCI project, our path toward improving EUSE systems again began with theories, then moved to an iterative series of refinements and applications of the theories, and ultimately produced a general method that we call GenderMag. The overall project goals were (1) to investigate whether gender differences reported in social science domains, such as psychology and education, applied to EUSE tools; and when the importance of these differences became clear, (2) to develop a theory-based method that would enable creators of EUSE environments and tools to identify features in their software that were not gender-inclusive.

Toward these ends, we built on social science theories using the research paradigm presented in Fig. 6. We began with social science literature containing theories potentially applicable to gender differences in how people problem-solve with computers. We then derived hypotheses about what these theories might predict in EUSE situations and empirically tested these hypotheses in controlled laboratory studies. Using the results of these studies to guide our designs, we prototyped new features in our EUSE tools and again evaluated them empirically, keeping in mind the foundational theories, and decided whether the EUSE setting required further potential refinements. The highly iterative process then began again with refined theories.

We illustrate this paradigm using two of the theories that strongly influenced the Gender HCI project: self-efficacy theory and information processing theory.

3.1   A GenderMag Foundation: Self-Efficacy Theory

Self-efficacy is a person's belief that they can succeed at a specific task (Bandura, 1986). It is a form of self-confidence specific to a situation or task; for example, someone may have high bike-riding self-efficacy and low computer self-efficacy. According to this theory, someone with high self-efficacy who encounters problems will persist through adversity, such as by trying different approaches and strategies to overcome the problems. In contrast, someone with low self-efficacy is more likely to stay with faulty approaches and strategies and to experience high levels of self-doubt. As a result, low self-efficacy individuals are often unsuccessful in their tasks, leading to lower and lower self-efficacy in an unfortunate

Fig. 6 The Gender HCI project's iterative research paradigm

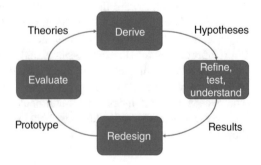

feedback loop. Research shows that self-efficacy is particularly important when it comes to challenging tasks and is a reasonably accurate predictor of success and behavior in such situations (Bandura, 1986).

Computer self-efficacy is a person's belief about their capabilities to use computers in a variety of situations (Compeau & Higgins, 1995). Previous studies have found that females statistically have lower computer self-efficacy than males. This holds true across a number of computing situations, from females majoring in computer science to female end users (Appel, Kronberger, & Aronson, 2011; Beyer, Rynes, Perrault, Hay, & Haller, 2003; Huffman, Whetton, & Huffman, 2013; Luger, 2014). Research has also reported females having lower computer self-efficacy even when objective measures show them to be just as competent at completing the task as males (Hargittai & Shafer, 2006).

Our own investigations of how self-efficacy relates to gender differences with debugging and programming tools also showed that females often had lower computer self-efficacy than males. More important, their low self-efficacy was tied to the way females used software features (Burnett et al., 2011, Hartzel, 2003). For example, females' self-efficacies were predictive of their successful use of debugging tools – even though there was no predictive relationship for males (Beckwith et al., 2005, Beckwith, Burnett, Wiedenbeck, Grigoreanua, & Wiedenbeck, 2006). Females were also (statistically) less willing to engage with or explore novel debugging features – despite these features being tied to improved debugging performance by both females and males (Beckwith et al., 2006, Beckwith, Inman, Rector, & Burnett, 2007). Further, Subrahmaniyan et al. showed that females *used different features* and *used features differently* than males (2008). Finally, the features most conducive to females' successes were features that are not commonly found in EUSE environments (Subrahmaniyan et al., 2008).

Informed by self-efficacy theory and in light of the above empirical results, we devised two new features to add to our EUSE prototype. The previous prototype, a spreadsheet system, had a testing feature, in which users could "check off" any spreadsheet cell value that they decided was right, or "X out" any spreadsheet cell value they decided was wrong. Based on a hypothesis that the previous "it's right" and "it's wrong" checkmark and X in the spreadsheet cells might seem like a stronger statement than low self-efficacy users would feel comfortable making, we introduced "seems right maybe" and "seems wrong maybe" options to the check box widget in each spreadsheet cell (Fig. 7). The intention of this change was to communicate the idea that a user didn't have to be confident about a testing decision in order to be "qualified" to make judgements (Grigoreanu et al., 2008).

Fig. 7 Clicking on the checkbox turns it into four choices whose tool tips say "it's wrong," "seems wrong maybe," "seems right maybe," "it's right." Our decision to add this feature to the prototype was based on self-efficacy theory

Fig. 8 (Top): 1-minute video snippets. (Bottom): Hypertext version. As with Fig. 7, our decision to add these features to the prototype was based on self-efficacy theory

The second feature we introduced to the prototype was to add strategy explanations in two formats: short video snippets and equivalent hypertext content (Fig. 8). The original prototype had included only feature-oriented tooltips to explain the system's functionalities. Our addition of video snippets was informed by work with the "vicarious experience" source of self-efficacy, which is self-efficacy based on watching someone similar to the user perform the task (Bandura, 1977; Zeldin & Pajares, 2000). In each video snippet, the female debugger works on a debugging problem, and a male debugger, referring to the spreadsheet, converses with her about strategy ideas (Grigoreanu et al., 2008), ultimately ending in the female succeeding. The hyperlink contained the same information as the video and was offered as an option for those who don't learn best pictorially, or who want to quickly scan to a particular part of the information as a time saver.

With the addition of these new features, both females' and males' (but especially females') usage of testing/debugging features increased, which translated into testing and debugging improvements. Females' confidence levels also improved to an appropriate level – where their self-judgments were roughly appropriate indicators of their actual ability levels. Males' confidence levels had already been appropriate indicators of their abilities, and remained so. Females' and males' (but especially females') post-session verbalizations showed that their attitudes toward the software environment were significantly more positive. Note that the gains for females came without disadvantaging the males, and, in fact, usually ended up helping them as well (Grigoreanu et al., 2008).

3.2   A GenderMag Foundation: Information Processing Theory

Another theory that has strongly influenced our gender investigations is the Selectivity Hypothesis of information processing styles (Meyers-Levy, 1989; Meyers-Levy & Maheswaran, 1991; Meyers-Levy & Loken, 2015). This theory proposes that males process information in a selective manner, attending to highly available and salient cues and then acting, whereas females process information in a comprehensive manner, gathering as much information from all available cues as possible to develop a full picture of the issue before acting. The theory also claims that males and females categorize and classify information into categories differently, with females creating more categories than males, and placing statements with conceptual similarity into these categories in more consistent ways than males (Meyers-Levy, 1989; Meyers-Levy & Loken, 2015; Meyers-Levy & Maheswaran, 1991).

We hypothesized that someone's information processing style should affect the way they approach a problem in the realm of debugging. Indeed, our studies have shown this link. For example, females tended to process information comprehensively using code inspection to get a relatively complete picture of the problem. This strategy often resulted in success for female participants. On the other hand, males had more success using dataflow and following particular dependencies one at a time, which coincides with selective information processing (Grigoreanu et al., 2009; Subrahmaniyan et al., 2008).

A close-up look at the most successful female participant and the most successful male participant from one of our studies helps to illustrate these distinct information processing styles. In (Grigoreanu et al., 2012), we investigated how male and female end users made sense of spreadsheet correctness when debugging. Participants were given 45 minutes to decide whether a (flawed) spreadsheet was correct, and, if it wasn't, to fix it.

The most successful female demonstrated the comprehensive information processing style, gathering a lot of information before taking fix action(s) (stars above the graph in Fig. 9), which often occurred in bursts. The lengths of her bursts of

Male

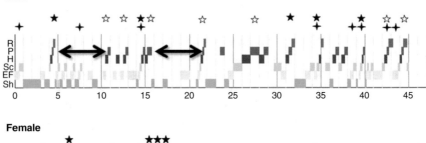

Female

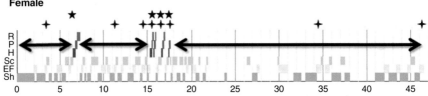

Fig. 9 Two end-user developers' information processing activities while debugging a spreadsheet over about 45 minutes. The bottom three rows of each graph (green, yellow, and orange) are information gathering activities, and the top three rows (red, pink, and blue) are acting upon that information. (Top graph): The most successful male participant. (Bottom graph): The most successful female participant

information gathering are indicated by the superimposed horizontal arrows. In all cases her fixes were successful, indicated on the graph by all the stars being filled in. This burst-y style, during which she spent a burst of time gathering a large batch of information and then acted upon that batch in a burst of activity, is consistent with a comprehensive style of information processing.

This strategy generally worked well for our female participant, but it had a downside as well. In times of uncertainty, the successful female would continue gathering information even though it did not yield results, as evident in Fig. 9 where she sometimes did not emerge from the information gathering stages for long periods of time. This resulted in her noticing bugs while foraging but not marking them or fixing them at the time, so she sometimes forgot to fix them.

In contrast to the female's style, the successful male's style was a classic example of selective processing. In fact, his *maximum* time spent gathering information (about 5 minutes in the graph) was less than the successful female's *minimum* time spent on gathering information. Instead, he iterated tightly between gathering a little information and trying out a fix. As Fig. 9 shows with hollow stars, many of his attempted fixes were unsuccessful, but he often realized that and went back to gather a little more information and then try again.

As with the female's use of her comprehensive processing strategy, our male participant's selective processing strategy worked well for him, but also had a downside. He fixated on one bug and focused on only that bug until it was fixed. This cost him time and also discouraged him from fixing or identifying other bugs that he came across while working on his target bug.

In total, the two participants fixed the same number of bugs. (The number of filled-in stars shows one extra for the male because he also implanted a new bug along the way that he also had to fix.) As these two participants illustrate, both styles have advantages and disadvantages, but can lead people differently to equal levels of success.

Insights into these information processing styles are then reasonably prescriptive: they suggest that an EUSE tool should support both styles. In Sect. 4, one example of how to do this will be seen in Table 2, in which expandable tooltips are used to support this diversity of information processing styles.

3.3   GenderMag: A Theory-to-Practice Method

We have used foundations like those mentioned above to develop a practical method for evaluating software features for gender inclusiveness issues. We call it GenderMag (Gender-Inclusiveness Magnifier) (Burnett et al., 2016).

3.3.1   The GenderMag Method

GenderMag is based on five theory-based facets of individual differences that statistically cluster according to gender. The five facets are: motivation, information processing, computer self-efficacy, risk-aversion, and tinkering. We discussed two of them (self-efficacy and information processing) above, and a discussion of all five facets can be found in (Burnett et al., 2016). Our criteria for selecting these particular five facets were that (1) they had been extensively researched in prior literature, (2) they were usable for ordinary software developers or UX designers without needing backgrounds in gender research, and (3) they had implications for software usage in problem-solving situations. We conducted several formative studies, a lab study, and a field study to ensure that the facets satisfied these criteria (Burnett et al., 2016, Burnett, Peters, Hill, & Elarief, 2016).

These facets are embedded in a set of four personas to bring them to life: Tim, Abby, Pat(ricia), and Pat(rick). Personas are archetypes of particular user groups of interest (Marsden, 2014; Turner & Turner, 2011). Thus, in our case, each persona captures facets of individual differences that statistically cluster by gender. The Tim persona has facet values that were most frequently seen in males across numerous studies, and Abby's facet values are those *least* frequently seen in males while still occurring frequently in females. Most of Pat(ricia)'s and Pat(rick)'s facet values are "between" Tim's and Abby's values. The only difference between the two Pat personas is their gender, to reinforce the point that the road to gender inclusiveness lies not in a person's gender identity, but in the facet values themselves.

As a concrete example, Fig. 10 demonstrates a portion of the data behind the Motivation facet values of each persona. As with all the facets, motivation is backed by multiple studies, but for simplicity of presentation, only one of them is

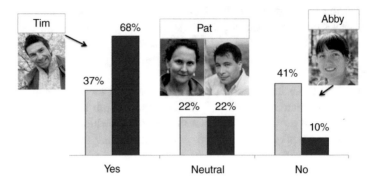

Fig. 10 A portion of the empirical foundations behind the personas' Motivation facet values (see text)

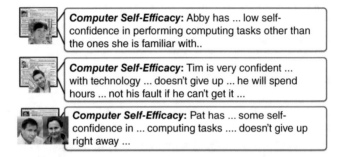

Fig. 11 The self-efficacy portions of Abby, Tim, and the two Pats, drawn from self-efficacy and empirical data (Burnett et al., 2016) (see text)

illustrated in the figure (Burnett et al., 2010). In that study, about 2/3 of males and 1/3 of females were motivated by exploring next-generation technology (covered by Tim), and about 1/5 of both males and females felt neutral about it (covered by the two Pats). The largest percentage of females and smallest percentage of males did not enjoy exploring next-generation technology (covered by Abby). Fig. 11 shows the persona side of such mappings, with text snippets of how another facet, self-efficacy, maps to each persona.

GenderMag intertwines these personas with a specialized Cognitive Walkthrough (CW). The CW is a long-standing inspection method for identifying usability issues for users new to a system or feature (Wharton, Rieman, Lewis, & Polson, 1994). We based the GenderMag CW on a streamlined version of the CW (Spencer, 2000) and further streamlined from there to increase the method's practicality.

More important, we embedded mentions of the personas and the appropriate facets to consider in each CW questions. Our reason for mentioning the personas was to address the problem of evaluators thinking about the way *they* would respond to the interface, not the way the persona would respond. (Some researchers term this unfortunate tendency that evaluators sometimes have as the "I methodology.") Our reason for embedding the facets in the questions was to keep evaluators focused on the five facet values, instead of falling back on their own biases and stereotypes.

3.3.2   Evaluation: GenderMag in the Field

GenderMag has just started being used in the field, but it has already produced encouraging and rather surprising results.

More specifically, we recently conducted a field study of four software teams in U.S. technology organizations who used GenderMag to evaluate their own software for gender-inclusiveness issues (Burnett et al., 2016). Their software spanned a range of types and maturity levels, and evaluation team members spanned a range of job titles, including software developers, UX researchers, computer science researchers, and software managers.

Despite these differences, the results consistently showed that all teams found gender-inclusiveness issues in their software. Most issues were those that would disproportionately affect users in the group represented by Abby, but one team also uncovered an issue that would disproportionately affect users in the group represented by Tim. (This field study occurred before the Pat personas had been released.) On average, the teams turned up gender-inclusiveness issues in 25% of the software features they evaluated (Fig. 12). In many cases, these issues had gone unnoticed for months or even years.

All the teams found the method to be useful. Agency G's two teams (GB and GS) found four issues that they deemed important enough to pursue fixing, even though their software had been in maintenance status for years. Team E fixed three issues right away, and Team W convinced the software's designers to fix three issues. Teams GB, GS, and W also made longer-term follow-up plans involving GenderMag. Perhaps most important, all of the teams ultimately realized that for software to be gender-inclusive, it needs to support a range of facet values, not just facet values matching the designers' own personal styles. In essence, they

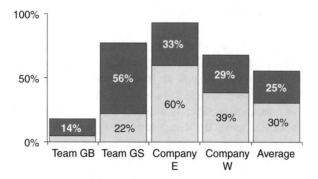

Fig. 12 Issues each team found as a percentage of the number of user actions and subgoals evaluated (Burnett et al., 2016). Dark blue: gender-inclusiveness issues. Light gray: other issues

realized that gender inclusiveness is not about sorting people into gender bins–it is about supporting the entire range of facet values (Burnett et al., 2016).

4 The Idea Garden

Our third example is the Idea Garden, a theory-based approach we developed to support end users' problem-solving during programming and debugging. Evidence abounds that, despite advances in EUSE environments and tools, users continue to encounter programming barriers. For example, Ko et al. identified six learning barriers faced by end users in using Visual Basic (Ko, Myers, & Aung, 2004). In the realm of spreadsheets, Chambers and Scaffidi found that spreadsheet users face barriers similar to those faced by Visual Basic learners as identified by Ko et al. (Chambers & Scaffidi, 2010). Our own research found the same barriers in other end-user programming platforms as well, such as CoScripter and Gidget (Cao, Fleming, & Burnett, 2011; Lee et al., 2014).

To help end users overcome barriers like these, the Idea Garden aims to help end users generate new ideas and problem-solve in a self-directed way. This goal contrasts with approaches that aim to remove such barriers. For example, we do not seek to change the programming language to make it simpler or more natural (Blackwell & Hague, 2001; Kelleher & Pausch, 2006; Myers, Pane, & Ko, 2004; Little et al., 2007), do not seek to automatically eliminate or solve problems for the user (Ennals, Brewer, Garofalakis, Shadle, & Gandhi, 2007; Hartmann, MacDougall, Brandt, & Klemmer, 2010; Lin, Wong, Nichols, Cypher, & Lau, 2009; Little et al., 2007; Miller et al., 2010; Repenning & Ioannidou, 2008), and do not seek to delegate programming responsibilities to someone other than the end users themselves (Brandt, Dontcheva, Weskamp, & Klemmer, 2010; Oney & Myers, 2009). Rather, we seek to help end users generate their *own* ideas to overcome the programming barriers they do encounter.

4.1 The Idea Garden's Foundations

Toward that end, we followed a theory-based approach to devise the Idea Garden. The principle theoretical foundation behind the Idea Garden is minimalist learning theory (Carroll, 1990, 1998; Carroll & Rosson, 1987; van der Meij & Carroll, 1998). Rooted in the constructivism of Bruner and Piaget, minimalist learning theory (MLT) is an education theory that explains how (and why) to design instructional materials for end users: the theory terms people like this "active" computer users. Active computer users are those whose primary motivation is to *do* some computer-based task of their own, not particularly to *learn* computing skills. Active users are so focused on the task at hand that they are often unwilling to invest time in taking tutorials, reading documentation, or using other training materials – even if such an investment would be rational in the long term. Helping users who face this paradox learn *despite* their lack of interest in learning per se is the goal of MLT. This theory is especially suited to the design of the Idea Garden features because the Idea Garden aims to help end users generate new ideas while they are working on their own, self-directed programming tasks.

MLT suggests several design principles that lend themselves to effective learning activities for active users. The Idea Garden follows these guidelines in the following ways:

(MLT-1) Permit self-directed reasoning: The Idea Garden suggests strategy alternatives and provides (intentionally) incomplete hints, all of which require the user to actively reason and problem solve in order to make substantive progress on the task at hand (as opposed to simply giving them the solution). The parts that are not problem-specific are "correct" in that they apply regardless of the granular details of the user's task. The incomplete parts of hints are so specific that they are unlikely to be exactly what the user needs and must be adapted to the user's specific problem or barrier. In addition, the Idea Garden uses negotiated-style interruptions, which inform users of pending messages but do not force them to acknowledge the messages (McFarlane, 2002). This allows users to decide for themselves whether to read and consider the messages, permitting self-directed reasoning. This interruption style contrasts with assertive instructional agents that violate users' self-directedness with immediate-style interruptions, such as Microsoft Office's paperclip ("Clippy"), which hijack the user's attention (McFarlane, 2002). Negotiated-style interruptions have been shown to be superior to immediate-style interruptions in end-user debugging situations (Robertson et al., 2004).

(MLT-2) Be meaningful and self-contained and *(MLT-3) Provide realistic tasks early on:* In the Idea Garden, hints are task-oriented, and many of them are closely coupled with the user's context. To follow MLT-2, hints are generally tied to tasks that the user has already chosen to initiate with the goal of giving meaning, value, and realism. Hints also uphold MLT-3 using examples of tasks that the user is likely to be working on or may have performed in the past.

(MLT-4) Be closely linked to the actual system: The Idea Garden is a layer on top of a host environment. The Idea Garden can be a layer on any end-user programming environment that allows the Idea Garden to: retrieve the user's data and code as it appears to the user (i.e., on the screen) and as it appears to the machine (i.e., after parsing); change the user's code (e.g., by inserting constants or lines of code); and annotate the programming environment and/or user's code with interactive widgets (e.g., tooltips, buttons, graphics, or font changes). Many programming environments, including Excel, CoScripter, Gidget, and Cloud9, satisfy these constraints, providing pluggable architectures into which Idea Garden features can be added (Cao et al., 2010, 2011; Jernigan et al., 2015, 2017; Loksa et al., 2016).

(MLT-5) Provide for error recognition and recovery: The Idea Garden is not intended to replace the programming environment's native error recovery system, so it leaves most of the detection of and recovery from errors to the host environment itself. Rather, the Idea Garden adds onto its host programming environment, expanding whatever help systems and error supports the host provides.

Using the MLT principles as our foundation, we define the Idea Garden as (Cao, Fleming, Burnett, & Scaffidi, 2014):

(Host) A subsystem that extends a "host" end-user programming environment to provide hints that...
(Theory) follow the 5 MLT principles (MLT-1 through MLT-5) and...
(Content/Presentation) non-authoritatively give intentionally imperfect guidance about problem-solving strategies, programming concepts, and design patterns, via negotiated interruptions.
(Implementation) In addition, the hints are presented via host-independent templates that are informed by host-dependent information about the user's task and progress.

4.2   The Idea Garden in Action

We have implemented the Idea Garden in three host programming environments: CoScripter (Cao et al., 2010, 2011), Gidget (Jernigan et al., 2015, 2017), and Cloud9 (Jernigan et al., 2017; Loksa et al., 2016). Although each version looks different, all follow the Idea Garden definition and MLT guidelines we have just presented. In the next subsections, we show examples of ways the five MLT guidelines can be instantiated, using these implementations.

4.2.1   CoScripter

The first environment in which we prototyped the Idea Garden was CoScripter, an end-user programming-by-demonstration environment for web scripting (Cao et al., 2010, 2011; Lin et al., 2009). Users demonstrate to CoScripter how they would carry out a task on the web by actually performing the task themselves. The system watches and translates users' actions into a script that they can later execute to perform the same task again, or can generalize to perform the task in a variety of situations. When working on these scripts, users can turn to Idea Garden hints if they get "stuck."

Recall that, to stay in accordance with MLT-1, Idea Garden hints have both "correct" and "incomplete" parts. Fig. 13 demonstrates with a representative hint from the CoScripter prototype. The "correct" part suggests using a repeat statement to iterate over cells in a column rather than addressing each cell as a separate case. The "incomplete" part gives a specific example of using this strategy that does not directly solve the user's problem, but that the user can use as a model for the correct solution.

The hint shown in Fig. 13 also demonstrates how the Idea Garden supports MLT-2, MLT-3, and MLT-4 as follows. The hint example started as a "repeat" template, then plugged in URLs ("http://maps.google.com/"), cell references ("'Address' column of row 1"), and widgets ("the first button") from the user's own code. This content's concrete connections to the user's own task are to fulfill the "meaningful" aspect of MLT-2 and also the "realistic task" aspect of MLT-3. In addition, the hint's example does not require background knowledge of the user

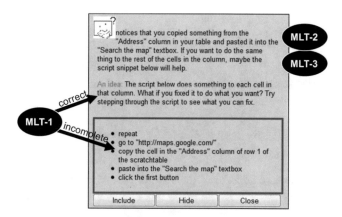

Fig. 13 The hint's content is triggered if the user's scripting suggests that they are trying to repeat the same action on more than one data element, adhering to MLT-2 and MLT-3. The hint does not pop up; its availability is indicated in situ (for MLT-4) by an icon that decorates the user's script at the relevant script segment. The user can click on the icon to see this hint. To uphold MLT-1, the hint's example has incomplete parts, so that the user must actively engage with it by modifying the script to make it work. MLT-5 is not shown in this example

beyond common copy/paste editing operations and programming constructs they have already used, thereby adhering to the "self-contained" aspect of MLT-2.

4.2.2   Gidget

Gidget, an online puzzle game that centers on debugging, hosted the second version of the Idea Garden. In the game, a robot named Gidget provides players with code to complete missions. According to the game's backstory, Gidget was damaged, and the player must help Gidget by diagnosing and debugging Gidget's faulty code. Game levels introduce or reinforce different programming concepts.

Gidget's adherence to MLT-1 through MLT-4 are similar to CoScripter's, so we do not repeat them here. However, the Gidget example shown in Fig. 14 demonstrates particularly well its adherence to MLT-5, the Idea Garden's integration with the host environment's built-in error identification and recovery systems. The superimposed callouts ("grab/piglet/" and "Oh no! …") show the way the host environment points out and helps with a logic error in the user's code. Fig. 14 shows Gidget handling the same error while the Idea Garden augments the environment with a tooltip based on the user's code. By acting as a layer on top of the native environment rather than a full replacement of its help system, the Idea Garden allows users to fully use Gidget's built-in error handling.

4.2.3   Cloud9

The third host environment for the Idea Garden was Cloud9, a web-based IDE. We used this version of the Idea Garden in two 2-week high school web

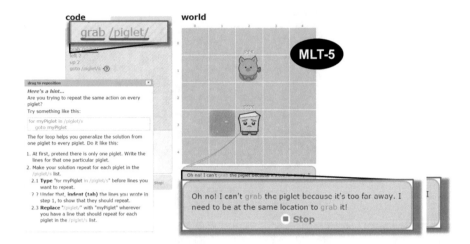

Fig. 14 How MLT-5 is supported in Gidget. The ⟨?⟩ (in the code pane, upper left) and the tooltip-like hint (lower left) are the Idea Garden's error recognition and recovery mechanisms, which supplement Gidget's built-in error/recovery features (outlined with pink boxes in the upper left ("grab/piglet/") and lower right ("Oh no! …")). The superimposed callouts are for readability

Fig. 15 The top portion of the Idea Garden panel in the Cloud9 IDE. To uphold MLT-4, the panel mimics the functionality of Cloud9's other expandable panels

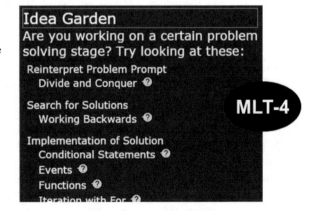

development camps that taught HTML and JavaScript, as a resource for students to turn to when they were stuck (Loksa et al., 2016). The Idea Garden runs within Cloud9 in the form of a plugin. The pluggable architecture of the environment gave us access to Cloud9's background processes, such as its parser, tokenizer, and listener, which allowed us to directly inspect and handle the user's code, as was also the case in the other two environments.

The Cloud9 implementation of the Idea Garden adheres to the MLT principles in ways similar to the other two host environments, but its appearance is different. Fig. 15 shows the Idea Garden as it appears in the expandable panel within the programming environment, designed to look and act similarly to the rest of Cloud9's expandable panels for MLT-4. Fig. 16 shows how the use of the

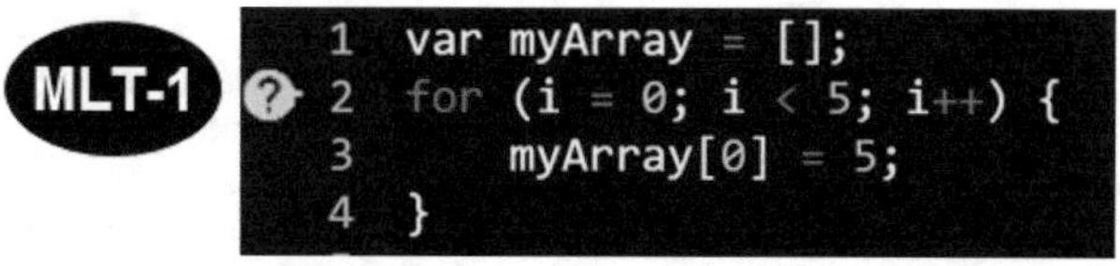

Fig. 16 An example of the Idea Garden decorating the code with an icon. Here, the icon links to the *Iteration with For* hint if the user decides to click on it

negotiated interruption style to inform users of potentially useful hints by decorating the environment with a ⊘ icon, as per MLT-1.

4.3   The Idea Garden's Principles

As we empirically investigated these instantiations of the Idea Garden with end users, we found that the *Content/Presentation* aspect of the definition (Sect. 4.1) – arguably the most important of the four aspects – was difficult to get right. The collection of MLT principles MLT-1 though MLT-5 were too high-level to adequately address this problem. We needed a lower-level set of principles that would expand upon MLT's guidelines while still being implementation-independent enough to support future Idea Gardens.

To address this need, we derived seven lower-level principles using prior Idea Garden studies and the theoretical foundations of Sect. 4.1 to better ground the Content/Presentation aspect (Jernigan et al., 2015), which we enumerate in Table 1. As we discussed in the introduction, a theory can explain, predict, or prescribe behaviors, and theory can be both consumed and produced. Here, we *consume* prescriptions and predictions from MLT and related theories, and *produce* our own prescriptive set of principles on how a system like the Idea Garden might be most effective.

Most of the principles build upon MLT's points as to how to serve active users. For instance, IG1-Content provides content that relates to what the user is *already doing*; IG2-Relevance displays content in a way that the user believes it to be *relevant to the task at hand*; IG3-Actionable gives the user something to *do* with the newfound information; and IG6-Availability ensures that users can access content within the context in which they are working to *keep their focus on getting the task done* rather than searching for solutions from external sources. Figs. 17 and 18 and Table 2 show concrete examples of how we implemented the Gidget-based Idea Garden according to these principles.

Detecting *antipatterns* enables support for two of the Idea Garden principles. Antipatterns, a notion similar to "code smells," are implementation patterns that suggest some kind of conceptual, problem-solving, or strategy difficulty, such as not using an iterator variable within the body of a loop or defining a function without calling it. We used antipatterns in all three Idea Garden implementations. The examples shown here are from the Gidget version.

Antipatterns define context for IG6.ContextSensitive, letting the hint be derived from and shown in the context of the user's problem. For IG2-Relevance, the hint

Table 1 The seven Idea Garden Principles and their explanations. A hyphenated name signifies a principle (e.g. IG1-Content), while a name with a dot signifies a subprinciple (IG1.Concepts)

Principle	Explanation
IG1-Content	Content that makes up the hints need to contain at least one of the following:
IG1.Concepts	Explains a programming *concept* such as iteration or functions. Can include programming constructs as needed to illustrate the concept.
IG1.Mini-patterns	*Design mini-patterns* show a usage of the concept that the user must adapt to their problem (minipattern should not solve the user's problem).
IG1.Strategies	A problem-solving strategy such as working through the problem backward.
IG2-Relevance	For Idea Garden hints that are context-sensitive, the aim is that the user perceives them to be relevant. Thus, hints use one or more of these types of relevance:
IG2.MyCode	The hint includes some of the user's code.
IG2.MyState	The hint depends on the user's code, such as by explaining a concept present in the user's code.
IG2.MyGoal	The hint depends on the requirements the user is working on, such as referring to associated test cases or pre/post-conditions.
IG3-Actionable	Because the Idea Garden targets MLT's "active users," hints must give them something to *do* (Carroll & Rosson, 1987; Carroll, 1990). Thus, Idea Garden hints must imply an action that the user can take to overcome a barrier or get ideas on how to meet their goals:
IG3.Explictly Actionable	The hint prescribes actions that can be physically done, such as indenting or typing something.
IG3.Implicitly Actionable	The hint prescribes actions that are "in the head," such as "compare" or "recall."
IG4-Personality	The personality and tone of Idea Garden entries must try to encourage constructive thinking. Toward this end, hints are expressed non-authoritatively and tentatively (Lee & Ko, 2011). For example, phrases like "try something like this" are intended to show that, while knowledgeable, the Idea Garden is not sure how to solve the user's exact problem.
IG5-Information Processing	Because research has shown that (statistically) females tend to gather information comprehensively when problem-solving, whereas males gather information selectively (Meyers-Levy, 1989), the hints must support both styles. For example, when a hint is not small, a condensed version must be offered with expandable parts.
IG6-Availability	Hints must be available in these ways:
IG6.Context Sensitive	Available in the context where the system deems the hint relevant.
IG6.ContextFree	Available in context-free form through an always-available widget (e.g., pull-down menu).
IG7-Interruption Style	Because research has shown the superiority of the negotiated style of interruptions in debugging situations (Robertson et al., 2004), all hints

(continued)

Table 1 (continued)

Principle	Explanation
	must follow this style. In negotiated style, nothing ever pops up. Instead, a small indicator "decorates" the environment (like the incoming mail count on an email icon) to let the user know where the Idea Garden has relevant information. Users can then request to see the new information by hovering or clicking on the indicator.

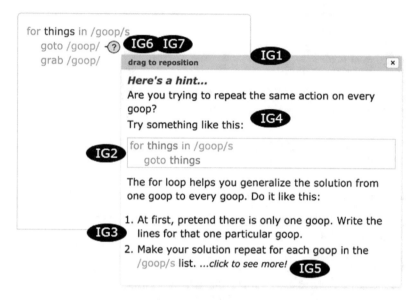

Fig. 17 An example of a context-sensitive Idea Garden hint in Gidget. Hovering over the ⑦ shows the hint, and the superimposed black ovals show where the seven principles are instantiated in the hint

communicates relevance (to the user's current problem) by being derived from the player's current code as soon as they enter it, such as using the same variable names (Fig. 17, IG2 and IG6). The Gidget-based Idea Garden brings these two principles together by constructing a context-sensitive hint whenever it detects a conceptual antipattern. The Idea Garden then displays the hint indicator (⑦ in the Gidget-based version) beside the relevant code to show the hint's availability.

4.4   Evaluation

We conducted an empirical study with teams of teenaged students to evaluate these principles (Jernigan et al., 2015) as instantiated in Gidget. Teams worked through Gidget's levels, and, if they had time, designed their own levels using the

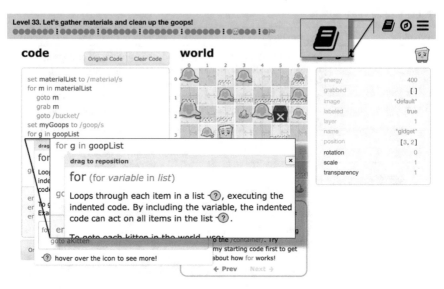

Fig. 18 As part of IG6 and IG7, the Idea Garden's hints appear as tooltips when the user hovers over a ⟨?⟩. The superimposed callouts are for readability

Table 2 How the seven Idea Garden principles were implemented, with examples in Gidget

Principle	Which part(s) of Idea Garden affected	Example in Gidget
IG1-Content	Body of hint: Code example (drawn from *antipattern*); strategy	Fig. 18, large callout; Fig. 17, middle
IG2-Relevance	Gist of hint ("Are you trying to...?"); Inclusion of user's own code and variable names	Fig. 17, gist and code example
IG3-Actionable	Suggested strategy in hint, using actionable words like "pretend" and "write"	Fig. 17, numbered steps
IG4-Personality	Tentative phrasing ("You might try.../...Try something like this")	Fig. 17, text
IG5-Information Processing	Expandable strategies in longer hints	Fig. 17, "Click to see more"
IG6-Availability	In-context availability through antipattern-triggered icons; Context-free availability via a UI widget that always gives access to all hints	Fig. 17, ⟨?⟩; Fig. 18, small callout of dictionary button
IG7-Interruption Style	Icon users can *choose* to interact with rather than hijacking control to display a hint	Fig. 17, ⟨?⟩

built-in editor. As it turned out, teams did not always need the Idea Garden; they solved many of their problems just by discussing them with each other, reading the reference manual, etc. However, when these measures did not suffice, they turned to the Idea Garden for more assistance.

As Table 3 shows, the Idea Garden enabled campers to problem-solve their way past the majority of these barriers (52%) without any guidance from the

Table 3 Barrier instances and teams' progress with/without getting in-person help. Teams did not usually need in-person help when an Idea Garden hint and/or an antipattern-triggered ⑦ was on the screen (top row). The third column, containing instances of barriers where teams did not make progress, is shown to ensure the rows sum to the correct values

IG Available and On-screen?	Progress without in-person help	Progress if team got in-person help	No evidence of progress
Yes (149+25 instances)	77/149 (52%)	25/25	72/(149+25)
No (155 instances)	53/155	91/155 (59%)	11/155

helper staff. Particularly noteworthy is the fact that their problem-solving progress with the Idea Garden alone (52% solved their problem using the Idea Garden alone, *without* in-person help from camp helpers) was almost as high as their progress with in-person help (59% solved their problem using only in-person help from camp helpers, *without* the Idea Garden).

Further, the results suggested that each principle complemented the others in coming together to support a diversity of problems, information processing and problem-solving styles, cognitive stages, and people.

For example, teams' successes across a diversity of concepts served to demonstrate this point while also validating the concept aspect of IG1-Content. Antipatterns were especially involved in teams' success rates with different kinds of barriers. Together, these aspects enabled the teams to overcome, without any in-person help, 41–68% of the barriers they encountered across *diverse barrier types*. Adding to this, teams could overcome these barriers in diverse ways by IG2-Relevance and IG6-Availability working together to provide relevant, just-in-time hints to afford teams diverse paths by which to use the ⑦ to make progress. This suggests that IG2 and IG6 help support *diverse EUP problem-solving styles*.

IG3-Actionable's explicit vs. implicit approaches also played to different strengths. Teams tended to use explicitly actionable instructions (e.g., "Indent…") to translate an idea into code, at the Bloom's Taxonomy of Educational Objectives "apply" stage (using information in new situations) (Anderson et al., 2001). In contrast, teams seemed to follow implicitly actionable instructions more conceptually and strategically ("recall how you…"), as with Bloom's "analyze" stage (drawing connections among different ideas). This suggests that the two aspects of IG3 can help support EUPs' learning across *diverse cognitive process stages*. Finally, IG5-InformationProcessing requires the Idea Garden to support both the comprehensive and selective information processing styles, as per previous research on gender differences in information processing styles. The teams used both of these styles, mostly aligning by gender with the previous research, implying that following IG5 helps support *diverse EUP information processing styles*.

Much of the success of the Idea Garden principles ties to the theories upon which they are grounded. Minimalist learning theory (MLT) defined our intended audience of active users and prescribed ways in which we could target them with the Idea Garden's resources. The guidelines laid down by MLT gave us a strong foundation from which to begin the research. Past successes with MLT-based systems also predicted our success with the early versions of the Idea Garden.

When it became clear that we needed to develop lower-level principles tailored to the Idea Garden, we again turned to theory to help us build some theory of our own. By beginning with the MLT foundations that had served us so well and then expanding to encompass theory from the realms of cognition and information processing styles, we were able to create a specialized set of principles to support a diverse range of problem solving styles and situations. For instance, Meyers-Levy's theories on information processing styles (Meyers-Levy, 1989) informed the way that we structured Idea Garden hints in order to benefit both selective and comprehensive learners.

Most important, however, basing the Idea Garden on a set of principles provided generality, which we evaluated by implementing the system for three different EUSE environments and evaluating each (Cao et al., 2015; Jernigan et al., 2015, 2017; Loksa et al., 2016). These general principles then contribute to the theory pool to further research in end-user problem solving and debugging. We hope that others in the EUSE research community will be able to draw from these principles as they develop new systems to support end users' problem solving endeavors.

5   Discussion and Concluding Remarks

This chapter has advocated for researchers in the EUSE research community to increase their connections to theory, both as consumers and producers. We see this approach as a complement to the many other EUSE design methods in our community, with each method having its own unique advantages and disadvantages.

One example of an atheoretic approach is the idea-tool-summative sequence, in which a researcher gains inspiration from some kind of problem they have seen or learned about in the literature, devises an approach to solve that problem, and evaluates its effectiveness empirically. Its strength lies in showing that the new tool works better than some comparative approach. However, its weakness is that it cannot easily get from the success of the tool to underlying causes of why exactly it worked better. As Ruthruff et al. showed, the underlying causes might be quite surprising to a researcher; for example, his study of alternative EUSE fault localization tools showed that, although one might have assumed that differences in effectiveness were due to differences in the algorithms' reasoning approaches, they actually had more to do with nuanced differences in the user interface than algorithmic differences (Ruthruff, Burnett, & Rothermel, 2006).

Other approaches emphasize theory building over theory consuming. For approaches following this philosophy, research begins with formative empirical work to understand the detailed needs of users in a particular domain, then builds new theories based upon the results of this research. Grounded theory work is an example of this kind of approach (e.g., Stol, Ralph, & Fitzgerald, 2016). The theories derived from this method are intended to be consumed in later tool building phases (whether by those researchers or by other researchers). The outcome of this approach is a highly detailed understanding of the particular domain. However, the resulting theories are often not particularly parsimonious or cohesive; perhaps for that reason, it is often challenging for researchers other than the original investigators to then consume the theories built by this method.

Practice-based computing (Wulf, Müller, Pipek, Randall, & Rohde, 2015) adds an emphasis on the contextual and social aspects of technology usage in practice. This method may or may not result in new theories, but its main emphasis is not theory. Rather, its distinguishing characteristic from most other approaches is its emphasis on in-the-wild settings for knowledge discovery. This method can reveal social aspects of technology appropriation and usage that many other methods may miss; but its findings may be so situated in the system(s) studied that reusing its findings in other types of systems can be challenging.

Although these other approaches all have advantages, we argue that theory consumption should be brought into the picture much more often and that it is currently underutilized in EUSE research. In a recent lecture, Herbsleb eloquently explained one example when he pointed out that certain theories of how people self-organize in groups reflect processes that have evolved in humans over thousands of years (Herbsleb, 2016). Rather than ignore these theories, it makes sense to leverage them (i.e., become good consumers of them) in designing our own tools.

Another example is information foraging theory (IFT), a theory devised to explain and predict how people seek information (Pirolli, 2007). The basic building blocks are that "predators" (people seeking information) look for "prey" (information relevant to their goals) through "patches" of information (such as different files) that contains "cues" (such as clickable links) about where to find the information they want. Such a simple set of concepts can be remarkably powerful when applied to software tools. For example, Fleming et al. used IFT to reveal commonalities among different sub-branches of software engineering research that could be leveraged toward faster progress (Fleming et al., 2013), and Piorkowski et al. (2016) used IFT to reveal a kind of "lower bound" in software tool usage that determines programmers' minimum costs in using a software tool.

Theory likewise brought a number of advantages to the projects we presented in this chapter. In Explanatory Debugging, the mental model theory of reasoning's notion of "runnable" mental models gave us a deep understanding of how Explanatory Debugging can effectively support the actionability necessary for debugging. This, in turn, led to the EluciDebug prototype and a set of general principles for Explanatory Debugging approaches. In the GenderMag work, the attention investment model, self-efficacy theory, and information processing theory gave us the ability to make reasonable predictions about what diverse users might attend to and follow through with (or not) and why. Because these theories went deeper than gender itself, they provided a basis for GenderMag to help software developers improve the inclusiveness of the software they build for a diversity of users – without the need to navigate the political waters of talking about one gender versus another. Finally, in the Idea Garden project, minimalist learning theory provided us a number of prescriptive ideas on how to not only enable, but also entice, untrained end users to incrementally succeed when faced with software development misbehaviors, difficulties, and barriers.

These theory-grounded projects demonstrate the idea that an EUSE research project can be both theory-informed and theory-producing – allowing EUSE researchers to participate in both the verification and creation of theories that can, in turn, further inform EUSE. As examples like these show, theories enable us to go beyond instances of successful approaches to cross-cutting principles and methods that can be used across a breadth of situations. Further, theories can give us ways to connect multiple research efforts, pattern-matching existing projects to a common theory to evolve to a deeper understanding of the domain. In essence, theories can provide powerful means by which EUSE researchers can better "stand on the shoulders" of the researchers who came before them.

Acknowledgements We thank our students and collaborators who contributed to our work, all the participants of our empirical studies, and the reviewers for their helpful suggestions. Our work in developing this chapter was supported in part by the National Science Foundation under grants CNS-1240957, IIS-1314384, and IIS-1528061, and by the DARPA Explainable AI (XAI) program grant DARPA-16-53-XAI-FP-043. Any opinions, findings and conclusions or recommendations expressed in this material are those of the author(s) and do not necessarily reflect those of the sponsors.

References

Aho, A., Lam, M., Sethi, R., Ullman, J. (2006). *Compilers: principles, techniques & tools*. Boston, MA, USA: Addison Wesley.

Anderson, L., Krathwohl, D., Airasian, P., Cruikshank, K., Mayer, R., Pintrich, P., et al. (Ed.). (2001). *A taxonomy for learning, teaching, and assessing: a revision of Bloom's taxonomy of educational objectives (Complete edition)*. Longman.

Appel, M., Kronberger, N., Aronson, J. (2011). Stereotype threat impair ability building: effects on test preparation among women in science and technology. *European Journal of Social Psychology, 41*(7), 904–913.

Bandura, A. (1977). Self-efficacy: toward a unifying theory of behavioral change. *Psychological Review, 8*(2), 191–215.

Bandura, A. (1986). *Social foundations of thought and action*. Englewood Cliffs, NJ: Prentice Hall.

Beckwith, L., Burnett, M., Wiedenbeck, S., Grigoreanua, V., Wiedenbeck, S. (2006). Gender HCI: what about the software? *Computer*, (Nov. 2006), 83–87.

Beckwith, L., Inman, D., Rector, K., Burnett, M. (2007). On to the real world: gender and self-efficacy in excel. In *IEEE symposium visual languages and human-centric computing* (pp. 119–126). USA: IEEE, Couer d'Alene, Idaho.

Beckwith, L., Sorte S., Burnett, M., Wiedenback, S., Chintakovid, T., Cook C. (2005). Designing features for both genders in end-user programming environments. In *IEEE symposium VLHCC* (pp. 153–160). USA: IEEE, Dallas, Texas.

Beyer, S., Rynes, K., Perrault, J., Hay, K., Haller, S. (2003). Gender differences in computer science students. In *SIGCSE: special interest group on computer science education* (pp. 49–53). Reno, Nevada, USA: ACM.

Blackwell, A., & Hague, R. (2001). AutoHAN: an architecture for programming the home. *IEEE symposium human-centric computing languages and environments* (pp. 150–157). Stresa: IEEE.

Blackwell, A. F. (2002). First steps in programming: a rationale for attention investment models. In *IEEE VL/HCC* (pp. 2–10). Arlington, Virginia, USA: IEEE.

Brandt, J., Dontcheva, M., Weskamp, M., Klemmer, S. (2010). Example-centric programming: integrating web search into the programming environment. In *ACM conference on human factors in computing systems* (pp. 513–522). Atlanta, Georgia, USA: ACM.

Bunt, A., Lount, M., Lauzon, C. (2012). Are explanations always important? A study of deployed, low-cost intelligent interactive systems. In *ACM IUI* (pp. 169–178). Austin, Texas, USA: ACM.

Burnett, M., Beckwith, L., Wiedenbeck, S., Fleming, S. D., Cao, J., Park, T. H., et al. (2011). Gender pluralism in problem-solving software. *Interacting with Computers, 23*, 450–460.

Burnett, M., Fleming, S., Iqbal, S., Venolia, G., Rajaram, V., Farooq, U., et al. (2010). Gender differences and programming environments: across programming populations. In *ACM-IEEE international symposium on empirical software engineering and measurement*. 10 pages. http://doi.acm.org/10.1145/1852786.1852824

Burnett, M., & Myers, B. (2014). Future of end-user software engineering: Beyond the silos. In *ACM/IEEE international conference on software engineering: future of software engineering track (ICSE companion proceedings)* (pp. 201–211). Hyderabad, India: ACM

Burnett, M., Peters, A., Hill, C., Elarief, N. (2016). Finding gender-inclusiveness software issues with GenderMag: a field investigation. In *ACM conference on human factors in computing systems (CHI)*. (pp. 760–787). Oxford, UK: Oxford University Press.

Burnett, M., Stumpf, S., Macbeth, J., Makri, S., Beckwith, L., Kwan, I., et al. (2016). GenderMag: a method for evaluating software's gender inclusiveness. *Interacting with Computers, 28*(6), 760–787. doi:10.1093/iwc/iwv046.

Cao, J., Fleming, S., Burnett, M. (2011). An exploration of design opportunities for "gardening" end-user programmers' ideas. In *IEEE symposium on visual languages and human-centric computing* (pp. 35–42).

Cao, J., Fleming, S., Burnett, M., Scaffidi, C. (2015). Idea Garden: situated support for problem solving by end-user programmers. *Interacting with Computers, 27*(6), 640–660.

Cao, J., Rector, K., Park, T., Fleming, S., Burnett, M., Wiedenbeck, S. (2010). A debugging perspective on end-user mashup programming. In *IEEE symposium on visual languages and human-centric computing* (pp. 149–156). Madrid, Spain: IEEE.

Carroll, J. (1990). *The nurnberg funnel: designing minimalist instruction for practical computer skill.* Cambridge, MA, USA: MIT Press.

Carroll, J. (Ed.). (1998). *Minimalism beyond the nurnberg funnel.* Cambridge, MA, USA: MIT Press.

Carroll, J., & Rosson, C. (1987). The paradox of the active user. In *Interfacing thought: cognitive aspects of human-computer interaction* (pp. 26–28). Cambridge, MA, USA: MIT Press.

Chambers, C., & Scaffidi, C. (2010). Struggling to excel: a field study of challenges faced by spreadsheet users. *IEEE symposium on visual languages and human-centric computing* (pp. 187–194). Pittsburg, USA: IEEE.

Compeau, D., & Higgins, C. (1995). Application of social cognitive theory to training for computer skills. *Information System Research, 6*(2), 118–143.

Craven, M. W., & Shavlik, J. W. (1997). Using neural networks for data mining. *Future Generation Computer Systems, 13*, (Nov. 1997), 211–229.

de Souza, C. S. (2017). Semiotic engineering: a cohering theory to connect EUD with HCI, CMC and more. In F. Paternò & V. Wulf (Eds.). *New perspectives in end-user development.* (pp. 269–306). Cham: Springer.

Ennals, R., Brewer, E., Garofalakis, M., Shadle, M., Gandhi, P. (2007). Intel mash maker: join the web. *SIGMOD Record, 36*(4), 27–33.

Fleming, S., Scaffidi, C., Piorkowski, D., Burnett, M., Bellamy, R., Lawrance, J., et al. (2013). An information foraging theory perspective on tools for debugging, refactoring, and reuse tasks. *ACM Trans. Soft. Engr. and Method. (TOSEM), 22*(2), 14:1.

Gregor, S. (2006). The nature of theory in information systems. *MIS Quarterly, 30*(3), 611–642.

Grigoreanu, V., Brundage, J., Bahna, E., Burnett, M., ElRif, P., Snover, J. (2009). Males' and females' script debugging strategies. In *Symposium on end-user development.* (pp. 205–224). Siegen, Germany: Springer.

Grigoreanu, V., Burnett, M., Wiedenbeck, S., Cao, J., Rector, K., Kwan, I. (2012). End-user debugging strategies: a sensemaking perspective. *Transactions on Computer-Human Interaction 19*, 1, ACM.

Grigoreanu, V., Cao, J., Kulesza, T., Bogart, C., Rector, K., Burnett, M., et al. (2008). Can feature design reduce the gender gap in end-user software development environments? In *IEEE symposium on visual languages and human-centric computing* (pp. 149–156). New York, New York, USA: ACM.

Hargittai, E., & Shafer, S. (2006). Differences in actual and perceived online skills: the role of gender. *Social Science Quarterly, 87*(2), 432–448.

Hartmann, B., MacDougall, D., Brandt, J., Klemmer, S. (2010). What would other programmers do: suggesting solutions to error messages. In *ACM conference on human factors in computing systems* (pp. 1019–1028). Atlanta, Georgia, USA: ACM.

Hartzel, K. (2003). How self-efficacy and gender issues affect software adoption and use. *Communications of ACM, 46*(9), 167–171.

Herbsleb, J. (2016). Building a socio-technical theory of coordination: why and how. In *ACM symposium foundations of software engineering* (pp. 2–10). Seattle, Washington, USA: ACM.

Huffman, A., Whetton, J., Huffman, W. (2013). Using technology in higher education: the influence of gender roles on technology self-efficacy. *Computers in Human Behavior, 29*(4), 1779–1786.

Jernigan, W., Horvath, A., Lee, M., Burnett, M., Cuilty, T., Kuttal, S., et al. (2015). A principled evaluation for a principled Idea Garden. In *Proceedings IEEE Visual Languages and Human-Centric Computing (VL/HCC '15)* (pp. 235–243). Atlanta, Georgia, USA: IEEE.

Jernigan, W., Horvath, A, Lee, M., Burnett, M., Cuilty, T., Kuttal, S., et al. (2017). General principles for a Generalized Idea Garden. *Journal of Visual Languages and Computing, 39*, 51–65.

Johnson-Laird, P. N. (1983). *Mental Models: Towards a Cognitive Science of Language, Inference, and Consciousness*. Cambridge MA, USA: Harvard University Press.

Kelleher, C., & Pausch, R. (2006). Lessons learned from designing a programming system to support middle school girls creating animated stories. *Symposium on visual languaes and human-centric computing* (pp. 165–172). Brighton: IEEE.

Ko, A., Abraham, R., Beckwith, L., Blackwell, A., Burnett, M., Erwig, M., et al. (2011). The state of the art in end-user software engineering. *ACM Computing Surveys 43*(3), Article 21, 44 pages.

Ko, A., & Myers, B. (2004). Designing the whyline: a debugging interface for asking questions about program behavior. In *ACM conference on human factors in computing systems* (pp. 151–158). Vienna, Austria: ACM.

Ko, A., Myers, B., Aung, H. (2004). Six learning barriers in end-user programming systems. In *IEEE symposium on visual languages and human-centric computing* (pp. 199–206). Rome, Italy: IEEE

Kulesza, T., Burnett, M. M., Wong, W. -K., Stumpf, S. (2015). Principles of explanatory debugging to personalize interactive machine learning. In *ACM conference on intelligent user interfaces* (pp. 126–137). Atlanta, Georgia, USA: ACM.

Kulesza, T., Stumpf, S., Burnett, M. M., Kwan, I. (2012). Tell me more? The effects of mental model soundness on personalizing an intelligent agent. In *ACM CHI* (pp. 1–10). Austin, Texas, USA: ACM.

Kulesza, T., Stumpf, S., Burnett, M. M., Wong, W. -K., Riche, Y., Moore, T., et al. (2010). Explanatory debugging: supporting end-user debugging of machine-learned programs. In *IEEE symposium on visual languages and human-centric computing* (pp. 41–48). Madrid, Spain: IEEE.

Kulesza, T., Stumpf, S., Burnett, M. M., Yang, S. (2013). Too much, too little, or just right? Ways explanations impact end users' mental models. In *IEEE symposium on visual languages and human-centric computing* (pp. 3–10). San Jose, California, USA: IEEE.

Kulesza, T., Stumpf, S., Wong, W. -K., Burnett, M. M., Perona, S., Ko, A. J., et al. (2011). Why-oriented end-user debugging of naive Bayes text classification. *ACM Transactions on Interactive Intelligent Systems, 1*, 1.

Lacave, C., & Díez, F. J. (2002). A review of explanation methods for Bayesian networks. *The Knowledge Engineering Review, 17*(2), 107–127.

Lee, M., Bahmani, F., Kwan, I., Laferte, J., Charters, P., Horvath, A., et al. (2014). Principles of a debugging-first puzzle game for computing education. *IEEE Symposium on Visual Languages and Human-Centric Computing*, Melbourne, Australia (pp. 57–64).

Lee, M., & Ko, A. (2011). Personifying programming tool feedback improves novice programmers' learning. In *Proceedings of ICER* (pp. 109–116). Providence, Rhode Island, USA: ACM Press.

Lieberman, H., Paterno, F., Wulf, V. (Eds.). (2006). *End-user development*. Dordrecht, The Netherlands: Kluwer/Springer.

Lim, B. Y., & Dey, A. K. (2009). Proceedings of the International Conference on Ubiquitous Computing. Orlando, Florida, USA: ACM.

Lin, J., Wong, J., Nichols, J., Cypher, A., Lau, T. (2009). End-user programming of mashups with Vegemite. In *ACM international conference on intelligent user interfaces* (pp. 97–106). Sanibel Island, Florida, USA: ACM.

Little, G., Lau, T., Cypher, A., Lin, J., Haber, D., Kandogan, E. (2007). Koala: capture, share, automate, personalize business processes on the web. In *ACM conference on human factors in computing systems* (pp. 943–946). San Jose, California, USA: ACM.

Loksa, D., Ko, A. J., Jernigan, W., Oleson, A., Mendez, C.J., Burnett, M. (2016). Programming, problem solving, and self-awareness: effects of explicit guidance. In *ACM conference on human factors in computing systems (CHI)*. (pp. 1449–1461). California, USA: ACM, San Jose

Luger, E. (2014). A design for life: recognizing the gendered politics affecting product design. In *CHI workshop: perspectives on gender and product design*. https://www.sites.google.com/site/technologydesignperspectives/papers.

Marsden, N. (2014). *CHI 2014 workshop on perspectives on gender and product design*. https://www.sites.google.com/site/technologydesignperspectives/papers.

McFarlane, D. (2002). Comparison of four primary methods for coordinating the interruption of people in human-computer interaction. *Human-Computer Interaction, 17*(1), 63–139.

Meyers-Levy, J. (1989). Gender differences in information processing: a selectivity interpretation. In P. Cafferata & A. Tubout (Eds.), *Cognitive and affective responses to advertising*. Lexington Books. (pp. 219–260). Lanham, Maryland, USA.

Meyers-Levy, J., & Loken, B. (2015). Revisiting gender differences: what we know and what lies ahead. *Journal of Consumer Psychology, 25*, pp. 129–149.

Meyers-Levy, J., & Maheswaran, D. (1991). Exploing differences in males' and females' processing strategies. *Journal of Consumer Research, 18*, 63–70.

Miller, R., Bolin, M., Chilton, L., Little, G., Webber, M., Yu, C. -H. (2010). Rewriting the web with chickenfoot. In A. Cypher, M. Dontcheva, T. Lau, & J. Nichols (Eds.), *No code required: giving users tools to transform the web* (pp. 39–63). Burlington, MA, USA: Morgan Kaufmann.

Myers, B. A., Pane, J. F., Ko, A. (2004). Natural programming languages and environments. *Communications of the ACM, 47*(9), 47–52.

Norman, D. A. (2002). *The design of everyday things*. Revised and Expanded Edition. New York, New York, USA: Basic Books.

Oney, S., & Myers, B. (2009). FireCrystal: understanding interactive behaviors in dynamic web pages. In *IEEE symposium on visual languages and human-centric computing* (pp. 105–108).

Piorkowski, D., Henley, A., Nabi, T., Fleming, S., Scaffidi, C., Burnett, M. (2016). Foraging and navigations, fundamentally: developers' predictions of value and cost. In *ACM symposium foundations of software engineering* (pp. 97–108). Seattle, Washington, USA: ACM.

Pirolli, P. (2007). *Information foraging theory: adaptive interaction with information*. Oxford, UK: Oxford University Press.

Repenning, A., & Ioannidou, A. (2008). Broadening participation through scalable game design. *International Conference on Software Engineering* (pp. 305–309). Leipzig: ACM.

Robertson, T., Prabhakararao, S., Burnett, M., Cook, C., Ruthruff, J., Beckwith, L., et al. (2004). Impact of interruption style on end-user debugging. In *ACM conference on human factors in computing systems (CHI)* (pp. 287–294). Vienna, Austria: ACM.

Rowe, M. B. (1973). *Teaching science as continuous inquiry.* New York, New York, USA: McGraw-Hill.

Ruthruff, J., Burnett, M., Rothermel, G. (2006). Interactive fault localization techniques in a spreadsheet environment. *IEEE Transactions on Software Engineering, 2*(4), 213–239.

Shaw, M. (1990). Prospects for an engineering discipline of software. *IEEE Software, 7,* 15–24.

Shneiderman, B. (1995). Looking for the bright side of user interface agents. *ACM Interactions, 2*(1), 13–15, January.

Sjøberg, D., Dybå, T., Anda, B., Hannay, J. (2008). Building theories in software engineering. In F. Shull, J. Singer, & D. I. K. Sjøberg (Eds.), *Guide to advanced empirical software engineering* (pp. 312–336). London, UK: Springer.

Spencer, R. (2000). The streamlined cognitive walkthrough method, working around social constraints encountered in a software development company. *ACM Conference on Human Factors in Computing Systems,* The Hague, The Netherlands (pp. 353–359).

Stol, K., Ralph, P., Fitzgerald, B. (2016). Grounded theory in Software Engineering research: a critical review and guidelines. In *ACM/IEEE international conference on software engineering* (pp. 120–131). Austin, Texas, USA: ACM.

Stumpf, S., Rajaram, V., Li, L., Wong, W. -K., Burnett, M. M., Dietterich, T., et al. (2009). Interacting meaningfully with machine learning systems: three experiments. *International Journal of Human-Computer Studies, 67*(8), 639–662. (Aug. 2009).

Subrahmaniyan, N., Beckwith, L., Grigoreanu, V., Burnett, M., Wiedenbeck, S., Narayanan, V., et al. (2008). Testing vs. code inspection vs. … what else? Male and female end users' debugging strategies. In *Proceedings of CHI* (pp. 617–626). Florence, Italy: ACM.

Szafron, D., Greiner, R., Lu, P., Wishart, D. (2003). *Explaining naive Bayes classifications.* Tech report TR03-09, University of Alberta.

Turner, P., & Turner, S. (2011). Is stereotyping inevitable when designing with personas? *Design Studies, 32,* 30–44, 1, January 2011.

van der Meij, H., & Carroll, J. M. (1998). Principles and heuristics for designing minimalist instruction. In J. M. Carroll (Ed.). *Minimalism beyond the nurnberg funnel* (pp. 19–53). Cambridge, MA: MIT Press.

Wharton, C., Rieman, J., Lewis, C., Polson, P. (1994). The cognitive walkthrough method: a practioner's guide. In J. Nielsen, & R. Mack (Eds.). *Usability inspection methods* (pp. 105–140). New York: John Wiley.

Wulf, V., Müller, C., Pipek, V., Randall, D., Rohde, M. (2015). Practice based computing: empirically-grounded conceptualizations derived from design cases studies. In V. Wulf, K. Schmidt, D. Randall (Eds.). *Designing socially embedded technologies in the real-world.* (pp. 111–150). London: Springer.

Yang, R., & Newman, M. W. (2013). Learning from a learning thermostat: lessons for intelligent systems for the home. In *ACM international joint conference on pervasive and ubiquitous computing* (pp. 93–102). Zurich, Switzerland: ACM.

Yang, Y., & Pedersen, J. O. (1997). A comparative study on feature selection in text categorization. *Twentieth International Conference on Machine Learning,* 412–420. San Francisco, CA, USA: Morgan Kaufmann Publishers Inc.

Zeldin, A. L., & Pajares, F. (2000). Against the odds: self-efficacy beliefs of women in mathematical, scientific, and technological careers. *American Educational Research Journal, 37,* 215–246.

Semiotic Engineering: A Cohering Theory to Connect EUD with HCI, CMC and More

Clarisse Sieckenius de Souza

Abstract Theories have an important role to play in research areas whose application faces rapid technological changes. They can provide longer-term intellectual references that shape deeper investigations and contribute to consolidate the identity of such research areas. A recent survey of EUD-related work published between 2004 and 2013 suggests that our field is remarkably techno-centered and could increase its scientific impact by diversifying some of its research approaches and practices. In this paper we show concrete examples of how Semiotic Engineering, originally a semiotic theory of human-computer interaction, can provide a unified theoretical framing for various EUD-related topics of investigation. Our contribution to the collection of chapters in this book is to demonstrate this particular theory's potential as a catalyst of new kinds of trans-disciplinary debate, as well as a source of inspiration for new breeds of technological developments.

Keywords Semiotic Engineering · computer-mediated social communication · programming as self-expression · EUD theory

1 Introduction

In ten years since the publication of the first end user development (EUD) book (Lieberman, Paternò, & Wulf, 2006), software produced by non-professional developers has grown in volume and diversified in kind. Commercial and non-commercial tools for data mashup creation and visualization (*e.g.* Tableau[1] and Klipfolio[2]),

---

[1]Tableau – http://www.tableau.com/

[2]Klipfolio – https://www.klipfolio.com/

C.S. de Souza (✉)
Semiotic Engineering Research Group (SERG), Departamento de Informática, PUC-Rio, Rio de Janeiro, Brazil
e-mail: clarisse@inf.puc-rio.br

© Springer International Publishing AG 2017
F. Paternò, V. Wulf (eds.), *New Perspectives in End-User Development*,
DOI 10.1007/978-3-319-60291-2_11

269

repetitive task automation and scripting (*e.g.* iMacros[3] and UiPath[4]), customized service integration (*e.g.* IFTTT[5] and Microsoft Flow[6]), IoT programming (*e.g.* IFTTT and Cayenne my Device[7]) and mobile application development (*e.g.* AppInventor[8] and AppsGeyser[9]) have been extensively used by non-expert end users. The programming style in many of these tools has been influenced by pioneering end user programming and computational thinking acquisition environments such as Scratch[10], Alice[11], AgentSheets[12] and KidSim[13]. Yet, in a recent study about the methods, the purposes and the impact of work published in EUD-related fields between 2004 and 2013, Tetteroo and Markopoulos (2015) conclude that the influence of EUD research on the work done by other scientific communities is smaller than expected. The authors report the prevalence of techno-centered approaches in the surveyed publications and the relative scarcity of work aimed at gaining deeper understanding about the central object of investigation in EUD, the contexts and conditions in which it occurs, how EUD tasks are successfully achieved, and why. By implicitly electing the HCI community as the main potential beneficiary of research done by the EUD community, the authors claim that "the impact of [EUD] research for the greater HCI community can increase" [Tetteroo and Markopoulos (2015), p. 60]. Indeed, a greater impact on HCI should create a healthy interdisciplinary feedback loop, given that most of the research done in EUD is founded in HCI theories, frameworks, approches and models.

This chapter is about EUD research based on *theory*, more specifically on a *semiotic theory*, and its potential to respond to some important aspects of Tetteroo and Markopoulos's call to action. Semiotic Engineering was originally proposed as a semiotic theory of *human-computer interaction* (de Souza, 2005a,b). This is the first and most apparent reason why we typify it a *cohering theory*, that is, a theory that can create stronger coherence between otherwise unevenly related fields such as, in our case, EUD and HCI. Additionally, as we will discuss in subsequent sections, Semiotic Engineering can also create and strengthen coherence with other relevant areas of research, besides HCI. Coherence is achieved because the theory defines that the activities performed by end users during, and by means of, software development are primarily related to a particular kind of computer-mediated

---

[3]iMacros – http://imacros.net/

[4]UiPath – http://www.uipath.com/

[5]IFTTT – https://ifttt.com/recipes

[6]Microsoft Flow – https://flow.microsoft.com/en-us/

[7]Cayenne - http://www.cayenne-mydevices.com/

[8]App Inventor - http://appinventor.mit.edu/explore/

[9]AppsGeyser - https://www.appsgeyser.com/

[10]Scratch – https://scratch.mit.edu/

[11]Alice - http://www.alice.org/index.php

[12]AgentSheets – http://www.agentsheets.com/

[13]Kidsim has been known as Stagecast Creator since 1997 – more about it at http://web.archive.org/web/20150517004640/http://www.stagecast.com/index.html

social communication, rather than to algorithmic problem solving and program coding, which although fundamentally important to EUD, come *second* to social communication. In other words, the theory explicitly privileges the social dimensions of programming instead of the logic and cognitive ones.

The communication-centered approach of Semiotic Engineering is not, in itself, an innovation. Most semiotic approaches and accounts of human-computer interaction, programming and computation do the same (see, for example, Andersen, 1997; Andersen, Holmqvist, & Jensen, 1993; Liu, 2000; Nadin, 1988, 2011, Tanaka-Ishii, 2010). Even outside the domain of semiotic expertise, more than two decades ago Terry Winograd, one of the foreground figures in HCI research, expressed his belief that communication is at the center of computing (Winograd, 1997):

> [...] the computer is not a machine whose main purpose is to get a computing task done. The computer, with its attendant peripherals and networks, is a machine that provides new ways for people to communicate with other people. The excitement that infuses computing today comes from the exploration of new capacities to manipulate and communicate all kinds of information in all kinds of media, reaching new audiences in ways that would have been unthinkable before the computer. (p. 150)

Theories can play an important role in research areas whose application faces rapid technological changes. They provide long-term intellectual references to guide and advanve investigations of persistent hardcore issues that contribute to define a field of studies. In this light, we will show that Semiotic Engineering stands as an attractive theoretical choice for EUD researchers who share Winograd's view although, as is the case of any theory, it is limited by nature and by design. It is limited by nature because it is produced by human minds and human minds can only produce limited accounts of reality. And it is limited by design because, as all theories do, Semiotic Engineering *focuses* on a particular dimension of a complex phenomenon. Focus, as we know, is achieved by abstraction, that is, by hiding away other dimensions that undeniably exist but fall outside the interest of theorists.

This chapter presents concrete examples of how Semiotic Engineering can bring current EUD-related discussions involving computer education, end user software engineering (EUSE), computer-mediated social communication (CMC) and self-expression through software under a unified theoretical framing. The examples are drawn from a 5-year project with three Brazilian schools in which we developed and used technologies especially designed to explore the power of social communication through programmable computer proxies. The chapter also illustrates how our own research in EUD has changed and evolved since our contribution to the 2006 edition of this book (de Souza & Barbosa, 2006).

In the sections that follow we will briefly outline the theory (Sect. 2), then highlight selected research results from the Scalable Game Design *Brasil* project (Sect. 3), and discuss the cohering power of Semiotic Engineering in view of perceived characteristics of EUD research (Sect. 4). Finally, we will conclude the chapter and share some thoughts about theory-driven research in our field and the importance of intellectual diversity for the growth and continuation of scientific research areas (Sect. 5).

2 Semiotic Engineering

Semiotic Engineering appeared in 1993 as a semiotic approach to interface language design (de Souza, 1993). It shared most of the semiotic perspectives on HCI and computing that had been previously expressed by Nadin (1988), Andersen (1997), Andersen et al., (1993), Kammersgaard (1988) and others, viewing human-computer interaction as a special case of computer-mediated human communication. Kammersgaard's work provides us with a good lead into the semiotic theory we developed. The author presents four perspectives in human-computer interaction. One of them is the *media perspective*, that is, viewing computers as a medium through which humans communicate with each other. In this perspective, humans do not interact *with* computers, but rather *through* computers, a communication-centered view that is at the core of the *Language-Action Perspective* (LAP). LAP gained much popularity after the publication of Winograd and Flores's influential book entitled "Understanding Computers and Cognition – New Foundations for Design" (Winograd, 2006; Winograd & Flores, 1986). While in their version of LAP Winograd and Flores chose Speech Acts (Searle, 1985) as a theoretical basis in the context of group technologies, Kammersgaard pointed at additional less obvious possibilities (Kammersggard, 1988):

> Seen from the media perspective, two types of communications are interesting. First of all, communication between (groups of) users that takes place through the computer application. Secondly, the one-way (mass) communication from designer to user which takes place when an application designed by one person is used by other persons. I will not go into further detail about this last type of communication, except to mention that Oberquelle, Kupka, & Maass (1983) talk about delegation of communicating behaviour from the designer to the machine and then treat the situation as seen from a dialogue partner perspective, whereas Andersen (1985) treats the designer as having the role of one sender in a collective of senders, who makes a contribution to each message sent through the medium. (p. 356, reference calls added)

Semiotic Engineering sprang from the idea that designers speaking to users through the machine, their delegated proxy, was neither a case of dialog partnership (*computers* and humans engaged in mutually intelligible conversation), nor necessarily or even mainly a matter of participation in collective human discourse delivered through computers. It was rather a matter of computer-mediated *metacommunication*, involving systems designers (as well as systems developers) and systems users. This was the touchstone of the entire theory (de Souza, 2005a) that developed from our earlier approach (de Souza, 1993). Metacommunication in this case refers to communication about the conditions, purposes and effects of communication with the system.

For a quick illustration of what metacommunication is, consider the sequence of CMC turns in Fig. 1. The context of communication is one where the user has seen that the clock app in her friend's cell phone shows the time in three different cities around the world. The user lives in Rio de Janeiro and now wishes to be

Fig. 1 Explanatory verbalizations for a piece of metacommunication between user and system acting as its designer's proxy

able to see the time in Rio and in Austin, Texas, on her cell phone's clock screen. Her son lives in Austin and she prefers to call him when he is at home. Being able to see the time of day in Austin directly on screen is better than having to do mental calculations with time zones before making the call. With this goal in mind, she therefore engages in interaction that is partly shown and commented in Fig. 1, where balloons of different shapes and colors denote system's and user's turns in communication.

The entire communication develops as the user interacts with the system, by pressing on certain areas of the phone screen, and the system responds to the user, by changing its states. The verbalizations in the balloons are not part of the actual interaction. They are just annotations we have added to the screen shot images in order to describe and explain the structure, the style and the intent of meanings exchanged by user and system during this short span of interaction. The system, who speaks for the people who have created it, opens the conversation (see the numbering of turns in Fig. 1) and then begins to respond to the user's interactive turns. Note that the user's sixth ("<6>") and seventh ("<7>") turns do not elicit new communication content from the system. This is because the user has not *sent* the messages expressed in the balloons to the system. In this particular kind of computer-mediated communication, the activation of the channel that carries the user's message to the system must be explicitly commanded by pressing on the appropriate interface control. If not, the message cannot reach its targeted recipient. This protocol can be the source of many blunders in human-computer interaction. Therefore, to say that smooth, pleasurable, effective and efficient communication in this context is the result of competent "semiotic engineering" of interface languages and communicative protocols is not a pretentious choice of terms. Indeed, since every system is different from all other systems, every system has a unique interface language and set of communicative protocols that users must learn through a process that can justifiably be characterized as the acquisition of an *artificial* language. For every new system, a new language of interaction must be engineered and deployed by the system's designers and developers, and acquired and mastered by the system's users.

2.1 A Specifically Defined Object of Investigation

Theories do not necessarily have to construct their individual object of investigation, but many of them do. The option with Semiotic Engineering has been to do so because the more natural alternative, to take "human-computer interaction" as its object of investigation, would blur a fundamentally important distinction that the theory was trying to make. At a time when user-centered design and usability studies were practically the dominant topics in HCI, designers and developers were completely out of the picture in *human-computer interaction* accounts. Users were at the center stage, as paradigmatically defined in Norman's widely known and used Seven Step Theory of Action (Norman, 1986). It proposed a characterization of human-computer interaction as the iterated traversal of two gulfs, the Execution Gulf and the Evaluation Gulf (see Fig. 2).

The radical view that users should be at the *center* of HCI investigations is powerfully expressed by the fact that all the actions involved in Norman's theory of HCI are performed by the user. In Fig. 2 we see that "the user" is the subject of all verbs and phrases defining the seven steps in interaction. There are no other "humans" in view in this model and, for many, there should not be, otherwise the users might have their central position *threatened* by the presence of other stakeholders in systems design and development. This fear has been voiced in one of the first reviews of the book introducing Semiotic Engineering (see below), because in our perspective, a system's interface is the producers' *proxy*, capable of enacting all and only the communicative exchanges encoded in software. Sometimes literally (speaking through natural language words and sentences) and sometimes metaphorically (speaking through non-verbal signs and patterned behavior as shown in Fig. 1), this *proxy* communicates to users, with greater or lesser effectiveness and efficiency, what, how, when, where, why and for what purposes

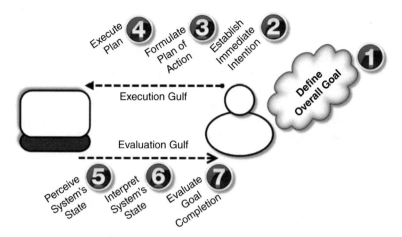

Fig. 2 Seven Steps in Norman's theory of action

and effects users can or should, in turn, communicate back with the system. The complete message from designers and developers is totally encoded in software before metacommunication begins and the process unfolds progressively as users engage in the action by interacting with the system.

Once we defined a specific object of investigation in a vastly complex field of studies such as HCI, the shift in focus was at least in part felt as a threat to the *field* (if the theory was adopted) or to the *theory* (if the field continued to reaffirm user-centered values and views that were dominant at the time). In his review of *The Semiotic Engineering of Human-Computer Interaction* (Gerd Waloszek, 2005), Waloszek gives us an example of this way of thinking:

> · I hear the alarm bells ring in the user-centered design (UCD) fraction. Are we in danger of reviving an idea that we believed to be long dead? Are we supporting the "users are stupid!" proponents, who put all blame on the users who are seemingly unable to decipher the designers' noble plans? This is an open question for me. Of course, there are two sides of the coin, the other of which would be to attribute the users' failures to the designers because they were unable to communicate their intentions properly through the user interface. Nevertheless, my personal feeling is that the designer's role is overemphasized in the picture that semiotic engineering sketches of HCI.

Waloszek's review was addressed to interaction design practitioners, not HCI researchers. By contrast, and as a lead into the importance of cohering theories, only a few years later Norman himself published an article about *systems thinking* (Norman, 2009) where he picked Semiotic Engineering as an example of a theory that "can help ensure consistency and coherence" (p. 54) in the broader picture of systems design, development and use. Of course this comes at the expense of *reframing* familiar concepts and having the appropriate means to operate with them while searching for new knowledge, be it at the level of users' tasks and actions, or at the level of services and experiences.

2.2   An Ontology and Theory-Specific Methodology

In order to keep its semiotic orientation and narrow focus on metacommunication, Semiotic Engineering created its own ontology and specific methods. This is not to say that all other ontologies, from more, or less, popular theories of HCI are incompatible with our theory. However, some of them are (such as the already mentioned Seven Step Theory of Action Norman, 1986) and most of them, although not incompatible (such as Activity Theory Kuutti, 1996), do not keep a sharp focus on metacommunication, its limits and possibilities, modalities, structure, qualities and strategies.

From the ontological point of view, Semiotic Engineering added participants on the interaction stage. Designers and developers became *the senders* of an interactive message delivered by systems interfaces. By the same token, contrary to the user-centered ontology, systems became *senders* and *receivers* of smaller pieces of locally connected communication with users. In other words, in this new ontology, designers, developers, users and systems share the same role in HCI, they all are (directly or indirectly) communication partners in the same event. Even more importantly, because communication involves intentions, in a Semiotic Engineering perspective, interaction design must explicitly address the designers' (and developers') goals expressed through systems interfaces, which in general amount to responding in the best possible way to the needs and expectations of the users. One of the effects of giving the same ontological status to systems producers and consumers is that it opens the way to the study of certain kinds of interaction where talking about "tasks," "goals" and preferences does not seem to be exactly right. For example, in computer art (Edmonds, 2007) the *user* plays a totally different role than defined in user-centered theories of HCI. The intent and expression of the designer can be just as important or even prevail. The same is arguably the case in security-sensitive systems, where users must follow protocols that they may not like and enjoy, but are safer *by design*.

The Semiotic Engineering ontology also included non-cognitive concepts that play an important role in distinguishing natural human communication and computer-mediated metacommunication. The most important one is *semiosis*, borrowed from Peircean semiotics (Peirce, 1992, 1998). In very brief and necessarily simplified terms, semiosis is the process by which (human) minds continually assign and revise meaning to whatever is perceived as potentially significant. For example, the sign ⬍ when first seen by users was probably *significant* in strict terms (*i.e.* it meant "something") yet *unknown*, or not well *understood*. Overtime, as sharing items on social networks became popular, users began to associate ⬍ with the idea of sending the item to others or posting it on various kinds of digital boards. However, the *meaning* of ⬍ is constantly changing, not only because new social computing technologies are constantly being deployed, but much more importantly because one's personal experience with (and hence the value assigned to) sharing items online resignifies and repurposes ⬍ in unanticipated ways. Therefore, in semiotic theory, semiosis is an *unlimited* process that actually determines all change and evolution, be it at the small individual scale, or at the very large cultural level. Moreover, for a number of theorists, semiosis is part of our genetic programming, that is, we cannot *not* signify or resignify the world around us (this is true even for non-semiotic theories, see for example Calvo & Peters, 2013).

The theoretical distinctions that Semiotic Engineering introduces in the study of computer-mediated human communication through software are particularly powerful in the context of EUD. As will be shown in the next section, it promotes, in Norman's terms, a *systems thinking* approach to EUD, even though – as we should emphasize one more time – the theory cannot account for all parts of the system. It can, however, transform our way of looking at EUD. If nothing else, we can now think about how end users can develop software for other end users to engage with, be it for the sake of the producers' interest, the consumers', or both. As a consequence of this shift in perspective, what users mean by their software and the way they communicate it come immediately into focus.

In order to operationalize the use of all concepts introduced in the new ontology of HCI proposed by Semiotic Engineering, we developed specific methods to investigate metacommunication through software. Because they can characterize how the designers' and developers' message to users is elaborated and expressed (*i.e.* emitted), as well as how it is interpreted and used (*i.e.* received) by the end users, in practice the two methods can be applied in HCI evaluation to determine the fundamental semiotic quality of systems in our perspective, *communicability* (de Souza & Leitão, 2009).

In keeping with the ⋖ example, systems whose interface signs include ⋖ speak for their human designers and developers, to their human users. Therefore, the meaning of ⋖ for human parties involved in various instances of metacommunication enabled by these systems will typically evolve. Users, as already mentioned, will naturally change their interpretation of sharing in view of experiences that they (or others) have with these (or other) technologies. But the same will happen with designers and developers. Once their product systems are deployed, their interpretation of sharing will, for the same reasons, change, too. A *system's* interpretation of ⋖ will however stay the same, until or unless it is reprogrammed by developers or users. This is to say that unlike human semiosis, computer semiosis is limited by its algorithmic nature (Nake & Grabowski, 2001).

Semiotic Engineering methods to study communicability and metacommunication concentrate on signs and semiosis, supporting the investigation of designers', systems' and users' meanings. They are interpretive methods that belong in the domain of qualitative methodology (Blandford, Furniss, & Makri, 2016). This is an important feature of the potential contributions of this theory to EUD, which will be presented and discussed in the following sections. Other qualitative methods, such as action research (Greenwood & Levin, 2007) for example, can also be used in investigations informed or guided by Semiotic Engineering. The use of metrics and quantitative methodology should however be used with caution (if at all), since the *counting* of meaning-related objects and events can be not only difficult but also questionable.

3 Social Communication Through Software Programming

The intersection between EUD-related topics and Semiotic Engineering dates back to the late 1990's, when a number of young researchers at PUC-Rio were doing their PhDs. Simone Barbosa's work on the interpretation of metaphors and metonymies expressed in user interface languages as a mechanism to extend or modify a system's behavior (Barbosa & de Souza, 2001) is a good example of what can be done with this theory. Another example is the evaluation framework derived from two principles we have proposed in order to assess the quality of scripting languages (or any other system of signs, such as visual ones in graphical user interfaces), namely the interpretive abstraction principle and the semiotic *continuum* principle (de Souza, Barbosa, & da Silva, 2001). In the 2006 EUD book (Lieberman et al., 2006) the chapter written by Simone Barbosa and myself (de Souza & Barbosa, 2006) followed the lines anticipated in the 2005 introduction to Semiotic Engineering (de Souza, 2005a). We argued that thanks to the principle of ongoing *semiosis* (see Sect. 2) the "usability" of interactive systems was intrinsically dependent on how they supported customization and extension carried out by the end users themselves. Besides the conceptual framing of EUD in the light of semiotic theory, our chapter provided a semiotic characterization and classification of customization and extension styles known at the time. To the best of our knowledge, what we proposed then is still applicable today, even after radical changes in technology.

In 10 years, our research in Semiotic Engineering has become even more tightly related to EUD, but following a completely different direction. In the sequel of the more *technical* kinds of metacommunication that we investigated in a previous phase, we began to investigate *subjective* aspects of metacommunication, that is, the presence of individual and collective beliefs, values, affect and intent in software design (see for example Semiotic Engineering work about culture and HCI Salgado, Leitão, & de Souza, 2012) and computer programming. The remainder of this section presents the highlights of our work in *Scalable Game Design Brasil* (SGD-Br), a 5-year computational thinking acquisition project in partnership with Alexander Repenning's *Scalable Game Design* initiative in Colorado, using AgentSheets (Repenning & Ioannidou, 2004, 2006; Repenning, Webb, & Ioannidou, 2010). The main feature of the Brazilian version of the project was an emphasis on *self-expression* and *social communication through programming* (de Souza et al., 2014; de Souza, Garcia, Slaviero, Pinto, & Repenning, 2011; Ferreira et al., 2012) rather than on the learning of computational thinking patterns. To be sure, the required cognitive skills for anyone to be able to express ideas through software he or she has created include the ability to think computationally. The interesting addition to the story is that expressive and communicative skills are just as important (de Souza, 2013).

The parallel between computational thinking and social communication through storytelling or writing is not new and has been explored in different ways. Kelleher's work with Storytelling Alice (Kelleher & Pausch, 2007) is well known for increasing young girls' interest in computer technology. In a different direction, Burke and Kafai's work has investigated how programming can help young students master narrative structures in discourse (Burke & Kafai, 2010, 2012). Additionally, the interdisciplinary work of Wolz and colleagues (2011) has shown how broader participation in computing can be increased by teaching strategies centered on social communication activity, more specifically on what they call interactive journalism. Although our project shares many of the underlying assumptions and motivations of these and other related works, the main difference is our focus on *semiotic* aspects of computer programming, that is, on the representations and meanings that computer programs manifest internally (when looking at their code) and externally (when looking at their interface and the interactions supported by it) and on how these can signify a programmer's intent, beliefs and values.

SGD-Br is a collaborative project carried out by the Semiotic Engineering Research Group (SERG) at the Pontifical Catholic University of Rio de Janeiro, in partnership with: the Center for Lifelong Learning and Design at the University of Colorado in Boulder; the Active Documentation & Intelligent Design Laboratory at Universidade Federal Fluminense; AgentSheets, Inc.; and 3 schools located in the metropolitan area of Rio de Janeiro. The project ran from Mach 2010 to February 2015, with an average duration of four semesters at each school. In Table 1 we show that a total of 235 students and 19 teachers learned to program games and simulations using AgentSheets. In all three schools, teachers have carried out activities that explicitly involved the expression of ideas through games and simulations. They were, however, free to choose other kinds of activity, which they did (for example, asking the students to build versions of traditional games like Space Invaders and Frogger).

Three kinds of technologies have been used in SGD-Br studies. The first is AgentSheets, the visual programming environment used for creating games and simulations. The second is a dedicated live documentation Web system called PoliFacets, which we developed to explore meanings and representations embedded in AgentSheets projects. The third is SideTalk, a Firefox extension to create metacommunication dialogs for scripted navigation. SideTalk is built on top

Table 1 SGD-Br facts

	School one	School two	School three	Totals
Duration	2010–2013	2012–2014	2012–2014	2010–2014
CTA programs	6	7	9	22
Number of trained teachers	6	5	8	19
Number of coached classes	4	3	3	10
Classes subjects	1 Geography	1 Informatics	1 Media Arts	
	1 Biology	1 Literature	1 Science	
	2 Math	1 Math	1 Programming	
Number of students	72	46	117	235

of IBM's CoScripter (Leshed, Haber, Matthews, & Lau, 2008) and was used mainly in one particular study with a small group of volunteer students and their teacher. We will briefly describe and illustrate each one of these technologies and provide references for readers who wish to know more about them.

3.1 AgentSheets

AgentSheets is a visual programming environment specifically designed to support computational thinking acquisition (Repenning & Ioannidou, 2004; Repenning et al., 2010). The programming involves: (a) creating one or more agents; (b) deciding on their appearance and behavior; and (c) creating one or more Worksheets, which are game/simulation spaces where agents are deployed. The program can be executed ("played") at different speeds (from slow to fast) or step by step. An agent's behavior is defined by a set of if/then rules triggered by a set of events. Rules are created and tested interactively with direct manipulation of visual objects representing agents, rule conditions, actions and play space (Repenning, 2011).

For an illustration, consider the image shown in Fig. 3. It shows the execution space (worksheet named Skies) once the program is "played." Fireworks (like two variations of it, discussed below) is a demonstration program, built by one of the SGD-Br researchers. The visual pattern on screen is a collection of agents shown in the Gallery of agents (right-hand side of Fig. 3). In this case there are two agents in the gallery, FireRed and SetOnFire. One of them has five

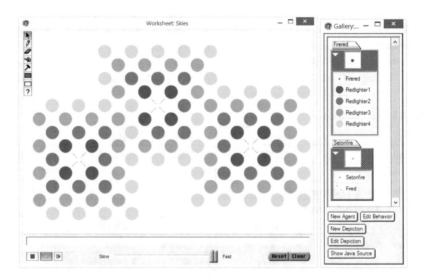

Fig. 3 AgentSheets worksheet after Fireworks execution and program agents gallery

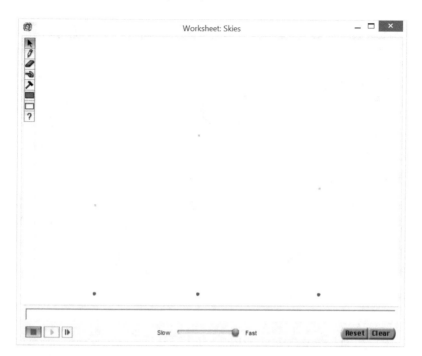

Fig. 4 AgentSheet's execution interface (Worksheet) in `Fireworks` initial state

depictions (visual forms), while the other has only two. All depictions and agents must have a name chosen by the user (upper and lower case used in this chapter to improve readability).

The initial state of the play space is shown in Fig. 4, where all we see is virtually a blank sheet with only three red dots at the bottom (three instances of the agent class FireRed). The worksheet configuration is changed during execution, according to the agents' behavior rules. Multiple instances of the two classes of agents, with different depictions, are shown in the program's final state (see the worksheet configuration in Fig. 3). In Fig. 5, we show the only two behavior rules for the `SetOnFire` agent. The empty rule triggered by AgentSheets `While running` event is created automatically. However, the non-empty rule triggered by the "On" event has been defined by the programmer. A pseudo-natural language translation of the rule might be: "if <no specific condition required>, then change <yourself> to <selected depiction>".

3.2 PoliFacets

PoliFacets is a Web system specifically designed to support the semiotic exploration of meanings and representations embedded in AgentSheets projects. The targeted users of PoliFacets are learners and teachers using AgentSheets to

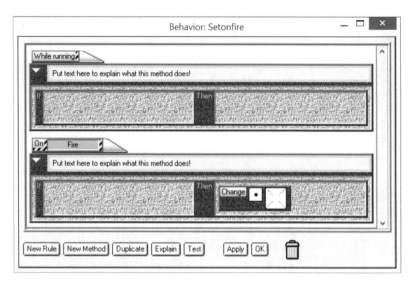

Fig. 5 AgentSheets' interface to create behavior rules

communicate ideas through games and simulations. The exploration of meanings and representations is done through navigating and interacting with the system, which thus becomes a live documentation of the *semiotic engineering* activity involved in the design and construction of games and simulations (Mota, Faria, & de Souza, 2012; Mota, Monteiro, Ferreira, Slaviero, & de Souza, 2013). There are six facets to explore: Description; Tags; In Practice; Worksheets; Rules; and Connections. The Description facet displays the programmer's free-text description and instructions to the player. The Tags facet displays an interactive tag cloud showing which commands have been used more and less frequently by the programmer (and where, if the user interacts with the cloud terms). The In Practice facet loads an applet for the user to "play." The programmer's description and instructions are shown above the applet. The Worksheets facet enables various kinds of interactions to explore how the programmer has structured the "play space" and where various instances of agents are displayed in a worksheet's initial state. The Rules facet presents a (pseudo) natural language translation of agents' behavior rules, that is, the program logic as conceived and encoded by the programmer. Finally, the Connections facet presents a series of graphs showing the (kinds of) relations between agents by virtue of their behavior rules. Relations can be appreciated from different agents' point of view.

Except for Descriptions, all facets are automatically generated. In Practice is generated by Ristretto, an AgentSheets component. The other four facets are generated by the PoliFacets parsing component. In Fig. 6, we show the the system's interface exhibiting part of the Description facet of the Fireworks program. Notice the thumbnail image of the programs initial (nearly

Fig. 6 PoliFacets' interface showing the Description facet of Fireworks

blank) worksheet beside the metadata information section, with the program's name, the author's ID, the date of creation, etc. The six facets can be accessed through the links displayed on the right-hand side of the screen.

We will illustrate the purpose and power of PoliFacets with a brief exploration of selected facets of three different programs whose output produces exactly the same visual pattern. We have already shown the agents in the first version, called Fireworks (see Figs. 3–5, above). In Fig. 7 we compare the introductory part of the Rules facet for Fireworks (top), AnotherFireworks (center) and YetAnotherFireworks (bottom). We can already see a significant difference in the programming (*i.e.* in the way the authors' messages are *signified*). Fireworks has only two active agents, no passive agents and no stacked agents. AnotherFireworks has three agents, two active and one passive, and no stacked agents (like Fireworks). Finally, YetAnotherFireworks has two agents, like Fireworks, but unlike any of the other two, it has stacked instances of both classes of agents.

An interesting case to explore is the Connections facet for Fireworks and YetAnotherFireworks. Although both have exactly two agents (with exactly the same names), the relations between them are different in the graphs compared in Fig. 8. The YetAnotherFireworks connections graph shown in the upper half of the image has an annotated edge between the two nodes. The red-color node is the agent "whose connections" are being explored. The black-color agent is the one with which it is related. The green-color edge between them indicates that the rule(s) establishing the connection between them can be found in the behavior of the red-colored agent, in focus. The annotation on the edge

Rules

There are 2 types or classes of agents in this game: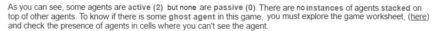

- Agent <u>setonfire</u> (active)
- Agent <u>firered</u> (active)

As you can see, some agents are **active (2)** but none are **passive (0)**. There are **no instances** of agents **stacked** on top of other agents. To know if there is some **ghost agent** in this game, you must explore the game worksheet, <u>(here)</u> and check the presence of agents in cells where you can't see the agent.

See rules in: <u>Natural Language</u> | <u>AgentSheets Code Language</u>

Rules

There are 3 types or classes of agents in this game: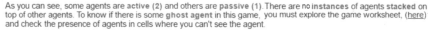

- Agent <u>setonfire</u> (active)
- Agent <u>onfire</u> (passive)
- Agent <u>firered</u> (active)

As you can see, some agents are **active (2)** and others are **passive (1)**. There are **no instances** of agents **stacked** on top of other agents. To know if there is some **ghost agent** in this game, you must explore the game worksheet, <u>(here)</u> and check the presence of agents in cells where you can't see the agent.

See rules in: <u>Natural Language</u> | <u>AgentSheets Code Language</u>

Rules

There are 2 types or classes of agents in this game: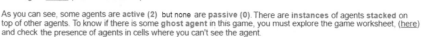

- Agent <u>setonfire</u> (active and stacked)
- Agent <u>firered</u> (active and stacked)

As you can see, some agents are **active (2)** but none are **passive (0)**. There are **instances** of agents **stacked** on top of other agents. To know if there is some **ghost agent** in this game, you must explore the game worksheet, <u>(here)</u> and check the presence of agents in cells where you can't see the agent.

See rules in: <u>Natural Language</u> | <u>AgentSheets Code Language</u>

Fig. 7 Snippets of three programs' `Rules` facets

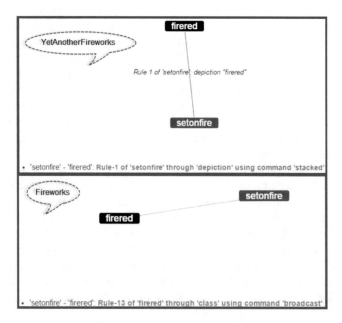

Fig. 8 A comparison between YetAnotherFireworks (1) and Fireworks (2) "Connections" facet

indicates how many rules are involved. Moreover, below the graph, there is an indication of the command(s) that have been used to create the connection.

The Fireworks connections graph at the lower half of Fig. 8 has a gray-colored edge connecting the two agents. This means that connections are established by behavior rules of the other agent, which is not in focus. Notice that there are no annotations on the edge. Below the YetAnotherFireworks graph on the upper half of Fig. 8 there is an indication of a different command (Stacked) than the one used to established connections between the same two agents in Fireworks (Broadcast).

Another meaningful comparison can be made using the Tags and the Worksheets facets of all three programs. In, Table 2 we show a synopsis of the outstanding differences between the *internal signs* of the three programs. The external signs exhibited when the programs are executed are virtually perceived as the same, in spite of slightly noticeable differences in the speed of execution, depending on the machine where the program is running. But for all practical effects, the player does (and sees the program do) the same actions in all three cases. Although the facets' images in Table 2 are definitely not readable or significant in detail, the broad-brush visual patterns that can be seen in the three columns with visual cues to the programs' facets support the comments on differences shown in the last row of the table. The details of differences in programming are lengthy and beyond the purpose of this paper. The interested reader is invited to explore them online in the collection of sample projects showcased in the PoliFacets website[14].

The points in evidence by way of the illustrations above is that, first, the *coding* of programs is laden with meanings that can tell us interesting things about the programmer's frame of mind, and that, second, a semiotic analysis combining internal and external program signs can be further explored in certain domains. For example, in Computer Art there are interesting discussions about the *conceptual* dimensions of images produced by a computer program (Boden & Edmonds, 2009; Nake, 2005). The kind of semiotic analysis carried out by PoliFacets with AgentSheets suggests that there may be room to develop exciting EUD art tools based on semiotic dimensions advanced by Semiotic Engineering and other related theories. The three programs above *paint* the same trivial pattern on the screen and they have been created by the same programmer. However, it they had been produced by different participants of an introductory "Art with AgentSheets" workshop for non-artist novice programmers, for example, PoliFacets would show that the programmer of YetAnotherFireworks *conceived* his artistic piece as something different from the other two programmers. While interacting with YetAnotherFireworks, the player sees a succession of manually designed worksheets, whereas in the other two programs the player sees the action

---

[14]PoliFacets sample projects can be accessed at http://www.serg.inf.puc-rio.br/polifacets/project/list.lua?lg=en&page=example. The user can use the search box to access "Fireworks," "AnotherFireworks" and "YetAnotherFireworks" more quickly. To run the programs, a Java-enabled browser is required.

Table 2 A comparison between facets of three programs

	Fireworks	Another fireworks	Yet another fireworks
Tags	9 commands	8 commands	8 commands
	new see empty	see new empty	switch to worksheet
Worksheets	1 worksheet	1 worksheet	11 worksheets
	Skies	OtherSkies	OtherSkies3 OtherSkies9 OtherSkies7 OtherSkies10 OtherSkies OtherSkies8 OtherSkies6 OtherSkies2 OtherSkies5 OtherSkies4 OtherSkies1

(continued)

Table 2 (continued)

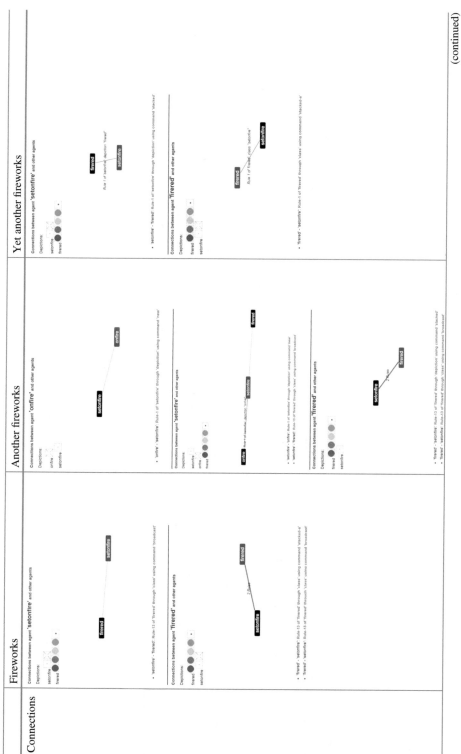

(continued)

Table 2 (continued)

	Fireworks	Another fireworks	Yet another fireworks
Rules	2 agents:	3 agents:	2 agents:
	Firered (5 depictions, 1 method, 14 rules)	Firered (5 depictions, 1 method, 14 rules)	Firered (5 depictions, 1 method, 2 rules)
	Setonfire (2 depictions, 2 methods, 3 rules total)	Setonfire (1 depiction, 2 methods, 2 rules total) onfire (1 depiction, 1 method, 1 empty rule)	Setonfire (2 depictions, 1 method, 1 rule)
Comments on differences	There are only 2 agents, whose appearances are changed as – in the course of execution – their relation with one another changes. [strict agent state (depictions) change strategy]	There are 3 agents. changes in mutual relations during execution lead to changes of appearances, self-destruction or creation of new agents. [mix of agent state (depictions) change and agent creation strategy]	There are 2 agents. changes in mutual relations during execution lead to a succession of global changes in the play space, introducing more *static* agents, at each change step. [frame animation strategy, with intensive use of *still images* in the play space]

algorithmically defined by `if/then` rules. Would this be an indication that the rule-based "art" of two participants is more *conceptual* than that of the other participant? Likewise, would the program using the smallest number of resources (agents, rules, or worksheets) be a *minimalist* version of the others? These are just hints at possibilities that could be further explored with more robust technologies of the same sort as AgentSheets and PoliFacets in end user programming and development activities involving creativity and art, in middle schools, high schools, or even elsewhere.

3.3   SideTalk

SideTalk first appeared under the name of Web Navigation Helper, used in a series of accessibility studies (Intrator, 2009; Intrator & de Souza, 2008; Monteiro, da Silva Alves, & de Souza, 2013). Later, as it began to be explored in SGD-Br research, it was revised and renamed to express the fact that it could be used for many different purposes beyond helping navigate the Web (Monteiro & de Souza, 2012; Monteiro, Tolmasquim, & de Souza, 2013). As already mentioned, SideTalk is an extension to Firefox built on top of CoScripter (Leshed et al., 2008). CoScripter is a macro recorder for the Web, which allows users to create scripts mainly to automate repetitive tasks like form filling, login and navigation in a frequently used workflow system, project testing and debugging. Automation does not preclude interaction. Script users can interact with the pages at various stages (which can be controlled by the script or not). With SideTalk, an end user can create and follow a parallel conversation with another user who is running a CoScript. The purpose of the parallel conversation can be to explain what happens while the script is executed, to instruct the script user about how to interact with a Web application, to make a commentary on Web content, and more. One of the useful things we can do with SideTalk is to guide a user's interaction with website designed for a foreign culture, with content in a foreign language. In Fig. 9 the superimposed images show SideTalk running in Firefox's sidebar, with a sequence of steps recorded with CoScripter (lower-layer image). The SideTalk home page, whose content is in Brazilian Portuguese, is loaded when the first step is executed. At this point, the author of the conversation under construction decides to create a *dialog* (as conversational steps are called in SideTalk) that will be shown to the conversation's end user, the author's *interlocutor* in this sort of metacommunication. The dialog creation window (upper-layer image) illustrates some of the functionality supported by the dialog editor.

In Fig. 10, we show superimposed images of a dialog creation screen (lower-layer image), captured while the author designs the metacommunication he wants to achieve with the targeted users, and a mediated web navigation snapshot (upper-layer image), captured while the user is running the script. Notice that the communication language on the sidebar, the actual the *side talk*, is different than on the

Fig. 9 SideTalk's sidebar and dialog creation interface

Fig. 10 SideTalk conversation, in design and use mode

main page. This script works as an *interpreter* for a foreign English-speaking visitor to the SideTalk website.

Although SideTalk, just like PoliFacets, is technically limited in a number of ways, it has the power to probe metacommunication in considerable depth. For

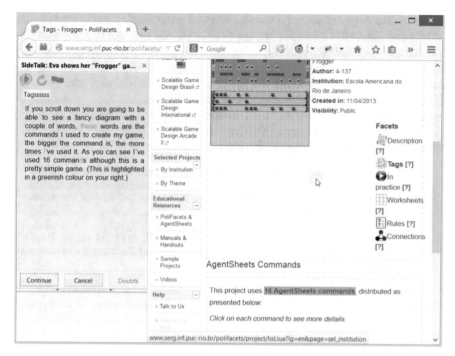

Fig. 11 A snapshot of student-teacher asynchronous conversation mediated by SideTalk

example, in SGD-Br, SideTalk has been used in combination with PoliFacets in a study carried out by Monteiro and colleagues (Monteiro, de Souza, & Tolmasquim, 2015). Six volunteer students from one of the partner schools designed SideTalk conversation to present their favorite AgentSheets project to their teacher. The presentation was based on the live documentation of their game, generated and supported by PoliFacets. The results of the study showed powerful evidence of *first-person discourse* embedded in AgentSheets programs. In Fig. 11 we show a snapshot of the mediating conversation that Eva, an 8th grader, designed for Mr. Tobias, her teacher. She wants to share with him *her view* of the Frogger game she has created. Notice her expressive choices while explicitly or implicitly commenting on PoliFacets interface (*Tagsssssss, fancy diagram*) or her own programming choices (*the bigger the command is, the more times I've used it, As you can see I've used 16 commands although this is a pretty simple game*).

The power of metacommunication in this context can be appreciated in at least three dimensions. The technical one is that Eva is using a program whose object is another program, that is, she is engaged in *metaprogramming*. The design of meta-communication steps and dialogs is entirely of her own, although she has been occasionally helped by an instructor while trying to correct a mistake or find the appropriate control to be used in SideTalk's dialog-creation interface. The psycho-logical dimension, already manifest in Fig. 11, is that Eva is proudly presenting her own meanings and achievements in different programming environments. She used AgentSheets to design her version of Frogger and now she is using SideTalk to comment on what PoliFacets is saying about her program. This unique triangulation context is full of possibilities for EUD (and non-EUD) activity. Finally, the social communication dimension can be appreciated by the teacher's reaction to the SideTalk conversations designed by his students. The detailed findings and discussions of this dimension can be found in Monteiro's work (Monteiro et al., 2015) (see also Monteiro & de Souza, 2012 for a related study). This is one of the comments made by the teacher, with his reaction to the use of SideTalk in this activity:

> I liked it a lot. I think the tool is fantastic. It has this personal touch to it. I think that 'cause they were addressing me specifically, and this was between me and them, it was a great opportunity for them to kind of have a closure of the class and kind of, you know, have a way of [...] connecting with me.

The teacher also commented on the pedagogical potential of asking the students to use SideTalk in combination with PoliFacets to present their programming projects. He said:

> I think that would help them make better games [...]. I think it has the potential to give them awareness, which could stimulate actually computational thinking 'cause they'd think deeper about what they did and why they did it.

4 On the Potential Contributions of Semiotic Engineering for Increasing EUD's Scientific Impact

In the introduction to this paper we contrasted evidence of great technological influence achieved by EUD-related research with the perception that its scientific influence on closely related areas – especially HCI – has been much less substantial (Tetteroo & Markopoulos, 2015). Although we do not discuss *why* (or even *if*) this perception is correct, we propose that Semiotic Engineering is a cohering theory that can be productively used to achieve two important kinds of effects. Firstly, it can inspire the development of new kinds of technologies. Secondly, with its origins in HCI and its commitments with CMC, this theory provides a pathway for EUD researchers to exchange knowledge and make significant contributions across disciplinary borders.

Since our chapter is about the development and use of theory in research that involves distinctly practical goals and settings, we begin this discussion by invoking Stokes's revision (Stokes, 2011) of the traditional contrast between basic and applied research crystallized in Vannevar Bush's famous postwar report about the role of science in peacetime (Bush, 1990). Stokes argues against the separation between basic and applied research and what he calls the *dynamic form* of this contrastive paradigm, visually depicted in Fig. 12 as a sequence of steps leading from basic science to technological innovation.

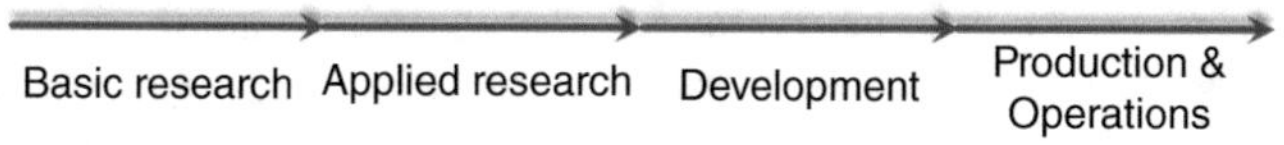

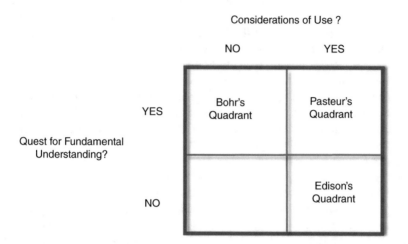

Fig. 12 The dynamic form of the separated basic and applied research paradigm

Fig. 13 The Quadrant Model for scientific research

Although Stokes was mainly interested in discussing public policies for funding research, his revision helps us to clarify what we mean by theory-oriented work and why we think it should be more stimulated in the field of EUD. He claims that research made to *understand* reality must not be (and most often *is not*) carried out without considerations of how its results might be used to *control* (or change) reality. According to Stokes, the *Quadrant Model of Scientific Research* (see Fig. 13) can not only accommodate research to *understand* reality and research to *control* reality more easily articulated with one another, but also organize a much richer territory within which scientists can position and reposition themselves as their scientific projects evolve over time.

The Quadrant Model in Fig. 13 might be used to map where EUD research has been more intense to date. Tetteroo and Markopoulos's conclusion that EUD research published between 2004 and 2013 is remarkably *techno-centered* suggests that there aren't (many) members of the EUD community positioned in the Bohr's Quadrant. Yet, the fact that most of the surveyed papers were classified as *applied research* (Tetteroo & Markopoulos, 2015, p. 62), following the traditional perspective inspired by Vannevar Bush, leaves considerable room for ambiguity regarding which of the remaining quadrants (Edison's or Pasteur's) would be home for EUD research produced in the past decade. Even without revisiting and reanalyzing Tetteroo and Makopoulos's data, we can make some considerations about the scientific impact of our work in other fields of study by simply looking at what it means to be in Edison's or Pasteur's Quadrant.

If most of our work is to be plotted inside Edison's Quadrant, this means that, in general, our community is not driven by a quest for fundamental understanding of the phenomena involved in end user development. Although a possibility, this would seem to be a strange choice in such a young field of studies as EUD. If verified, this situation would imply that, just like Edison, EUD researchers in this case would be using fundamental understanding that they have *imported* from other fields of knowledge. HCI theories, for example, typically orient their understanding of who the users are, what they do when they interact with computer technologies, what makes such technologies usable, and so on. Software Engineering and Information Systems Development knowledge, in turn, typically orient their understanding of which programming languages and styles can be used and what kinds of systems integration possibilities should be explored. The impact of research positioned in Edison's Quadrant is to create new life-changing products, environments and possibilities. The greater and better the change, the deeper and stronger the impact.

If, however, most of our work is to be plotted inside Pasteur's Quadrant, this means that even though we are driven by use considerations (and at times extensively so), our research is also concerned with setting the grounds and foundations for future EUD research. Therefore, although we might be possibly importing concepts and methods from other fields of studies, we would also be committed to proposing *new* concepts and methods that contribute to consolidate and advance EUD as a field. Compared to the case with Edison's Quadrant, the depth and strength of impact achieved by this mode of research can now be additionally assessed in terms of intellectual influence, that is, by how its proposed new ways of describing and thinking about EUD-enabled reality influence the perspective of other scientists, while doing their own work.

Our perception therefore is that an increase of EUD research impact outside its borders is probably more a matter of explicitly positioning our research in the so-called *Pasteur's Quadrant* (Stokes, 2011) than a matter of preferred research methods or practical engineering orientation (Tetteroo & Markopoulos, 2015). Moreover, we claim that Semiotic Engineering is a *cohering theory* with which EUD research can *connect with* HCI, CMC and other areas of investigation. We have presented a compact description of the theory in Sect. 2 and shown how it has been used to address practical challenges in Sect. 3. Could it help increase the scientific impact of EUD? Why? How has it contributed to this end up to now?

Although the first publication about Semiotic Engineering appeared in 1993 (de Souza, 1993), only in 2005 was the complete theory presented in a book, which included an entire chapter dedicated to software customization, extension and programming carried out by end users (de Souza, 2005a). The theory is therefore about as young as EUD and, from the start, committed to making an explicit articulation between HCI and EUD. During the first decade of EUD as a field, Semiotic Engineering was also in the process of maturing and becoming more widely known. The progress made by the theory since 2005 can be appraised by the publication of three additional books, whose topics are very closely related to topics of investigation in EUD. In 2009 the Semiotic Engineering methods book (de Souza & Leitão, 2009) was published. The Semiotic Inspection Method and the Communicability Evaluation Methods allow for a detailed analysis of meta-communication from a sender's (designer and developer) and a receiver's (user's) perspective. In 2012, Salgado and co-authors published a book about the semiotic engineering of cross-cultural interactive systems (Salgado et al., 2012). The interest of this work is that the notion of *culture* can also be used to frame studies about systems that aim to shorten the distances between professional and non-professional *cultures* of software development, a topic that lies at the heart of EUD. Finally, in 2016, the first Semiotic Engineering book that explicitly addresses software engineering activities (de Souza, Cerqueira, Afonso, Brandão, & Ferreira, 2016), such as systems modelling and programming, was published. In it the authors propose a suite of tools for investigating how human meanings get to be inscribed in software. This amounts to tracing the presence of related signs across different stages of software design, development and use. Intentionality, meaning and representations are at the center of the *SigniFYI Suite* presented in this book, which suggests that the tools included in the suite might shed an attractive light onto certain kinds of EUD studies (especially those related to EUSE).

The paragraph above contains part of our answers to the other two questions above ("why" and "how"). The work done in Semiotic Engineering to-date suggests that the theory could indeed support an increase of the scientific impact of EUD by helping some of the research done in our field to be framed and positioned more clearly as work that is not exclusively engaged in building new technology. A coherent use of the above-mentioned Semiotic Engineering concepts, methods and tools while developing technology can help researchers articulate their theory or model of EUD-related objects and phenomena in such a way that other researchers in the field can use them, regardless of whether *their* technology is of the same kind (and even regardless of whether they are developing any technology at all). Two examples of how we have done it are presented in Sect. 3, but much more can be done by a creative community of research.

The answer to *why* this theory can increase the scientific impact of EUD-related research is nonetheless incomplete if we do not discuss the *role of theories* in expanding the influence and applications of a field of studies. In her analysis of existing HCI theories, Rogers (2012) comments on the proliferation of theories and theoretical approaches in that field, in connection with how their roles have changed over time. According to the author, one of the lessons learned with theories used in the early stages of HCI development is that "you cannot simply lift theories out of an established field (*i.e.*, cognitive psychology), that have been developed to explain specific phenomena about cognition, and then reapply them to explain other kinds of seemingly related phenomena in a different domain (*i.e.*, interacting with computers)" (Rogers, 2012, p. 22). When the HCI community realized this, a multitude of theories that aimed at overcoming the limitations shown with early cognitive theories were developed. However, the transfer of knowledge from theory to practice has been far less clear and direct than one would have expected. Today, in the midst of what Rogers describes as "a messy and ever-changing, technologically augmented world", HCI theories play an important transdisciplinary role, by enabling HCI researchers to establish productive debates with colleagues from other fields whose objects of investigation are most certainly affected by computer technologies. Following this line of thought, we see an analogous situation in the future of EUD, that is, theoretical work that addresses directly the specific contexts, conditions and activities of EUD can eventually contribute to transdisciplinary discussions, which will naturally increase the impact of our field beyond its borders.

In the field of design studies and design research, authors interested in the role of theories have raised additional points that are also relevant for EUD. Di Sessa and Cobb (2004) underline the importance of theories in achieving *ontological innovation*, that is, in establishing "new categories of existence in the world" (diSessa & Cobb, 2004, p. 84). With ontological innovation, theories induce new ways of thinking and new possibilities for action. Venable (2006), in turn, surveys a large number of publications about design science and research, including Herbert Simon's ground-breaking *Sciences of the Artificial* (Simon, 1996). He sees the role of theories as that of supporting technological innovation as well as the process of design, evaluation, problem diagnosis and problem solving, by means of *utility* theoretical constructs that relate solution spaces and problem spaces in the field of interest. Venable defines *utility theories* as those whose assertions state that certain classes of technology can improve certain classes problem situations because of certain facts, principles or other consistently and sufficiently articulated justification.

Rogers, diSessa and Cobb, and Venable speak of the relations between theories and innovation in fields of studies that are very closely related to EUD. If Tetteroo and Markopoulos are correct in concluding that EUD-related research is remarkably focused on (re)engineering activities (Tetteroo & Markopoulos, 2015), this is an important *cultural feature* of our community. Consequently, the chances of adoption of any theory in EUD are proportional to the perception of their role in the design and development of new technologies. We can take the example of the Cognitive Dimensions of Notations (CDN) framework (Blackwell & Green, 2003) to check if, as a well known and often used theoretical approach in EUD, it confirms the above-mentioned points made by Rogers, diSessa and Cobb, and Venable.

CDN is a theoretical framework that supports mainly the analysis (but also the design) of representations that users of information artifacts must understand and manipulate while using them. According to its creators, CDN sets out a small *vocabulary* of relevant terms with which evaluators and designers can articulate cognitive aspects involved in the use of notations for a variety of tasks carried out with information artifacts (Green & Petre, 1996). Evidence of its power to support cross-disciplinary debates mentioned by Rogers (2012) comes not only from the research community interested in the psychology of programming (which, according to Blackwell has been "something of a research ghetto within mainstream HCI" Blackwell, 2006), but also from examples of its adoption in other research areas such as Software Engineering (Mehra, Grundy, & Hosking, 2005) and Programming Languages (Jones, Blackwell, & Burnett, 2003), especially Visual

Programming Languages (Green, 2006). We also have evidence of its role in achieving ontological innovation, as defined by diSessa and Cobb (diSessa & Cobb, 2004). One example is how it has inspired Hundhausen's "Communicative Dimensions" framework (Hundhausen, 2005). This work is explicitly proposed as an extension to the CDN framework, now focusing on other sorts of dimensions that must be attended to in the context of information visualization environments, where end users create representations aimed at, in Hundhausen's words, "[mediating] conversations about a scientific domain of interest". CDN's ontological innovation lies in prompting researchers to think of other dimensions that might play an equally critical role in the use of information artifacts. Since Hundhausen's work aims at informing the design of end user visualization environments, his contribution plays a similar role as Venable's utility theories (Venable, 2006).

The purpose of mentioning CDN in this argumentation is to underline the influence that theory-based *EUD* research might have in other research communities if we use *cohering* theoretical references (which, given the examples above, is clearly the case of CDN) and explicitly show their role in our own EUD research (*techno-centered*, or not). Semiotic Engineering is an alternative theoretical basis for EUD. Compared to the CDN framework, it refers to other dimensions, which are in fact "communicative dimensions," like those of Hundhausen's framework (Hundhausen, 2005). A critically important difference, for better or worse, is that the goal of Semiotic Engineering extends beyond that of CDN. It is far more than a vocabulary that corresponds to a set of relevant cognitive dimensions of notations, which is also how and why it is different from Hundhausen's communicative dimensions of notations framework and hence apt to achieving new kinds of ontological innovations and promoting new kinds of transdisciplinary conversations. While the use of Semiotic Engineering requires more investment in learning its principles, ontology, models and methods than the use of CDN, the return on such investment has been signposted throughout this entire paper. On the theoretical front, our theory has been originally proposed as an HCI theory that requires that end users be able to customize and extend software that they use (de Souza, 2005a). Hence the connections between HCI and EUD are *native* to Semiotic Engineering, unlike most other approaches except Meta-Design (Arias, Eden, & Fischer, 2015; Fischer & Giaccardi, 2006; Maceli, & Atwood, 2011, 2013), whose influence is so extensive in EUD that Tetteroo and Markopoulos take it as an EUD-related "field" (Tetteroo & Markopoulos, 2015). Meta-Design, just like Semiotic Engineering, proposes that the main challenge for productive use of systems is that the users' interpretation of systems, contexts and opportunities for action are constantly evolving. Both perspectives conclude that we should therefore design for meaningful evolution. However, similarly to the case with CDN, compared to Semiotic Engineering, Meta-Design is not a *theory* in the same sense, but a powerful conceptual framework and a design process model.

In addition to the basic ontological foundations that bind three distinct areas of research – HCI, CMC and EUD – Semiotic Engineering, as we have shown in Sect. 3, has already inspired technological innovations that can be advantageously explored by EUD researchers. More recently, Semiotic Engineering studies have shown that PoliFacets has also a great potential as a support tool for EUSE education (Monteiro et al., 2017). However, we believe that a possibly more enduring scientific impact that Semiotic Engineering should help achieve stems from the idea that end user programming and development can be widely practiced and promoted as a means of self-expression and social communication, rather than as a means for solving problems, personalizing technologies, or increasing personal efficacy. This perspective, in our view, is likely to raise substantial interest from other disciplines such as Psychology, Sociology, Communication Studies and even Philosophy. Note that, for these disciplines to have a good grasp of what is involved in social communication and self-expression through software proxies, the EUD research community has a critically important role to play in conceptualizing, exposing and operationalizing knowledge about this particular phenomenon and how various kinds of technologies influence the way how people experience and explore EUD in "technologically augmented worlds" (Rogers, 2012).

5 Concluding Remarks

The motivation for this chapter is the perception that the scientific impact of EUD research is lesser than one would expect. In their survey of one decade of publications in EUD-related fields, Tetteroo and Markopoulos (Tetteroo & Markopoulos, 2015) concluded that little work is dedicated to understanding what end user development, as a distinctive human activity, is, and what are the various contexts and conditions that lead to success or failure in this sort of activity. Since this kind of research typically involves the adoption (or development) of a theoretical stand, our goal with this chapter is to show that Semiotic Engineering (de Souza, 2005a) is a promising alternative to stimulate theoretically-based EUD research. In Sects. 2 and 3 we briefly outlined the theory and gave examples from a research project where we have developed and used technology that was designed in accordance with Semiotic Engineering principles and whose results have contributed to develop central aspects of the theory. In Sect. 4 we addressed the underlying assumption of the chapter, namely, that theory-based research has a positive influence on the scientific impact of a field of studies. The argumentation in favor of this view started by invoking Stokes (2011) revision of the traditional classification of research as basic or applied, the former being typically the home of theory-centered work, and the latter the home of technology-centered work. Stokes convincingly argues that considerations about use (i.e. application) are present in a large portion of theory development and have considerable influence on how the theory is shaped and evolved. We then proposed that theory-based research in EUD is not incompatible with this community's drive towards engineering and reengineering systems. In fact, we should emphasize in these final remarks that EUD theories could benefit extensively from being tested (even if partially) in technological developments. Could this increase the impact of our field outside its disciplinary borders?

The second part of our argumentation in Sect. 4 brought up a discussion of perceived roles of theory in two areas of research that are tightly connected with EUD, namely, HCI and Design. We took one of the elements of Rogers's view on HCI theories (Rogers, 2012) – the ability to create transdisciplinary conversations – and the notion of "ontological innovation' from diSessa and Cobb's discussion of the roles of theory in Design Studies (diSessa & Cobb, 2004) to show that theory-based work has the potential to increase the scientific influence of a field of studies. Moreover, using Venable's characterization of "utility theories" (Venable, 2006) as the ones that are most productive in Design research and science, we reinforced the argument put forth using Stokes's revision of the traditional basic vs. applied classification of research and proposed that there is a window of opportunity for our community if we begin to stimulate the development of EUD theories or EUD-related theoretical work.

Throughout the discussion, we showed how Semiotic Engineering is favorably positioned to be used as a theoretical basis for EUD research. The main points in the argument were the following. First, Semiotic Engineering is a theory of HCI where the end-users' ability to modify and extend the technologies with which they interact is of fundamental importance. This is because of the centrality of semiosis in communication and interpretation, as was explained in Sect. 2. This radical coupling of HCI and EUD at the root of Semiotic Engineering is in itself a key factor for the success of transdisciplinary conversations between researchers from the two fields. Second, in consonance with other semiotic approaches to HCI, Semiotic Engineering states that systems' interfaces are actually the systems' creators proxies with which end users communicate during interaction. This view is entirely different from greatly influential theories of user-centered design, such as Norman's Seven-Step Theory of Action (Norman, 1986). The effect of the change in perspective is to connect the fields of HCI and Social Communication through deeper theorizations on specific kinds of computer-mediated human communication. This connection can not only fulfill the social role of theories in scientific debate put forth by Rogers (2012), but also achieve its share of ontological innovation on both sides of the disciplinary border. To be sure, bringing designers and users together at interaction time (de Souza, 2005b) expands the ontology of most theories of human-computer interaction, as well as of theories of social communication. Third, and as a result of Semiotic Engineering being used in practical projects such as Scalable Game Design Brasil (SGD-Br), the theory has expanded its original boundaries and begun to explore programming and software development, more explicitly and deeply, as a means of self-expression. Studies with middle school children and teachers indicate that our project's principle – that logic and algorithmic problem solving can come second to learning why and how programs are a means of self-expression – has obtained very promising preliminary confirmation. There is thus an open avenue for interdisciplinary research involving two directly implicated fields – EUD and Computer Education – as well as other connected fields, such as Psychology (cf. Turkle's "Second Self" studies Turkle, 2005) and, of course, Semiotics. Once again, we can see Semiotic Engineering's potential to involve EUD researchers in transdisciplinary debate and to achieve ontological innovation inside and outside the borders of EUD. Moreover, since our studies about programming as self-expression have been carried out with technologies that have been specifically designed to this end, we have evidence of the theory's capacity of being used as a "utility theory" in Venable's sense (Venable, 2006), possibly enabling new kinds of conversations with Design researchers as well. Our technologies might thus be taken as instances of a class of technologies, for which there are probably other instances and sub-classes yet to be discovered. This can be especially fitting for a community that, in accordance to Tetterro and Markopoulos (Tetteroo & Markopoulos, 2015), has a strong attraction to engineering and reengineering systems and technologies. Fourth and finally, Semiotic Engineering has also been used, more recently, in research about professional software development (de Souza et al., 2016), which shows that the theory might also be useful in EUSE studies. In fact, one of our latest studies shows that PoliFacets is richly equipped to support end-user software engineering education initiatives in high schools and colleges (Monteiro et al., 2017).

The argument presented in Sect. 4 therefore sustains our claim that Semiotic Engineering can contribute to increase the scientific impact of EUD in the next decade. We emphasize, however, that this is not the only way to do theory-based work in EUD. Green's Cognitive Dimensions of Notations framework (Blackwell, 2006; Blackwell & Green, 2003; Green & Petre, 1996) and Fischer's Meta-Design approach (Arias et al., 2015; Fischer & Giaccardi, 2006; Maceli, & Atwood, 2011, 2013) are two examples of very successful foundations used not only in EUD but also in other fields, such as HCI. The achievements they already have in record reinforce our argument that an investment in paying more attention to theoretical aspects of EUD research can bring us more impact in return. However, given that the first paper on Semiotic Engineering was published at about the same time as the first papers on CDN and Meta-Design, one might ask: why have the latter been more widely used in EUD research than Semiotic Engineering?

The answer, as mentioned in Sect. 4, is that, in comparison, Semiotic Engineering is a much larger and consequently more complex body of knowledge than CDN or Meta-Design. Therefore, not only has it taken longer to mature and required much more time and effort to be fully exposed to the broader research community, but it naturally requires that those who are interested in using it spend more of their resources in learning its concepts and methods before putting them into practice. The positive side of this theory's breadth and complexity is how many different things can be done with it. There is, however, a deeper reason why we might encourage more EUD work based on Semiotic Engineering. It is the importance of intellectual diversity for the survival of a field of studies.

In their book dedicated to analyzing how the human body and mind has been replicated and extended in the history of science and technology, Franchi and Güzeldere (Franchi & Güzeldere, 2005) discuss the dispute between Cybernetics and Artificial Intelligence, which shared much of the centuries-old ideal of building automata that would look like humans, think like humans and act like humans.

The dispute was eventually won by Artificial Intelligence and Cybernetics shrank into insignificance compared to the success of the winner. According to the authors, one of the main reasons why Cybernetics lost the battle for AI was that the entire project of the field, although reaching out for intensive interdisciplinary involvement and collaboration, tried to impose certain kinds of research methods and conceptualizations that, at the time, seemed to be the only ones compatible with the grand view of the discipline in the eyes of its founders. It so happened, however, that the excluded researchers from various disciplines – those who would prefer to use different methods, different perspectives and look at different aspects of human mind and body – gradually proved their points in their respective disciplines. Consequently, the disciplinary project of Cybernetics was suddenly confronted with the misjudgment regarding the choice theoretical and methodological foundations. Interestingly, Franchi and Güzeldere conclude their chapter by asking whether AI was not in risk (at least at the time of their book's publication) of facing a similar fate, given its focus on engineering and computing.

As our chapter has shown, we already have considerable intellectual diversity in EUD, considering that ours is a young field of studies and also a relatively small community of researchers. The message I want to send with the chapter is that we can make more extensive and reflective use of such diversity. By so doing we will most probably contribute to increase the scientific impact of EUD research outside its borders and, thinking of Franchi and Güzeldere's analysis of Cybernetics and AI, keep our field alive and intellectually healthy for years to come.

Acknowledgements I thank CNPq, FAPERJ and The AMD Foundation for financial support to the research reported in this paper. I am also grateful to Alex Repenning, AgentSheets Inc. and all the participants, researchers and partner schools involved in SGD-Br. I am additionally thankful to Ernest Edmonds and Alan Blackwell for comments, suggestions and interesting discussions about some of the ideas exposed in this paper. Finally, I am greatly obliged to the anonymous reviewers whose insightful comments have helped me improve this chapter significantly.

References

Andersen, P. B. (1997). *A theory of computer semiotics: semiotic approaches to construction and assessment of computer systems*. Cambridge: Cambridge University Press.

Andersen, P. B. (1985). *Semiotics and informatics: computers as media Proceedings of the Conference on Information Technology for Information Use*. Copenhagen: The Royal School of Librarianship.

Andersen, P. B., Holmqvist, B., Jensen, J. F. (1993). *The computer as medium*. Cambridge: Cambridge University Press.

Arias, E. G., Eden, H., Fischer, G. (2015). *The envisionment and discovery collaboratory (EDC): explorations in human-centered informatics with tabletop computing environments*. San Rafael, California: Morgan & Claypool Publishers.

Barbosa, S. D. J., & de Souza, C. S. (2001). Extending software through metaphors and metonymies. *Knowledge-Based Systems, 14*(1), 15–27.

Blackwell, A. (2006). Psychological issues in end-user programming. In H. Liberman, F. Parternò, V. Wulf (Eds.). *End user development* (pp. 9–30). Dordrecht, Netherlands: Springer.

Blackwell, A., & Green, T. (2003). Notational systems–the cognitive dimensions of notations framework. In J. Carroll (Ed.), *HCI models, theories, and frameworks: toward an interdisciplinary science* (pp. 103–133). San Francisco, Calif: Morgan Kaufmann.

Blandford, A., Furniss, D., Makri, S. (2016). "Qualitative HCI research: going behind the scenes." *Synthesis Lectures on Human-Centered Informatics*, 9(1), 1–115.

Boden, M. A., & Edmonds, E. A. (2009). What is generative art? *Digital Creativity*, 20, 21–46.

Burke, Q., & Kafai, Y. B. (2010). Programming & storytelling: opportunities for learning about coding & composition. In *Proceedings of the 9th International Conference on Interaction Design and Children (IDC '10)* (pp. 348–351). New York, NY, USA: ACM. doi:10.1145/1810543.1810611.

Burke, Q., & Kafai, Y. B. (2012). The writers' workshop for youth programmers: digital story-telling with scratch in middle school classrooms. In *Proceedings of the 43rd ACM technical symposium on Computer Science Education (SIGCSE '12)* (pp. 433–438). New York, NY, USA: ACM. doi:10.1145/2157136.2157264.

Bush, V. (1990). *Science: the endless frontier: a report to the president on a program for post-war scientific research*. Washington, DC: National Science Foundation. 192 p.

Calvo, R. A., & Peters, D. (2013). The irony and re-interpretation of our quantified self. In H. Shen, R. Smith, J. Paay, P. Calder & T. Wyeld (Eds.), *Proceedings of the 25th Australian computer-human interaction conference: augmentation, application, innovation, collaboration (OzCHI '13)* (pp. 367–370). New York, NY, USA: ACM. doi:10.1145/2541016.2541070.

de Souza, C., Barbosa, S., da Silva, S. (2001). Semiotic engineering principles for evaluating end-user programming environments. *Interacting with Computers*, 13, 467–495.

de Souza, C. S. (1993). The semiotic engineering of user interface languages. *International Journal of Man-Machine Studies, Academic Press*, 39, 753–773.

de Souza, C. S. (2005a). *The semiotic engineering of human-computer interaction*. Cambridge, MA: The MIT Press.

de Souza, C. S. (2005b). Semiotic engineering: bringing designers and users together at interaction time. *Interacting with Computers*, 17(3), 317–341.

de Souza, C. S. (2013). Semiotic perspectives on interactive languages for life on the screen. *Journal of Visual Languages & Computing*, 24(3), 218–221.

de Souza, C. S., & Barbosa, S. D. J. (2006). A semiotic framing for end-user development. In H. Lieberman, F. Paternò, V. Wulf (Eds.). *End user development* (pp. 401–426). Netherlands: Springer.

de Souza, C. S., Cerqueira, R. F. G., Afonso, L. M., Brandão, R. M. R., Ferreira, J. S. J. (2016). *Software developers as users: semiotic investigations in human-centered software development*. Cham: Springer International Publishing.

de Souza, C. S., Garcia, A. C. B., Slaviero, C., Pinto, H., Repenning, A. (2011). *End-user development: third international symposium, IS-EUD 2011, Torre Canne (BR), Italy, June 7–10, 2011. Proceedings* (pp. 155–170). Berlin, Heidelberg: Springer Berlin Heidelberg.

de Souza, C. S., & Leitão, C. F. (2009). Semiotic engineering methods for scientific research in HCI. *Synthesis Lectures on Human-Centered Informatics*, 2(1), 1–122.

de Souza, C. S., Salgado, L. C., Leitão, C. F., Serra, M. M. (2014). Cultural appropriation of computational thinking acquisition research: seeding fields of diversity. In *Proceedings of the 2014 conference on Innovation & technology in computer science education (ITiCSE '14)* (pp. 117–122). New York, NY, USA: ACM. doi:10.1145/2591708.2591729.

diSessa, A. A., & Cobb, P. (2004). Ontological innovation and the role of theory in design experiments. *The Journal of the Learning Sciences*, 13(1), 77–103.

Edmonds, E. A. (2007) *Reflections on the Nature of Interaction CoDesign*, 3, 139–143.

Ferreira, J. J., de Souza, C. S., de Castro Salgado, L. C., Slaviero, C., Leitão, C. F., de F. Moreira F. (2012), Combining cognitive, semiotic and discourse analysis to explore the power of notations in visual programming. In *2012 IEEE Symposium on Visual Languages and Human-Centric Computing (VL/HCC)., September, 2012* (pp. 101–108). Los Alamitos, CA: IEEE Computer Society.

Fischer, G., & Giaccardi, E. (2006). Meta-design: a framework for the future of end-user development. *End user development* (pp. 427–457). Netherlands: Springer.

Franchi, S., & Güzeldere, G. (2005). Machinations of the mind: cybernetics and artificial intelligence from automata to cyborgs. In S. Franchi, & G. Güzeldere (Eds.). *Mechanical bodies, computational minds* (pp. 15–149). Cambridge, MA: The MIT Press.

Gerd Waloszek. (2005). Book review: the semiotic engineering of human-computer interaction. https://experience.sap.com/archived/review_semiotic_eng/ Accessed 24 May 2016.

Green, T. (2006). Aims, achievements, agenda—where CDs stand now. *Journal of Visual Languages & Computing, 17*(4), 288–291.

Green, T. R. G., & Petre, M. (1996). Usability analysis of visual programming environments: a 'cognitive dimensions' framework. *Journal of Visual Languages & Computing, 7*(2), 131–174.

Greenwood, D. J., & Levin, M. (2007). *Introduction to action research. Social research for social change* (2nd Edition) Thousand Oaks, CA: Sage Publications, Inc.

Hundhausen, C. D. (2005). Using end user visualization environments to mediate conversations: a 'communicative dimensions' framework. *Journal of Visual Languages and Computing, 16*(3), 153–185.

Intrator, C. (2009). *Using web scripts to improve accessibility*. MSc dissertation. Departamento de Informática. PUC-Rio. 103 p. http://www2.dbd.puc-rio.br/pergamum/tesesabertas/0711270_09_pretextual.pdf.

Intrator, C., & de Souza, C. S. (2008). Using Web scripts to improve accessibility. In *IHC 2008 - VIII Simpósio Brasileiro de Fatores Humanos em Sistemas Computacionais, 2008, Porto Alegre. Proceedings of the VIII Brazilian Symposium on Human Factors in Computing Systems* (v. 378. pp. 292–295). New York: ACM.

Jones, S. P., Blackwell, A., Burnett, M. (2003). A user-centred approach to functions in Excel. In *Proceedings of the eighth ACM SIGPLAN international conference on Functional programming (ICFP '03)* (pp. 165–176). New York: ACM.

Kammersggard, J. (1988). Four different perspectives on human–computer interaction. *International Journal of Man-Machine Studies, 28*, 343–362.

Kelleher, C., & Pausch, R. (2007). Using storytelling to motivate programming. *Communications of the ACM, 50*, 58–64.

Kuutti, K. (1996). Activity theory as a potential framework for human-computer interaction research. In *Context and consciousness: activity theory and human-computer interaction* (pp. 17–44). Cambridge, Mass.: MIT Press.

Leshed, G., Haber, E. M., Matthews, T., Lau, T. (2008). CoScripter: automating & sharing how-to knowledge in the enterprise. In *Proceedings of the SIGCHI Conference on Human Factors in Computing Systems (CHI '08)* (pp. 1719–1728). New York, NY, USA: ACM. doi:10.1145/1357054.1357323.

Lieberman, H., Paternò, F., Wulf, V. (Eds.) (2006). *End user development*. Netherlands, Dordrecht: Springer.

Liu, K. (2000). *Semiotics in information systems engineering*. Cambridge: Cambridge University Press.

Maceli, M., & Atwood, M. E. (2011). From human crafters to human factors to human actors and back again: bridging the design time–use time divide. In *International symposium on end user development* (pp. 76–91). Berlin Heidelberg: Springer.

Maceli, M., & Atwood, M. E. (2013). "Human crafters" once again: supporting users as designers in continuous co-design. In *International symposium on end user development* (pp. 9–24). Berlin Heidelberg: Springer.

Mehra, A., Grundy J., Hosking, J. (2005). A generic approach to supporting diagram differencing and merging for collaborative design. In *Proceedings of the 20th IEEE/ACM international conference on automated software engineering (ASE '05)* (pp. 204–213). New York: ACM.

Monteiro, I. T., da Silva Alves, A., de Souza, C. S. (2013). Using mediated communication to teach vocational concepts to deaf users. In C. Stephanidis, & M. Antona (Eds.). *Universal access in human-computer interaction. applications and services for quality of life: 7th international conference, UAHCI 2013, held as part of HCI international 2013, Las Vegas, NV, USA, July 21–26, 2013, Proceedings, Part III* (pp. 213–222). Berlin Heidelberg: Springer.

Monteiro, I. T., & de Souza, C. S. (2012). The representation of self in mediated interaction with computers. In *Proceedings of the 11th Brazilian Symposium on Human Factors in Computing Systems (IHC '12)* (pp. 219–228). Porto Alegre, Brazil: Brazilian Computer Society.

Monteiro, I. T., de Souza, C. S., Tolmasquim, E. T. (2015). My program, my world: insights from 1st-person reflective programming in EUD education. In P. Díaz, V. Pipek, C. Ardito, C. Jensen, I. Aedo, A. Boden (Eds.), *End-user development: 5th international symposium, IS-EUD 2015, Madrid, Spain, May 26–29, 2015. Proceedings* (pp. 76–91). Cham: Springer.

Monteiro, I. T., de Castro Salgado, L. C., Mota, M. P., Sampaio, A. L., de Souza, C. S. (June 2017). Signifying software engineering to computational thinking learners with AgentSheets and PoliFacets. *Journal of Visual Languages & Computing, 40*, 91–112. doi:10.1016/j.jvlc.2017.01.005.

Monteiro, I. T., Tolmasquim, E. T., & de Souza, C. S. (2013). Going back and forth in metacommunication threads. In *Proceedings of the 12th Brazilian symposium on human factors in computing systems (IHC '13). Brazilian computer society, Porto Alegre, Brazil* (pp. 102–111).

Mota, M. P., Faria, L. S., de Souza, C. S. (2012). Documentation comes to life in computational thinking acquisition with agentsheets. In *Proceedings of the 11th Brazilian Symposium on Human Factors in Computing Systems (IHC '12)* (pp. 151–160). Porto Alegre, Brazil: Brazilian Computer Society.

Mota, M. P., Monteiro, I. T., Ferreira, J. J., Slaviero, C., de Souza, C. S. (2013). On signifying the complexity of inter-agent relations in AgentSheets games and simulations. In *Proceedings of the 31st ACM international conference on design of communication* (pp. 133–142). New York: ACM.

Nadin, M. (1988). Interface design and evaluation – semiotic implications. In H. R. Hartson, & D. Hix (Ed.), *Advances in human-computer interaction ablex* (v. 2, pp. 45–100).

Nadin, M. (2011). Computation, information, meaning. *Anticipation and Games International Journal of Applied Research on Information Technology and Computing, 2*, 50–76.

Nake, F. (2005). Computer art: a personal recollection. In *Proceedings of the 5th conference on Creativity & cognition (C&C '05)* (pp. 54–62). New York, NY, USA: ACM. doi:10.1145/1056224.1056234.

Nake, F., & Grabowski, S. (2001). Human–computer interaction viewed as pseudo-communication. *Knowledge-Based Systems, 14*, 441–447.

Norman, D. A. (1986). Cognitive engineering. In D. Norman, & S. Draper (Eds.), *User centered systems design* (pp. 31–629). Hillsdale, N.J.: L. Erlbaum Associates.

Norman, D. A. (2009). THE WAY I SEE IT: Systems thinking: a product is more than the product. *Interactions, 16*, 52–54.

Oberquelle, H., Kupka, I., Maass, S. (1983). A view of human—machine communication and co-operation. *International Journal of Man-Machine Studies, 19*, 309–333.

Peirce, C. S. (1992). *The Essential Peirce*. Selected Philosophical Writings Volume 1 (1987–1893) edited by Nathan Houser and Christian Kloesel. Bloomington IN: Indiana University Press.

Peirce, C. S. (1998). *The Essential Peirce*. Selected Philosophical Writings Volume 2 (1893–1913) edited by Nathan Houser and Christian Kloesel. Bloomington IN: Indiana University Press.

Repenning, A. (2011). Making programming more conversational. *2011 IEEE Symposium on Visual Languages and Human-Centric Computing (VL/HCC)* (pp. 191–194). Los Alamitos, CA: IEEE Computer Society.

Repenning, A., & Ioannidou, A. (2004). Agent-based end-user development. *Communications of the ACM, 47*(9), 43–46.

Repenning, A., & Ioannidou, A. (2006). What makes end-user development tick? 13 design guidelines. In H. Lieberman, F. Paternò, V. Wulf, (Eds.). *End user development* (pp. 51–85). Netherlands: Springer.

Repenning, A., Webb, D., Ioannidou, A. (2010). Scalable game design and the development of a checklist for getting computational thinking into public schools. In *Proceedings of the 41st ACM technical symposium on Computer science education (SIGCSE '10)* (pp. 265–269). New York, NY, USA: ACM. doi:10.1145/1734263.1734357.

Rogers, Y. (2012). HCI theory: classical, modern, and contemporary. *Synthesis Lectures on Human-Centered Informatics 5.2*, 1–129.

Salgado, L. C. C., Leitão, C. F., de Souza, C. (2012). *A journey through cultures: metaphors for guiding the design of cross-cultural interactive systems*. London; New York: Springer.

Searle, J. R. (1985). *Expression and meaning: studies in the theory of speech acts*. Cambridge: Cambridge University Press.

Simon, H. A. (1996). *The sciences of the artificial*. 3rd Edition Cambridge, MA: The MIT Press.

Stokes, D. E. (2011). *Pasteur's quadrant: basic science and technological innovation*. Washington, DC: Brookings Institution Press.

Tanaka-Ishii, K. (2010). *Semiotics of programming*. Cambridge: Cambridge University Press.

Tetteroo, D., & Markopoulos. (2015). A review of research methods in end user development. In P. Díaz, V. Pipek, C. Ardito, C. Jensen, I. Aedo, A. Boden (Eds.), *End-user development: 5th international symposium, IS-EUD 2015, Madrid, Spain, May 26–29, 2015* (pp. 58–75). Cham: Springer.

Turkle, S. (2005). *The second self: computers and the human spirit. Twentieth Anniversary Edition*. Cambridge, MA: The MIT Press.

Venable, J. (2006). The role of theory and theorising in design science research. In S. Chatterjee & A. Hevner (Eds), *Proceedings of the First International Conference on Design Science in Information Systems and Technology (DESRIST 2006)* (pp. 1–18). Claremont, CA: Claremont Graduate University.

Winograd, T. (1997). The design of interaction. In P. Denning (Ed.). *Beyond calculation: the next fifty years of computing* (pp. 149–161). New York: Springer.

Winograd, T. (2006). Designing a new foundation for design. *Communications of the ACM, 49*, 71–74.

Winograd, T., & Flores, F. (1986). *Understanding computers and cognition: a new foundation for design*. Boston, Mass.: Addison-Wesley.

Wolz, U., Stone, M., Pearson, K., Pulimood, S. M., Switzer, M. (2011). Computational thinking and expository writing in the middle school. *Transactions on Computing Education, 11*, 9:1–9:22.

End-User Development and Social Big Data – Towards Tailorable Situation Assessment with Social Media

Christian Reuter, Marc-André Kaufhold and Thomas Ludwig

Abstract The amount of data being available is increasing rapidly. Based on the technological advances with mobile and ubiquitous computing, the use of social media is getting more and more usual in daily life as well as in extraordinary situations, such as crises. Not surprisingly, this increasing use is one reason why data on the internet is also developing that fast. Currently, more than 3 billion people use the internet and the majority is also registered with social media services such as Facebook or Twitter. While processing this kind of data by the majority of non-technical users, concepts of End-User Development (EUD) are important. This chapter researches how concepts of EUD might be applied to handle social big data. Based on foundations and an empirical pre-study, we explore how EUD can support the gathering and assessment process of social media. In this context, we investigate how end-users can articulate their personal quality criteria appropriately and how the selection of relevant data can be supported by EUD approaches. We present a tailorable social media gathering service and quality assessment service for social media content, which has been implemented and integrated into an application for both volunteers and the emergency services.

Keywords Social media · information quality · tailoring · End-User Development · emergencies

C. Reuter (✉) · M.-A. Kaufhold · T. Ludwig
University of Siegen, Siegen, Germany
e-mail: christian.reuter@uni-siegen.de

M.-A. Kaufhold
e-mail: marc.kaufhold@uni-siegen.de

T. Ludwig
e-mail: thomas.ludwig@uni-siegen.de

© Springer International Publishing AG 2017
F. Paternò, V. Wulf (eds.), *New Perspectives in End-User Development*,
DOI 10.1007/978-3-319-60291-2_12

1 Introduction

The amount of data has experienced exponential growth – data generation has been estimated at 2.5 Exabytes (=2,500,000 Terabytes) per day. The sources are manifold and include not only technical sensors, but also social sensors, such as posts to social media such as Facebook or Twitter. To handle this big data, new applications, frameworks, and methodologies arose that allow efficient data mining and information fusion from social media and new applications and frameworks (Bello-Orgaz, Jung, & Camacho, 2016). Usually, the data is called user-generated content, which is according to the definition of the Organization for Economic Co-operation and Development (OECD) (2007), "content that has been made publicly available via the internet".

Not only in daily life but also in recent emergencies, such as the 2012 hurricane Sandy or the 2013 European floods, both the people affected and volunteers alike used social media to communicate with each other and to coordinate private relief activities (Kaufhold & Reuter, 2016). Since the involvement of citizens is, still, mostly uncoordinated and the content is therefore not necessarily created in a structured way, a vast amount of resulting data has to be analyzed. Appropriate methods of valuation are essential for the analysis, whereby a consistent evaluation of the quality of information can be complex (Friberg, Prödel, & Koch, 2010). Especially in cases where a selection, whether by emergency managers or citizen volunteers, has to be made from a variety of information sources and formats under time-critical constraints, it is helpful if the evaluation can be simplified by applying situationally relevant quality criteria. Thus, our research question is how the concepts of End-User Development (EUD) can be applied to support individuals in extracting relevant social media information in the extraordinary and unique settings of emergencies.

This chapter explores the challenges arising from the integration of citizen-generated content and the analysis of information from social media focusing on EUD. Based on a review of related work in big data analysis, social media and EUD (Sect. 2), we present a design case study (Wulf, Müller, Pipek, Randall, & Rohde, 2011, 2015) on social media use in emergencies and its assessment by the tailorable weighting of information quality criteria. Accordingly, an empirical study on the use of citizen-generated content and social media by emergency services and the challenges, focusing on individual and dynamic quality assessments of social media data, informed the implementation of tools for platform-independent social media gathering (Social Media API) and quality assessment (Social-QAS) (Sect. 3). Furthermore, we have prototypically integrated and evaluated Social-QAS in two reference applications (Sect. 4). Finally, we draw conclusions (Sect. 5).

2 Big Data, Social Media and End-User Development

2.1 Big Data, Social Media and Data Analysis

Although – or because – big data is a buzzword, there is no unified definition of the term big data across various origins (Ward & Barker, 2013). According to the

Gartner IT Glossary, big data is "high-volume, high-velocity and high-variety in formation assets that demand cost-effective, innovative forms of information processing for enhanced insight and decision making." Dijcks (2012) distinguishes between different types of data: traditional enterprise data, machine-generated/ sensor data and finally social data, which are also known as *social big data*: it "will be based on the analysis of vast amounts of data that could come from multiple distributed sources but with a strong focus on social media" (Bello-Orgaz *et al.*, 2016). Reviewing current literature, Olshannikova, Olsson, Huhtamäki, and Kärkkäinen (2017) contribute with the definition of social big data as "any high-volume, high-velocity, high-variety and/or highly semantic data that is generated from technology-mediated social interactions and actions in digital realm, and which can be collected and analyzed to model social interactions and behavior." Ward and Barker (2013) explicitly research for a definition of big data and suggest that it: "is a term describing the storage and analysis of large and/or complex data sets using a series of techniques including, but not limited to: NoSQL, MapReduce and machine learning."

Ganis and Kohirkar (2012) consider that most big data is from social media: "Where is all of this big data coming from? It's produced within the many social media applications by a wide variety of sources (people, companies, advertisers, etc.)." Additionally, Bassett (2015) outlines that the existence of social media as big data was underplayed in the past, and, to bridge the gap to the domain of emergency management, Watson, Finn, and Wadhwa (2017) exemplify promising benefits of big data to support situational awareness and decision making especially before and during emergencies.

Data from social media contains complex dependencies and relationships within itself and this, combined with its – not to mention the characteristics of crises and emergencies – heterogeneous nature and imposes strong limitations on the data models that can be used as well as on the scope of information that can be discovered. In the case of current social media, the amount of data is increasing steadily as the data set is constantly supplemented. Data analysis or mining in the context of social media must continuously transform raw social media data into a processable form by selectively using specific characteristics needed for the upcoming analysis process. In the following, we will specify characteristics for the analysis process.

Big Data Paradox: Social media data has a huge amount of records consisting of different data types, like profiles, posts, groups, relationships and other. Therefore, enormous computing and storage capacities are required to process the data (Batrinca & Treleaven, 2014). However, little data exists for individuals, and conventional data mining techniques do not process relationships between profiles.

Obtaining Sufficient Samples: A wide range of data is accessible so that trends, indicators and patterns can be detected based on statistical information (Zafarani, Abbasi, & Liu, 2014). However, collecting data from social media has several limitations. In many cases one gets only a limited amount of data in a restricted period of time (Reuter & Scholl, 2014).

Context and User Dependency: A large part of data from social media is generated and consumed by users and, from the interactions between different actors and the environment, new metadata such as time, location, groups, hashtags and other variables arise. When analyzing data it is important to mention that the data that is being processed originates from a variety of sources (e.g. third-party applications) which have their own use context and purpose (Mislove *et al.*, 2007).

Structured and Unstructured Data: Profile data, the number of likes or retweets are structured data and can easily be compared with each other. In contrast, user-generated text is usually in an unstructured form and varies in quality and quantity (Stieglitz, Dang-Xuan, Bruns, & Neuberger, 2014). This is a challenge because data mining requires the identification of *high-quality* information in the large data sets (Agichtein, Castillo, Donato, Gionis, & Mishne, 2008).

Importance of Metadata: Metadata represent an essential part of the social media's information content. They provide the interaction context of users such as a specification of time and location. Because a large set of metadata is available in almost any situation, it may be possible to draw conclusions on the user intention and situation. The in-situ context influences user behavior significantly and is formed by activities, time, place and conversations of the respective user (Church & Oliver, 2011).

Historicity of Data: The historicity of data can be represented not only by the data and metadata itself but also through the interactions between social media. A snapshot can be created in the virtual space of social media including all dependencies. Here it is vital that the collected data is stored persistently because the access to data from social media such as Twitter is volatile, particularly at high-traffic events such as crises.

Type of content: Social media is strongly characterized by the use of images, videos and sounds and by text comments and annotations from users and therefore important contextual information may be present. Hence, data mining of social media usually includes natural language processing (NLP). A major problem with NLP on social media is non-standard language (Ritter, Clark, Mausam, & Etzioni, 2011; Xu, Ritter, & Grishman, 2013). Social media reports frequently contain non-standard grammar (punctuation, capitalization, syntax) and vocabulary (including non-standard spelling) (Eisenstein, 2013).

2.2   The End-User Development Perspective in Data Analysis

Referring to situation assessment during emergencies, it is important to have information available at the right time, the right place and in the right format (Ley, Pipek, Reuter, & Wiedenhoefer, 2012). Endsley (1995) makes a distinction between *situation awareness* as a "state of knowledge" and *situation assessment* as the "process of achieving, acquiring, or maintaining" that knowledge; he defines information gathering as a selection procedure which results in the construction of a mental model pursuant to individual goals. Since several emergencies are extraordinary and time-critical, they require a demand for unpredictable information. It is therefore essential to have instantaneous access to as many sources as possible. Still, it is not easy to dispose of all the necessary information (Turoff, Chumer, van de Walle, & Yao, 2004). Simultaneously, it is very important to prevent a possible information overload so that the decision making is not affected (Hiltz & Plotnick, 2013).

In crisis management, situation assessment and decision making are supported by information systems (van de Walle & Turoff, 2008). Of course, it can come to difficulties, particularly when dealing with seldom used technologies within emergencies and while assessing social media. Adjustments of these technologies and especially of the considered information are essential and play a big role at 'use-time' (Fischer & Scharff, 2000; Pipek & Wulf, 2009; Stevens, Pipek, & Wulf, 2009).

EUD supports flexible adjustments by making it possible for end-users to tailor and rearrange information systems independently (Lieberman, Paterno, & Wulf, 2006). EUD can be defined as all "methods, techniques, and tools that allow users of software systems, who are acting as non-professional software developers, at some point to create modify or extend a software artefact" (Lieberman *et al.*, 2006). One essential part of EUD, with regard to the change of a "stable" aspect of an artefact, is adapting (Henderson & Kyng, 1991). Nonetheless, for some people it is "tailoring," for others it is "use." An essential part of software with regard to its establishment in practice definitely is tailorability. EUD uses mashups to combine services or information from various sources (Cappiello, Daniel, Matera, Picozzi, & Weiss, 2011). The metaphor of a "bazaar" has therefore been used (Doerner, Draxler, Pipek, & Wulf, 2009). While component-based architectures in software engineering enable tailorable systems (Won, Stiemerling, & Wulf, 2006), intuitive notions as well as interaction designs are needed to support end-user articulations (Hess, Reuter, Pipek, & Wulf, 2012). Pipek (2005) argues that tailoring might lead towards appropriation support to support the users.

2.3   Existing Approaches in EUD and Emergency Management

There are existing approaches and models (Costabile, Member, Fogli, Mussio, & Piccinno, 2007; Doll & Torkzadeh, 1988; Grammel, 2009) to deal with data analysis using EUD: Wong and Hong (2007) argue that there is "a tremendous amount of web content available today, but it is not always in a form that supports end-users' needs." Addressing this, their EUD tool enables end-users to create mashups that re-purpose and combine existing web content and service. In the domain of social networks, Heer and Boyd (2005) present a case study of the design of Vizster, an interactive visualization system for end-user exploration of online social networks. Resulting techniques include connectivity, highlighting and linkage views for viewing network context, X-ray mode and profile search for exploring member profile data, and visualization of inferred community structures. Coutaz and Crowley (2016) present their "lived-with" experience with an EUD prototype deployed at their home.

Considering the domain of visual programming, Borges and Macías (2010) present a visual language and a functional prototype, called VISQUE, providing an easy-to-use mechanism to create SQL queries for non-programmer professionals, such as engineers, scientists and freelancers. With VISQUE the users can build the queries through a web-based visual interface to explore and analyze data without the need of SQL skills. Ardito *et al.* (2014) conducted a study to identify end-user requirements for accessing and customizing web-services and APIs. Based on their findings, the authors present a prototype, which enables people without programming skills to create a dashboard of widgets. With the help of a wizard the users can create a widget to combine data from different services and APIs and choose a visualization format. In addition, FaceMashup (Massa & Spano, 2015) is an EUD environment that "empowers social network users, supporting them in creating their own procedures for inspecting and controlling their data."

Taking the case of emergency management, where social media is used for about 15 years (Reuter & Kaufhold, 2017), in addition to information that is provided automatically (meteorological data, water levels, etc.), there are two other kinds of information sources provided by people: emergency services in the field from whom information can be requested (Ludwig, Reuter, & Pipek, 2013) and other individuals and organizations not actively dealing with the emergency. In the case of a house coal for example, the (target) number of residents can be requested from the registration office, but the estimation of the fire's size and of the (actual) number of affected people can only be performed on-site. Unlike sensor data, information provided by citizens is not always objective. Sometimes citizen-generated content is accurate – illustrated at a comparison of Wikipedia and Britannica encyclopedia articles (Giles, 2005). In some cases, however, the subjectivity of citizen-provided reports can generate some sort of vigilantism (Rizza, Pereira, & Curvelo, 2013). Additionally, the misinterpretation of a situation – whether deliberate or not – can lead to potential misinformation; this can result from the reporter paying too little attention to some aspects of the situation or from an incorrect representation of the facts (Thomson, Ito, Suda, & Lin, 2012). However, some information cannot be obtained from other sources (Zagel, 2012). This subjectivity makes data analysis rather complex.

There are approaches concerning the selection and use of data from social media; these, however, do not support a complete quality assessment (Reuter, Ludwig, Ritzkatis, & Pipek, 2015): *Twitcident* (Terpstra, Vries, de Stronkman & Paradies, 2012) allows the user to select tweets by keywords, message types or users and display them on a map. Nevertheless, quality assessment based on meta-information such as the time of creation is not possible. *Alert.io*[1] offers individual trainable tonality analyses and thus first approaches to the integration of machine learning in the form of a learning process to be carried out by the end-user. *HootSuite*[2] emphasizes the design of the analysis by adapting and extending software artifacts. *Tweet4act* (Chowdhury, Amer-Yahia, Castillo, Imran, & Asghar, 2013) enables the tracing and classification of information on Twitter

---

[1]https://mention.com/en/

[2]www.hootsuite.com

by matching every Tweet against an emergency-specific dictionary to classify them into emergency periods. With *TwitInfo* (Marcus *et al.*, 2011) information concerning a specific event can be collected, classified and visualized graphically including additional information about the (not adaptable) quality of the actual information. *Netvizz* is a "data collection and extraction application that allows researchers to export data in standard file formats from different sections of the Facebook social networking service" (Rieder, 2013) to allow quantitative and qualitative research in the application, mainly based on pre-defined categories. *Ushahidi* (McClendon & Robinson, 2012) enables citizens to exchange information. Additionally, emergency services can get access to the information. The direct communication and the spread of unfiltered information can cause an information overload, which forces the user to evaluate the information manually according to its quality.

To sum up, one can say that many studies and approaches about citizen-generated content exist, but concerning EUD in quality assessment of social big data, they are missing a tailorable tool for assessing social media information.

3   EUD in Social Big Data Gathering and Assessment

Based on the results of our literature review, an empirical pre-study and further analysis, we developed two tailorable services processing social media content. First, this section summarizes the key findings of the pre-study. Second, it introduces the "Social Media API" (SMA), which allows end-users to gather, process, store and re-access social media content and, third, it serves as a foundation of the "Social Quality Assessment Service" (Social-QAS) that facilitates the assessment of social media content by the tailorable weighting of information quality criteria.

3.1   Pre-Study: Social Media Assessment by Emergency Services

To gain a deeper understanding of the impact of citizen-generated content in social media on emergency services, we analyzed the data from a previous empirical study on the work practices of the emergency services (focus on fire departments and police) in two different regions of Germany. The results of this pre-study have already been published (Reuter *et al.*, 2015; Reuter & Ritzkatis, 2014) and we aggregate the main results within this chapter.

The question: "Who is going to evaluate this now [...] and is it really going to help us to assess the situation?" (I03) often appears in emergency situations. The sheer amount of citizen-generated content makes its use especially difficult: "Above all, 290 [messages] of 300 are trash. You can only get something from ten reports" (I02). The mass of information quickly raises the problem of how to handle it: "You have to read them all. Of course, it would be helpful if there was a preselection" (I02).

For this reason, automatic selection is recommendable: "It would be nice if there was a selection that separates the important from the unimportant" (I03). Nevertheless, information has to appear in a certain quantity to render it trustworthy for the emergency services: "It's a problem if I only have one source. It is certainly more reliable to have five sources than just one" (I15). External sources are especially susceptible to providing misinformation (I14, I15) and have to be verified (I15) because of this: You "have to be careful with the content because it does not always reflect reality" (I14) – "In such cases it becomes obvious that someone is trying to lead us up the garden path [...] and we have to evaluate the information for ourselves" (I02). In these cases, misinformation is not always intended; potentially it can result from the subjective perception of the situation, which can appear very different to a neutral observer. In conclusion, the use of citizen-generated content from social media fails because of the need for assessment by the emergency services: "There is simply a bottleneck which we cannot overcome" (I02).

Overall it is noticeable that "the more precise information, the more relevant it is" (I02). This kind of precision can be achieved by assessment. There has to be some form of guarantee that the selected information is useful for the emergency services (I02, I03). Global selection also proves to be difficult because "it does not seem possible to me that we can select in advance what is important for the section leader. He might need the same information as the chief of operations – or not" (IM01). This therefore necessitates the possibility of flexible assessment criteria (I19). Due to the time-critical aspect of emergency situations, it is imperative that the personal selection of information be supported since every member of the emergency team has to decide "relatively quickly between the important and the unimportant" (I19).

The first impression has to include some amount of significance and has to be helpful for the situation assessment: "If someone takes a photo of a window, I know that he was really there. But where is that window exactly?" (I16). This shows that pictures need additional meta-information just as normal textual information does. Pictures can be especially useful for assessing crowds of people at huge events: "If someone had noticed that a relevant number of people were congregating in certain areas, you could have closed the entrance immediately with the help of the security" (I06). Even though this entails gathering a lot of information, "most people [...] do not [know] what counts and what kind of information we need" (I02). There is therefore a risk that the information has no additional value and cannot be used in the emergency situation: "I do not believe that someone who is not connected in some way to the police or the fire service is capable of providing useful information in these stress situations" (I02). It is unusual for an untrained citizen to have knowledge of this sort. "You have to be very careful with this kind of information" (I14).

Ultimately, it is a member of the emergency team who has to assume responsibility for actions and who also has to decide if the information is utilized or not (I15). Misinterpretation is possible both by humans and through computer support.

It does not matter how good the assessment mechanism is: there "remains a risk and the person in charge has to bear it, it is as simple as that" (I15). That is the reason why the emergency services are so careful when using external information. In conclusion, it can be stated that "assessing information, assessing it correctly and dealing with it […] is a challenging task" (I15). Every single piece of information is an input to evaluate the whole situation: "You add more and more flesh to the skeleton you start off with so that in the end, you have a picture; not just a silhouette but a whole figure and any actions executed by the police are mostly based on that figure" (I16). Situation assessment influences the actions which in return influence the situation.

3.2   EUD in Social Big Data Gathering

Before assessing any social media data, ways of gathering relevant information must be established with the flexibility to support EUD applications, such as Social-QAS (Sect. 3.3). Thus, the "Social Media API" (SMA) allows its user to gather, process, store and re-query social media data (Reuter et al., 2016). Although it was developed as enabling technology for emergency management applications initially, its implementation enables the support of a variety of use cases in different fields of application, e.g. it allows its users to examine the impact of a product image within the field of market research (Reuter et al., 2016). Because it serves as the foundation of Social-QAS, we discuss its key challenges and concepts, implementation and tailorability in the following sections.

3.2.1   Key Challenges and Concept

To enable access to social big data and allow subsequent analysis, our first step was to specify a service for gathering and processing social media content. During the analysis, we agreed upon the following requirements, which are partly derived from Sect. 2.2 and enriched with considerations from conceptual and implementation viewpoints.

1. *Multi-Platform Support:* Relevant data during emergencies is spread across different social media services. Furthermore, depending on the participants, different services are used. As a result, it is required that a request allows access to multiple platforms. To obtain sufficient samples and reach most users, a further requirement is therefore to allow the gathering and posting of citizen-generated information spread widely on social media services.
2. *Extensible and Unified Data Format:* Both the multi-platform support and cross-platform usage imply the requirement of a standardized data format that is capable of mapping the diverse attributes, whether structured or unstructured content, of different social media content and providers. The possible emergence or relevance

of new attributes, which define the activity's and users' context, requires the extensibility of the data format.

3. *Gathering Service*: The historicity and volatility of social media content require the continuous capturing of citizen-generated information in nearly real time in order to accumulate a rich representation and allow post-analysis of the emergency. We therefore need to specify a service that constantly gathers the data over a defined period of time.

4. *Integration of Rich Metadata:* Literature not only identifies textual content but also images, sounds and videos as important information carriers during emergencies. Furthermore, location- and time-based information are very important metadata, because they provide interesting context-data to the information itself. Therefore, a requirement is that location- and time-based data are provided with the information itself.

5. *Flexible Query of Data:* Not only in the acquisition but also in the retrieval of already gathered data from database, sufficient filtering parameters are required to enable situated data analysis and provide a high degree of flexibility to support tailorable client applications or services.

3.2.2 Implementation of a Cross-Platform Social Media API

To gather and process social media content, we developed a REST web service called "Social Media API". With *gathering* we refer to the ability to uniquely or continuously collect social media activities (e.g. messages, photos, videos) from different platforms (Facebook, Google+, Instagram, Twitter and YouTube) in a unified manner using multiple search or filter criteria. *Processing* means that the API is capable of accessing, disseminating, enriching, manipulating and storing social media activities. The SMA is realized as a service following the paradigm of a web-based, service-oriented architecture (SOA). It is a Java Tomcat application using the Jersey Framework for REST services and the MongoDB database for document-oriented data management. Several libraries facilitate the integration of social media platform APIs such as Facebook Graph API or Twitter Search API. All gathered social media entities are processed and stored according to the ActivityStreams 2.0 specification (World Wide Web Consortium, 2016) in JSON format (JavaScript Object Notation). The SMA uses service interfaces, allowing a standardized implementation of further social media if their APIs provide suitable access to their data.

It comprises four main services, each providing a multitude of service functions: The *Gathering Service* comprises endpoints for gathering and loading social media activities. The main components are the Search service, enabling onetime search requests, and Crawl Service, which continuously queries new social media activities across a specified timeframe. Using the *Enrichment Service*, gathered social media activities are enriched with further computed and valuable metadata. Moreover, the *Dissemination Service* is a unified endpoint for publishing, replying

Table 1 Excerpt of source-based data attributes

Attributes	Facebook	Google+	Instagram	Twitter	YouTube
Date, Time	✓	✓	✓	✓	✓
Sender	✓	✓	✓	✓	✓
Age	✗	✓ (Age range)	✗	✗	✓ (Age range)
Location	✓	✓	✗	✓	✓
Real name	✓	✓	✓	✓	✓
Title	✗	✓	✓ (Caption)	✗	✓
Tags	✗	✗	✓	✗	✓
Replies	✓ (Comments)	✓ (Replies)	✓ (Comments)	✗	✓ (Google+)
Content	✓	✓	✓ (Caption)	✓	✓ (Description)
Mentions	✓	✗	✗	✓	✗
Views	✗	✗	✗	✗	✓
Likes	✓ (Likes)	✓ (Plusoners)	✓ (Likes)	✗	✓ (Likes)
Dislikes	✗	✗	✗	✗	✓ (Dislikes)
Retweets	✗	✗	✗	✓	✗
Shares	✓	✓ (Resharers)	✗	✗	✗

to or deleting (multiple) social media activities (simultaneously). The *Data Service* provides structured database management operations. For instance, it encapsulates remote MongoDB operations to insert, load, update or delete data.

While working with SMA, based on the available type of social media, different data attributes are accessible (Table 1). The implementation or support of different attributes depends on the individual policies of social media providers. For instance, while it is certainly possible to add the age to a Facebook user account, the Facebook Graph API, which provides applications and developers access to Facebook data, does not allow retrieving the age of Facebook users. On the one hand, the flexibility of the document-oriented approach allows the social media users to store distinct structured documents with different numbers of attributes. Using ActivityStreams 2.0, the majority of attributes is stored according to a standardized specification. On the other hand, in terms of divergent metadata, the comparability and therefore analysis of social media activities is restricted. Therefore, it is not possible to apply all quality assessment methods in the same way. Also, because not all attributes can be mapped to the ActivityStreams 2.0 specification, we needed to add a custom property mapping our special metadata.

Furthermore, as already discussed in Sect. 2.2, during implementation some technical and business-oriented limitations became apparent (Reuter & Scholl, 2014): Quota limits restricted the access to social media data and most data is publicly available for a limited time only. Consequently, especially with non-expensive approaches, it is possible to capture and process merely small portions of the high-volume social data. Concerning the historicity of data, another challenge arose: As social media activities are likely to be updated regarding, for instance, the number of comments, number of likes or the content itself, inconsistencies between the online data and the stored data occur.

Besides the available data, there are two kinds of additional valuable data: First, some data is only available in certain social media, but computable for others. For instance, embedded hyperlinks, mentions or tags can be extracted from activities to get a comparable amount of data from each social media. Second, some required data regarding the assessment of quality is not available in any social media. Therefore, the SMA computes classification attributes (negative sentiment, positive sentiment, emoticon conversion, slang conversion), content attributes (number of characters, number of words, average length of words, words-to-sentences ratio, number of punctuation signs, number of syllables per word, entropy) and metadata attributes (hyperlinks, language, location, media files, tags) manually.

3.2.3   Tailorability: Filtering Data during Gathering and Post-Processing

A key challenge of a tailorable SMA is the provision of suitable service endpoints with sufficient filter parameters that behave consistently over heterogeneous social media. Table 2 summarizes our implemented filter parameters of the *Crawl* and *Search* services. The flexibility of filtering depends on the providing APIs to a certain degree: While some social media APIs support location (Twitter, YouTube) and temporal (Facebook, Twitter, YouTube) filtering, it has to be realized manually for the other ones. However, given the quota limitations of social media, manual filtering always implies the prior gathering of results that do not match the filter criteria and is therefore less efficient than using native filter parameters. Another issue is the keyword parameter, because social media process keywords differently and support various types and notations of logical query operators (e.g. and, or, not, phrases). Here, the need for a unified query language and layer becomes apparent, which translates the unified query parameters into the platform-specific parameters.

Table 2 Parameters for social media search

Parameter	Type	Description
keyword	String	Required. The search term.
platforms	String	Required. A csv-list (Facebook, Google+, Instagram, Twitter, YouTube).
since	Long	Search Service. Lower bound of the searched timeframe (Unix time).
until	Long	Search Service. Upper bound of the searched timeframe (Unix time).
start	String	Crawl Service. Starting point of the crawl job (Unix time, default: now).
end	String	Crawl Service. Termination of the crawl job (Unix time, default: null).
latitude	Double	Latitude for geo search (decimal degree).
longitude	Double	Longitude for geo search (decimal degree).
radius	Double	Radius for geo search (km).

After data is gathered and stored into the database, the access becomes an important factor to allow loading and post-processing of data. Given the job id, social media activities of past crawl or search jobs can be loaded and filtered by count (amount of data returned) and offset (position of the first result to be returned) parameters. Alternatively, a list of activity ids allows loading the desired social media activities explicitly. However, to enhance the tailorability of SMA in order to increase the flexibility for consuming client applications, the implementation of additional parameters is planned, e.g. keyword, platform, location and time-based filtering, or language. In this case, the efficiency and flexibility of filtering is dependent on the underlying database management solution. Based on the SMA, the application Social Data Service has been implemented, which aims to allow the generation of data sets (Reuter *et al.*, 2016).

3.3   EUD in Social Big Data Assessment

As our literature review suggests, citizens may provide emergency-relevant information via social media, but challenges regarding the quality of information, especially under time-critical constraints, persist. Moreover, our pre-study and further literature report on the relevance of quality-relevant metadata during emergencies, e.g., author reputation, location and time. That is why the "Social Quality Assessment Service" (Social-QAS) aims on facilitating the assessment of social media content by the tailorable weighting of information quality criteria. This section refers to content that has already been published in a research paper (Reuter *et al.*, 2015), but is required to introduce the application's concept, depict its evaluation and elaborate the chapter's discussion.

3.3.1   Key Challenges and Concept

Our literature review and the empirical study have proved that the quality assessment of mass information and extractions of relevant information is a great challenge. Of course, various circumstances call for various assessment methods. That is why the possibility to combine these methods could help to improve the quality assessment practice (Ludwig, Reuter, & Pipek, 2015). Our concept allows the assessment of (social media) content with 15 assessment methods (Table 3), which are subdivided into four categories pursuant to their technical execution:

1. The *rating of metadata* consists of five assessment methods (author frequency, temporal proximity, local proximity, number of followers/likes, amount of metadata), in which either the discrepancy from the entered research criteria or the absolute appearance is defined by rating the difference.

2. The *rating based on the content* allocates two assessment methods (frequency of search keyword, stop words), which identify the occurrence of particular words (or their synonyms) from a list.
3. The *rating based on the classification of the message* supplies six assessment methods (sentiment analysis, fear factor, happiness factor, named entity recognition, emoticon, slang), which determine the occurrence of words applying word lists. Thus, information is sorted in different categories.
4. The *rating based on scientific methods* provides two assessment methods (Shannon Information Theory (Entropy), term frequency, inverse document frequency).

Table 3 Implemented quality assessment methods (Reuter *et al.*, 2015)

#	Method/Criterion	Description
A	**Assessment of metadata**	
1	Author frequency (Reputation)	Number of messages from the same author in the message set. The level of knowledge about the situation depends on the number of messages an author writes.
2	Temporal proximity (Currency)	Temporal proximity of the messages to the center of the search period. The information's importance depends on the proximity to the search moment.
3	Local proximity	Distance between the place where the message was created and the incident's place. Short distance stands for higher probability that the message is about the current disaster.
4	Followers/likes (Credibility)	It is assumed that credibility and the number of likes/followers conferred on a particular message/author grow proportionally.
5	Metadata (pictures/links)	It can be helpful to complement textual information with an image or other media material. With this assessment criterion the amount of data can be ascertained.
B	**Assessment based on content**	
6	Frequency of search keyword (Interpretability)	The keyword indicates the issue; it does not appear randomly in the message. The message is also searched for synonyms.
7	Stop words	Stop words such as "so" do not allocate any information as long as they do not increase the validity of the message. That is why the decrease of stop words increases message utility.
C	**Assessment based on classification of the message**	
8	Sentiment analysis (Impartiality)	The message is analysed concerning its emotional property. Emotional content, especially fear, can falsify the meaning.
9	Negative sentiment (Fear Factor)	Words that are related to the subject of fear are identified in the message; The Fear Factor determines the degree of expression of fear.
10	Positive sentiment (Happiness Factor)	Words that are related to the subject of joy are identified in the message; The Happiness Factor determines the degree of expression of joy.

(continued)

Table 3 (continued)

#	Method/Criterion	Description
11	Named entity recognition (NER)	Number of entities in the message. The relation between the information's content and another information source is indicated by an entity. The more entities, the higher the information quality.
12	Emoticon conversion	The possibility to make a message readable for different audiences by converting emoticons into language expressions.
13	Slang conversion	The possibility to make a message readable for different audiences by converting slang words into standard language.
D	**Assessment based on scientific methods**	
14	tf-Idf (term frequency – Inverse document frequency)	The appearance of individual search keywords (term frequency) with the frequency of appearance in all messages (inverse document frequency). Helpful if more than one single keyword is used since the occurrence of a fragment of the whole term, which only appears frequently in few documents, is weighted higher than the occurrence of a fragment, which appears in many documents but less frequently. $$tf(t,d) = \frac{f(t,d)}{\max\{f(w,d) \, : \, w \in d\}}$$
15	Shannon information theory (Entropy)	Shannon theory of information. The average amount of information contained in each message received. $$I(p_x) = \log_a\left(\frac{1}{p_x}\right) = -\log_a(p_x)$$

A subjective quality of information can be defined if the (non-specified) end-user of an application based on Social-QAS has the option to select various assessment methods. In addition to that, this selection and the classification enable further use of the quality assessment service within several scenarios. Generally speaking: Initially, the individual messages are analyzed absolutely regarding the specific method. Then the score of each message is determined. The message with the highest absolute score is rated with "1.0" (100%), the one with the lowest absolute score gets a "0.0" (0%). After that, an overall score is received by weighting the single scores. Further, to address both the requirements of querying multiple sources and enabling the subjectivity of quality assessment, the individual user gets the option to choose the desired social media sources.

3.3.2 Implementation of Social-QAS

The actual quality assessment service is conceived as a service that follows the paradigms of a web-based, service-oriented architecture (SOA). The use of such architecture enables a central rating and makes it possible to integrate it into

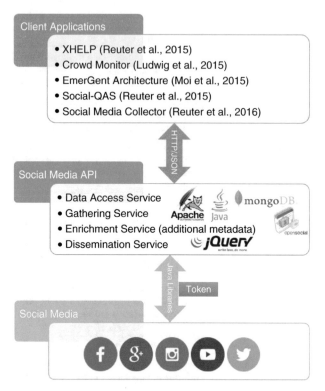

Fig. 1 Overall architecture of client applications such as Social-QAS that use the Social Media API to access different social media over a unified interface

various applications by allocating assessment results with the original data in JSON format (JavaScript Object Notation). The interface is called "via HTTP-GET" and the URL is complemented with query parameters, which are separated by "&". The client's processing load is supposed to decrease by the server-sided information rating. Via SMA, as illustrated in Fig. 1, the APIs of the particular social network providers are used to extract data from the social networks (Reuter & Scholl, 2014). In this context, especially Twitter and Facebook appear to be essential APIs: these APIs allocate many possibilities to both export and import data concerning the related social network.

To collect the semantic content of the message, one can apply a Named Entity Recognizer (NER) (No.11). The Stanford NER[3] is available as Java library for free. The corpus "deWac generalized classifier" was used for the NER because it works exceptionally well with German messages from social networks. The library Classifier4J[4] was utilized for the creation of a Bayes Classifier (No. 8) that enables

---

[3]http://nlp.stanford.edu/software/CRF-NER.shtml

[4]http://classifier4j.sourceforge.net/

the division of information into various categories since it can be skilled with lists of words. The list of synonyms (No. 6) was created by applying the Open Thesaurus web services[5]. One requires a geographical reference in order to visualize the information; however, in many cases the information does not contain any geographical metadata so that it has to be geocoded. The Gisgraphy Geocoder[6] is usable by web services and geocodes location information for any map material. To accelerate the process, there is a list of locations which have already been geolocated and whereof the coordinates can be defined without geolocation. GSON[7] is used for conversion since it allocates an automatic generation of a JSON object based on a java object model.

3.3.3   Tailorability: Integration of Social-QAS into a Web Application

To test the implemented service, we have integrated Social-QAS into a web-based application specified for emergency services as well as a Facebook-app "XHELP" to support volunteer moderators during disasters. In the following we will outline prototypically the implementation into XHELP, which allows information to be both acquired and distributed cross-media and cross-channel (Reuter *et al.*, 2015).

Inside this application, it is possible to search for information by using different quality parameters in order to perform a quality assessment (Fig. 2). For this, the user chooses an assessment criterion with the help of a slider. Integrating the user in this way meets the requirements for a flexible and manageable quality assessment, as identified in the pre-study.

The search results are presented in a table and on a visual situation map. An abundance of meta-information such as the degree of completion of particular methods is illustrated as tool tips in the table. Simultaneously, the situation map makes it possible to directly determine the proximity of the information to the search location (Fig. 3). Thus, the user may select one mode in which s/he wishes to view the results; this method improves the flexibility of the application. This user interface is only one of several possibilities how Social-QAS can be applied.

To sum up, Social-QAS unifies the following functionalities (Reuter *et al.*, 2015): Assessment takes place on the basis of metadata as well as on the basis of content. The user decides upon the weighting of each method. When all the assessments of every method have been combined, the subjective quality of a message develops. Social-QAS is very flexible since it makes it possible to expand the sources and assessment methods very easily. Due to the SOA-based implementation it is possible to integrate it and use it in other applications.

---

[5]http://www.openthesaurus.de/

[6]http://www.gisgraphy.com/

[7]https://code.google.com/p/google-gson/

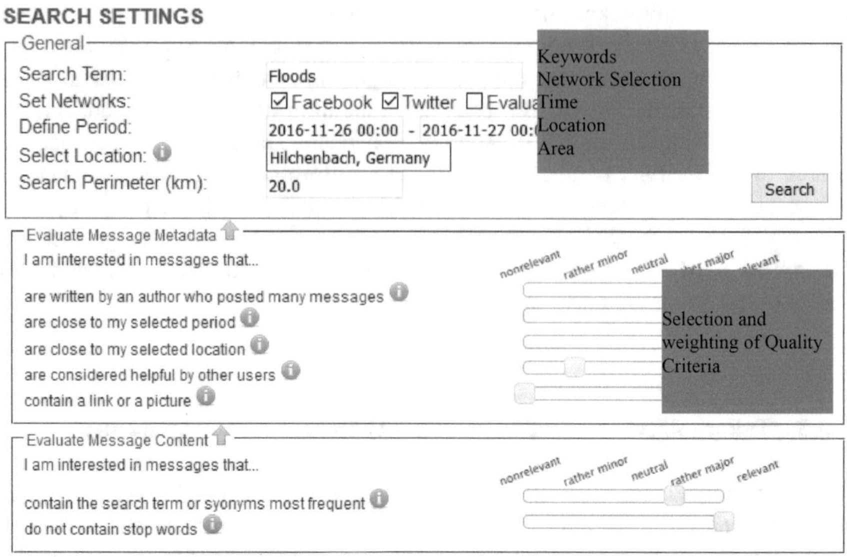

SEARCH SETTINGS

General

Search Term: Floods

Set Networks: ☑Facebook ☑Twitter ☐Evalua

Define Period: 2016-11-26 00:00 - 2016-11-27 00:(

Select Location: ⓘ   Hilchenbach, Germany

Search Perimeter (km):   20.0

Keywords
Network Selection
Time
Location
Area

Search

Evaluate Message Metadata ⬆

I am interested in messages that...

are written by an author who posted many messages ⓘ

are close to my selected period ⓘ

are close to my selected location ⓘ

are considered helpful by other users ⓘ

contain a link or a picture ⓘ

nonrelevant   rather minor   neutral   her major   levant

Selection and
weighting of Quality
Criteria

Evaluate Message Content ⬆

I am interested in messages that...

contain the search term or syonyms most frequent ⓘ

do not contain stop words ⓘ

nonrelevant   rather minor   neutral   rather major   relevant

Fig. 2 Quality Assessment Service integrated into an application

Fig. 3 Search results (left), degree of completion (lower left) and map presentation (right)

4 Evaluation: Tailorable Quality Assessment

To answer the question how tailorable assessment services can be provided to users properly and how users can articulate the assessment criteria appropriately, Social-QAS has been evaluated by potential end-users.

4.1 Methodology

The philosophy behind the evaluation process was derived from the notion of "situated evaluation" (Twidale, Randall, & Bentley, 1994), in which qualitative methods are applied to draw conclusions about real-world use of a technology using domain experts. The purpose is to derive subjective views from experts about how useful and relevant the technology might be in use instead of measuring the relationship between evaluation goals and outcomes.

In order to obtain as much knowledge as possible about the potential of the service and the quality assessment of citizen-generated information, the evaluation consisted of a scenario-based walkthrough with a subsequent semi-structured interview. The participants were directed to tell us their thoughts according to the think-aloud protocol (Nielsen, 1993), enabling underlying reasoning and subjective impressions to be gathered. Each evaluation took about 45 minutes and was per-formed with 20 people in all (E1-E20). While, besides general knowledge on the use of social media, 15 participants were skilled technology experts, four participants had been initiators and moderators of Facebook pages during the European floods in 2013, and one was member of a voluntary fire brigade. Any participant who was not a volunteer using social media very actively had a role definition introduced to them, enabling them to place themselves in the position of a volunteer.

The scenario was supposed to show the participants a disaster's character and what volunteers do in crises (unless the participant was already an experienced volun-teer). They worked on the basis of hurricane Xaver, which destroyed big parts of the German coast in December 2013. The participants got a general role description in order to know how to deal with the information demands of affected citizens with the help of Social-QAS embedded in XHELP (see Sect. 3.3.3). After that, the partici-pants had the chance to get to know the application by solving a concrete problem: they were supposed to filter and search specific information about water levels. An evaluation mode was added to the search function for this purpose. The results of the search were assumed beforehand on preselected data records in order to be sure that the participants' results were comparable. In the following, semi-structured inter-views were meant to support reflection on the evaluation process, on handling and the overall application's value. The questions were specialized in overall impressions concerning quality assessment, the advantages and disadvantages of Social-QAS, coverage of information demands, influence on information flow, potential overload and problems of cross-platform information acquisition. The interviews were evalu-ated and classified systematically. "Open" coding was employed, i.e. distributing data into adequate categories to reflect the issues raised by respondents relying on repeated readings of the data and its grouping into "similar" statements. The most remarkable classifications will be presented in the following.

4.2 Results I: How Much Tailoring? Quality Assessment Criteria

Many users considered the number of assessment criteria to be too high for effective use under the time-critical constraints of emergencies (E09, E07, E19). Nonetheless, the respondents agreed with the opinion that different situations require different assessment criteria (E12, E13, E08); and that a certain adjustment of the criteria to the situation is necessary: "There are many criteria, but I think that this is important, because different questions require different search keywords" (E13). Accordingly, the suggestion was made that the assessment criteria could be adjusted in such a way that allows the goal to be achieved more quickly (E12). Furthermore, other possibilities – for example the opportunity to search for a hyponym (E19) – were requested in addition to the various settings. The evaluation demonstrated that the biggest challenge to be overcome is the identification of criteria of appropriate quality. Although currency was an important criterion for all respondents, only a few understood the meaning of coordinate quality. The explanation of coordinate quality as a measure for the local proximity helped them to understand its meaning. One participant raised the question of the correlation between the author's number of subscribers and his reputation (E4).

4.3   Results II: Broad Information Basis and Information Overload

In order to achieve a situational overview of an emergency setting, users especially regarded the opportunity to consider different information sources simultaneously to be an added value (E19, E15, E18): "Because public networks are used such a lot, it is much better to relate them to each other. That could really help to meet the information need" (E17). The number of sources should be steadily supplemented with further useful sources. What is more, not only social networks but also e.g. news sites should be taken into consideration. Furthermore, the interviewed persons were afraid of being confronted by a flood of information while searching for information in social networks during a large-scale emergency (E16, E19). This fear was soon quelled by sorting the results in Social-QAS. Most users did not want to go through the entire list of search results, but preferred to only look at the first few results on the list. Still it should remain possible for the user to see the additional results at will since some scenarios potentially require an inspection of the additional results.

4.4   Results III: Automatic and Tailorable Quality Assessment Necessary

The quality assessment of information proceeds automatically. Users accept this automatism as they have the possibility to control the assessment and are able to comprehend why something was assessed in a particular way (E08, E11). "As always, when something is evaluated, that does not replace your own opinion" (E10). Yet the general possibility to combine criteria was considered a benefit: "The default settings do not matter. That means if I do nothing, my search results will not change" (E13). "As a consequence, diverse combinations are possible, of course, which seems to me to be helpful" (E07). To counter negative impacts on actions, manual post-processing should be implemented, allowing the correction or recognition of defective entries.

Considering the possibilities and suggestions for improvement shown (E13, E19, E14), there is potential to improve the information flow in emergency situations. This could especially be realized by the classification of emergency situations and a preset of weightings based on this. Crucial temporal and organizational bottlenecks could be avoided by collecting information from local people (real volunteers) or the internet (digital volunteers) (Reuter, Heger, & Pipek, 2013) (E07, E16): "The benefits are that I can find things quickly, [...] because it is possible to search specifically for something and that is really displayed on the different platforms, just how I want it. And I can weight very easily using the assessment criteria" (E18).

5 Discussion and Conclusion

From the perspective of EUD, many systems for analyzing social media offer more or less customization possibilities and are aimed at end-users who have little or no technical knowledge. However, the adaptability is largely limited to visualization elements, e.g. in form of a central dashboard. There, the presented figures are prepared in such a way that the end-user can scale and analyze along fixed dimensions. At another level of customization, there are systems such as HootSuite, which provide strong software extensibility by providing their own SDK. Expert users are able to create new functionalities available to all end-users. These extensions do not affect the design of the analysis process, thus, the end-user cannot tailor it to the individual preferences. The system alert.io with the structure of a learning process of tonality analysis shows approaches to such extensibility. An end-user trains this component based on his or her own situation understanding so that the machine learning algorithm can work independently on new data from a certain size of the experience data base.

This article demonstrates how it is possible to combine EUD and social big data. It discusses how situation assessment practices of crisis management actors, namely emergency services (Ludwig et al., 2015) and informal volunteers (Reuter et al., 2015), can be encouraged by tailorable quality assessment of citizen-generated information from social media. At the beginning, the results of an empirical study involving emergency services concerning the use of citizen-generated content and social media within their current work practices are summarized. With the help of literature and empirical findings we identified the need for different quality criteria and applied them on information from social media. We implemented an own Social Media API and a quality assessment service.

We come to three results that extend the current state of the art:

(1) An analysis of dealing with citizen-generated content in emergencies by means of an empirical study, which emphasizes the range and quality assessment of citizen-generated content in emergencies (Reuter & Ritzkatis, 2014).
(2) A concept for a tailorable social media gathering (Sect. 3.2.1) and quality assessment service (Sect. 3.3.1) for social media as well as a running

implementation which is SOA-oriented, tailorable and can be applied in various applications (Reuter *et al.*, 2015, 2016).

(3) A reference implementation of the gathering service (Sect. 3.2.2) as well as quality assessment service (Sect. 3.3.2) inside an existing web-based application for emergency services (Ludwig *et al.*, 2015) and an existing web-app for volunteers (Reuter *et al.*, 2015) (Sect. 3.3.3).

The contribution of this chapter is to show the process from data selection to use from an EUD perspective including pre-study, design, implementation and evaluation in order to generate findings to the field.

To sum up, it is useful to be flexible by tailoring options for source platform selection and quality assessment criteria since situation assessment revealed itself to be very subjective. Consequently, personal feelings, experience and the situation itself influence the information requirement. Our findings turned out to be interesting for other application fields as well. While gathering or analyzing information and implementing information systems to encourage the task, there is always one question that is hard to answer: How can we realize information systems, which enable the automatic selection of relevant data and, simultaneously, grant end-users the option to adapt this automation, thus allowing tailorable quality assessment pursuant to their requirements?

In terms of big data, some restrictions are apparent: Although social media provide high-volume, high-velocity and a high-variety (McAfee & Brynjolfsson, 2012) of social data (Dijcks, 2012), the access is limited allowing client applications such as Social Media API and Social-QAS to merely gather small portions of data (Reuter & Scholl, 2014). Even with continuously gathering new data and filling the database, the volume and velocity of data processing in client applications like those will be small compared to the daily data creation in social media (Kaisler, Armour, Espinosa, & Money, 2013). Therefore, in high-volume scenarios, valuable information according to the user-selected quality criteria may be missed. In future work, it is important to examine how the end-user can be better integrated into the analysis process by applying machine learning to ensure the adaptability and alignment of the analysis of social media in the dynamic context of end-users.

Our work still has some limitations. Not all the criteria that are relevant for quality assessment are included within Social-QAS. Furthermore, according to the context, the number of criteria might overburden the cognitive skills of end-users. It is, therefore, important to define standards and to allow end-users to adapt them, whereby different tailoring power might then require different skills, according to MacLean, Carter, Lövstrand, and Moran (1990); thus local developers may be required (Gantt & Nardi, 1992).

Acknowledgements The research project EmerGent' was funded by a grant of the European Union (FP7 No. 608352). This article is built upon existing and published research; the empirical study has been presented at Mensch & Computer conference (Reuter & Ritzkatis, 2014), in some parts the concept enhances, refocuses and improves a paper presented at the 2015 international symposium on EUD (Reuter *et al.*, 2015).

References

Agichtein, E., Castillo, C., Donato, D., Gionis, A., Mishne, G. (2008). Finding high-quality content in social media. In *Proceedings of the 2008 international conference on web search and data mining* (pp. 183–194). Palo Alto: ACM Press. doi:10.1145/1341531.1341557.

Ardito, C., Costabile, M. F., Desolda, G., Lanzilotti, R., Matera, M., Picozzi, M. (2014). Visual composition of data sources by end users. In *Proceedings of the 2014 international working conference on advanced visual interfaces - AVI '14* (pp. 257–260). New York: ACM Press. doi:10.1145/2598153.2598201.

Bassett, C. (2015). Plenty as a response to austerity? Big data expertise, cultures and communities. *European Journal of Cultural Studies, 18*(4–5), 548–563. doi:10.1177/1367549415577394.

Batrinca, B., & Treleaven, P. C. (2014). Social media analytics: a survey of techniques, tools and platforms. *AI & Society, 30*(1), 89–116. doi:10.1007/s00146-014-0549-4.

Bello-Orgaz, G., Jung, J. J., Camacho, D. (2016). Social big data: recent achievements and new challenges. *Information Fusion, 28*, 45–59. doi:10.1016/j.inffus.2015.08.005.

Borges, C. R., & Macías, J. A. (2010). Feasible database querying using a visual end-user approach. In *Proceedings of the 2nd ACM SIGCHI symposium on engineering interactive computing systems - EICS '10* (pp. 187–192). New York: ACM Press. doi:10.1145/1822018.1822047.

Cappiello, C., Daniel, F., Matera, M., Picozzi, M., Weiss, M. (2011). Enabling end user development through mashups: requirements, abstractions and innovation toolkits. In M. F. Costabile, Y. Dittrich, G. Fischer, A. Piccinno (Eds.). *Proceedings of the international symposium on end-user development (IS-EUD)* (pp. 1–16). Torre Canne: Springer.

Chowdhury, S., Amer-Yahia, S., Castillo, C., Imran, M., Asghar, M. R. (2013). Tweet4act: using incident-specific profiles for classifying crisisrelated messages. In T. Comes, F. Fiedrich, S. Fortier, J. Geldermann, T. Müller (Eds.). *Proceedings of the information systems for crisis response and management (ISCRAM)* (pp. 834–839). Baden-Baden, Germany: ISCRAM Digital Library.

Church, K., & Oliver, N. (2011). Understanding mobile web and mobile search use in today's dynamic mobile landscape. In *Proceedings of the 13th international conference on human computer interaction with mobile devices and services* (pp. 67–76). Stockholm: ACM.

Costabile, M. F., Fogli, D., Mussio, P., Piccinno, A. (2007). Visual interactive systems for end-user development: a model-based design methodology. *IEEE transactions on systems, man, and cybernetics - part a: systems and humans, 37*(6), 1029–1046. doi:10.1109/TSMCA.2007.904776.

Coutaz, J., & Crowley, J. L. (2016). A first-person experience with end-user development for smart homes. *IEEE Pervasive Computing, 15*(2), 26–39. doi:10.1109/MPRV.2016.24.

Dijcks, J. (2012). Oracle: Big data for the enterprise. *Oracle white paper*, (June), 1–14.

Doerner, C., Draxler, S., Pipek, V., Wulf, V. (2009). End users at the bazaar: designing next-generation enterprise-resource-planning systems. *IEEE Software, 26*(5), 45–51.

Doll, W. J., & Torkzadeh, G. (1988). The measurement of end-user computing satisfaction. *MIS Quarterly, 12*(2), 259. doi:10.2307/248851.

Eisenstein, J. (2013). What to do about bad language on the internet. In L. Vanderwende (Ed.). *Proceedings of NAACL-HLT 2013* (pp. 359–369). Atlanta: The Association for Computational Linguistics.

Endsley, M. R. M. R. (1995). Toward a theory of situation awareness in dynamic systems. *Human Factors: The Journal of the Human Factors and Ergonomics Society, 37*(1), 32–64. doi:10.1518/001872095779049543.

Fischer, G., & Scharff, E. (2000). Meta-design – Design for designers. In D. Boyarski, W. Kellogg (Eds.). *Proceedings of the international conference on designing interactive systems* (pp. 396–405). New York: ACM.

Friberg, T., Prödel, S., Koch, R. (2010). Analysis of information quality criteria in crisis situation as a characteristic of complex situations. In M. Lacity, S. March, F. Niederman (Eds.). *Proceedings of the 15th international conference on information quality*. Little Rock: AIS Electronic Library (AISeL).

Ganis, M., & Kohirkar, A. (2012). Ensuring the accuracy of your social media analysis. *Cutter IT Journal, 25*(10), 13–18.

Gantt, M., & Nardi, B. (1992). Gardeners and gurus: patterns of cooperation among CAD users. In P. Bauersfeld, J. Bennett, G. Lynch (Eds.). *Proceedings of the conference on human factors in computing systems (CHI)* (pp. 107–117). Monterey: ACM Press. doi:10.1145/142750.142767.

Giles, J. (2005). Internet encyclopaedias go head to head. *Nature, 438*(December), 900–901. doi:10.1038/438900a.

Grammel, L. (2009). Supporting end users in analyzing multiple data sources. In R. DeLine, M. Minas, M. Erwig (Eds.). *2009 IEEE Symposium on Visual Languages and Human-Centric Computing (VL/HCC)* (pp. 246–247). Corvallis: IEEE. doi:10.1109/VLHCC.2009.5295248.

Heer, J., & Boyd, D. (2005). Vizster: visualizing online social networks. In M. Ward, J. Stasko (Eds.). *IEEE symposium on information visualization, 2005. INFOVIS 2005* (pp. 32–39). Minneapolis: IEEE. doi:10.1109/INFVIS.2005.1532126.

Henderson, A., & Kyng, M. (1991). There's no place like home: continuing design in use. In J. Greenbaum & M. Kyng (Eds.), *Design at work cooperative design of computer systems* (pp. 219–240). Lawrence Erlbaum Associates.

Hess, J., Reuter, C., Pipek, V., Wulf, V. (2012). Supporting end-user articulations in evolving business processes: a case study to explore intuitive notations and interaction designs. *International Journal of Cooperative Information Systems (IJCIS), 21*(4), 263–296.

Hiltz, S., & Plotnick, L. (2013). Dealing with information overload when using social media for emergency management: emerging solutions. In T. Comes, F. Fiedrich, S. Fortier, J. Geldermann, T. Müller (Eds.). *Proceedings of the information systems for crisis response and management (ISCRAM)* (pp. 823–827). Baden-Baden, Germany: ISCRAM Digital Library.

Kaisler, S., Armour, F., Espinosa, J. A., Money, W. (2013). Big data: issues and challenges moving forward. In R. H. Sprague (Ed.). *2013 46th hawaii international conference on system sciences* (pp. 995–1004). Wailea: IEEE. doi:10.1109/HICSS.2013.645.

Kaufhold, M.-A., & Reuter, C. (2016). The self-organization of digital volunteers across social media: the case of the 2013 european floods in germany. *Journal of Homeland Security and Emergency Management (HSEM), 13*(1), 137–166.

Ley, B., Pipek, V., Reuter, C., Wiedenhoefer, T. (2012). Supporting improvisation work in inter-organizational crisis management. In *Proceedings of the conference on human factors in computing systems (CHI)* (pp. 1529–1538). Austin, TX: ACM Press.

Lieberman, H., Paterno, F., Wulf, V. (2006). *End-user development*. Dordrecht: Springer. doi:10.1007/1-4020-5386-X.

Ludwig, T., Reuter, C., Pipek, V. (2013). What you see is what I need: mobile reporting practices in emergencies. In O. W. Bertelsen, L. Ciolfi, A. Grasso, G. A. Papadopoulos (Eds.). *Proceedings of the European conference on computer supported cooperative work (ECSCW)* (pp. 181–206). Paphos: Springer. Retrieved from http://link.springer.com/chapter/10.1007/978-1-4471-5346-7_10.

Ludwig, T., Reuter, C., Pipek, V. (2015). Social haystack: dynamic quality assessment of citizen-generated content during emergencies. *Transactions on human computer interaction (ToCHI), 22*(4), 17:1–17:27. doi:10.1145/2749461.

MacLean, A., Carter, K., Lövstrand, L., Moran, L. (1990). User-tailorable systems: pressing the issues with buttons. In J. C. Chew, J. Whiteside (Eds.). *Proceedings of the conference on human factors in computing systems (CHI)*. Seattle: ACM Press.

Marcus, A., Bernstein, M., Badar, O., Karger, D. R., Madden, S., Miller, R. C. (2011). Twitinfo: aggregating and visualizing microblogs for event exploration. In D. Tan, G. Fitzpatrick, C. Gutwin, B. Begole, W. A. Kellogg (Eds.). *Proceedings of the conference on human factors in computing systems (CHI)* (pp. 227–236). Vancouver, Canada: ACM Press.

Massa, D., & Spano, L. D. (2015). FaceMashup: enabling end user development on social networks data BT. In P. Díaz, V. Pipek, C. Ardito, C. Jensen, I. Aedo, A. Boden (Eds.). *5th international symposium on end-user development (IS-EUD)* (pp. 204–210). Cham: Springer International Publishing. doi:10.1007/978-3-319-18425-8_17.

McAfee, A., & Brynjolfsson, E. (2012). Big data: the management revolution. *Harvard Business Review, 90*(10), 61–67.

McClendon, S., & Robinson, A. C. (2012). Leveraging geospatially-oriented social media communications in disaster response. In L. Rothkrantz, J. Ristvej, Z. Franco (Eds.). *Proceedings of the information systems for crisis response and management (ISCRAM)* (pp. 1–11). Vancouver, Canada: ISCRAM Digital Library.

Mislove, A., Marcon, M., Gummadi, K. P., Druschel, P., Bhattacharjee, B. (2007). Measurement and analysis of online social networks. In C. Dovrolis, M. Roughan (Eds.). *Proceedings of the internet measurement conference* (pp. 29–42). San Diego: ACM Press.

Nielsen, J. (1993). *Usability engineering.* San Francisco, CA: Morgan Kaufmann.

Olshannikova, E., Olsson, T., Huhtamäki, J., Kärkkäinen, H. (2017). Conceptualizing big social data. *Journal of Big Data, 4*(1), 1–19. doi:10.1186/s40537-017-0063-x.

Organisation for Economic Co-operation and Development (OECD). (2007). Participative web: user-created content. http://www.oecd.org/internet/ieconomy/38393115.pdf.

Pipek, V. (2005). *From tailoring to appropriation support: negotiating groupware usage (PhD-Thesis)* (Faculty of Science - Department of Information Processing Science - University of Oulu, Ed.). Oulu: Oulu University Press.

Pipek, V., & Wulf, V. (2009). Infrastructuring: toward an integrated perspective on the design and use of information technology. *Journal of the Association for Information Systems (JAIS), 10*(5), 447–473.

Reuter, C., & Kaufhold, M.-A. (2018). Fifteen years of social media in emergencies: a retrospective review and future directions for crisis informatics. *Journal of contingencies and crisis management (JCCM), 26*(1).

Reuter, C., Heger, O., Pipek, V. (2013). Combining real and virtual volunteers through social media. In T. Comes, F. Fiedrich, S. Fortier, J. Geldermann, T. Müller (Eds.). *Proceedings of the information systems for crisis response and management (ISCRAM)* (pp. 1–10). Baden-Baden: ISCRAM Digital Library.

Reuter, C., Ludwig, T., Kaufhold, M.-A., Pipek, V. (2015). XHELP: design of a cross-platform social-media application to support volunteer moderators in disasters. In B. Begole, J. Kim, K. Inkpen, W. Woo (Eds.). *Proceedings of the conference on human factors in computing systems (CHI)* (pp. 4093–4102). Seoul: ACM Press.

Reuter, C., Ludwig, T., Kotthaus, C., Kaufhold, M.-A., von Radziewski, E., Pipek, V. (2016). Big data in a crisis? Creating social media datasets for emergency management research. *I-Com: Journal of Interactive Media, 15*(3), 249–264. doi:10.1515/icom-2016-0036.

Reuter, C., Ludwig, T., Ritzkatis, M., Pipek, V. (2015). Social-QAS: tailorable quality assessment service for social media content. In P. Díaz, V. Pipek, C. Ardito, C. Jensen, I. Aedo, A. Boden (Eds.). *Proceedings of the international symposium on end-user development (IS-EUD)* (pp. 156–170). Madrid: Lecture Notes in Computer Science.

Reuter, C., & Ritzkatis, M. (2014). Adaptierbare Bewertung bürgergenerierter Inhalte aus sozialen Medien. In M. Koch, A. Butz, J. Schlichter (Eds.). *Mensch & computer: interaktiv unterwegs – Freiräume gestalten* (pp. 115–124). München: Oldenbourg-Verlag.

Reuter, C., & Scholl, S. (2014). Technical limitations for designing applications for social media. In M. Koch, A. Butz, J. Schlichter (Eds.). *Mensch & computer: workshopband* (pp. 131–140). München: Oldenbourg-Verlag.

Rieder, B. (2013). Studying facebook via data extraction: the netvizz application. *Proceedings of the 5th annual ACM web science conference* (pp. 346–355). New York: ACM. doi:10.1145/2464464.2464475.

Ritter, A., Clark, S., Mausam, Etzioni, O. (2011). Named entity recognition in tweets: an experimental study. In P. Merlo, R. Barzilay, M. Johnson (Eds.). *EMNLP '11 Proceedings of the conference on empirical methods in natural language processing* (pp. 1524–1534). Edinburgh: Association for Computational Linguistics.

Rizza, C., Pereira, Â., Curvelo, P. (2013). Do-it-yourself justice-considerations of social media use in a crisis situation: the case of the 2011 vancouver riots. In T. Comes, F. Fiedrich, S. Fortier,

J. Geldermann, T. Müller (Eds.). *Proceedings of the information systems for crisis response and management (ISCRAM)* (pp. 411–415). Baden-Baden: ISCRAM Digital Library.

Stevens, G., Pipek, V., Wulf, V. (2009). Appropriation infrastructure: supporting the design of usages. In V. Pipek, M. B. Rosson, V. Wulf (Eds.). *Proceedings of the second international symposium on end-user development (IS-EUD)* (pp. 50–69). Heidelberg: Springer, LNCS.

Stieglitz, S., Dang-Xuan, L., Bruns, A., Neuberger, C. (2014). Social media analytics. *Wirtschaftsinformatik, 56*(2), 101–109.

Terpstra, T., Vries, A., de, Stronkman, R., Paradies, G. L. (2012). Towards a realtime twitter analysis during crises for operational crisis management. In L. Rothkrantz, J. Ristvej, Z. Franco (Eds.). *Proceedings of the information systems for crisis response and management (ISCRAM)* (pp. 1–9). Vancouver: ISCRAM Digital Library.

Thomson, R., Ito, N., Suda, H., Lin, F. (2012). Trusting tweets: the fukushima disaster and information source credibility on twitter. In L. Rothkrantz, J. Ristvej, Z. Franco (Eds.). *Proceedings of the information systems for crisis response and management (ISCRAM)* (pp. 1–10). Vancouver: ISCRAM Digital Library.

Turoff, M., Chumer, M., van de Walle, B., Yao, X. (2004). The design of a dynamic emergency response management information system (DERMIS). *The Journal of Information Technology Theory and Application (JITTA), 5*(4), 1–35. Retrieved from http://aisel.ais-net.org/jitta/vol5/iss4/3.

Twidale, M., Randall, D., Bentley, R. (1994). *Situated evaluation for cooperative systems situated evaluation for cooperative systems*. Lancester.

van de Walle, B., & Turoff, M. (2008). Decision support for emergency situations. *Information Systems and E-Business Management, 6*(3), 295–316. doi:10.1007/s10257-008-0087-z.

Ward, J.S., & Barker, A. (2013). Undefined by data: a survey of big data definitions. *Computing Research Repository*, abs/1309.5.

Watson, H., Finn, R. L., Wadhwa, K. (2017). Organizational and societal impacts of big data in crisis management. *Journal of contingencies and crisis management (JCCM), 25*(1), 15–22. doi:10.1111/1468-5973.12141.

Won, M., Stiemerling, O., Wulf, V. (2006). Component-based approaches to tailorable systems. In H. Lieberman, F. Paternó, V. Wulf (Eds.). *Enduser development* (pp. 115–141). Dordrecht: Springer.

Wong, J., & Hong, J. I. (2007). Making mashups with marmite. In *Proceedings of the SIGCHI conference on human factors in computing systems - CHI '07* (pp. 1435–1444). New York: ACM Press. doi:10.1145/1240624.1240842.

World Wide Web Consortium. (2017). Activity vocabulary. Retrieved July 3, 2016, from https://www.w3.org/TR/activitystreams-vocabulary/

Wulf, V., Müller, C., Pipek, V., Randall, D., Rohde, M. (2015). Practice based computing: empirically-grounded concpetualizations derived from design cases studies. In V. Wulf, K. Schmidt, D. Randall (Eds.). *Designing socially embedded technologies in the real-world*. London: Springer.

Wulf, V., Rohde, M., Pipek, V., Stevens, G. (2011). Engaging with practices: design case studies as a research framework in CSCW. In *Proceedings of the conference on computer supported cooperative work (CSCW)* (pp. 505–512). Hangzhou: ACM Press.

Xu, W., Ritter, A., Grishman, R. (2013). Gathering and generating paraphrases from twitter with application to normalization. In *Proceedings of the sixth workshop on building and using comparable corpora* (pp. 121–128). Sophia: Association for Computational Linguistics.

Zafarani, R., Abbasi, M. A., Liu, H. (2014). *Social media mining: an introduction*. Cambridge: Cambridge University Press.

Zagel, B. (2012). Soziale Netzwerke als Impulsgeber für das Verkehrs-und Sicherheits management bei Großveranstaltungen. In A. Koch, T. Kutzner, T. Eder (Eds.). *Geoinformationssysteme* (pp. 223–232). Berlin/Offenbach: VDE Verlag GMBH.

End-User Development and Learning in Second Life: The Evolving Artifacts Framework with Application

Anders I. Mørch, Valentina Caruso and Melissa D. Hartley

Abstract We explore the relationship of end-user development (EUD) and learning in a case study informed by a new conceptual framework (evolving artifacts). The case is an online distance education program for training in-service teachers in special education in the 3D virtual world Second Life (SL). The "box," a specific building block in the SL environment became a multipurpose tool for EUD in the study. The professor of the course designed the learning environment by creating and combining 3D boxes and then used boxes as containers to share course materials to the class. Some of the in-service teachers created boxes to personalize their learning activity. The conceptual framework for analysis integrates EUD concepts and concepts from sociocultural and constructivist learning theories (duality of learning; adaptation). We present an analysis of the participants' spoken utterances and turn taking around the use of the boxes through the lens of two different EUD and learning situations (technology-adaptation and knowledge-adaptation). We show how participants take up these features to become engaged in the activity. One of the situations required the learners to adopt EUD techniques (technology-adaptation), and the professor used EUD techniques to enable knowledge-adaptation.

Keywords 3D virtual world · adaptation · empirical analysis · end-user tailoring · EUD · evolving artifacts framework · in-service teacher · knowledge adaptation · Second Life · qualitative study · special education · tailorable component · teacher education · technology adaptation

A.I. Mørch (✉)
University of Oslo, Oslo, Norway
e-mail: anders.morch@iped.uio.no

V. Caruso
Swiss Federal Institute for Vocational Education and Training (SFIVET), Lugano, Switzerland
e-mail: valentina.caruso@iuffp.swiss

M.D. Hartley
West Virginia University, Morgantown, WV, United States
e-mail: melissa.hartley@mail.wvu.edu

© Springer International Publishing AG 2017
F. Paternò, V. Wulf (eds.), *New Perspectives in End-User Development*,
DOI 10.1007/978-3-319-60291-2_13

1   Introduction

Second Life (SL) is a multi-user virtual environment (MUVE) and a virtual world (VW) in which individuals interact in real time as avatars with other people and virtual objects in a three-dimensional space (Sardone & Devlin-Scherer, 2008). MUVEs offer course organizers new opportunities to design advanced learning environments composed of computer-based tools and virtual spaces for interaction and to stage authentic learning activities with resources that would be difficult to match in a traditional classroom setting.

Second Life provides a platform for teaching distance education courses as synchronous interactions (Baker, Wentz, & Woods, 2009). Faculty members in a teacher preparation program at a research university in the US have been teaching in SL for 5 years, and it has been the educational platform for six online graduate courses, at both the Master's and Doctoral level. It has also been incorporated into undergraduate, campus-based courses for role-play simulation. The present study reports on a course designed for preservice and in-service special education teachers and held entirely in Second Life (Caruso, Mørch, Thomassen, Hartley, & Ludlow, 2014; Mørch, Hartley, & Caruso, 2015); specifically, we focus on the participants' involvement with end-user development (EUD) and the relationship of EUD to learning activities. The professor created the flexible learning environment using the embedded Second Life build feature (a design environment), and the participants used this virtual campus to collaboratively create and enact role-play scenarios as part of their online learning activities. Fig. 1 shows part of the virtual campus.

A specific building block in the SL environment is the "box." The box originated as way of packaging and purchasing goods in the SL marketplace (building units, furniture, clothing, etc.); in our study, this tool was used for EUD by a professor and a group of fulltime in-service teachers following an evening master's degree program. The professor created the virtual campus, learning resources and information sharing containers using boxes, and the in-service teachers used, created and sometimes further developed (tailored) these containers in the collaborative learning activities (Caruso, Hartley, & Mørch, 2015; Mørch, 2016).

Fig. 1 Two buildings of the Second Life™ virtual campus used in the distance education program (Left: Main Classroom; right: Small Group Building)

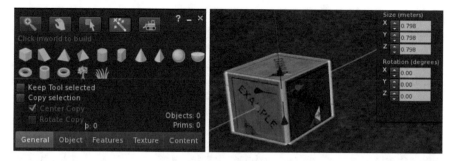

Fig. 2 Left: Selecting a basic 3D shape (prim) in the SL builder. Right: setting two of the attribute values (size and rotation) of the cube prim ("box")

Our informants used the term "box" when they described the tool. The technical term is "default prim" or "cube prim," a primitive object or just "object." Other prim types are named after basic 3D shapes (prism, sphere, cylinder, torus, tube, ring) (Fig. 2, left). Prims are the basic building blocks in SL and can be created, modified and stored with simple commands. Prims are created in a design environment (builder) invoked by Ctrl-B (Fig. 2, left and right). In the builder, objects can be linked to form composite prims or grouped objects to model more complex building parts. The surface texture and other attributes (e.g. size and rotation) of an object can also be edited in the builder (Fig. 2, right). Later (runtime) edits are possible on any object on land with building permit by right clicking on the object and selecting "Edit" from the pop-up menu, referred to as direct activation in the EUD literature (Wulf & Golombek, 2001). All of these features were used in the study reported here.

We adopt a "components approach" to EUD (Bandini & Simone, 2006; Mørch et al., 2004; Mørch & Zhu, 2013; Won, Stiemerling, & Wulf, 2006). The components approach combined with tools for end-user tailoring (Mørch, 1997; Mørch, 2011) differs from the "programming approach" in that end users create and modify software artifacts using high-level (user oriented; domain specific) operations rather than programming operations. However, using the Linden Scripting Language (LSL), boxes can also be modified by writing code. Such modification was not observed in this course, but the professor has used LSL in another course to create a non-player character (NPC) in a roleplay.

Our long-term goal is to use EUD to practice generic (domain general) skills in order to complement the domain-specific concepts and skills taught in classes. The skills and concepts taught in the special education class we report from include: negotiation, conflict resolution, persuasion, and resistance (Caruso et al., 2014; Mørch et al., 2015). On the other hand, generic skills include: learning to learn, academic basics (reading and writing; computational skills), communication, adaptability, personal development, and group effectiveness (Carnevale, 1991; Kearns, 2001). We argue adaptability is the generic skill best matched for EUD and learning. It is defined as follows: (1) The ability to bridge the gap between what is and what ought to be, (2) the ability to produce a novel idea, and then turn it into a practical one (Carnevale, 1991; Kearns, 2001).

The skill most often thought of in conjunction with EUD and learning is computational thinking, i.e., programming and algorithmic problem solving (Grover & Pea, 2013; Repenning, Webb, & Ioannidou, 2010; Wing, 2006) and certain areas of mathematics, such as geometry (Papert, 1980) and vector calculus (El-Nasr & Smith, 2006). The full mastery of EUD in SL requires skills in programming and applied mathematics, but in the work presented here we aim to go beyond computational thinking and use EUD for practicing adaptability in conjunction with preparing for learning domain-specific skills.

We address the following research questions: (1) How do the multiple functionalities of the SL "box" support end-user development, and (2) what is the role of EUD in the learning activity?

The rest of the chapter is organized as follows. The conceptual framework is presented in Sect. 2. The design of the virtual learning environment is described in Sect. 3, and the research methods for data collection and analysis of the case study are given in Sect. 4. Sect. 5 presents five data extracts for exemplification. The findings are discussed in Sect. 6 in terms of the conceptual framework. At the end, we identify some limitations and unresolved issues with our approach and suggest some directions for further research.

2   The Evolving Artifacts Framework (EAF)

We present a conceptual framework for research design and analysis that integrates concepts in EUD and concepts from sociocultural and constructivist learning theories. The three areas of research have developed independently, but have some things in common: learning with the use of tools and application of evolutionary principles and ideas beyond biology. We draw on their similarities to identify a set of concepts and techniques for end-user development as a learning activity (adapt to learn; sense making) and learning as the creation and modification of knowledge (learn to adapt; tool mediation). Researchers in the learning sciences (e.g., Cobb, 1994) have argued for integrating sociocultural and constructivist learning based on complementarity of individual and social processes. In this chapter we propose the complementarity of EUD (tool adaptation) and learning domain-specific concepts (knowledge adaptation).

2.1   Evolving Artifacts in End-User Development: Frameworks, Tools, and Techniques

End-user development is defined as the methods, techniques, and tools that allow users who are acting as non-professional software developers, to create, modify or extend a software artifact (Lieberman, Paterno, & Wulf, 2006). One branch of EUD focuses on enabling and studying these activities in evolutionary application development (Fischer, 1998; Mørch, 2011; Stevens, 2017), i.e. continuous processes of creating and modifying software artifacts that may also involve professional developers and changes made on different time scales (design time vs. use time). Key notions are meta-design, end-user tailoring and appropriation.

2.1.1 Meta-Design

Meta-design is a conceptual approach for system development with end users that pioneered the adoption of evolutionary ideas in EUD (Fischer, 1998). Through this approach, developers create at *design-time* an environment in which users, as "owners of problems," are empowered during *use-time* with methods and tools to create the solutions themselves and engage actively in the continuous development of systems rather than being restricted to the use of existing systems (Fischer, 2009). More recently, researchers have broadened meta-design to include different application domains, including virtual worlds (Fischer, Fogli, & Piccinno, 2017). Second Life is an example of a meta-design environment (Koehne, Redmiles, & Fischer, 2011). SL provides a set of components (building blocks and tools) for a range of different tasks that define flexible design spaces for end-user developers to create locally adapted solutions and participate in the continuous development of the shared environment (Caruso et al., 2015).

Fischer (1998) refers to two types of system development processes (evolutionary growth and reseeding) inspired by two types of organism evolution, ontogenetic (individual; lifespan) and phylogenetic (species; genes). End user developers are the main contributors during evolutionary growth, whereas seeding and reseeding involves professional system developers. Mørch, Nygård, and Ludvigsen (2009) refer to the two processes as adaptation and generalization, and Andersen and Mørch studied the interdependencies of adaptation and generalization and refer to the overall process as mutual development (Andersen & Mørch, 2009). In the case study we report from here, reseeding or generalization means to maintain the Second Life software and spawn new versions, which is a design-time activity organized by Linden Lab with initial release in 2003 and downloaded by end users during use-time. Evolutionary growth or adaptation is the creation and modification of specific artifacts in SL during use-time by end user developers. Both types of evolution have shaped the SL box tool and other SL artifacts; we have focused our research on end-user developed solutions.

2.1.2 End-User Tailoring and Direct Activation

Researchers in EUD have created instances of meta-design by specific tools and techniques for continuous application development (Cabitza & Simone, 2017; Fogli & Provenza, 2012; Mørch, 1997). Mørch (1997) has suggested tools for tailoring generic applications at three levels – customization, integration and extension. These levels provide a gradual transition into the computational complexity of an application via increased power for each level. Fogli and Provenza (2012) apply a meta-design model to create EUD environment for citizens to take active part in an e-government service in Italy. These tools and environments empower domain expert users to create solutions themselves (Costabile et al., 2008) and learning while doing it (Caruso et al., 2015).

The SL user interface consists of visual components. The notions of direct activation by event handling (Mørch, 1995; Wulf & Golombek, 2001) and components approach (Bandini & Simone, 2006; Mørch et al., 2004; Mørch & Zhu, 2013; Won et al., 2006) support tailorability. It entails that tools for EUD are part of the runtime environment at the granularity of components and invoked by a mouse-keyboard combination. Direct activation supports a "gentle slope to complexity" (Ludwig, Dax, Pipek, & Wulf, 2017), which means that the practice situation indicates to the user when there is need to tailor, e.g., associated with a breakdown or problem. A breakdown triggers the need for "repair," whereby a tailor descends to a lower level of detail to make the necessary changes (Ludwig et al., 2017). Direct activation is supported in Second Life by right clicking on a modifiable 3D object. The edit command in the pop-up menu opens a property sheet for customization, allowing object features, textures and content to be changed (see Fig. 2).

2.1.3 Appropriation

Appropriation of everyday objects will typically not involve actions to "create, modify or extend a software artifact." For example, appropriation is defined in the arts in Wikipedia to use pre-existing objects or artifacts in new ways and combinations with little or no transformation applied to them. On the other hand, both appropriation and EUD can be characterized as continuous processes of evolving artifacts. Software appropriation has been researched in computer supported cooperative work (CSCW) and human computer interaction (HCI) and defined as combining adoption and adaptation: adoption of a specific technology in an organizational context and adaptation of the technology to that context (Dourish, 2003; Tchounikine, 2017).

Pipek (2005) argues that appropriation should be considered in terms of design in use and tailoring. He describes appropriation as "an ongoing design process that end users perform largely without any involvement of professional developers" (Pipek, 2005, p. 5). Based on two long-term empirical studies, he identified advanced user activities with collaboration tools (groupware) in two workplace settings and proposed appropriation support to aid the activities. Pipek characterized this appropriation as "a collaborative effort of end users ... to make sense of the software in their work context" (Pipek, 2005, p. 5). The appropriation support combines communication, demonstration, negotiation, and tailoring.

More recently Stevens (2017) has proposed appropriation as a sociotechnical framework (infrastructure) for EUD. He traces the roots of the concept back to German idealism in the works of Hegel and Marx and studies its uptake in 20th century Activity Theory of Leontiev and Engeström, who connect appropriation with expansive learning, thus forming a dialectic of mental and material appropriation activities (Engeström, 1999). The dialects of acting on the external world, as a form of production and reproduction, and changing one's inner nature as a form of learning and self-expression, are elements of Marx' theory that provided later scholars with ideas for new research methods for studying human activity as a dialectic process (Stevens, 2017).

2.2   Evolving Artifacts and Human Learning

EUD and learning from a sociocultural and constructivist perspective share a focus in the use of tools (cultural tools in sociocultural learning; learning through concrete experiences in constructivist learning) and application of evolutionary ideas. However, there are also important differences between the two perspectives, one being that constructivist theory suggests to focus on individual learning motivated by personal interest while sociocultural theory is more concerned with the ways in which learning is culturally dependent and involve social interaction and scaffolding (Scott & Palincsar, 2013). We present two theoretical ideas, Vygotsky's Genetic law of cultural development and Piaget's process of Adaptation, which we integrate with concepts from EUD to define two types of adaptation: technology-adaptation (EUD) and knowledge-adaptation (learning).

2.2.1   The Genetic Law of Cultural Development (Duality of Learning)

Vygotsky's "genetic law of cultural development," referred to here as "duality of learning" to avoid confusion with the contemporary meaning of genetics (genes and DNA), states that "every function in the child's cultural development appears twice: first, on the social level, and later, on the individual level; first *between* people (*inter-psychological*), and then *inside* the child (*intra psychological*). This applies equally to voluntary attention, to logical memory, and to the formation of concepts. All the higher functions originate as actual relations between human individuals" (Vygotsky, 1934/1978, p. 57, emphasis original).

Wertsch (1991) suggested that the interaction between individual and social processes is not linear but interdependent and that tool-mediated human activity is central to the interdependence. The activities that tools facilitate are the co-construction of knowledge and the internalization of knowledge for the individuals (Säljö, 1999; Wertsch, 1991). Leontiev (1981), a junior colleague of Vygotsky, used the term "appropriation" to characterize this process of internalization to simplify the task of understanding the history of development of specific artifacts that have taken centuries and decades to evolve in order to appropriate such objects into their own system of activity (Newman, Griffin, & Cole, 1989).

The connection between appropriation as a form of advanced technology use and the social construction of knowledge has been studied in teacher education research, for example, in examining the appropriation that occurs when learners (teachers in training) adapt information technology in a way that is meaningful to them (Cook, Smagorinsky, Fry, Konopak, & Moore, 2002; Grossman, Smagorinsky, & Valencia, 1999). Appropriation involving modification to software (EUD) has been studied in computer science education research where the aim is to teach computational thinking (Grover & Pea, 2013; Repenning et al., 2010; Wing, 2006) and in CSCW to provide a sociotechnical infrastructure for tool modification (EUD) and flexible use practices (e.g. participatory design, collaborative sense making, and learning) in workplace settings (Stevens, 2017). However, to the best of our knowledge, EUD has been little investigated in research in special education.

2.2.2 Piaget's Adaptation: Assimilation, Accommodation and Equilibration

Constructivism is a theory that puts forward the hypothesis that knowledge is not passively received but actively built on an individual's prior experiences. It also considers the main function of cognition as adaptive in order to organize and make sense of the experiential world (Bruner, 1961; Piaget, 1952; Von Glasersfeld, 1989). Piaget's constructivism suggests that learning happens whereby learners integrate new experiences with prior knowledge through two complementary processes of adaptation, assimilation and accommodation, driven by a tension-laden internal dynamic referred to as equilibration (Piaget, 1952).

In *assimilation*, people take information from the outside world and convert it to fit in with their existing ideas and concepts. These mental categories are known as schemas, and are used to understand the world around them. When people encounter information that is completely new or that challenges their existing ideas, they often have to form a new schema to *accommodate* the information or alter their existing mental categories (Piaget, 1952). The desire for *equilibration* (inner sense of balance of knowing) motivates learners in periods of restless mind (cognitive conflict) to adjust old ideas and imprecise concepts and to learn new and better ones. Piaget's tension-laden process of evolving knowledge artifacts can be compared with and form part of Vygotsky's broader social-individual (outer-inner) dynamic of learning and knowledge development in the context of human activity.

2.2.3 Duality of Adaptation: Technology Versus Knowledge

By synthesizing two sets of ideas on adaptation, we suggest that adaptation takes place in two realms by two processes: in the social realm by technology adaptation, and later, in the individual realm, by knowledge adaptation. This is not a strict linear process, but one that iterates between two sides, where each side draws on the other to cope with own shortcomings (e.g., lack of knowledge to accompany technology-adaptation and lack of stable intermediate forms in knowledge-adaption). Furthermore, knowledge adaptation does not have to be an individual activity;

collaborators can create and adapt knowledge together and conversational data allows researchers to study knowledge adaptation in a semi-naturalistic setting.

In sum: The key concepts of the evolving artifacts frameworks are the following, 1) technology-adaptation: customization, integration, extension, 2) knowledge-adaptation: assimilation, accommodation, 3) complementarity, and 4) bridging concepts (in alphabetical order): cognitive conflict, collaboration, direct activation, externalization, internalization, knowledge refinement, practice iteration, scaffolding, social tension, and tool mediation. These concepts have informed our research design and we have used some of them as sensitizing concepts to classify the data material we report in Sect. 5. We also refer to aspects of meta-design (time scales: design-time vs. use-time) and appropriation (gentle slope; sociotechnical infrastructure) in our discussions in Sect. 6.

2.3 Constructionism

Constructionism developed by Papert and colleagues (Papert & Harel, 1991) is probably the best known theory of knowledge construction in EUD and builds on the constructivist ideas developed by Piaget (self-directed learning involving tangible objects and motivated by personal interest rather than predefined curricular goals) and supported by visual programming environments, pioneered by Logo (Papert, 1980). Several constructionist environments have been created after Logo, such as Boxer (diSessa & Abelson, 1986), Alice (Conway, Audia, Burnette, Cosgrove, & Christiansen, 2000), Agentsheets (Repenning, Ioannidou, & Zola, 2000), Scratch (Maloney, Resnick, Rusk, Silverman, & Eastmond, 2010), and Blockly from Google. The boundary between these environments and the "components approach" is not clear-cut. For example, LEGO WeDo and App Inventor are construction kits that contain a large number of building blocks for composition, programming, and modification, thus combining component-based design and programming. Furthermore, contemporary constructionist environments provide learners with a wealth of scaffolding by online help and instruction, online peer communities, libraries of examples, and video tutorials (Roque, Rusk, & Resnick, 2016), thus bridging the gap between constructionism (self directed) and sociocultural (facilitated) learning theory.

In sum, our approach to EUD (component-based design and modification) and theoretical perspective (Evolving Artifacts) differ from Constructionism in two ways: 1) at the technology level in the same way as Minecraft (and Second Life) differs from Scratch (modification vs. programming; learning domain-oriented concepts vs. computational thinking), and 2) at the theoretical level by a conceptual framework based on evolutionary ideas. However, the two perspectives overlap with respect to the following: end users are learners who actively contribute to own learning through advanced technology use while interacting with fellow learners, facilitators and culture specific scaffolds.

3 Designing the Learning Environment: Buildings & Activities

The third author of this study is the "professor;" who created the learning environment from scratch using Second Life's build feature (a design environment). This was accomplished based on skills acquired through a workshop offered by Sloan Consortium (now called Online Learning Consortium), in which she learned how to build a "box" and how to put content inside of a box. Below we describe two types of functionality that can be built with the SL box as basic building blocks: virtual buildings and learning activities and tools (Caruso et al., 2015).

3.1 Designing Virtual Buildings

After taking the workshop, the professor-as-designer spent time playing in SL to practice making virtual buildings. She built the buildings (two of them are shown in Fig. 1) by creating multiple boxes and linking them together, as shown in Fig. 3: left). There were restrictions on the size of an individual object; therefore, multiple boxes were put together to create a building of the size needed.

Fig. 3 Left: Building a box in Second Life; right: changing the size attributes of a box

In order for the main classroom to appear as one large lecture hall, the interior walls of the boxes were set to "phantom" and made transparent, as shown in the left part of Fig. 3. When an object is set to phantom in SL as opposed to merely "transparent," one can walk through the object. The main classroom had six boxes linked together in order to create the look and feel the designer wanted. Once the walls were created, faculty built one large floor from a box so that the texture on the floor would look uniform.

After the interior walls were created, the professor changed each "texture" of the exterior of each box to give the objects the appearance of a building. It was the intent to make the buildings look similar to the architectural design of the downtown campus, including vaulted windows (see Fig. 1). The professor built the floor for the foyer by building a box and adjusting the dimensions. She then linked the boxes and the floor together. Several other pieces were also created in a similar manner and finally linked together.

In addition to the main classroom, it was necessary to build small-group buildings for collaborative work. Each group building included a group table with chairs, as well as a lounge area with a sofa and chairs. The group buildings were 60 (virtual) meters apart to avoid sound interference between groups while talking. Combining two boxes and making the interior walls of the boxes transparent and "phantom" created the small group buildings, and the texture of the boxes was changed to account for floors and walls (including windows) without building separate boxes. After the prototype group building had been created, multiple copies were made by duplication of the original; in total, five group rooms per instructor were created.

3.2 Designing Learning Activities and Tools

The learning environment was designed to maximize collaboration and student engagement. When envisioning the main classroom, the online instructors wanted a space where students could meet as a large group ($N = 25$) and engage in interactive lectures. The professor had visited other instructors' classes in SL and thought that flipping through slides in SL while students sat in a seat and watched was less engaging than students physically moving their avatar to participate, which is more in line with constructivist learning ideals such as active learning (Karagiorgi & Symeou, 2005). Therefore, a decision was made to design the space so that students would walk from display board to display board (Fig. 4, left).

The display boards were used to show lesson content by uploading PowerPoint slides as jpeg textures, and there were individual activities throughout the lesson. After the interactive lecture, students worked in groups for the remainder of the session. During this time, students worked collaboratively to solve problems. In addition to solving problems, students were asked to create a role-play scenario for their classmates to practice skills surrounding one of the topic areas taught in the class (e.g., interpersonal problem solving, effective communication,

Fig. 4 Left: Professor lecturing and walking students through slides; right: a student facilitating a role-playing session using a "box" for information sharing (the box is on the table)

negotiation, persuasion, conflict, resistance). The right-hand side of Fig. 4 shows a group of students engaged in a role-play, using a box attached to a table to share information.

Incorporating role-playing through virtual simulations is grounded in the constructivist notion of learning through concrete experiences and then reflecting upon those experiences (Bruner, 1961; Piaget, 1952). Role-playing scenarios typically encountered in special education training were enacted during class sessions, in order prepare future teachers to experience controlled situations and allow them to rehearse professional responses using effective communication strategies. In addition to participating in role-play creation and play, they were also asked to facilitate their classmates' participation in their role-play, which we show by example in Sect. 5.

As part of this assignment, students had to learn how to build boxes to disseminate their materials, create notecards and put them inside the boxes, and allow their boxes to be "purchased" for zero Linden dollars. These were the same kind of boxes the professor used to create the learning environment, but in this case, the students did not have to connect boxes. Instead, some of the in-service teachers played around with self-created boxes and customized them to personalize it to their collaborative work, serving as a "group identity" (Greenberg, 1991). To add content to their box, they dragged a notecard from their inventory into the Contents section of the Edit window.

4 Methods and Research Design

Thirty-four in-service teachers took part in the study, participating in seven live 2-hour class sessions and nine collaborative group work sessions spanning four weeks. Each class consisted of a combination of teacher-led and student-centered activities, including interactive lectures of theoretical concepts (30 minutes), individual activities (15 minutes), group activities in separate rooms (30 minutes), and role-play activities (10 minutes). Learning was embedded within the activities, and members of the group were assigned roles (leader, facilitator, secretary, time keeper, organizer) during collaborative group work sessions.

We used a qualitative research analysis, combining a case study (Yin, 2003) and virtual ethnography (Boellstorff, Nardi, Pearce, & Taylor, 2012; Hine, 2000). A cases study is a particular instance of something used or analyzed in order to illustrate a thesis or principle. In accordance with virtual ethnography (Boellstorff et al., 2012; Hine, 2000), all sessions were observed at a distance in the virtual world and video-recorded with screen capture software (BSR, Camtasia, SnagIt) by the first two authors (in total 15 hours of raw video data). Afterwards, two interviews were conducted with one student who volunteered, and with the professor, by using chat and voice (headset), in SL.

In order to manage and classify the data material, each session and interview were stored in a separate file and entirely transcribed. We thematically categorized the data (Guest, 2012) in two rounds: first according to an open coding and iterative classification process (data-driven), and then informed by our research questions and by two empirical concepts (technology-adaptation and knowledge-adaptation). We focused on one group's activities as they unfold throughout the collaborative work and roleplay. This group was chosen because its members were the most active in using EUD techniques in their collaborative work. Then we counted the occurrences of domain-specific concepts in the transcripts ("conflict" had 34 instances in the session we report from). Inspired by the interaction analysis method (Jordan & Henderson, 1995) we base our claims on the participants' utterances (chat and voice), verbal interactions, turn taking, and tone of voice ("body language"). We integrate the participants' EUD actions with their verbal and non-verbal data using screen images and comments. We have reproduced five extracts below, which are snapshots of the learning trajectory organized into two themes: technology-adaptation (Extracts 1–3) and knowledge-adaptation (Extracts 4–5).

5   Data Extracts and Findings

Each subsection below is organized as follows: (1) short context description, (2) illustrative example of "raw" data (spoken utterances, set in italics), and (3) brief summary of findings. The transcript notation used in the data presentations includes these symbols: (..) short pause; ((text)) comment by researcher; [..] excluded (not audible) speech; :: interruption of talk by extraneous sources at the participant site.

5.1   Data Extract 1: Creating a Box and Personalize the Learning Activity

In Extract 1, in-service teachers are working in small groups. We follow the group consisting of Heather, Janet, Mandy, and Stacy (fictitious names of participants). After creating a scenario for the role-play activities, they need to write the instructions on a notecard intended for one of the other groups to act out. The notecard is put in a box. When the extract below begins, the group is ready to create their box:

Stacy:	OK, now we need somebody to make the box.
Heather:	Y'all go together and do that. I kind of... can we build it in here? ((A default box appears on the screen in yellow color))
Stacy:	I'm not sure if we can or not.
Heather:	I think we can build it here ((in their group room)), we just have to put it in our inventory before we leave. I have one (..) started; I'll try to get it so you can see it. ((Typing on keyboard)) (..)
Janet:	Exactly. ((chat))
[14:18] Stacy:	Ok. ((chat)) (..) ((long pause, then the box' color changes several times))
Heather:	That's a fancy box. Is it changing:: the scenery on it or are you changing that? (..)
Mandy:	Yeah, can you see it? ((Positive tone of voice))
Heather:	Yeah, I can ((laughs)) (..)
Mandy:	OK, tell me when you... we get something that you like. ((Happy voice))

The group attempts to collaboratively create a box for sharing documents with another group, but Stacy is unsure if they can build it in their group room or somewhere else. The box eventually appears in the room in a default state based on Heather's actions ("I have one … started; I'll try to get it so you can see it."), and she believes it can be saved in her inventory (a local storage for each person's items). Then, Mandy modifies the box into the pattern shown in Fig. 5, thus connecting the box with their case.

Fig. 5 The participants in the four-person group shown in data extracts 1–4 collaborate to build and customize a box for information sharing (the fancy colored box in the lower right-hand corner). The professor provided the two other boxes for seeding the environment with learning resources

What the in-service teachers build is not rocket science in EUD; they set parameters in the box's property sheet, but they struggle with the physical location and operations on the object (shared view vs. local actions). But when they figure out how to make changes that are visible to them all, it gives them great pleasure. It also gives them a sense of ownership of the box they made, which is evident by the tone of their interactions, as shown in the last four turns.

5.2 Data Extract 2: Customizing the Box for Content Sharing

The content to be put in boxes refers to notecards with instructions for the role-players of another group. To accomplish this, the groups needs to make one more adjustment to the box to allow for content sharing, as shown in Extract 2:

Mandy:	How do I make the box (..) ahm:: have a price of nothing? What do I…?
Stacy:	There should be a spot on there ((in the property sheet)) that says… with a… I think it's down toward the bottom where it says ahm, the price or whatever and you have to set it to zero dollars. Let me see if I can…
Mandy:	Oh pay… about object (..) I'll have to make it for sale.
Stacy:	Yeah.
[14:25] Mandy:	Features, ahm:: (..) I'll have to look it up. I'm trying to build. If you guys want to talk, I'll still listen (..) All right. I did have the note (..) So:: what exactly do we want to put in this box? I'm guessing do we need to put a little snippet of (..) what part of this case we're going to talk about and what skill we want them to practice on?

Stacy looks at the property sheet for the box after doing an edit command on the object, and suggests an attribute to be set ("the price or whatever"). She struggles at first to understand why they have to set the value to "zero dollars," which was described in the instructions from the professor. Mandy suggests they have to make the object for sale, and goes on modifying the box ("I'm trying to build. If you guys want to talk, I'll still listen"). The other in-service teachers comment on her work, test the box, and report what they see. By setting the value of the content to $0L in the box's property sheet, they allow the content to be shared without payment (a feature inherited from the box' commodity packaging origin). Now, they can start to work on their role-play script to be disseminated to another group and start educational role-playing and concept application.

5.3 Data Extract 3: Exploring Online Scaffolding

The participants we observed were newcomers to SL, and the professor prepared multiple ways of scaffolding the learning activities. She created a "getting started handbook" (Hartley, Ludlow, & Duff, 2016) and several instructional videos for specific situations. The use of the handbook is shown in the following extract:

[14:28] Mandy:	In our handbook that we have did it say how to put a card in there (..) or was it on-line that the instructions were there?
Heather:	I'll see if I can help too. I remember doing it for that activity but let me go play around, see what I can find (..) Mandy, what did you put under ahm:: content permission?
Heather:	Go under content and click on permissions and see what you have selected there.
Mandy:	It has all checked ahm:: (..) Maybe I need to put share there (..) Anyone (..) ok (..) see if that works and you can buy it now (..)(..)
Heather:	How did you pick it up, Mandy? ((a new box appears on their lap))
Mandy:	I have no idea. I just started cracking up laughing because I have no idea why it's on my lap ((laughs)).
Heather:	Somebody else has it. Janet, you have it on you.
Janet:	How do I get it off, it's squashing me! ((the box is on her lap))
Heather:	If you right click it'll say drop ((laughs)) (..) It's floating above the window (..) (..) There are two tie-dye boxes floating above the window. ((box is in the air))
Mandy:	Yeah, I see them.

Extract 3 shows the necessity of giving the participants some examples and instructions for scaffolding their activities. When the professor incorporates an online handbook and short video instructions, she ensures that in-service teachers feel more confident with the virtual environment. They refer to the online handbook to set permission for sharing documents, and as a result they make changes to some attribute values in the property sheet of the box. It is worth noticing that the work to do this takes some time and is partly done individually according to own time preferences. For examples Heather needs to "play around," and Mandy asks, "if that works," after setting a value in the property sheet. It is clear from the tone of their voice that they enjoy the activity, which gives them time to reflect on and learn to understand what it means to create and modify boxes.

5.4 Data Extract 4: Using Domain-Specific Concepts in Planning a Roleplay

The pre-service teachers were asked to create a role-play scenario for their classmates to practice one or more interpersonal problem solving skills during the role-play activity. In addition, each member was assigned a specific role in coordinating the activities: leader, organizer, timekeeper, secretary, and facilitator. In Extract 4 the group of students are planning the role-play activity (note: Franklin is a child described in the scenario and the role players argue for best placement for him using the concepts taught in class):

Stacy:	Is our situation going to be like Franklin and other – and other teachers or is it going to be like teachers talking about Franklin or:: (...) what? You know, what kind of scenario? I think we've got to think of what kind of scenario first and then think of what kind of skill we should practice.
[14:14] Janet:	True ((chat))
Janet:	I think that we could do something like ahm:: the teachers talking about what they can do to help him, like what is the best help. I mean, because that's kind of what we've struggled on too, what is the best help for Franklin? Do we try and seek counseling for him, do we just punish him for making dirty pictures and making shanks at home, like what is the best for Franklin?
[14:14] Stacy:	Ok, that sounds good ((chat))
Stacy:	So do you think that might fall under negotiation? (...) Because they're... teachers are kind of negotiating with each other about (...) what would be best for him.
[14:15] Janet:	I think that or conflict ((chat))

By planning the role-play activities in collaboration, in-service teachers were highly motivated to take part in the group discussions, thus making sense of the theoretical concepts taught in the course. This is in the beginning of planning the role-play and they are raising the issue of what should be the key concepts to be taught, and considers negotiation and conflict. The extract also illustrates how the role-play in Second Life provided the pre-service teachers with a significant level of immersion and realism, since they interpreted their roles by practicing real collaboration skills and exploring learning situations more safely than in the real world.

5.5 Data Extract 5: Using Domain-Specific Concepts in Skills Practice

In Extract 5, reproduced below, we are at the end of a debrief session of a roleplay facilitated by one of members in the group shown above (Heather). This session occurs one week after the session reported in Extracts 1–4. The debrief starts immediately after time is up for role-playing. The students are no longer playing scripted roles, and we get an idea of what they learned from it:

Heather:	Okay, do you guys have any, um, we need to head back to class, you guys were doing, like, amazing, but is there anything, real quickly, you would say, um, about (..) You kind of talked about different persuasion strategies which could work, um, what the cause of conflict is, just real quickly, about why the team members cannot reach an agreement, from page two-ninety-seven to two-ninety-nine. Then we can head back to class, 'cause I know the other group is finished already.
Jenny:	((long pause)) I think some of it was [passed]

(continued)

(continued)

Andy:	*::I was gonna say with individuals, if not conflict between individuals with the same goals, because we all have the same goal (..) and we all have different opinions of what's best for this student.*
Peter:	*Yeah, I'd mean, I agree, I think it's – it's conflicts (..) it could probably easily be considered like you said, conflict with the same goal, 'cause everyone's looking out for the student, but one side, they're lookin' out, okay, what's best for the student, is it to remove him from my ((emphasized)) classroom and everyone else wants the best for him, but it- it's the same goal, but they (..) still using different placements.*
Heather:	*Awesome! ((Chat))*

The in-service teachers show evidence of knowing about the skills associated with persuasion and conflict, in two ways: Referring to the pages in the text book where it was presented (Heather), and used when reflecting upon their application of the concepts in the role play. The reflection is about what kind of conflict, if any, did this persuasion strategy lead to and what was the cause of it. The three participants (Jenny, Andy, Peter) elaborate on each other's answer ("I think some of it was" → "conflict between individuals with the same goals" → "it's the same goal, but they still using different placements"), which is acknowledged as "awesome" and "I agree" by the facilitator at the end of the in-group debrief.

5.6 Summary of Findings

The results of the study indicate that the learning we observed in Second Life was highly motivating for the in-service teachers. They took part in collaborative and role-play activities and were deeply engaged; they applied the theoretical concepts taught by the professor in lecture, which in turn aided the participants' learning of key concepts in the subject domain through skills practice. The collaborative activities included advanced technology use, such as modification of 3D boxes for information sharing in Second Life. We focused our analysis of two situations of collaboration and learning, technology adaptation and knowledge adaptation.

The situations revealed two trajectories of evolving artifacts, which were not directly connected but we suggest they are complementary, in the following manner. Technology adaptation required mastery of adaptability skills (i.e., "the ability to bridge the gap between what is and what ought to be" in terms of modifying an SL box from a generic one toward one that is personalized to a group of learners), but it did not involve domain specific concepts or skills to serve as a kind of design rationale for the adapted box. On the other side, knowledge adaptation by which in-service teachers learned domain-specific concepts and skills in special education in an iterative, incremental, three-step fashion (i.e., interacting with professor during theory presentation; collaborative planning of roleplay involving theoretical concepts and skills practice; practicing required skills doing role playing) did not provide any means for practicing adaptability hands-on to ensure deep learning. We hypothesize these "shortcomings" of either side are "off loaded" to the other. At this stage our findings are tentative and must be further explored, as this is the first application of a new conceptual framework for learning with computer tools. We elaborate our findings in the next section.

6 Discussion

Drawing on the findings reported in the previous section and using the conceptual framework presented in Sect. 2, we discuss the research questions raised in Sect. 1.

6.1 How Do the Multiple Functionalities of the SL "Box" Support End-User Development?

A specific building block in the SL environment, the "box," became the focus for our study as it supported end-user development in Second Life in two different ways: (1) building the learning environment with boxes as building blocks and (2) collaboratively adapting boxes for information sharing with other groups. We discuss our findings in terms of the evolving artifacts framework (and in some areas supplemented by and compared with meta-design and appropriation).

The findings show that professional educators (a professor of education and a class of in-service teachers) are able to design and appropriate advanced 3D objects through an engaging process of collaboration in the 3D virtual environment Second Life, despite little knowledge of computer science. This was possible by an environment created according to principles of meta-design, which according to Fischer (2009) include that "owners of problems" act as designers. In our case the owners of problems are a professor and the in-service teachers, who act in their capacity as domain-expert users (Costabile et al., 2008). The in-service teachers created notecards for preparing learning activities such as role-play scenarios, and they used and sometimes customized boxes for sharing the notecards with peers (Extract 1–2).

The basic building block used by the professor to create the learning environment is the "box tool" (Mørch, 2016), allowing both buildings and learning resources to be created (see Sect. 3). Buildings required connecting boxes (a form of tailoring by integration) whereas modifying them required tailoring by customization (Mørch, 1997). The generic nature of the box tool did not prevent in-service teachers from taking part in EUD. The boxes were also specific enough and provided a "gentle slope" to complexity (Ludwig et al., 2017) so that in-service teachers could further adapt them by customization, which was an enjoyable activity that gave the in-service teachers a sense of ownership of their case (Extract 1), connection with their learning activity (Extract 2), and means to reflect on their learning activity (Extract 3).

In some instances customizing the box tool gave the users some unforeseen challenges (as shown in Extracts 2–3). We firmly believe that this form of appropriation was beneficial for them in terms of self-confidence in accomplishing an online learning activity in real time (this is evident in that they had a lot of fun and were able to "play around," see Extract 3). The professor created scaffolding structures using video and signposts in the virtual world to explain that in some places objects cannot be modified (inventory) and in other locations they can (when attached to modifiable building units or land with building permitted, or in a sandbox).

The notions of direct activation (Mørch, 1995; Wulf & Golombek, 2001) and the components approach to EUD (Bandini & Simone, 2006; Mørch et al., 2004; Mørch & Zhu, 2013; Won et al., 2006) suggest that tools for EUD should be available where the need for tailoring occurs in order to minimize interruption of the ongoing activity and to enter a new activity. Our data indicates that the participants understood these notions. Direct activation is supported in SL by right clicking on an editable 3D object and selecting the edit command (or by keyboard shortcut Ctrl-3). The edit command opens a property sheet for basic operations (move, resize, rotate, modify texture, etc.). The group consisting of Heather, Janet, Mandy, and Stacy (Extracts 1–2) were able to customize their own notecard-sharing box in their group room and enjoyed the activity. Further research ought to investigate ways to stimulate engagment in deeper complexity and increased flexibility in technology adaptation in Second Life, and to compare two conditions of object modification (direct activation vs. sandbox) in order to determine the optimal balance of ease of use and space for experimentation without unanticipated consequences.

6.2   What Is the Role of EUD in the Learning Activity?

The evolving artifacts framework presented in this chapter takes inspiration from meta-design, appropriation, and constructionism (Sect. 2). In this section we compare appropriation and evolving artifacts as conceptual frameworks for addressing RQ2.

6.2.1   Appropriation Versus Evolving Artifacts

One of the aims of writing this chapter was to develop a new framework for EUD and learning. Appropriation is one possible way to start because it encompasses sociotechnical development (Dourish, 2003; Pipek, 2005; Stevens, 2017; Tchounikine, 2017) and learning (Billet, 1998; Grossman, 1999; Newman et al., 1989; Wertsch, 1998). Dourish (2003) defined appropriation in the field of computer supported cooperative work (CSCW) as the process by which people adopt and adapt technologies, fitting them into their working practices. Dourish (2003) also says "it is similar to customization, but concerns the adoption patterns of technology and the transformation of practice at a deeper level." Wertsch defined appropriation as learning from a socio-cultural perspective as "the process of taking something that belongs to others and make it one's own" (Wertsch, 1998, p. 53). Implied by this perspective is the idea that knowledge is constructed during appropriation, and that students play an active role in the process (Cook et al., 2002; Grossman et al., 1999). The process of constructing knowledge originates in social and cultural sources, and then it is integrated into one's prior knowledge (Billet, 1998).

The gaps bridged by appropriation by the scholars cited are technology adaptation and social organization on one hand (CSCW), and cultural development and learning on the other (sociocultural perspective). The problem with appropriation as an overarching framework is when it attempts to integrate two types of development activities that operate on different time scales (short term vs. long term; specific vs. general; ontogeny vs. phylogeny) with the risk of aligning incompatible activities (Billet, 1998). This problem is articulated by Newman et al. (1989) in terms of sociocultural learning as follows: "task of understanding the history of development of specific artifacts that have taken millennia to evolve in order to appropriate such objects into their own system of activity."

Arguable it is easier to bridge two forms of ontogeny, tool adaptation and knowledge adaptation, in the activities of a small group of learners as we have attempted with our case study, despite shortcomings associated with weak connections between the two sets of actions and interactions (complementarity rather than subsumption). Two premises of the evolving artifacts framework that should be considered before it is put to further use are as follows: (1) knowledge adaptation is enhanced by hands-on adaptability experience, i.e., learning to bridge prior and new (taught) knowledge by end-user development, thus making learning concrete, and (2) technology adaptation (in the broadest sense of the term, not limited to computers) is a fundamental human activity (design) that gives rise to joy, meaning, and knowledge by accounting for the choices made during the activity. The latter corresponds to a type of design rationale referred to in CSCW as "accountable artifacts" (e.g., Dourish, 2003; Stevens, 2017).

6.2.2 The SL Box as Evolving Artifact

The Box became an evolving artifact for the participants in several situations, starting with the basic box tool as shown in Fig. 2, used by the professor for creating building units and information sharing containers (Figs. 1 and 3). Some of those information-sharing containers (Figs. 4: right and 5) served as models for in-service teachers to create their own personalized containers (Fig. 5). The actual time span during which in-service teachers were engaged in box adaptation was about 10–15 minutes, a short and intense activity, which is captured by Extracts 1–3.

The trajectory of the conversation in these extracts starts with a focus on Second Life idiosyncrasies (build, boxes, inventory, property sheet) in Extract 1, followed by adopting the vocabulary of real-life metaphors built into SL and extending to other application domains (price of nothing, make it for sale, zero dollars) in Extract 2, and in Extract 3 the participants are more comfortable and use also experimental and humorous phrases such as "play around," "it's squashing me," and "floating above the window." Once the technology and metaphors had been appropriated, the students' conversation switched almost instantaneously into the terminology of the skills practice and boxes as artifacts were put in the background for the rest of the session (Caruso et al., 2014; Mørch et al., 2015).

6.2.3   Domain-Specific Skills Practice as Evolving Artifact

Our data captures conversations between the professor and in-service teachers and among in-service teachers in their group work. Their conversation is "public" in the sense that it does not directly represent the thoughts of individual learners but meaning making at the group level, i.e., collaborative learning. The professor applied multiple strategies to support collaborative learning: combing theory and practice, repeating the activities, and providing "before" and "after" methods with the role-play (Mørch et al., 2015). Theoretical concepts such as persuasion and conflict were first taught in interactive lectures, then in-service teachers became engaged in collaborative group work to create a role-play scenario (Extract 4), and finally applied in role-playing, which ends with a debrief (Extract 5). The debrief takes place in two rounds: within the group organized by a peer group (Extract 5), and for the whole class organized by the professor. This combination of abstract and concrete learning activities, application of skills in several rounds and debriefing (skills practice iteration) provides for multiple ways of prior knowledge to surface in the learners' conversations. It also gives the learners multiple opportunities to interact with flexible technology and to refine their knowledge over time.

During the group collaboration activity, the in-service teachers went through a process of making sense of the theoretical concepts presented by the professor (Extract 4). This indicates that the concepts were "assimilated" among the contributing members of the group. We did not observe "accommodation," i.e. that learners adjust old ideas and imprecise concepts in order to create better ones, with the methods we used. However, in the final extract (Extract 5) the participants in the roleplay show evidence of knowing about the skills associated with "conflict" in their discussions as they elaborate on each other's answer in response to the facilitator's question in the debrief session, and in a sense the participants build on each other's experiences of the whole situation, the participants' roles, the rules of the game, and the interactions among the role-players (revealed in our video data by tone of voice, temper, and position).

7   Conclusions, Shortcomings, and Directions for Further Research

This study shows that the "box," a specific and flexible (multipurpose) tool in Second Life is used in three different ways: (1) the environment developer (the professor) created the learning environment by combining boxes to create the virtual campus with buildings and learning resources (tailoring by integration) and editing the user interface of the boxes (customization), (2) active users (more technically inclined in-service teachers) modified boxes by customization, and (3) ordinary users (in-service teachers) used the boxes for information sharing without any modifications. There are two interesting findings, one that can be read out of our data and another which is indicative at this stage and requires more work to establish: (1) The modification of boxes allowed in-service teachers to personalize their learning activity, which engaged them in the learning process, and (2) by off-loading those aspects of knowledge adaptation that individuals cannot be con-sciously aware of, EUD makes the whole learning process more transparent and meaningful to the participants and observers. Furthermore, modification of boxes is simplified by direct activation of a builder (design environment) and editor (property sheet) by right clicking on modifiable 3D objects. The boxes can be modified over an extended period of time by storing them in a repository con-nected with their copy of the SL software, thus making the modifications be per-sistent across all sessions in this environment.

This empirical study is primarily descriptive and adopts a qualitative approach to data collection and analysis, focusing on giving empirical evidence for claims through the voices of the participants, and by giving concrete examples of possibilities and limitations of the technology in a real context (outside a usability laboratory). The overarching theoretical perspective is the evolving artifacts framework (EAF), which entails that humans learn by evolving artifacts in two realms (outer and inner; social and individual; technology and knowledge). We have explored the role of end-user development in the "outer realm," and found that it increases engagement in the learn-ing activity, and we hypothesize that EUD complements the more abstract knowledge adaptation by concrete (hands on) activity and experimentation.

7.1 Theoretical and Methodological Shortcomings

Further work should integrate insights from contemporary theories of collaborative learning to enrich the conceptual framework for knowledge adaptation. We have used Piaget's notions of assimilation and accommodation that focus on knowledge adaptation at the individual level, but our data and methods for knowledge adapta-tion are discursive and focus on situations of collaborative learning. These two shortcomings can be addressed in the following ways: (1) extend the theoretical framework with concepts and models for knowledge adaptation as a social process (e.g. collaborative inquiry models; from ontogenetic to sociogenetic development), and (2) extend the researchers' toolbox with methods for capturing knowledge adaptation at the individual level, such as to identify students' prior knowledge and differences in prior and new knowledge as a result of flexible tool mediation (EUD) and instructor's facilitation (e.g. pre and posttests; treatment and control groups).

7.2 Technology Improvements

(1) Compare two conditions of object modification (in-place and sandbox) in order to determine the optimal balance of ease of use and space for experimentation

without unanticipated consequences, (2) identify the pros and cons of the various ways to support (or not support) direct activation of tailoring tools in EUD-enabled learning environments, (3) compare the "components approach" and the "programming approach" to EUD to identify their respective strengths and weaknesses to (fail to) support constructivist ideals and design principles, and (4) identify the key characteristics of computer tools to support active learning, and (5) compare EUD with other computational approaches toward that end.

Acknowledgements The first author (Mørch) received funding from Dept. of Education, University of Oslo, to explore Second Life as a platform for distance education courses. The second author (Caruso) was a visiting researcher at Dept. of Education, University of Oslo with a 6 months stipend from University of Palermo while the research was carried out. The third author (Hartley) built the virtual campus on a private island provided by WVU's College of Education & Human Services.

References

Andersen, R., & Mørch, A. I. (2009). Mutual development: a case study in customer-initiated software product development. In *Proceedings IS-EUD 2009* (pp. 31–49). Berlin: Springer.

Baker, S. C., Wentz, R. K., Woods, M. M. (2009). Using virtual worlds in education: second life as an educational tool. *Teaching of Psychology, 36*(1), 59–64.

Bandini, S., & Simone, C. (2006). EUD as integration of components off-the-shelf: the role of software professionals' knowledge artifacts. In H. Lieberman, F. Paterno, V. Wulf (Eds.). *End-user development* (pp. 347–369). Berlin: Springer.

Billett, S. (1998). Appropriation and ontogeny: identifying compatibility between cognitive and sociocultural contributions to adult learning and development. *International Journal of Lifelong Education, 17*(1), 21–34.

Boellstorff, T., Nardi, B., Pearce, C., Taylor, T. L. (2012). *Ethnography and virtual worlds: a handbook of methods*. Princeton, NJ: Princeton University Press.

Bruner, J. S. (1961). The act of discovery. *Harvard Educational Review, 31*, 21–32.

Cabitza, F., & Simone, C. (2017). Malleability in the hands of end users. In F. Paternò & V. Wulf (Eds.). *New perspectives in end-user development* (pp. 137–164). Cham: Springer.

Carnevale, P. (1991). *America and the new economy*. San Francisco, CA: Jossey Bass.

Caruso, V., Hartley, M. D., Mørch, A. I. (2015). End-user development in Second Life: meta-design, tailoring, and appropriation. In *Proceedings IS-EUD 2015* (pp. 92–108). Berlin: Springer.

Caruso, V., Mørch, A. I., Thomassen, I., Hartley, M., Ludlow, B. (2014). Practicing collaboration skills through role-play activities in a 3D virtual world. *The new development of technology enhanced learning* (pp. 165–184). Berlin: Springer.

Cobb, P. (1994). Where is the mind? Constructivist and sociocultural perspectives on mathematical development. *Educational Researcher, 23*(7), 13–20.

Conway, M., Audia, S., Burnette, T., Cosgrove, D., Christiansen, K. (2000). Alice: lessons learned from building a 3D system for novices. In *Proceedings CHI 2000* (pp. 486–493). New York, NY: ACM Press.

Cook, L. S., Smagorinsky, P., Fry, P. G., Konopak, B., Moore, C. (2002). Problems in developing a constructivist approach to teaching: one teacher's transition from teacher preparation to teaching. *The Elementary School Journal, 102*(5), 389–413.

Costabile, M. F., Fogli, D., Lanzilotti, R., Mussio, P., Parasiliti Provenza, L., Piccinno, A. (2008). Advancing end user development through meta-design. In *End user computing challenges and technologies: emerging tools and applications* (pp. 143–167). Hershey, PA: IGI Global.

DiSessa, A., & Abelson, H. (1986). Boxer: a reconstructible computational medium. *Communications of ACM, 29*(9), 859–868.

Dourish, P. (2003). The appropriation of interactive technologies: some lessons from placeless documents. *Computer Supported Cooperative Work, 12,* 465–490.

El-Nasr, M. S., & Smith, B. K. (2006). Learning through game modding. *Entertainment Computing, 4*(1), Article 7.

Engeström, Y. (1999). Innovative learning in work teams: analyzing cycles of knowledge creation in practice. In Y. Engeström, R. Miettinen, R.-L. Punamäki (Eds.). *Perspectives on activity theory* (pp. 337–404). Cambridge: Cambridge University Press.

Fischer, G. (1998). Seeding, evolutionary growth and reseeding: constructing, capturing and evolving knowledge in domain-oriented design environments. *Automated Software Engineering, 5*(4), 447–464.

Fischer, G. (2009). End-user development and meta-design: foundations for cultures of participation. In *Proceedings IS-EUD 2009* (pp. 3–14). Berlin: Springer.

Fischer, G., Fogli, D., & Piccinno, A. (2017). Revisiting and broadening the meta-design framework for end-user development. In F. Paternò & V. Wulf (Eds.). *New perspectives in end-user development* (pp. 61–98). Cham: Springer.

Fogli, D., & Provenza, L. P. (2012). A meta-design approach to the development of e-government services. *Journal of Visual Languages and Computing, 23,* 47–62.

Greenberg, S. (1991). Personalizable groupware: accommodating individual roles and group differences. In *Proceedings ECSCW'91* (pp. 17–31). Dordrecht: Kluwer.

Grossman, P. L., Smagorinsky, P., Valencia, S. (1999). Appropriating tools for teaching English: a theoretical framework for research on learning to teach. *American Journal of Education, 108*(1), 1–29.

Grover, S., & Pea, R. (2013). Computational thinking in K-12: a review of the state of the field. *Educational Researcher, 42*(1), 38–43.

Guest, G. (2012). *Applied thematic analysis.* Thousand Oaks, CA: Sage Publications.

Hartley, M. D., Ludlow, B. L., Duff, M. C. (2016) Using Second Life in Teacher Preparation: https://drive.google.com/file/d/0B_iZGKQ6INBxS3hYTHlNbTR3THc/view

Hine, C. (2000). *Virtual ethnography.* London: Sage Publications.

Jordan, B., & Henderson, A. (1995). Interaction analysis: foundation and practice. *The Journal of the Learning Sciences, 4,* 39–103.

Karagiorgi, Y., & Symeou, L. (2005). Translating constructivism into instructional design: potential and limitations. *Educational Technology & Society, 8*(1), 17–27.

Kearns, P. (2001). *Generic skills for the new economy. Australian National Training Authority.* Kensington Park: NCVER Ltd.

Koehne, K., Redmiles, D., Fischer, G. (2011). Extending the meta-design theory: engaging participants as active contributors in virtual worlds. In *Proceedings EUD-2011* (pp. 264–269). Berlin: Springer.

Leontiev, A. N. (1981). *Problems of the development of the mind.* Moscow: Progress Publishers.

Lieberman, H., Paterno, F., Wulf, V. (Eds.) (2006). *End-user development.* Berlin: Springer-Verlag.

Ludwig, T., Dax, J., Pipek, V., & Wulf, V. (2017). A practice-oriented paradigm of end-user development. In F. Paternò & V. Wulf (Eds.). *New perspectives in end-user development* (pp. 23–42). Cham: Springer.

Maloney, J., Resnick, M., Rusk, N., Silverman, B., Eastmond, E. (2010). The Scratch programming language and environment. *Transations on Computing Education, 10*(4), 1–15.

Mørch, A. (1995). Application units: basic building blocks of tailorable applications. In B. Blumenthal, J. Gornostaev, C. Unger (Eds.). *Selected papers from the 5th East-West Conference on Human-Computer Interaction* (pp. 45–62). London: Springer.

Mørch, A. (1997). Three levels of end-user tailoring: customization, integration, and extension. In M. Kyng, & L. Mathiassen (Eds.). *Computers and design in context* (pp. 51–76). Cambridge, MA: MIT Press.

Mørch, A. I. (2011). Evolutionary application development: tools to make tools and boundary crossing. In H. Isomäki, & S. Pekkola (Eds.). *Reframing humans in information systems development* (pp. 151–171). London: Springer.

Mørch, A. I. (2016). End-user development and learning in second life: the "box" as multipurpose building block. In A. Blackwell, B. Plimmer, G. Stapleton (Eds.). In *Proceedings of 2016 IEEE symposium on visual languages and human-centric computing* (pp. 208–212). Washington, DC: IEEE.

Mørch, A. I., Hartley, M. D., Caruso, V. (2015). Teaching interpersonal problem solving skills using roleplay in a 3D virtual world for special education: a case study in second life. In *Proceedings ICALT 2015* (pp. 464–468). Washington, DC: IEEE Computer Society.

Mørch, A. I., Nygård, K. A., Ludvigsen, S. R. (2009). Adaptation and generalisation in software product development. In H. Daniels et al. (Eds.). *Activity theory in practice: Promoting learning across boundaries* (pp. 184–205). London: Taylor & Francis Books.

Mørch, A. I., Stevens, G., Won, M., Klann, M., Dittrich, Y., Wulf, V. (2004). Component-based technologies for end-user development. *Communications of ACM, 47*(9), 59–62.

Mørch, A. I., & Zhu, L. (2013). Component-based design and software readymades. In *Proceedings EUD-2013* (pp. 278–283). Berlin: Springer.

Newman, D., Griffin, P., Cole, M. (1989). *The construction zone: working for cognitive change in school.* Cambridge: Cambridge University Press.

Papert, S. (1980). *Mindstorms: children, computers, and powerful ideas.* New York, NY: Basic Books.

Papert, S., & Harel, I. (1991). *Constructionism.* Norwood, NJ: Ablex Publishing Corporation.

Piaget, J. (1952). *The origins of intelligence in children.* New York, NY: International University Press.

Pipek, V. (2005). *From Tailoring to appropriation support: negotiating groupware usage* (PhD Thesis). University of Oulu, Finland.

Repenning, A., Ioannidou, A., Zola, J. (2000). AgentSheets: end-user programmable simulations. *Artificial Societies and Social Simulation, 3*(3), 14. http://jasss.soc.surrey.ac.uk/3/3/forum/1.html

Repenning, A., Webb, D., Ioannidou, A. (2010). Scalable game design and the development of a checklist for getting computational thinking into public schools. In *Proceedings SIGCSE 2010* (pp. 265–269). New York, NY: ACM.

Roque, R., Rusk, N., Resnick, M. (2016). Supporting diverse and creative collaboration in the Scratch online community. In U. Cress et al. (Eds.). *Mass collaboration and education* (pp. 241–256). Berlin: Springer.

Säljö, R. (1999). Learning as the use of tools: a sociocultural perspective on the human-technology link. In K. Littleton, & P. Light (Eds.). *Learning with computers* (pp. 144–161). New York, NY: Routledge.

Sardone, N. B., & Devlin-Scherer, R. (2008). Teacher candidates' views of a multi-user virtual environment. *Technology, Pedagogy and Education, 17*(1), 41–51.

Scott, S., & Palincsar, A. (2013). Sociocultural Theory. http://www.education.com/reference/article/sociocultural-theory/ (Updated on Jul 15, 2013; read on Des 8, 2016).

Stevens, G. (2017). *Understanding and designing appropriation infrastructure* (PhD thesis), Faculty of Economic Disciplines, University of Siegen, Germany. Forthcoming.

Tchounikine, P. (2017). Designing for appropriation: a theoretical account. *Human-Computer Interaction, 32*(4), 155–195.

Von Glasersfeld, E. (1989). Constructivism in education. In T. Husen, & T. N. Postlethwaite (Eds.). *The international encyclopedia of education vol.* 1, (162–163). Oxford: Pergamon Press.

Vygotsky, L. (1978). *Mind in society: the development of higher psychological processes.* Cambridge, MA: Harvard University Press.

Wertsch, J. V. (1991). *Voices of the mind: a sociocultural approach to mediated action.* Cambridge, MA: Harvard University Press.

Wertsch, J. V. (1998). *Mind as action.* Oxford: Oxford University Press.

Wing, J. M. (2006). Computational thinking. *Communications of ACM, 49*(3), 33.

Won, M., Stiemerling, O., Wulf, V. (2006). Component-based approaches to tailorable systems. In H. Lieberman, F. Paterno, V. Wulf (Eds.). *End-user development* (pp. 115–141). Berlin: Springer.

Wulf, V., & Golombek, B. (2001). Direct activation. A concept to encourage tailoring activities. *Behaviour & Information Technology, 20*(4), 249–263.

Yin, R. K. (2003). *Case study research: design and methods.* London: Sage Publications.

End-User Development for Serious Games

Zeno Menestrina and Antonella De Angeli

Abstract End-User Development (EUD) is a topic that finds application in varied domains but so far it has only been marginally considered in digital games research. However, there are several games that would benefit from a EUD approach, in particular for those games designed for a purpose other than entertainment, such as learning or training. These processes are permeated by large individual variation; as a consequence, the teacher must have a control over the game to use it like any other educational resource. In this chapter we present the state of the art in research on EUD for serious games from academic and industrial perspectives. We discuss a case study investigating the design process and evaluation of the Actors' Programming Environment (APE), a EUD tool for modelling the behaviour of Non-Player Characters (NPCs). Starting from the literature review and empirical experience gathered over a time span of two years, the chapter provides a set of guidelines for the design of EUD tools for serious games, reflecting on their importance and complexity. It concludes with a set of heuristics that may advance research in the topic.

Keywords Serious game · end-user development · high-level programming · interaction design

1 Introduction

Since the first book on End User Development (EUD) (Lieberman, Paternò, & Wulf, 2006), the principles and practices of EUD have found application in several domains, spanning from service engineering (Mehandjiev & De Angeli, 2012;

Z. Menestrina (✉)
University of Trento, Trento, Italy
e-mail: zeno.menestrina@unitn.it

A. De Angeli
University of Lincoln, Lincoln, United Kingdom
e-mail: antonella.deangeli@unitn.it; adeangeli@lincoln.ac.uk

© Springer International Publishing AG 2017   359
F. Paternò, V. Wulf (eds.), *New Perspectives in End-User Development*,
DOI 10.1007/978-3-319-60291-2_14

Namoun, Nestler, & De Angeli, 2010) to healthcare (Martín, Alcarria, Sánchez-Picot, & Robles, 2015; Tetteroo et al., 2015). Surprisingly, EUD practices and tools have only marginally affected research on video games and the rich market surrounding it. As a matter of fact, a few software applications have been developed over the years to supplement professional game editors. Examples are Unreal Engine or CryEngine, which allow users to contribute to the game content and extend the gameplay experience. However, these applications are often similar to the ones used by developers and require a steep learning curve. In other cases, such as Minecraft, the customization is at the core of the game and the modification of the virtual environment is a basic game mechanic. Although these solutions are very effective, the level of customization is limited.

In the wider framework of EUD, scant attention has been devoted to implement simplified tools that are directly aimed at the end-users. Yet, there are several applications of game research and development that would benefit from an EUD approach, in particular games designed for specific purposes other than entertainment. In the last decades, games have been studied not only as entertainment products, but also as specific educational or training tools. This growing field of research is addressed by the label *serious games* (Breuer & Bente, 2010) and has covered many fields of application, from military training (Lim & Jung, 2013) to healthcare (De Mauro, 2011; Göbel, Hardy, Wendel, Mehm, & Steinmetz, 2010; Vidani, Chittaro, & Carchietti, 2010) and emergency management (Chittaro & Ranon, 2009; El Mawas & Cahier, 2013). The discussion has focused on different topics, such as their educational value (Egenfeldt-Nielsen, 2006; Gee, 2007) or development (Khaled & Ingram, 2012; Linehan, Kirman, Lawson, & Chan, 2011), but research on EUD remains a niche. We posit that an increased use of EUD tools in serious games would benefit their efficacy, fostered by the adaptation of the content around the players' skills and teachers' needs (Mehm, Konert, Göbel, & Steinmetz, 2012).

Due to their structure, video games require special attention when considering EUD. According to Schell (2014), video games can be decomposed in four elements: technology, aesthetics, story and mechanics. The *technology* is the artefact mediating the gameplay experience. It is linked to implementation requirements, and usually cannot be easily modified by the user. The *aesthetics* regards the user's sensory experience of the game (e.g., graphics and sounds) and can be open to basic or advanced customisation. Both technology and aesthetics are typical components of software products; what differentiates games are story and mechanics. The *story* relates to the sequence of events that unfold in the game; changing the behaviour of a character or adding a new event in a game level has consequences for the story. The *mechanics* are the procedures of the game; defining new rules or adding new features to the player interaction has consequences on the mechanics.

In this chapter we focus on serious games, which for this writing are considered as simulation environments where people exercise/acquire skills by playing in a virtual word, and the EUD tools that might be provided to the stakeholders to personalize the content of the game according to their requirements. This chapter first introduces the application of EUD to serious games, discussing the challenges and potentials, and underlining the necessity of a EUD approach in this research field. Secondly, following the call made by Tetteroo to collect experiences from EUD deployment studies (Tetteroo et al., 2015), we present a case study on the development of a EUD tool for emergency management training. The experience shared from the case study and the literature review highlights the need for a deeper reflection on the use of EUD principles in the game domain. We propose a set of reflections, in form of guidelines, to support designers to work in an agile way on the design of EUD tools for serious games and aimed at stimulating a discussion and encourage further research on this topic.

The chapter grounds its argument on a review of serious games literature and focuses on the application of EUD in serious game research (Sect. 2). This knowledge is compared with a rich set of data collected during a 2-year industrial research project aimed at the development of an interactive virtual simulation outfitted with a set of tools for the customization of the digital environment (Sect. 3). Reflections on the case study and the design of EUD tools for serious games are elaborated (Sect. 4) and followed by a discussion of results and limitations of our work (Sect. 5). The chapter closes with some final considerations (Sect. 6).

2   Related Work

This section provides a broad and comprehensive vision on software products targeted to the creation and/or modification of game elements by end-users. It focuses on the application of EUD tools and methods, describing solutions related to entertainment games and serious games from a research and development perspective. The section closes with a reflection on the design issues that these tools exhibit.

2.1   Serious Games

Early attempts at creating learning games with software programs (Breuer & Bente, 2010) date back to the 80s. The interest has expanded over the years finding application in different contexts (Dondlinger, 2007; Egenfeldt-Nielsen, 2006) and being identified by a variety of keywords, such as *entertainment education*, *edutainment*, *game-based learning* or *digital game-based learning* (Breuer & Bente, 2010). Even if these keywords describe slightly different products (e.g., edutainment specifically concerns children, whereas entertainment education refers to a larger user population), they all reflect a continuous interest on the instructional application of games that has recently consolidated under the umbrella definition of *serious game*.

Serious games have explicit educational, training or informational purposes, going beyond pure entertainment. This keyword has quite a broad meaning, covering various research directions and applications. Carter and colleagues (2014) note that the most explored branch of games research within human-computer interaction research relates to the *operative paradigm*, defined as games "that leverages knowledge gained from the study of games or play to exert control upon the world, such as encouraging exercise or learning.". Several researchers have studied the efficacy of these tools in relation to their purpose, providing various meta-analysis on the operative studies (Boyle et al., 2016; Sitzmann & Ely, 2010; Wouters & van Oostendorp, 2013). Most notably a vast number of these works has focused on instructional serious games, mostly used in schools. However, these games have been applied to and studied in many other markets. Zayda (Zyda, 2005) provided in 2005 a categorization of serious games in five domains: healthcare, public policy, strategic communication, defence, training and education. Only three years later, Alvarez and Michaud (Alvarez & Michaud, 2008) extended this classification, identifying seven serious games application domains: defence, training and education games, advertising, information and communication, health, culture, and activism.

These studies are useful to identify the various applications of serious games, but also to show their continuous expansion of use. Like video games, serious games have been developed in various directions, for different markets and purposes. An increased use of EUD tools could have many potential benefits, including, but not restricted to, the adaptability of the game content around the players abilities and needs (Mehm et al., 2012), and the direct involvement of the instructors in the design (Torrente, Moreno-Ger, Fernández-Manjón, & Sierra, 2008). EUD tools could encourage wider distribution and increased longevity, by enabling users to update, change or enrich a game according to different pedagogies, technologies, representations, cultures, contexts and learners (Protopsaltis et al., 2011). These tools also could contribute to cost reduction, allowing the repurposing of a product for diverse contexts without constraining the educational value (Torrente et al., 2015).

2.2 EUD for Digital Games

The EUD framework proposed by Liebermann and colleagues (2006), as well as the *end-user modifiability* paradigm proposed by Fisher (Fischer & Girgensohn, 1990), start with the assumption that a software artefact arrives sooner or later at a state in which it is no longer suitable to fully meet the needs of its user. The activities that the user performs may evolve, but these new circumstances lead to new service requirements, and usually the system stays static unless the software developers intervene to extend its features. To solve this problem, Liebermann and Fischer assert that the user should be empowered to master the system. In other words, the software artefact should be modifiable and should include features to allow the end-user to make changes without requiring specific computing expertise. The skills of the user must be taken into account; the system must remain accessible and user-friendly, keeping the investment in learning to a minimum and raising the scope of application to its maximum potential (Fischer, Giaccardi, Ye, Sutcliffe, & Mehandjiev, 2004). In regard to digital games, various tools have been designed to edit the game elements, to modify or expand the digital environment (e.g., adding new mechanics).

2.2.1   Research

Video games are products divided into multiple genres and sub-genres; this heterogeneity is based on variations on story, aesthetics, mechanics and technology (Schell, 2014). It is clear that a game like Candy Crush (a puzzle game played on mobile platforms) has in common with StarCraft (a real time strategy game played on a computer) little more than a shared definition of video game. In serious games this diversification is further accentuated by a game's purpose, which can range from the training of pilots, to the teaching of the multiplication tables to children. Considering all these factors, serious games cannot be attributed to a single type or label, in the same way that research on EUD tools for serious games is diversified by different points of view.

A strain of research investigates the design of EUD tools from a *game-oriented* perspective. The game elements are placed in the foreground, and the EUD tools developed around them. In this sense, the tools are developed ad hoc and could not be applied to any other game without appropriate changes. The most explored type of game is interactive storytelling, which can be roughly defined as a game where the player interacts with a multiple-choice story. As the name suggests, the player "lives" a story, influencing the progression of the narrative while interacting with a virtual world, usually based on the communication with Non-Player Characters (NPCs). NPCs are computer-generated agents that move in the virtual world and whose presence makes the virtual world and the narrative more realistic, challenging and effective. The scope varies from professional training to conflicts management, but these games are largely based on similar mechanics. Works such as Scribe (Medler & Magerko, 2006), Art-E-Fact (Iurgel, 2004), StoryTec (Gobel, Salvatore, & Konrad, 2008; Mehm et al., 2012) and Scenejo (Weiss, Müller, Spierling, & Steimle, 2005) provide development environments for the creation and customization of interactive stories for users with basic programming knowledge. Their use is simple and intuitive, however these platforms allow the development of a pre-defined type of game, and thus fix a strong constraint to the EUD potential.

Within the game-oriented perspective, Hackel and colleagues (Heckel, Youngblood, & Hale, 2009) and Van Est (van Est, Poelman, & Bidarra, 2011) propose EUD tools in the context of professional training. The former proposes Behaviourshop, a character builder for the construction of behavioural models of NPCs. The latter proposes Shai, an editor for event management designed to allow trainers to define chains of events in virtual training (e.g., event 1: the car crash against a wall, event 2: oil starts to leak from the tank) and control it at runtime (scene 3a: The car takes fire and explode, or the trainer decide to activate scenes 3b: the leakage continues, but nothing else happens). Both systems were evaluated with positive feedbacks from the end-users; nonetheless, situated within these fairly elaborate systems, the tools are quite complex, and require a modicum of technical proficiency, e.g., basic understanding of Artificial Intelligences (AIs).

Tetteroo and colleagues (2015) experimented with EUD to provide a personalized experience in the physical world while applying serious games to physiotherapy rehabilitation. Their study shows interesting results; however, the focus is not on the tool but on users, highlighting issues such as the lack of confidence in using content generated by others. Even if their research applies to a quite different technological environment – tangible interfaces – compared to the previous studies, the design of the EUD tool is oriented to a specific game and a specific purpose.

Another strain of research investigates the design of EUD tools from a *tool-oriented* perspective. The focus is not on the customization of a specific game, but on the structure of the EUD tool and its use for multiple applications. In this regard, Lagerstorm and colleagues (Lagerström, Soute, Florack, & Markopoulos, 2014) propose a development kit for simple tangible outdoor games (e.g., enhanced tag game) focussing on the customization and the player interaction on the physical objects. The customization system is related to a particular design space, but without tying the work of users to a single application. The design is *tool-oriented*, placing the game in the background and emphasising the EUD properties; the game is designed accordingly.

In this regard, Protopsaltis et al. (2011) proposes the mEditor, a tool for repurposing scenario-based games. With mEditor the user can manage most of the game content as *black boxes*, and use the blocks to create modified scenarios to fit individual needs and situations. As with EUD in interactive storytelling, the specificity of use restricts the richness of customization. This is not necessarily a negative design aspect; it is the responsibility of the designers to find a right balance between the skills and needs of end users. An example in this regard is Mokap (Torrente et al., 2015), successor of e-Adventure (Torrente, Del Blanco, Marchiori, Moreno-Ger, & Fernández-Manjón, 2010; Torrente et al., 2008), that offers a complete development environment for educational games, providing advanced EUD tools to the user, yet keeping the system easy to use. Another product with a similar purpose is AgentCubes (Ioannidou, Repenning, & Webb, 2009), that offers a development environment and a simplified visual programming language to the players.

Depending on the application, EUD tools for serious games can integrate high-level programming languages, leveraging a common research interest into new user-friendly development paradigms (Paternò, 2013). High-level programming languages differentiate from EUD as they are usually aimed at the development of complete programs and not to the partial customization of a product. The use of high-level programming languages in EUD tools for serious games depends on the needs, and abilities, of the users. If we take a simple example, such as changing the colour palette of the game, this can be achieved via a one-click wizard or single page where colours are set. Using a high-level language to change colours would increase the complexity without providing particular benefits. On the other hand, the modification of an NPC's behaviour could require a deeper level of customization, which might be facilitated by the use of a (more or less complex) programming language. In general, high-level abstractions aim at providing tools with an expressiveness similar to the one offered by more technical products, but requiring a lower cognitive load. The design of these tools is oriented towards end users and their capabilities. Two leading products in the game domain are Scratch (Resnick et al., 2009; Resnick & Rosenbaum, 2013) developed at the MIT with the objective of exposing children to computing through a modular programming language, and developed by Lego to program the robots of the Mindstorm series, also targeted at children. These products are grounded in comprehensive studies on the design of high-level interactions. The classical programming approach is replaced by a modular structure, and the division into categories and colours makes navigation between modules clearer, to aid users in building their mental model of the language.

2.2.2 Development

In contemporary video game industry, diverse authoring tools are on offer for editing virtual environments, e.g., constructing new levels, modifying NPC behaviour and even changing the rules of a game. However, compared to the wide choice of video games, those that implement some sort of EUD features represent a small percentage. The most popular game series usually allow for the creation, editing and sharing of mods. Mods can be defined as formal or functional changes to a video game (e.g., new game levels, characters and quests, and also new mechanics) created by professionals or by gamers. Examples of authoring tools include the Unreal Engine, CryEngine, F.E.A.R. Software Development Kit or The Elder Scrolls Construction Set. These development environments provide features that are similar to the ones used by the game developers. The interaction approach is low-level and the complexity of these tools requires strong knowledge of programming and advanced topics such as AI architecture. For this reason, passionate users, willing to acquire a full understanding of the tools in order to extend the game according to their own desires, are the primary users. Players with limited programming knowledge use mods developed by the most expert members of a game community. Generally, the design of these tools is not fully in line with the principles of EUD. The tools allow appropriation by a user only if she is willing to learn how to use their complex functionalities. There is no mediation between the potential of the tool (i.e., what the player can do on the game content) and its simplicity of use; the user is forced directly from the role of player into the role of programmer.

In other cases, customization is one of the basic mechanics of a game. In games such as Minecraft, Scribblenauts or DayZ the modification of the game world is one of the main features, allowing the player to add new elements to enrich the virtual world. They are simpler to use in comparison to the game editors previously described, but the level of customization is also drastically reduced. A player can usually add new game elements, such as buildings or vehicles, but she has no control over more complex aspects of the game, such as changing the behaviour of a specific NPC or adjusting a particular game mechanic (e.g., setting the running speed of the main character). An exception is Minecraft that can also be used as a hybrid between a game and a development environment: the game is a simplified development environment that allows the creation of new content that goes beyond the scope of the game itself (e.g., users were able to create working Turing machines). Whatever the capabilities of the tools provided, it is clear that the type and quality of results achieved by users depends on their desire to learn and practice the most complex tools provided by the system.

Serious games that provide authoring tools have similar usability problems. Some products only allow the setting of certain parameters of the system (e.g., the difficulty of the training session). This simplifies the interaction with the tool but also makes the virtual environment rather static. In other cases, the available authoring tools are particularly rich, but their subsequent complexity makes it difficult for the end-user to build a clear mental model of the actions made on the system. XVR Sim, for example, is a virtual reality software aimed at training operational and tactical skills of safety and security professionals. The product provides a trainer with all the elements to set up a training scenario, like placing objects in the environment (e.g., vehicles and human avatars), setting animations and managing specific events (e.g., if a player enters the room, then turn on the light). However, XVR lacks an automatic control on the game; if a user wants to define the behaviour of a NPC or a decisional tree for the game events, these must be simulated manually. For example, if the trainer wants a NPC to move to a particular place under specific circumstances (e.g., if you see a fire, then reach the emergency exit and find help, else proceed on your tasks), she has to move it by hand because the system will not automatically check the state of the world. Overall, the interface of XVR allows easy manipulation of the basic game elements, but it has a quite complex interaction for a deeper control on the system.

VBS2 Behaviour Modeling Discovery Machine is another example of a serious game with authoring tools. Aimed at the preparation of the army for the management of terrorist attacks in urban conflict zones, this product is provided with a series of interfaces for modelling the behaviour of NPCs. The interaction is limited to the setting of a long list of parameters that the user can customize for a specific NPC. Using dropdown lists as the core interaction simplifies the use of the interface. The user is guided extensively in the setting of the behavioural model and the parameters are constrained to the values proposed by the system. While this basic interaction simplifies use, it limits the customization in that the complexity of the final result, a list of dozens of parameters, makes it difficult for the end-user to link it to the constructed model.

2.2.3 Reflections

A common problem to various EUD systems for serious games concerns the *balance of language*, an expression that does not specifically refer to a programming language, but to the overall functionalities proposed by the system. The balance of language concerns the issues related to designing tools that are sufficiently expressive yet ease to use. This concept can be connected to the gentle slope of MacLean and colleagues (1990) that correlated the tailoring mechanisms of the system to the skills needed to use them. The balance of language underlines the risk of creating a EUD tool that places users in a position of the slope not suited to their skills, negatively (easy tool, but little expression) or positively (expressive tool, but too technical). In considering this balance, several questions arise: how rich is the language of the tool? Is it rich enough to allow a sufficient level of customization for the user? Is it too rich, making the interaction complex for a non-technical user? These questions summarize a fundamental dilemma in the development of EUD tools.

The research described in the literature review introduced this dilemma. The interactive storytelling approach (Gobel et al., 2008; Iurgel, 2004; Medler & Magerko, 2006; Weiss et al., 2005) proposed fairly simple interfaces, but these strongly limit the outcomes of the user interaction. More technical tools, such as Shai and BehaviorShop (van Est et al., 2011; Heckel et al., 2009), allow a higher degree of customization, but they also require an in-depth learning of the system. In other cases, such as Scratch (Resnick et al., 2009; Resnick & Rosenbaum, 2013), and even Minecraft, the proposed systems are simple and versatile. However, when the user acquires in-depth knowledge she can obtain more complex results, but the interaction is much less efficient as compared to more technical tools (e.g., Scratch can be recommended for the introduction to programming, but environments such as Unity3D are more efficient for the development of digital games).

The literature review suggests an interest in research and development for providing tools that allow the users to become "authors" of the game they play. Overall, the design of these products lacks a solid foundation, in part caused by the limited nature of research, which leaves many uncertainties and wide margin for action. As Tetteroo (2015) suggests, there is a need to expand this discussion and bring new studies on EUD tools for serious games. The collection of new empirical evidence will raise the discussion to a higher level, elaborating on the general principles that inform the design of these tools. We contribute to this challenge with a case study focussed on the design of a EUD tool for the customization of the behaviour of NPCs in simulations aimed at emergency management training.

3 Case Study

Our case study concerns the Plausible Representation of Emergency Situations for Training Operations (PRESTO), an industrial research project aimed at training professionals in the context of emergency management (Busetta, Ghidini, Pedrotti, De Angeli, & Menestrina, 2014). The aim of PRESTO was to build a platform for the development of serious games in the form of interactive virtual simulations. The platform had to be enriched with a set of EUD tools to tailor the game according to particular training objectives for the purpose of improving re-use and adaption. In this type of serious game the training sessions involve two main stakeholders: the trainers and the trainees. The former are managers of the game, who set the goals and monitor the gameplay sessions; the latter are players who interact with the virtual environment to accomplish training goals.

The EUD tools designed for PRESTO were aimed at defining the story of the training sessions, through the management of the chain of events (e.g., if "Firefighter Samantha" does not check in time for gas leaks, there will be an explosion) and the behaviour of the characters (e.g., "Doctor John" panics while seeing the fire). An AI controlled the virtual environment, and the instructor was the director of the game. The EUD tools allowed defining the progression of the events in the scenario and the behaviour of the NPCs that populated it. Once the parameters were set, the AI staged the training session.

We participated in this project as design researchers in two phases. The first was focussed on the development of a EUD prototype for the customization of the behaviour of the NPCs populating the virtual environment. The second phase started approximately one year later, when we were tasked with the evaluation of the tool, which since our proposal had undergone several iterations, expansions and modifications. These two interventions were characterised by generalised difficulty in interacting with real users of the tools, a difficulty that arose from the novelty of the product. In fact, the use of serious games in a training context is still nascent, and although in years their application has indeed increased, a well-defined reference professional figure was not yet established itself in the target market of PRESTO.

3.1   First Intervention – Design of APE

The first intervention for the PRESTO project focussed on the development of a EUD tool for the customization of the behaviour of NPCs used in virtual simulations for emergency management training. The tool was called the Actors' Programming Environment (APE) (Menestrina, De Angeli, & Busetta, 2014). The main goal of this tool was to modify, or even build from scratch, the behavioural models of game NPCs. A behavioural model can be roughly described as the definition of the available sets of actions (what can they do?) and strategies (how do they do it?) of a specific NPC. These behavioural models can be used in the training sessions to fulfil the following goals:

- Meet specific educational goals (e.g., add a wounded character who needs aid);
- Change the environment according to new requirements (e.g., alter the behaviour of "Firefighter Samantha" because emergency tactics of this NPC are not updated);
- Diversify the gameplay experience (e.g., modify the behaviour of some civilians to confront trainees with unexpected events).

The modification of the behaviour of NPCs can have an impact both on story and mechanics of the game. For example, adding a panicked person in a fire simulation can have consequences on the story, because the player will have first to rescue the person and only then deal with the fire. Adding a firefighter (controlled by the system) can have consequences on the mechanics, as the player can exploit this new character to implement cooperative tactics.

The design of APE was based on the metaphor of the theatrical performance. NPCs were considered virtual actors whose actions depended on a script, while the instructor played the role of director. In the game, each NPC was defined by a set of roles and behaviours, depending on the capabilities of the actor. The role defined who was the character and what that character was capable of. The behaviours reflected "how" the character would act in specific circumstances. In this way a character could, for example, have the role of a fireman associated to a heroic behaviour, which would push it to bravely face situations of extreme risk in order to save human lives. That same firefighter could also have a secondary role of paramedic, which would provide the competences for first response to the injured.

APE was divided into two interfaces, the *RoleAssignment* and the *ScriptEditor*. The former was used to define the roles that a certain NPC could play, thus determining possible actions (e.g., the role fireman has the capability of managing a fire, the doctor cannot, but she can examine patients). The latter was used to set the behaviours that would be translated in action plans (e.g., in normal conditions the nurse proceeds with the work routine, consisting of actions A, B and C; in case of fire, the nurse puts into practice the emergency management plan, consisting of actions D, E and F). While the RoleAssignment was represented by a rather simple interface in which the user chose the roles from a list, the ScriptEditor was based on a visual programming language (Fig. 1). The ScriptEditor was visually divided into two parts: on the left there was a toolbox containing various actions, categorized according to their type; on the right side there was the canvas, used to compose the action plans. In order to build elaborated behavioural patterns, the actions in the toolbox were moved into the canvas and interconnected via three basic controls – sequence, selection and iteration – which could be combined to form more complex structures. There was also a fourth structure dealing with the termination condition of behaviours with no specific goal fulfilment (e.g., "wave your hands" has no specific interruption and needs a termination such as "until you see someone coming").

The system facilitated the user interaction by automatically creating the control structures based on how the actions were placed in the canvas. The actions placed on different columns were considered to be sequential; for example, an action in the second column was performed only after those in the first. The actions placed in the same column but different rows were treated as exclusive disjunctions: a conditional structure was immediately created and the condition could be set through a wizard. Termination conditions automatically appeared in the cells in which there were actions with no default termination. The deletion, addition or insertion of an action in the canvas caused the automatic rearrangement of

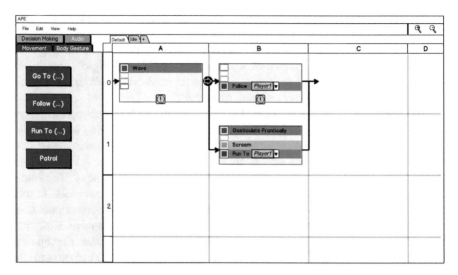

Fig. 1 Example of a simple behaviour using the ScriptEditor: the NPC waves the hands until Player1 approaches the scene (condition set through a wizard); if the NPC is calm she will follow Player1, else she will run to Player1 screaming and gesticulating

the behavioural structure. The only control structures that could not be generated automatically by the system were loops, which needed to be inserted manually by the user. Different wizards managed the setting of specific information, such as conditional and loop structures. Features similar to the ones of common spreadsheets (e.g., add a column, remove a cell) supported the editing of the elements in the canvas. The spreadsheet metaphor was selected after testing various prototypes; the structure in rows and columns was considered the clearest in the representation of flow for behavioural models. Additional functionalities of APE were quite similar to the ones used in spreadsheets (insert a new column, delete a row, copy a cell). In this design we operated under the assumption that recalling the interface of this commonly used system (e.g., Excel, Google Spreadsheet) would have simplified the user interaction and reduced the learning curve.

As an operative example, let us consider the following user scenario: the user wants to add a new character to a training session that entails the evacuation of a burning building. The user opts for a civilian trapped in the building. Using the RoleAssignment, she assigns the character the role of "civilian," able to move around, communicate, and interact with objects, but with no competence in the management of emergencies. At this point the user can create the behavioural model through the ScriptEditor: she places the action "go to [a corner of the room]" in the cell corresponding to the first column and first row. Then she adds the action "go to [door]" in the second column, first row. Finally she places the action "ask for help" in the same column, but in the row below. The system automatically creates a conditional structure between these two columns. The user sets, via a wizard, the condition to reach the door if the character "perceives [a firefighter] [inside the building]," otherwise it will ask for help. To finalize the behaviour the user adds a *do-while* cycle around this last column, with the condition that it will loop until the character "perceives [a firefighter] [inside the building]." With this behaviour the civilian will go to a corner of the room, continuing to ask for help until the arrival of the firefighters in the building, then they will rush to the door. If the user wants to change the behaviour at a later time, she can load the script to the canvas and add or delete elements.

Due to the difficulty in engaging real users, we opted for an expert based evaluation conducted by four interaction designers. Their feedback supported the development of a high-fidelity interactive prototype, which was released as the result of the first design intervention to the PRESTO development team.

3.2   Second Intervention – Evaluation of APE

The second intervention in the PRESTO project started one year after the development of APE. This intervention focused on the evaluation of the tool, which since the original proposal underwent several iterations, expansions and modifications by the development team who added several additional features[1]. In the original version, the termination, conditional and loop controls could be set up with only one condition, while the new version introduced Boolean expressions (AND, OR, NOT), allowing the user to set more conditions for a single control. The system also integrated the management of internal variables: for example, an NPC could detect the other NPCs that were in its field of view and could perform specific actions based on this information. The loop control, previously limited to *do-while*, was extended including *for* loops. Furthermore, the developers implemented the feature to set *triggering events* in the form of control structures used to impose a new behaviour above the one currently active. For example, if the "Firefighter Samantha" saw a wounded civilian, it paused the current behaviour and activated a rescue plan. Finally, the new APE had nested control structures through which a user could create complex structures, for example conditional sub-levels (e.g., if () {if () {} else {}} else {}) or mixed controls (e.g., while () {if () {for () {}}}). These changes made APE a much richer tool, allowing users to have a deeper control on behavioural models. However, it also became a more complex system, and where the first version required a minimum programming bases, such as knowing the meaning of an *if-then-else* statement, the new version of APE required a more developed understanding of programming.

APE was used during the course "Agent-Oriented Software Engineering" at the University of Trento ($N = 25$). The objective was to introduce the students to the PRESTO architecture, expose them to a new application area of serious game, and

---

[1]More details about these features can be found at https://youtu.be/QdEKQ0BeIAA.

test the functionalities of the system. This evaluation approach was chosen for students' background akin to that of the target users. In this regard, the development team identified as pre-requisites for the user a thorough knowledge of emergency management (skills not required for this evaluation phase) and an intermediate programming knowledge. These individuals were characterized by a constant use of computers and by being able to master the standard elements of programming languages, such as control structures and Boolean expressions. The project's goal was the development of a set of new behaviours for different NPCs (2–3 receptionists, 2–3 doctors, 1 nurse) to be used in a light version of the environment provided by PRESTO comprising a virtual simulation of a hospital ward. Starting from default behaviours, the students were required to model the different actors and make them as realistic as possible. We observed students using the APE interface during four lab sessions (each lasting 2 hour). Additionally, we held two extra sessions of tutoring (each lasting 2 hours), one of which included a focus group concerned with the experience with the system (a summary of the activities is shown in Table 1). Students were informed that their performance would be evaluated as part of the course-work, which prompted them to be extremely proactive in asking for changes to the interfaces, which were implemented on the fly. The pivotal objective of the entire course and the meetings that followed was the collection of feedback, suggestions and detection of bugs. Communication took place both face to face during the course and through continuous and rapid email exchanges with the students. This mode of communication enabled a dynamic re-design and release of seven updates of the tool during the evaluation period.

Table 1 Summary of the activities organized by researchers and developers during the course

Date	Activity	Description
5/6/12-May-2016	Introduction to JACK and CoJACK (Ritter et al., 2012)	The developers provided the theoretical basis related to the architecture of the AI of PRESTO.
13-May-2016	Introduction to APE	The researchers introduced the basic structure of APE.
19/20/26/27-May-2016	Lab session	Researchers and developers provided a manual for the use of APE and PRESTO, and the interfacing of the two. The students worked individually or in groups; researchers and developers provided support and collected feedbacks for the improvement of the system.
28/29-May-2016	Tutoring and focus group	The researchers organized two tutoring sessions in order to support the students in the advanced phase of the course and collected additional feedbacks during a focus group.
2-June-2016	Deadline	Submission of the coursework.

4   Analysis

The course and subsequent meetings provided many insights that emerged from the students' experiences. After collecting the main feedbacks and implementing changes to the system we could identify three different categories of challenges:

- *interaction*: the problem was related to the APE interface and the interaction with its components;
- *semantic*: the problem was related to the interpretation of the meaning of a particular element of the system or a specific action on the system;
- *integration*: the problem was related to gaps in the integration of APE in the PRESTO architecture and in perceiving the two modules as parts of a single system.

The users highlighted some positive aspects and criticalities. The focus of this section is not to evaluate the effectiveness of the product, which was generally perceived as simpler than classic programming languages but still far from being a EUD tool, but to present our reflections on the collected data. This information has been processed in form of guidelines applicable to the design of other EUD tools. We processed the user data with an analysis based on design guidelines coming from the works of Nielsen (Nielsen, 1994), identified with the label NIE, Namoun et al. (2010), identified with the label NAM, McIver & Conway (1996), identified with the label MCI, and Green & Petre (1996), identified with the label GRE. We clustered the information collected from labs and tutoring hours according to a set of principles provided in these works and we examine them in the next subsections. Table 2 shows the relation between our guidelines and these works. As previously discussed in the related work session, the heterogeneity of the game context makes it difficult to produce frameworks or models that are valid for every possible application, and these guidelines serve solely as reflection points to support design.

4.1   Simplify the Semantics

The terminology and language used within a EUD tool should help the users understand the meaning of their actions without requiring computing knowledge. This heuristic implies that the language should not be technical, favouring domain-specific terminologies to computing-orientated ones. This is a general design principle applicable to many EUD applications that are often developed by the software authors to interface the computing codes they have implemented. However, as modern serious games increasingly tend to introduce powerful AI engines in their architectures, the need for a simple semantics increases in relevance. The rhetoric of AI research unfolds on an explicit parallel between human

Table 2 The relation between the proposed guidelines and related works

Proposed guidelines	Related works
Simplify the semantics	User language and terminology – NAM
	Match between system and the real world – NIE
	Closeness of mapping – GRE
Balance the syntax	Make the syntax readable and consistent – MCI
	Error prevention – NIE
	Error-proneness – GRE
Support the understanding of errors (and recover from them)	Help users recognize, diagnose, and recover from errors – NIE
	Provide better error diagnosis – MCI
Provide a small and orthogonal set of feature	Provide a small and orthogonal set of feature – MCI
Design a coherent system	Visibility of system status – NIE
	Premature commitment – GRE
Balance the abstraction level	Abstraction gradient – GRE
Balance between difficulty and motivation	Balance between difficulty and motivation – NAM
Provide a complete documentation	System help – NAM
	Help and documentation – NIE

and machine intelligence and behaviour. This parallel manifests in the language used in AI, which reflects a strong anthropomorphic metaphor. However, AI research and development is highly technical and concepts such as behavioural models, roles and goals, can be of little meaning to untrained users.

Throughout the evaluation, we witnessed several problems that specifically addressed the semantic level, as the interface exposed the complexity of the AI architecture directly to the user. Due to this characteristic, users found it hard to understand some logic, operations, and functionalities. A key example was linked to the system ontology, which successfully conveyed knowledge to the machine while carrying little meaning to human beings. The machine-readable ontology was directly exposed in the interface and instigated important communication breakdowns. In the design of the first iteration of APE (Fig. 1) we paid attention to using a simple and intuitive language, but the toolbox of the last version of APE was populated by goals that had overly technical (e.g., "start gone to entity" or "get location id") or general (e.g., "perform") labels. Even if these terms had a specific meaning to the system, the need for a revision of the language became clear. One possible solution for our case would be a double vocabulary for the system providing different labels according to the use, one that is hidden from the user and used by the system and the developers, and another that is visible in the interface and defined according to language understandable by the user.

4.2 Balance the Syntax

McIver writes that the "language should aim to boost the conceptual signal and reduce the syntactic noise" (McIver & Conway, 1996). In the development of EUD tools, a solution would be the use of simple and limited subsets of a language, aimed at "a careful design which prevents a problem from occurring in the first place" (Nielsen, 1994). However, as the balance of language underlines, the expressiveness is necessarily related to the complexity of the overall system. An example of this issue can be found in Scratch. Scratch is based on a visual language, in which the various elements of the language are represented by blocks that can be dragged on a canvas and wedged according to certain syntactic criteria (e.g., logical operators are characterized by a specific shape and can be placed only in cells that can receive that shape). This "puzzle box" system constrains the user interaction, preventing any syntactical error in the creation of the code (i.e., if the placement of a block goes against the syntactic criteria, the block cannot be dropped in the canvas). This approach, however, is not efficient for writing complex programs and can result in very elaborate structures of blocks that are more difficult to read than other representations of code.

In APE, the spreadsheet metaphor implicitly constrained the interaction, reducing the possibility to make mistakes and simplifying the language. These aspects were greatly appreciated by our users, and yet this penalized the expressiveness. A balance between richness, simplicity and constraints should be taken into account at the design phase of any EUD tool. Moreover, this balance should not be set a priori by designers and developers, but studied in relation to the needs of users and focussed on the required manipulation of the system. The users may need to change the game elements in a precise and detailed way (e.g., changing structural mechanics), or calibrate only a few parameters and these diverse options would effect different consequences for the design.

4.3 Support the Understanding of Errors (and Recover from Them)

The users must be able to easily understand whether they are making errors and be able to recover from them. The design of EUD systems should take particular note of this point, especially given a lack of technical training of users. The system should prevent errors, which could be done by constraining the interaction to a simple set of actions. When such constraints are not possible, for example when a simple set of actions would not provide enough customization, the system should give the user a clear overview of the error and the reasons for that error. Similarly, the system should allow for quick and intuitive means to remedy errors. Furthermore, the quantity of information available to the user should be proportional to the type of interaction. It should not provide overly technical details, as these would be beyond the effective knowledge of the users and largely unnecessary for a EUD approach. Conversely, the notifications must not be too abstract, to avoid preventing the user from maintaining a clear understanding of their actions.

One example in APE is the design of the deletion features, which proved difficult. During the evaluation the users requested to be able to remove multiple blocks at once. This improvement would have increased the efficiency of editing, yet it would also have increased the risk of undesired deletions. One way to solve this issue was to provide an *undo/redo* functionality and allow the users to navigate between the last actions on the system. Another feature that was added was a notification system used to inform the users about any possible missing data, in which case a pop-up would appear providing information about the problem (e.g., information missing for the goal "start gone to location" at cell B1).

4.4   Provide a Small and Orthogonal Set of Feature

The language should have a small set of non-overlapping features, with distinct syntactic representations, a factor that is particularly important to avoid ambiguity. Every element should have a specific unambiguous meaning, and any overlapping features should be carefully analysed (e.g., keyboard shortcuts are usually allowed even if the same effects can be obtained through different interactions). This heuristic is related with 4.2 and is particularly advisable for the design of a lean language, where the overall set of features is minimized in an effort to reduce the cognitive load for the user.

An example of this is related to the deletion feature. The delete of the items inside the spreadsheet of APE could be done through right click, and selecting "delete" from a context menu, or a combination of "X" and "left click." While the former was positively evaluated, the latter was found less intuitive and too quick as it allowed users to rapidly delete every item with the potential to initiate undesired deletions.

4.5   Design a Coherent System

A primary design guideline states that the user should be able to easily understand the status of the system (Nielsen, 1994). This requirement can be complex when designing EUD for serious games, as they tend to be developed as additional interfaces on top of a complex architecture. The EUD tools consist of interfaces used by the players to interact with the game: the input is on the tool, but the real output is on the game. If the tool and the game are not well integrated, the users can struggle understanding the cause-effect relation of their actions on the system.

This then can lead to the undesired need to drastically change the work done on the tool (e.g., the user assumes to have created a specific behaviour, but the NPC acts in a completely different way). A seamless integration of authoring tools and the actual system should be a must in order to help the user achieve, and maintain a complete overview.

Several users during the evaluation remarked on the difficulty of understanding the causes of NPCs acting differently compared to their expectations. The main reason was the "gap" between APE and the PRESTO architecture that played the virtual simulation. In fact, the two were not perfectly integrated and this made it difficult to understand the status of the overall system. As a result, when the NPCs did not behave according to the expectations, it was not clear whether this was due to the programming of the behaviour via APE, or the execution of the behaviour in the virtual simulation. This issue also increased the risk of a premature commitment, obliging the users to develop the complete behaviour of the NPCs before any possible testing.

4.6 Balance the Abstraction Level

Green and Perte (1996) suggest focusing the design on the level of abstraction of the system, considering the possibility to encapsulate details. Encapsulating elements of the system for a more high-level management means also to hide details from the users. The question then arises concerning what level of control the user needs to have over the system.

An example of this requirement can be seen in the nesting system introduced in the second version of APE. In the first version, the control structures could be used in a linear way, without being able to combine them into complex structures (e.g., a *for* loop enveloping an *if-then-else* condition, with another *for* loop inserted in the *else* branch). To allow more control over the system, the second version of APE enabled users to generate sub-canvas and create endless combinations of control structures. This change brought a clear advantage in the level of customization of behaviours, but it greatly complicated the understanding of the outcome of the system.

4.7 Balance between Difficulty and Motivation

Building on MacNeal, Namoun et al. (2010) suggests a "gentle slope of difficulty" (MacLean et al., 1990) meaning that the users should be taught new features in a progressive way. The user should not have access to advanced actions without having first acquired the basic skills, and interaction with the system should be gradual to reduce the possibility of error and avoid an overabundance of information. Considering the complexity of serious games, the customization of the game content could potentially be demanding.

APE allowed using every feature from the beginning that often caused misunderstandings. The users were able to do everything immediately, however sometimes it was easier to undertake an action than to understand its meaning and effect on the system. Working on an AI platform, this quick interaction was risky. A possible solution could be designing the system with different levels of editing. For example, dividing between "basic" and "advanced" features would help the users in their progression through the interaction with the system.

4.8   Provide a Complete Documentation

The user should be supported in understanding and using the system. In the previous heuristics we particularly emphasized the need for a lean design. However, when EUD tools cannot be simple, it is necessary to provide a clear documentation, with a level of detail proportional to the use (e.g., a digest version of the architecture of the AI).

In our case, even if every user defined APE as "easy to use," their main issue was to understand the structure of the AI they were using. Even as every student was able to use APE, many struggled to fully understand what they could do with it (e.g., they had some issues in understanding the meaning of the different goals they could use to populate the canvas). From this, it becomes clear that a complete documentation on the overall system is another fundamental aspect.

5   Discussion

Serious games and EUD tools are complex systems, the design of which is anything but trivial. If we consider the objectives of the two systems, to create digital games for training or learning purposes and allow non-technical users to modify these games, the problem is very delicate. This issue does not only concern the complexity of the systems, but also their diversity. When we talk about serious games, we do not refer to a specific product, but applications that can be diversified depending on the type (e.g., virtual simulation or puzzles) and purpose of use (e.g., military training or math teaching) (Breuer & Bente, 2010). In addition, it is important to consider that many elements characterize video games (Schell, 2014). Other media, such as movies, have aesthetics, a story and a technological support, but have no mechanics. Other software applications have aesthetics, technological support, but no story; they have mechanics, but usually not complex as in video games where mechanics tend to influence not only the user interaction, but also the general behaviour of the system and the game rules. All these factors affect the design of video games, and therefore also any EUD tool connected to them.

Compared to other application domains, serious games are characterized by a wider variety of perspectives. Technology, aesthetics, story and mechanics are always part of the design, making the customization of serious games a complex and delicate process. For example, the mechanics of a game may involve several factors, from the general rules (e.g., fire extinguishers can be used to extinguish the fire) to the behaviour of the NPCs (e.g., an unconscious person can not use a fire extinguisher), and have varied levels of detail (e.g., a fire extinguisher lasts fifteen). In addition, the mechanics can have an impact on other dimensions, such as the story (e.g., civilians are now capable of performing first aid), going to affect the whole gaming experience in different ways. Defining how, and to what extent, users can change these aspects has no simple solution, which depends on many factors, such as the context of use, the type of game and players.

The case presented in this chapter is but one of many potential applications of EUD tools in the serious games domain, yet it reveals a number of interesting design challenges. The PRESTO case study exemplifies the difficulty of finding a right balance of the language. The first design intervention produced a relatively simple tool, which nevertheless had several limitations in the customization as compared to the tools used by the developers, who felt the need to expand it. The second version of the software provided much richer functionalities, but the users highlighted issues related to the technical expertise required to handle them. The general feeling was that the new version of APE moved our users from *tinkerers* ("workers who enjoys exploring the computer system, but may not fully understand it" MacLean et al., 1990) in the direction of becoming programmers of the system. Finding a fair balance between the richness of the language and ease of use is not an immediate process and requires a clear understanding of the context and how the tool is used in practice.

The design of video games, even more than other interactive software, provides great possibilities in the development of EUD tools, allowing the modification of a wider set of elements. Moreover, considering the serious purpose, this kind of systems requires customization features to adjust its content to the training or educational needs. Given this complexity, defining generic rules that could be applied to each case study may not be possible at the current state of the knowledge on the subject, limited as it is compared to the breadth of the application domain. Our case study focused on the customization of behavioural models in the context of emergency management. It is debatable to what extent our reflections will be of value for similar tools applied to different serious games (e.g., military training). Such a question applies not only to the purpose of the game, but also that of the EUD tool: would the same considerations still hold for the design of a different customization tool? These questions can likely be answered, but only through a broader discussion on the topic, one that collects other experiences and efforts to define generally applicable solutions. In this regard, our guidelines are not aimed at providing a definitive set of rules for the design of EUD tools for serious games, but to structure the reflections, to contribute to the discussion and expand the research made by the academic community on this topic.

5.1 Limitations

The PRESTO case study had a major limitation concerning the involvement of users. This limitation is likely to emerge in other projects, particularly when the development outcome is an artefact that is not yet used in current working practices, and for which there is not an established professional figure to act as informer. In the PRESTO project we put in place several strategies to counteract the lack of direct user involvement, by relying for example on expert designers and user-surrogates in the forms of students. The involvement of students could not be considered equal to an evaluation with the end users, but it certainly led to important results that informed the re-design of APE. In fact, the feedbacks clearly expressed that, even if the tool was found to be relatively simple, the design partially deviated from the principles of EUD, placing it in a middle ground between those used by developers and those used by novices.

What was particularly interesting in our experience was the definition of a new end user by the development team. At the end of the first design intervention we built a tool aimed at providing professional trainers with limited computing knowledge the possibility to adapt a simulation scenario. In the following year, the development team enriched this tool and they were well aware it no longer suited the original target users. At this point, the users were represented by a sub-set of the original target, which was expected to be computing literate and domain expert, and training was proposed to enable them to execute this role.

This fact highlighted a clear issue in the relationship between developers and designers. Even if the former were familiar since the beginning with the design of APE, their decisions were strongly influenced by technical requirements of PRESTO (e.g., implementation of a new AI for the management of game events and the behaviours of NPC). The principles of EUD were not a main concern in the development of their part of the project, pushing the overall design in the direction of an authoring tool. APE gradually lost part of its purpose, as it was not designed for a general user, but for a sub-set of the reference group.

6   Conclusion

The chapter focused on EUD and its potential application in the context of serious games. The development of customization tools for serious games targeted to non-technical users can have significant benefits, allowing the modification of the game elements in accordance with the training or the educational goals. The academic community has shown interest on the topic, but the discussion boast few examples compared to the wide possibilities of application. The discussion on the subject is complex and more studies are essential.

In this regard, we presented an analysis of the literature, broadening to the work proposed by the game industry in an effort to provide a complete overview.

Moreover, we presented a case study, aimed at the development of a tool for the customization of AIs for NPCs populating virtual simulations in the context of emergency management. Where our previous work provided a general description of PRESTO (Busetta et al., 2014) and a preliminary study of APE (Menestrina et al., 2014), this chapter focused on the design of the tool, analysing pros and cons in regard to the EUD objectives. Combining the work of other researchers, from the heuristics of Nielsen (1994) to the design recommendations by Namoun (2010), we structured the reflections on the case study providing a set of guidelines aimed at highlighting critical elements and offering various suggestions on the development of EUD tools for serious games.

References

Alvarez, J., & Michaud, L. (2008). *Serious games. Advergaming, edugaming, training and more.* Montpellier, France: IDATE.

Boyle, E. A., Hainey, T., Connolly, T. M., Gray, G., Earp, J., Ott, M., et al. (2016). An update to the systematic literature review of empirical evidence of the impacts and outcomes of computer games and serious games. *Computers & Education, 94*, 178–192.

Breuer, J. S., & Bente, G. (2010). Why so serious? On the relation of serious games and learning. *Eludamos. Journal for Computer Game Culture, 4*(1), 7–24.

Busetta, P., Ghidini, C., Pedrotti, M., De Angeli, A., Menestrina, Z. (2014). Briefing virtual actors: a first report on the PRESTO project. In *Proceedings of the AI and games symposium at AISB*. London, UK: SSAISB.

Carter, M., Downs, J., Nansen, B., Harrop, M., Gibbs, M. (2014). Paradigms of games research in HCI: a review of 10 years of research at CHI. In *Proceedings of the first ACM SIGCHI annual symposium on computer-human interaction in play* (pp. 27–36). New York, NY, USA: ACM.

Chittaro, L., & Ranon, R. (2009). Serious games for training occupants of a building in personal fire safety skills. In *Conference in games and virtual worlds for serious applications, VS-GAMES'09* (pp. 76–83). New York, NY, USA: IEEE.

De Mauro, A. (2011). Virtual reality based rehabilitation and game technology. *EICS4Med, 1*, 48–52.

Dondlinger, M. J. (2007). Educational video game design: a review of the literature. *Journal of Applied Educational Technology, 4*(1), 21–31.

Egenfeldt-Nielsen, S. (2006). Overview of research on the educational use of video games. *Digital Kompetanse, 1*(3), 184–213.

El Mawas, N., & Cahier, J.-P. (2013). Towards a knowledge-intensive serious game for training emergency medical services. In *Proceedings of the 10th international conference on information systems for crisis response and management, ISCRAM '13* (pp. 135–139). ISCRAM Conference, Baden-Baden, Germany.

van Est, C., Poelman, R., Bidarra, R. (2011). High-level scenario editing for serious games. In *GRAPP* (pp. 339–346). GRAPP Conference,Vilamoura, Portugal.

Fischer, G., Giaccardi, E., Ye, Y., Sutcliffe, A. G., Mehandjiev, N. (2004). Meta-design: a manifesto for end-user development. *Communications of the ACM, 47*(9), 33–37. doi:10.1145/1015864.1015884.

Fischer, G., & Girgensohn, A. (1990). End-user modifiability in design environments. In *Proceedings of the SIGCHI conference on human factors in computing systems, CHI '90* (pp. 183–192). New York, NY, USA: ACM. doi:10.1145/97243.97272.

Gee, J. P. (2007). *Good video games + good learning: collected essays on video games, learning, and literacy*. New York, NY, USA: Peter Lang.

Göbel, S., Hardy, S., Wendel, V., Mehm, F., Steinmetz, R. (2010). Serious games for health: personalized exergames. In *Proceedings of the international conference on multimedia* (pp. 1663–1666). New York, NY, USA: ACM.

Göbel, S., Salvatore, L., Konrad, R. (2008). StoryTec: a digital storytelling platform for the authoring and experiencing of interactive and nonlinear stories. In *International conference on automated solutions for cross media content and multi-channel distribution, AXMEDIS'08* (pp. 103–110). New York, NY, USA: IEEE.

Green, T. R. G., & Petre, M. (1996). Usability analysis of visual programming environments: a "cognitive dimensions" framework. *Journal of Visual Languages & Computing*, 7(2), 131–174.

Heckel, F.W.P., Youngblood, G. M., Hale, D. H. (2009). BehaviorShop: an intuitive interface for interactive character design. In *AIIDE* (pp. 46-51). AAAI, Palo Alto, CA, USA.

Ioannidou, A., Repenning, A., Webb, D. C. (2009). AgentCubes: incremental 3D end-user development. *Journal of Visual Languages & Computing*, 20(4), 236–251.

Iurgel, I. (2004). From another point of view: art-E-fact. *Technologies for interactive digital storytelling and entertainment* (pp. 26–35). Berling, Heidelberg, Germany: Springer-Verlag.

Khaled, R., & Ingram, G. (2012). Tales from the front lines of a large-scale serious game project. In *Proceedings of the SIGCHI conference on human factors in computing systems, CHI '12* (pp. 69–78). New York, NY, USA: ACM.

Lagerström, S., Soute, I., Florack, Y., Markopoulos, P. (2014). Metadesigning interactive outdoor games for children: a case study. In *Proceedings of the 2014 conference on interaction design and children, IDC '14* (pp. 325–328). New York, NY, USA: ACM.

Lieberman, H., Paternò, F., Klann, M., Wulf, V. (2006). End-user development: an emerging paradigm. In H. Lieberman, F. Paternò, V. Wulf (Eds.). *End user development* (pp. 1–8). Netherlands: Springer.

Lieberman, H., Paternò, F., Wulf, V. (2006). *End user development (human-computer interaction series)*. New York: Springer-Verlag New York, Inc.

Lim, C.-W., & Jung, H.-W. (2013). A study on the military serious game. *Advanced Science and Technology Letters*, 39, 73–77.

Linehan, C., Kirman, B., Lawson, S., Chan, G. (2011). Practical, appropriate, empirically-validated guidelines for designing educational games. In *Proceedings of the SIGCHI conference on human factors in computing systems, CHI '11* (pp. 1979–1988). New York, NY, USA: ACM.

MacLean, A., Carter, K., Lövstrand, L., Moran, T. (1990). User-tailorable systems: pressing the issues with buttons. In *Proceedings of the SIGCHI conference on Human factors in computing systems, CHI '90* (pp. 175–182). New York, NY, USA: ACM.

Martín, D., Alcarria, R., Sánchez-Picot, Á., Robles, T. (2015). An ambient intelligence framework for end-user service provisioning in a hospital pharmacy: a case study. *Journal of Medical Systems*, 39(10), 1–10.

McIver, L., & Conway, D. (1996). Seven deadly sins of introductory programming language design. In *Proceedings of the international conference software engineering: education and practice, SE:EP '96* (pp. 309–316). Washington, DC, USA: IEEE.

Medler, B., & Magerko, B. (2006). Scribe: A tool for authoring event driven interactive drama. In *Technologies for interactive digital storytelling and entertainment* (pp. 139–150). Berling, Heidelberg, Germany: Springer-Verlag.

Mehandjiev, N., & De Angeli, A. (2012). End user mashups: analytical framework. In *Proceedings of the 2nd international workshop on adaptive services for the future internet and 6th international workshop on web APIs and service mashups* (pp. 36–39). New York, NY, USA: ACM.

Mehm, F., Konert, J., Göbel, S., Steinmetz, R. (2012). An authoring tool for adaptive digital educational games. In *21st century learning for 21st century skills* (pp. 236–249). Berling, Heidelberg, Germany: Springer-Verlag.

Menestrina, Z., De Angeli, A., Busetta, P. (2014). APE: end user development for emergency management training. In *Sixth international conference of the games and virtual worlds for serious applications, VS-GAMES '14* (pp. 1–4). New York, NY, USA: IEEE.

Namoun, A., Nestler, T., De Angeli, A. (2010). Service composition for non-programmers: Prospects, problems, and design recommendations. In *IEEE 8th European Conference on Web Services (ECOWS)*, 123–130.

Nielsen, J. (1994). Heuristic evaluation. In *Usability inspection methods* (pp. 25–62). Fremont, CA, USA: Nielsen Norman group.

Paternò, F. (2013). End user development: survey of an emerging field for empowering people. In *ISRN software engineering*. London, UK: Hindawi.

Protopsaltis, A., Auneau, L., Dunwell, I., de Freitas, S., Petridis, P., Arnab, S., et al. (2011). Scenario-based serious games repurposing. In *Proceedings of the 29th ACM international conference on design of communication, SOGDOC '11* (pp. 37–44). New York, NY, USA: ACM.

Resnick, M., Maloney, J., Monroy-Hernández, A., Rusk, N., Eastmond, E., Brennan, K., et al. (2009). Scratch: programming for all. *Communications of the ACM, 52*(11), 60–67.

Resnick, M., & Rosenbaum, E. (2013). Designing for tinkerability. In *Design, make, play: growing the next generation of STEM innovators* (pp. 163–181). Abingdon-on-Thames, UK: Routledge.

Ritter, F. E., Bittner, J. L., Kase, S. E., Evertsz, R., Pedrotti, M., Busetta, P. (2012). CoJACK: A high-level cognitive architecture with demonstrations of moderators, variability, and implications for situation awareness. *Biologically Inspired Cognitive Architectures, 1*, 2–13.

Schell, J. (2014). *The art of game design: a book of lenses*. San Francisco, CA, USA: Morgan Kaufmann.

Sitzmann, T. (2011). A meta-analytic examination of the instructional effectiveness of computer-based simulation games. *Personnel Psychology, 64*(2), 489–528.

Tetteroo, D., Vreugdenhil, P., Grisel, I., Michielsen, M., Kuppens, E., Vanmulken, D., et al. (2015). Lessons learnt from deploying an end-user development platform for physical rehabilitation. In *Proceedings of the SIGCHI conference on human factors in computing systems, CHI '15* (pp. 4133–4142). New York, NY, USA: ACM.

Torrente, J., Del Blanco, Á., Marchiori, E. J., Moreno-Ger, P., Fernández-Manjón, B. (2010). <e-Adventure>: introducing educational games in the learning process. In *Education engineering, EDUCON* (pp. 1121–1126). New York, NY, USA: IEEE.

Torrente, J., Moreno-Ger, P., Fernández-Manjón, B., Sierra, J. L. (2008). Instructor-oriented authoring tools for educational videogames. In *Eighth IEEE international conference on advanced learning technologies, ICALT'08* (pp. 516–518). New York, NY, USA: IEEE.

Torrente, J., Serrano-Laguna, Á., Fisk, C., O'Brien, B., Alesky, W., Fernández-Manjón, B., et al. (2015). Introducing mokap: a novel approach to creating serious games. In *Proceedings of the 5th international conference on digital health* (pp. 17–24). New York, NY, USA: ACM.

Vidani, A. C., Chittaro, L., Carchietti, E. (2010). Assessing nurses' acceptance of a serious game for emergency medical services. In *Second international conference of the games and virtual worlds for serious applications, VS-GAMES '10* (pp. 101–108). New York, NY, USA: IEEE.

Weiss, S., Müller, W., Spierling, U., Steimle, F. (2005). Scenejo - an interactive storytelling platform. In *Virtual storytelling. Using virtual reality technologies for storytelling* (pp. 77–80). Berlin, Heidelberg, Germany: Springer-Verlag.

Wouters, P., & van Oostendorp, H. (2013). A meta-analytic review of the role of instructional support in game-based learning. *Computers & Education, 60*(1), 412–425.

XVR Sim. http://www.xvrsim.com/. Accessed 1 January 2017.

Zyda, M. (2005). From visual simulation to virtual reality to games. *Computer, 38*(9), 25–32.

Integrating End Users in Early Ideation and Prototyping: Lessons from an Experience in Augmenting Physical Objects

Paloma Díaz, Ignacio Aedo and Andrea Bellucci

Abstract Creating rewarding and resonant user experiences usually requires a *designerly* approach, that is, to explore multiple ideas and later converge to a specific design outcome that can be eventually implemented. Engaging novice designers as well as end users in fuzzy ideation processes can cause participants' discouragement and disengagement when they do not understand the goal of the various design tasks and the contribution of such tasks to the whole development process. To mitigate this problem, we propose two software tools (called CoDICE and ECCE) to support the ideation, design and early prototyping of augmented experiences. The tools make it possible to apply generative techniques to promote creativity whilst providing a virtual space where ideas and designs can be persistently documented and developed further. The creation of physical prototypes is supported to close the loop, thus enabling end users to ideate, design and prototype their own augmented experiences. Tools were tested with end users who valued (i) to have a process flow to follow, (ii) to be able to explore multiples ideas and interrelate them and, finally, (iii) to create their own working prototypes.

Keywords Co-design · software engineering · design thinking · digital cultural heritage

1 Introduction

The current status of ubiquitous and tangible computing is opening a new panorama for interactive applications in different domains, including quotidian activities, health, work, leisure or cultural heritage. Moving the software development

P. Díaz (✉) · I. Aedo · A. Bellucci
Computer Science Department, Universidad Carlos III de Madrid, Madrid, Spain
e-mail: pdp@inf.uc3m.es

I. Aedo
e-mail: aedo@ia.uc3m.es

A. Bellucci
e-mail: andrea.bellucci@uc3m.es

© Springer International Publishing AG 2017
F. Paternò, V. Wulf (eds.), *New Perspectives in End-User Development*,
DOI 10.1007/978-3-319-60291-2_15

to the physical world and integrating tangible objects and wereables make it possible to envision resonant applications that blur the boundaries between the real and the virtual to provide more enjoyable, intrinsically motivating and memorable experiences. To identify what is motivating or memorable for end-users we have to integrate them into the whole development process. Developing such augmented and tangible technologies that intertwine human practices and values, interaction spaces and complex digital artifacts is rather difficult and multifaceted since designers have to envision cohesive interaction ecosystems that augment our capacities and experiences (Buchanan, 1992; Kaptelinin & Nardi, 2006; Simon, 1996; Zimmerman, Forlizzi, & Evenson, 2007). Three agents (namely people, technologies, and spaces) and their interrelationships have to be taken into account to identify affordances and constraints that emerge from the agents and their interaction (Terrenghi, Quigley, & Dix, 2009). Also, understanding how technology can be employed to improve our capacities and our experiences can be considered as a wicked problem that, as defined by Rittel and Weber (1973), doesn't have a unique solution nor a linear way to solve it. When designers are shaping the future and not solving a well-defined problem, requirements are unclear and evolve over time as more powerful technologies become available and end users become familiar with them. End users and stakeholders might also have competing values and priorities. For instance, within the domain of cultural heritage, whilst curators might be chiefly interested in knowledge transmission, the cultural institutions main goal might be creating stronger links with visitors that will imply using technology in novel ways not necessarily oriented towards improving their knowledge but to provide more engaging experiences. Visitors also have their own ideas about how to augment cultural heritage to make it more enjoyable and personally meaningful.

In this context, design becomes an exploratory and iterative process aimed at understanding how technology can augment and improve user experiences. In this chapter we focus on the design of such augmented digital experiences, assuming that their design is a serendipitous process that expands over time. Deliberation and argumentation become essential to provide rationale on the design decisions in order to understand why and how technologies augment human experiences as suggested in (Buchanan, 1992).

Since there is no panacea solution that works in any context, it is not enough to count on end-user platforms that enable end users to prototype augmented experiences. As stated by Sanders and Stappers (2008), end users have to engage in co-design tasks that span throughout the whole development process to provide their unique perspective on how technology can enhance their lives. Therefore, their active participation in early ideation and exploration tasks can also be considered as part of the end-user development process. In this chapter we will describe how we dealt with the need to support a more serendipitous (Liang, 2012) and reflective practice (Schön, 1983) within the context of the meSch EU project (mesch-project.eu), aimed at integrating smart objects in cultural heritage sites. In order to encourage and make it easier the participation of end users in the ideation tasks, we developed a set of tools that follow a goal-oriented co-design process based on three steps: ideation, design and early prototyping. The first two steps are supported by CoDICE (COdesigning DIgital Cultural Encounters), a multi-device environment that offers interfaces for situated, collocated and distributed ideas co-generation and co-elaboration (Díaz, Aedo, & van der Vaart, 2015). Early prototyping of small-scale ecologies of devices is supported by using ECCE (Entities, Components, Couplings and Ecosystems), a tool that reduces the complexity of implementing smart objects by providing a EUD interface (Bellucci, Díaz, Aedo, & Malizia, 2014). This chapter describes how such tools were used to engage end users in group working to ideate, design and prototype augmented experiences. We will assume the definition of Lieberman, Paternò, Klann, and Wulf (2006) of end users as "*non professional software developers*" that in our case will be able to design and prototype digital futures even though they are not experts in creative design nor in physical or ubiquitous computing.

2   Context and Related Works

Co-design is a social creativity endeavor that involves designers and other professional and non-professional participants in the process of ideation, design and building of design artifacts (Sanders & Stappers, 2008). In this chapter we understand co-design as a process made up of divergent design tasks that are aimed at ideating and exploring solutions, and convergent design tasks aimed at reflecting upon different alternatives to choose the ones that should be prototyped to test whether they fit the end users and stakeholders expectations (Rhea, 2003). The next subsections explore these processes and analyze related works in the literature.

2.1   Co-design Tools

To enable end users to describe their problems and ideas in a natural and expressive way, generative techniques like collages, affinity diagrams, journey maps, personas, storyboards, inspirational cards and so on, are often used in co-design workshops (Sanders, Brandt, & Binder, 2010). A comprehensive guide of techniques can be found at (Hanington & Martin, 2012). These techniques are called generative since they guide the members of the co-design team in the exploration of the problem and the co-creation of solutions through a cyclic and evolving process (Sanders & Stappers, 2008). The unrestricted nature of these techniques facilitates the exploration of open-ended questions like ideating future interaction scenarios, but as posited by several researchers (Rhea, 2003; Sanders & Stappers, 2008) they tend to end up into fuzzy processes in which some participants, and particularly novice designers and end users, often are unaware of the goal of each design task and the way different tasks are interconnected (Garde & van der Voort, 2012; Kleinsmann & Valkenburg, 2008; Sanders & Westerlund, 2011). This situation can provoke participants' discouragement and disengagement.

However, richness of perspectives and knowledge is a key feature of co-design that can only be achieved when end users are integrated not only to evaluate and take decisions but also during the ideation process (Sanders & Stappers, 2008). The goal of the work reported in this chapter is related with using technological tools to support co-design as a collaborative and reflective practice. This goal goes beyond empowering individual end users to quickly prototype their own ideas and aims at encouraging them to participate in collaborative ideas generation, ideas assessment and decision making in order to build a common understanding of both, the problem and the potential courses of action (Bergman, Lyytinen, & Mark, 2007; Buchanan, 1992; O'Neill, Johnson, & Johnson, 1999).

The use of software tools for free ideation processes might impose limitations such as circumscribed thinking, premature fixation, and bounded ideation (Robertson & Radcliffe, 2009). These problems might be caused by the erroneous conception of software tools as design facilitators that mediate and guide the ideation process. For instance, tools like Two Thousand Points of Interaction (Harboe, Doksam, Keller, & Huang, 2013) or The designers' outpost (Klemmer, Newman, Farrell, Bilezikjian, & Landay, 2001) provide user interfaces to support the generation of design products like affinity diagrams. This kind of software tools are more limited in terms of expressivity than typical creativity techniques since the tool forces designers to use very specific constructs that have limited functionality. On the contrary and in order to promote a more active participation from end uses and stakeholders, most generative techniques rely upon more natural expression means like free drawing and crafting with physical materials (such as paper, pens or dough) or even performing scenarios. Such techniques do not force participants to learn to use a new tool to express their ideas nor they limit them to use specific constructs. Participants only need to focus on the goal of the ideation task and put their imagination to work.

Using software tools for free ideation can limit their efficacy by producing circumscribed thinking as discussed in (Luebbe, Edelman, Steinert, Leifer, & Weske, 2010; Robertson & Radcliffe, 2009) since the media used to externalize ideas shapes the way people think, For example, the experiments by (Robertson & Radcliffe, 2009) using CAD tools showed that participants not only might be limited to express their ideas because they are forced to use the constructs offered by the software tool but they also tended to use only the easiest constructs. Our proposal to avoid this kind of circumscribed thinking is to consider software tools not as mediators but as additional virtual co-design spaces that coexists with other spaces, including the physical design space and the ideation tasks carried out by participants using generative techniques as proposed in (Sanders & Westerlund, 2011). In this way, co-designers will be able to use any technique in a free ideation process and then use the virtual co-space of the software tools to document, validate and generate a design rationale about their augmented experiences. The goal is to promote and facilitate the exploration of ideas and their evaluation in a reflective process, but at the same time letting co-designers and end-users use any techniques that boost their creativity and active participation.

2.2 Prototyping Augmented Experiences

Once the best ideas are selected by the co-design team they have to be implemented. The implementation has to be a very agile process enabling to quickly generate physical prototypes that support further exploration in terms of affordances, possibilities and limitations (Nielsen, 1993). However, prototyping interactions among interconnected devices is a complex task that requires specialized technical skills, such as knowledge of electronics, different programming languages and developing platforms. Even software developers become end users in this context, since they rarely have the variety of knowledge required to prototype such ecologies of interconnected devices that include mobile devices with sensors and actuators embedded in physical objects.

To ease the labor of designers, researchers are focusing on novel programming approaches and end-user toolkits that speed-up the prototyping of device ecosystems and enable new interaction scenarios. The majority of such tools banks on web-based technologies to build device- and platform-agnostic interfaces. For instance, Weave provides an authoring environment for interweaving off-the-shelf wereables and mobile devices (Chi & Li, 2015). It uses JavaScript for the definition of cross-device behaviors and HTML for the user interface components. Panelrama (Yang & Wigdor, 2014) targets web applications and allows to build cross-device interactions by extending the HTML language with additional tags for the definition of distributed interfaces. XDStudio (Nebeling, Mintsi, Husmann, & Norrie, 2014) provides a visual tool for interactively designing cross-device interfaces. It allows to simulate target devices, thus allowing the authoring of cross-device behaviors on a single device, and also to deploy the generated interfaces on the devices. All these tools, however, expect the user to be proficient with scripting languages, such as JavaScript, and therefore they are not suitable for designers with no programming expertise. As for the case of contemporary interaction designers with programming experience, the aforementioned tools offer limited support to the design and development of custom interactive devices; that is, they support off-the-shelf smartphones and wearables and do not allow to program custom physical objects augmented with sensors and actuators.

WatchCONNECT (Houben & Marquardt, 2015) explores sensor-based interactions focusing on smart watches. It represents an exception to the previous toolkits since it provides a custom and extendable platform for prototyping interactions between smart watches and other off-the-shelf devices. However, the toolkit focuses on gestural interaction with wearable devices and does not support, for example, the implementation of other types of custom tangibles. It also seems to support only interactions between one single wearable device and another display-enabled device, thus limiting the creation of extended ecosystems.

Other environments embrace visual programming for prototyping physical interaction and offer tools that address more closely the needs of users with little technical knowledge. For instance, Scratch4Arduino (Rosenbaum, Eastmond, & Mellis, 2010) exploits the Scratch visual environment (Maloney, Resnick, Rusk, Silverman, & Eastmond, 2010) to program Arduino hardware through the composition of logical blocks on the screen. However, Scratch4Arduino is meant for educational purposes and to ease the transition to a classical textual programming language, thus it does not provide support for the rapid prototyping of multi-device interaction. More advanced tools for this task are Node-RED (nodered.org) and MIT App Inventor (Pokress & Veiga, 2013). Node-RED implements a visual data-flow language to interweave smart things. It provides high configurability and extensibility and it is powered by a crowd-based development that allows to reuse code created by others. However, users still need to have programming knowledge to create useful programs, it does not support interactions with mobile devices and does not offer direct support for interconnecting devices. App Inventor offers a visual environment for building mobile user interfaces via drag-and-drop of graphical elements and programming device behaviors (including sensors) via a Scratch-like approach. It is limited to mobile devices and it does not support cross-device interfaces. Therefore, integrating different devices in the same environment would still require considerable effort.

Our approach, which aims to ease and speed-up the creation of physical interfaces, resonates with the vision of sketching "*interactive materials*" proposed by Obrenovic and Martens (2011) with their Sketchify. This tool enables designers to rapidly prototype interactive systems by combining pen-based mock-ups of the user interface with interactive elements, that includes a wide range of i/o devices (e.g., Nintendo Wiimote) as well as external software services and environments (e.g., MAX/MSP). While sharing similar motivations, design goals and rationale, our prototyping tool ECCE differs from Sketchify in that ECCE supports the rapid prototyping of small-scale device ecosystems, including off-the-shelf device and custom-made tangibles, thus enabling cross-device interactions similarly to aforementioned systems such as Weave (Chi & Li, 2015) or XDStudio (Nebeling et al., 2014). Moreover, CoDICE supports two previous tasks to prototyping, namely divergent and convergent design, so that using the tools here proposed alternatives can be explored and properly documented including the rationale behind the design decisions taken. In this way, not only the design outcomes are digitized but they also include information about how or when they can be used, by whom, their limitations as well as their evolution as suggested by (Carroll & Rosson, 2003; Krippendorf, 2005).

3   The Co-design Process with Codice-Ecce

The work reported in this chapter aims at linking three processes involved in co-design (ideation, design and early prototyping) through the use of a set of software tools that will enable end users to participate in the whole process. In particular, four design spaces are supported or partly supported by software tools as depicted in Fig. 1 and described in the next paragraphs.

The *Situated design* space is where co-designers explore the physical objects or places that will be augmented to try to understand how to provide a better experience. For instance, if an augmented object is going to be used in a museum it might be worth running a workshop in that place to look for inspiration and understand

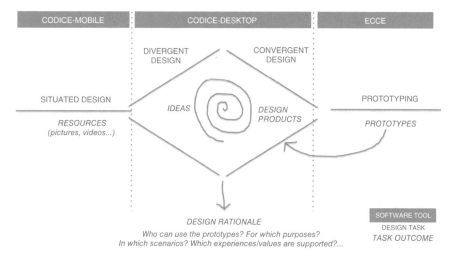

Fig. 1 Design spaces, tasks and tolos

Fig. 2 CoDICE-mobile can be used to collect inspirational material in onsite visits or to digitalize the outcomes of design workshops like paper-based stories, affinity diagrams or performances of interaction scenarios

the limitations and possibilities of the physical space. For this kind of design task CoDICE-mobile can be used to collect material while visiting the physical environment as shown in Fig. 2. *Resources* captured with CoDICE-mobile can be tagged and automatically uploaded to a central server, so that they will be available for subsequent design tasks. Any other kind of document that might be useful during the design process, such as existing multimedia material and reports, can be directly uploaded to the server using CoDICE-desktop. *Resources* are independent and persistent entities that can be tied to more than one *idea* and *design product*.

The *Divergent Design* space is where co-design teams engage in free brainstorming and exploration assuming two of the classical tenets of brainstorming (Osborn, 1979): generate lots of ideas and defer judgment. This is the space where co-designers can hold and share their ideas before evaluating whether they should be implemented or not. In this space, co-design teams will use the techniques they prefer to explore and externalize their ideas. In order to keep such ideas in a persistent and meaningful way so they can be revisited and studied further, CoDICE-desktop offers a web platform to document them using four entities (namely physical objects, encounters, personas and augmented objects) that will be described in the next section. With these four entities teams can start envisioning whose objects will be augmented, how the augmentation experience will be, the target users and the technologies that will be used, respectively.

CoDICE-desktop virtual space makes it possible to keep track of all the ideas that emerge during the co-design workshops, even those that didn't succeed. In this way, if interesting ideas are not developed further due to temporal constraints, they can be revisited later. Also ideas that failed can be kept along with the reasons that made them not viable, so that co-design teams can learn from their mistakes. Fig. 3 shows an idea that was discarded by a co-design team as described in the use case reported

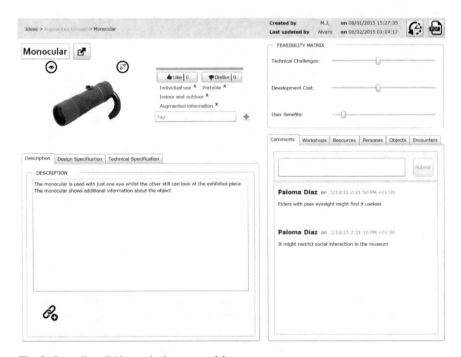

Fig. 3 Recording all ideas, whether successful or not

in (Díaz et al., 2015). The idea was to implement a monocular to look closer at objects and get more information on them. Two facts, shortly reported as comments in the interface, remind co-designers about the discussions on this artifact that supported this decision (see the right lower panel in Fig. 3): people with low vision, like the elder visitors, might have problems to enjoy it; and the artifact had to be used on an individual basis and the museum audience was mainly composed of families who were usually more interested in experiencing the visit as a social activity.

In the *Convergent Design* space ideas are assessed and those positively evaluated are moved to the CoDICE-desktop virtual design space to be elaborated further. More concrete information on the prototypes, scenarios of use and requirements is provided, including a design rationale that justifies and explains why decisions were made. Information on known uses and evolutions can also be included so the history and genetic evolution of artifacts (Krippendorf, 2005) can be fully documented. With this purpose, the conceptual entities of CoDICE are envisioned as long-term entities whose information is constantly updated, even once artifacts are implemented and deployed in real environments. Indeed, information on known uses of the artifact can be added to its description. Fig. 4 shows

Fig. 4 Evolution of an idea reported as a design product. Area 1 includes general information on the concept; Area 2 contains descriptions of the artifact including multimedia files such as the *youtube* video and the image in the "validation" tab; Area 3 includes comments about this component and its relations with other components such as the personas that will use this prototype, the scenarios in which it can be used, its requirements, its evolutions; Area 4 includes a navigation tool, information about the updates of this element and a link to create a pdf file with all the information provided for this component

an example of an artifact ideated and developed through several meSch co-design workshops, called the Loupe. The description of the final prototype includes a picture, user generated ratings and tags, visual and technical description, validation information, design rationale and known uses. Comments on the design artifact can also be added by the co-design team, as well as links with related entities like the personas who will use the artifact, the scenarios of use, the identified requirements and its evolutions if any.

Finally, in the *Early Prototyping* space co-design teams can create an early prototype to test how their ideas will work in the real world. To facilitate the generation of ecologies of devices by end users and reduce the programming complexity, the ECCE toolkit is used. With this tool, end users can choose the components of their artifact and define the rules that determine their behavior using a visual interface. The goal is not to support the generation of complete high-quality prototypes. ECCE Toolkit, instead, aims at enabling end users to generate a quick-and-dirty physical prototypes they can tinker with to get feedback on their ideas and designs, fix problems and improve the characteristics of their designs in an iterative cycle as shown in Fig. 1.

Next subsections describe in a detailed way the tools used in this process before introducing the co-design workshops where the integration of both CoDICE and ECCE was used to enable teams both to reflect on their ideas and to give shape to them through early prototypes.

3.1   Ideation and Design with CoDICE

CoDICE is a software platform developed within the meSch EU project to support the co-design of digital ecosystems in which physical objects are augmented using smart objects to support more engaging user experiences. One the main pillars of the project is the use of a co-design approach to envision such futures and, hence, for a period of two years a number of co-design workshops and activities involved cultural heritage professionals (CHP), end users, designers, software engineers and developers in this endeavor. Whilst these workshops were being held, we designed a technological tool that may assist co-designers in their work. Thus, CoDICE development was informed by requirements and needs identified in the literature and also by the experience gained in the co-design workshops run by the meSch consortium. The latter source of inspiration made it possible to understand which kind of software platform could be deployed in the wild to assist multidisciplinary teams, who work both in collocated and distributed ways, without imposing constraints that will make the tool useless. During these workshops it emerged that there was a need to properly document the outcomes and their interrelationships as suggested in the literature (Garde & van der Voort, 2012; Kleinsmann & Valkenburg, 2008; Sanders & Westerlund, 2011). In this way all the team members understand why they are participating in a specific task and why their contribution is relevant.

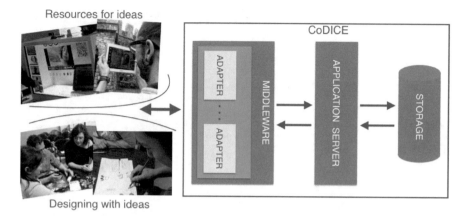

Fig. 5 CoDICE architecture

CoDICE assists such heterogeneous teams in co-design tasks through three virtual design spaces that can be used in a collocated or distributed way: situated design, ideation and convergent design. In the context of the tool, end users are heterogeneous groups of technical and non-technically skilled people who want to take part in a collaborative process to ideate new ways to interact with smart objects.

The platform is conceived as a multi-device toolkit that makes it possible to support situated, collocated and distributed tasks using different devices as shown in Fig. 5. With this purpose it implements a client-server architecture: the server makes use of a web service to store the information using in a SQL database; and two clients are implemented to support different design spaces and tasks, CoDICE-mobile that supports Situated resources gathering and CoDICE-desktop that is used in the other two design spaces, Divergent and Convergent design. CoDICE-mobile is a quite simple app that is only used to collect information and upload it to the server. For that reason, the remaining of this subsection is only focused on CoDICE-desktop, the virtual space where ideation (or divergent design) and convergent design take place.

In order to ease communication among team members during the design tasks, a number of Design Boundary Objects (DBOs) are identified. DBOs are defined as conceptualizations that encapsulate a shared representation of the design outcomes and their design rationale (Bergman et al., 2007). Examples of DBOs proposed in the literature include Personas, Scenarios or proto-architectures (Bergman et al., 2007; Carroll & Rosson, 2003; Cooper, 1999). Boundary objects should be flexible and expressive enough as to accommodate the needs of different participants and at the same time be able to convey useful design knowledge. After several iterations in the meSch workshops the final structure of DBOs supported by CoDICE-desktop are represented in Fig. 6 using an entity-relationship model. The model reads as follows. For the Ideas spaces (upper area in the Figure), physical *Objects* can be enhanced through *Encounters* that make use of *Augmented concepts* to improve the user experience of *Personas*. This BDOs (defined in Table 1)

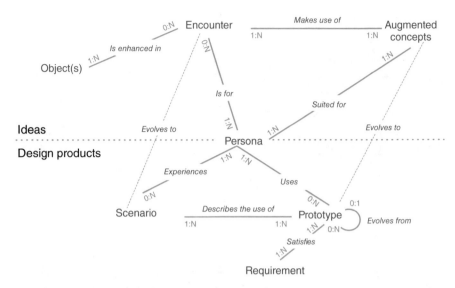

Fig. 6 CoDICE final conceptual model. DBOs are linked through relations (arrows) whose cardinality reflects whether they are mandatory or not (1 or 0 respectively) and whether they can be linked to 1 or more components (1 and *N* respectively)

Table 1 DBOs provided by CoDICE to document ideas and designs

BDO idea/design concept	Description	Goal
Object	Physical object or collection of objects to be augmented	To analyze the real objects in terms of features, interaction affordances and constraints, and the emotions and feelings they inspire
Encounter/scenario	Augmentation scenario	To envision augmented experiences with cultural heritage objects or sites focusing on the values and benefits they will bring
Augmented concept/prototypes	Augmented concept	To ideate digital artifacts or ecologies that will support the augmented encounters with the physical objects
Persona	User stereotypes	To identify potential users of an augmented object for which encounters are devised focusing on their needs, expectations and goals
Requirements	Implementation requirements	To specify the features of the prototypes in terms of functional, usability, user, data and technical requirements

and their relations set up the ideation space, offering design entities to document each agent involved in an augmented experience. The lower part of the figure represents what happens during convergent design. Once the ideas are assessed, those *Encounters* and *Augmented Concepts* that are considered worth to be explored further will evolve into *Scenarios* and *Prototypes* (see dashed lines in the Figure), respectively, to provide more details in the Design Products space. In this space, *Prototypes* might evolve into other *prototypes* and they are linked with a number of *requirements*. Relationships are labelled and each end has two cardinalities indicating the minimum and maximum of instances of that conceptual entity that must take part in the relationship. In general terms, 0 cardinalities are added to support more flexible and evolving processes where entities not linked yet to other entities can be stored since they are considered yet useful for design purposes. For instance, I can define a Persona for which I haven't yet found a useful Encounter. N cardinalities reflect the fact that some ideation and design outcomes can be linked to more than one occurrence of other outcomes. For example, the relationship among Scenario and Prototype in the Design Products area of the Figure imply that an interaction scenario can involve the use of more than one prototype and that the same prototype can be used in different scenarios.

For each of DBO, described in Table 1, CoDICE-desktop provides a web user interface (see Figs. 3 and 4) to include information on them as well as to link them, so that the relationships in the data model in Fig. 6 can be directly navigated. The evolution of *Ideas* into *Design Products* is guided by a wizard that forces to comply with the 1:N relationships. For instance, an *Augmented Concept* (that is, a potential new artifact) cannot be transformed into a *Prototype* if at least one *Persona* and one *Encounter* have been defined for such an artifact (that is, the artifact idea is expected to be useful for at least one type of user and implements at least one interaction scenario). Moreover, the wizard asks users provide a justification on their decision to move that element to the design space by asking them to fill a SWOT (Strengths, Weaknesses, Opportunities and Threats) matrix. This matrix, along with the use of Scenarios and relationships among prototypes and personas are included to support the generation of a design rationale about the product under development. Some additional concepts are included to facilitate the organization of co-design session materials, including *Resources* to add any kind of reusable content or file, *Workshops* to keep track of different co-design sessions and *Projects* to organize information concerning different developments. Finally, when *Prototypes* are defined a whole document including all the information about their conception, design, and evolution can be automatically produced. This document includes the design rationale as well as information on known uses so that the co-design team can produce a complete description of their design. All these DBOs and concepts are not related with the cultural heritage domain and, therefore, they can be used to model any augmentation of a physical object.

The tool was used to document the different prototypes generated by the co-design teams in the meSch project (Díaz et al., 2015). During its development, the tool was continuously evaluated with the projects partners who had different backgrounds and provided their view on how the tool could support the co-design processes. In this chapter we focus on the experiment we carried out outside the boundaries of the project in order to understand in a broader sense the tool utility for end users who are not experts in ideating, designing and prototyping augmented experiences with physical objects.

3.2 Early Prototyping with ECCE

The intrinsic technical complexity of building interactive systems that make use of heterogeneous interconnected devices limits their current design. Without the appropriate development tools, the implementation of advanced designs is a privilege of experienced developers. We designed the ECCE (Entities, Components, Couplings and Ecosystems) Toolkit (Bellucci et al., 2014) to lower the skill barrier and shift implementation efforts from low-level technical details to more sophisticated design nuances. The ECCE Toolkit implements a graphical web-based interface for authoring physical/digital multi-device interactions (see Fig. 7). The interface allows designers to create device ecosystems by creating new devices (both off-the-shelf and custom tangibles), defining their interactive capabilities and program the interaction among interconnected devices. To this end, the authoring tool provides three main modules:

1. The *Entities & Components Editor* assists the design of the user interface as well as the physical assemblage of sensor and actuators. ECCE supports smartphones, tablets or interactive tabletops and surfaces as well as custom-built electronic-incorporated objects, e.g., sensor-based devices with microcontrollers.
2. The *Couplings Editor* enables end users to define interactions among devices by means of event-based behaviors, taking into account the capabilities of the components, physical or digital, on each device.
3. The *Ecosystem Code Generator* automatically generates the *Entity Runtime* source code (web applications as well as microcontrollers code) by parsing XML-descriptors created with the authoring tool. The runtime code is deployed

Fig. 7 The Web interface of the ECCE Authoring Environment to create an ecosystem: (1) add/edit new entities via the Entity & Components Editor and (2) define their behavior (Couplings Editor). By selecting an existing entity, a preview gives users a prompt feedback regarding the entity design. (3) Automatically generate the runtime code of the entities as well as the server logic (Ecosystem Code Generator)

on target devices according to its development environment and capabilities. The *Ecosystem Code Generator* also instantiates the logic of the *Ecosystem Server* that embeds the functionality to setup and to transparently manage data routing among heterogeneous networked devices.

The *Entities & Components Editor* (Figs. 8 and 9, respectively) module allows to add new devices to the ecosystem by (i) using off-the-shelf mobile devices such as tablets or smartphones, laptops and multi-touch surfaces such as tabletops, see-through displays or projected surfaces, or (ii) building custom sensor-based inter-active objects with micro-controllers. In the *Entities & Components Editor*, each entity is designed as the aggregation of different components both physical and digital. Examples of physical components that are supported by the toolkit are (i) sensors such as accelerometers, gyroscopes, distance, luminosity sensors, load or flex, (ii) physical input devices such as potentiometers, joysticks or RFID readers, and (iii) actuators such as speakers, motors or LEDs. Digital components – the ele-ments of the graphical interface – can be defined for entities that feature a display screen. They are labels, digital buttons, sliders, video streams and the like. New entities can be created by selecting from a list of predefined entities (Fig. 7). Common off-the-shelf devices are provided (e.g., Apple iPad, Apple iPhone 4/5/6,

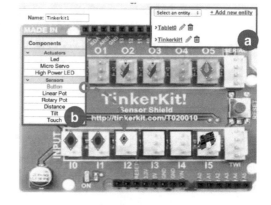

Fig. 8 Screenshot of the web interface for the definition of Tinkerkit-based interactive entities. Users can (a) select an entity from the main page and (b) edit the entity by drag-and-drop sensors and actuators from a palette of components to the desired input or output sockets

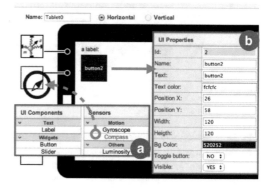

Fig. 9 Screenshot of the web interface for editing off-the-shelf devices with a display screen. User can (a) add sen-sors and interface elements from a palette, and (b) config-ure the properties of digital elements on the screen

Google Nexus 4/5/6/7, Samsung Galaxy Tab 10.1, Samsung S4/S5) as well as the possibility to create custom configurations, for instance by defining the screen resolution and available sensors. With respect to custom-made devices, the current implementation supports the design of custom objects building on top of the Tinkerkit hardware toolkit, which provides an Arduino shield to connect ready-to-use sensors and actuators.

The *Entities & Components Editor* provides a coherent definition of all the objects in the ecosystem in terms of their components (e.g., sensors and actuators) and attributes. Those descriptions are store in XML archives, which provides the backbone for the development of physical and digital models that are independent of the underlying hardware. The *Couplings Editor* exploits the descriptions to link components with the definition of the rules that manage the interplay between physical and digital components. Again, a graphical interface is provided for the end-user configurability of behaviors (see Fig. 10). ECCE has been developed to allow a wide range of integration of physical and digital components following an event-driven approach. At this stage of development, cross-device behaviors can be implemented with two sensors/actuators couplings: (i) a direct mapping that provides a one-to-one mapping of the input value of a sensor into an output value of an actuator/output device (e.g., LED or servomotor), and (ii) trigger-action rules that have been demonstrated to be powerful enough to enable a wide range of smart behaviors for device ecosystems (Ur, McManus, Pak Yong Ho, & Littman, 2014). The trigger-action programming approach is not new in the development of interactive systems and it has been mostly adopted by earlier systems, for instance e-Gadgets (Markopoulos et al., 2004), to provide a tool for untrained user to program interconnected device in smart

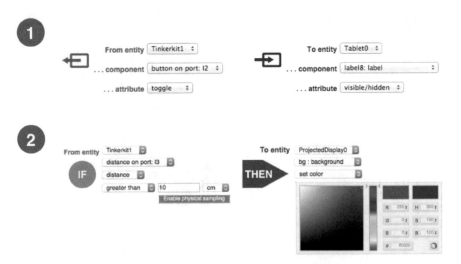

Fig. 10 Screenshot of the interface for configuring cross-device behaviors. (1) A direct mapping: The button on port I2 (see Fig. 3) is used to toggle the visibility of a label on the graphical interface of a tablet. (2) A trigger-action: if I am at more than 10cm from the distance sensor change the background of the projected display to "red."

environments, such as the case of smart home systems. Recent commercial systems such as IFTTT.com have enhanced the capabilities of trigger-action programming by providing APIs to seamlessly interconnect physical devices with a wide variety of web services. In our case, the use of trigger-action programming aims at lowering the development threshold for non tech-savvy user and thus support open-ended scenarios for creative design. All the XML-based descriptions are parsed by the *Ecosystem Code Generator*, which creates the logic of the *Ecosystem Server* in terms of data structures that hold the description of interactive objects, their interactions and network-agnostic data routing. It also generates the source code for Tinkerkit-based objects to be uploaded on the microcontrollers. The *Ecosystem Server* acts as a central communication unit. All the messages from one object to another pass through it and it maintains the data structures for validating the interaction rules between physical and virtual objects. The server receives events from remote sensors and dispatches the event to the corresponding target entity.

4 Using Codice-ECCE To Ideate and Design Smart Objects

Both CoDICE and ECCE had been evaluated separately to assess their usability as reported in Díaz et al. (2015) and Bellucci et al. (2014) respectively. In this chapter we report the evaluation of the combined use of the two tools by end users who ideated, designed and prototyped augmented experiences with physical objects. Though the tools were inspired by the observations done in the co-design workshops of the meSch project, they do not include any specific components or functionalities related with cultural heritage, so they can be used to ideate augmented experiences for any purpose. Hence, the goal was to assess how end users perceived the use of such tools to ideate and early prototype augmented physical objects. We were interested in covering design processes that expanded over time to identify the benefits of using the tools to organize ideas, make them evolve into design artifacts and, finally, materialize them through prototypes. With this purpose we involved a group of end users with no capabilities to implement augmented experiences who could perform the task as a multi-session assignment. Participants were 8 students of a Master course on "Formal methods for multimedia and the web" who had different backgrounds, all of them technical, but none of them had used or programmed micro-controlled objects nor were they familiar with design thinking methods, so they could be considered as end users. During a three-weeks period they were asked to use the tools to ideate, design and prototype an innovative augmented experience with a physical object. For the first two tasks (ideation and design) they used CoDICE as the documentation tool whilst prototyping was done using ECCE. Participants used their own computers and worked both in collocated sessions as well as in a distributed way. They organized themselves in groups of two or three. Self-organization instead of random assignation was chosen given the fact that and that most of the work had to be done outside the course lectures, so facilitating distributed work was a key factor.

4.1 Procedure

The experiment expanded over three weeks, with one additional week to prepare an oral presentation of the final prototype. Each week, there was a 2 hours session of collocated work in a classroom where students could bring their own laptops or tablets. The first session was devoted to the ideation process and the second and third to move ideas to the design space and to implement a prototype (see Fig. 11). All the ideas and designs were documented using CoDICE. ECCE was employed to create the final prototype together with Arduino and Tinkerkit platforms and a number of sensors, actuators and mobile devices. At the end of the workshop, participants filled a questionnaire indicating their perception of the utility of the tool and of its main features. The time allocated for collocated meetings was 4.5 hours (slots of 1.5 hours per week) so most of the work had to be done in a distributed way. This made it possible to test the technologies in a realistic environment in which co-designers can reflect upon their work and elaborate it further once the collocated sessions are completed.

In order to ideate digital futures three objects were made available in the room to facilitate inspiration: (i) a Mayan funerary mask, (ii) the Chichén Itzá pyramid and (iii) glyphs of the Mayan script that were combined to write words or sentences. Cards with information on the objects and their cultural meaning were also provided. During the ideation process, they were no restrictions at all: students could choose as many objects as wanted and groups were encouraged to freely ideate digital augmentations without being constrained by cost, feasibility or other issues. They were also asked to ideate any kind of augmented use, not necessarily related with cultural heritage. For the example, participants in Fig. 11 designed an augmented mask that hides a security code.

Participants were suggested a specific design flow to follow during the three sessions. The first step was to think about the physical object itself using the CoDICE *Object* entity. Then they were suggested to imagine scenarios of use for that idea and to document them using the CoDICE *Encounter* entity and to identify potential user profiles or *Personas* that might benefit from such an encounter and finally to describe their proto-prototypes using the *Augmented concept* entity.

Fig. 11 Designing and prototyping new artifacts using CoDICE and ECCE

During the second co-located session, participants moved some of their ideas to the design space. They were asked to choose just one of the *Augmented concepts* they created in the previous session and make it evolve to the design space, so they could work further on it and prepare the implementation process. After using the wizard that asks them to provide a SWOT matrix justifying their decision, a *Prototype* design entity was created where they could add technical and detailed information, refine use *Scenarios* and identify *Requirements*.

In the last session, prototypes were created. Participants used ECCE to implement at least once of the design ideas they chose making use of the hardware at their disposal.

One week later, they met again to present their work highlighting the ideation and design process they followed to propose such artifact.

At the end of this last session, participants were given a questionnaire. Two open-ended questions provided information on whether or not participants understood the purpose and value of the two software tools and if they would use the tools again for designing smart objects. Then set of closed questions was used to assess the potential utility of the tools and the design flow established in the experiment.

4.2   Data Collection and Findings

At the end of the three weeks, 6 augmented concepts were ideated from which 3 evolved into prototypes all of which were implemented with ECCE. All the proposals included the description of at least one use scenario where the prototype will be used and one persona who will benefit from it (see Table 2). All the prototypes were justified through a SWOT matrix.

Concerning the data collected in the questionnaires, the first open question was to describe the goal and use of the tools. All participants acknowledged to understand in which context both tools could be used for and described their purpose in a very precise way. Most of them focused on the fact that the tools helped them to be systematic and to collaborate. As one of the said *"The purpose of CoDICE-ECCE is to support the process of converting a smart object idea into a working prototype in a collaborative environment. It makes this process less chaotic and more systematic by providing the tools to document and share ideas and design decisions easily with collaborators (CoDICE). Additionally, ECCE allows non-experts to augment and interconnect objects easily in order to rapid-prototype those smart object ideas."*

Table 2 Number of related DBOs defined per prototype

Prototype	Scenarios	Personas	Requirements
Interactive pyramid	1	1	3
Karicha simulation	1	3	4
Interactive mask	1	1	3

The second part of the questionnaire was aimed at analyzing the utility of the tools from the point of view of end users. In particular, we measured three issues about the tools and the design flow. For each aspect, participants answered a set of questions using a 5 points Likert scale, being 5 "Strongly Agree" and 1 "Strongly Disagree." The three issues analyzed were:

1. The **perceived utility** of the tools is related with how useful participants find the functionalities currently offered. Focusing on usefulness as in the TAM model (Davis, 1989) would have assumed that participants were professional designers and not end users, since it requires a capability to assess how the tools improve the quality of your work. Participants do not have any scale or expertise to measure such quality but they can rate how useful the software tools were to reach their goals. Since the tools are developed in an iterative way this kind of questions make it possible to understand if those tools who are not considered useful should be removed or whether this perception is based on a problem with the design session organization. For example, the use of different types of multimedia resources in a design process might not be considered useful if the designer moderator does not stress the need to use different techniques during the ideation process and the participants feel more comfortable using descriptions they can include in the tool fields instead of drawings or performing scenarios.

2. The **performance expectancy** is the degree participants feel they could use to tools do perform specific tasks (Venkatesh, Morris, Davis, & Davis, 2003). In this case, we focused on the design tasks participants were asked to perform that include: generating and exploring multiple ideas; interrelating concepts; documenting their ideas; justifying their decisions, and transforming ideas into design concepts and designs into prototypes. This set of questions makes it possible to understand whether participants perceived they were accomplishing their goals using the tools and whether there are problems with the interfaces or the design flow used in the experiment.

3. **Attitude towards the tools** understood as the individual affective reaction to using the tools, that is, how participants liked performing the different tasks proposed (Venkatesh et al., 2003). In this case, all questions started by "I valued …" so that participants were asked to rate their level of satisfaction with performing such task.

Other factors included in the UTAUT model (Venkatesh et al., 2003) like facilitating conditions or social influence were not considered since participants are students and given their lack of expertise in professional contexts their opinions might not be too informative. As summarized in Table 3, all the questions about the three dimensions were positively rated above 3 (neutral value). For the first dimension (M=4.05, Median=4.0, SD=0.78), a one-sample Wilcoxon Signed-rank test shows that Likert scores are significantly different from a neutral value ($p < 0.05$, 95% CI [4.0, 4.5]). The one-sample Wilcoxon Signed-rank test shows similar results also for the second dimension (M=4.08, Median=4.0, SD=0.96, $p < 0.05$, 95% CI [4.0, 4.5]) as well as the for the third dimension (M=4.02, Median=4, SD=0.81, $p < 0.05$, 95% CI [4.0, 4.5]).

Table 3 Perceived utility of the tools and tasks performed with them

(1) Utility of the tools		
How useful participants found the functionalities of the tools whilst performing the assignment		
Tool Functionality	*Mean*	*Mode*
Adding different kinds of resources	3,6	4
Documenting ideas	4,4	4
Separation between ideas and designs	3,9	4
Transition from ideas to designs	4,4	5
Documenting design concepts	4,4	5
Transition from designs to prototypes	4,0	4
Implementing interactive prototypes	3,8	4
(2) Performance expectancy		
How well participants could perform the different tasks involved in the assignment		
Task	*Mean*	*Mode*
Explore multiple ideas before deciding to implement one of them	4,4	5
Generate and share documentation about my ideas	3,9	5
Justify my design decisions	3,6	4
Interrelate concepts (vg, personas with augmented concepts)	4,4	5
Transform my ideas into design concepts	4,3	4
Transform my ideas into prototypes	4,0	4
(3) Attitude towards		
How participants valued the different tasks perfomed with the tools		
Task	*Mean*	*Mode*
Exploring multiple ideas before deciding to implement one of them	4,0	4
Generating and share documentation about my ideas	4,1	5
Justifying my design decisions	3,5	4
Interrelating concepts (vg, personas with augmented concepts)	4,4	5
Transforming my ideas into design concepts	4,0	4
Transforming my ideas into prototypes	3,8	4

Concerning the first dimension, the questions explicitly mentioning documentation (documenting ideas, design concepts and moving ideas to design concepts) were the ones rated more positively. This is a relatively surprising finding as most students of technical courses do not usually appreciate spending time in documentation tasks.

The second group of questions tried to explore whether participants felt they could do all the tasks involved in the assignment using the tools. Again all the results were above the neutral value, being "Justify my design decisions" the one rated less positively (with a mean value of 3.6) but still had a mode value of 4. Finally, for the questions about attitude towards the tasks performed, positive values were obtained for all the questions. In this case, "justifying decisions" task was again the one with the lowest score. The fact that such justification was under the name of "design rationale" a concept participants were not familiar with, and that the interface was not in their mother tongue, might have created some misconception about what we meant by justifying my decisions. In any case, both results might suggest the need to stress the relevance that design rationale has in the co-design process. Given the fact that co-design teams did not work on designs done by other teams, they might have not appreciated how valuable it is making it explicit how and why artifacts are proposed. However, when they did the oral presentations of their artifacts they used the links among entities and the SWOT matrix to justify their decisions.

4.3 Lessons Learnt

All participants acknoweledged that they understood the goal of the tools and they said that they will use them again in case of having to design an augmented experience. Taking into account their comments, three benefits can be highlighted.

CoDICE helped them to organize ideas and the process. As one of the participants said "*Starting from a lot of ideas, CoDICE helped us to organize them in the best way, working step-by-step you could see how the project evolved.*" Since they had a limited set of entities to organize their ideas and there was a certain process flow, participants knew how different design tasks (like defining scenarios and personas) were connected. This is a problem that has been identified in co-design workshops in which novice designers tend to be disoriented when they do not understand the purpose of each activity they are involved in (Garde & van der Voort, 2012; Kleinsmann & Valkenburg, 2008). In our case, the ability to link the different outcomes of such activities into a comprehensive space like the one provided by CoDICE makes it possible to have a clear idea of the whole picture and to understand the development process and the forces that drove it.

Our participants acknowledged in their definitions of the tool the fact that they could interrelate the objects, places, scenarios and personas involved in the use of a specific artifact. This is particularly important in many application domains where the same object can be experienced in a different way by different people. The fact that there are different entities for each of these concepts in CoDICE pushed participants to look more closely into each of them. Additionally, most participants tried to reuse the concepts they defined by linking them with other entities, for instance assigning the same persona with several artifacts. Though given the constraints of the experiment there were no many associations among concepts, this is a need we identified in (Díaz et al., 2015) were professional designers and end users (in that case curators) needed to detach scenarios from physical objects, personas and design artifacts to reuse scenarios, personas or objects. In that case, we used the example of two artifacts (the *Loupe* and the *Monocular*) implementing the same scenario (*Layered information*) as well as an artifact (the *Loupe*) used in two different scenarios (*Wayfinding* and *Layered information*). Analyzing the same artifact in different scenarios of use can also provide ideas about its utility as well as limitations. For example, in the case of the Loupe, the use in a scenario about wayfinding with children demonstrated that the augmented artifact became a goal per se. Children were eager to find out the next step with the Loupe and were distracted from the real objective: following a route in a museum to learn about a specific topic.

It's worth noting here that the use of CoDICE helped to move the focus from the implementation to the ideas space. Since all our participants had a technical background they were eager to discuss the technical features of the prototype, but being forced to think about the object affordances, personas or scenarios made them realize they had to explore the problem first and then think about the implementation. Indeed, according to their own comments at the end of the workshop they did appreciate the possibility of discussing all kind of ideas. As one of them said *"Even though I found documenting every step of the design process a little boring I understand its usefulness, especially when collaborating with other people and when a long time passes from session to session (when the rationale behind decisions is easily forgotten if not registered). CoDICE provides many tools to avoid this information loss."*

Tinkering with early prototypes created with ECCE made it possible to test ideas very quickly. Our participants considered that being able to create their own prototypes with ECCE was also a very rewarding and productive task. Even if some of the participants stated they would have liked to create more complex prototypes – a task that was precluded by the limited functionality that ECCE provides in terms of composition of sensors and actuators – participants still acknowledged that moving from ideas to something that worked in a very short time was very useful for them. This finding has been already highlighted by other agile design methods, such experience prototyping (Buchenau & Suri, 2000). When the aim is to cover early prototyping of ideas, complexity has to give way to simplicity. The design of physical artefacts like smart objects deals with issues that go beyond graphical interfaces and focus on the physicality and affordances of the devices among others, which can only be tested if the devices are given a physical shape. Spending too much time implementing different aspects of a physical prototype, however, can compromise the exploration of more than one idea. ECCE applies an end-user approach to make it easier the creation of physical prototypes thus supporting broad exploration. The tradeoff is the reduced complexity of the potential prototypes.

A relevant challenge in co-design is to engage participants into broad exploration processes that not only focus on the first idea but give room and opportunities to diverge and explore from multiple perspective problems and solutions before converging into specific ways of action and reflecting over the outcomes (Adams, Daly, Mann, & Dall'Alba, 2011; Garde & van der Voort, 2012; Sanders & Westerlund, 2011). The combination of CoDICE that makes it possible to keep in a persistent and meaningful way ideas and ECCE that allows to give shape to such ideas offered a co-design space where multiple ideas could be explored both from a conceptual and physical way.

Participants valued the capacity to work in a collaborative and distributed way and share all the information among different groups. The fact that the co-design workshop can expand beyond the limits of co-located sessions was considered quite useful since it replicates the way developers and designers work in real projects. As one of our participants said *"The main benefit is that it allows you to make collaborative brainstorming, without the need to be all together in the same room. It allows to have something persistent at the end of a co-design workshop and allows ideas to be shared."*

Another issue that was considered particularly interesting was sharing the same workspace, so that the entities defined by other groups could be reused or just examined to look for inspiration. Indeed, when they first opened the tools they already had an item for each of the conceptual entities as an example to understand better why the entities should be used for but also as an element they could reuse in their own designs. We all are creative but we do not have all the same level of creativity or feel equally comfortable when taking part in creative activities. The possibility of revisiting ideas in a distributed way, help those who are not so bold to make their own contributions in the comfort area of their own laptop. In this way, the tools here presented can help to deal with another typical problem in co-design workshops: the lack of documentation of participants Also, being able to revisit all ideas promotes a more reflective practice that is not limited by the time constraints of co-located sessions.

5   Conclusions

In this chapter we have discussed the use of two tools, CoDICE and ECCE, that enable end users to ideate, design and prototype physical smart artifacts that augment user experiences. Compared to end-user tools, the approach here described focuses not only on the implementation phase but on the whole process that starts from an idea and evolves into a number of design outcomes that eventually are implemented. Moreover, it stimulates end users to explore not only one idea but different options applying a brainstorming process as defined by Osborn (1979). In this way, the tools provide virtual spaces to keep in a persistent way divergent and convergent design outcomes so that judgment can be deferred and design rationale can be elaborated for each of the design decisions taken. In this way, co-designers can engage in serendipitous processes required to create meaningful experiences with interactive technologies (Liang, 2012). These design spaces are also complemented with a tool that facilitates the creation of early prototypes to physically test ideas following an experience prototyping approach (Buchenau & Suri, 2000).

The experience gained through the use of the tools in real projects (Díaz et al., 2015) and workshops shows that software tools can be used to involve end users in ideation and early prototyping activities without compromising creativity. Our approach consists on integrating software tools as an alternative design space that coexists with creative design workshops were generative techniques are used. Such an alternative space was used to document ideation and design outcomes and to turn such outcomes into working prototypes that could be tested. In the evaluation reported in this chapter, the use of the tool forced participants to explore several ideas. In our experience as interaction design teachers in computer science, this is a very important activity that needs to be stressed with technical students who usually prefer to think in the solution rather than spending a lot of time exploring the problem. From this point of view, we found the workshop and the use of the tools quite useful from an educational point of view.

The use of the tools in projects and workshops showed that being a bit systematic always pays off for co-designers with a technical as well as a non technical background. Creativity techniques usually applied in co-design workshops are very uplifting and fun but not always the participants understand their goal and purpose in the design process, so they can feel frustrated and discouraged (Sanders & Westerlund, 2011), particularly if the designer in charge of the session is not experienced enough as to engage all of them in a meaningful way. The space shaped by the ideas and design concepts in CoDICE and the rules that determine the process flow helped to avoid this kind of disorientation in novice co-designers. They had clear goals to follow with a process that forces them to start from ideas before moving to design concepts. Also the possibility of linking scenarios, personas, objects and artifacts provided a view on how all these concepts are interrelated and why they have to be defined. Moreover, since there are validation rules that avoid moving a concept from the ideas space to the design space if it is not linked with some other components that justify this evolution, our designers were reminded of the need to think not only on augmented objects but also on the scenarios these objects will be used or the types of users who might enjoy them.

The capability of keeping track of all the ideas, even if they are not implemented, in an integrated and meaningful way helps to revisit and justify decisions and understand why some ideas were discarded. For instance in the case study in (Díaz et al., 2015), the designer documenting prototypes remembered why one the potential scenarios for a prototype didn't work even though apparently was a good idea, and she could keep this information in a persistent way, so none will try it again.

However, as all kind of software tools to support creative processes, they are not devoid of problems. Of course they shape and constraint the way designers think about their artifacts, since a number of limited entities are managed; but still these limitations can be worth if the co-design teams is not highly innovative and does not feel comfortable with too fuzzy processes. Highly creative and expert designers do not like the idea of documenting their design and providing a rationale on their decisions, but novice designers and end users need a way to confirm what they think is a good idea, and trying to put prototypes in context, relating them with people and scenarios of uses, can be a useful way to look at ideas from different perspectives.

Acknowledgements meSch is funded by EC FP7 "ICT for access to cultural resources" (ICT Call 9: FP7-ICT-2011-9) under the Grant Agreement 600851.

References

Adams, R. S., Daly, S. R., Mann, L. M., Dall'Alba, G. (2011). Being a professional: three lenses into design thinking, acting, and being. *Design Studies, 32*(6), 588–607.

Bellucci, A., Díaz, P., Aedo, I., Malizia, A. (2014). Prototyping device ecologies: physical to digital and viceversa. In: *Proceedings of the 8th international conference on tangible, embedded and embodied interaction* (pp. 373–376). New York, NY, USA: ACM.

Bergman, M., Lyytinen, K., Mark, G. (2007). Boundary objects in design: an ecological view of design artifacts. *Journal of the Association for Information Systems, 8*(11), 546.

Buchanan, R. (1992). Wicked problems in design thinking. *Design Issues, 8*(2), 5–21.

Buchenau, M., & Suri, J. F. (2000). Experience prototyping. In: *Proc. of the 3rd conference on designing interactive systems: processes, practices, methods, and techniques* (pp. 424–433). New York, NY, USA: ACM.

Carroll, J. M., & Rosson, M. B. (2003). Design rationale as theory. In: *HCI models, theories and frameworks: toward a multidisciplinary science* (pp. 431–461). San Francisco, CA, USA: Morgan Kaufmann Publishers Inc.

Chi, P. Y. P., & Li, Y. (2015). Weave: scripting cross-device wearable interaction. In: *Proceedings of the 33rd annual ACM conference on human factors in computing systems* (pp. 3923–3932). New York, NY, USA: ACM.

Cooper, A. (1999). *The inmates are running the asylum.* Indianapolis, IN, USA: Macmillan Publishing Inc. Co.

Davis, F. D. (1989). Perceived usefulness, perceived ease of use, and user acceptance of information technology. *MIS Quarterly, 13*(3), 319–340.

Díaz, P., Aedo, I., van der Vaart, M. (2015). Engineering the creative co-design of augmented digital experiences with cultural heritage. In: *International symposium on end user development* (pp. 42–57). Switzerland: Springer International Publishing.

Garde, J. A., & van der Voort, M. C. (2012). Participants' interpretations of PD workshop results. In: *Proceedings of the 12th participatory design conference: exploratory papers, Workshop descriptions, Industry cases* (pp. 5–8). New York, NY, USA: ACM.

Hanington, B., & Martin, B. (2012). *Universal methods of design: 100 ways to research complex problems, develop innovative ideas, and design effective solutions.* Beverly, MA, USA: Rockport Publishers.

Harboe, G., Doksam, G., Keller, L., Huang, E. M. (2013). Two thousand points of interaction: augmenting paper notes for a distributed user experience. In: *Distributed user interfaces: usability and collaboration, Human–computer interaction series* (pp. 141–149). London, UK: Springer.

Houben, S., & Marquardt, N. (2015). Watchconnect: a toolkit for prototyping smartwatch-centric cross device applications. In: *Proceedings of the 33rd annual ACM conference on human factors in computing systems* (pp. 1247–1256). New York, NY, USA: ACM.

Kaptelinin, V., & Nardi, B. A. (2006). *Acting with technology: activity theory and interaction design.* Massachussetts, MA USA: MIT Press.

Kleinsmann, M., & Valkenburg, R. (2008). Barriers and enablers for creating shared understanding in co-design projects. *Design Studies, 29*(4), 369–386.

Klemmer, S. R., Newman, M. W., Farrell, R., Bilezikjian, M., Landay, J. A. (2001). The designers' outpost: a tangible interface for collaborative web site. In: *Proceedings of the 14th annual ACM symposium on user interface software and technology (UIST '01)* (pp. 1–10). New York, NY, USA: ACM.

Krippendorff, K. (2005). *The semantic turn: a new foundation for design.* Boca Raton, FL, USA: CRC Press.

Liang, R. H. (2012). Designing for unexpected encounters with digital products: case studies of serendipity as felt experience. *International Journal of Design, 6*(1), 41–58.

Lieberman, H., Paternò, F., Klann, M., Wulf, V. (2006). End-user development: an emerging paradigm. In: H. Lieberman, F. Paternò, V. Wulf (Eds.). *End-user development, Human-Computer Interaction Series* 9, (1–7). Netherlands: Springer.

Luebbe, A., Edelman, J., Steinert, M., Leifer, L., Weske, M. (2010). Design thinking implemented in software engineering tools. *8th Design Thinking Research Symposium (DTRS8)*. Sydney: University of Technology.

Maloney, J., Resnick, M., Rusk, N., Silverman, B., Eastmond, E. (2010). The scratch programming language and environment. *ACM Transactions on Computing Education (TOCE), 10*(4), 16.

Markopoulos, P., Mavrommati, I., Kameas, Λ. (2004). End-user configuration of ambient intelligence environments: Feasibility from a user perspective. In: EUSAI 2004, European Symposium on Ambient Intelligence. Lecture notes in computer science vol 3295 (pp. 243–254). Springer, Heidelberg.

Nebeling, M., Mintsi, T., Husmann, M., Norrie, M. (2014). Interactive development of cross-device user interfaces. In *Proceedings of the 32nd annual ACM conference on human factors in computing systems* (pp. 2793–2802). New York, NY, USA: ACM.

Nielsen, J. (1993). Iterative user-interface design. *Computer, 26*(11), 32–41.

Obrenovic, Ž., & Martens, J. B. (2011). Sketching interactive systems with sketchify. ACM Transactions on Computer-Human Interaction (TOCHI), *18*(1):1–38.

O'Neill, E., Johnson, P., Johnson, H. (1999). Representations and user-developer interaction in cooperative analysis and design. *Human-Computer Interaction, 14*(1), 43–91.

Osborn, A. F. (1979). *Applied imagination: principles and procedures of creative problem-solving*. 3rd ed. New York, NY, USA: Scribner.

Pokress, S.C., & Veiga, J.J.D. (2013). *MIT App inventor: enabling personal mobile computing*. arXiv preprint arXiv:1310.2830.

Rhea, D. (2003). Bringing clarity to the "Fuzzy Front End". In: B. Laurel (Ed.). *Design research: methods and perspectives* (pp. 145–154). Cambridge, USA: MIT Press.

Rittel, H. W., & Webber, M. M. (1973). Planning problems are wicked. *Polity, 4*, 155–69.

Robertson, B. F., & Radcliffe, D. F. (2009). Impact of CAD tools on creative problem solving in engineering design. *Computer-Aided Design, 41*(3), 136–146.

Rosenbaum, E., Eastmond, E., Mellis, D. (2010). Empowering programmability for tangibles. In *Proceedings of the fourth international conference on tangible, embedded, and embodied interaction* (pp. 357–360). New York, NY, USA: ACM.

Sanders, E. B. N., Brandt, E., Binder, T. (2010). A framework for organizing the tools and techniques of participatory design. In *Proc. of the 11th Biennial Participatory Design Conference* (pp. 195–198). New York, NY, USA: ACM.

Sanders, E. B. N., & Stappers, P. J. (2008). Co-creation and the new landscapes of design. *Co-design, 4*(1), 5–18.

Sanders, E. B. N., & Westerlund, B. (2011). Experiencing, exploring and experimenting in and with co-design spaces. In *Proc. nordic design research conference* (pp. 298–302). Helsinki, Finland: Aalto University.

Schön, D. A. (1983). *The reflective practitioner: how professionals think in action* 5126, New York, NY, USA: Basic Books.

Simon, H. A. (1996). *The sciences of the artificial*. Cambridge, MA, USA: MIT Press.

Terrenghi, L., Quigley, A., Dix, A. (2009). A taxonomy for and analysis of multi-person-display ecosystems. *Personal and Ubiquitous Computing, 13*(8), 583–598.

Ur, B., McManus, E., Pak Yong Ho, M., Littman, M. L. (2014, April). Practical trigger-action programming in the smart home. In *Proceedings of the SIGCHI conference on human factors in computing systems* (pp. 803–812). New York, NY, USA: ACM.

Venkatesh, V., Morris, M. G., Davis, G. B., Davis, F. D. (2003). User acceptance of information technology: toward a unified view. *MIS Quarterly, 27*(3), 425–478.

Yang, J., & Wigdor, D. (2014). Panelrama: enabling easy specification of cross-device web applications. In: *Proceedings of the 32nd annual ACM conference on human factors in computing systems* (pp. 2783–2792). New York, NY, USA: ACM.

Zimmerman, J., Forlizzi, J., Evenson, S. (2007). Research through design as a method for interaction design research in HCI. In: *Proceedings of the SIGCHI conference on Human Factors in Computing Systems* (pp. 493–502). New York, NY, USA: ACM.

An End-User Development Framework to Support Quantified Self in Sport Teams

Stefano Valtolina and Barbara R. Barricelli

Abstract In the IoT domain, communities of domain experts, having different skills in specific areas of endeavor, need effective and easy-to-use ways for managing physical devices and their data streams. The configuration of networks of sensors, the design of the business logic of IoT applications based on proper policies, and the visualization and analysis of relevant events can be successfully carried out if different competencies are brought into play. Starting from a definition of End-User Development designed around the pervasive requirements of IoT applications, we describe an End-User Development model and a related three-layered architecture used for the development of the SmartFit framework. SmartFit is designed to be used in non-professional sport teams and is constituted by three different environments, respectively for IoT Engineers, Coaches and Trainers, and Athletes.

Keywords Interaction design · Internet of Things · End-user Development · lifelogging · quantified-self

1 Introduction

Nowadays networks of sensors and mobile apps allow to digitally monitoring the physical world and take real-time actions on data upon the occurrence of specific relevant events. These conditions enable the Internet of Things (IoT) to have a profound impact on our daily lives, including technologies for home, health, and environment monitoring. IoT is deeply changing the way we interact with physical objects and the environment. Success in designing and developing tools and services based on IoT requires a broad approach that includes expertise in sensing hardware, networked systems, human-computer interaction, usability, and data

S. Valtolina (✉) · B.R. Barricelli
Università degli Studi di Milano, Milan, Italy
e-mail: valtolina@di.unimi.it

B.R. Barricelli
e-mail: barricelli@di.unimi.it

© Springer International Publishing AG 2017
F. Paternò, V. Wulf (eds.), *New Perspectives in End-User Development*,
DOI 10.1007/978-3-319-60291-2_16

management. IoT adoption could be further encouraged by the application of a multifaceted and interdisciplinary approach that often transcends technology and focus on requirements regarding privacy, user experience, public policies, and regulatory issues.

These requirements can be explicated by domain experts who are not technical experts but know well their context of work, have the competence for controlling dataflows, and are able to detect interesting events or anomalous situations. Experts in healthcare, wellness, fitness, and ambient intelligence are examples of domain professionals that can take advantage by adopting an IoT ecosystem of tools and services for detecting, handling, and advising people on the occurrence of critical events (e.g., a patient taking an inappropriate behavior, an athlete asking more of her/himself than is reasonable). Beside physical sensors, for phenomena like temperature and humidity detection, domain experts need also to control personal sensors able to gather biological data (e.g., heartbeat, quality of sleep).

IoT ecosystems include devices that interact in rich and complex ways. One of the main risks in designing tools for domain experts is to force them in spending time and efforts in tasks aimed at configuring software and hardware components that are in constant flux. This is a typical task for IoT engineers, whereas domain experts have to focus on other aspects of the process, aimed at taking critical decisions on the base of the monitored flow of data.

This leads to the establishment of a network of interdisciplinary stakeholders bound together by common objectives but playing different roles and having competencies according to their work activities and processes. The involved stakeholders constitute three distinct Communities of Practice (CoPs), having different expertise, that need to design and develop efficient and effective software for complex IoT ecosystems; this requires new approaches to software development including tools and practices that reflect the changing needs of designers and developers. This chapter presents an evolution of what published in (Barricelli & Valtolina, 2016) and (Barricelli & Valtolina, 2017).

Specifically, in this chapter we present and discuss our sociotechnical study on the design and development of IoT ecosystems to be used to monitor sleep, food intake, exercise, mood, and other behaviors that characterize people health landscape. In this field, one of the clearest and complete examples can be identified in the management of sport teams.

Coaches and trainers have to monitor what their athletes are or are not doing; for example, sleep is not an active time but it is just as essential as the training activities an athlete will do in track and field. Indicators of nutritional compliance and psychological states, such as the mood, in combination with burned calories can bring to change the training plans. Finally, a good heart rate monitor or other sensor can get simple data such as the recovery rate after active rest sessions that can be used for setting up the day's load. Moreover, the promise of a cheaper, better, and efficient healthcare monitor brings us to take into account non-professional sport teams that need to gather data from heterogeneous devices and apps, unlike of professional teams that they can count on specialized laboratories and medical centers.

The peculiar structure of non-professional sport organizations is characterized by the existence of small teams with athletes who live different kind of lives, being professionals in different domains and meeting only for some hours a week. Keeping track of their habits, in terms of physical activity, nutrition, and sleep, would help the coaches in understanding the variety of the team members and in finding successful plans of training. For managing such application domain, we need to adopt End-User Development (EUD) techniques for supporting non-experts in computer science in designing services and dataflows (Costabile, Fogli, Mussio, & Piccinno, 2007; Fischer, Giaccardi, Ye, Sutcliffe, & Mehandjiev, 2004; Petre & Blackwell, 2007).

In a non-professional sport organization, we need to take into account two classes of problems that involve stakeholders with different competencies. The first problem concerns the need of collecting and combining data from heterogeneous devices able to gather the athletes' physiological states, nutrition behavior, and mood. Several challenges should be faced for handling data that are heterogeneous in structure (different types), in spatial and/or temporal granularity, and in thematic. Therefore, there is the need of services to be applied during data acquisition in order to properly identify the relevant streams when significant events occur and to undertake the proper actions. For this reason, we need to involve a figure like the IoT engineer able to understand the meaning of data acquired and how to combine and handle them according to the type of the gathered data or the sampling or granularity with which they are acquired. This task cannot be carried out by coaches and trainers who are not experts in handling stream of data but who, on the other hand, are the only domain experts able to detect significant or critical events once the dataflow has been generated. To do so they need a tool for composing control rules able to trigger warnings in case specific conditions are met.

The idea is to empower the domain experts for making them become unwitting developers. Therefore, in such context, EUD activities need to support IoT engineers for controlling and configuring more than one sensor/device (even of different brands) in order to combine, aggregate, and port data coming from different data sources. Then, we need to devise EUD strategies for supporting domain experts in defining business polices and rules for detecting relevant and critical events. This chapter aims at presenting an architecture designed around a EUD methodology addressed to provide different CoPs, respectively of IoT engineers and domain experts, with proper environments that according to their competencies can be used for configuring, manipulating, and accessing the flow of data and events that charactering their IoT domain.

2   Design Model

The knowledge associated with the design of the highly dynamic data processing that characterizes an IoT system is tacitly distributed among the various design communities (Fischer, 1999, 2000; Rittel & Webber, 1973). Specifically, in lifelogging and quantified-self applied to the management of non-professional sport teams, the communities are: IoT engineers, Coaches and Trainers, and Athletes.

IoT sensors/devices engineers are in charge of connecting, maintaining, and setting up the devices and sensors to be used by the IoT ecosystems and its users (coaches, trainers, and athletes). Their system enables the design of data flows by dragging and dropping data sources and applying visual operators to them for filtering, transforming, aggregating and composing the gathered data. The role of coaches and trainers is to collaborate in guiding, instructing, and training the members of a sport team. To exploit at best, the potentials of IoT in their practice requires a specialized interactive system for designing rules able to define what actions have to be performed in response to specific events. They act as End-User Developers by designing the rules to be used to supervise athletes' performances and lifestyle and they also analyze the gathered data in their interactive system. Finally, athletes can be seen as the ones who generate the data gathered by the IoT sensors and devices on the basis of which coaches and trainers created the rules for ehancing their lifestyle and sport performances. A tailored interactive system can be used to have a view on their behavior and performances at any time during the day.

Several solutions have been proposed to bridge the communication gap that exists among the different CoPs and to design usable interactive systems (Costabile et al., 2007; Zhu, Mussio, & Barricelli, 2010). In the last 4 years, we defined and widely applied the Hive-Mind Space (HMS) model (Zhu et al., 2010), an evolution of the SSW methodology (Costabile et al., 2007). HMS, depicted in Fig. 1, is aimed to support multidisciplinary design teams' collaboration and to foster their situated innovation by means of several EUD methods. The model provides localized habitable environments for diverse stakeholders and tools for tailoring the system, allowing the co-evolution of systems and practices. Layered levels of participation give access to different degrees of tailoring and system

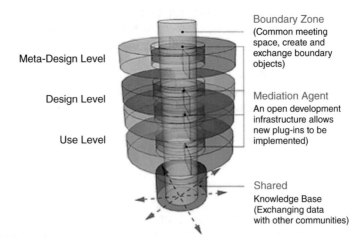

Fig. 1 The hive-mind space model

complexity. Boundary objects and boundary zones are used within the HMS model to facilitate the communication amongst stakeholders as well as their participation. HMS follows a bottom-up approach that breaks down static social structures to support richer ecologies of participation. It provides means for structuring communication and appropriation over time and it extends the "boundary object" concept with open mediation mechanisms to tackle unforeseen communication gaps among different design communities. The HMS model supports three different levels of participation and design activities: (i) Meta-design level, where software engineers maintain the system and design environments for domain experts; (ii) Design level, where domain experts design environments for end users; (iii) Use level, where end users use the environments and tools. For the CoPs we consider in the specific IoT application domain, at Meta-design Level the IoT engineers CoP operates, at Design Level there is the Domain Experts Cop, while Use Level is dedicated to General Users CoP. The HMS model can be adapted for supporting the design of IoT ecosystems at design and meta-design level relying on the concept of space and time data model as described in Sect. 3. In our solution we identify a stream with both its temporal and spatial dimensions that can be exploited from one side for the identification of the useful information needed to face a given event and from the other side for the analysis and forecast of useful activities for notifying people.

The HMS introduces a central communication channel serving as a boundary zone that supports the exchange and management of boundary objects. In our solution, there are two types of boundary objects. The first type is exchanged among the IoT engineers and the coaches and trainers for assessing what data have to be extracted from the sensors' streams and how they need to be aggregated and filtered. The second type are the rules created by coaches and trainers that are discussed with representatives of the athletes. In the current version of the SmartFit Framework, the boundary zone is implemented as an asynchronous private messages tool but will be further developed for offering more powerful features (e.g. synchronous communication). In this way, according to the HMS model, our solution provides: (1) sensors and services configuration that are not fixed but can be easily adapted and enlarged to meet the users' needs; (2) new solutions can be drafted, which leave enough space for proposing creative add-ons during design for use as well as during use. Our model follows a bottom-up approach that breaks down static social structures to support richer ecologies of participation. Fig. 2 presents the dataflow that characterizes the case study described in Sect. 3. It offers three different levels of participation and design activities: (i) Dataflow design level; (ii) Rules design level; (iii) Rules deployment, where the rules are deployed and end users use the environments and tools. In the rest of chapter, we will focus only on the environments used by IoT engineers (at Dataflow design level) and the coaches and trainers (at Rule design level), because better describe the EUD activities that are behind the creation of rules.

In what follows, we present the SmartFit case study by which we experiment the potentials of our solutions both at meta-design and design level. All the

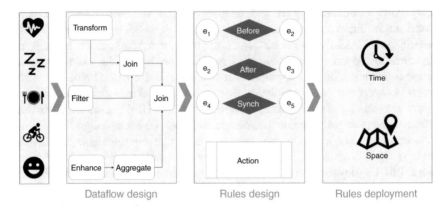

Fig. 2 The different environments in the eWellness application domain

interactive systems used by IoT Engineers, Coaches and Trainers, together with the IoT devices, constitute the SmartFit Framework. SmartFit aims at offering a set of graphical visual environment for exploiting the potentials of an IoT environment in the domain of non-professional athletes training.

3 Dataflow Design

At dataflow design level, IoT Engineers need to configure the network of sensors and services for managing the data-flow to be served at the rules design level. The outcome of this environment is the detection of a set of relevant events that coaches and trainers need to manipulate for monitoring the physical activities or daily behavior of their athletes. We identify an event with its temporal, spatial, and thematic dimensions that can be exploited both for the identification of the useful information needed to face a given event and for the analysis and forecast of useful activities to be notified to the users.

3.1 State of the Art for Visual Design of ETL Operators

Dataflow design systems supporting a wide range of operations have been proposed in different contexts depending on the kinds of data to handle (structured and semi-structured). In (Gorawski & Gorawska, 2014; Theodorou, Abelló, Thiele, & Lehner, 2014; Vassiliadis, Simitsis, & Skiadopoulos, 2002; Zhou, Yang, & Xu, 2012) there is a good treatment of ETL (Extract, Transform, Load) operations at the conceptual level for feeding a Data warehouse. Moreover, approaches for the semi-automatic generation of ETL operations depending on the user needs and context of use are proposed in (Theodorou et al., 2014).

ETL operations refer to a process in database usage and are usually coupled with graphical visual dataflows for helping the user in the identification of the original data sources, the application of the operations for extracting, cleaning, transforming and combining their data. These approaches have been mainly developed for producing relational data to feed conventional Data Warehouse (DW) System. Moreover, approaches for the semi-automatic generation of ETL operations depending on the user needs and context of use are proposed in (Mesiti, Valtolina, Ferrari, Dao, & Zettsu, 2015) and (Mesiti & Valtolina, 2014). ETL operations are usually coupled with graphical visual dataflow for helping the user in the identification of the original data sources and the application of the operations for extracting, cleaning, transforming and combining their data. Once the ETL specification is completed, some strategies are proposed for the optimization of the data-flow and for the efficient execution of the loading schedule. These approaches have been mainly developed for producing relational data to feed conventional DW systems. In (Mesiti & Valtolina, 2014) an approach is presented for feeding arbitrary target sources (either relational or based on a NoSQL system). Commercial systems such as Talend Studio,[1] StreamBase Studio,[2] Waylay.io,[3] Node.Red[4] offer graphical interfaces for designing workflows and dataflows as graphs of connected nodes representing tasks and data-sources. While Talend works on static data coming from fixed data-sources, StreamBase, WayLay and Node.Red can receive and analyze continuous data streams and are specifically designed for IoT. These environments provide rich user interface support for the full application lifecycle but they are desktop-based systems and in some cases, specific conditions can be only created by adopting strategies based on programming languages paradigms (as for StreamSQL in StreamBase Studio) or by personalizing existing templates having well-defined trigger policy (as in Waylay.io or Node.Red).

These systems offer a composition paradigm based on the use of graphs for representing the flow of data that are generated by sensors and services. This notation fits very well the mental model of IoT experts who are used to adopt a visual representation where nodes representing data inputs, outputs, and functions are connected with edges that define the data flow between components (Blackstock & Lea, 2014; Guinard, Trifa, Mattern, & Wilde, 2011). Nevertheless, these systems are not able to support multidisciplinary requirements of the stakeholders at all different levels of the IoT design chain. What is missing in these solutions is a clear separation from the IoT engineers' task that concerns the need to configure a network of data sources, by the task itself that is aimed at supporting domain experts in expressing policies and rules for managing the dataflow and for detecting relevant events. For these latter, a graph-based notation introduces severe problems that downgrade performance and satisfaction due the need to adopt a too technical and programming-oriented

---

[1]www.talend.com

[2]www.streambase.com

[3]www.waylay.io

[4]https://nodered.org/

behavior (Namoun, Nestler, & De Angeli, 2010). For this reason, we need to separate the data-flow design environment by a task automation tool that aims at enabling non-technical domain experts to associate "condition" with "action" according to an ECA (Event-Condition-Action) paradigm to use at rule design level (Ng, 2015).

Finally, another problem affecting visual programming environments such as Talend Studio, StreamBase Studio, Waylay.io, or Node.Red concerns the fact that their visual notation is not adequate for meeting the real characteristics of the knowledge base that IoT engineers have to use for configuring the data-flow. In other words, it is important to foster domain-specificity, a quality that is fundamental in IoT platforms (Casati, 2011). In order to allow IoT engineers to make sense of the services, sensors, and objects that are available for composition, it is indeed important to restrict the platform to a well-defined domain, represented through adequate notations the users are comfortable with. The idea is to provide a unified description schema of the knowledge base able to describe resources and their semantic relationships. For this reason, our tool is designed for simplifying the developing of data extraction features able to acquire data according to their spatio-temporal-thematic dimensions.

3.2   Visual Dataflow Design System

We designed a meta-design environment for helping the IoT engineers to detect relevant events by exploiting three dimensions of the data-flow: Space, Time, and Theme. Relying on the concept of event, we can characterize an event stream that a source (either sensor or service) can produce.

As an example, let us consider a sport scenario where a trainer wishes to monitor the physical conditions of her/his athletes for suggesting better exercises or for warning them about anomalous situations. For example, a possible anomalous situation is the overtraining syndrome (Budgett, 1990) that can be described as a consequence of high intensity and/or large volume training associated with insufficient recovery, potentially leading to impairment of both physical performance and training capacity. Many factors have been described to enhance the risk of overtraining states, including a variable resting heart rate, inadequate nutrition and/or weight loss, sleep patterns, environmental conditions, and psychological stressors.

For simplifying we consider to put together the following sensors and services: (i) An electronic bracelet for gathering data about the heartbeat, the quality of sleep (hours of sleep, number of awakenings for night, and minutes of restless sleep), the burned calories and the physical (number of steps or kilometers walked); (ii) a calorie counter app, (iii) a mood tracker app and finally. At the first stage of design, before to understand the problem of the overtraining syndrome and how to check critical situations, we need a strategy for putting together heterogeneous data coming from different devices and apps. At this stage, we need to involve IoT engineers who understand the schemas of the data sources; they are able to combine the data for producing a flow of events that the trainer or coach can monitor and according to which they define a set of conditions at rule design level that, if met, can trigger a warning. The data collected by these types of sensors and services can be characterized by the time dimension (when the parameters have been detected), the space dimension (where they have been detected) and the theme is the meaning associated to a value or a set of values.

In our approach, EUD activities take place during the meta-design where the system enables IoT Engineers to design data-flows for transforming, enriching, and combining data. These EUD activities are exploited for executing efficiently and effectively ETL operators. So far, several operations have been developed for processing and combining the streams produced by the sensors (Mesiti & Valtolina, 2014).

According to this design strategy, we developed a web-based system, named *StreamLoader*, that offers facilities for the development of data-flows specifically tailored for heterogeneous sensor and service data through the definition of a graph of operations that load, filter, transform, aggregate, and compose different kinds of stored and stream data relying on the context in which they are acquired. Following, in describing these operations in details, with data-stream we mean the flow of data coming from a specific sensor or service that is described by its data-schema.

The *Transform* operation allows the users to apply a transformation function on the properties of the data schemas. At the current stage, the following transformation functions have been considered: (i) for changing the unit of measure (e.g. from yards to meters); or (ii) for checking that data conform to given validation rules (e.g. dates conforming to given patterns). However, further functions can be easily integrated in our framework. The *Aggregation* operation allows the users to aggregate every t time interval, the data-stream of a sensor or a service on a set of properties by applying an aggregation function: *count, avg, sum, min, max* on the other properties. The temporal granularity t of the aggregation function needs to be compatible with the one of the data-stream (both have to be expressed in minutes or hours or other time measure unit). The *Union* operation allows the users to union the data-streams produced by different sensors in the same time window and produce a new stream of data. The *Join* operation allows the users to make in correspondence two data-streams when their temporal and spatial granularity are identical and the join predicate is verified. The evaluation of the join is window-based, that is, it is performed on the data collected from the two streams in a given temporal interval and produce a joint data-stream having a new associated theme. The *Enrich* operation allows the users to include extra information to the data-schema by adding a new property coming from the data-schema of other sources. The binding between the current data-stream and one from which the property is inherited is realized through a join function. The spatio-temporal granularity of the two data-streams need to be compliant. The *Virtual Property* operation allows the users to include a new property to the schema according to a given specification. This specification is an arithmetic expression allowing to determine the value of the property relying on the values of the other properties of the data-schema.

The final result is a flow of data that can be used in a dedicated environment by domain experts (e.g., Coaches, Trainers), not necessarily expert in IoT technologies, for defining rules to monitor specific situations and to adopt suitable actions according to the occurrence of particular conditions.

In our example, the data-streams might concern the user's physical conditions, which will be used for suggesting what exercises are better to perform, or which precautions to follow for improving the quality of live. To help the trainer in taking proper decisions and precautions, *StreamLoad* has to provide a set of data-flows about heartbeats, quality of sleep, physical activities, burned calories and caloric intake and mood status. By using *StreamLoader*, in order to provide such data-flows, IoT engineers have to manage the data-schema of each sensor or app involved. First, the schema of each sensor needs to be mapped to an internal data model in which, when available, the temporal, spatial and thematic dimensions are pointed out. This guarantees the adoption of a common model within our system (tough at this level we cannot guarantee the adoption of the same semantics). Then, some operations are composed for filtering, combining, aggregating and enhancing the data-streams produced by the sensors/apps in order to lead to the specific calculus interested in the analysis. We remark that these operations are specified at the logical level and the user does not bother where they are actually executed.

Consider the situation described in our example, the IoT engineer has to combine data in order to produce a flow concerning the physical activity about an athlete. This athlete uses an electronic bracelet for gathering the heartbeat, the number of steps and meters walked and a mobile app that registers the burned calories and the kilometers traveled on foot or by bike. Fig. 3 presents the *StreamLoader* interface and the case in which the six streams, three from the bracelet and three from the mobile app, are managed. In Figure the rectangles represent the streams and for each one is indicated the type of data (e.g., heartbeat, distance, num. of steps) and in round brackets its unit of measure. On the bottom of the screenshot is visualized further information about data source of the selected stream (Bracelet_HR01 – *Heartbeat Rate* in Fig. 3).

First of all, the IoT manager has to transform the meters walked gathered by the bracelet in kilometers. Then s/he has to combine, through the *Union* operator, the kilometers walked that are retrieved by the two data-sources (for example calculating the average in the same time window). Finally, s/he has to join the streams in a unique data-flow that represents the athlete's physical activity. Then, the coach or trainer will create the rule needed to check when the quantity of the distance covered (number of steps or kilometers traveled) in combination with the heartbeat or the burned calories can be considered intensive, moderate or light training activities. The *Join* operator is based on the temporal dimension that is defined by using the detected timestamp according to a given measurement unit of the sampling time. In the same way, it is possible to produce other data-flows related to the nutrition behavior, quality of sleep and mood status. Alternatively, it is also possible to handle the data in order generate new information. For example, through *Virtual property* operation, the

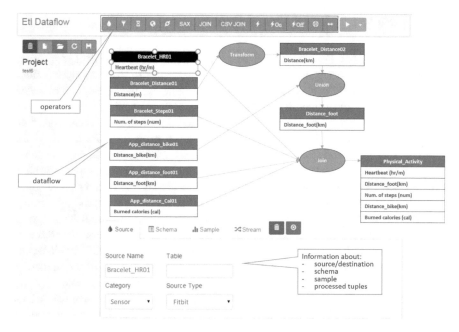

Fig. 3 The meta-design system for dataflow design

data-stream related to the heartbeat could be enriched by adding a new property that is used for describing the standard deviation that is, the amount of half-hourly variation or dispersion of the heartbeats.

The thematic of the data-flow generated in the *StreamLoader*, is provided by the name used for creating a data-stream. For example, in Fig. 3, the name "Physical Activity" is associated to the schema representing the final data-flow and it is used for communicating the real meaning of the data-flow to deliver to the Rule Editor. The semantic of the data-flows in an understandable way for the trainer that has to take proper decisions and precautions according to the monitored data-flows. The thematic can assist domain experts to select correct data-flows to provide proper rules according to their needs.

4   Rules Design

The meta-design environment described earlier and used by IoT Engineers, constitutes the base for providing coaches and trainers with the possibility to manipulate the flow of events in order to monitor the physical activities or daily behavior of their athletes. The design environment for manipulating these events aims at offering a graphical visual strategy for exploiting the potentials of an IoT environment in the deployment of rules.

4.1 State of the Art of Visual Rule Editors

Systems like JBoss Drools,[5] OpenRules,[6] and IBM WebSphereJRules[7] provide platforms for supporting users in creating complex rules to trigger proper actions when specific conditions occur. In these environments, the coding of complex rules is generally performed by skilled technicians through ad-hoc Rule Engines. Once specified, rules need first to be translated in executable code and then enforced by means of Rule Engines. These engines offer different solutions for editing, managing, and executing rules and in some cases they also provide functions for graphically modeling the execution data-flows by applying a set of rules. Nevertheless, what it missing is the possibility to graphically specify these rules. Moreover, in real contexts of use, the definition of rules is performed by domain experts that are not experienced technician and prefer to use natural language or graphical notations. In order to offer an easier way for editing rules, in (Kaczor, Nalepa, Łysik, & Kluza, 2011) the integration of Drools and the XTT2 rule representation and the HQEd visual rule editor is proposed. The results of the modeling are translated in Drools Language (DRL) files, which can be executed by the Drools engine. However, the weakness of these approaches is that the XTT2 language has not been standardized and has several limitations as reported in (Kaczor & Nalepa, 2012) despite the high expressivity of DRL. Another paper presents a solution for graphical modelling of rules (Bona, Re, Aiello, Tamburo, & Alessi, 2011) that are then automatically translated in the programming language supported by the adopted rule engine. In this case, the graphical editor is integrated in Drools Guvnor that provides a guided text editor for writing rules that are then translated into the Drools rule engine compliant language. The expressivity of the visual language, however, is reduced with respect to drools textual language especially for what concerns the specification and processing of complex events. Other visual strategies typically used in IoT field for modelling Event-Condition-Action rules can be described through the most famous systems that apply them: IFTTT,[8] Atooma,[9] and Yahoo's Pipes.[10] In (Lucci & Paternò, 2014) authors discuss how the first two design strategies support users without programming knowledge to define their context-dependent applications. In the paper, the design strategies provided by such tools are investigated in term of their expressiveness and usability. These tools allow users to define sets of desired behaviors in response to specific events. This is made mainly through rules definition-wizards that rely on the sensors/devices states. Rules can be typically chosen among existing ones or can be tweaked through customization. These activities put in place a task automation layer across

---

[5]http://www.drools.org/

[6]http://openrules.com/

[7]http://www-01.ibm.com/software/integration/business-rule-management/jrules-family/

[8]https://ifttt.com

[9]http://www.atooma.com/

[10]https://pipes.yahoo.com/pipes

all sensors/devices in the IoT environment. The visual strategy aims at creating automated rules by using graphical notation for programming statements such as: "IF this DO that" or "WHEN trigger THEN action."

A second type of applications stems from the outstanding work done with Yahoo's Pipes. Such applications offer solutions based on graphical environments for data transformation and mashup. The idea is to provide a visual pipeline generator for supporting end users in creating aggregation, filtering, and porting of data originated by sources. The visual strategies adopted by following IFTTT or Yahoo's Pipes compliant solutions are promising techniques but, in our opinion, they present some lacks. The former offers a very simple and easy to learn solution based on the definition of ad hoc rules that can notify the end users when something happens – e.g. when their favorite sites are updated, when they check-in in some places or their friends do, or warn them when specific weather conditions are going to take place. However, the language is not enough expressive for the specification of more sophisticated rules based on time and space conditions. On the other hand, the latter offers a too complex solution for supporting the end user in expressing their preferences. Pretending that end users can deal with APIs of several sensors/devices put at risk the success of the visual approach. Moreover, events in each stream of an IoT scenario, are time and space dependent and so the related rules need to take into account these type of conditions. Nevertheless, in the described systems, time and space dimensions are almost neglected.

4.2 Visual Rule Editor

Once the relevant events for a given analysis have been identified by IoT engineers, rules should be defined for specifying the action to be actuated when specific events occur. All the possible events and the access to the data gathered via the IoT devices connected to the SmartFit network are made available to the domain expert in the Visual Rule Editor. They are ready to be used for creating rules and in case the domain expert needs specific changes in the events, an asynchronous communication tool is available. The objective of the Visual Dataflow Design System is to generate a flow of events which is the result of IoT engineers' activities aimed to collect, transform, and aggregate heterogeneous data streams coming from different sensors. Instead, the Visual Rule Editor focuses on allowing domain experts (coaches and trainers) to monitor such flow of events for detecting significant situations by means of the specification of suitable rules.

The rules generated by domain experts using the Rule Editor extends the IF-THIS-THEN-THAT approach and supports the definition of rules in a more articulated way. Moreover, time and space dimensions are exploited and adopted for expressing more loose rules in the statements. Specifically, the time dimension allows domain experts to set rules that can be fired at some specific time, delayed in case of certain conditions are verified, and may be repeated until some event happens. The time dimension can also be used for creating temporal rules by using temporal operators that point out temporal correlations among spatio-temporal events. In (Behrend, Dorau, & Manthey, 2009) the authors propose a set of functionalities to be implemented with triggers written in SQL:1999 standard that cover three types of temporal categories – absolute, periodic, and relative – and allow to base delay or periodic repetition on valid time or transaction time events, respectively. According to this proposal of functionalities, we can provide domain experts with a new set of temporal operators opt ∈{*before, after, when*}. The different combinations of temporal conditions on rules that can be specified using these temporal operators according to the Allen's work on temporal logic (Allen, 1983). To implement the Drools rules editing in an interface would force the user to select among a set of different type of presets that are not very recognizable without effort. In fact, Drools has a set of 13 temporal operators: After, Before, Coincides, During, Finishes, Finished by, Includes, Meets, Met by, Overlaps, Overlapped by, Starts, and Started by. All 13 operators have different meaning but some of them are not very distinguishable from one another. In our editor, we only use the temporal operations Before, After and When and this reduces the complexity of generation of temporal rules, in respect to typical rule languages as the one used by Drools.

Let us propose an example for proving the reduced complexity in our Rule Language is the creation of a complex temporal condition:

An event n starts from15 to 20 minutes before that the event m starts; the two events are overlapped and n ends 2 minutes after m ends.

The sample rule in Drools can be expressed by the following instruction:

$n : n(this before[15m, 20m] $m) && $n : n(this finishes [2m] $m)

In our Rule Editor, the creation of such conditions not only can be performed by using a less number of operators without to lose expressivity but, it takes place by asking the user to select only a set of parameters so s/he can write the conditions by adopting a more natural language. As explained later, by using the Rule Editor interface the domain expert is driven in the composition of this rule:

The event n starts from 15 to 20 minutes before the event m and ends 2 minutes after

The framed parameters are the only parts of the sentence customized by the user by using a select widget. The writing of this sentence enables to trigger proper temporal operations in order to execute the rule into the Rule Editor. The interaction with the system is extremely easy, fast, and results in the creation of a natural language sentence that is very easy for the user to understand, even if s/he reads them a long time after it has been created. On the contrary, the same temporal condition, if expressed in Drools, would force the user in understanding which one of the available operators to use.

With regard to the space dimension, by exploiting the thesaurus of named locations, it is possible to create rules for specifying that an event happens in the same place or close to a place where another event happens. The closeness is checkable by comparing the coverage areas of each location as indicated in the thesaurus. Say that an event happens within 300 m where another event happens, means that, if the coverage areas are polygons, then the maximum distance between the closer vertexes is less than 300 m. Instead, on case a coverage area is a circle, the maximum distance is calculated from the geographical point of its center plus the length of the radius.

4.3   Rule Editor Interface

The Rule Editor user interface leverages the issues required for expressing complex conditions leading to a system that can be easily used by non-expert users. As depicted in Fig. 4 the interface is based on select widgets that are populated by using the attributes that characterize the JSON of the flow of events produced by the IoT Engineers with the *StreamLoader* environment. Through a visual notation, domain experts can specify conditions and temporal operations for implementing the business rules that characterize their activities. The Rule Editor aims at allowing non-technical people to specify rules by using simple drop-down menus. The conditions can be composed by combining groups of statements connected by using the AND/OR operators. The order of the conditions can be changed by the user just by dragging and dropping the statements into the right position. Domain experts can filter data on a certain period of time set by using the "validity interval" parameter (see Fig. 4).

Fig. 4 Example of the composition of a rule named "Bad sleep" which aims at monitoring if the hours of sleep are less than 7 AND the number of awakenings for night is greater than 5 AND the minutes of restless sleep is greater than 90

Fig. 5 Example of the composition of a rule named "Bad Mood" which aims at monitoring if the athelte's mood is either "sad" or "angry" or "anxious."

By considering the scenario presented in the previous section, an example of Composite Rule creation is given in Fig. 4 where the trainer has defined a rule named "Bad sleep" for monitoring the athletes' quality of sleep. The creation starts from taking into account the data-flow that concerns the quality of sleep and that reports the 3 days average of the hours of sleep, number of awakenings for night, and minutes of restless sleep. The created rule checks if the hours of sleep are less than 7 AND the number of awakenings for night is greater than 5 AND the minutes of restless sleep is greater than 90. Another possible rule can check if at day the burned calories are less than 1,000 and the caloric intake is greater than 1,500 in order to monitor an inadequate nutrition status.

An example of use of OR operator is presented in Fig. 5. In this case, the trainer wants to check the athletes' mood status. The rule "Bad Mood" is meet is the collected mood is either "sad" or "angry" or "anxious." Another possible example could be used for detecting when a day is characterized by bad environment conditions, that is, when the Wind Chill is less than –20 (that is, low temperature and a strong wind) OR greater than 30 (that is, hot temperature and absence of wind). Finally, a rule can be defined for checking a variable resting heart rate (Fig. 6). In this case, the trainer has to define two rules on the base of these conditions: (i) minutes of sedentary activities more than 50 minutes each hour (ii) standard deviation of the heartbeats more than 10 each half-hour. However, the two rules have to be connected by a temporal condition in order to monitor if the athlete has a variance of the heart rate during resting time. In other word, we need to monitor the heartbeat standard deviation WHEN the physical activities are low. Temporal conditions are defined using the automatically assigned names of the Rules as elements to be composed (e.g., E1, E2 in Fig. 6). An example of complex temporal condition can be E1 (sedentary activity duration more than 50 minutes) starts before

Fig. 6 Example of the composition of a rule named "a variable resting heart rate." In the screenshot the trainer is creating a temporal condition which aims at monitoring that the event E1(sedentary activity duration more than 50 minutes) starts before of the event E2 (standard deviation of the heartbeats more than 10) and ends after E2 ends

of the E2 (standard deviation of the heartbeats more than 10) and ends after E2 ends. In other words, the trainer wants to check if her/his athletes when they do not do light, moderate or intense physical activities, have an anomalous variable heart rate. Moreover, the trainer can add spatial conditions by specifying that a rule is met only is the event happens in a given named location or if it happens close (by indicating the distance) to the place where another event happens. Once a set of basic rules are defined, the Rule Editor can provide trainers with the possibility to compose different rules for specifying more complex monitoring. Suppose to take the previous scenario in which the trainer wants to monitor a possible anomalous situations related to onset of the overtraining syndrome. As said before, many factors can affect the onset of overtraining states, including a variable resting heart rate, inadequate nutrition, sleep patterns, environmental conditions, and psychological stressor. By reusing the rules previously specified for monitoring the bad quality of sleep, bad nutrition, bad mood, and the occurrence of a variable resting heart rate, the trainer can define a new rule, named "Overtraining," for checking if all rules are met. Moreover, in this new rule, the trainer has to specify that the bad environment check is a rule that must not be met because the bad mood or the variability of the heartbeats should not depend by unfavorable climatic conditions.

The rules: *bad quality of sleep, bad nutrition, bad mood*, and *bad environment conditions*, are checked on data-flows collected once daily. Instead, the last factor, the variable resting heart rate, is checked several times a day, that is, every time the occurrence of sedentary activity happens when a high heartbeats standard deviation happens. In this case, the trainer can put in AND all the rules, specifying that the bad environment conditions must not be met and that the last one has to be met more than 3 times a day. Moreover, once a set of rules is created, it is stored in a repository for further reuse or for sharing it among members of a community of trainers and coaches.

Once the composition of a rule or a set of rules is carried out, a translator module permits to translate the rules expressed by the visual specification in DRL (the Drools Language) files. When the domain expert executes the rule, a request is sent to a micro-service implemented in GO that translates a JSON file representing the rule into DRL so that it can be can be executed by the Drools engine. Once the Drools engine detects that a rule is satisfied according to its conditions, it sends a notification to the domain experts. The notification reports the rule and the flow of events that meet the condition expressed in the rule.

5   Conclusions and Future Work

In our design model, we aim at involving multidisciplinary design teams in the design of the network configuration of sensors and services by means of EUD techniques. A key difference of our work with respect to standard data-flow management systems and their graphical interface is related with the need of handling data streams. As reported in (Eckerson & White, 2003), the problem of extracting, transforming data constitutes 60–80% of business intelligent projects. Now we are working for setting up a user test evaluation for our eWellness system thanks to collaboration with the Centro Sportivo Italiano (Italian Sport Centre).

A group of sport teams will be involved in order to perform a set of activities concerning the design of data-flows and related rules from monitoring the athletes' activities. What we want to study is how far our approach is able to offer new possibilities both at the design and use time and to understand how the idea to combine the design and end users' environments appears to be successful and effective solution for both domain and technical experts.

References

Allen, J. F. (1983). Maintaining knowledge about temporal intervals. *Communications of the ACM, 26*(11), pp. 832–843.

Barricelli, B.R., & Valtolina, S. (2017). A visual language and interactive system for end-user development of internet of things ecosystems. *Journal of Visual Languages & Computing*, ISSN 1045-926X, doi:10.1016/j.jvlc.2017.01.004.

Barricelli, B.R., & Valtolina, S. (2016). End-user development for lifelogging and ewellness. In *Proceedings of the international working conference on advanced visual interfaces* (pp. 292–293, AVI '16). New York, NY: ACM.

Behrend, A., Dorau, C., Manthey, R. (2009). Sql triggers reacting on time events: an extension proposal. In *Advances in databases and information systems* (pp. 179–193). Berlin, Heidelberg: Springer.

Blackstock, M., & Lea, R. Toward a distributed data flow platform for the web of things (distributed node-red), in *Proceedings of the 5th international workshop on web of things, WoT '14*, (New York, NY), pp. 34–39, ACM, 2014.

Bona, D.D., Re, G.L., Aiello, G., Tamburo, A., Alessi, M. (2011). A methodology for graphical modeling of business rules. In *2011 Fifth UKSim European symposium on computer modeling and simulation (EMS)* (pp. 102–106). Los Alamitos, CA: IEEE.

Budgett, R. (1990). Overtraining syndrome. *British Journal of Sports Medicine, 24*(4), pp. 231–236.

Casati, F. (2011). *How end-user development will save composition technologies from their continuing failures*. Berlin: Springer pp. 4–6.

Costabile, M.F., Fogli, D., Mussio, P., Piccinno, A. (2007, November). Visual interactive systems for end-user development: a model-based design methodology. *IEEE Transactions on Systems, Man, and Cybernetics - Part A: Systems and Humans, 37*, 1029–1046.

Eckerson, W., & White, C. (2003). *Evaluating etl and data integration platforms*. Seattle, WA; The Data Warehousing Institute.

Fischer, G. Symmetry of igorance, social creativity, and meta-design, in Proceedings of the 3rd Conference on Creativity & Cognition, C&C '99, (New York, NY), pp. 116–123, ACM, 1999.

Fischer, G. (2000). Social creativity, symmetry of ignorance and meta-design. *Knowledge-Based Systems Journal, 13*(7–8), pp. 527–537.

Fischer, G., Giaccardi, E., Ye, Y., Sutcliffe, A. G., Mehandjiev, N. (2004, September). Meta-design: a manifesto for end-user development. *Communications of the ACM, 47*, pp. 33–37.

Gorawski, M., & Gorawska, A. (2014). Research on the stream etl process. In *Beyond databases, architectures, and structures* (pp. 61–71). Cham: Springer.

Guinard, D., Trifa, V., Mattern, F., Wilde, E. (2011). *From the internet of things to the web of things: resource-oriented architecture and best practices*. Berlin: Springer pp. 97–129.

Kaczor, K., & Nalepa, G.J. (2012). Critical evaluation of the xtt2 rule representation through comparison with clips. *Knowledge Engineering and Software Engineering (KESE8), 381*, 46.

Kaczor, K., Nalepa, G. J., Łysik, Ł., Kluza, K. (2011). Visual design of drools rule bases using the xtt2 method. In *Semantic methods for knowledge management and communication* (pp. 57–66). Montpellier, France: Springer.

Lucci, G., & Paternò, F. (2014). *Understanding end-user development of context-dependent applications in smartphones*. Berlin: Springer pp. 182–198.

Mesiti, M., & Valtolina, S. (2014). Towards a user-friendly loading system for the analysis of big data in the internet of things. In *Computer software and applications conference workshops (COMPSACW), 2014 IEEE 38th international* (pp. 312–317). Los Alamitos, CA: IEEE.

Mesiti, M., Valtolina, S., Ferrari, L., Dao, M., Zettsu, K. (2015). An editable live ETL system for ambient intelligence environments. In *WF-IoT* (pp. 393–394). Los Alamos, CA: IEEE.

Namoun, A., Nestler, T., De Angeli, A. (2010). *Conceptual and usability issues in the composable web of software services*. Berlin: Springer 396–407.

Ng, J.W. (2015). Task as a service: extending cloud from an application development platform to a tasking platform. In *2015 IEEE World Congress on Services (SERVICES)* (pp. 294–301). Los Alamitos, CA: IEEE.

Petre, M., & Blackwell, A.F. (2007, September). Children as unwitting end-user programmers. In *IEEE symposium on visual languages and human-centric computing, 2007. VL/HCC 2007* (pp. 239–242). Los Alamos, CA: IEEE.

Rittel, H. W. J., & Webber, M. M. (1973). Dilemmas in a general theory of planning. *Policy Sciences, 4*(2), 155–169.

Theodorou, V., Abelló, A., Thiele, M., Lehner, W. A framework for user-centered declarative etl, in *Proceedings of the 17th international workshop on data warehousing and OLAP*, DOLAP '14, (New York, NY), pp. 67–70, ACM, 2014.

Vassiliadis, P., Simitsis, A., Skiadopoulos, S. (2002).Conceptual modeling for etl processes. In *Proceedings of the 5th ACM international workshop on Data Warehousing and OLAP* (pp. 14–21). New York, NY: ACM.

Zhou, H., Yang, D., Xu, Y. (2012). *An ETL strategy for real-time data warehouse*. Berlin: Springer pp. 329–336.

Zhu, L., Mussio, P., Barricelli, B.R. Hive-mind space model for creative, collaborative design, in *Proceedings of the 1st DESIRE Network Conference on Creativity and Innovation in Design, DESIRE '10*, (Lancaster), pp. 121–130, Desire Network, 2010.

Web Augmentation as a Promising Technology for End User Development

Iñigo Aldalur, Marco Winckler, Oscar Díaz and Philippe Palanque

Abstract This chapter presents Web Augmentation (WA) technologies as tools and techniques for end-user development. WA technologies differ from other web development technologies as they target at improving existing Web pages and not at creating new Web sites. These improvements can deeply alter the way users use and interact with Web sites. This chapter revisits the concept of WA and provides an overview of the main features that characterize WA technologies. This characterization is used to position and compare the various contributions that have been made in WA. To make things more concrete we provide an illustration of WA technology through a case study using a dedicated tool called WebMakeup. Despite all their advantages, WA technologies present some limitations that might result in challenges on the user side. These aspects are also presented and discussed, highlighting directions for future work in that domain.

Keywords End-user development · web augmentation · web adaptation

1 Introduction

Nowadays, many applications which, formerly, would have been designed for the desktop such as calendars, travel reservation systems, purchasing systems, library card catalogs, maps viewers or even games have made the transition to the Web,

I. Aldalur · O. Díaz
University of the Basque Country (UPV/EHU), San Sebastián, Spain
e-mail: inigo.aldalur@ehu.eus

O. Díaz
e-mail: oscar.diaz@ehu.eus

M. Winckler (✉) · P. Palanque
University of Toulouse, Toulouse, France
e-mail: winckler@irit.fr

P. Palanque
e-mail: palanque@irit.fr

© Springer International Publishing AG 2017
F. Paternò, V. Wulf (eds.), *New Perspectives in End-User Development*,
DOI 10.1007/978-3-319-60291-2_17

433

largely successfully. Many Web sites are created every day to help users to find information and/or to provide services they need. However, there are cases where rather than a new Web site, what users need is to combine information or services that are already available but scattered on the WWW. Some examples follow: (1) users who want to have additional links on a Web page to improve the navigation (for example to create a personalized menu that gathers in one location multiple personal interests), (2) users who need to integrate contents from diverse Web sites (for example to include a Google's map into a Web page that originally only shows addresses as flat text) in order to improve their performance in identifying distance from their personal location or (3) simply to remove content from Web pages (such as contact details they consider irrelevant) to improve reading and selection performance as identified by Hick's law (1952). Because these needs might be perceived as idiosyncratic, volatile (being short-lived or occasional) or dissenting with the interests of the Web site, they might well not be considered (or even not known) by Web developers (Frajberg, Urbieta, Rossi, & Schwinger, 2016). This is because Web sites are, by definition, designed for the masses and that at design time only few users are available.

Previous work on End-User Development (EUD) (Iturrioz, et al. 2014; Lieberman, Paterno, & Wulf, 2005) has demonstrated that, if appropriate tools are provided, end users might be able to create what they need (or at least define more precisely part of what they need). DENIM is a pioneer example that illustrates how tools can be used for involving users into the design of the Web sites to be developed (Newman, Lin, Hong, & Landay, 2003). A more demanding scenario is when the target is not in-home Web sites but Web pages that have already been created by third parties. The options are here, either to redevelop what has already been done by the third party or to try to convince the third party to tune its development to fit a particular user need. This deeply collides with the principle of Web development that target the masses and not the individual.

The term Web Augmentation (WA) is used to describe tools that can be used to improve (hence the word "augment") existing Web pages (found for instance whilst browsing the Web) to create better fit user's needs and activities. Some of the most popular WA tools work by extending the functionalities of the Web browser used by the user via plug-ins that can run client-side scripts to manipulate the structure of Web pages loaded in the browser. In that case the augmentation will be applied to all the visited Web page featuring specific characteristics. The potential of WA techniques can be illustrated by some advanced applications such as lightweight integration of information extracted from the Web, context-sensitive navigation across diverse Web site, context-dependent multimodal adaptation (Ghiani, Manca, Paternò, & Porta, 2014) or refactoring Web sites for accessibility (Garrido et al., 2013). Another example is a spellchecking plug-in that would automatically check the text entered by the user on any Web page. The degree of expertise required for using WA tools varies dramatically (Han & Tokuda, 2010). For example, some tools only require basic knowledge of how to install plug-ins in the Web browsers while others may require integrating sophisticated scripting code created by the user.

In this chapter, we examine the potential of WA technology for supporting end-user development for the Web. In Sect. 2, we discuss the relationship between WA and end-user development. Sect. 3, proposes a classification of WA technologies, positions existing tools with respect to this classification and provides a study of research contributions for each main category of the classification. To make things concrete, Sect. 4 illustrates how the WebMakeup WA tool relates to the classification using a case study based on augmentation of the dblp computer science researchers' publications repository. In Sect. 5, we explain some of the users and usage difficulties specific to the adaptation of Web applications. Sect. 6 concludes the paper and highlights possible directions for future work.

2 Web Augmentation and End-User Development

Web Augmentation (WA) is *not* End-User Development (EUD) for the Web but some of the features provided by WA tools can be used for that purpose. To highlight similarities and differences, we revisit their definitions.

Many authors have tried to define precisely the term end-user programming (Burnett & Scaffidi, 2011; Wulf, Paterno, & Lieberman, 2006). In this chapter, we adhere to the definition provided by Ko et al. (2011) who state that *end-user programming is programming to achieve the result of program primarily for personal, rather than public use.* That definition has many implications. First, it is important to note the absence of any reference to an application domain and/or technology highlighting the large scope for the use of EUD tools. Next, the term "programming" refers to a general activity, which might encompass the development of software from scratch and/or making modification to an existing software. Finally, the term "end-user" does not refer to the user's skills in so for as a professional developer is engaged in end-user programming when writing code to fulfill a personal need, such as visualize the data structure to help diagnose a bug. Moreover, even if the definition implies a particular intention behind the development of the program, it does not exclude the possibility of sharing the program with other users.

There are fewer attempts to define precisely the term Web Augmentation. This term was originally coined by Bouvin (1999) to describe a tool that *through integration with a Web browser, a HTTP proxy or a Web server adds content or controls not contained within the Web pages themselves to the effect of allowing structure to be added to the Web page directly or indirectly, or to navigate such structure. The purpose of such a tool is help users organize, associate, or structure information found on the Web. This activity may be done by a single user or in collaboration with others.* More recently, Díaz, Arellano and Azanza (2013) said that *WA is to the Web what Augmented Reality is to the physical world: layering relevant content/layout/navigation over the existing Web to customize the user experience.* These definitions highlight WA as a non-intrusive approach: augmentations are "layers" on top of an existing content. These augmentation layers might be needed to cater for situational and idiosyncratic needs, difficult for designers to foresee. Technically, augmentations do not need the participation of the Web sites used for the augmentation since the augmentation occurs on the Web browser. Web augmentation technology only acts on the user interaction and does not change the original Web page stored on the Web server. It is interesting to note that whilst Bouvin does not assign any particular intention for the use of WA tools, Díaz explicitly mentions that augmentation layers might aim at improving the user experience with the Web page.

For our purposes, WA describes *tools that allow people to modify Web pages to improve user performance and satisfaction.* This definition connects WA to EUD as EUD *is programming to achieve the result of program primarily for personal, rather than public use.* Indeed, WA realizes this vision in the web sphere as far as it helps to support users' needs that have not been originally been identified or taken into account during the design of the Web site.

3   Overview of EUD Tools for the Web

The evolution of Web technology is changing the way users interact with Web sites. At first, users could only consume contents provided by Web sites. Later, users could actively contribute with content by using tools such as CMS and wikis. More recently, WA tools empower people in different ways making these tools real EUD tools: (1) to create their own web sites, (2) to combine information from diverse Web sites into a single hub (using mashups), and even (3) to modify Web pages created by others (using WA tools e.g. MADCOW (Bottoni et al., 2004) and DiLAS (Agosti et al., 2005)). This highlights the broad range of approaches that Web-centered EUD tools explore. Fig. 1 introduces a set of dimensions to classify these tools while the positioning of existing tools with respect to this classification is shown in Table 1.

Although the focus is on WA tools, we also introduce mashup tools because this provides some elements of comparison between the existing approaches for EUP of the Web.

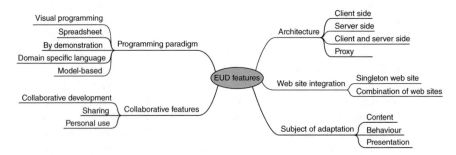

Fig. 1 *Five EUD features* of WA tools and their attributes

Table 1 EUD tools for the Web positioned with respect to the classification in Fig. 1

Tools	Year	Type	Architecture			Subject of adaptation			Web site Integration	Collaboration features	Programing Paradigm	Ref.
			C	S	P	Co	Be	Pr				
Marmite	2007	M	C			Co			Combination	Personal use	Visual program.	Wong and Hong (2007)
MARGMASH	2007	WA	C			Co			Combination	Personal use	By demonstration	Díaz, Pérez and Paz (2007)
CoScripter	2008	M	C			Co	Be		Singleton	Collaborative dev.	By demonstration	Leshed, Haber, Matthews and Lau (2008)
Reform	2009	WA	C			Co			Combination	Personal use	By demonstration	Toomim et al. (2009)
SemanticWebPipes	2009	M		S		Co			Combination	Sharing	Visual program.	Phuoc, Polleres, Hauswirth, Tum-marello and Morbidoni (2009)
Mashroom	2009	M	C			Co			Combination	Personal use	Spreadsheets	Wang, Yang and Han (2009)
Deep	2010	M	C			Co		Pr	Combination	Personal use	By demonstration	Guo, Han and Tokuda (2010)
MashSheet	2010	M	C			Co			Combination	Collaborative dev.	Spreadsheets	Hoang, Paik and Benatallah (2010); Hoang, Paik and Dong (2011)
Atomate	2010	M	C			Co			Combination	Collaborative dev.	Model-based	Kleek, Moore, Karger, André and Schraefel (2010)
RUMU	2010	WA		S		Co		Pr	Singleton	Personal use	Visual program.	Poley (2010)
CSN framework	2011	WA	C			Co	Be		Combination	Sharing	By demonstration	Firmenich, Winckler and Rossi (2011)
OntoCompo	2011	M	C			Co	Be		Singleton	Personal use	Model-based	Brel, Dery-Pima, Renevier-Go-nin and Riveill (2011)
Mixer	2011	WA	C			Co			Combination	Sharing	By demonstration	Gardiner, Tomasic, Zimmerman, Aziz and Rivard (2011)
IVO	2011	M	C	S		Co	Be		Singleton	Sharing	By demonstration	Realinho, Dias and Romão (2011)
MashupEditor	2011	M			P	Co			Combination	Sharing	By demonstration	Ghiani, Paternò and Spano (2011); Ghiani, Paternò, Spano and Pintori (2016)
DashMash	2011	M	C/S			Co	Be		Combination	Personal use	Visual program.	Cappiello, Daniel, Matera, Picozzi and Weiss (2011); Cappi-ello et al. (2011)

(continued)

Table 1 (continued)

Tools	Year	Type	Architecture			Subject of adaptation			Web site Integration	Collaboration features	Programing Paradigm	Ref.
			C	S	P	Co	Be	Pr				
MAIDL	2011	M		C/S		Co			Combination	Personal use	By demonstration	Chaisatien, Prutsachainimmit and Tokuda (2011)
VisPro	2011	M		C/S		Co			Combination	Personal use	Visual program.	Bottaro et al. (2011)
SOA4All Studio	2011	M		C/S		Co	Be		Combination	Sharing	Visual program.	Wajid, Namoun, and Mehandjiev (2011)
Cowpath	2012	WA	C				Be		Combination	Sharing	DSL	Díaz, Sosa, Arellano and Trujillo (2012)
WebCrystal	2012	WA	C			Co		Pr	Combination	Personal use	By demonstration	Chang and Myers (2012)
Baya	2012	M	C			Co			Combination	Sharing	Visual program.	Chowdhury, Rodríguez, Daniel and Casati (2012); Daniel, Rodríguez, Chowdhury, Nezhad and Casati (2012)
ResEval Mash	2012	M		C/S		Co			Combination	Sharing	Visual program.	Imran et al. (2012)
CrowdDesign	2012	M		C/S		Co	Be		Combination	Sharing	Visual program.	Nebeling, Leone and Norrie (2012)
Chudnoskyy et al.	2012	M	C			Co			Combination	Sharing	Visual program.	Chudnovskyy et al., 2012
MOWA	2013	WA	C			Co			Combination	Sharing	Model-based	Challiol, Firmenich, Bosetti, Gordillo, & Rossi, 2013
Sticklet	2013	WA	C			Co			Combination	Sharing	DSL	Arellano & Díaz, 2013; Díaz et al., 2013
Social Overlays	2013	WA	C			Co		Pr	Singleton	Sharing	Visual program.	Dong, Ackerman, Newman and Paruthi (2013)
openHTML	2013	WA		S		Co		Pr	Singleton	Collaborative dev.	By demonstration	Park, Saxena, Jagannath, Wieden-beck and Forte (2013)
Ardito et al. (a)	2013	M		S		Co		Pr	Combination	Sharing	Visual program.	Ardito et al. (2013)
MobiMash	2013	M		S		Co	Be		Combination	Personal use	Visual program.	Cappiello, Matera and Picozzi (2013)
DireWolf	2013	M		S		Co	Be		Combination	Collaborative dev.	Visual program.	Kovachev, Renzel, Nicolaescu and Klamna (2013)
Rana et al.	2013	M		S		Co			Combination	Personal use	Visual program.	Rana, Morshed, and Synnes (2013)

(continued)

Table 1 (continued)

	Year				Co	Be	Pr				
CapView	2013	M		S	Co	Be	Pr	Combination	Personal use	Visual program.	Radeck, Blichmann and Meißner (2013)
WebMakeup	2014	**WA**	C		Co	Be		Combination	Sharing	Visual program.	Díaz, Arellano, Aldalur, Medina and Firmenich (2014)
CrowdMock	2014	**WA**	C		Co	Be		Combination	Collaborative dev.	Visual program.	Firmenich, Firmenich, Rivero and Antonelli (2014)
Ardito et al. (b)	2014	M		S	Co			Combination	Sharing	Visual program.	Ardito et al. (2014); Ardito, Costabile, Desolda, Latzina and Matera (2015)
MultiMasher	2014	M		S	Co			Combination	Sharing	Visual program.	Husmann, Nebeling, Pongelli and Norrie (2014)
NaturalMash	2014	M	C	S	Co			Combination	Sharing	By demonstration	Aghaee and Pautasso (2014)
SmartComposition	2014	M	C	S	Co			Combination	Sharing	Model-based	Krug, Wiedemann and Gaedke (2014)
Tayeh et al.	2014	**WA**	C		Co			Singleton	Personal use	Visual program.	Tayeh and Signer (2014, 2015)
FaceMashup	2015	M		S	Co			Singleton	Personal use	Visual program.	Massa and Spano (2015)
IWC	2015	M		S	Co	Be		Combination	Sharing	By demonstration	Nicolaescu and Klamma (2015)
MAMSAAS	2015	M		S	Co			Combination	Sharing	Visual program.	Wang and Wainer (2015)
EasyApp	2016	M	C	S	Co	Be		Combination	Personal use	Visual program.	Zhai et al. (2016)
MOWA/WOA	2016	**WA**	C		Co	Be	Pr	Combination	Collaborative dev.	By demonstration	Bosetti, Firmenich. Rossi and Winckler (2016); Firmenich, Bosetti, Rossi, Winckler and Barbieri (2016)
Mijián et al.	2016	**WA**	C		Co	Be		Singleton	Sharing	Visual program.	Mijián, Garrigós, and Firmenich (2016)

M: Mashup; WA: WA; C: client side; S: server side; C/S: both client and server sides; P: proxy; Co: content; Be: behavior; Pr: presentation; DSL: domain specific language.

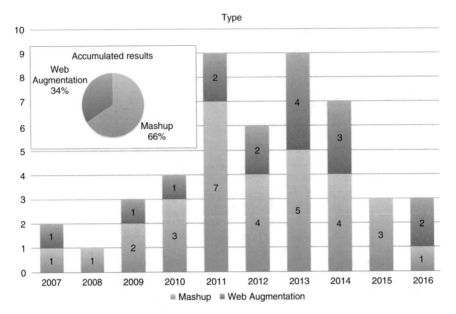

Fig. 2 Contributions presenting tools: Mashup versus WA technology

Mashup technology is an interesting alternative for final users to combine existing resources and services in a new Web application (Aghaee & Pautasso, 2011). Mashups are often very specialized and only operate with specific types of contents (quite often structured data sources). For example, FaceMashup (Massa & Spano, 2015) is a EUD tool for mashup that allows users to manipulate social network APIs to combine data and sharing them with other users through the social networks. It is interesting to notice that some WA tools such as CSN Framework (Firmenich et al., 2011) borrow from mashups the ability to integrate contents but they are even more flexible allowing to compose any kind of DOM element from a Web page.

Tool wise, Fig. 2 highlights how mashups (66%) have received more attention throughout w.r.t. WA tools (34%). This seems to suggest that integrating different data sources is being considered more important than customizing existing Web sites. Though this might be true in a general sense, when it comes to empowering end-users, data integration might be more costly and hence, more difficult to end users to achieve. By contrast, WA is not so demanding, and hence more affordable to end-users. This makes WA tools more likely to be adopted by end users.

The rest of this section explains the classification presented in Fig. 1 and provides examples of the corresponding Web technology.

3.1 Architecture

Tools might rest on the client side, the server side or both. Client-side tools are executed as Web browsers' extensions (or plug-ins) and processing happens on the user's local computer. Common programming languages used to implement client-side applications include HTML, CSS, and Javascript. Conversely, server side technology runs on a remote machine, and only the outcome of the execution returns to the user's local computer. Common programming languages include Ruby, Python, PHP, C# … Server side technologies can store persistent data. However, data can only be accessed than through HTTP requests for a particular URL.

Miján et al. (2016) and WebCrystal (Chang & Myers, 2012) illustrate the client-side approach. WebCrystal is a Firefox plug-in that allows the inspection of code corresponding to visual objects. WebCrystal provides users feedback using a textual description and a customized code snippet that can be copied-and-pasted to rebuild the user-selected properties. Additionally, Miján et al. resort to a set of personalization rules to be applied in the client-side with minimum alterations defined without requiring either advanced programming skills or advanced configuration.

Whilst Web browsers can store data in the local cache, server-side technology is used by many tools such as DireWolf (Kovachev et al., 2013), FaceMashup (Massa & Spano, 2015), Ardito et al. (2013) and MultiMasher (Husmann et al., 2014) as a means to support data persistence. DireWolf provides several extensible components for adapting Web sites and it implements a service for data persistence such as user device profiles and shared application states.

As for client-server tools, most requests a kept in the client with sporadic calls to the server. For example, DashMash (Cappiello et al., 2011) has a client-side module for mashup creation and a server module responsible for integrating and storing data from different types of services. In the mobile world, IVO (Realinho et al., 2011) follows a similar architecture. For mashups, MashupEditor (Ghiani et al., 2011, 2016) allows for adaptations to be created on the client (using a dedicated editor). Next, a proxy server store those adaptations that can be later reused during the creation of the mashup.

From the accumulated results in Fig. 3, it is clear that the client-side approach is the most popular architecture (49%). The Client-server option (21%) boosted in 2011, presumably due to the popularity of the Web 2.0 and the focus on sharing and the need to have common repositories. The server-side option (28%) rose from 2013 onwards, arguably on the search for a business model for mashup platforms.

3.2 Subject of Adaptation

Web sites might be adapted in different ways: including brand-new content, changing the behavior associated to DOM elements or altering the appearance (style and layout). Most tools provide functions to add/remove/replace contents. Adding content from other sources is often used as a means for making information readily available whilst removing content is useful to improve focus, preventing users from distraction. Mixer resorts to WA to improve the organization of Web pages simply

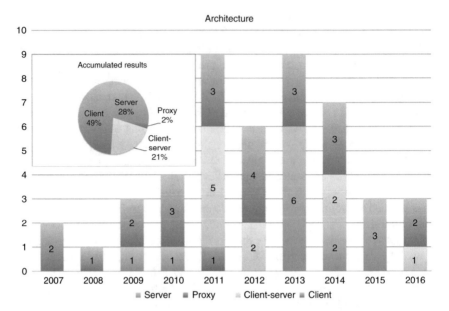

Fig. 3 Distribution over the years of tools and what part of the Web architectures they were exploiting

by letting users to move contents around and include/exclude contents needed. Mashups are also used to add content from different websites. SmartComposition (Krug et al., 2014) is another content-based approach that is primarily used to build mashups but it also features unique functions that allow to reorganize contents to fit into different screen sizes. Chudnovskyy et al. (2012) take a step forward by assisting users with recommendations and automatic composition.

Whilst modifying CSS code (color, font, etc.) is relatively simple, few tools account for this kind of adaptation. RUMU (Poley, 2010) is a web-based WYSIWYG editor that resorts to a semantic language to change the page style and simplifying web design. OpenHTML (Park et al., 2013) is also a web editor to introduce laymen into HTML and CSS.

Finally, changing the behavior of Web sites is far from trivial. It often requires adding some Javascript code to DOM elements like show or hide web nodes, click on certain button, change the content of an element, etc. Changing the behavior of web sites might be necessary, for example, for automating repetitive tasks. Inter-Widget Communication (IWC) (Nicolaescu & Klamma, 2015) is a semi-automatic, end-user friendly approach to extend widgets employing the programming-by-demonstration paradigm. IWC is built by composing interactive widgets. IWC leaves users with the tedious task of manual wiring widgets to create mashups. SOA4All (Wajid et al., 2011) is a visual development environment that addresses adaptation of Web applications through the connection of different service components into an assembly line.

3.3   Web Site Integration

This dimension tells if users work with one (singleton) or more (combination of) Web sites in a single project. Whilst many EUD tools are designed to augment a particular type of singleton Web site (e.g. OpenHTML), some tools allow to mix content from diverse Web sites.

Mashups tools like Baya (Chowdhury et al., 2012), Deep (Guo et al., 2010), MamSaas (Wang & Wainer, 2015) and Marmite (Wong & Hong, 2007) are typical examples of tools that allow to extract data from different Web sites and recombine them in a form that better fulfill user's needs. Nonetheless, other strategies combine Web sites that don't necessarily involve structured data sets. For example, Ardito et al. (2015) is a platform for end users to compose personal information spaces by assembling pieces of information from different sources. Such personal information spaces can be enacted in different devices and shared with other users. MamSaas is a layered architecture to deploy and identify mashup components as well as link and execute mashups for quick application development. MOWA (Bosetti et al., 2016) is another EUD tool for WA that enables end users to create a custom guided tour of a city based on contents collected from diverse Web sites. Its aim is to augment existing Web applications with mobile features. Using MOWA end users can pinpoint in a map content from a different Web site and then generate a custom script. This mobile Web application prompts the users add points of their interests while they move around the city.

Finally, CrowdDesign (Nebeling et al., 2012) can also be classified as a EUD tool in so far as it supports mashup based on the integration of scripts coming from diverse sources. CrowdDesign works as a storage for scripts and user interface components shared by a community of developers. CrowdDesign also features a visual authoring environment that allows users to combine contents and scripts available at the platform to create a more personal version of Web sites.

3.4   Collaborative Features

Whilst a WA strategy can be adopted only for personal purposes, sharing is an important aspect of end-user development (Lieberman et al., 2005; Repenning et al., 2011). We distinguish between sharing and collaborative development.

Sharing. Some tools focus on personal use, i.e. results cannot be reused and/or shared with other users. Tayeh and Signer (2014) is a case in point. These authors provide a tool for the linking and the integration of arbitrary documents and multimedia content dynamically. Rana et al. (2013) and EasyApp (Zhai et al., 2016) are also tools for personal use. Both tools provide a systematic way of designing, developing and deploying personalized apps. Reform is a Firefox extension that contributes with architecture for web enhancement that allows end users to integrate existing enhancements with new websites. Despite the fact that it allows end users to communicate with developers for requesting new features, they do not allow sharing developments. CapView (Radeck et al., 2013) is a mashup platform that provides instant feedback for user development actions. CapView helps non-programmers form components with recommendations provided by the system and it manipulates a mashup through visually composing component features.

Moving away for the personal realm, Social Overlays (Dong et al., 2013) and the CSN framework (Firmenich et al., 2011) illustrate the use of repositories for script sharing. Social Overlays focuses on repairing either the behavior or the appearance of Web sites. Updates made by individuals are visible to the community which use a voting mechanism to decide if the updates are relevant and if so, be incorporated as part of the Web site offerings. CSN features a plug-in that allows users to adapt Web pages by triggering different types of scripts. It has different features depending on the user profile: developer or end user. Developers can write new augmentation scripts to extend the set of original sets of scripts available in the framework. Such scripts can then be obtained by other users who on their turn can execute them to adapt the Web sites. Finally, it is interesting to notice that a few tools allow to publish the code in social networks (e.g. Sticklet Arellano & Díaz, 2013; Díaz et al., 2013) whilst others allow to export files for personal use on an individual basis (e.g. WebMakeup).

Collaborative development. CrowdMock (Firmenich et al., 2014) does not provide a voting mechanism but it permits to amend/complete augmentation script by people other than the author. CoScripter (Leshed et al., 2008) resorts to programming by demonstration to enable users to record all the information related to user interaction to edit a Website. The outcome is a script macro that can be automatically stored in a Web server from where they can be delivered to other users and they can use a collaborative scripting environment for recording, automating, and sharing web-based processes.

Fig. 4 helps to apprehend differences and similitudes between WA and mashups as for "collaboration features" and "subject of adaptation" support. As for the

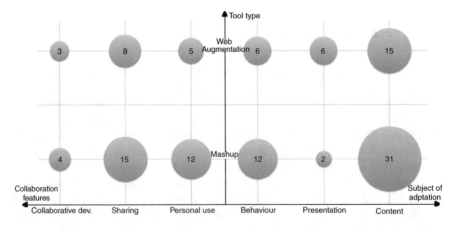

Fig. 4 Mapping WA tools and Mashups across "Collaboration features" and "Subject of adaptation"

former, both scenarios (i.e. WA and mashups) pay attention to the idiosyncratic scenario ("Personal use"), while the potential of reuse (i.e. sharing) is felt to be more intensive for mashups than for WA developments. Also, mashups and WA coincide in their interest in handling content (31 vs. 15) while WA underscores in addressing presentation concerns (2 vs. 6). This is according to expectations since WA adapts existing web sites whose presentation might need to be tuned to better meet users' needs. By contrast, behavior modification has received more attention in the mashup realm.

3.5 Programming Paradigm

EUD tools resort to diverse programming paradigm: visual languages, spread-sheets, programming by demonstration, domain specific languages (DSL) and model-based automation (Aghaee & Pautasso, 2011).

Visual programming is mainly found in mashup tools that allow drag-and-drop to connect components to create a mashup. Examples include VisPro (Bottaro et al., 2011), ResEval Mash (Imran et al., 2012), MobiMash (Cappiello et al., 2013), SemanticWeb Pipes (Phuoc et al., 2009) and WebMakeup (Arellano & Díaz, 2013; Díaz et al., 2014). VisPro creates mashups by dragging and dropping widgets from a library. ResEval Mash is a domain-specific mashup tool that explores dedicated mashuping, in this case in the domain of research evaluation. MobiMash resorts to visual notations to create mobile mashups. The particularity of SemanticWeb Pipes is to blend mashups and the Semantic Web. Here, ontologies are used for better matching widgets parameters that build up the mashup. WebMakeup is an editor that delivers Chrome plugs-in for augmentation purposes. A DSL is defined that sets the expressiveness of the augmentation. WebMakeup helps construct DSL expressions on top of the page being augmented. Once constructed, WebMakeup generates and installs the corresponding Chrome extension.

Programming by demonstration is most popular for data extraction and visualization, where service composition and orchestration play an ancillary role. NaturalMash (Krug et al., 2014), WOA (Firmenich et al., 2016), Margmash (Díaz et al., 2007) and MAIDL (Chaisatien et al., 2011) illustrate this approach

NaturalMash is a WYSIWYG mashup tool. NaturalMash stands out for its formative support where the tool is able to collect user feedback. WOA enables users to create/extract Web contents in the form of objects that they can manipulate to create Personal Web experiences. Margmash creates augmentations out of personalized information, which are gathered from diverse Web sites. Margmash behaves as a lightweight wrapper that guides end users on both data gathering and data recombination. MAIDL permits the rapid creation of mobile mashup out of components.

Model-based Automation is concerned with the automatic creation of mashups out of knowledge about the user and the context of use. This technique's weakness is the risk of generating irrelevant mashups w.r.t. the given requirements. Ontocompo (Brel et al., 2011) and Atomate (Kleek et al., 2010) illustrate this approach. Ontocompo makes use of an ontology to generate new applications based on existing ones. Atomate is a personal information assistant engine that automatically carries out tasks for the user. Atomate combine RSS/ATOM feeds from social networking into a simple RDF model representing people, places and things.

DSLs strive to abstract from general-purpose programming language. The challenge here is to find a compromise between expressiveness and learnability. DSLs in the augmentation realm can be illustrated by Cowpath (Díaz et al., 2012) and Sticklet (Díaz et al., 2013). Cowpath focuses on "Web trails", i.e. recurring navigation paths across distinct Web sites. Rather than switching between tabs and typing once and again the same URLs, Cowpath augments the affected websites with additional hyperlinks that "pave the way" of these Web trails. On the other hand, Sticklet explores the use of a dedicated assistant that help users to come with Sticklet expressions to augment Web sites.

Spreadsheets-like programming are often considered ease-of-use, intuitive and with enough expressive power to represent and manage complex data. When it comes to mashups, Mashroom (Wang et al., 2009) and MashSheet (Hoang et al., 2010, 2011) explore this approach. Mashroom builds Web applications by combining content coming from different Web sites. To this end, it resorts to an expressive data structure and a set of defined mashup operators. The data structure allows users to express complex data objects while mashup operators are visualized in the formula bar. MashSheet extends conventional spreadsheet paradigms to facilitate Web services "mashup" in a spreadsheet environment. MashSheet is a collection of operators that supports orchestrating Web services, manipulating and visualizing data created by the services.

Fig. 5 depicts the distribution of research contributions with respect to the "programming paradigm" feature over the years. Visual programming is by far the most popular approach (53%), where the other approaches fall behind: programming by demonstration (30%), Model-based (9%), DSL (4%) and spreadsheets (4%). Worth mentioning, the boost of programming-by-demonstration in 2011 although it faded over the years.

4 Web Augmentation: A Case Study with WebMakeup

This section illustrates WA at work using WebMakeup (Díaz et al., 2014). This tool supports the modification of the content, the presentation, and the behavior of Web pages. Moreover, it also supports the integration of dynamic content from other web sites. So far, WebMakeup only work for the Chrome browser. A video is available at https://vimeo.com/204338864.

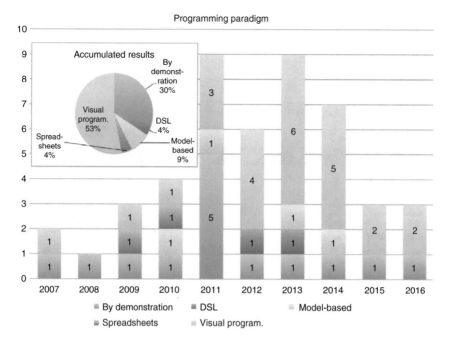

Fig. 5 "Programming paradigm" in research contributions over the years

4.1 Architecture

WebMakeup is a plug-in freely available at the Chrome Web Store[1]. Once installed, it can be activated at any time by selecting the icon in the top-right side of the address bar as shown by Fig. 6a. By selecting the option "New" from the pop-up menu, two vertically aligned tabs called "Piggy Bank" and "Patterns" appear (see Fig. 6b).

WebMakeup is a client-side application developed using JavaScript. Scripts created by the user are stored in the Web browser, so persistence can be ensured as far as the user does not clear the local cache.

4.2 Subject of Adaptation

WebMakeup allows users to modify the contents, the presentation and the behavior of existing Web pages through the manipulation of the DOM elements that

---

[1] Available at: https://chrome.google.com/webstore/detail/alnhegodephpjnaghlcemlnpdknhbhjj

a

b

Fig. 6 WebMakeup main menus. (a) Launching WebMakeup to create a new augmentation layer on top of DBLP. (b) Tab menus vertically aligned at right-side (collapsed)

conform the Web page. Only after selecting a DOM element, it is possible to manipulate it: remove, re-arrange or change its behavior.

4.2.1 Selecting DOM Elements in a Web Page

As shown in Fig. 7a) WebMakeup highlights the underlying DOM through two visual elements: the pointer, which becomes a small camera, and the background color, which is turned into green. By clicking on the green zone, the corresponding DOM element is selected and transformed into a widget. Widgets are framed

a

b

Fig. 7 Selection of the DOM element using WebMakeup. (a) Selection of DOM elements using mouse over operation on a Web page. (b) DOM element selected (after click) showing options for inspecting it

by "decorators," i.e. frames that include three button (see Fig. 7b): the red-circle button removes the DOM element at hand; the green-circle button changes the visibility of the DOM element from hide to show, and vice versa; finally, the yellow-circle button unselects the DOM element, removing the decorator frame.

In this way, users can remove elements from Web pages to accomplish diverse personalization needs. For example, removing short papers from the DBLP page might help highlight other types of publications. However, the red-circle button (see Fig. 7b) only removes the corresponding DOM element from the current

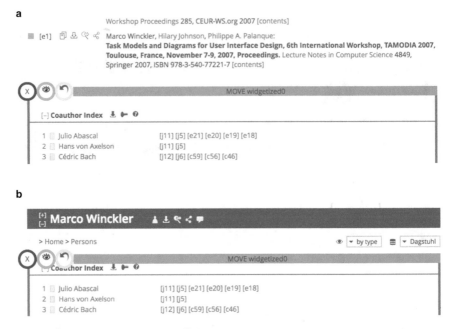

Fig. 8 Moving DOM elements around the Web page using WebMakeup. (a) Initial position of the co author index. (b) Final position of the co author index

session. For changes to become permanent (i.e. enforceable in future visits to the DBLP Web site), users should "deploy" the WebMakeup script by clicking on the namesake option in the scrollable menu (third item at Fig. 6a).

4.2.2 Re-arranging Contents around the Web Page

Another way to highlight content is to place it in a more suitable position. Fig. 8 provides an example. Here, the DOM elements accounting for the coauthor index is moved upwards from the bottom section of the page. This operation is achieved by selecting the corresponding DOM node (see Fig. 8a), click on the MOVE legend and next drag & drop to the new position (see the resulting page at Fig. 8b). The new position might prevent scrolling for users that mind co-authors.

4.2.3 Creating New Behaviors

WebMakeup allows supporting new behaviors (e.g. setting blink relationships between DOM elements). As an example, consider the Amazon page of the book "A Game of Thrones." Two widgets are created after two DOM nodes: the *title* DOM and a widget with information of the book price and how it can be bought.

a

b

Fig. 9 Behavior definition in WebMakeup joining different widgets with wires. (a) Associating between widgets. (b) Resulting web site after deploying the adaptation

Both widgets joined through the yellow point from the triggering widget to the triggered widget (see Fig. 9a). It is possible to choose which event (ex. click, doubleclick and mouseEnter) will trigger the show/hide behavior. At the end, the user can decide if the current book will be bought and clicking on the triggering

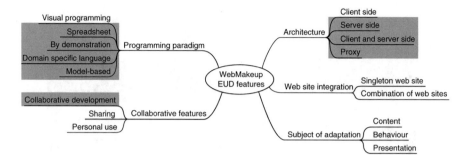

Fig. 10 Summary of WebMakeup with respect to the classification presented in Fig. 1

element (the book title), the triggered widget will show the desired information (see Fig. 9b). Clicking on the book title again, the triggered element will be hidden.

4.3 Collaborative Features

WebMakeup scripts are stored locally in the Web browser. WebMakeup does not support collaborative development. Nonetheless, users can export scripts into a file and next share them through email or other means. Consumers should have WebMakeup installed and use the "import" option (Fig. 6a). Also in the scrollable menu, the entry "CarryOn" permits consumers to tune imported scripts to their own likes.

4.4 Programming Paradigm

WebMakeup does not require users to write a single line of code to modify Web pages. All programming is achieved through selecting DOM elements and interacting with widget decorators. For that, WebMakeup is classified as visual programming. Fig. 10 highlight this and other EUD features of WebMakeup, w.r.t. those presented at Fig. 1, by shadowing those not covered.

5 User and Usage Challenges with WA Tools

Each tool cited in this chapter has its own idiosyncrasies and their use will reveal very specific challenges. But beyond the use of a particular tool, WA challenges users to revise what they know about the web and how to program applications. When it comes to WA, users should be aware of a number of aspects, namely:

- WA is mainly a browser-based technology. Regardless of the technology employed to store and run the augmentation scripts, the adaptation only affects how a web site is displayed in the user's personal machine. Users must understand that their adaptation is personal and that will not be visible by other visitors of the same web site.
- WA is mainly a single browse technology. Changes performed by the user will only occur on the browser where the augmentation has been performed. The same user performing the same actions on another computer will not see the augmentation. It thus requires replication of the augmentation multiple times if the users are using multiple execution platforms (e.g. desktop computers, smartphones.
- Similar to other EUD technologies, WA require the adaption of the code produced by someone else. This has multiple implications for assessing the code of Web pages before to adapt them (Gross & Kelleher, 2010; Gross, Yang, & Kelleher, 2011).
- WA is constricted within the DOM hierarchy. Users should be aware of manipulation of DOM elements imposes a certain order of access to contents. For instance, elements might appear visually together but be arranged in separated DOM nodes. This might imply having different ancestors. This, in turn, prevents these "alongside elements" from being selected as a single DOM element. This constrain is imposed by the DOM element hierarchy (Bosetti et al., 2016). Notice that the DOM hierarchy itself does not need to be made visible but manipulated through metaphors and witty interactive tools. But no matter the tool, it is constricted within the DOM hierarchy.
- WA is fragile upon Web-site upgrades. Web sites evolve overtime and with the evolution of a web site some elements resulting from the augmentations may disappear and/or be replaced by other elements that directly affect the way WA scripts operate. Thus, whilst some scripts will be resilient to maintenance of web sites, other scripts will stop working once a Web site is upgraded. This makes the use of WA a more suitable technique when user's needs are volatile (Frajberg et al., 2016). WebMakeup illustrates the feasibility of having dynamic updates for contents but the bindings between WA scripts and the web site remain fragile and prone to become obsolete when the underlying web site evolves. This a major challenge as, by definition, web applications are meant to evolve. Beyond, as the users do not own the web application, the loss of a web augmentation is not predictable.
- WA does not create brand-new applications but enhances existing ones. The inclusion of contents from other web sites raises some pragmatic questions about the type of relationship created between web sites (Firmenich, Firmenich, Winckler, Rossi, & Distante, 2015). The simplest approach is the clone&own of elements. This implies that changes in the source element will not propagate to its clones. Alternatively, it is also possible to keep a dynamic binding with the source element so that changes in the source ripple throughout its clones.

6 Conclusion

This chapter has presented the principles behind Web Augmentation and highlighted how this technology shares multiple similar objectives as End User Development. Indeed, as it allows users to recycle, reuse and exploit material that can be obtained from other web sites it supports the construction (by the end users themselves) of more usable and more adapted web application. One of the biggest challenges is how treat dynamic states of Web applications, which means contents that evolves over time. Whilst this remains an unsolved issue that should be addressed by future research, it is possible to envisage various copy and paste strategies to address the problem.

In our study of WA tools, we have observed a prominence of tools that run exclusively on the client side. This is not surprising as one of the advantages of using a client-side approach is the faster execution that has a huge impact on the user performance while interacting with the web application making it possible to provide immediate feedback to the users. Moreover, users do not need to understand sever side functioning and to deal with complex installations on a remote web server (for which they, most of the time, have no access rights). Whilst client-side approach is not a panacea, we suggest that this is still a suitable strategy for giving end users more autonomy on the scripts they want to develop.

As demonstrated in the chapter, there are multiple technologies for performing web augmentation. We have presented some precise examples through the use of a particular tool called WebMakeup. For sake of simplicity, we have only provided here simple examples that can be easily reproduced. Nonetheless, we have demonstrated that using such simple adaptation of contents, behavior and presentation, web sites can be profoundly modified to better fit with users' needs.

Despite our efforts, it is important to note that none of the references provided refer to studies with a large number of users. Because of that, we cannot measure the impact of such as a strategy on the end-user community. Nonetheless, the tools we have presented are functional and a dedicated community maintains most of them. We believe that these WA tools deserve more publicity and that a wider and more systematic communication towards end users would deeply impact usability of web application and, more generally, of the Web as a whole.

Acknowledgements This work is co-supported by the Spanish Ministry of Education, and the European Social Fund under contract TIN2014-58131-R and the stay scholarship EEBB-I-16-11126. Aldalur has a doctoral grant from the Spanish Ministry of Science & Education. This project is also supported by the STIC AmSud project WAMAW-OUR.

References

Aghaee, S., & Pautasso, C. (2011). End-user programming for web mashups – open research challenges. In *Current trends in web engineering – workshops, doctoral symposium, and tutorials, held at ICWE 2011, Paphos, Cyprus, June 20–21, 2011. Revised Selected Papers* (pp. 347–351).

Aghaee, S., & Pautasso, C. (2014). End-user development of mashups with naturalmash. *Journal of Visual Languages and Computing*, 25(4), 414–432.

Agosti, M., Albrechtsen, H., Ferro, N., Frommholz, I., Hansen, P., Orio, N., Panizzi, E., Pejtersen, A. M., and Thiel, U. DiLAS: a Digital Library Annotation Service. *Proceedings of the International Workshop on Annotation for Collaboration – Methods, Tools and Practices (IWAC 2005), La Sorbonne, Paris, France, November 23–24 2005*, pages 91–101.

Ardito, C., Bottoni, P., Costabile, M.F., Desolda, G., Matera, M., Piccinno, A., et al. (2013). Enabling end users to create, annotate and share personal information spaces. In *End-user development – 4th international symposium, IS-EUD 2013, Copenhagen, Denmark, June 10–13, 2013. Proceedings* (pp. 40–55).

Ardito, C., Costabile, M. F., Desolda, G., Lanzilotti, R., Matera, M., Piccinno, A., et al. (2014). User-driven visual composition of service-based interactive spaces. *Journal of Visual Languages and Computing*, 25(4), 278–296.

Ardito, C., Costabile, M.F., Desolda, G., Latzina, M., Matera, M. (2015). Hands-on actionable mashups. In *End-user development – 5th international symposium, IS-EUD 2015, Madrid, Spain, May 26–29, 2015. Proceedings* (pp. 295–298).

Arellano, C., & Díaz, O. (2013). Lightweight end-user software sharing. In *End-user development – 4th international symposium, IS-EUD 2013, Copenhagen, Denmark, June 10–13, 2013. Proceedings* (pp. 241–246).

Bosetti, G., Firmenich, S., Rossi, G., Winckler, M. (2016). Web Objects Ambient: an integrated platform supporting new kinds of Personal Web experiences. In *Proceedings of the International Conference of Web Engineering (ICWE 2016), Lugano, Switzerland, June 6–9, 2016. Proceedings* (pp. 563–566). Heidelberg: Springer Verlag. Lecture Notes in Computer Science 9671, ISBN 978-3-319-38790-1.

Bottaro, A., Marino, E., Milicchio, F., Paoluzzi, A., Rosina, M., Spini, F. (2011). Visual programming of location-based services. In *Human interface and the management of information. interacting with information – Symposium on human interface 2011, held as part of HCI international 2011, Orlando, FL, USA, July 9–14, 2011, Proceedings, Part I* (pp. 3–12).

Bottoni, P., Civica, R., Levialdi, S., Orso, L., Panizzi, E., Trinchese, R. (2004). MADCOW: a multimedia digital annotation system. In *Proceedings of the working conference on Advanced visual interfaces (AVI '04)* (pp. 55–62). New York: ACM. doi:10.1145/989863.989870.

Bouvin, N.O. (1999). Unifying strategies for WA. In *Proceedings of the 10th ACM conference on hypertext and hypermedia*.

Brel, C., Dery-Pinna, A., Renevier-Gonin, P., Riveill, M. (2011). Ontocompo: a tool to enhance application composition. In *Human-computer interaction – INTERACT 2011 – 13th IFIP TC 13 international conference, lisbon, Portugal, September 5–9, 2011, Proceedings, Part IV* (pp. 588–591).

Burnett, M.M., & Scaffidi, C. (2011). End-user development. In Mads Soegaard and Rikke Friis Dam (Eds.), *Encyclopedia of human-computer interaction*. http://www.interaction-design.org/encyclopedia/end-user_development.html.

Cappiello, C., Daniel, F., Matera, M., Picozzi, M., Weiss, M. (2011). Enabling end user development through mashups: Requirements, abstractions and innovation toolkits. In *End-user development – third international symposium, IS-EUD 2011, Torre Canne (BR), Italy, June 7–10, 2011. Proceedings* (pp. 9–24).

Cappiello, C., Matera, M., Picozzi, M. (2013). End-user development of mobile mashups. In *Design, user experience, and usability. web, mobile, and product design – Second international conference, DUXU 2013, held as part of HCI international 2013, Las Vegas, NV, USA, July 21–26, 2013, Proceedings, Part IV* (pp. 641–650).

Cappiello, C., Matera, M., Picozzi, M., Sprega, G., Barbagallo, D., Francalanci, C. (2011). Dashmash: a mashup environment for end user development. In *Web engineering – 11th international conference, ICWE 2011, Paphos, Cyprus, June 20–24, 2011* (pp. 152–166).

Chaisatien, P., Prutsachainimmit, K., Tokuda, T. (2011). Mobile mashup generator system for cooperative applications of different mobile devices. In *Web Engineering – 11th international conference, ICWE 2011, Paphos, Cyprus, June 20–24, 2011* (pp. 182–197).

Challiol, C., Firmenich, S., Bosetti, G.A., Gordillo, S.E., Rossi, G. (2013). Crowdsourcing mobile web applications. In *Current trends in web engineering – ICWE 2013 international workshops ComposableWeb, QWE, MDWE, DMSSW, EMotions, CSE, SSN, and PhD Symposium, Aalborg, Denmark, July 8–12, 2013. Revised Selected Papers* (pp. 223–237).

Chang, K.S., & Myers, B.A. (2012). Webcrystal: understanding and reusing examples in web authoring. In *CHI conference on human factors in computing systems, CHI '12, Austin, TX, USA – May 05–10, 2012* (pp. 3205–3214).

Chowdhury, S.R., Rodríguez, C., Daniel, F., Casati, F. (2012). Baya: assisted mashup development as a service. In *Proceedings of the 21st world wide web conference, WWW 2012, Lyon, France, April 16–20, 2012 (Companion Volume)* (pp. 409–412).

Chudnovskyy, O., Nestler, T., Gaedke, M., Daniel, F., Fernández- Villamor, J.I., Chepegin, V.I., et al. (2012). End-user-oriented telco mashups: the OMELETTE approach. In *Proceedings of the 21st world wide web conference, WWW 2012, Lyon, France, April 16–20, 2012 (Companion Volume)* (pp. 235–238).

Daniel, F., Rodríguez, C., Chowdhury, S.R., Nezhad, H.R.M., Casati, F. (2012). Discovery and reuse of composition knowledge for assisted mashup development. In *Proceedings of the 21st world wide web conference, WWW 2012, Lyon, France, April 16–20, 2012 (Companion Volume)* (pp. 493–494).

Díaz, O., Arellano, C., Aldalur, I., Medina, H., Firmenich, S. (2014). End-user browser-side modification of web pages. In *Web information systems engineering – WISE 2014 – 15th international conference, Thessaloniki, Greece, October 12–14, 2014, Proceedings, Part I* (pp. 293–307).

Díaz, O., Arellano, C., Azanza, M. (2013). A language for end-user WA: caring for producers and consumers alike. *TWEB, 7*(2), 9.

Díaz, O., Pérez, S., Paz, I. (2007). Providing personalized mashups within the context of existing web applications. In *Web information systems engineering WISE 2007, 8th international conference on web information systems engineering, Nancy, France, December 3–7, 2007, Proceedings* (pp. 493–502).

Díaz, O., Sosa, J.D., Arellano, C., Trujillo, S. (2012). Web-based tool integration: a WA approach. In *Web engineering – 12th international conference, ICWE 2012, Berlin, Germany, July 23–27, 2012. Proceedings* (pp. 431–434).

Dong, T., Ackerman, M.S., Newman, M.W., Paruthi, G. (2013). Social overlays: collectively making websites more usable. In *Human-computer interaction – INTERACT 2013 – 14th IFIP TC 13 international conference, Cape Town, South Africa, September 2–6, 2013, Proceedings, Part IV* (pp. 280–297).

Firmenich, S., Bosetti, G., Rossi, G., Winckler, M., Barbieri, T. (2016). Abstracting and structuring web contents for supporting personal web experiences. In *Web Engineering – 16th international conference, ICWE 2016, Lugano, Switzerland, June 6–9, 2016. Proceedings* (pp. 77–95).

Firmenich, D., Firmenich, S., Rivero, J.M., Antonelli, L. (2014). A platform for WA requirements specification. In *Web engineering, 14th international conference, ICWE 2014, Toulouse, France, July 1–4, 2014. Proceedings* (pp. 1–20).

Firmenich, D., Firmenich, S., Winckler, M., Rossi, G., Distante, D. (2015). User interface adaptation using WA techniques: towards a negotiated approach. In *International conference on web engineering 2015 (ICWE)* LNCS (vol. 9114, pp. 147–164). Heidelberg: Springer Verlag.

Firmenich, S., Winckler, M., Rossi, G. (2011). A framework for concern-sensitive, client-side adaptation. In *Web engineering – 11th international conference, ICWE 2011, Paphos, Cyprus, June 20–24, 2011* LNCS (vol. 6757, pp. 198–213). Heidelberg: Springer Verlag.

Firmenich, S., Winckler, M., Rossi, G., Gordillo, S. (2011). A crowdsourced approach for concern-sensitive integration of information across the web. *Journal of Web Engineering (JWE), 10*(4), 289–315. Rinton Press.

Frajberg, D., Urbieta, M., Rossi, G., Schwinger, W. (2016). Volatile functionality in action: methods, techniques and assessment. In *Proceedings of the international conference of web engineering (ICWE 2016), Lugano, Switzerland, June 6–9, 2016. Proceedings* (pp. 59–76).

Heidelberg: Springer Verlag. ISBN 978-3-319-38790-1, Lecture Notes in Computer Science 9671.

Gardiner, S., Tomasic, A., Zimmerman, J., Aziz, R., Rivard, K. (2011). Mixer: mixed-initiative data retrieval and integration by example. In *Human-computer interaction – INTERACT 2011 – 13th IFIP TC 13 international conference, Lisbon, Portugal, September 5–9, 2011, Proceedings, Part I* (pp. 426–443).

Garrido, A., Firmenich, S., Rossi, G., Grigera, J., Medina-Medina, N., Harari, I. (2013). Personalized web accessibility using client-side refactoring. *IEEE Internet Computing, 17*(4), 58–66.

Ghiani, G., Manca, M., Paternò, F., Porta, C. (2014). Beyond responsive design: context-dependent multimodal augmentation of web applications. In *MobiWIS*, LNCS (vol. 8640, pp. 71–85). Heidelberg: Springer Verlag.

Ghiani, G., Paternò, F., Spano, L.D. (2011). Creating mashups by direct manipulation of existing web applications. In *End-user development – Third international symposium, IS-EUD 2011, Torre Canne (BR), Italy, June 7–10, 2011. Proceedings* (pp. 42–52).

Ghiani, G., Paternò, F., Spano, L. D., Pintori, G. (2016). An environment for end-user development of web mashups. *International Journal of Human-Computer Studies, 87*, 38–64. Elsevier.

Gross, P. A., & Kelleher, C. (2010). Non-programmers identifying functionality in unfamiliar code: strategies and barriers. *Journal of Visual Languages and Computing, 21*(5), 263–276.

Gross, P.A., Yang, J., Kelleher, C. (2011). Dinah: an interface to assist nonprogrammers with selecting program code causing graphical output. In *Proceedings of the international conference on human factors in computing systems, CHI 2011, Vancouver, BC, Canada, May 7–12, 2011* (pp. 3397–3400).

Guo, J., Han, H., Tokuda, T. (2010). Towards flexible mashup of web applications based on information extraction and transfer. In *Web information systems engineering – WISE 2010 – 11th international conference, Hong Kong, China, December 12–14, 2010. Proceedings* (pp. 602–615).

Han, H., & Tokuda, T. (2010). Towards flexible and lightweight integration of web applications by end-user programming. *IJWIS, 6*(4), 359–373.

Hick, W. E. (1952). On the rate of gain of information. *Quarterly Journal of Experimental Psychology, 4*(1), 11–26. doi:10.1080/17470215208416600.

Hoang, D.D., Paik, H., Benatallah, B. (2010). An analysis of spreadsheet based services mashup. In *Database technologies 2010, twenty-first australasian database conference (ADC 2010), Brisbane, Australia, 18–22 January, 2010, Proceedings* (pp. 141–150).

Hoang, D.D., Paik, H., Dong, W. (2011). Mashsheet: mashups in your spreadsheet. In *Web information system engineering – WISE 2011 – 12th international conference, Sydney, Australia, October 13–14, 2011. Proceedings* (pp. 332–333).

Husmann, M., Nebeling, M., Pongelli, S., Norrie, M. C. (2014). Multimasher: providing architectural support and visual tools for multi-device mashups. In *Web information systems engineering – WISE 2014 – 15th international conference, Thessaloniki, Greece, October 12–14, 2014, Proceedings, Part II* (pp. 199–214).

Imran, M., Soi, S., Kling, F., Daniel, F., Casati, F., Marchese, M. (2012). On the systematic development of domain-specific mashup tools for end users. In *Web engineering – 12th international conference, ICWE 2012, Berlin, Germany, July 23–27, 2012. Proceedings* (pp. 291–298).

Iturrioz, J., Azpeitia, I., Díaz, O. (2014). Generalizing the "like" button: empowering websites with monitoring capabilities. In *Proceedings of the 29th annual ACM symposium on applied computing (SAC '14)* (pp. 743–750). New York: ACM.

Kleek, M.V., Moore, B., Karger, D.R., André, P., Schraefel, M.C. (2010). Atomate it! End-user context-sensitive automation using heterogeneous information sources on the web. In *Proceedings of the 19th International Conference on World Wide Web, WWW 2010, Raleigh, North Carolina, USA, April 26–30, 2010* (pp. 951–960).

Ko, A. J., Abraham, R., Beckwith, L., Blackwell, A., Burnett, M., Erwig, M., et al. (2011). The state of the art in end-user software engineering. *ACM Computing Surveys*, *43*(3), Article 21, 44 pages.

Kovachev, D., Renzel, D., Nicolaescu, P., Klamma, R. (2013). Direwolf – distributing and migrating user interfaces for widget-based web applications. In *Web engineering – 13th international conference, ICWE 2013, Aalborg, Denmark, July 8–12, 2013. Proceedings* (pp. 99–113).

Krug, M., Wiedemann, F., Gaedke, M. (2014). Smartcomposition: a component based approach for creating multi-screen mashups. In *Web engineering, 14th international conference, ICWE 2014, Toulouse, France, July 1–4, 2014. Proceedings* (pp. 236–253).

Leshed, G., Haber, E.M., Matthews, T., Lau, T.A. (2008). Coscripter: automating & sharing how-to knowledge in the enterprise. In *Proceedings of the 2008 Conference on Human Factors in Computing Systems, CHI 2008, 2008, Florence, Italy, April 5–10, 2008* (pp. 1719–1728).

Lieberman, H., Paterno, F., Wulf, V. (Eds.) (2005). *End-user development*. Human-Computer Interaction Series, Kluwer/Springer.

Massa, D., & Spano, L.D. (2015). Facemashup: enabling end user development on social networks data. In *End-user development – 5th international symposium, IS-EUD 2015, Madrid, Spain, May 26–29, 2015. Proceedings* (pp. 204–210).

Miján, J.L., Garrigós, I., Firmenich, I. (2016). Supporting personalization in legacy web sites through client-side adaptation. In *Web engineering – 16th international conference, ICWE 2016, Lugano, Switzerland, June 6–9, 2016. Proceedings* (pp. 588–592).

Nebeling, M., Leone, S., Norrie, M. C. (2012). Crowdsourced web engineering and design. In *Web engineering – 12th international conference, ICWE 2012, Berlin, Germany, July 23–27, 2012. Proceedings* (pp. 31–45).

Newman, M. W., Lin, J., Hong, J. I., Landay, J. A. (2003). DENIM: an informal web site design tool inspired by observations of practice. *Human—Computer Interaction*, *18*(3), 259–324.

Nicolaescu, P., & Klamma, R. (2015). A methodology and tool support for widget based web application development. In *Engineering the web in the big data era – 15th international conference, ICWE 2015, Rotterdam, The Netherlands, June 23–26, 2015, Proceedings* (pp. 515–532).

Park, T.H., Saxena, A., Jagannath, S., Wiedenbeck, S., Forte, A. (2013). Openhtml: designing a transitional web editor for novices. In *2013 ACM SIGCHI conference on human factors in computing systems, CHI '13, Paris, France, April 27 – May 2, 2013, Extended Abstracts* (pp. 1863–1868).

Phuoc, D.L., Polleres, A., Hauswirth, M., Tummarello, G., Morbidoni, C. (2009). Rapid prototyping of semantic mash-ups through semantic web pipes. In *Proceedings of the 18th international conference on world wide web, WWW 2009, Madrid, Spain, April 20–24, 2009* (pp. 581–590).

Poley, E. (2010). RUMU editor: a non-wysiwyg web editor for non-technical users. In *Proceedings of the 28th international conference on human factors in computing systems, CHI 2010, extended abstracts volume, Atlanta, Georgia, USA, April 10–15, 2010* (pp. 4357–4362).

Radeck, C., Blichmann, G., Meißner, K. (2013). Capview – functionality aware visual mashup development for non-programmers. In *Web engineering – 13th international conference, ICWE 2013, Aalborg, Denmark, July 8–12, 2013. Proceedings* (pp. 140–155).

Rana, J., Morshed, S., Synnes, K. (2013). End-user creation of social apps by utilizing web-based social components and visual app composition. In *22nd international world wide web conference, WWW '13, Rio de Janeiro, Brazil, May 13–17, 2013, Companion Volume* (pp. 1205–1214).

Realinho, V., Dias, A.E., Romão, T. (2011). Testing the usability of a platform for rapid development of mobile context-aware applications. In *Human-computer interaction – INTERACT 2011 – 13th IFIP TC 13 international conference, Lisbon, Portugal, September 5–9, 2011, Proceedings, Part III* (pp. 521–536).

Repenning, A., Ahmadi, N., Repenning, N., Ioannidou, A., Webb, D.C., Marshall, K.S. (2011). Collective programming: making end-user programming (more) social. In *End-user development – third international symposium, IS-EUD 2011, Torre Canne (BR), Italy, June 7–10, 2011. Proceedings* (pp. 325–330).

Taych, A.A.O., & Signer, B. (2014). Open cross-document linking and browsing based on a visual plug-in architecture. In *Web information systems engineering – WISE 2014 – 15th international conference, Thessaloniki, Greece, October 12–14, 2014, Proceedings, Part II* (pp. 231–245).

Tayeh, A.A.O., & Signer, B. (2015). A dynamically extensible open cross document link service. In *Web information systems engineering – WISE 2015 – 16th international conference, Miami, FL, USA, November 1–3, 2015, Proceedings, Part I* (pp. 61–76).

Toomim, M., Drucker, S.M., Dontcheva, M., Rahimi, A., Thomson, B., Landay, J.A. (2009). Attaching UI enhancements to websites with end users. In *Proceedings of the 27th international conference on human factors in computing systems, CHI 2009, Boston, MA, USA, April 4–9, 2009* (pp. 1859–1868).

Wajid, U., Namoun, A., Mehandjiev, N. (2011). Alternative representations for end user composition of service-based systems. In *End-user development – third international symposium, IS-EUD 2011, Torre Canne (BR), Italy, June 7–10, 2011. Proceedings* (pp. 53–66).

Wang, G., Yang, S., Han, Y. (2009). Mashroom: end-user mashup programming using nested tables. In *Proceedings of the 18th international conference on world wide web, WWW 2009, Madrid, Spain, April 20–24, 2009* (pp. 861–870).

Wang, S., & Wainer, G.A. (2015). A mashup architecture with modeling and simulation as a service. In *Web information systems engineering – WISE 2015 – 16th international conference, Miami, FL, USA, November 1–3, 2015, Proceedings, Part I* (pp. 247–261).

Wong, J., & Hong, J.I. (2007). Making mashups with marmite: towards end-user programming for the web. In *Proceedings of the 2007 conference on human factors in computing systems, CHI 2007, San Jose, California, USA, April 28 – May 3, 2007* (pp. 1435–1444).

Wulf, V., Paterno, F., Lieberman, H. (2006). *End user development*. Rotterdam: Kluwer/ Springer.

Zhai, Z., Cheng, B., Wang, Z., Liu, X., Liu, M., Chen, J. (2016). Design and implementation: the end user development ecosystem for cross-platform mobile applications. In *Proceedings of the 25th international conference on world wide web, WWW 2016, Montreal, Canada, April 11–15, 2016, Companion volume* (pp. 143–144).

Printed in the United States
By Bookmasters